FRONTIERS IN APPLIED GENERAL EQUILIBRIUM MODELING

This volume brings together fifteen papers by many of the most prominent applied general equilibrium modelers to honor Herbert Scarf, the father of equilibrium computation in economics. It deals with new developments in applied general equilibrium, a field that has broadened greatly since the 1980s. The contributors discuss some traditional as well as some newer topics in the field, including nonconvexities in economy-wide models, tax policy, developmental modeling, and energy modeling. The book also covers a range of new approaches, conceptual issues, and computational algorithms, such as calibration, and new areas of application, such as the macroeconomics of real business cycles and finance. An introductory chapter written by the editors maps out issues and scenarios for the future evolution of applied general equilibrium.

Timothy J. Kehoe is Distinguished McKnight University Professor at the University of Minnesota and an advisor to the Federal Reserve Bank of Minneapolis. He has previously taught at Wesleyan University, the Massachusetts Institute of Technology, and the University of Cambridge. He has advised foreign firms and governments on the impact of their economic decisions. He is co-editor of *Modeling North American Economic Integration*, which examines the use of applied general equilibrium models to analyze the impact of the North American Free Trade Agreement. His current research focuses on the theory and application of general equilibrium models.

T. N. Srinivasan is Samuel C. Park, Jr., Professor of Economics at Yale University. He has previously taught at the Indian Statistical Institute, Delhi, and at numerous American universities. He has authored or edited three books, including *Reintegrating India with the World Economy*. He is a Fellow of the American Academy of Arts and Sciences and the Econometric Society, a member of the American Philosophical Society, and a Foreign Associate of the National Academy of Sciences. He was named Distinguished Fellow of the American Economic Association in 2003. His current research interests include international trade, development, agricultural economics, and microeconomic theory.

John Whalley is Professor of Economics at the University of Western Ontario, a Fellow of the Royal Society of Canada and the Econometric Society, and a foreign member of the Russian Academy of Natural Sciences. He also holds affiliations with Peking University, NBER, CESifo, and Warwick University. He is well known for his early work on applying general equilibrium as well as tax policy, trade policy, and environmental and development policy. His current research interests include WTO issues and globalization.

Frontiers in Applied General Equilibrium Modeling

In Honor of Herbert Scarf

Edited by

TIMOTHY J. KEHOE

University of Minnesota and
Federal Reserve Bank of Minneapolis

T. N. SRINIVASAN

Yale University

JOHN WHALLEY

University of Western Ontario

CAMBRIDGE
UNIVERSITY PRESS

PUBLISHED BY THE PRESS SYNDICATE OF THE UNIVERSITY OF CAMBRIDGE
The Pitt Building, Trumpington Street, Cambridge, United Kingdom

CAMBRIDGE UNIVERSITY PRESS
The Edinburgh Building, Cambridge CB2 2RU, UK
40 West 20th Street, New York, NY 10011-4211, USA
477 Williamstown Road, Port Melbourne, VIC 3207, Australia
Ruiz de Alarcón 13, 28014 Madrid, Spain
Dock House, The Waterfront, Cape Town 8001, South Africa

http://www.cambridge.org

First published 2005

Printed in the United States of America

Typeface Times Roman PS 10/12.5 pt.   *System* LaTeX 2_ε [TB]

A catalog record for this book is available from the British Library.

Library of Congress Cataloging in Publication Data
Frontiers in applied general equilibrium modeling / edited by Timothy J. Kehoe,
T.N. Srinivasan, John Whalley.
p.   cm.
Includes bibliographical references and index.
ISBN 0-521-82525-3 (hardback)
1. Equilibrium (Economics) – Mathematical models.   I. Kehoe, Timothy Jerome, 1953–
II. Srinivasan, T.N., 1933–   III. Whalley, John.
HB145.F76   2005
339.5'01'5195 – dc22   2004045758

ISBN 0 521 82525 3 hardback

Contents

Contributors

Lisandro Abrego is affiliated with the International Monetary Fund. His publications include journal articles and book contributions on applied general equilibrium modeling of international trade and environmental economics issues. (*labrego@imf.org*)

Aloisio Araujo is currently affiliated with the Instituto de Matematica Pura e Aplicada and Fundacao Getulio Vargas. His recent research interests include bankruptcy in incomplete markets and signaling models without single crossing. (*aloisio@impa.br*)

Kenneth J. Arrow is Professor of Economics Emeritus at Stanford University. He has written on different aspects of economic theory and related applications, including social choice, general equilibrium, asymmetric information, production functions, risk-bearing, medical economics, inventory theory, and environmental economics. (*arrow@stanford.edu*)

François Bourguignon is Chief Economist and Senior Vice President at the World Bank in Washington. He is on leave from the Ecole des Hautes Etudes en Sciences Sociales in Paris and from Delta, a research center he co-founded in 1988. His work is both theoretical and empirical and bears mostly on the distribution and redistribution of income in both developed and developing countries. He has consulted in many major international organizations. He is widely published and has been the editor of *European Economic Review* and *World Bank Economic Review* for several years.

Shantayanan Devarajan is the Chief Economist of the World Bank's South Asia Region. He has published in the areas of public economics, trade, natural resources and the environment, and general equilibrium modeling. He was the Director of the *World Development Report 2004, Making Services Work for Poor People*. At the World Bank since 1991, Mr. Devarajan was previously on the faculty of Harvard University's John F. Kennedy School of Government. (*sdevarajan@worldbank.org*)

Steven P. Dirkse is the Director of Optimization at GAMS Development Corporation. He enjoys working on problems of a computational nature, particularly those involving complementarity. He is one of the authors of the well-known PATH solver for complementarity problems.

Michael C. Ferris is Professor of Computer Sciences and Industrial Engineering at the University of Wisconsin at Madison. His research develops and uses computational methods and modeling for optimization and complementarity, involving application areas from economic analysis, structural mechanics, transportation, and medical treatment planning.

James Heckman is the Henry Schultz Distinguished Service Professor of Economics at the University of Chicago as well as Director of the Economics Research Center at the Department of Economics at the University of Chicago, Director of the Center for Social Program Evaluation at the Harris School of Public Policy at the University of Chicago, and Senior Research Fellow at the American Bar Foundation. Dr. Heckman has received numerous honors for his research. Among the most notable, he is a Fellow of the Econometric Society, a Fellow of the American Statistical Association, and a member of both the American Academy of Arts and Sciences and the National Academy of Sciences of the United States. He received the John Bates Clark Award of the American Economic Association in 1983. Most recently, he shared the 2000 Nobel Memorial Prize in Economic Sciences with Daniel McFadden for his work on selective sampling and the formulation of rigorous counterfactuals in policy analysis. Some of his recent books include *Inequality in America: What Role for Human Capital Policy?*, co-edited with Anne O. Krueger, and *Law and Employment: Lessons from Latin America and the Caribbean*, co-authored with C. Pages (forthcoming).

Dale W. Jorgenson is the Samuel W. Morris University Professor at Harvard University and Director of the Program on Technology and Economic Policy at the Kennedy School of Government. Professor Jorgenson is the author of more than 200 articles and 25 books. His collected papers on general equilibrium modeling have been published in two volumes by the MIT Press.

Kenneth L. Judd is Senior Fellow at the Hoover Institution on War, Revolution, and Peace in Stanford, California. He has worked on problems in public finance and imperfect competition, has published several papers on applying computational methods to economics problems, and is the author of *Numerical Methods in Economics*. (*judd@hoover.stanford.edu*)

Timothy J. Kehoe is currently Distinguished McKnight University Professor in the Department of Economics at the University of Minnesota. His research focuses on the theory and applications of general equilibrium, especially in international trade and macroeconomics. He advised the Spanish government on the impact of joining the European Community in 1986 and the Mexican government on the impact of joining the North American Free Trade Agreement in 1994. More recently, he has advised the governments of Panama and Ecuador on trade liberalization strategy.

Lars Ljungqvist is Professor of Economics at the Stockholm School of Economics and a Research Fellow at CEPR and IZA.

Alan S. Manne is Professor Emeritus of Operations Research at Stanford University. His fields of specialization include energy-environmental policy analysis, development planning, and industrial scheduling.

Rosa Matzkin is Research Professor of Economics at Northwestern University. Her research focuses on the discovery of new restrictions of economic theory, as well as on known restrictions, to develop nonparametric estimation and testing methods in various econometric models. Her methods are useful for models of consumer demand, price determination, and choice among a finite number of alternatives, among other things. (*matzkin@northwestern.edu*)

Alexander Meeraus is the founder and president of GAMS Development Corporation. He specializes in model language design and model building, encompassing a large class of academic, public service, and commercial uses of optimization, including economic policy design, class scheduling, finance, and supply chain applications. (*ameeraus@gams.com*)

Makoto Nakajima received his Ph.D. from the University of Pennsylvania in 2004. He is currently Assistant Professor of Economics at the University of Illinois, Urbana-Champaign. His research interests include macroeconomics and computational methods.

Lars Nesheim is affiliated with the Centre for Microdata Methods and Practice, Department of Economics, University College London, and the Institute for Fiscal Studies. His research interests include hedonic models, educational sorting models, and applied equilibrium models with unobservable heterogeneity.

Mário Páscoa is Professor in the Faculty of Economics at Universidade Nova de Lisboa (UNL) in Portugal. His current research interests are collateral and bubbles, endogenous collateral, and bankruptcy laws, and he has completed research in monopolistic competition, large games, demand theory, core and manipulability, incomplete markets, default, bankruptcy, and ponzi schemes. (*pascoa@fe.unl.pt*)

Edward C. Prescott is the W. P. Carey Professor at Arizona State University and is Senior Monetary Analyst at the Minneapolis Federal Reserve Bank. He received the Nobel Memorial Prize in Economic Science in 2004 for his contribution to real business cycle theory. He was awarded the Irwin Plein Nemmers Prize in Economics in 2002 for his discovery and analysis of the time-inconsistency problem. (*http://minneapolisfed.org/research/prescott/*)

José-Víctor Ríos-Rull is affiliated with the University of Pennsylvania, Centro de Altisimos Estudios Rios Perez, CEPR, and NBER. His research interests are macroeconomics, the mechanisms that determine family formation and dissolution, and the endogenous theory of policy. (*Vr0j@econ.upenn.edu*)

Anne-Sophie Robilliard is a Research Fellow with DIAL, a research unit of IRD (Institut de Recherche pour le Developpement), a Paris-based public science and technology research institute. She holds a Ph.D. in economics from the University of Paris-I (Sorbonne). Before joining IRD, she was a Postdoctoral Fellow at IFPRI

(International Food Policy Research Institute). Her research focuses on the modeling of poverty and income distribution as well as on poverty dynamics in rural areas. (*robilliard@dial.prd.fr*)

Sherman Robinson joined the University of Sussex as a Professor of Economics in 2004, moving from the International Food Policy Research Institute (IFPRI) where he had been Director of the Trade and Macroeconomics Division. Before joining IFPRI in 1993, he was Professor of Agricultural and Resource Economics at the University of California, Berkeley. (*sherman.robinson@sussex.ac.uk*)

Thomas J. Sargent is William Berkley Professor of Economics and Business at New York University and Senior Fellow at the Hoover Institution, Stanford University. He is interested in dynamic macroeconomic theory, theories of persistent unemployment, monetary history, and refinements of rational expectations theory, such as robustness and recursive least squares adaptation.

Herbert Scarf is the Sterling Professor of Economics at Yale University. His publications and research interests include general equilibrium theory and its applications, cooperative game theory, inventory management, and the study of production sets with indivisibilities. (*herbert.scarf@yale.edu*)

T. N. Srinivasan is Samuel C. Park, Jr., Professor of Economics at Yale University. His research interests include international trade, economic development, and microeconomic theory. He is a Fellow of the American Academy of Arts and Sciences and the Econometric Society, a member of the American Philosophical Society, and a Foreign Associate of the National Academy of Sciences. He was recently named Distinguished Fellow of the American Economic Association. His publications include *Agriculture, Growth and Redistribution of Income: Policy Analysis with a General Equilibrium Model of India*, co-authored with N.S.S. Narayana and K. Parikh, and his most recent book, *Reintegrating India with the World Economy*, co-authored with Suresh Tendulkar. (*t.srinivasan@yale.edu*)

John Whalley is Professor of Economics at the University of Western Ontario and Research Associate of NBER. He is also Guest Professor at Peking University and coordinator of the Global Economy Research Group for CESifo, Munich. He is a Fellow of the Royal Society of Canada and a foreign member of the Russian Academy of Natural Sciences, as well as a Fellow of the Econometric Society and Joint Managing Editor of *The World Economy*.

Charles A. Wilson is Professor of Econometrics at New York University. He has publications in general equilibrium theory, international trade, and overlapping generations. He has also worked on various applications of game theory, with publications in the economics of information, auctions, and experimental economics.

Kun-Young Yun is Professor of Economics at Yonsei University, Seoul, Korea. He has coauthored two books on tax reform with Professor Dale Jorgenson, and was recently elected to the National Assembly of the Republic of Korea in 2004.

Acknowledgments

Herbert Scarf has been the guiding spirit in several ways for each of us. Kehoe and Whalley did their doctoral dissertations under Scarf and have continued to be involved with him. Then a graduate student at Yale, Srinivasan had the privilege of hearing Scarf present his paper (Scarf 1960) on examples of global instability of competitive equilibrium at the summer meetings of the Economic Society at Stanford in 1959. Since joining the faculty of the Department of Economics at Yale in 1980, Srinivasan has constantly learned from and interacted with Scarf, including jointly teaching a course on Applied General Equilibrium twice in the past several years. All of us owe a deep intellectual debt to him.

We thank John Geanakoplos, Director, Cowles Foundation, for financial support from the Foundation for the conference. Dee Smitkowski, Business Manager, and Nora Wiedenbach, Administrative Assistant at Cowles, did a wonderful job of organizing the conference and corresponding with authors and discussants of papers. We thank them.

We thank Alan Deardorff, Eduardo Engel, John Geanokoplos, Michael Keane, Anne Krueger, Kirit Parikh, Thomas Rutherford, Herbert Scarf, Jaime Serra, and John Shoven for their comments as discussants at the conference.

Introduction

Timothy J. Kehoe, T. N. Srinivasan, and John Whalley

This volume honors Herbert Scarf and his contributions to economics. It deals with new developments in applied general equilibrium (AGE) modeling, a field in which Scarf's contributions have played a decisive role. All but two of the chapters in the volume were presented at a conference held at Yale University in April 2002. The chapter by Herbert Scarf and Charles Wilson was written afterward; it demonstrates the uniqueness of equilibrium in an important class of international trade models. The chapter by Lars Ljungqvist and Thomas Sargent is an outgrowth of Sargent's discussion at the conference of the paper presented there by Edward Prescott. The chapters presented here build on a well-known earlier volume in applied general equilibrium, edited by Herbert Scarf and John Shoven in 1984 (Scarf and Shoven 1984), which in turn grew out of Scarf's pioneering contributions in general equilibrium computation in the 1960s and early 1970s (Scarf 1967a, Scarf and Hansen 1973). Kenneth Arrow's chapter in this volume points out that the ability to deploy AGE models is the product of research advances, going back at least 130 years, in which progress in economic theory and vastly improved availability of economic data have played crucial roles. According to Arrow, equally crucial inputs were improvements in computing power and the development of algorithms for computing equilibrium, in which Scarf's (1967b) algorithm based on simplicial subdivisions was the crucial step.[1]

Since the 1980s, applications of AGE have broadened. They now include international trade, public finance, development, energy, and climate change and broader environmental concerns, as well as other fields. A range of new approaches and conceptual issues, not to mention computational algorithms, has evolved. These include calibration and expanded areas of application, such as macroeconomics of real business cycles and finance. In addition, the techniques of AGE modeling – namely calibrating and benchmarking observed data on economies into an initial

---

[1] In an as yet unpublished paper, Scarf (2002) provides a fascinating account of his involvement in the computation of economic equilibria and the contribution of his interaction with faculty and students at Yale in the late sixties and seventies.

1

equilibrium data set and then doing counterfactual policy analysis – have spread into other areas, such as game theory and even partial equilibrium models of industrial organization.

After the initial phase of demonstrating the potential of using AGE models for policy analysis, searching questions were raised as to the performance and robustness of AGE as a basic tool in policy and other work. Most of the policy applications had been performed ex ante, in anticipation of a policy change being enacted, such as the implementation of NAFTA or of the Uruguay Round agreement on international trade. These applications provided valuable estimates of the likely consequences of a policy change. For the methodology of AGE to become a widely accepted and useful policy tool, however, cross checking of the projections of models with actual outcomes, after the policy change has been put in place, is essential. Such cross checking (which is an analogue of cross checking of out-of-sample predictions of an econometric model with its actual realizations) has to allow for the fact that projections of an AGE model are conditional in that they are based on particular assumptions about values of variables exogenous to the model, and, as such, the projections could deviate from the actual outcomes if the realized values of exogenous variables differed from their assumed values. Also, in actual implementation, aspects of a policy could differ from those assumed in the model, and other policies not included in the model could be implemented at the same time. Nonetheless, with appropriate allowance for these factors, it should be possible to look backward, after the model's policy change has been implemented, and evaluate how accurate and useful the model projections were. Timothy Kehoe's evaluation of models of NAFTA in this volume is one such attempt.

This volume builds on existing AGE literature and consciously aims to go well beyond it and to look to the future. Scarf's research agenda of making the elegant theoretical general equilibrium models fully operational, implementable with actual data, and useful to practitioners such as policy makers is relevant to all theoretical models of economics. All analytical structures should, in principle, have their numerical analogues implementable with data. The practical issues are how to do this and what conclusions can be drawn from simulations or projections from the numerical model. Similar issues of how models are parameterized or calibrated arise even when models other than the general equilibrium model are used.

The chapters in this volume illustrate both the progress in AGE modeling since the 1980s and applications to new areas, as well as challenges that remain to be addressed. We start with a discussion of the origins of applied general equilibrium modeling and Herbert Scarf's contributions to this field. We then provide brief descriptions of the individual chapters.

ORIGINS OF APPLIED GENERAL EQUILIBRIUM MODELING

Numerical applications of general equilibrium began with the work of Arnold Harberger (1962) and Leif Johansen (1960). Harberger used a model with two production sectors, one corporate and one noncorporate, calibrated to U.S. data from the 1950s, to calculate the incidence of the U.S. corporate income tax. Johansen used a model with nineteen production sectors, calibrated to Norwegian data from 1950, to identify the sources of economic growth in Norway over the period 1948–53. Both linearized the model and solved it analytically without worrying whether an equilibrium of the original nonlinear model actually existed near the benchmark equilibrium. Neither Harberger nor Johansen raised the possibility of multiple equilibria in the model or attempted to check for multiplicity in any way. Interestingly, in many of the more recent contributions to AGE, proofs of existence are also forgone, and instead a computational algorithm is presented, which, in practice, converges to an approximate equilibrium, given some specified measures for closeness of approximation. The check for multiplicity, if at all attempted, is often rudimentary – it is simply whether the algorithm, starting from different initial positions, converges to the same or different final positions.

The first rigorous approach to developing a computational algorithm that was guaranteed to find equilibria to any desired degree of approximation dates to the pioneering work of Herbert Scarf, first published in 1967. Although Scarf himself did not ever put together an AGE model and solve it for its equilibrium using his algorithm, he clearly had applications in mind. In fact, describing his involvement in the computation of equilibrium, Scarf (2002) has this to say about the numerical example with six commodities and eight activities in his 1967 paper (Scarf 1967a):

The example was meant to suggest to my colleagues, at Yale and elsewhere, that these novel numerical techniques might be useful in assessing consequences for the economy of a change in the economic environment, or in a major policy variable – to engage in comparative statics where the equilibrium model was too large to solve graphically or by hand.

He adds that:

... it was some time before this suggestion was taken seriously. We were in the 1960s, in the era of large Keynesian macro models in which specific scarce resources and relative prices were not included; there was, in the air, a suggestion that the economy could actually be fine-tuned by prescient economic advisors.

It turned out that building large macro econometric models would no longer engage academic macroeconomists, although private economic forecasters and some public agencies continue to use such models. Whether this development is to be applauded or regretted, it is a fact. In contrast, the use of AGE models has grown far beyond what Scarf might have foreseen in 1967.

We would like to supplement the intellectual history of AGE modeling, narrated by Arrow in his paper, with an account of the contributions of Scarf and his students at Yale to this history, drawing on the account in Scarf (2002). Kenneth Arrow and Gerard Debreu (1954) and Lionel McKenzie (1959) provided a careful definition of a competitive equilibrium, a rigorous proof of its existence under certain sufficient conditions, and a characterization of the equilibrium (often called the two fundamental theorems of neoclassical welfare economics) and its extension to cover transactions over time and involving uncertainty. The first fundamental theorem established that the set of competitive allocations without lump sum redistribution is a subset of Pareto efficient allocations. The second theorem shows that with lump sum redistributions, any Pareto efficient allocation can be sustained as a competitive equilibrium, thus the set of competitive allocations and the set of Pareto efficient allocations are the same, once lump sum redistributions are allowed. In 1881, Francis Edgeworth had developed the idea of the core as the set of allocations upon which no coalition of agents in the economy can improve, in the sense of doing better for all of its members by an alternate allocation in an economy of its own with its own endowments and technology. The core is obviously a subset of the set of Pareto efficient allocations, but in general, the core is much smaller than the Pareto efficient set. Debreu and Scarf (1963) proved a deeper result than the first welfare theorem by showing that the core converges to the set of competitive allocations – without lump sum income redistributions – as the economy is replicated.

The issue of whether there is a mechanism that will lead an economy to a competitive equilibrium is related to the development of an algorithm to compute equilibrium. Léon Walras, the founding father of general equilibrium theory, had proposed in 1874 a process that he called *tâtonnement*, or groping, to find an equilibrium. Paul Samuelson later formalized this *tâtonnement* process as a system of differential equations. This process raises the price of a good in positive excess demand and lowers the price of a good in negative excess demand. Research in the late 1950s by Kenneth Arrow, H. D. Block, and Leonid Hurwicz (1959) and by Hirofumi Uzawa (1960) established that the Walrasian *tâtonnement* process for an exchange economy was globally stable provided either that the market excess demands exhibited gross substitutability or that they satisfied the weak axiom of revealed preference. Unfortunately, although gross substitutability in the excess demand of each individual consumer ensures that it holds also for the aggregate market excess demand, it is not satisfied for individual demand functions that exhibit some complementarity, however modest. On the other hand, although the weak axiom is satisfied by individual excess demands, it need not be satisfied by aggregate excess demands. In 1960, Scarf produced the first examples of global instability of the competitive equilibrium woven around preferences that exhibit complementarity. Scarf's examples come as no surprise now, because a later series of papers by Hugo Sonnenschein (1973), Rolf Mantel (1974) (a student of Scarf), and Gerard Debreu (1974) showed that, with a sufficient number of consumers, aggregate excess demand is essentially arbitrary and hence the behavior of the *tâtonnement* can be made to follow arbitrary curves. At the time, however, Scarf's (1960) paper had considerable influence in discouraging enthusiasm for the *tâtonnement* process. It also had the effect of focusing Scarf's own attention on the need for developing an algorithm for calculating competitive equilibria.

Scarf had first thought that computation of competitive equilibria could be found by finding allocations in the core of an economy and then replicating. He had developed an algorithm for finding allocations in the core (Scarf 1967c) using techniques similar to those developed by Carlton Lemke and Joseph Howson (1964) for finding Nash equilibria for two-person non-zero-sum games. Scarf then developed an alternative algorithm avoiding the core and closely related to Sperner's argument demonstrating Brouwer's fixed point theorem. This later work was the beginning of homotopy, or path-following, computational algorithms for calculating equilibria. Scarf himself later made important contributions to the theory and implantation of these algorithms, most notably in his joint work with Curtis Eaves (Eaves and Scarf 1976).

Some students of Scarf at Yale – Terje Hansen, Timothy Kehoe, Rolf Mantel, Michael Todd, and Ludo van der Heyden – wrote Ph.D. theses on computation or on theoretical topics related to computation. But Scarf encouraged even more of his students to search for ways in which to apply general equilibrium theory and these novel computational techniques. Indeed, there is what many would characterize as the Yale school of economists, who use AGE models to do economic policy analysis. Students of Scarf in this group include Andrew Feltenstein, Timothy Kehoe, Ana Matirena-Mantel, Marcus Miller, Donald Richter, Jaime Serra-Puche, John Shoven, John Spencer, and John Whalley. A feature that characterizes the research of the Yale school of AGE modeling – and distinguishes it from some other AGE modelers – is its heavy interaction with the general equilibrium theory of Arrow, Debreu, McKenzie, and Scarf. Members of the Yale school rely on rigorous theory to guide the development of their models, and they carefully modify and develop new theory when the existing theory is not adequate for their particular applications.

As applications of AGE modeling progressed, they were taken up by governments and international organizations around the world. The World Bank, the World Trade Organization, the International Monetary Fund, and government agencies in the United States, Australia, Canada, Mexico, the United Kingdom, the Netherlands, and many other countries all had general equilibrium models. The field of AGE modeling as an operational tool in government and policy circles was launched.

CONTRIBUTIONS IN THIS VOLUME

We have grouped the contributions into parts in order to bring coherence to our discussion and to draw on any overlaps among them. Part 1 has two chapters. The first, by Kenneth Arrow, is an expanded version of his talk at the conference dinner. It is a fascinating recapitulation of the intellectual history of general equilibrium theory and its use in AGE. The chapter of Herbert Scarf and Charles Wilson follows Arrow's chapter. It is on pure general equilibrium theory as applied to the classic Ricardian model of international trade. It provides elegant proofs for the uniqueness (assumed by most trade economists) of equilibrium for the model under the well-known sufficient condition of gross substitution in aggregate demand. One of the proofs relies on the fixed point index theorem developed by Timothy Kehoe (1980) in his Ph.D. thesis, written under Scarf's supervision. Kehoe's work had been inspired by the results obtained by Eaves and Scarf (1976).

Part 2 consists of two chapters on developments in computation methods. The first, by Kenneth Judd, presents an alternative algorithm for solving dynamic stochastic models, combining convergent methods for solving finite systems of equations with convergent dynamic programming. The second, by Michel Ferris, Steven Dirkse, and Alexander Meeraus, describes a new suite of methods for solving problems that combine facets of optimization and complementarity using a unifying framework of mathematical programs with equilibrium constraints.

Part 3 is devoted to applications in macroeconomics and finance. It consists of four chapters. Edward Prescott reviews the role of nonconvexities at the micro level in macro business cycles. In contrast to a long tradition of viewing business fluctuations as disequilibrium phenomena, in contemporary stochastic dynamic general equilibrium macroeconomic models, of which Prescott's is one, the cycles emerge from the stochastic processes that are essential elements of the models. Thus random, but persistent, changes in the factors that determine the level of output give rise to fluctuations that approximate those observed in real economies. The chapter by Lars Ljungqvist and Thomas Sargent both complements and challenges the results presented by Prescott. It shows that models in which unemployment is frictional have very different implications for the data than do models, such as that of Prescott, in which lotteries transform the economic environment into a standard Arrow–Debreu–McKenzie general equilibrium setting. The chapter by Makoto Nakajima and José-Víctor Ríos-Rull focuses on borrowing and lending by individual agents with endogenous default and credit limits and explores the extent to which aggregate events are amplified or smoothed by bankruptcy filings. The parameters of this model are estimated using U.S. data and the model replicates aggregate fluctuation of the U.S. economy. The chapter by Alosio Araujo and Mário Páscoa also models default penalties and collateral and credit restrictions. It extends the received theory of general equilibrium with incomplete markets that has been used to analyze the stochastic volatility of asset prices and the risk premium puzzle to incorporate default, credit risk, and institutions to deal with them. This chapter, which is theoretical, shows that Ponzi schemes and asset price bubbles may occur. The authors provide sufficient conditions for the nonexistence of bubbles in equilibrium.

Part 4 consists of three chapters on applications of AGE to public finance, development, and climate change. Dale Jorgensen and Kun-Young Yun employ an aggregate dynamic general equilibrium model of the U.S. economy to analyze the economic impact of alternative tax reform proposals. Equilibrium is characterized by an intertemporal price system that clears markets for labor, capital services, consumption goods, and investment goods. Starting from the base case solution of a unique steady state for the tax policy existing in 1996 and the associated transition to that steady state from initial conditions of 1996, they solve for the unique transition path following tax reform to compare social welfare associated with each policy proposal with that in the base case. Jorgenson and Yun find a substantial welfare gain from a reform that they call efficient taxation of income. This reform treats income sources symmetrically, reduces marginal rates, and retains progressivity. The chapter by François Bourguignon, Anne-Sophie Robilliard, and Sherman Robinson provides a methodology for linking a household-based micro simulation model of income generation from labor force participation and occupational choices, given wages and prices, with a sectoral AGE model that determines the commodity and factor prices in equilibrium.[2] The proposed methodology is illustrated with household survey data and sectoral data from Indonesia. The model is used to assess the impacts on income distribution of a terms-of-trade shock that reduces the export price of crude oil and processed oil products and of a shock that reduces external capital inflow by 30 percent. The simulations using the authors' methodology are compared to those from the use of a traditional methodology in which 9,800 sample households are aggregated into ten household types. The comparison suggests that the differences may be quite substantial, in one case even reversing the sign of the impact of the shock on inequality. The chapter by Alan S. Manne uses a ten-region, multiperiod (fifteen decades, starting from the base year of 2000), and multisector model to illustrate the controversial issues in the debate over the United Nations Framework on Climate Change of 1992 and the later Kyoto Protocol of 1997. It provides a perspective on emissions and on taxes to restrain these emissions. The implications of the use of alternative rates for discounting the future and the possible presence (or absence) of equity–efficiency trade-offs are explored.

Part 5 consists of an encyclopedic contribution by James Heckman, Rosa Matzkin, and Lars Nesheim. This chapter tackles the problem of estimation of hedonic models that price differentiated goods or services (such as that of labor) using an equilibrium framework. Because most goods and services traded in an economy are differentiated, understanding the structure of demand and supply of differentiated goods is essential for a normative analysis of policy proposals in such areas as education, occupational safety, and job training as well as a positive analysis of incorporating quality changes into price indices. This task seems daunting because the specification of preferences and technology in models with differentiated goods involves the characteristics of these goods rather than the goods themselves. Although potential applications of hedonic models are myriad, the authors point out that their application and development, except in certain special cases, have been hindered by computational difficulties, failure to exploit the implications of equilibrium in the hedonic model, and the widely held (but erroneous) belief that identification of structural parameters in a hedonic model is not possible using data from a single

---

[2] The authors are aware of and state explicitly that the methodology involves several ad hoc assumptions. For this and other reasons it is an open question whether the linked model is fully coherent.

market. Heckman, Matzkin, and Nesheim present analytical and computational results for two classes (scalar additive and nonadditive) of hedonic models that fill the gaps in the literature. They simulate and estimate examples of equilibrium and provide evidence on the performance of several estimation techniques. In many ways, the chapter is groundbreaking. It is distinct from other chapters in this volume in its systematic and internally consistent use of the concept of economic equilibrium (loosely speaking, prices clearing markets) and its precise implications for the distribution of the relevant latent variables so that alternative methods of estimation of underlying structural parameters can be conceived of and their performance assessed.

Part 6 is devoted to performance and policy use of AGE models. It consists of three chapters. The chapter by Timothy Kehoe is an evaluation post-NAFTA of the performances of three different multisectoral static AGE models that had been constructed to project ex ante the impact of NAFTA. His findings are sobering – these models drastically underestimated the impact of NAFTA on North American trade and failed to capture much of the relative impact on different sectors. Kehoe concludes that a new theoretical mechanism for generating large increases in trade in product categories with little or no previous trade (as, in fact, happened post-NAFTA) and an approach to capturing changes in productivity are needed for AGE models to project ex ante future outcomes reasonably well.

Since the 1980s, the inequality in the distribution of wages, particularly across workers of varying skills, has increased in the industrializaed countries. Two, not necessarily competing, sources for this trend have been proposed. One is the growth in trade of industrialized countries with labor-abundant less developed countries. The other is skill-biased technical change. Lisandro Abrego and John Whalley evaluate the relative contributions of the two sources to the observed increases in wage inequality in the United Kingdom between 1979 and 1995. They find that the contribution of the second source has been underestimated by other analysts and the contribution of the first is small. Interestingly, changes in factor endowments have played a major role in partially offsetting the contributions of the two sources.

Shantayanan Devarajan and Sherman Robinson survey the experience of the policy use of AGE models. The models have been used for assessing policies relating to international trade, public finance, agriculture, income distribution, and energy and environmental policy. The authors draw a distinction between "stylized models," which tend to be small, narrowly focused, and capture a particular mechanism through which policy influences derived outcomes, and "applied models," which are much larger, capture important institutional characteristics of the economy being modeled, and encompass a wider spectrum of issues. In stylized models, the link between policy changes and their outcomes is transparent, whereas in the applied models, the link is often difficult to see. Such lack of transparency can dissuade policy makers from using these models, even though they are based on a more realistic description of the economy and a better recognition of often complex policy linkages. The authors list a set of desiderata for ensuring the success of the policy use of AGE models and recommend the complementary use of applied and stylized models to enhance the effectiveness of both in policy debates.

KEY ISSUES IN APPLIED GENERAL EQUILIBRIUM MODELING

As AGE modeling has grown over the years, it has frequently displaced more conventional econometric modeling in policy analysis, but it has also encountered fresh problems. Its great strength has been its ability to provide numerical assessments of the equity and efficiency implications of micro policy change, something hard to do with conventional econometric models. On the one hand, in situations of simultaneous changes in several policies, in which interaction among policies of different countries could be significant, there is no alternative to AGE for assessing the effects of policy changes. On the other hand, many questions arise, and indeed have been raised, over the empirical plausibility of AGE model results.

These questions range from the observations that the particular equilibrium structure and functional forms used will, to a large degree, predetermine the results and that the key parameter values used (especially elasticities) are known with little certainty to the claim that there has been little or no ex post validation of model projections. When taken together with the claim that, in practice, actual models are often uneasy compromises compared to their theoretically pure parents, such questions have led some to doubt that anything of value can be found from the numerical calculations resulting from these models.

The relevant point for comparison in evaluating this work is the next best alternative and not some absolute standard devised in a mistaken analogy to the natural sciences. Policy makers find model calculations useful because for the questions they ask the only other alternative is guess-work, which is unlikely to be well informed. In contrast, well-specified AGE models are internally consistent and force anyone who is not satisfied with their results to think through the reasons for dissatisfaction. Is the source of dissatisfaction the unsatisfactory structure of the model, the values of its parameters, or the interpretation of model results? The interactive process of modeling, generating results, and analyzing the potential reasons that the results can or cannot be accepted raises the level of argument in policy process. Such a discussion avoids the pretense of providing or being able to provide definitive answers to policy questions. This is necessary if policy makers are to find AGE models a useful tool.

Nonetheless, there can be no denying that work on AGE modeling has both raised and faced many challenges and that these point the way forward for the field. Calibration inevitably implies subjective judgment by the calibrator. How is this to be squared with econometric rigor?

Ex post validation and the use of models for ex post analysis, rather than only ex ante policy evaluation, are another challenge. The claims made for the empirical validity of or support for calibrated dynamic, stochastic, general equilibrium models of the business cycle are contentious.[3]

Elasticity parameters and the poor state of parameter estimation in empirical economics are another problem area. Statistical work in economics, following Karl Popper and Milton Friedman, still is strongly associated with hypothesis testing rather than estimation, but AGE models are dense with parameters, the values of which have to be calibrated if econometric estimates are unavailable. Often no estimates exist of required parameters, so they are guessed; or multiple estimates exist that are contradictory. In the econometric literature different estimation procedures, different data series, and different theoretical concepts are used, making it very difficult to use estimates drawn from the literature.

Another problem is the potential for misuse of models. The rather baroque structure of some of the models leads to a problem in clearly identifying the links between policy changes and their outcomes. This nontransparency leads nonmodelers even to suggest that models have been deviously constructed backward in such a way as to support and corroborate particular prior positions on an issue, and as such models are viewed by them as little more than tools of propaganda. While the modelers would no doubt dismiss such claims as verging on the hysterical, they can undermine the political legitimacy of model results. AGE models, while becoming central to policy analysis around the world, have critics as well. This poses challenges for the years ahead.

ON TO NUMERICAL SIMULATION

AGE modeling is being used ever more widely. In economic theory the inability to obtain unambiguous general results even under fairly strong assumptions on the model's structure has led to the use of illustrative calculations based on quasi-plausible parameters. Economics is evolving like other disciplines (astrophysics, life sciences) so that the numerical representation of theoretical constraints and the resulting implications are becoming major issues.

How does a theoretical structure or model behave under plausible numerical representation and parameterizations? If theory is silent as to the sign of the effect of a change, what does the simulation suggest? Is the effect big or is it small, and by what criteria? Why do the observed sign and size of effect occur? Are these effects plausible? How are we sure there are no coding or conceptual errors? Can results be replicated? How robust are they?

---

[3] There is a deeper problem with the use of estimated parameters from the literature on AGE models. Many estimated parameters, including some of the elasticities, are not what Robert Lucas calls "deep" – invariant parameters of tastes and technology. This means that their estimates are subject to the Lucas critique that they are policy-regime specific, so that values estimated with data from one regime cannot be used for analysis of data from a different regime. Even if the data are treated as representing an equilibrium, the restrictions on parameters that an equilibrium implies are rarely imposed in estimation. The paper by Heckman, Matzkin, and Nesheim in this volume stresses the important role in estimation played by such conditions.

These then become the primary issues for the emerging field of computational economics – which is loosely related to the field of AGE modeling – a field that is slowly becoming dominant in such areas as macroeconomics and will, in our view, increasingly engulf all of economics. The goal is to use numerical methods to assess the implications of analytical structures, both in policy and analysis and for understanding the world around us. Because this work is necessarily subjective in design and execution, the credibility of modelers is key. Their ability to communicate what they have done, why they have done it, and what they conclude is absolutely central.

Some years ago, Peter Wiles (1962) aptly characterized the then debate on computational methods in economics as the unsolved problem of "the perfect computation of perfect competition." Herbert Scarf's algorithm and thesis advising solved it and achieved in large measure the perfection that Wiles imagined. The challenge for the next generation of AGE modelers is to take Scarf's achievement one stage further. We are confident that the chapters in this volume will set the stage for meeting it.

REFERENCES

K. J. Arrow, H. D. Block, and L. Hurwicz (1959), "On the Stability of Competitive Equilibrium, II," *Econometrica* 27: 82–109.

K. J. Arrow and G. Debreu (1954), "Existence of Equilibrium for a Competitive Economy," *Econometrica* 22: 265–90.

G. Debreu (1974), "Excess Demand Functions," *Journal of Mathematical Economics* 1: 15–23.

G. Debreu and H. E. Scarf (1963), "A Limit Theorem on the Core of an Economy," *International Economic Review* 4: 235–46.

B. C. Eaves and H. E. Scarf (1976), "The Solution of Systems of Piecewise Linear Equations," *Mathematics of Operations Research* 1: 1–27.

A. C. Harberger (1962), "The Incidence of the Corporate Income Tax," *Journal of Political Economy* 70: 215–40.

L. Johansen (1960), *A Multi-sectoral Study of Economic Growth*. Amsterdam: North-Holland.

T. J. Kehoe (1980), "An Index Theorem for General Equilibrium Models with Production," *Econometrica* 48: 1211–32.

L. McKenzie (1959), "On the Existence of General Equilibrium for a Competitive Market," *Econometrica* 27: 54–71.

C. E. Lemke and J. T. Howson (1964), "Equilibrium Points of Bi-matrix Games," *SIAM Journal of Applied Mathematics* 12: 413–23.

R. R. Mantel (1974), "On the Characterization of Aggregate Excess Demand," *Journal of Economic Theory* 7: 348–53.

H. E. Scarf (1960), "Some Examples of Global Instability of the Competitive Equilibrium," *International Economic Review* 1: 157–72.

(1967a), "The Approximation of Fixed Points of a Continuous Mapping," *SIAM Journal of Applied Mathematics* 15: 1328–43.

(1967b), "On the Computation of Equilibrium Prices." In *Ten Economic Studies in the Tradition of Irving Fischer*, edited by W. J. Fellner. New York: Wiley, 207–30.

(1967c), "The Core of an *n* Person Game," *Econometrica* 35: 50–69.

(2002), "The Computation of Economic Equilibria," Yale University.

H. E. Scarf with T. Hansen (1973), *The Computation of Economic Equilibria.* New Haven, CT: Yale University Press.

H. E. Scarf and J. B. Shoven (1984), *Applied General Equilibrium Analysis.* Cambridge: Cambridge University Press.

H. Sonnenschein (1973), "Do Walras' Identity and Continuity Characterize the Class of Community Excess Demand Functions?" *Journal of Economic Theory* 6: 345–54.

H. Uzawa (1960), "Walras' Tatonnement in the Theory of Exchange," *Review of Economic Studies* 27: 182–94.

P. J. Wiles (1962), *The Political Economy of Communism.* Cambridge, MA: Harvard University Press.

1 Personal Reflections on Applied General Equilibrium Models

Kenneth J. Arrow

The applied (or computable) general equilibrium (CGE) model is one of today's standard tools of policy analysis. As with all economic policy tools and prescription drugs, its use requires great caution. Nevertheless, in all cases where the repercussions of proposed policies are widespread, there is no real alternative to CGE. If it is not used explicitly, the tools used will contain implicit implications for remote implications, if only to deny them.

The ability to deploy CGE models is the outcome of research going back at least 130 years and involving very disparate lines of inquiry. Economic theory and the vastly improved availability of economic data have played basic roles. But other research inputs have been equally crucial: improvements in computing power and the development of algorithms for computing equilibria. The decisive step in the last direction has been the pioneering work of Herbert Scarf. If one examined a time series of development and publication of applied general equilibrium models, I am sure that there would be a marked régime change following Scarf's paper (1967) and especially his monograph (with the collaboration of Terje Hansen) (1973).

Let me give a partial account of and reflections on the development of applied general equilibrium models. This is not a true scholarly account but relies primarily on my own impressions over the years. It originated as an after-dinner speech and should be regarded as a written version of one. In Section 1, I define the subject matter. Section 2 defends the need for complete systems in economic analysis and, in particular, policy formation. Section 3 shows how the principles developed for static models generalize, at least ideally, into an understanding of the roles of time and uncertainty. Section 4 goes into other topics historically associated with complete empirical models, the model as a basis for statistical inference, and the new types of time-series data. Finally, Section 5 reviews very briefly the crucial role of solution algorithms in the usefulness of CGE.

1.1. THE DEFINIENDUM

Let us spell out the complete name of the subject of this inquiry: applied general competitive equilibrium model. What does each word in that mouthful mean?

1.1.1. "Applied"

Over the years, general equilibrium models have been applied to many different applied questions. In my view, the intellectual history goes back to studies of economic fluctuations, or "business cycles," as we used to call them. When I was a graduate student (from the viewpoint of current students, that would be just at the end of the Stone Age), the most important problem of economics, in the view of many of our faculty, was the occurrence of business cycles. Admittedly, this was at Columbia in the early 1940s, which was rather different than Chicago or Harvard in its emphases. What was not taught by my professors was the exciting European work on complete systems of the economy (dynamic macroeconomic models, as we would say today), of which the intellectual forebear was the Norwegian, Ragnar Frisch (see, for example, 1931, 1933), and the great practioner and empirical exponent was Jan Tinbergen (his first major work was a study of the Dutch economy (1937), and his most famous work was the study of business cycle theories and their testing, mostly on United States data, done under the auspices of the League of Nations (1939)). These are, I believe, the first applied general (i.e., complete) models in the literature. Their logic is more in the tradition that developed into macroeconomics than in the more microeconomic analysis that has underlain most of what we now call applied general equilibrium analysis.

As is not surprising, the focus of application shifted with shifts in the focus of economic inquiry generally. Short-term economy-wide forecasts have never lost their important role. In the postwar period, Lawrence Klein was an early leader (Klein 1952, Klein and Goldberger 1955). But other interests grew, particularly in economic growth. At a more microeconomic level, there have been elaborate studies of the effects of tax and welfare policies (the pioneer study using Scarf's algorithm was that of Shoven and Whalley 1972), of changes in foreign trade (see, for example, the conference volume edited by Srinivasan and Whalley 1986), on economic development (conference volume edited by Mercenier and Srinivasan 1994), or of the effects of climate change and of policies to meet climate change (e.g., Manne, Mendlelsohn, and Richels 1995, Bovenberg and Goulder 1996).

1.1.2. "General"

As I have already hinted, the word "general" is the most important one in the definition. It is a recognition that the economy is highly interdependent. More precisely, it is the claim that the equations defining the economy do not decompose in any useful way. The most famous and vigorous proponent of this view is, of course, Léon Walras (1874–7). His demand, repeated in all his successively more complicated models, was the need for as many equations as unknowns. Elementary as this demand is, it was not fulfilled in the classical economists, Adam Smith or David Ricardo. This is true even though their interests were definitely in a general equilibrium direction; they had little or no interest in individual markets but rather sought a general principle for determining relative prices of different commodities. John Stuart Mill, in this as other matters, is interestingly inconsistent. In his theory of domestic values, he strongly reasserted Ricardo's system, with its incomplete treatment, though on many specific points he showed an understanding of the logical problems of the system. In fact, some of his remarks, such as the proposition that rent of land in one use is a cost for an alternative use, are definitely steps toward a general equilibrium viewpoint. But in his theory of international values, he very explicitly recognizes that Ricardo's theory of comparative advantage simply does not answer the relevant questions. It does not provide a complete system. Mill's own theory of reciprocal demand is a true general equilibrium theory of international trade. I return to the need for a complete system in Section 1.2 below.

1.1.3. "Equilibrium"

Familiar though the concept of equilibrium is to economists, it has many subtleties, too many for extended comment here. Still, I can't help mentioning three. (1) For goods with some degree of durability (most manufactured goods), a failure of the equality of supply and demand may simply show up in inventory changes. The disequilibrium will show up as "unintended inventories." Unfortunately, this is not a variable that can be observed. (2) Disequilibria in some markets seem to be clearly observed. I refer to unemployed labor and idle capital equipment. Much effort has gone into models that maintain that all unemployment is voluntary and therefore explained by the supply curve of labor. I think this is clearly false. Unemployment of capital goods appears as variations in the capacity utilization rate, unfortunately a measure with no clear meaning. Nevertheless, this phenomenon is also real. (3) Under imperfect competition, the usual (Nash) definition of equilibrium no longer amounts to equating supply and demand. Indeed, the possibility of price discrimination means that there is not even a unique price for a given economy. (4) Restrictions on foreign trade frequently take the form of quotas. The last two items lead to the next word,

1.1.4. "Competitive"

Certainly, the essential perspective on the world of CGE models is indeed a world of perfect competition. That does not mean that individual relations in the models do not reflect imperfections. There may be a wage floor, to permit the possibility of unemployment. There might be (though there rarely is) a recognition of quotas as restrictions on foreign trade. In the "dual economy" models of economic development, the ratio of urban to rural wages may be taken as fixed. Of course, taxes are explicitly modeled.

A counterpart of the emphasis on competition is that prices are the equilibrating variables. To the extent that price rigidities exist, of course, quantities take their role as equilibrating variables. That is usually taken as the hallmark of Keynesian models (see Patinkin [1982, Part One]). The models oriented to practical short-term forecasting have this characteristic much more than the typical CGE.

The importance of imperfect competition has been emphasized by some economists since the days of Cournot (1838). The emphasis rose with the works of the 1930s (Chamberlin 1933, Robinson 1933) and intensified to become a major part of the literature with the modernized Cournot theory, known as "non-cooperative games" (Nash 1950 and the vast literature in which Nash equilibrium is used to characterize issues ranging from classical industrial organization to financial crises). The most important novel development in microeconomics in recent years has been the recognition (by economic agents and by economists) of asymmetric information as a basic element in economic interaction. This development is closely related to that of game theory (especially in the work of Harsanyi 1967–8) but has been compatible with some forms of competitive equilibrium (for example, Radner 1968, Grossman 1976, and Rothschild and Stiglitz 1976). I think it fair to say that none of these developments have been reflected in CGE models. The reason is clear. Economists have not developed any successful way of going from the individual decisions and outcomes of small-group interactions to the economy as an interacting whole. Hence useful theoretical analysis of a general economy-wide model and CGEs share a common root in traditional competitive analysis.

1.1.5. "Model"

Every analysis is a model.

1.2. WHY COMPLETE SYSTEMS?

1.2.1. Tinbergen

The Tinbergen studies mentioned earlier are, I believe, the first examples of estimated complete systems. The League of Nations study was certainly by far the most elaborate piece of empirical work in economics to that time. It required a team of researchers centered in Geneva. Some idea of the intellectual inputs may be gleaned from the fact that two of the researchers were Tjalling Koopmans and Leonid Hurwicz (both later associated with the Cowles Foundation for Research in Economics or its predecessors).

A typical equation explained one of the endogenous variables in terms of other contemporary endogenous variables, their lagged values, and exogenous variables. Tinbergen's basic approach was to use proximate determinanats (e.g., of consumption). The more indirect effects were expressed by the system taken as a whole. Because all relations were linear, the only algorithm required to solve the system for the purposes of prediction (including prediction of the effects of alternative policies) was one of the standard methods for solving linear equations. (In the days of desk calculators, that was not such a trivial task, as I can painfully testify.)

1.2.2. Completeness for Determinateness

Tinbergen, like most (virtually all?) mathematically minded economists, simply took it as obvious that making any kind of prediction requires completeness. Having fewer equations than unknowns simply means that the variables are undetermined, though they will lie in a lower dimensional space. What is usually meant by an alternative to a complete system is not a genuinely incomplete system. It is rather one in which the system is completed by assuming that some variables will not change or will change in very simple ways, not analyzed according to usual economic principles. For example, in foreign trade models, the assumption of a "small open economy" means that foreign prices remain unchanged despite the policy change.

1.2.3. Consistency of Viewpoint

A simple implication of general equilibrium theory is the linkage of different markets through budget constraints and through consistency of motivation for behavior in different sectors. Thus, in the analysis of demand functions for different commodities, we should insist (a) that the demands for all commodities depend on the same variables (prices and income or endowments) and (b) that these functions satisfy an adding-up condition. Usually, these conditions taken together imply that the relations must be nonlinear.

Milton Friedman has frequently criticized the Walrasian approach as being too abstract for scientific and policy use. How does he manage to produce macro-economic policy recommendations? We certainly can identify two of his key relations, which are developed independent of each other. One is the quantity theory of money: the demand for money (in real terms) is proportional to real income,

$$M/p = aY,$$

where M is money holding, p is price, and Y is real income. The second is his famous theory of the demand for consumption goods, that it is proportional to *permanent* income,

$$C = bY^p,$$

where C is consumption and Y^p is permanent income. Can these relations be made consistent with a budget constraint? It is hard to think of this in any static system. Presumably, at any one moment of time, there is a holding of assets, perhaps money and some kind of security, say short-term loans. These, together with current income, are to be allocated among the two assets and current consumption. Demand for increments in the security will constitute saving. If the above relations really represent the demand for money and for consumption, the investment implied by the budget constraints will be an odd relation indeed. Although Friedman does present a complete system in an attempt to isolate his differences with Keynesianism (Friedman 1974, pp. 29–30), it is very hard to identify the individual equations with demand equations or indeed to see what budget constraint is being satisfied. (In this presentation, he does not differentiate between current and permanent income.)

1.2.4. The Price of Completeness

Everything comes at a price, and completeness is no exception. As a matter of general principle, some areas are better studied than others, perhaps those more capable of being studied or perhaps those that seem most important. A complete system means that there must be some basis for every part of the economy. Some parts have been less studied, and therefore the relations used in the model have less basis.

The construction of an applied model is usually motivated by interest in some particular area, such as foreign trade or tax or welfare policy. The model will usually be very detailed in the area of interest and sketchy elsewhere. Less attention will be paid to other areas, given resource limitations (intellectual and economic) on the modeling process.

The unevenness of coverage was pointed out long ago by Marc Nerlove (1965) when surveying some macroeconomic models, but the same principle will apply to models with a more microeconomic orientation. The seriousness of this problem depends precisely on how important the completeness condition is. If the repercussion effects on the sector of interest through the incompletely analyzed sectors are secondary to the effects within the sector, then errors induced in this way will be small. But that is precisely the case where completeness is not really needed.

1.3. THE EXTENSION INTO TIME AND UNCERTAINTY

Let me turn in this part to theoretical rather than empirical models. They have to some extent already motivated some empirical work, but they offer opportunities still incompletely explored.

1.3.1. Equilibrium over Time

Most CGE models have tended to be static in nature; in this they reflect not only a need for simplification but also the presence of observable markets. Still there was elaborated as long ago as 1929 (Lindahl 1929; 1939, Chapter 1) a concept of equilibrium of markets not only in the present but also in the future. This theory was elaborated by Hicks (1939) in the form in which it is generally known. Hicks's work had a profound effect on the entire next generation of economic theorists.

Households and firms consider the future as well as the present; that is, utility functions depend on future as well as present consumption magnitudes, and production relations involve inputs and outputs at different times. The economic agents have expectations of future prices and use them in making plans. These plans in turn determine actions in current markets, including, of course, purchase and sale of securities.

The fullest version is logically equivalent to what is now known as "rational expectations"; that is, expectations of future prices are in fact correct. Models like this are certainly beginning to be used in applied work (Manne et al. 1995, Bovenberg and Goulder 1996, and others).

1.3.2. Equilibrium with Uncertainty

The simple idea of Lindahl and Hicks of labeling commodities by date to permit a joint equilibrium for present and future invited an analogous construction for handling uncertainty. The incorporation of uncertainty into general equilibrium had long been recognized among those who cared about such things as a major unsolved problem. In fact, it required only using the concept of the *state of the world*, as used by probability theorists in defining a random variable. All that was needed was to index commodities by the state of the world in which they were to be produced and/or delivered (see Arrow 1953 for a one-period exchange economy and the complete generalization by Debreu 1959, Chap. VII).

1.3.3. The Curse of Dimensionality

One obvious problem with extending models over time and especially under uncertainty is the sheer increase in the dimensionality of the commodity space. The modeler is concerned about thinking through the numerous equations; the numerical analyst is worried about computations whose elementary steps rise rapidly, perhaps exponentially, with the number of commodities. Obviously, we will always pursue models up to the point where they become too expensive in time and other costs, so it will always appear that computational limits are blocking analysis. There are, of course, alternatives; a prominent one is taking the fixed point in the space of individuals (Negishi's formulation, 1960). Of course, the literal number of individuals, now and in the future, is very large, but the analyst groups them into a few large classes, within each of which there is identity of preferences and endowments. If we take the "dynastic" approach, so that all individuals live forever, then the number of individuals and therefore the dimensionality of the problem remains unchanged when the model is extended in time or to take care of uncertainty. This approach has been exploited in macroeconomic models (Stokey and Lucas 1989).

1.3.4. Securities Markets

In the treatment of uncertainty, there has been a serious philosophical and practical issue. Is it even possible to enumerate all the possible events, especially when an event is regarded as a path in time? In practice, both theoretical and emprical, the observables are considered to be securities whose payoffs depend on the chance events. Under suitable Markovian assumptions as to the evolution of uncertainty, the dimensionality of the commodity space at each time can be held constant.

1.4. THE COMPLETE MODEL: STATISTICAL INFERENCE AND DATA SOURCES

1.4.1. Simultaneous Equations Estimation

One of the most interesting and certainly important consequences of the emphasis on complete systems was the realization of the implications of this viewpoint for statistical inference.

Mathematical statistics in the 1930s was wracked by considerable controversy on fundamentals between R. A. Fisher on one hand and Jerzy Neyman and E. S. Pearson on the other. But both really agreed on the way a statistical problem should be formulated: given a stochastic model with some unknown parameters and a body of data which was assumed to satisfy the model, make some statements about the parameters (estimates or tests of hypotheses). It was in that context that Frisch (1938) observed that the existence of simultaneous relations among variables introduced new elements and that standard regression analysis was not adequate. A clear formulation and analysis was presented in the path-breaking work of Trygve Haavelmo (1943, 1944) and elaborated in the later work of the Cowles Commission by Tjalling Koopmans, Theodore Anderson, Herman Rubin, and others (Koopmans 1950).

1.4.2. Time Series and National Income Accounting

The proliferation of large-scale models, whether macroeconomic or CGE, has been driven to a considerable extent by the availability of national income data. Tinbergen's works in the 1930s lacked this basis and made do with a lot of proxy variables, based on the same theoretical principles. Klein's model (1952) was,

I think, the first to exploit the national income data which the United States government was then producing. It is tempting and certainly cheap to use a public good such as national income data. One consequence has been to force the models into a bed of Procrustes. National income data depend on a particular model of the economy (at least in a broad way) and omit large areas. For example, externalities are not well represented. There are also problems of aggregation. Either it is necessary to modify the national income data to reflect these additional elements, as proposed a long time ago by William Nordhaus and James Tobin (1972), or we simply have to use additional variables not in the national income data.

1.5. SOLUTION ALGORITHMS

1.5.1. Solving Systems of Nonlinear Equations

Even the simplest macroeconomic models generally had some nonlinear element. I have not tried to reread the early literature to see how they were solved, but some kind of successive linear approximations, essentially some variation of Newton's method, seems to have been standard.

1.5.2. Algorithms: Need They Always Converge?

Somewhere about 1970, I remember talking with a student at Harvard who was using a CGE model for a developing country (all of four equations, if I recall corrrectly). He was very good at numerical analysis and proceeded by adding an error term to each of the four equations. He then sought to minimize the sum of the squares of the errors, eventually reaching zero. In the middle of his work, I showed him one of Scarf's working papers which had just come to me. Having already programmed his method, he wasn't happy about reconsidering. In fact, he succeeded in solving his system in his way. He had an algorithm that certainly might have failed. But it did have the property that you knew you had solved the problem when you did. In solving a set of equations, that is of course trivial.

I believe that in fact a good many systems were solved by *ad hoc* methods of one kind or another, methods where convergence was not assured

1.5.3. Convenient Function Forms

Of course, a standard approach is to pick functional forms that permit easy manipulation. Sometimes it is possible to solve even nonlinear equations in a fairly explicit manner. But the straitjacket can be very restrictive indeed.

1.5.4. The Liberating Power of the Scarf Algorithm

What the Scarf algorithm did was to give a license to develop CGE models according to economic logic and empirical validity. The author did not have to modify the model to consider tractability or computability. Once completed, the model might be solved in some way that, if it worked, would be less demanding computationally. But the author or authors knew that there was a way that would always work and that, with steadily and rapidly increasing computational power, would likely be practically feasible. It was this knowledge that generated the subsequent explosion in applied general equilibrium models.

REFERENCES

Arrow, K. J. 1953. Le rôle des valeurs boursières dans la répartition la meilleure des risques. Pp. 41–7 in *Économétrie*. Colloques Internationaux du Centre National de la Recherche Scientifique, vol. XI. Paris: France.

Bovenberg, A. L., and L. H. Goulder. 1996. Optimal environmental taxation in the presence of other taxes: General equilibrium analyses. *American Economic Review* 86: 985–1000.

Chamberlin, G. H. 1933. *Theory of Monopolistic Competition*. Cambridge, MA: Harvard University Press.

Cournot, A. A. 1838. *Recherches sur les principes mathématiques de la théorie des Richesses*. Paris: Hachette.

Debreu, G. 1959. *Theory of Value*. New York: Wiley.

Friedman, M. 1974. A theoretical framework for monetary analysis. Pp. 1–62 in *Milton Friedman's Monetary Framework*, ed. R. G. Gordon. Chicago: University of Chicago Press.

Frisch, R. 1931. The interrelation between capital production and consumer-taking. *Journal of Political Economy* 39: 646–54.

    1933. Propagation problems and impulse problems in dynamic economics. Pp. 171–205 in *Economic Essays in Honour of Gustav Cassel*. London: Allen & Unwin.

    1938. Statistical vs. theoretical relations in macrodynamics. Circulated as part of R. Frisch, T. Haavelmo, T. C. Koopmans, and J. Tinbergen, Autonomy of economic relations, Memorandum of Universitets Socialokonomiske Institut, Oslo, 6 November 1948. Mimeographed.

Grossman, S. 1976. On the efficiency of competitive stock markets where traders have diverse information. *Journal of Finance* 31: 573–84.

Haavelmo, T. 1943. The statistical implications of a system of simultaneous equations. *Econometrica* 11: 1–12.

    1944. The probability approach in econometrics. In supplement to *Econometrica* 12: iii–118.

Harsanyi, J. C. 1967–8. Games with incomplete information played by "Bayesian" players. *Management Science* 14: 154–82, 320–34.

Hicks, J. R. 1939. *Value and Capital*. Oxford: Clarendon Press.

Klein, L. 1952. *Economic Fluctuations in the United States 1921–1941*. New York: Wiley.

Klein, L., and A. S. Goldberger. 1955. *An Econometric Model of the United States 1929–1952*. Amsterdam: North-Holland.

Koopmans, T. C., ed. 1950. *Statistical Inference in Dynamic Economic Models*. New York: Wiley.

Lindahl, E. 1929. Prisbildungsproblemets Uppläggning från Kapitalteorisk synpunkt. *Ekonomisk Tidskrift* 31: 31–81.

1939. *Studies in the Theory of Money and Capital*. London: Allen & Unwin.

Manne, A. S., R. Mendelsohn, and R. Richels. 1995. MERGE: A model for evaluating regional and global effects of GHG reduction policies. *Energy Policy* 23: 17–34.

Mercenier, J., and T. N. Srinivasan. 1994. *Applied General Equilibrium and Economic Development: Present Achievements and Future Trends*. Ann Arbor, MI: University of Michigan Press.

Nash, J. F., Jr. 1950. Equilibrium in *n*-person games. *Proceedings of the National Academy of Sciences* 36: 48–9.

Negishi, T. 1960. Welfare economics and the existence of an equilibrium for a competitive economy. *Metroeconomica* 12: 92–7.

Nerlove, M. 1965. Two models of the British economy. *International Economic Review* 6: 442–91.

Nordhaus, W. D., and J. Tobin. 1972. Is growth obsolete? In *Economic Growth*. New York: National Bureau of Economic Research.

Patinkin, D. 1982. *Anticipations of the General Theory? And Other Essays on Keynes*. Chicago: University of Chicago Press.

Radner, R. 1968. Competitive equilibrium under uncertainty. *Econometrica* 36: 31–58.

Robinson, J. 1933. *The Economics of Imperfect Competition*. London: Macmillan.

Rothschild, M., and J. Stiglitz. 1976. Equilibrium and competitive insurance markets. *Quarterly Journal of Economics* 90: 629–49.

Scarf, H. 1967. The approximation of fixed points of a continuous mapping. *SIAM Journal of Applied Mathematics* 15: 1328–43.

Scarf, H. 1973. *The Computation of Economic Equilibria*. With the collaboration of T. Hansen. New Haven, CT: Yale University Press.

Shoven, J., and J. Whalley. 1972. A general equilibrium calculation of the effects of differential taxation of income from capital in the U.S. *Journal of Public Economics* 1: 281–322.

Srinivasan, T. N., and J. Whalley. 1986. *General Equilibrium Trade Policy Modeling*. Cambridge, MA/London: MIT Press.

Stokey, N., and R. E. Lucas, Jr. 1989. *Recursive Methods in Economic Dynamics*. With E. C. Prescott. Cambridge, MA: Harvard University Press.

Tinbergen, J. 1937. *An Econometric Approach to Business Cycle Models*. Paris: Herman.

1939. *Statistical Testing of Business-Cycle Theories*. 2 vols. Geneva: League of Nations.

Walras, L. 1874–7. *Éléments d'économie politique pure*. 2 vols. Lausanne: Corbaz.

2 Uniqueness of Equilibrium in the Multicountry Ricardo Model

Herbert E. Scarf and Charles A. Wilson

ABSTRACT: We present two arguments, one based on index theory, demonstrating that the multicountry Ricardo model has a unique competitive equilibrium if the aggregate demand functions exhibit gross substitutability. The result is somewhat surprising because the assumption of gross substitutability is sufficient for uniqueness in a model of exchange but not, in general, when production is included in the model.

It is well known that the competitive equilibrium is unique in a pure exchange economy when the market excess demand function satisfies the assumption of gross substitutability. However, if we introduce an arbitrary constant-returns-to-scale technology, a unique equilibrium is ensured only if the market excess demand function satisfies the weak axiom of revealed preference. Because gross substitutability does not imply the weak axiom, we can construct examples using an activity analysis model of production in which there are several equilibria even though the market demand functions display gross substitutability. The first such example can be found in Kehoe [4].

There are few results on how the assumption of the weak axiom may be relaxed, and uniqueness still prevail, as we impose conditions on the technology. One notable example is the case where there is only one primary factor of production and each productive activity produces a single good, using other produced goods as inputs in addition to the primary factor. In this case, the nonsubstitution theorem implies that the technology alone uniquely determines the equilibrium price. In the present paper we consider the Ricardo model in which there are many primary factors, the labor in each country, but in which each good is produced using labor alone. We demonstrate that the assumption of gross substitutability on the market excess demand is sufficient to guarantee the uniqueness of the competitive equilibrium for the multicountry Ricardo model. Two distinct proofs are discussed. The first is based on the induced properties of the excess demand for labor and requires that the gross substitutability condition holds everywhere. The second applies index theory directly to the market demand function for goods and requires only that the gross substitutability condition be satisfied at the equilibrium price.

24

To emphasize the applicability of our results to standard models of international trade, our analysis assumes a fixed supply of labor. In Wilson [5], both proofs of the uniqueness of equilibrium are extended to include models that incorporate a variable supply of labor, so long as the excess demand for labor and goods satisfies the gross substitutability assumption. That paper also extends the proof of Hildenbrand and Kirman [2] and provides a direct proof of the existence of equilibrium in a Ricardo model with gross substitutes that does not appeal to a fixed point theorem.

2.1. UNIQUENESS IN THE MODEL OF EXCHANGE

All of the arguments in this chapter are essentially more complicated versions of simple and well-known arguments for pure exchange economies. For this reason, we first review how they work in a model of pure exchange.

For any positive integer k, let R^k denote k-dimensional Euclidean space, and let $R^k_{++} \equiv \{x \in R^k : x_i > 0 \text{ for all } i\}$ denote the interior of the nonnegative orthant. Let $S^k_{++} = \{x \in R^k_{++} : \sum_{i=1}^k x_i = 1\}$ denote the interior of the unit simplex of dimension $k - 1$. For any $x, y \in R^k$, we define $x \geq y$ to mean that $x_i \geq y_i$ for all $i = 1, \ldots, k$, and $x > y$ to meant that $x \geq y$ and $x_i > y_i$ for some i.

Definition 2.1: A function $f : R^n_{++} \to R^n$ is a *market excess demand function* if it is homogeneous of degree zero in prices and satisfies the Walras law:

$$f(\pi) = f(\lambda \pi) \quad \text{for all } \pi \in R^n_{++} \quad \text{and} \quad \lambda > 0;$$

$$\sum_{i=1}^n \pi_i f_i(\pi) = 0.$$

Definition 2.2: The market excess demand satisfies *gross substitutability* if at all prices $\pi \in R^n_{++}$ and for each good i,

$$\frac{\partial f_i(\pi, w)}{\partial \pi_k} > 0 \quad \text{for all } k \neq i.$$

Notice that the market excess demand function and therefore the gross substitutability condition are defined only when all prices are strictly positive. (The gross substitutability condition is inconsistent with homogeneity of prices if one or more prices are zero.)

To guarantee the existence of an equilibrium with strictly positive prices (and to guarantee that this would be the only equilibrium were we to allow for zero prices), we impose the following boundary condition. Using homogeneity of the demand function, we may normalize prices so that $\pi \in S^n_{++}$.

Definition 2.3: A market excess demand function satisfies the *boundary condition* if for any sequence of price vectors $\{\pi^t\} \in S^n_{++}$, we have

$$\min[\pi^t_1, \ldots, \pi^t_n] \to 0 \quad \text{implies} \quad \max[f_1(\pi^t), \ldots, f_n(\pi^t)] \to \infty.$$

An elementary example satisfying all of these conditions arises when each household has a strictly positive endowment of each good and a Cobb–Douglas utility function. (Because the gross substitutability condition is linear, it is clearly satisfied when the individual excess demand functions are aggregated to obtain the market excess demands.)

The standard argument for uniqueness of equilibrium in a model of exchange with gross substitutes is extraordinarily simple.

Theorem 2.1: *Suppose the market excess demand function satisfies gross substitutability. Then the equilibrium $\pi \in R^n_{++}$ is unique up to a scalar multiple.*

Proof: Suppose that π and π^* are two equilibrium price vectors that are not proportional. Then we may use the assumption of homogeniety to normalize π^* so that there is a nonempty proper subset of goods I for which

$$\pi_i = \pi_i^* \quad \text{if } i \in I$$
$$\pi_i < \pi_i^* \quad \text{if } i \notin I.$$

But then for any good $i \in I$, the gross substitutability assumption implies that

$$0 = f_i(\pi) > f_i(\pi^*) = 0,$$

which is a contradiction. ∎

2.1.1. General Equilibrium with Production

We describe the production side of the economy by an activity analysis matrix

$$A = \begin{bmatrix} a_{11} & \cdots & a_{1j} & \cdots & a_{1k} \\ \vdots & \ddots & \vdots & \ddots & \vdots \\ a_{n1} & \cdots & a_{nj} & \cdots & a_{nk} \end{bmatrix}.$$

Each column of A represents a feasible production plan, with negative entries referring to inputs into production and positive entries to outputs. The activities can be used simultaneously at arbitrary nonnegative activity levels $x = (x_1, \ldots, x_k)$ so that the production possibility set available to the economy as a whole is given by

$$Y = \{y = Ax \text{ for } x \geq 0\}.$$

Free disposal of commodities is described by the presence of n columns in A that form the negative of a unit matrix.

A competitive equilibrium is given by a price and activity level pair (π, x) such that

- $f(\pi) = Ax$ and
- $\pi A \leq 0$ with equality for column j if $x_j > 0$.

In order to guarantee the existence of an equilibrium the following assumption is typically made:

Assumption: There exists a nonzero price vector $\pi \geq 0$ such that $\pi A \leq 0$.

Under this assumption and the ones previously made about the market excess demand functions it is straightforward to demonstrate the existence of a competitive equilibrium.

2.1.2. Uniqueness in the Ricardo Model

Let there be m countries and n goods with the output in country j of good i for a single unit of that country's labor given by $a_{ij} > 0$. Suppose that each country j has a fixed endowment of labor L_j and let $f_i^j(p, w_j)$ denote the demand for good i in country j, given the price vector $p \in R_{++}^n$ and the country's wage w_j. Let $f_i(p, w) \equiv \sum_j f_i^j(p, w)$ represent the aggregate demand for good i. If we suppose that each $f^j = (f_1^j, \ldots, f_n^j)$ is homogeneous of degree 0 and satisfies the budget constraint $\sum p_i f_i^j(p, w_j) = w_j L_j$, then f will also be homogeneous of degree 0 in prices and wages and satisfy the Walras law

$$\sum_{i=1}^{n} p_i f_i(p, w) \equiv \sum_{j=1}^{m} w_j L_j.$$

To ensure that each good is produced by some country in equilibrium we assume that the market demand is strictly positive at all prices.

Definition 2.4: The market aggregate demand f satisfies *gross substitutability* if at all prices $(p, w) \in R_{++}^n \times R_{++}^m$ and for each good i and country j,

$$\frac{\partial f_i(p, w)}{\partial p_k} \geq 0 \quad \text{for all } k \neq i$$

$$\frac{\partial f_i(p, w)}{\partial w_j} > 0.$$

If good i is produced in country j in the equilibrium with wage rate w, then

$$p_i a_{ij} = w_j \quad \text{and} \quad p_i a_{ik} \leq w_k \text{ for all other countries } k.$$

It follows that

$$p_i = \min[w_k / a_{ik}],$$

so that the equilibrium wage vector w uniquely determines the equilibrium price vector p. Because of this fact about the Ricardo model, we will occasionally find it convenient to refer to an equilibrium in terms of wages alone.

Theorem 2.2: *Suppose the market demand function satisfies gross substitutability; then the equilibrium wage vector w is unique up to a scalar multiple.*

Suppose w and w^* are both equilibrium wage vectors that are not proportional. Then we may normalize w^* so that there is a nonempty proper subset of countries J for which

$$w_j = w_j^* \quad \text{if } j \in J$$
$$w_j > w_j^* \quad \text{if } j \notin J.$$

We have the following simple observation about the two equilibria which is valid for all Ricardo models, regardless of assumptions on the market demand functions.

Observation: A good that is produced by a country $j \in J$ in the equilibrium with wages w^* will be produced only by the countries in J in the equilibrium with wages w.

Proof of Theorem 2.2: We see from this observation that there are some goods that are produced exclusively by the countries in J in the equilibrium with wages w. Let us define I to be the set of these goods; i.e.,

$$I \equiv \{i : p_i < w_k/a_{ik} \text{ for all } k \notin J\}.$$

Also, let I^* be the set of goods for which the countries in J are least-cost producers under wages w^*:

$$I^* \equiv \left\{i : p_i^* = \min_{j \in J} w_j^*/a_{ij}\right\}.$$

Some of the goods in I^* may be produced by countries not in J in the equilibrium with wages w^*.

The observation tells us that

$$I^* \subseteq I.$$

We have

$$p_i = p_i^* \quad \text{for } i \in I^*$$

and

$$\text{if } i \notin I^* \text{ then } p_i^* < \min_{j \in J} w_j^*/a_{ij} = \min_{j \in J} w_j/a_{ij} = p_i.$$

Because goods in I are produced only by countries in J at wage vector w, it must be true at equilibrium that the cost of purchasing the world demand for the goods in I is less than or equal to the wages received by the countries in J under w:

$$\sum_{i \in I} p_i f_i(p, w) \leq \sum_{j \in J} w_j L_j.$$

Moreover, because the countries in J produce only goods in I^* at wage vector w^*, it follows that the value of the world demand for the goods in I^* is greater than or equal to the wages received by the countries in J under w^*:

$$\sum_{j \in J} w_j^* L_j \leq \sum_{i \in I^*} p_i^* f_i(p^*, w^*).$$

But because $w_j = w_j^*$ for $j \in J$, we have

$$\sum_{i \in I} p_i f_i(p, w) \leq \sum_{j \in J} w_j L_j = \sum_{j \in J} w_j^* L_j \leq \sum_{i \in I^*} p_i^* f_i(p^*, w^*).$$

This inequality is valid for all Ricardo models regardless of the assumptions made about the market excess demand functions. If we now make the assumption of gross substitutability, then

$$f_i(p, w) > f_i(p^*, w^*) \quad \text{for all } i \in I^*,$$

and we obtain the inequalities

$$\sum_{i \in I} p_i f_i(p, w) \geq \sum_{i \in I^*} p_i f_i(p, w) = \sum_{i \in I^*} p_i^* f_i(p, w) > \sum_{i \in I^*} p_i^* f_i(p^*, w^*).$$

The contradiction between the last pair of inequalities completes the proof of uniqueness of the competitive equilibrium under gross substitutability. ∎

2.2. INDEX THEORY

Index theory is a sophisticated method of analysis used to study the solutions of systems of nonlinear equations

$$g_i(x_1, \ldots, x_n) = 0 \quad \text{for } i = 1, \ldots, n.$$

Under mild assumptions on the problem, we can associate an index, ± 1, with each solution of the system of equations, depending on the local behavior of the functions at that point. The main theorem of index theory states that the sum of the indices over the entire set of solutions is equal to $+1$. This global result permits us to assert the uniqueness of the solution of the system of equations on the basis of local behavior; for example, if each solution has an index of $+1$, then there can be only one solution.

We shall provide a simple illustration of the main theorem in the very special case of an exchange economy with two goods. A thorough and accessible presentation of index theory may be found in the volume by Garcia and Zangwill [1].

2.2.1. Exchange Economies with Two Goods

Consider a pure exchange economy with two goods. Because the boundary condition implies that the set of equilibrium prices is strictly positive, we may normalize the second price to be unity and consider the excess demand for the first good

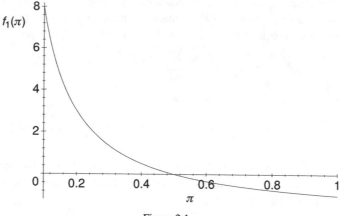

Figure 2.1.

as a function of its own price. Let $f_1(\pi)$ denote the excess demand for good 1, given the price vector $(\pi, 1)$. Our boundary condition and the Walras law imply that $\lim_{\pi \to 0} f_1(\pi) = \infty$ and $\lim_{\pi \to \infty} \pi f_1(\pi) = -\infty$. Figure 2.1 illustrates a market excess demand function for good 1 with a single equilibrium at $\pi = 1/2$.

Notice that at the equilibrium price the market excess demand for good 1 crosses the π axis from above, so we must have $f_1'(\pi) < 0$ at this equilibrium.

Figure 2.2 illustrates a case with three equilibria.

At the first and third equilibria we have, as before,

$$f_1'(\pi) < 0,$$

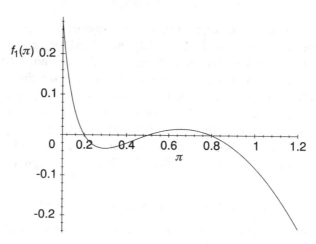

Figure 2.2.

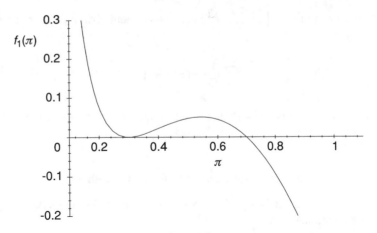

Figure 2.3.

but at the middle equilibrium we have the reverse inequality,

$$f_1'(\pi) > 0.$$

More generally, suppose there are n equilibria,

$$\pi^1 < \pi^2 < \cdots < \pi^n.$$

Then if the excess demand is continuous and satisfies the boundary condition and the demand function is never tangent to the π axis, then the first crossing of f_1 must be from above, the second from below, and ultimately the last crossing must be from above. There must, therefore, be one more crossing of f_1 from above than from below.

Our argument is valid for any excess demand that does not have a *degenerate* equilibrium π at which the excess demand function is tangent to the π axis. At a degenerate equilibrium π, where

$$\frac{df_1(\pi)}{d\pi} = 0,$$

the number of equilibria changes dramatically with small perturbations in the demand function, as illustrated in Fig. 2.3. We therefore exclude this nongeneric class of economies from our analysis by restricting our attention to *regular* economies, in which none of the equilibria are degenerate.

For any nonzero number x, let sign$[x]$ be $+1$ if $x > 0$ and -1 if $x < 0$. Then, for a regular economy, we define

$$\text{Index}(\pi) = \text{sign}[-f'(\pi)]$$

for each equilibrium π. If $\{\pi^1, \ldots, \pi^k\}$ is the set of equilibrium prices our analysis implies that

$$\sum_{j=1}^{k} \text{Index}(\pi^j) = 1.$$

It follows that a necessary and sufficient condition for there to be a single equilibrium is that each equilibrium have an index of $+1$.

2.2.2. The Index for a Model of Exchange with n Goods

This illustrative result can be extended to an excess demand function with n goods. We use the notation

$$f_{ij} = \partial f_i / \partial \pi_j.$$

The assumption that the excess demands are homogeneous of degree zero implies that

$$\sum \pi_j f_{ij} \equiv 0$$

so that the Jacobian matrix

$$J(f) = \begin{bmatrix} f_{11} & \cdots & f_{1n} \\ \vdots & \ddots & \vdots \\ f_{n1} & \cdots & f_{n,n} \end{bmatrix}$$

is singular. In order to define the index of an equilibrium we examine an arbitrary principal minor of the Jacobian, say,

$$D(f) = \begin{bmatrix} f_{11} & \cdots & f_{1,n-1} \\ \vdots & \ddots & \vdots \\ f_{n-1,1} & \cdots & f_{n-1,n-1} \end{bmatrix}$$

Definition 2.5: An excess demand function f is regular if $f(\pi) = 0$ implies that $D(f)$ is nonsingular.

Definition 2.6: The index associated with an equilibrium price vector is defined to be

$$\text{sign}[\det(-D(f))].$$

We have the following major result from index theory, which links the indices of all of the equilibria of a model of exchange.

Theorem 2.3 (Index Theorem): *If $\pi^1, \pi^2, \ldots, \pi^k$ are the competitive equilibrium of a* regular *exchange economy that satisfies the boundary condition, then*

$$\sum_{j=1}^{k} \text{Index}(\pi^j) = 1.$$

2.2.3. Uniqueness in a Model of Exchange with Gross Substitutes

To demonstrate uniqueness of the equilibrium in an n-good pure exchange economy with gross substitutes we simply show that the index of each equilibrium is positive, i.e., that

$$\det \begin{bmatrix} f_{11} & \cdots & f_{1,n-1} \\ \vdots & \ddots & \vdots \\ f_{n-1,1} & \cdots & f_{n-1,n-1} \end{bmatrix} < 0.$$

The assumption of gross substitutability implies that the matrix

$$-\begin{bmatrix} f_{11} & \cdots & f_{1,n-1} \\ \vdots & \ddots & \vdots \\ f_{n-1,1} & \cdots & f_{n-1,n-1} \end{bmatrix}$$

has positive entries on the main diagonal and negative entries elsewhere, so that it is a Leontief matrix. But it is also a *productive* Leontief matrix, because homogeneity of prices implies that

$$\sum_{j=1}^{n-1} \pi_j(-f_{ij}) = \pi_n f_{i,n} > 0 \quad \text{for } i = 1, \ldots, n-1.$$

The classical result that a productive Leontief matrix has a positive determinant implies that the index is positive, and therefore, the equilibrium is unique.

2.2.4. Index Theory with Production

We shall now discuss the index theorem for an equilibrium model in which production is described by an activity analysis matrix. The first presentation of index theory for this model appears in Kehoe's Ph.D. thesis (1979) and in the subsequent paper [3] in *Econometrica*.

As before, let the market excess demand functions be $f_i(\pi)$, and let A be the activity analysis matrix. The equilibrium is given by a price vector π and a set of activity levels $x \geq 0$, such that

- $f_i(\pi) = Ax$ and
- $\pi A \leq 0$ with equality for those activities that are used at a positive level.

Let S be the subset of activities used at a positive level in the particular equilibrium in question and let s be the number of these activities. The equilibrium conditions yield the set of $n + s$ equations in $n + s$ variables

$$f_i(\pi) - \sum_{j \in S} a_{ij} x_j = 0$$

$$\sum_i \pi_i a_{ij} = 0 \quad \text{for } j \in S,$$

as well as inequalities stating that the remaining activities make a nonpositive profit. The Jacobian of the system of equations is the $(n + s) \times (n + s)$ matrix

$$J = \begin{bmatrix} F & -A_S \\ A_S^T & 0 \end{bmatrix},$$

where F is the $n \times n$ matrix of derivatives of the excess demand functions,

$$F = \begin{bmatrix} f_{11} & \cdots & f_{1j} & \cdots & f_{1n} \\ \vdots & \ddots & \vdots & \ddots & \vdots \\ f_{j1} & \cdots & f_{jj} & \cdots & f_{jn} \\ \vdots & \ddots & \vdots & \ddots & \vdots \\ f_{n1} & \cdots & f_{nj} & \cdots & f_{nn} \end{bmatrix},$$

and A_S represents the subset of activities used in this equilibrium.

As in the model of exchange, this Jacobian J is singular. In order to have a well-defined index for this equilibrium we need to assume that the problem is *nondegenerate* in the sense that the rank of J is $n + s - 1$. We then calculate the sign of the determinant of the principal minor obtained by striking out the jth row and column of the matrix $-J$, where j is one of the first n rows (and columns). If the determinant is positive the index is $+1$; if the determinant is negative the index is -1.

We then have the important, general theorem that if the model is nondegenerate, then the sum of the indices over all of the equilibria is $+1$. It follows that the equilibrium is unique if every equilibrium has an index of $+1$.

2.2.5. Index Theory and the Ricardo Model

In the Ricardo model the price vector $\pi = (p, w)$ has two components: p, the goods prices, and w, the wage rates. We assume that there are n goods and m countries. The activity analysis matrix takes the form

$$
\begin{bmatrix} A \\ C \end{bmatrix} = \begin{bmatrix}
a_{11} & \cdots & 0 & \cdots & a_{1m} & \cdots & 0 \\
0 & \cdots & 0 & \cdots & 0 & \cdots & 0 \\
\vdots & \ddots & \vdots & \ddots & \vdots & \ddots & \vdots \\
0 & \cdots & a_{n1} & \cdots & 0 & \cdots & a_{nm} \\
-1 & \cdots & -1 & \cdots & 0 & \cdots & 0 \\
\vdots & \ddots & \vdots & \ddots & \vdots & \ddots & \vdots \\
0 & \cdots & 0 & \cdots & -1 & \cdots & -1
\end{bmatrix},
$$

with A being that part of the activity analysis matrix involving outputs and C the rows referring to the m countries.

With general market demand functions the Jacobian of demand with respect to prices p and wages w is given by

$$
\begin{bmatrix}
\partial f_1/\partial p_1 & \cdots & \partial f_1/\partial p_n & \partial f_1/\partial w_1 & \cdots & \partial f_1/\partial w_m \\
\vdots & \ddots & \vdots & \vdots & \ddots & \vdots \\
\partial f_n/\partial p_1 & \cdots & \partial f_n/\partial p_n & \partial f_n/\partial w_1 & \cdots & \partial f_n/\partial w_m \\
0 & \cdots & 0 & 0 & \cdots & 0 \\
\vdots & \ddots & \vdots & \vdots & \ddots & \vdots \\
0 & \cdots & 0 & 0 & \cdots & 0
\end{bmatrix}.
$$

The zeros in the last m rows arise because there is no demand for leisure.

Since the market demand functions are homogeneous of degree zero, we have, for each good i,

$$
\sum_j p_j \partial f_i/\partial p_j + \sum_j w_j \partial f_i/\partial w_j = 0.
$$

As before we assume that at equilibrium the s activities in the set S are used. Then the matrix used to calculate the index of the equilibrium is of size $n + m + s$. It has the form

$$
\begin{bmatrix}
-F & -L & -A_S \\
0 & 0 & -C_S \\
A_S^T & C_S^T & 0
\end{bmatrix},
$$

where

$$
f_{ij} = \partial f_i/\partial p_j,
$$

L is a matrix of size $n \times m$ with entries $l_{ij} = \partial f_i/\partial w_j$, and

$$
\begin{bmatrix} A_S \\ C_S \end{bmatrix}
$$

is the set of activities used at equilibrium. The index of the equilibrium is the sign of the determinant of a principal minor of this matrix obtained by striking out the jth row and column, where $1 \le j \le n$. We assume that the model is nondegenerate, so that the index is well defined.

With more detail the index matrix is given by

$$
\begin{bmatrix}
-\partial f_1/\partial p_1 & \cdots & -\partial f_1/\partial p_i & \cdots & -\partial f_1/\partial p_n & -l_{11} & \cdots & -l_{1j} & \cdots & -l_{1m} & \cdots & 0 & \cdots \\
\vdots & \ddots & \vdots & \ddots & \vdots & \vdots & \ddots & \vdots & \ddots & \vdots & \ddots & \vdots & \ddots \\
-\partial f_i/\partial p_1 & \cdots & -\partial f_i/\partial p_i & \cdots & -\partial f_i/\partial p_n & -l_{i1} & \cdots & -l_{ij} & \cdots & -l_{im} & \cdots & -a_{ij} & \cdots \\
\vdots & \ddots & \vdots & \ddots & \vdots & \vdots & \ddots & \vdots & \ddots & \vdots & \ddots & \vdots & \ddots \\
-\partial f_n/\partial p_1 & \cdots & -\partial f_n/\partial p_i & \cdots & -\partial f_n/\partial p_n & -l_{n1} & \cdots & -l_{nj} & \cdots & -l_{nm} & \cdots & 0 & \cdots \\
0 & \cdots & 0 & \cdots & 0 & 0 & \cdots & 0 & \cdots & 0 & \cdots & 0 & \cdots \\
\vdots & \ddots & \vdots & \ddots & \vdots & \vdots & \ddots & \vdots & \ddots & \vdots & \ddots & \vdots & \ddots \\
0 & \cdots & 0 & \cdots & 0 & 0 & \cdots & 0 & \cdots & 0 & \cdots & 1 & \cdots \\
\vdots & \ddots & \vdots & \ddots & \vdots & \vdots & \ddots & \vdots & \ddots & \vdots & \ddots & \vdots & \ddots \\
0 & \cdots & 0 & \cdots & 0 & 0 & \cdots & 0 & \cdots & 0 & \cdots & 0 & \cdots \\
\vdots & \ddots & \vdots & \ddots & \vdots & \vdots & \ddots & \vdots & \ddots & \vdots & \ddots & \vdots & \ddots \\
0 & \cdots & a_{ij} & \cdots & 0 & 0 & \cdots & -1 & \cdots & 0 & \cdots & 0 & \cdots \\
\vdots & \ddots & \vdots & \ddots & \vdots & \vdots & \ddots & \vdots & \ddots & \vdots & \ddots & \vdots & \ddots \\
\end{bmatrix},
$$

where column $m + n + i$ and row $m + n + i$ indicate that good i is produced in country j. The index associated with the equilibrium is $+1$ if the determinant of the principal minor obtained by striking out the row and column associated with a particular good is positive; the index is -1 if the sign is negative.

We simplify the index matrix, while retaining the sign of all principal minors, by multiplying columns and rows $1, \ldots, n, n + 1, \ldots, n + m$ by

$$
p_1, \ldots, p_n, w_1, \ldots, w_m
$$

and using the fact that if good i is produced in country j then $p_i a_{ij} = w_j$.

After this simplification the index matrix becomes

$$
\begin{bmatrix}
v_{11} & \cdots & v_{1i} & \cdots & v_{1n} & -e_{11} & \cdots & -e_{1j} & \cdots & -e_{1m} & \cdots & 0 & \cdots \\
\vdots & \ddots & \vdots & \ddots & \vdots & \vdots & \ddots & \vdots & \ddots & \vdots & \ddots & \vdots & \ddots \\
v_{i1} & \cdots & v_{ii} & \cdots & v_{in} & -e_{i1} & \cdots & -e_{ij} & \cdots & -e_{im} & \cdots & -w_j & \cdots \\
\vdots & \ddots & \vdots & \ddots & \vdots & \vdots & \ddots & \vdots & \ddots & \vdots & \ddots & \vdots & \ddots \\
v_{n1} & \cdots & v_{ni} & \cdots & v_{nn} & -e_{n1} & \cdots & -e_{nj} & \cdots & -e_{nm} & \cdots & 0 & \cdots \\
0 & \cdots & 0 & \cdots & 0 & 0 & \cdots & 0 & \cdots & 0 & \cdots & 0 & \cdots \\
\vdots & \ddots & \vdots & \ddots & \vdots & \vdots & \ddots & \vdots & \ddots & \vdots & \ddots & \vdots & \ddots \\
0 & \cdots & 0 & \cdots & 0 & 0 & \cdots & 0 & \cdots & 0 & \cdots & w_j & \cdots \\
\vdots & \ddots & \vdots & \ddots & \vdots & \vdots & \ddots & \vdots & \ddots & \vdots & \ddots & \vdots & \ddots \\
0 & \cdots & 0 & \cdots & 0 & 0 & \cdots & 0 & \cdots & 0 & \cdots & 0 & \cdots \\
\vdots & \ddots & \vdots & \ddots & \vdots & \vdots & \ddots & \vdots & \ddots & \vdots & \ddots & \vdots & \vdots \\
0 & \cdots & w_j & \cdots & 0 & 0 & \cdots & -w_j & \cdots & 0 & \cdots & 0 & \cdots \\
\vdots & \ddots & \vdots & \ddots & \vdots & \vdots & \ddots & \vdots & \ddots & \vdots & \ddots & \vdots & \ddots \\
\end{bmatrix},
$$

with

$$e_{ij} = p_i w_j \partial f_i / \partial w_j,$$
$$v_{ij} = -p_i p_j \partial f_i / \partial p_j,$$

and

$$\sum_j v_{ij} = \sum_j e_{ij}.$$

And finally we divide columns $n + m + i$ of the activity analysis matrix, and the rows of its transpose, by the corresponding wage rate, obtaining the following matrix, which is sufficently important to warrant a formal definition:

Definition 2.7: We define the index matrix I to be

$$\begin{bmatrix}
v_{11} & \cdots & v_{1i} & \cdots & v_{1n} & -e_{11} & \cdots & -e_{1j} & \cdots & -e_{1m} & \cdots & 0 & \cdots \\
\vdots & \ddots & \vdots & \ddots & \vdots & \vdots & \ddots & \vdots & \ddots & \vdots & \ddots & \vdots & \ddots \\
v_{i1} & \cdots & v_{ii} & \cdots & v_{in} & -e_{i1} & \cdots & -e_{ij} & \cdots & -e_{im} & \cdots & -1 & \cdots \\
\vdots & \ddots & \vdots & \ddots & \vdots & \vdots & \ddots & \vdots & \ddots & \vdots & \ddots & \vdots & \ddots \\
v_{n1} & \cdots & v_{ni} & \cdots & v_{nn} & -e_{n1} & \cdots & -e_{nj} & \cdots & -e_{nm} & \cdots & 0 & \cdots \\
0 & \cdots & 0 & \cdots & 0 & 0 & \cdots & 0 & \cdots & 0 & \cdots & 0 & \cdots \\
\vdots & \ddots & \vdots & \ddots & \vdots & \vdots & \ddots & \vdots & \ddots & \vdots & \ddots & \vdots & \ddots \\
0 & \cdots & 0 & \cdots & 0 & 0 & \cdots & 0 & \cdots & 0 & \cdots & 1 & \cdots \\
\vdots & \ddots & \vdots & \ddots & \vdots & \vdots & \ddots & \vdots & \ddots & \vdots & \ddots & \vdots & \ddots \\
0 & \cdots & 0 & \cdots & 0 & 0 & \cdots & 0 & \cdots & 0 & \cdots & 0 & \cdots \\
\vdots & \ddots & \vdots & \ddots & \vdots & \vdots & \ddots & \vdots & \ddots & \vdots & \ddots & \vdots & \ddots \\
0 & \cdots & 1 & \cdots & 0 & 0 & \cdots & -1 & \cdots & 0 & \cdots & 0 & \cdots \\
\vdots & \ddots & \vdots & \ddots & \vdots & \vdots & \ddots & \vdots & \ddots & \vdots & \ddots & \vdots & \ddots
\end{bmatrix}.$$

The columns to the right of the E matrix depend on the activities in use at the equilibrium. Each such column has two nonzero entries: -1 in a row corresponding to a good being produced and $+1$ in a row corresponding to a country which produces that good. The negative transpose of these columns appears below the block of zeros.

The assumption of gross substitutability,

$$\partial f_i / \partial p_j > 0, \quad \text{for } i \neq j,$$

and

$$\partial f_i / \partial w_j > 0,$$

implies that $e_{ij} > 0$ and that V is a Leontief matrix. V is a *productive* matrix because

$$\sum_j v_{ij} = \sum_j e_{ij} > 0.$$

We have the following theorem implying uniqueness of the equilibrium:

Theorem 2.4: *Under the assumption of gross substitutability, the determinant of the principal minor of I obtained by striking out its jth row and column, where $1 \le j \le n$, is* positive *and the index of the equilibrium is therefore* +1.

The basic idea of the proof is to observe that the determinant of the principal minor obtained by striking out the jth row and column of I is *precisely* the derivative of det I with respect to the jth diagonal entry v_{jj}. In order to work with these derivatives we generalize the matrix I by allowing its diagonal entries to vary.

Let $I(\xi)$ be the matrix

$$
\begin{bmatrix}
\xi_1 & \cdots & v_{1i} & \cdots & v_{1n} & -e_{11} & \cdots & -e_{1j} & \cdots & -e_{1m} & \cdots & 0 & \cdots \\
\vdots & \ddots & \vdots & \ddots & \vdots & \vdots & \ddots & \vdots & \ddots & \vdots & \ddots & \vdots & \ddots \\
v_{i1} & \cdots & \xi_i & \cdots & v_{in} & -e_{i1} & \cdots & -e_{ij} & \cdots & -e_{im} & \cdots & -1 & \cdots \\
\vdots & \ddots & \vdots & \ddots & \vdots & \vdots & \ddots & \vdots & \ddots & \vdots & \ddots & \vdots & \ddots \\
v_{n1} & \cdots & v_{ni} & \cdots & \xi_n & -e_{n1} & \cdots & -e_{nj} & \cdots & -e_{nm} & \cdots & 0 & \cdots \\
0 & \cdots & 0 & \cdots & 0 & 0 & \cdots & 0 & \cdots & 0 & \cdots & 0 & \cdots \\
\vdots & \ddots & \vdots & \ddots & \vdots & \vdots & \ddots & \vdots & \ddots & \vdots & \ddots & \vdots & \ddots \\
0 & \cdots & 0 & \cdots & 0 & 0 & \cdots & 0 & \cdots & 0 & \cdots & 1 & \cdots \\
\vdots & \ddots & \vdots & \ddots & \vdots & \vdots & \ddots & \vdots & \ddots & \vdots & \ddots & \vdots & \ddots \\
0 & \cdots & 0 & \cdots & 0 & 0 & \cdots & 0 & \cdots & 0 & \cdots & 0 & \cdots \\
\vdots & \ddots & \vdots & \ddots & \vdots & \vdots & \ddots & \vdots & \ddots & \vdots & \ddots & \vdots & \vdots \\
0 & \cdots & 1 & \cdots & 0 & 0 & \cdots & -1 & \cdots & 0 & \cdots & 0 & \cdots \\
\vdots & \ddots & \vdots & \ddots & \vdots & \vdots & \ddots & \vdots & \ddots & \vdots & \ddots & \vdots & \ddots
\end{bmatrix},
$$

with

$$\xi_i \ge v_{ii}.$$

According to our previous discussion, the index associated with the equilibrium is equal to

$$\text{sign}[\partial \det I(\xi)/\partial \xi_j] \quad \text{when } \xi_i = v_{ii}, i = 1, \ldots, n$$

The proof of our theorem will be complete if we can show the stronger statement that $I(\xi)$ is increasing in each of the variables ξ_i when $\xi_i \ge v_{ii}$.

It is useful to observe that the equilibrium has associated with it a bipartite graph G with $m + n$ vertices, one for each good and one for each country. There is an edge connecting good i and country j if in this equilibrium good i is produced in country j.

The graph may very well be disconnected; if it is, we partition G into connected subgraphs $G_1, \ldots, G_p$. For example, if the model involves four goods and three countries and the particular equilibrium uses the activities

$$
\begin{bmatrix} A_S \\ C_S \end{bmatrix} = \begin{bmatrix}
a_{11} & 0 & 0 & 0 & 0 \\
0 & a_{21} & 0 & 0 & 0 \\
0 & 0 & a_{31} & 0 & 0 \\
0 & 0 & 0 & a_{42} & a_{43} \\
-1 & -1 & -1 & 0 & 0 \\
0 & 0 & 0 & -1 & 0 \\
0 & 0 & 0 & 0 & -1
\end{bmatrix},
$$

then goods 1, 2, 3 are produced in country 1 alone and good 4 is produced in countries 2 and 3. The graph has two components: (goods 1, 2, 3 and country 1) and (good 4 and countries 2, 3).

Now let us demonstrate, by induction on the size of the Ricardo model, that

$$
\partial \det I(\xi)/\partial \xi_j > 0 \quad \text{when } \xi_i \geq v_{ii}.
$$

This result implies that the function

$$
\det I(\xi_1, \ldots, \xi_n)
$$

is increasing in each variable when $\xi_i \geq v_{ii}$. Because $\det I(\xi_1, \ldots, \xi_n)$ is zero when $\xi_i = v_{ii}$ for all i, it must be positive for $\xi_i > v_{ii}$.

In our induction argument we will use the fact that the corresponding matrix is strictly positive for Ricardo models – satisfying the assumption of gross substitutability – with a smaller number of goods and countries.

Let us take $j = 1$, because the other arguments are identical. The derivative

$$
\frac{\partial I(\xi)}{\partial \xi_1}
$$

is the determinant of the principal minor obtained by striking out the first row and column of $I(\xi)$. Columns $n + m + 1, \ldots, n + m + s$ of $I(\xi)$ each contain two nonzero entries, indicating that a particular good is produced in a particular country. Those columns describing the several countries producing good 1 will be replaced, in the principal minor, by columns containing a single entry of $+1$ in the row of that country; the columns involving goods other than good 1 will contain both $+1$ and -1. And similarly for the rows.

For example, if $I(\xi)$ has the form

$$
\begin{bmatrix}
\xi_1 & \cdots & v_{1i} & \cdots & v_{1n} & -e_{11} & \cdots & -e_{1j} & \cdots & -e_{1m} & \cdots & -1 & 0 & \cdots \\
\vdots & \ddots & \vdots & \ddots & \vdots & \vdots & \ddots & \vdots & \ddots & \vdots & \ddots & \vdots & \vdots & \ddots \\
v_{i1} & \cdots & \xi_i & \cdots & v_{in} & -e_{i1} & \cdots & -e_{ij} & \cdots & -e_{im} & \cdots & \vdots & -1 & \cdots \\
\vdots & \ddots & \vdots & \ddots & \vdots & \vdots & \ddots & \vdots & \ddots & \vdots & \ddots & \vdots & \vdots & \ddots \\
v_{n1} & \cdots & v_{ni} & \cdots & \xi_n & -e_{n1} & \cdots & -e_{nj} & \cdots & -e_{nm} & \cdots & 0 & 0 & \cdots \\
0 & \cdots & 0 & \cdots & 0 & 0 & \cdots & 0 & \cdots & 0 & \cdots & 0 & 0 & \cdots \\
\vdots & \ddots & \vdots & \ddots & \vdots & \vdots & \ddots & \vdots & \ddots & \vdots & \ddots & \vdots & \vdots & \ddots \\
0 & \cdots & 0 & \cdots & 0 & 0 & \cdots & 0 & \cdots & 0 & \cdots & 1 & 1 & \cdots \\
\vdots & \ddots & \vdots & \ddots & \vdots & \vdots & \ddots & \vdots & \ddots & \vdots & \ddots & \vdots & \vdots & \ddots \\
0 & \cdots & 0 & \cdots & 0 & 0 & \cdots & 0 & \cdots & 0 & \cdots & 0 & 0 & \cdots \\
\vdots & \ddots & \vdots & \ddots & \vdots & \vdots & \ddots & \vdots & \ddots & \vdots & \ddots & \vdots & \vdots & \vdots \\
1 & \cdots & \cdots & \cdots & 0 & 0 & \cdots & -1 & \cdots & 0 & \cdots & 0 & 0 & \cdots \\
0 & \cdots & 1 & \cdots & 0 & 0 & \cdots & -1 & \cdots & 0 & \cdots & 0 & 0 & \cdots \\
\vdots & \ddots & \vdots & \ddots & \vdots & \vdots & \ddots & \vdots & \ddots & \vdots & \ddots & \vdots & \vdots & \ddots
\end{bmatrix},
$$

then columns and rows $k, k + 1$ indicate that good 1 and good i are both produced in country j. After column and row 1 are struck out, the minor is given by

$$
\begin{bmatrix}
\ddots & \vdots & \ddots & \vdots & \vdots & \ddots & \vdots & \ddots & \vdots & \ddots & \vdots & \vdots & \ddots \\
\cdots & \xi_i & \cdots & v_{in} & -e_{i1} & \cdots & -e_{ij} & \cdots & -e_{im} & \cdots & \vdots & -1 & \cdots \\
\ddots & \vdots & \ddots & \vdots & \vdots & \ddots & \vdots & \ddots & \vdots & \ddots & \vdots & \vdots & \ddots \\
\cdots & v_{ni} & \cdots & \xi_n & -e_{n1} & \cdots & -e_{nj} & \cdots & -e_{nm} & \cdots & 0 & 0 & \cdots \\
\cdots & 0 & \cdots & 0 & 0 & \cdots & 0 & \cdots & 0 & \cdots & 0 & 0 & \cdots \\
\ddots & \vdots & \ddots & \vdots & \vdots & \ddots & \vdots & \ddots & \vdots & \ddots & \vdots & \vdots & \ddots \\
\cdots & 0 & \cdots & 0 & 0 & \cdots & 0 & \cdots & 0 & \cdots & 1 & 1 & \cdots \\
\ddots & \vdots & \ddots & \vdots & \vdots & \ddots & \vdots & \ddots & \vdots & \ddots & \vdots & \vdots & \ddots \\
\cdots & 0 & \cdots & 0 & 0 & \cdots & 0 & \cdots & 0 & \cdots & 0 & 0 & \cdots \\
\ddots & \vdots & \ddots & \vdots & \vdots & \ddots & \vdots & \ddots & \vdots & \ddots & \vdots & \vdots & \vdots \\
\cdots & \cdots & \cdots & 0 & 0 & \cdots & -1 & \cdots & 0 & \cdots & 0 & 0 & \cdots \\
\cdots & 1 & \cdots & 0 & 0 & \cdots & -1 & \cdots & 0 & \cdots & 0 & 0 & \cdots \\
\ddots & \vdots & \ddots & \vdots & \vdots & \ddots & \vdots & \ddots & \vdots & \ddots & \vdots & \vdots & \ddots
\end{bmatrix}.
$$

But now column k contains a single nonzero entry, 1, in row j and row k contains a single nonzero entry, -1, in column j. If we expand the minor by these two entries in turn we obtain the smaller minor

$$\begin{bmatrix} \ddots & \vdots & \ddots & \vdots & \vdots & \ddots & \ddots & \vdots & \ddots & \vdots & \ddots \\ \cdots & \xi_i & \cdots & v_{in} & -e_{i1} & \cdots & \cdots & -e_{im} & \cdots & -1 & \cdots \\ \ddots & \vdots & \ddots & \vdots & \vdots & \ddots & \ddots & \vdots & \ddots & \vdots & \ddots \\ \cdots & v_{ni} & \cdots & \xi_n & -e_{n1} & \cdots & \cdots & -e_{nm} & \cdots & 0 & \cdots \\ \cdots & 0 & \cdots & 0 & 0 & \cdots & \cdots & 0 & \cdots & 0 & \cdots \\ \ddots & \vdots & \ddots & \vdots & \vdots & \ddots & \ddots & \vdots & \ddots & \vdots & \ddots \\ \ddots & \vdots & \ddots & \vdots & \vdots & \ddots & \ddots & \vdots & \ddots & \vdots & \ddots \\ \cdots & 0 & \cdots & 0 & 0 & \cdots & \cdots & 0 & \cdots & 0 & \cdots \\ \ddots & \vdots & \ddots & \vdots & \vdots & \ddots & \ddots & \vdots & \ddots & \vdots & \vdots \\ \cdots & 1 & \cdots & 0 & 0 & \cdots & \cdots & 0 & \cdots & 0 & \cdots \\ \ddots & \vdots & \ddots & \vdots & \vdots & \ddots & \ddots & \vdots & \ddots & \vdots & \ddots \end{bmatrix}.$$

But now the column and row corresponding to any other good produced in country j will also have a single ± 1 in them and can also be removed without changing the value of the determinant of the minor obtained by striking out the first row and column. We have the following crucial observation.

Observation: The determinant of the minor obtained by striking out the rows and columns of $I(\xi)$ for any particular good will be unchanged if we then strike out the rows and columns for *all other goods that are produced in any country that produces that particular good.*

At this point we consider two cases, each with its own example.

Case 1. The subgraph of goods and countries containing good 1 is not the entire graph. In this case, after repeated application of the observation, we arrive at the determinant $I(\xi)$ for the corresponding solution to the Ricardo model in which all of the goods and countries in the subgraph containing good 1 are discarded. This is a smaller problem – which also satisfies the assumption of gross substitutability – and by induction the corresponding determinant is positive. It follows that

$$\partial \det I(\xi)/\partial \xi_i > 0 \quad \text{when } \xi_i > v_{ii}.$$

As an example of this case, consider the model with four goods and three countries in which goods 1, 2, 3 are produced in the first country and good 4 is produced in the second and third countries. The activity analysis matrix is

$$\begin{bmatrix} a_{11} & 0 & 0 & 0 & 0 \\ 0 & a_{21} & 0 & 0 & 0 \\ 0 & 0 & a_{31} & 0 & 0 \\ 0 & 0 & 0 & a_{42} & a_{43} \\ -1 & -1 & -1 & 0 & 0 \\ 0 & 0 & 0 & -1 & 0 \\ 0 & 0 & 0 & 0 & -1 \end{bmatrix}.$$

and the graph has two components: (goods 1, 2, 3 and country 1) and (good 4 and countries 2, 3).

The index matrix $I(\xi)$ is

$$\begin{bmatrix} \xi_1 & 0 & 0 & 0 & -e_{11} & -e_{12} & -e_{13} & -1 & 0 & 0 & 0 & 0 \\ 0 & \xi_2 & 0 & 0 & -e_{21} & -e_{22} & -e_{23} & 0 & -1 & 0 & 0 & 0 \\ 0 & 0 & \xi_3 & 0 & -e_{31} & -e_{32} & -e_{33} & 0 & 0 & -1 & 0 & 0 \\ 0 & 0 & 0 & \xi_4 & -e_{41} & -e_{42} & -e_{43} & 0 & 0 & 0 & -1 & -1 \\ 0 & 0 & 0 & 0 & 0 & 0 & 0 & 1 & 1 & 1 & 0 & 0 \\ 0 & 0 & 0 & 0 & 0 & 0 & 0 & 0 & 0 & 0 & 1 & 0 \\ 0 & 0 & 0 & 0 & 0 & 0 & 0 & 0 & 0 & 0 & 0 & 1 \\ 1 & 0 & 0 & 0 & -1 & 0 & 0 & 0 & 0 & 0 & 0 & 0 \\ 0 & 1 & 0 & 0 & -1 & 0 & 0 & 0 & 0 & 0 & 0 & 0 \\ 0 & 0 & 1 & 0 & -1 & 0 & 0 & 0 & 0 & 0 & 0 & 0 \\ 0 & 0 & 0 & 1 & 0 & -1 & 0 & 0 & 0 & 0 & 0 & 0 \\ 0 & 0 & 0 & 1 & 0 & 0 & -1 & 0 & 0 & 0 & 0 & 0 \end{bmatrix}.$$

The derivative of the determinant of $I(\xi)$ with respect to ξ_1 is

$$\det \begin{bmatrix} \xi_2 & 0 & 0 & -e_{21} & -e_{22} & -e_{23} & 0 & -1 & 0 & 0 & 0 \\ 0 & \xi_3 & 0 & -e_{31} & -e_{32} & -e_{33} & 0 & 0 & -1 & 0 & 0 \\ 0 & 0 & \xi_4 & -e_{41} & -e_{42} & -e_{43} & 0 & 0 & 0 & -1 & -1 \\ 0 & 0 & 0 & 0 & 0 & 0 & 1 & 1 & 1 & 0 & 0 \\ 0 & 0 & 0 & 0 & 0 & 0 & 0 & 0 & 0 & 1 & 0 \\ 0 & 0 & 0 & 0 & 0 & 0 & 0 & 0 & 0 & 0 & 1 \\ 0 & 0 & 0 & -1 & 0 & 0 & 0 & 0 & 0 & 0 & 0 \\ 1 & 0 & 0 & -1 & 0 & 0 & 0 & 0 & 0 & 0 & 0 \\ 0 & 1 & 0 & -1 & 0 & 0 & 0 & 0 & 0 & 0 & 0 \\ 0 & 0 & 1 & 0 & -1 & 0 & 0 & 0 & 0 & 0 & 0 \\ 0 & 0 & 1 & 0 & 0 & -1 & 0 & 0 & 0 & 0 & 0 \end{bmatrix}.$$

After systematically striking out the rows and columns in the component of the graph containing good 1 we arrive at the determinant

$$\det \begin{bmatrix} \xi_4 & -e_{42} & -e_{43} & -1 & -1 \\ 0 & 0 & 0 & 1 & 0 \\ 0 & 0 & 0 & 0 & 1 \\ 1 & -1 & 0 & 0 & 0 \\ 1 & 0 & -1 & 0 & 0 \end{bmatrix}$$

for a Ricardo model with a single good – good 4 – and countries 2, 3. Of course,

$$\xi_4 > e_{42} + e_{43}.$$

Case 2. The subgraph containing good 1 is the entire graph. In this case repeated application of the observation will lead us to a point where we strike the rows and columns for the last good. This results in the determinant

$$\det \begin{bmatrix} 0 & 1 \\ -1 & 0 \end{bmatrix},$$

whose determinant is clearly $+1$.

An example of this case arises in a model with four commodities and three countries in which goods 1, 2, and 3 are produced in country 1, goods 2 and 4 are produced in country 2, and good 4 is produced in country 3. The matrix of activities used in equilibrium is

$$\begin{bmatrix} a_{11} & 0 & 0 & 0 & 0 & 0 \\ 0 & a_{21} & 0 & a_{22} & 0 & 0 \\ 0 & 0 & a_{31} & 0 & 0 & 0 \\ 0 & 0 & 0 & 0 & a_{42} & a_{43} \\ -1 & -1 & -1 & 0 & 0 & 0 \\ 0 & 0 & 0 & -1 & -1 & 0 \\ 0 & 0 & 0 & 0 & 0 & -1 \end{bmatrix}.$$

In this example, the graph of goods and countries is completely connected.

The index calculation is based on the matrix

$$\begin{bmatrix} \xi_1 & 0 & 0 & 0 & -e_{11} & -e_{12} & -e_{13} & -1 & 0 & 0 & 0 & 0 & 0 \\ 0 & \xi_2 & 0 & 0 & -e_{21} & -e_{22} & -e_{23} & 0 & -1 & 0 & -1 & 0 & 0 \\ 0 & 0 & \xi_3 & 0 & -e_{31} & -e_{32} & -e_{33} & 0 & 0 & -1 & 0 & 0 & 0 \\ 0 & 0 & 0 & \xi_4 & -e_{41} & -e_{42} & -e_{43} & 0 & 0 & 0 & 0 & -1 & -1 \\ 0 & 0 & 0 & 0 & 0 & 0 & 0 & 1 & 1 & 1 & 0 & 0 & 0 \\ 0 & 0 & 0 & 0 & 0 & 0 & 0 & 0 & 0 & 0 & 1 & 1 & 0 \\ 0 & 0 & 0 & 0 & 0 & 0 & 0 & 0 & 0 & 0 & 0 & 0 & 1 \\ 1 & 0 & 0 & 0 & -1 & 0 & 0 & 0 & 0 & 0 & 0 & 0 & 0 \\ 0 & 1 & 0 & 0 & -1 & 0 & 0 & 0 & 0 & 0 & 0 & 0 & 0 \\ 0 & 0 & 1 & 0 & -1 & 0 & 0 & 0 & 0 & 0 & 0 & 0 & 0 \\ 0 & 1 & 0 & 0 & 0 & -1 & 0 & 0 & 0 & 0 & 0 & 0 & 0 \\ 0 & 0 & 0 & 1 & 0 & -1 & 0 & 0 & 0 & 0 & 0 & 0 & 0 \\ 0 & 0 & 0 & 1 & 0 & 0 & -1 & 0 & 0 & 0 & 0 & 0 & 0 \end{bmatrix}.$$

The derivative of the determinant of $I(\xi)$ with respect to ξ_1 is

$$
\det
\begin{bmatrix}
\xi_2 & 0 & 0 & -e_{21} & -e_{22} & -e_{23} & 0 & -1 & 0 & -1 & 0 & 0 \\
0 & \xi_3 & 0 & -e_{31} & -e_{32} & -e_{33} & 0 & 0 & -1 & 0 & 0 & 0 \\
0 & 0 & \xi_4 & -e_{41} & -e_{42} & -e_{43} & 0 & 0 & 0 & 0 & -1 & -1 \\
0 & 0 & 0 & 0 & 0 & 0 & 1 & 1 & 1 & 0 & 0 & 0 \\
0 & 0 & 0 & 0 & 0 & 0 & 0 & 0 & 0 & 1 & 1 & 0 \\
0 & 0 & 0 & 0 & 0 & 0 & 0 & 0 & 0 & 0 & 0 & 1 \\
0 & 0 & 0 & -1 & 0 & 0 & 0 & 0 & 0 & 0 & 0 & 0 \\
1 & 0 & 0 & -1 & 0 & 0 & 0 & 0 & 0 & 0 & 0 & 0 \\
0 & 1 & 0 & -1 & 0 & 0 & 0 & 0 & 0 & 0 & 0 & 0 \\
1 & 0 & 0 & 0 & -1 & 0 & 0 & 0 & 0 & 0 & 0 & 0 \\
0 & 0 & 1 & 0 & -1 & 0 & 0 & 0 & 0 & 0 & 0 & 0 \\
0 & 0 & 1 & 0 & 0 & -1 & 0 & 0 & 0 & 0 & 0 & 0
\end{bmatrix}.
$$

If we strike out rows and columns corresponding to country 1, then goods 2 and 3, then country 2 and good 4, we obtain the determinant

$$
\det
\begin{bmatrix}
0 & 1 \\
-1 & 0
\end{bmatrix}
> 0.
$$

This concludes the proof of Theorem 2.4 and demonstrates the uniqueness of the competitive equilibrium.

Wilson [5] provides an alternative argument for this result.

REFERENCES

[1]   C. B. Garcia and W. I. Zangwill, *Pathways to Solutions, Fixed Points and Equilibria*, Englewood Cliffs, NJ: Prentice–Hall, 1981.
[2]   Werner Hildenbrand and Alan P. Kirman, chap. 3 in *Equilibrium Analysis*, Amsterdam: North-Holland, 1988.
[3]   Timothy Kehoe, "An Index Theorem for General Equilibrium Models with Production," *Econometrica* 48, no. 5 (July 1980): 1211–32.
[4]   ———, "Multiplicity of Equilibria and Comparative Statics," *The Quarterly Journal of Economics* 100, no. 1 (February 1985): 119–47.
[5]   Charles Wilson, "Notes on Ricardian Models with Gross Substitutes," 2003, available from www.wilsonc.econ.nyu.edu.

3 Solving Dynamic Stochastic Competitive General Equilibrium Models

Kenneth L. Judd

ABSTRACT: The Scarf algorithm was the first practical, almost surely convergent method for computing general equilibria of competitive models. The current focus of much computational research is computing equilibrium of dynamic stochastic models. While many of these models are examples of Arrow–Debreu equilibria, Scarf's algorithm and subsequent homotopy methods cannot be applied directly, because they have an infinite number of commodities. Many methods have been proposed for solving dynamic models and some work well on simple examples. However, all have convergence problems and are not likely to perform as well in models with heterogeneous agents, multiple goods, joint production, and other features often present in general equilibrium models. This paper discusses weaknesses of standard methods for solving dynamic stochastic models. We then present an alternative Negishi-style approach that combines convergent methods for solving finite systems of equations with convergent dynamic programming methods to produce more reliable algorithms for dynamic analyses. The dynamic programming step presents the key challenge, because most practical dynamic programming methods have convergence problems, but we argue that shape-preserving approximation methods offer a possible solution.

The Scarf (1967) algorithm was the first practical, surely convergent method for computing general equilibrium prices and, equivalently, systems of nonlinear equations in $\mathbb{R}^n$. This was followed by the development of almost surely convergent homotopy methods for solving nonlinear equations.[1] This work gave us reliable and efficient methods for solving finite-dimensional systems of equations. Economists are now interested in analyzing dynamic models and there is currently substantial effort on computing equilibrium of dynamic stochastic models. While many of these models are examples of Arrow–Debreu general equilibrium models, Scarf's algorithm and subsequent homotopy methods cannot be applied directly, because dynamic stochastic models involve an infinite number of commodities. Following

---

[1]   See Eaves (1972), Garcia and Zangwill (1982), and Allgower and Georg (1990) for presentations of homotopy methods.

The author thanks Herb Scarf and Donald Brown for their valuable comments.

the spirit of Scarf (1967), the focus of this paper is on current efforts to find efficient and convergent methods for solving dynamic economic models.

There is substantial activity on computing equilibria of dynamic stochastic models. See, for example, the papers included in the Taylor and Uhlig (1990) symposium, the description of projection methods in Judd (1992), and the surveys in Judd (1996, 1998) and Judd, Kubler, and Schmedders (2003). However, these methods do not meet the Scarf standard. Most current methods revolve around systems of Euler equations. These methods generally work well for simple cases, but sometimes fail to converge (or converge only after substantial tinkering) even for simple one-good, one-agent problems. Convergence is even less likely if applied to models with heterogeneous agents, multiple goods, multiple factors, and other features often present in general equilibrium problems.

We will proceed with the same goal displayed in Scarf (1967). Before Scarf, economists solved general equilibrium models with Newton's method and other available algorithms for solving systems of nonlinear equations. These often worked but were not globally convergent; for example, the basic convergence theorem for Newton's method assumes that one has a good initial guess. Dixon and Parmenter (1996) discuss these early methods in computable general equilibrium modeling. Of course, there were methods that would converge, but they were impractical. Scarf (1967) points out that

Sperner's lemma suggests no procedure for the determination of an approximate fixed point other than an exhaustive search of all subsimplices until one is found with all vertices labeled differently. Clearly some substitute for an exhaustive search must be found if the problem is to be considered tractable.

The chief contribution of Scarf (1967) is the presentation of a tractable method for finding the critical subsimplex. We face a similar problem today when we attempt to compute equilibrium of competitive dynamic models because the available methods either have convergence problems or are impractical.

This paper examines possible numerical strategies that combine convergent methods for solving finite systems of equations with convergent dynamic programming methods to produce algorithms that will be more reliable for solving competitive equilibria of dynamic stochastic models. We do not present a general convergence theorem but lay out the necessary critical features for efficient convergent methods. Specifically, we examine the Negishi approach to computing competitive equilibria of dynamic stochastic general equilibrium. The basic idea is simple: for each set of Negishi weights over a finite number of agents (or agent types) we solve a dynamic programming problem. The solutions of the dynamic programming problems imply price and consumption processes for each agent. Equilibrium requires that the value of the endowments equals the value of consumption plans. If we can solve the dynamic programming problem for arbitrary Negishi weights, then any conventional nonlinear equation method can be used to find a finite vector of Negishi weights where each agent is on his intertemporal budget constraint.

While this is a theoretically straightforward and standard idea (for example, Ginsburgh and Keyzer, 1997, discuss its application in some deterministic dynamic models), its implementation for stochastic dynamic problems presents numerical difficulties. In particular, there are few dynamic programming methods suitable for the special demands of this application. This paper discusses these numerical issues and the availability of numerically efficient and reliable algorithms for solving the critical dynamic programming step. We have the same goal that motivated Scarf's algorithm: finding a reliable, robust, and relatively efficient algorithm for solving dynamic general equilibrium. Many of the surely convergent dynamic programming solution methods are too slow for this application, because the Negishi method requires solutions to many dynamic programming problems. Furthermore, one needs accurate approximations not only of the value function but also of the gradients of the value function and the allocation policies they imply.

Unfortunately, standard solution methods for dynamic programming problems either are impractical or have convergence problems that make them unreliable. The key fact is that most dynamic programming methods either suffer from a curse of dimensionality or are unstable because of difficulties in preserving shape. Concavity of production and utility functions is a standard assumption in competitive equilibrium analysis. These concavity properties imply concavity of the value function of any social planner's dynamic programming problem. Most dynamic programming algorithms do not exploit this property of the value function and will often produce nonconcave value functions for concave problems. Failure of shape preservation can lead to instabilities in solving dynamic programming problems. We argue that any convergent algorithm will need to be aware of these shape preservation issues and will need to use shape-preserving approximation methods in the dynamic programming step of the Negishi algorithm.

There is, as usual, a trade-off between speed and safety. The good news is that easy shape-preserving approximation methods are available for problems with one continuous dimension. These methods could also easily address problems with one continuous dimension (such as capital) and many discrete states (such as productivity levels), which naturally reduce to finite collections of problems with one continuous dimension. We present an example that shows that the reliability of shape-preserving approximation in one dimension comes at little cost. However, the cost of shape-preserving strategies for higher dimensional problems is nontrivial. There are some complex methods for two- and three-dimensional problems and some costly methods available for preserving concavity in higher dimensions. While I am not now aware of any practical and efficient method for multidimensional shape-preserving approximation, it is currently an active field of research in numerical analysis. As shape-preserving approximation methods are developed in the mathematical literature, economists can apply them to determine their practical value. In the meantime, economists will probably need to rely on Euler equation methods. Even though many problems can be solved by Euler equation methods, it is always valuable to develop reliable alternatives.

Section 3.1 presents a simple dynamic general equilibrium model, describes the conventional methods of solution, and discusses their weaknesses. Section 3.2 reviews the basic Negishi method for the static general equilibrium model. Section 3.3 presents the Negishi formulation for a general dynamic model. Section 3.4 discusses standard methods for solving dynamic programming problems and their weaknesses. Section 3.5 presents some simple shape-preserving approximation methods. Section 3.5.2 examines the performance of a shape-preserving method for a simple dynamic programming example.

3.1. A DYNAMIC GENERAL EQUILIBRIUM MODEL AND STANDARD SOLUTION METHODS

To motivate the arguments below, we examine a simple dynamic stochastic model and the most popular methods for solving it. These methods are often thought to be very successful, but this perception is possibly due to the very simple models to which they have been applied and the extra, nonsystematic steps sometimes used to attain this success. There is little reason to believe that they will be successful in more general models.

To ease the notational burden we will examine the case of a single-sector, multiple-agent model. Let $u^i(c)$, $i = 1, \ldots, m$, be agent i's utility function over consumption $c \in \mathbb{R}$ in each period, and assume a common constant discount factor β. Let $k_{i,t} \in \mathbb{R}$ be agent i's ownership of capital at the beginning of period t and let $K_t = \sum_{i=1}^{m} k_{i,t}$ denote the aggregate capital stock at the beginning of period t. We assume that output is CRTS in capital and labor. Let $F(K, \theta)$ be output (including the undepreciated capital stock) when total capital is K, labor input per capita is one, and productivity level is θ. We assume that each agent supplies one unit of labor inelastically[2]; therefore, the marginal product of labor is $(F(K, \theta) - K F_K(K, \theta))/m$. Assume that capital moves according to

$$K_{t+1} = F(K_t, \theta_t) - \sum_i c_{i,t}$$

$$\ln \theta_{t+1} = \rho \ln \theta_t + \varepsilon_{t+1},$$

where ε_{t+1} is distributed i.i.d. over t. Since this model is recursive, equilibrium consumption of agent i at time t can be expressed as a function of the wealth distribution at time t, $k_t = (k_{1,t}, k_{2,t}, \ldots, k_{m,t})$, and the current productivity, θ_t; we let

$$c_{i,t} = C^i(k_t, \theta_t)$$

denote the equilibrium consumption policy functions. Most current methods for solving dynamic general equilibrium models focus on Euler equation representations

---

[2] We assume inelastically supplied labor to reduce the notational burden; it is not essential to any of our arguments.

of equilibrium. The Euler equations for this model are

$$u_i'(C^i(k, \theta)) = \beta E \left\{ u_i'(C_i(k^+, \theta)) r(K^+, \theta^+) | \theta \right\}, \quad i = 1, 2, \ldots, m \quad (1)$$
$$k_i^+ \equiv Y_i(k, \theta) - C_i(k, \theta), \quad i = 1, 2, \ldots, m$$
$$K \equiv \sum_i k_i, \; K^+ \equiv \sum_i k_i^+$$
$$\theta^+ = \theta^\rho e^\varepsilon$$
$$Y_i(k, \theta) \equiv k_i r(K, \theta) + w(K, \theta), \quad i = 1, 2, \ldots, m$$
$$r(K, \theta) \equiv F_K(K, \theta)$$
$$w(K, \theta) \equiv (F(K, \theta) - K.F_K(K, \theta)) m^{-1},$$

where, if (k, θ) is today's state, $Y_i(k, \theta)$ is a type i agent's income today, $w(K, \theta)$ is today's wage, $r(K, \theta)$ is today's rate of return on capital, k_i^+ is a type i agent's wealth tomorrow, K^+ is tomorrow's aggregate capital, θ^+ is tomorrow's productivity level, and $r(K^+, \theta^+)$ is tomorrow's rate of return on capital. Equation (1) is a set of functional equations that must be satisfied in equilibrium. We will proceed, as does the dynamic general equilibrium literature, under the assumption that the stable solutions to (1) are locally unique.

Solution methods typically use parameterized families of functions to approximate $C^i(k, \theta)$. For example, linear approximations take the form

$$\widehat{C}^i(k, \theta; a) = \sum_{j=0}^n a_i \phi_i(k, \theta),$$

where the set $\{\phi_i | i = 1, 2, \ldots\}$ is a basis for the space of continuous functions over (k, θ). This formulation reduces the infinite-dimensional problem to a finite-dimensional search for good choices of the a coefficients. There are many different strategies available here. The tensor product method with orthogonal polynomials[3] approximates each consumption function as

$$\widehat{C}^i(k, \theta; a) = \sum_{j_1=0}^{n_k} \cdots \sum_{j_m=0}^{n_k} \sum_{\ell=0}^{n_\theta} a_{j_1 \ldots j_n \ell}^i \; \phi_{i_1}(k_1) \cdots \phi_{i_n}(k_m) \; \psi_\ell(\theta), \quad i = 1, \ldots, n,$$

where the $\phi_i(k)$ are orthogonal polynomials over some interval $[k_m, k_M]$ and the $\psi_i(\theta)$ are orthogonal polynomials over the range of θ. Other possibilities explored in the literature include complete orthogonal polynomials (Judd and Gaspar, 1997), multivariate splines (Judd et al., 1999, 2000), exponential polynomials (den Haan and Marcet, 1990), and Padé functions (Judd and Guu, 1997). One could use neural networks, wavelets, or trigonometric polynomials, or one could construct problem-specific bases (e.g., see the discussion of hybrid perturbation–projection methods in Judd 1998). The basic idea is to find some family of functional forms that produces

---

[3] For more details, such as the possible notions of orthogonality, see Judd (1992) or (1998).

a parsimonious approximation of $C(k, \theta)$ and is asymptotically complete in a space of functions which includes the equilibrium solution $C^i(k, \theta)$.

Once we have chosen some approximation scheme, we then need to fix the a coefficients. There are many methods for determining the a coefficients. We will briefly discuss them and their limitations.

Time iteration uses the Euler equation in an economically intuitive fashion to solve for $\widehat{C}(k, \theta; a)$. Time iteration picks a finite set Z of (k, θ) points. Suppose the iteration j approximation for type i consumption is $\widehat{C}^i\left(k^+, \theta; a^j\right)$. In iteration $j + 1$ we take each $(k, \theta) \in Z$ and solve the system of equations

$$u_i'(c_i) = \beta\, E\left\{u_i'\left(\widehat{C}^i(k^+, \theta; a^j)\right) r\left(K^+, \theta^+\right) | \theta\right\}, \quad i = 1, 2, \ldots, n \qquad (2)$$
$$k_i^+ \equiv Y_i(k, \theta) - c_i, \qquad\qquad\qquad\qquad i = 1, 2, \ldots, n$$
$$K^+ \equiv \sum_i k_i^+$$

for $c_i, i = 1, \ldots, m$. For a fixed (k, θ) point, (2) is a nonlinear equation in the consumption vector $c = (c_1, \ldots, c_m)$. Intuitively, it is similar to a static general equilibrium model where the random price of consumption tomorrow is the marginal utility tomorrow constructed by assuming that tomorrow agent i will use the $\widehat{C}^i(k^+, \theta; a^j)$ consumption rule. Note that the choice of c_i affects agent i's wealth tomorrow but does not affect tomorrow's decision rule. Solving (2) for several choices of $z_\ell \in Z$ generates solutions c^ℓ. These results are then used as data used to find a^{j+1}, either through interpolation or regression, so that the consumption functions $\widehat{C}^i(k, \theta; a^{j+1})$ approximate the c^ℓ solutions.

Successive approximation methods proceed more directly, using less computation per step. Specifically, successive approximation also begins with some set of points Z, but now solves for the c_i values in

$$u_i'(c_i) = \beta\, E\left\{u'\left(\widehat{C}^i(k^+, \theta; a^j)\right) r\left(K^+, \theta^+\right) | \theta\right\}, \quad i = 1, 2, \ldots, m \qquad (3)$$
$$k_i^+ \equiv Y_i(k, \theta) - \widehat{C}^i\left(k, \theta; a^j\right), \qquad\qquad i = 1, 2, \ldots, m$$
$$K^+ \equiv \sum_i k_i^+$$

for a finite number of points (k, θ). The system (3) basically solves for consumption choices today, taking tomorrow's marginal utilities as given, if agents use the consumption rule $\widehat{C}^i(k^+, \theta; a^j)$ both today and tomorrow. This set of equations for c_i^j is simpler to solve than the equations in time iteration, because c_i do not appear on the right-hand side. However, if we were to have multiple goods, then there would be several Euler equations relating the current gradient of utility to future utility, creating a small general equilibrium problem for current allocation and production decisions. As with time iteration, the c data are used to find the coefficients a so that, for each i, $\widehat{C}^{i,j+1}(k, \theta; a)$ fit the c_i data.

Successive approximation was used in the rational expectations model of Miranda and Helmburger (1988), who observed that it was an efficient method for computation. It was also motivated in den Haan and Marcet (1990) by learning arguments from Marcet and Sargent (1989). Successive approximation is often quite stable, converging to the equilibrium. For the case of a simple growth problem, Judd (1998, pp. 557–8) shows that successive approximation is locally convergent except for some extreme choices of tastes and technology.

Projection methods (see Judd, 1992), such as Galerkin and collocation methods, offer a more general approach motivated by numerical considerations instead of economic tatonnement stories. They begin by first defining the residual functions

$$R^i(k, \theta, a) = u_i'\left(\widehat{C}_i(k, \theta; a)\right) - \beta\, E\left\{u'\left(\widehat{C}_i(k^+, \theta^+; a)\right) r(K^+, \theta^+)|\theta\right\} \qquad (4)$$

$$k_i^+ \equiv Y_i(k, \theta) - C_i(k, \theta), \qquad\qquad i = 1, 2, \ldots, n$$

$$K^+ \equiv \sum_i k_i^+.$$

A projection method then constructs a finite set of projections conditions,

$$P_{ij}(a) \equiv \int_{\theta_m}^{\theta_M} \int_{k_m}^{k_M} \cdots \int_{k_m}^{k_M} \widehat{R}^l(k, \theta; a)\, \psi_j(k, \theta)\, \omega(k, \theta)\, dk_1 \cdots dk_n\, d\theta,$$

where $i = 1, \ldots, n$ and $j = 1, \ldots, m$, $\omega(k, \theta)$ is a weighting function, and the $\psi_j(k, \theta)$ are a set of test functions. Finally, a nonlinear equation solver is used to solve the projection equations for the coefficients a. This approach has the potential of being much faster than time iteration and successive approximation. For example, Newton's method converges quadratically. Newton-style methods may not be practical if a is large, but some combination of a block Gauss–Seidel method with Newton methods used within the blocks can bring some of the advantages of Newton's method to the solution of the large system. Time iteration and successive approximation methods are examples of projection methods because they use particular choices for projections and nonlinear equation solving methods.

These methods have proven successful for simple problems but will likely have difficulties for more general problems. There are three obvious difficulties. First, the issue of multiplicity raises several difficulties. Time iteration and successive approximations both revolve around solving a large number of small artificial problems similar to static general equilibrium models. Solving these equations at any particular (k, θ) point in Z is not a difficulty because one could use surely convergent methods, but multiple equilibria present coordination difficulties. Suppose that there were multiple equilibria to the dynamic model. Then there would possibly be multiple equilibria at some of the (k, θ) points we use. Since these problems are solved independently, there is no guarantee that the equilibrium selection will be consistent. This will not be a difficulty with the Negishi method we present below, because the constancy of the Negishi weights imposes strong connections across choices in various (k, θ) states. In any case, the possibility of multiple equilibria in

the dynamic economy means that we need to find all of the equilibria in the Euler
equation problems and make consistent choices, a very difficult problem.

There is an even more fundamental difficulty presented by multiple equilibria.
All of these methods assume the existence of a selection for equilibrium consumption
$C(k, \theta)$ which is smooth in (k, θ). In more general models, we would be making
the same assumption for price functions. This is not justified by general equilibrium
theory. Each (k, θ) point corresponds to a different dynamic general equilibrium
problem, where k is the initial endowment and θ is the initial productivity state.
Regularity theory (see Debreu, 1976) tells us that the equilibrium manifold is smooth
in endowments for *generic* endowments, but not for *all* endowments. The standard
Euler equation formulation of the problem assumes that there is a smooth manifold
that is an equilibrium selection map over *all* initial endowments. Since this is not
true for some simple static general equilibrium problems, it is not a safe assumption
for dynamic models.

Second, economists are often interested in the ergodic character of equilibrium. Unfortunately, ergodic properties will probably not be approximated well by
standard methods. The approximations to consumption functions $C(k, \theta)$ will have
errors that will accumulate over time. For example, we know that consumption
and wealth will be perfectly correlated across individuals in the true equilibrium.
Approximations to $C(k, \theta)$ will not have this property, and these errors will mean
that the computed ergodic distributions for consumption and wealth may not be
close to the true long-run distributions.

Third, we have no convergence theory for these methods. We would like to know
that the sequence of $\widehat{C}_i(k, \theta; a^j)$ approximate solutions converge to the true $C_i(k, \theta)$
as we increase j and the degree of the approximating polynomials (or splines or
trigonometric polynomials, etc.) This is a difficult problem in infinite-dimensional
nonlinear functional analysis.

Euler equation methods have been reliable for simple models but they have not
been tested on more complex models. Because the focus of this paper is on reliability,
we look elsewhere.

3.2. RELIABLE AND EFFICIENT COMPUTATION OF GENERAL EQUILIBRIUM

We first review the basic ideas from the computational general equilibrium literature used in the next section's discussion of dynamic problems. Standard general
equilibrium theory focusses on computing a zero of the excess demand function
$E(p)$. The Scarf algorithm (see Scarf, 1967, 1973 [with Hansen], and 1992) and
homotopy methods can be applied directly to solving $E(p) = 0$.

If the number of goods and prices is large, the system $E(p) = 0$ is large. If
the number of agents is much smaller than the number of goods, it is often desirable to use, instead, the Negishi method (also known as the planning method).
The Negishi method exploits the first theorem of welfare economics, which states

that any competitive equilibrium of an Arrow–Debreu model is Pareto efficient. Let $u^i(c^i)$ be agent i's utility function over consumption $c^i \in \mathbb{R}^n$ and let $e^i \in \mathbb{R}^n$ be his endowment.[4] Therefore, for any equilibrium, there is a set of nonnegative social welfare weights, λ^i, $i = 1, \ldots, m$, such that the equilibrium allocation of final consumption, c^i, $i = 1, \ldots, m$, is the solution to the social welfare problem

$$\max_{c^1, c^2, \ldots} \sum_{i=1}^{m} \lambda^i u^i(c^i) \tag{5}$$

$$\text{s.t.} \sum_{i=1}^{n} (e^i - c^i) = 0$$

The Negishi approach finds a set of social welfare weights, λ^i, $i = 1, \ldots, m$, such that the solution to (5) is an equilibrium allocation. Without loss of generality, we assume $\lambda \in \Delta \equiv \left\{ \lambda \geq 0 \,\middle|\, \sum_{i=1}^{m} \lambda^i = 1 \right\} \subset \mathbb{R}^m$.

The Negishi approach proceeds in a two-stage fashion. Given a vector of social welfare weights, λ, we compute the unique[5] allocation $(c^1, c^2, \ldots, c^m)$ that solves (5). As long as tastes are strictly concave and C^2, this is an easy optimization problem that can exploit the fastest optimization methods. Let $X(\lambda) = \left(X^1(\lambda), X^2(\lambda), \ldots, X^m(\lambda) \right) : \Delta \to \mathbb{R}^{m \times n}$ be the optimal allocation given the Negishi weight vector $\lambda \in \Delta$. Since u is concave, $X(\lambda)$ is continuous. The allocation $X(\lambda)$ implies a pattern of marginal rates of substitution that must equal the equilibrium prices if $X(\lambda)$ were an equilibrium allocation. These prices are defined by

$$p_j = \frac{u_j^1(X^1(\lambda))}{\sum_{\ell=1}^{n} u_\ell^1(X^1(\lambda))} \equiv P_j(\lambda). \tag{6}$$

In an equilibrium, each agent i can afford his allocation, $X^i(\lambda)$, at the prices $P(\lambda)$. To check this we define the excess budget function

$$B_i(\lambda) \equiv P(\lambda) \cdot (e^i - X^i(\lambda)), \quad i = 1, \ldots, m.$$

If $B_i(\lambda)$ is nonnegative, then agent i can afford $X^i(\lambda)$ at prices $P(\lambda)$ and have $B_i(\lambda)$ in unspent funds. The weights λ correspond to an equilibrium if and only if $B_i(\lambda) = 0$ for each i. Therefore the Negishi approach reduces the equilibrium problem to solving the system of nonlinear equations

$$B_i(\lambda) = 0, \quad i = 1, \ldots, m - 1 \tag{7}$$

$$\sum_{i=1}^{m} \lambda_i = 1$$

---

[4]   We examine an endowment problem to keep the notation simple; all ideas apply to economies with production.

[5]   For the purposes of this paper, we will assume strict concavity of all utility functions.

for $\lambda \in \Delta$. Existence theory tells us that a solution exists. Once we have a $\lambda \in \Delta$ that solves (7), we then take $P(\lambda)$ to be the equilibrium prices and $X(\lambda)$ the equilibrium consumption allocation.

The Negishi approach has substantial advantages if there are fewer agents than goods, even though it adds new variables, λ, to the problem. The reason is that the equilibrium (and numerically more difficult) part of the problem, (7), is a nonlinear equation with m unknowns independent of the number of goods. Of course, the consumption bundles c^i are also computed each time we evaluate $B(\lambda)$, but that is done by a collection of m concave optimization problems over n variables. If m is substantially smaller than n, as would be the case in dynamic problems with a finite, but long, horizon, then the nonlinear equation problem is much smaller in the Negishi approach than in a more direct approach focused on solving $E(p) = 0$. If solutions to (5) can be computed in closed form, then this approach reduces to $m - 1$ equations in $m - 1$ unknowns in a simplex. More typically, we need to use numerical methods to compute solutions to (5). This is not a substantial difficulty as long as the optimization method for solving (5) produces accurate answers.

Therefore, the Negishi approach replaces a possibly large system of excess demand conditions for equilibrium prices with a possibly much smaller set of nonlinear equations combined with a collection of well-behaved concave optimization problems. This approach works well for finite-dimensional problems. It also works well in deterministic dynamic problems since there are good methods for solving deterministic, concave dynamic problems; see Ginsburgh and Keyzer (1997) for a discussion of this case. We now focus on the Negishi approach for dynamic, stochastic problems.

3.3. A NEGISHI APPROACH TO STOCHASTIC, DYNAMIC GENERAL EQUILIBRIUM

We next present the Negishi approach to a simple stochastic dynamic model. Let $u^i(c^i)$ be agent i's utility function over n_c consumption goods,[6] $c^i \in \mathbb{R}^{n_c}$, in each period. We assume a common constant discount factor β. Let $\theta_t \in \mathbb{R}^{n_\theta}$ be the productivity state in period t. We assume that productivity follows a stochastic law of motion; for specificity, we assume $\ln \theta_{t+1} = \rho \ln \theta_t + \varepsilon_{t+1}$, where the productivity shocks ε_t are i.i.d. Let K_t denote the vector of n_k aggregate capital stocks at time t, and let $k_{i,0} \in \mathbb{R}^{n_k}$ be agent i's initial endowment of capital stocks at the beginning of period $t = 0$. Assume that the convex production possibility set in period t in productivity state θ_t is defined by $F\left(y_t, K_{t+1}, \widetilde{K}_t, \theta_t\right) \leq 0$, where K_{t+1} is the capital available at the beginning of period $t + 1$ and $\widetilde{K}_t \leq K_t$ is the amount of capital

---

[6] This formulation can include leisure. Let one of the components of c be labor supply, l. Then the marginal utility of l is negative and the "consumption expenditure" on l is negative. This allows us to use our compact notation.

actually used in production in period t. General equilibrium welfare theory again applies, telling us that for any equilibrium there is a set of nonnegative social welfare weights, λ^i, $i = 1, \ldots, n$, such that the equilibrium is, for some set of nonnegative weights λ, the solution to the social welfare problem

$$W(K_0, \theta_0) = \max_{c_t^i, y_t, \tilde{k}_t} \sum_{i=1}^{m} \lambda_i E \left\{ \sum_{t=0}^{\infty} \beta^t \, u^i \left(c_t^i \right) \right\} \tag{8}$$

$$F\left(y_t, K_{t+1}, \tilde{K}_t, \theta_t\right) \leq 0$$

$$\tilde{K}_t \leq K_t$$

$$\sum_i c_t^i - y_t \leq 0$$

$$\ln \theta_{t+1} = \rho \ln \theta_t + \varepsilon_{t+1}.$$

For any given set of nonnegative weights λ, the problem in (8) is a dynamic programming problem. The Bellman equation for (8) is

$$W(K, \theta) = TW(K, \theta) \tag{9}$$

$$\equiv \max_{c^i, \tilde{K}} \sum_i \lambda_i \, u^i \left(c^i \right) + \beta E \left\{ W(K^+, \theta^+) | \theta \right\}$$

$$F\left(y_t, K^+, \tilde{K}, \theta\right) \leq 0$$

$$\tilde{K} \leq K$$

$$\sum_i c_t^i - y_t \leq 0$$

$$\ln \theta_{t+1} = \rho \ln \theta_t + \varepsilon_{t+1},$$

where T is the Bellman operator. Because T is a contraction operator (under mild assumptions on u and F), there is a unique fixed point in the space of bounded functions for the Bellman equation, $W = TW$. In particular, the sequence $W^j = TW^{j-1}$ converges to the solution W. In our discussion we will assume that we solve (9) via value function iteration; that is, the W^j iterates are constructed by

$$W^{j+1}(K, \theta) = TW^j(K, \theta). \tag{10}$$

Define

$$Z(K, \theta) = \left(C(K, \theta), \tilde{K}(K, \theta), Y(K, \theta), \mathcal{K}(K, \theta) \right)$$

to be the vector of the equilibrium decision rules: the consumption allocation function $C^i(K, \theta)$ for each consumer, the capital utilization policy $\tilde{K}(K, \theta)$, the output function $Y(K, \theta)$, and the gross saving function $\mathcal{K}(K, \theta)$ denoting the next period's aggregate capital stock. $Z(K, \theta)$ solves

$$Z(K, \theta) \equiv \arg \max_{c^i, \tilde{K}, y, K^+} \sum_i \lambda_i \, u^i(c^i) + \beta E \left\{ W(K^+, \theta^+) | \theta \right\} \tag{11}$$

$$F\left(y, K^+, \tilde{K}, \theta\right) \leq 0$$

$$\tilde{K} \leq K$$

$$\sum_i c^i - y \leq 0$$

$$\ln \theta^+ = \rho \ln \theta + \varepsilon_{t+1}.$$

The solution to this problem implies a pattern of marginal rates of substitution, which in turn implies a sequence of prices. Let good 1 be the numeraire; then the prices for goods at time t is p_t, the vector of marginal rates of substitution with respect to the numeraire. Let $\Psi^i(K)$ be the current value at time s of consumer i's expenditure in terms of commodity 1 at time s if the economy has aggregate capital stock K at time s. Since marginal utilities are proportional to prices, $\Psi^i(K)$ satisfies the recursive expression

$$\Psi^i(K, \theta) = u_1^i(c^i)^{-1} \left(u_c^i(c^i) \cdot c^i + \beta E \left\{ u_1^i \left(c^{i,+} \right) \Psi^i(K^+, \theta^+) \right\} | \theta \right) \tag{12}$$

$$c^i \equiv C^i(K, \theta)$$

$$K^+ \equiv \mathcal{K}(K, \theta)$$

$$c^{i,+} \equiv C^i(\mathcal{K}(K, \theta), \theta^+),$$

where u_c is the vector of marginal utilities with respect to the various consumption goods. Equation (12) is a linear integral equation in the unknown function $\Psi^i(K, \theta)$.

The lifetime budget constraint of agent i includes the value of his initial wealth. Let $\psi_0(\lambda)$ be the price of capital relative to the numeraire at time $t = 0$. For each agent i define the excess budget function

$$B^i(\lambda) = \Psi^i(K, \theta_0) - \psi_0(\lambda) k_{i,0}. \tag{13}$$

Equilibrium is defined by the solution to

$$B^i(\lambda) = 0, \quad i = 1, \ldots, m. \tag{14}$$

λ is any λ such that $0 = B(\lambda) \equiv (B^i(\lambda))_{i=1}^m$. Equation (14) defines the Negishi approach to computing equilibrium.

We will assume that $B(\lambda)$ is well behaved; that is, we assume that it has a finite number of zeroes and is smooth with respect to the parameters of the model. These regularity properties require some additional assumptions. The recent paper by Shannon (1999) gives a general statement on sufficient conditions for regularity of infinite-dimensional models of general equilibrium. Her result covers many interesting instances of our model.

Determinacy Assumption: $B(\lambda)$ is Lipschitz continuous with finitely many zeroes.

In general, we won't be so lucky. The Schumaker method then adds a knot to the interval $[x_1, x_2]$ and constructs a spline with the desired properties. Schumaker provides formulas for a $\xi \in (x_1, x_2)$ such that there is a quadratic spline with nodes at ξ, x_1, and x_2 that satisfies (16). The general Hermite interpolation problem has data $\{(y_i, s_i, x_i) \mid i = 1, \ldots, n\}$. If the data are concave, then we can apply Schumaker's method to $[x_i, x_{i+1}]$ and preserve concavity. If we have Lagrange data, $\{(y_i, x_i) \mid i = 1, \ldots, n\}$, we must first add estimates of the slopes (Schumaker provides some simple estimates) and then proceed as we do with Hermite data. As long as the data are consistent with global concavity, we can produce a globally concave function. However, it is always better to use the true slopes if they are available.

3.5.2. Performance in a Simple Example

There is a legitimate concern that shape preservation comes at significant cost. Judd and Solnick (1994) presents evidence that shape preservation is practical in one-dimensional problems. They consider the optimal growth problem

$$\max \quad \sum_{t=0}^{\infty} \beta^t u(c_t)$$
$$k_{t+1} = f(k_t) - c_t,$$

where c_t is consumption in period t, $u(c)$ is the utility function at each date, k_t is the capital stock at the beginning of period t, and $f(k)$ is the aggregate production function in each period. They assume the specifications

$$u(c) = \frac{c^{1-\gamma}}{1 - \gamma}$$
$$f(k) = k + \frac{(1 - \beta)}{\alpha \beta} k^\alpha,$$

which imply that the steady state capital stock is $k = 1$.

Judd and Solnick (1994) solved this problem using several techniques: discretization of the state space, piecewise linear approximation for the value function, cubic spline approximation of the value function, polynomial interpolation of the value function, and Schumaker shape-preserving quadratic spline approximation for the value function. They used the following parameter values: $\alpha = 0.25$, $\beta = 0.95, 0.99$, $\gamma = 10, 2, 0.5$ over the interval $k \in [0.4, 1.6]$. They ran the discretization method using mesh sizes $\Delta k = 0.01, 0.001, 0.0001$, and 0.00001. We take the solution to the $\Delta k = 0.00001$ discretization, which implies 120,001 discrete states over $[0.4, 1.6]$ as the truth, and compare other solutions to this one. They used both level and slope information when they applied the Schumaker shape-preserving method. The other methods use only level information. The polynomial interpolation method used Chebyshev zeroes (adapted for the interval $[0.4, 1.6]$) because that is the optimal interpolation grid for polynomials.

TABLE 3.1. L_2 Norm of Relative Errors in Consumption

	(β, γ)					
N	(0.95,–10.)	(0.95,–2.)	(0.95,–0.5)	(0.99,–10.)	(0.99,–2.)	(0.99,–0.5)
	Discretized Model					
12	7.6e–02	2.8e–03	5.3e–03	7.9e–01	1.8e–01	1.1e–02
1200	1.0e–04	2.1e–05	5.4e–05	2.9e–03	5.4e–03	1.3e–04
	Linear Interpolation					
12	1.5e–03	9.8e–04	5.6e–04	1.5e–03	1.0e–03	6.3e–04
120	1.1e–04	3.7e–05	1.3e–05	1.4e–04	8.4e–05	4.2e–05
	Cubic Spline					
12	8.7e–05	1.5e–06	1.8e–07	1.3e–04	4.9e–06	1.1e–06
120	5.3e–09	5.6e–10	1.3e–10	4.2e–07	4.1e–09	1.5e–09
	Polynomial					
4	DNC	5.4e–04	1.6e–04	1.4e–02	5.6e–04	1.7e–04
12	3.0e–07	2.0e–09	4.3e–10	5.8e–07	4.5e–09	1.5e–09
	Shape-Preserving Quadratic Hermite Interpolation					
4	4.7e–04	1.5e–04	6.0e–05	5.0e–04	1.7e–04	7.3e–05
12	3.8e–05	1.1e–05	3.7e–06	5.9e–05	1.7e–05	6.3e–06
40	3.2e–06	5.7e–07	9.3e–08	1.4e–05	2.6e–06	5.1e–07
120	2.2e–07	1.7e–08	3.1e–09	4.0e–06	4.6e–07	5.9e–08

Table 3.1 reports the relative errors in the consumption function for various methods. N is the number of intervals used in spline methods and the degree of the polynomial used in the polynomial method. Table 3.1 shows that linear interpolation is roughly an order of magnitude more accurate than the discrete method, and shape-preserving interpolation is at least another order of magnitude better. Cubic spline and polynomial interpolation methods were often better. However, they encountered the shape problems we hypothesized above. In fact, Table 3.1 shows that the fourth-order polynomial interpolation method did not converge (DNC). In general, if the range of k is large or the curvature high then polynomial interpolation fails to preserve shape and value function iteration is unstable. Judd and Solnick also show that the time penalty of shape-preserving approximation is negligible.

These results make two important points. First, discretizing the state space is a very expensive way to proceed. Any of the interpolation methods achieved the same accuracy using much less computer time. This disadvantage surely grows with dimension. Second, the advantages of the shape-preserving method come at small computational cost. The shape-preserving method was faster than linear interpolation methods that achieved the same accuracy, and they were often faster than polynomials and cubic splines with the same number of free parameters. The key question is how this generalizes to higher dimensions. Economists should follow the progress approximation theorists make in their continuing work on this problem.

S. Johnson, J. R. Stedinger, C. A. Shoemaker, Y. Li, and J. A. Tehada–Guibert (1993), "Numerical Solution of Continuous–State Dynamic Programs Using Linear and Spline Interpolation," *Operations Research* 41: 484–500.

K. L. Judd (1992), "Projection Methods for Solving Aggregate Growth Models," *Journal of Economic Theory* 58: 410–52.

(1996), "Approximation, Perturbation, and Projection Methods in Economic Analysis," in *Handbook of Computational Economics*, edited by H. Amman, D. Kendrick, and J. Rust. Amsterdam: Elsevier.

(1998), *Numerical Methods in Economics*, Cambridge, MA: MIT Press.

K. L. Judd and J. Gaspar (1997), "Perturbation Methods for Discrete-Time Dynamic Deterministic Model," *Macroeconomic Dynamics* 1: 45–75.

K. L. Judd and S.-M. Guu (1993), "Perturbation Solution Methods for Economic Growth Models," in *Economic and Financial Modeling with Mathematica*, edited by Hal Varian. New York: Springer-Verlag.

(1997), "Asymptotic Methods for Aggregate Growth Models," *Journal of Economic Dynamics and Control* 21: 1025–42.

K. L. Judd, Felix Kubler, and Karl Schmedders (1999), "A Solution Method for Incomplete Asset Markets with Heterogeneous Agents," Hoover Institution working paper.

(2000), "Computing Equilibria in Infinite Horizon Finance Economies. I. The Case of One Asset," *Journal of Economic Dynamics and Control* 24: 1047–78.

(2003), "Computational Methods for Dynamic Equilibria with Heterogeneous Agents," in *Advances in Economics and Econometrics*, edited by Mathias Dewatripont, Lars Peter Hansen, and Stephen Turnovsky. Cambridge, UK: Cambridge University Press, pp. 243–90.

K. L. Judd and Andrew Solnick (1994), "Numerical Dynamic Programming with Shape-Preserving Splines," Hoover Institution, mimeo.

Boris I. Kvasov (2000), *Methods of Shape-Preserving Spline Approximation*, Singapore: World Scientific.

Finn E. Kydland and Edward C. Prescott (1982), "Time to Build and Aggregate Fluctuations," *Econometrica* 50: 1345–70.

J. P. M. Magill (1977), "A Local Analysis of *N*-Sector Capital Accumulation under Uncertainty," *Journal of Economic Theory* 15: 211–9.

A. Marcet and T. J. Sargent (1989), "Convergence of Least Squares Learning Mechanisms in Self Referential, Linear Stochastic Models," *Journal of Economic Theory* 48: 337–68.

M. J. Miranda and P. G. Helmburger (1988), "The Effects of Commodity Price Stabilization Programs," *American Economic Review* 78: 46–58.

J. Rust, J. F. Traub, and H. Wozniakowski (2002), "Is There a Curse of Dimensionality for Contraction Fixed Points in the Worst Case?" *Econometrica* 70: 285–329.

H. E. Scarf (1967), "The Approximation of Fixed Points of a Continuous Mapping," *SIAM Journal of Applied Mathematics* 15: 328–43.

(1992), "The Computation of Equilibrium Prices: An Exposition," in *Handbook of Mathematical Economics*, edited by K. Arrow and M. Intriligator. Amsterdam: North-Holland.

H. Scarf, with T. Hansen (1973), *Computation of Economic Equilibria*, New Haven, CT: Yale University Press.

L. L. Schumaker (1983), "On Shape-Preserving Quadratic Spline Interpolation," *SIAM Journal of Numerical Analysis* 20: 854–64.

C. Shannon (1999), "Determinacy of Competitive Equilibria in Economies with Many Commodities," *Economic Theory* 14: 29–87.

G. Tauchen and R. Hussey (1991), "Quadrature-Based Methods for Obtaining Approximate Solutions to the Integral Equations of Nonlinear Rational Expectations Models," *Econometrica* 59: 371–96.

J. B. Taylor and H. Uhlig (1990), "Solving Nonlinear Stochastic Growth Models: A Comparison of Alternative Solution Methods," *Journal of Business and Economic Statistics* 8: 1–18.

M. Trick and S. Zin (1997), "Adaptive Spline Generation through Linear Programming: Applications to Stochastic Dynamic Programming," *Macroeconomic Dynamics* 1: 255–77.

S.-P. Wang and K. L. Judd (2000), "Solving a Savings Allocation Problem by Numerical Dynamic Programming with Shape-Preserving Interpolation," *Computers and Operations Research* 27: 399–408.

4 Mathematical Programs with Equilibrium Constraints: Automatic Reformulation and Solution via Constrained Optimization

Michael C. Ferris, Steven P. Dirkse, and Alexander Meeraus

ABSTRACT: Constrained optimization has been extensively used to solve many large-scale deterministic problems arising in economics, including, for example, square systems of equations and nonlinear programs. A separate set of models has been generated more recently, using complementarity to model various phenomena, particularly in general equilibria. The unifying framework of mathematical programs with equilibrium constraints (MPEC) has been postulated for problems that combine facets of optimization and complementarity. This paper briefly reviews some methods available to solve these problems and describes a new suite of tools for working with MPEC models. Computational results demonstrating the potential of this tool are given that automatically construct and solve a variety of different nonlinear programming reformulations of MPEC problems.

4.1. INTRODUCTION

Nonlinear complementarity problems arise in many economic applications, most notably in the applied general equilibrium area [1, 29]. The past decade has seen an enormous increase in our ability to solve large-scale complementarity problems, due not only to the phenomenal increase in computer speed, but also to advances made in algorithms and software for complementarity problems. This paper attempts to review some of those advances and revisits some older techniques for the purpose of solving optimization problems with complementarity constraints, typically termed mathematical programs with equilibrium constraints (MPECs) in the literature [22, 26, 32].

Three advances in the past two decades have increased the capability of modelers to solve large-scale complementarity problems. The first is the implementation of large-scale complementarity solvers such as MILES [38], PATH [8], and SMOOTH

This material is based on research partially supported by the National Science Foundation, Grant CCR-9972372, the Air Force Office of Scientific Research, Grant F49620-01-1-0040, Microsoft Corporation, and the Guggenheim Foundation. The authors are grateful to Todd Munson, Nick Sahinidis, and Sven Leyffer for their advice and help with regard to algorithmic aspects. Both Tom Rutherford and Francis Tin-Loi have provided invaluable test problems and insight into specific applications without which this paper would not have been possible.

[30] that exploit significant advances in techniques of linear algebra and nonlinear optimization. The second is the advent of modeling systems that are able to directly express complementarity problems as part of their syntax [3, 13, 15, 39] and to pass on the complementarity models to the solver. Included in this are so-called mini-languages, such as MPSGE [40], which allow particular important application domains to express their problems in a convenient manner. Furthermore, the ability of modeling systems to provide accurate first- and second-order derivatives vastly improves the reliability of the solver. The third advance is due to the interactions that the first two foster. The ability of a modeler to generate realistic, large-scale models enables the solvers to be tested on much larger and more difficult classes of models. In many cases, new models point to deficiencies in particular facets of a solver, which frequently lead to further enhancements and improved reliability [16, 21]. Furthermore, the ability to solve larger and more complex complementarity problems furthers the development of new applied economic models.

Although it is clear that the state of the art in solution mechanisms for MPECs is currently far less satisfactory than that in complementarity problems, the intent of the present paper is to outline tools and approaches that may facilitate solution of MPECs. The intent of providing these tools is to highlight the potential for new questions that can be asked of this more general model format and to foster the development of a much broader and more realistic suite of examples for algorithmic design and improvement. The aim of the paper is to initiate a dialogue between modelers and algorithm developers.

The main approach to the solution of optimization problems with complementarity constraints used in this paper is a reformulation of the problem as a standard nonlinear program, thus enabling their solution using existing nonlinear programming algorithms. Attempts to do this in the past have been widespread and much of this paper builds on the lessons and examples that previous researchers have exhibited. We start the paper in Section 4.2 by outlining several reformulations of the MPEC as a standard nonlinear program. Inherent in such an approach are the techniques used to process the complementarity constraints, and it is natural to ask whether such approaches can be used to solve complementarity problems, essentially the underlying feasibility problem. Such techniques were somewhat discredited in the 1970s and 1980s, mainly due to the lack of robustness in finding feasible (hence complementary) solutions. The past decade has given rise to new formulations of the complementarity relationships that warrant further investigation, along with significant advances in the robustness and variety of nonlinear programming solvers. Section 4.3 outlines the tools that we provide to perform the conversion automatically. Assuming the modeler provides a GAMS description of the MPEC, the tools generate a large variety of different but equivalent nonlinear programming formulations of the model in a variety of input formats. Some preliminary computational results of using these tools then follow. Section 4.4 describes a set of experiments to outline how these approaches work on a small subset of complementarity problems known to be difficult to solve. We then proceed to describe some techniques for dealing with problems that have multiple complementary solutions. In particular, an example of how to determine all the Nash equilibria is given. The complete set of problems from MPEClib are then processed with a number of nonlinear programming solvers. The chapter concludes by outlining several issues that merit further investigation.

4.2. FORMULATIONS OF THE MODEL

We consider the optimization problem

$$\min_{x \in \mathbf{R}^n, y \in \mathbf{R}^m} f(x, y) \tag{1}$$

subject to the constraints

$$g(x, y) \in K \tag{2}$$

and

$$y \text{ solves } \mathrm{MCP}(h(x, \cdot), \mathbf{B}). \tag{3}$$

The objective function (1) needs no further description, except to state that the solution techniques we intend to apply require that f, g, and h are at least once differentiable, and for some solvers twice differentiable.

The constraints (2) are intended to represent standard nonlinear programming constraints. In particular, we assume that K is the Cartesian product of K_i, so that equality constraints arise whenever $K_i = \{0\}$ and less-than (greater-than) inequality constraints arise when $K_i = \{\xi : \xi \leq 0\}$ ($\{\xi : \xi \geq 0\}$). Because these constraints will be unaltered in all our reformulations, we use this notation for brevity.

The constraints that are the concern of this paper are the equilibrium constraints (3). Essentially, these are parametric constraints (parameterized by x) on the variable y. They signify that y is a solution to the mixed complementarity problem (MCP) that is defined by the function $h(x, \cdot)$ and the bound set $\mathbf{B}$. Due to this constraint (frequently called an equilibrium constraint), problems of this form are typically termed mathematical programs with equilibrium constraints [26, 32]. We now define the precise meaning of this statement.

We partition the y variables into free, $\mathcal{F}$, lower bounded, $\mathcal{L}$, upper bounded, $\mathcal{U}$, and doubly bounded, $\mathcal{B}$, variables. That is,

$$\mathbf{B} := \{y = (y_{\mathcal{F}}, y_{\mathcal{L}}, y_{\mathcal{U}}, y_{\mathcal{B}}) : a_{\mathcal{L}} \leq y_{\mathcal{L}}, \ y_{\mathcal{U}} \leq b_{\mathcal{U}}, \ a_{\mathcal{B}} \leq y_{\mathcal{B}} \leq b_{\mathcal{B}}\},$$

where it is assumed (without loss of generality) that $a_{\mathcal{B}} < b_{\mathcal{B}}$. Thus the box $\mathbf{B}$ represents simple bounds on the variables y.

The constraints (3) can now be given a precise meaning. They are entirely equivalent to the system of equalities and inequalities

$$\begin{aligned} a_{\mathcal{L}} \leq y_{\mathcal{L}}, \ h_{\mathcal{L}}(x, y) \geq 0 \quad &\text{and} \quad (y_{\mathcal{L}} - a_{\mathcal{L}})^T h_{\mathcal{L}}(x, y) = 0 \\ y_{\mathcal{U}} \leq b_{\mathcal{U}}, \ h_{\mathcal{U}}(x, y) \leq 0 \quad &\text{and} \quad (y_{\mathcal{U}} - b_{\mathcal{U}})^T h_{\mathcal{U}}(x, y) = 0 \end{aligned} \tag{4}$$

and for each $i \in \mathcal{B}$ exactly one of the following must hold:

$$
\begin{aligned}
a_i < y_i < b_i, \quad & h_i(x, y) = 0 \\
y_i = a_i, \quad & h_i(x, y) \geq 0 \\
y_i = b_i, \quad & h_i(x, y) \leq 0.
\end{aligned}
\tag{5}
$$

Note in particular that $y \in \mathbf{R}^m$ and h maps into a space of the same dimension m. Informally, the constraints represent orthogonality between the variables y and the function h. Formally, the bounds on the variable y determine the constraints that are satisfied by h. Some special cases are of particular interest and help illuminate the formulation. Whenever the variable is free ($a_i = -\infty$ and $b_i = +\infty$), it follows from (5) that $h_i(x, y) = 0$. Thus if all the y variables are free, then the complementarity problem is simply a system of nonlinear equations, and the MPEC is a nonlinear program. While there may be cases in which $a_i = -\infty$ and $b_i = +\infty$ is desirable, they are not of interest to the techniques developed here; we simply amalgamate such functions h_i into g.

For a second example, suppose a lower bound a_i is zero, then by (4) it follows that h_i is constrained to be nonnegative, and furthermore that the product $y_i h_i(x, y)$ must be zero. This latter conclusion follows from the simple fact that each term in the inner product given in (4) is nonnegative, and a sum of nonnegative terms can be zero only if each of the terms themselves are zero. We use this simple fact throughout this paper without further reference; it always allows us to treat the complementarity "inner product" term either in aggregate form or split up into separate components. The variable y_i is said to be complementary to the function h_i. It is these cases and further generalizations with finite lower and/or upper bounds that are of interest here.

Of course, the relative number of complementarity constraints compared to the number of general nonlinear constraints (i.e., those involving g) can have significant effects on the type of method that should be chosen to solve the problem. Implicit methods [32] work well when the complementarity constraints dominate and satisfy certain regularity conditions. They are typically limited by the ability to solve the resulting nonsmooth problem in the variable x. When the number of complementarity constraints are small, then nonlinear programming techniques should be more applicable. In this paper, we attempt to solve both types of problem using nonlinear programming reformulations.

Unfortunately, the constraints imposed by (5) depend on the solution value of y. For this reason, it is often convenient to introduce new variables $w_\mathcal{B}$ and $v_\mathcal{B}$ and rewrite (5) in an equivalent manner as

$$
\begin{aligned}
w_\mathcal{B} - v_\mathcal{B} &= h_\mathcal{B}(x, y) \\
a_\mathcal{B} \leq y_\mathcal{B} \leq b_\mathcal{B}, \quad & w_\mathcal{B} \geq 0, \quad v_\mathcal{B} \geq 0 \\
(y_\mathcal{B} - a_\mathcal{B})^T w_\mathcal{B} = 0, \quad & (b_\mathcal{B} - y_\mathcal{B})^T v_\mathcal{B} = 0.
\end{aligned}
\tag{6}
$$

We often introduce auxiliary variables for the constraints (4) as well to remove the need for a nonlinear solver to evaluate the derivatives of $h_\mathcal{L}$ and $h_\mathcal{U}$ more than once. Thus, (4) can be equivalently written as

$$w_\mathcal{L} = h_\mathcal{L}(x, y), \ a_\mathcal{L} \le y_\mathcal{L}, \ w_\mathcal{L} \ge 0 \quad \text{and} \quad (y_\mathcal{L} - a_\mathcal{L})^T w_\mathcal{L} = 0$$
$$v_\mathcal{U} = -h_\mathcal{U}(x, y), \ y_\mathcal{U} \le b_\mathcal{U}, \ v_\mathcal{U} \ge 0 \quad \text{and} \quad (b_\mathcal{U} - y_\mathcal{U})^T v_\mathcal{U} = 0. \tag{7}$$

Note that the size of the model will increase due to the additional artificial variables.

We collect all the "auxiliary definitions" together to simplify the ensuing discussion. Thus, we define a set $\mathcal{H}$ by

$$(x, y, w, v) \in \mathcal{H} \iff$$
$$g(x, y) \in K, \ w_\mathcal{L} = h_\mathcal{L}(x, y), \ v_\mathcal{U} = -h_\mathcal{U}(x, y), \ w_\mathcal{B} - v_\mathcal{B} = h_\mathcal{B}(x, y)$$
$$\text{and} \quad y \in \mathbf{B}, \ w_\mathcal{L} \ge 0, \ v_\mathcal{U} \ge 0, \ w_\mathcal{B} \ge 0, \ v_\mathcal{B} \ge 0.$$

Collecting all these observations together gives the first nonlinear programming formulation that we will consider:

$$\min_{(x,y,w,v)\in\mathcal{H}} f(x, y)$$
$$\text{subject to} \ (y_i - a_i)w_i = \mu, \ i \in \mathcal{L} \cup \mathcal{B} \tag{8}$$
$$(b_i - y_i)v_i = \mu, \ i \in \mathcal{U} \cup \mathcal{B}.$$

All the reformulations we give in this paper are parameterized by a scalar value μ. For $\mu = 0$, the above formulation corresponds precisely to the MPEC given as (1), (2), and (3) with the inner products treated componentwise. For positive values of μ the complementarity product terms are forced to be equal to μ; as μ is decreased to zero the corresponding solutions lie on what is typically called the "central path" in the interior point literature [50].

It is clear that all of the terms involved in the inner products of (6) and (7) are themselves nonnegative, and hence the equality with 0 can be replaced by a less-than inequality,

$$\min_{(x,y,w,v)\in\mathcal{H}} f(x, y)$$
$$\text{subject to} \ (y_i - a_i)w_i \le \mu, \ i \in \mathcal{L} \cup \mathcal{B} \tag{9}$$
$$(b_i - y_i)v_i \le \mu, \ i \in \mathcal{U} \cup \mathcal{B}.$$

Again, for $\mu = 0$, this corresponds to the MPEC given as (1), (2), and (3). For positive values of μ this corresponds to a componentwise relaxation of the original problem.

The following formulation aggregates all the complementarity constraints:

$$\min_{(x,y,w,v)\in\mathcal{H}} f(x, y)$$
$$\text{subject to} \ (y_\mathcal{L} - a_\mathcal{L})^T w_\mathcal{L} + (b_\mathcal{U} - y_\mathcal{U})^T v_\mathcal{U} + (y_\mathcal{B} - a_\mathcal{B})^T w_\mathcal{B} \tag{10}$$
$$+ (b_\mathcal{B} - y_\mathcal{B})^T v_\mathcal{B} \le \mu.$$

A partial aggregation can also be carried out:

$$\min_{(x,y,w,v)\in\mathcal{H}} f(x,y)$$
$$\text{subject to} \quad (y_{\mathcal{L}} - a_{\mathcal{L}})^T w_{\mathcal{L}} \leq \mu, (b_{\mathcal{U}} - y_{\mathcal{U}})^T v_{\mathcal{U}} \leq \mu \tag{11}$$
$$(y_B - a_B)^T w_B \leq \mu, (b_B - y_B)^T v_B \leq \mu.$$

There is of course a similar aggregation for (8) that immediately leads to the problem

$$\min_{(x,y,w,v)\in\mathcal{H}} f(x,y)$$
$$\text{subject to} \quad (y_{\mathcal{L}} - a_{\mathcal{L}})^T w_{\mathcal{L}} + (b_{\mathcal{U}} - y_{\mathcal{U}})^T v_{\mathcal{U}} + (y_B - a_B)^T w_B \tag{12}$$
$$+ (b_B - y_B)^T v_B = \mu.$$

It is well known that the above formulations (for $\mu = 0$) have poor theoretical properties in terms of the classical constraint qualifications.

Instead of using the auxiliary variables $w_{\mathcal{L}}$ and $v_{\mathcal{U}}$, we can substitute the relevant functions into the formulations explicitly. To facilitate a more succinct description, we introduce a new set $\tilde{\mathcal{H}}$ that collects the definitions together:

$$(x, y, w, v) \in \tilde{\mathcal{H}} \iff$$
$$g(x, y) \in K, y \in \mathbf{B}, h_{\mathcal{L}}(x, y) \geq 0, \ h_{\mathcal{U}}(x, y) \leq 0$$
$$\text{and} \quad w_B - v_B = h_B(x, y), w_B \geq 0, v_B \geq 0.$$

We rewrite four of the above reformulations with such an elimination:

$$\min_{(x,y,w,v)\in\tilde{\mathcal{H}}} f(x,y)$$
$$\text{subject to} \quad (y_i - a_i)h_i(x, y) = \mu, \ i \in \mathcal{L} \tag{13}$$
$$(b_i - y_i)h_i(x, y) = -\mu, \ i \in \mathcal{U}$$
$$(y_i - a_i)w_i + (b_i - y_i)v_i = \mu, \ i \in \mathcal{B}$$

$$\min_{(x,y,w,v)\in\tilde{\mathcal{H}}} f(x,y)$$
$$\text{subject to} \quad (y_i - a_i)h_i(x, y) \leq \mu, \ i \in \mathcal{L} \tag{14}$$
$$(b_i - y_i)h_i(x, y) \geq -\mu, \ i \in \mathcal{U}$$
$$(y_i - a_i)w_i \leq \mu, \ (b_i - y_i)v_i \leq \mu, \ i \in \mathcal{B}$$

$$\min_{(x,y,w,v)\in\tilde{\mathcal{H}}} f(x,y)$$
$$\text{subject to} \quad (y_{\mathcal{L}} - a_{\mathcal{L}})^T h_{\mathcal{L}}(x, y) \leq \mu, (b_{\mathcal{U}} - y_{\mathcal{U}})^T h_{\mathcal{U}}(x, y) \geq -\mu \tag{15}$$
$$(y_B - a_B)^T w_B \leq \mu, (b_B - y_B)^T v_B \leq \mu$$

$$\min_{(x,y,w,v)\in\tilde{\mathcal{H}}} f(x,y)$$
$$\text{subject to} \quad (y_{\mathcal{L}} - a_{\mathcal{L}})^T h_{\mathcal{L}}(x, y) - (b_{\mathcal{U}} - y_{\mathcal{U}})^T h_{\mathcal{U}}(x, y) \tag{16}$$
$$+ (y_B - a_B)^T w_B + (b_B - y_B)^T v_B = \mu.$$

A different approach involves a penalization of the complementarity conditions. We add a weighted sum of the complementarity conditions to the objective function, removing the complementarity conditions from the constraints in (10). With decreasing μ, the weight on the complementarity conditions becomes progressively larger:

$$\min_{(x,y,w,v)\in\mathcal{H}} f(x, y) + \frac{1}{\mu}\{(y_\mathcal{L} - a_\mathcal{L})^T w_\mathcal{L} + (b_\mathcal{U} - y_\mathcal{U})^T v_\mathcal{U} \\ + (y_\mathcal{B} - a_\mathcal{B})^T w_\mathcal{B} + (b_\mathcal{B} - y_\mathcal{B})^T v_\mathcal{B}\}. \tag{17}$$

A similar scheme works with (16):

$$\min_{(x,y,w,v)\in\tilde{\mathcal{H}}} f(x, y) + \frac{1}{\mu}\{(y_\mathcal{L} - a_\mathcal{L})^T h_\mathcal{L}(x, y) - (b_\mathcal{U} - y_\mathcal{U})^T h_\mathcal{U}(x, y) \\ + (y_\mathcal{B} - a_\mathcal{B})^T w_\mathcal{B} + (b_\mathcal{B} - y_\mathcal{B})^T v_\mathcal{B}\}. \tag{18}$$

A simple calculation (suggested in [19]) allows one to see that for two scalars r and s,

$$\phi(r, s) = 0 \iff r \geq 0, \ s \geq 0 \quad \text{and} \quad rs = 0,$$

where

$$\phi(r, s) := \sqrt{r^2 + s^2} - (r + s).$$

Note that ϕ is not differentiable at the origin, which may lead to solution difficulties. To overcome the nondifferentiability problems, a variety of smoothing approaches have been suggested. Essentially, they replace the solution of the MPEC by a parameterized NLP(μ) and solve a sequence of problems for decreasing values of $\mu > 0$. The perturbation μ guarantees differentiability of all constraint functions by replacing ϕ by

$$\phi_\mu(r, s) := \sqrt{r^2 + s^2 + \mu} - (r + s).$$

Note that $\phi_\mu(r, s) = 0$ if and only if $r > 0$, $s > 0$ and $rs = \mu/2$. Thus, the complementarity condition is satisfied in the limit as μ goes to zero. The formulation given below was proposed in [12]:

$$\min_{(x,y,w,v)\in\mathcal{H}} f(x, y) \\ \text{subject to} \ \phi_\mu(y_i - a_i, w_i) = 0, \ i \in \mathcal{L} \cup \mathcal{B} \tag{19} \\ \phi_\mu(b_i - y_i, v_i) = 0, \ i \in \mathcal{U} \cup \mathcal{B}.$$

It is also possible to rewrite the complementarity constraints as a system of nonlinear equations, namely,

$$\min(y_\mathcal{L} - a_\mathcal{L}, h_\mathcal{L}(x, y)) = 0 \\ \min(b_\mathcal{U} - y_\mathcal{U}, -h_\mathcal{U}(x, y)) = 0 \\ \min(y_\mathcal{B} - a_\mathcal{B}, h_\mathcal{B}(x, y)) = 0 \\ \min(b_\mathcal{B} - y_\mathcal{B}, -h_\mathcal{B}(x, y)) = 0. \tag{20}$$

While we provide mechanisms to form the nonlinear program using this construction, a modeler should note that the following formulation involves nonsmooth functions and thus appropriate solvers need to be invoked:

$$\min_{(x,y,w,v)\in\mathcal{H}} f(x, y)$$

$$\text{subject to } \min(y_i - a_i, w_i) \le \mu, i \in \mathcal{L} \cup \mathcal{B} \tag{21}$$

$$\min(b_i - y_i, v_i) \le \mu, i \in \mathcal{U} \cup \mathcal{B}.$$

A smoothed version of (20) was proposed in [5]. In this case, $\min(r, s)$ is replaced by

$$\psi_\mu(r, s) = r - \mu \log(1 + \exp((r - s)/\mu)).$$

Updating the four equations in (20) using this replacement is an alternative way to enforce complementarity as μ is driven to 0:

$$\min_{(x,y,w,v)\in\mathcal{H}} f(x, y)$$

$$\text{subject to } \psi_\mu(y_i - a_i, w_i) = 0, i \in \mathcal{L} \cup \mathcal{B} \tag{22}$$

$$\psi_\mu(b_i - y_i, v_i) = 0, i \in \mathcal{U} \cup \mathcal{B}.$$

It is easy to see that the functions ϕ_μ, min, and ψ_μ enforce the nonnegativity of their arguments in the limit without needing the additional bounding constraints. In the following we simply remove the bounding constraints in the definition of $\tilde{\mathcal{H}}$, leaving the following:

$$(x, y, w, v) \in \mathcal{H}^* \iff$$

$$g(x, y) \in K, \ w_\mathcal{L} = h_\mathcal{L}(x, y), \ v_\mathcal{U} = -h_\mathcal{U}(x, y), \ w_\mathcal{B} - v_\mathcal{B} = h_\mathcal{B}(x, y).$$

It is unknown at this time whether the bound statements help or hinder the solution process, but the tool we describe in the next section allows the modeler to make such choices, as shown by the examples below:

$$\min_{(x,y,w,v)\in\mathcal{H}^*} f(x, y)$$

$$\text{subject to } \phi_\mu(y_i - a_i, w_i) = 0, i \in \mathcal{L} \cup \mathcal{B} \tag{23}$$

$$\phi_\mu(b_i - y_i, v_i) = 0, i \in \mathcal{U} \cup \mathcal{B},$$

$$\min_{(x,y,w,v)\in\mathcal{H}^*} f(x, y)$$

$$\text{subject to } \min(y_i - a_i, w_i) = \mu, i \in \mathcal{L} \cup \mathcal{B} \tag{24}$$

$$\min(b_i - y_i, v_i) = \mu, i \in \mathcal{U} \cup \mathcal{B},$$

$$\min_{(x,y,w,v)\in\mathcal{H}^*} f(x, y)$$

$$\text{subject to } \psi_\mu(y_i - a_i, w_i) = 0, i \in \mathcal{L} \cup \mathcal{B} \tag{25}$$

$$\psi_\mu(b_i - y_i, v_i) = 0, i \in \mathcal{U} \cup \mathcal{B}.$$

Elimination of the artificial variables $w_\mathcal{L}$ and $v_\mathcal{U}$ within ϕ_μ gives the following formulation:

$$\min_{x \in \mathbf{R}^n, y \in \mathbf{R}^m, w_B, v_B} f(x, y)$$

subject to $g(x, y) \in K, \quad w_B - v_B = h_B(x, y)$

$\phi_\mu(y_i - a_i, h_i(x, y)) = 0, \quad i \in \mathcal{L}$ (26)

$\phi_\mu(b_i - y_i, -h_i(x, y)) = 0, \quad i \in \mathcal{U}$

$\phi_\mu(y_i - a_i, w_i) = 0, \quad \phi_\mu(b_i - y_i, v_i) = 0, \quad i \in \mathcal{B}.$

We can further eliminate w_B and v_B and treat finite upper and lower bounds using an approach suggested in [2]:

$$\min_{x \in \mathbf{R}^n, y \in \mathbf{R}^m} f(x, y)$$

subject to $g(x, y) \in K$

$\phi_\mu(y_i - a_i, h_i(x, y)) = 0, \quad i \in \mathcal{L}$ (27)

$\phi_\mu(b_i - y_i, -h_i(x, y)) = 0, \quad i \in \mathcal{U}$

$\phi_\mu(y_i - a_i, \phi_\mu(-h_i(x, y), b_i - y_i)) = 0, \quad i \in \mathcal{B}.$

Finally, the doubly bounded variables are sometimes treated using an alternative approach due to Scholtes:

$$\min_{x \in \mathbf{R}^n, y \in \mathbf{B}, w, v} f(x, y)$$

subject to $g(x, y) \in K, \quad w_B = h_B(x, y)$

$w_{\mathcal{L}} = h_{\mathcal{L}}(x, y), \quad v_{\mathcal{U}} = -h_{\mathcal{U}}(x, y), \quad w_{\mathcal{L}} \geq 0, v_{\mathcal{U}} \geq 0$ (28)

$(y_i - a_i)w_i = \mu, \quad i \in \mathcal{L}$

$(b_i - y_i)v_i = \mu, \quad i \in \mathcal{U}$

$(y_i - a_i)w_i \leq \mu, \quad (b_i - y_i)w_i \geq -\mu, \quad i \in \mathcal{B}.$

Note this is only exact when $\mu = 0$. Elimination of $w_{\mathcal{L}}$ and $v_{\mathcal{U}}$ then provides the following formulation:

$$\min_{x \in \mathbf{R}^n, y \in \mathbf{B}, w_B} f(x, y)$$

subject to $g(x, y) \in K, \quad w_B = h_B(x, y), \quad h_{\mathcal{L}}(x, y) \geq 0, \quad h_{\mathcal{U}}(x, y) \leq 0$ (29)

$(y_{\mathcal{L}} - a_{\mathcal{L}})^T h_{\mathcal{L}}(x, y) - (b_{\mathcal{U}} - y_{\mathcal{U}})^T h_{\mathcal{U}}(x, y) = \mu$

$(y_i - a_i)w_i \leq \mu, \quad (b_i - y_i)w_i \geq -\mu, \quad i \in \mathcal{B}.$

It is further possible to eliminate w_B with or without aggregation on the remaining complementarity constraints:

$$\min_{x \in \mathbf{R}^n, y \in \mathbf{B}} f(x, y)$$

subject to $g(x, y) \in K, \quad h_{\mathcal{L}}(x, y) \geq 0, \quad h_{\mathcal{U}}(x, y) \leq 0$ (30)

$(y_{\mathcal{L}} - a_{\mathcal{L}})^T h_{\mathcal{L}}(x, y) - (b_{\mathcal{U}} - y_{\mathcal{U}})^T h_{\mathcal{U}}(x, y) \leq \mu$

$(y_i - a_i)h_i(x, y) \leq \mu, \quad (b_i - y_i)h_i(x, y) \geq -\mu, \quad i \in \mathcal{B},$

$$\min_{x \in \mathbb{R}^n, y \in \mathbf{B}} f(x, y)$$

subject to $g(x, y) \in K, h_{\mathcal{L}}(x, y) \geq 0, h_{\mathcal{U}}(x, y) \leq 0$

$$(y_i - a_i)h_i(x, y) = \mu, i \in \mathcal{L} \tag{31}$$
$$(b_i - y_i)h_i(x, y) = -\mu, i \in \mathcal{U}$$
$$(y_i - a_i)h_i(x, y) \leq \mu, (b_i - y_i)h_i(x, y) \geq -\mu, \ i \in \mathcal{B}.$$

4.3. TOOLS FOR MPEC SOLUTION

4.3.1. Modeling Language Tools

MPECs can be modeled in GAMS or AMPL using quite natural syntax. For example, in GAMS we would define the functions f, g, and h with standard "equation" syntax, along with the bounds on the variable y. A full example is given in Appendix A. To define the actual MPEC model, the following statement is used:

```
model mpecmod / deff, defg, defh.y /;
```

Here it is assumed that the objective (1) is defined in the equation deff, the general constraints (2) are defined in defg and the function h is described in defh. The complementarity relationship is defined by the bounds on y and the orthogonality relationship shown in the model declaration using ".". More details for GAMS MPEC models can be found in [9], while similar formulations exist in AMPL [13].

In order to solve these models we propose to automatically reformulate the problems as nonlinear programs using a "convert" tool. We provide a solver, "nlpec," that automatically calls the convert tool and reports the results in the original GAMS environment. The specific syntax used by a modeler follows:

```
option mpec=nlpec;
solve mpecmod using mpec minimizing obj;
```

4.3.2. The Convert Tool

Many solvers have been developed that require a particular form of input, or have been implemented to interact with a particular modeling system. The convert tool is an evolving program whose purpose is to overcome these restrictive input formats.

Models that are formulated as a GAMS program are typically defined in terms of equations and variables that run over sets that are specified by the modeler. At compilation time, all of these equations are resolved into scalar equations and variables in order to be passed on to a particular solver. Sparse linear algebra and computational efficiency issues are considered, and a solver sees a clean model along with routines that specify derivative information.

At this scalar level it is very easy to convert the model into another input format. For example, the GAMS model can be written out as a scalar AMPL model (using the option "ampl"). Thus, the original GAMS model can be solved by any solver that accepts AMPL input. In a similar fashion, the BARON link to GAMS uses the convert tool to convert a GAMS model into BARON's required scalar input. Details of the other conversions possible can be found at http://www.gamsworld.org/translate.htm.

We modified the tool further to allow MPECs to be reformulated as nonlinear programs at the scalar level. In fact, we currently have 23 different reformulations whereby the original MCP or MPEC is rewritten as a scalar GAMS nonlinear programming model (i.e., without any sets), but with the complementarity constraints rewritten using one of the constructs of the previous section.

The tool is somewhat more sophisticated than just a simple converter. The mapping between the original variables and the new scalar variables is maintained, so that a solution of the original problem can be recovered from the solution of the converted problem. In this way, we can easily develop new "black box" algorithms for MPECs built simply by changing formulation, starting point, and the sequence of parametric solves.

4.3.3. Options and Parametric Solution

At the current time, 23 reformulations are provided by the convert tool. The following table indicates the internal code that we use for each reformulation of the previous section. To specify using the reformulation (8) for example, the modeler uses the option "er = 1" in the file "nlpec.opt":

1	2	3	4	5	6	7	8	9	10	11	12
(8)	(9)	(28)	(12)	(16)	(29)	(30)	(31)	(17)	(18)	(13)	(26)

13	14	15	16	17	18	19	20	21	22	23
(27)	(24)	(21)	(25)	(22)	(15)	(14)	(11)	(10)	(19)	(23)

Details of all the current options of "nlpec" are given in Table 4.1.

TABLE 4.1. *Options for the solver NLPEC*

Option	Value	Default	Description
er	integer	1	Reformulation to be generated.
initmu	real	0	Initial value of the parameter μ. A single solve of the nonlinear program is carried out for this value.
numsolves	integer	0	Number of extra solves carried out in a loop. This should be set in conjunction with the updatefac option.
updatefac	real	0.1	The factor that multiplies μ before each of the extra solves triggered by the numsolves option.
finalmu	real	–	Final value of the parameter μ. If specified, an extra solve is carried out with μ set to this value.
initslo	real	0	The lower bound for any artificials that are added.
initsup	real	inf	The upper bound for any artificials that are added.

It is assumed throughout all the testing that the modeler will have provided starting point values for the variables x and y. In all the formulations that add artificial variables (w and v) we initialize their values as follows:

$$w_B = \max\{0, h_B(x, y)\}$$
$$v_B = \max\{0, -h_B(x, y)\}$$
$$w_L = \max\{0, h_L(x, y)\}$$
$$v_U = \max\{0, -h_U(x, y)\}.$$

The tool provides the ability to change the constant chosen here as 0, and also allows an upper bound to be placed on the starting value for these artificial variables. Appropriate choices for these values is a topic for future research.

Another approach of interest when the complementarity constraints dominate the problem is to solve the complementarity problem first to generate initial values for the nonlinear programming solver. This approach has been used successfully in [18] and is a technique that is easily available to a modeler using the tools outlined here.

In many cases, it is useful to generate a sequence of problems, parameterized by μ, that converge to the solution of the original problem as μ goes to zero. The convert tool generates nonlinear programs that involve the scalar μ. We have provided some extra options to the solver "nlpec" that allow updates to μ and multiple solves in a loop.

We have used a variety of option files (see Fig. 4.1) for our computational tests and describe them now as examples of the flexibility of this scheme. Option file 1 results in seven nonlinear programs to be solved, the first with a value of $\mu = 0.01$, followed by five more solves with values of μ multiplied each time by 0.1. The final solve has $\mu = 0$. Option file 2 has six solves, the first with $\mu = 1.0$, the second with $\mu = 0.1$, each subsequent solve multiplying μ by 0.1.

initmu = 0.01	initmu = 1	initmu = 1
numsolves = 5	numsolves = 5	numsolves = 3
finalmu = 0		
(a) Option file 1	(b) Option file 2	(c) Option file 3
initmu = 1	initmu = 1	initmu = 0.2
numsolves = 4	numsolves = 5	finalmu = 0.1
	finalmu = 0	
(d) Option file 4	(e) Option file 5	(f) Option file 6

Figure 4.1. Option files used for computational results.

The resulting sequence of solves from option files 3, 4, 5, and 6 should be clear.

4.3.4. Nonlinear Optimization Codes

A large number of NLP solvers are available for the solution of the reformulated MPEC and MCP models. We have chosen a subset of these for computational testing. While all of the solvers chosen enjoy a strong reputation, they were also chosen to represent different algorithmic approaches.

For the MCP problems, we can choose to do no reformulation and solve the original model using the MCP solver PATH [8, 15, 29, 35]. PATH implements a generalization of Newton's method with linesearch applied to an equivalent formulation of a complementarity problem as a nonsmooth system of equations. The subproblems are solved using a variant of Lemke's method, a pivotal method for LCP. The pathsearch is controlled by the Fisher merit function and resorts to a gradient step of that function if the subproblem solution fails to give appropriate descent. Some safeguards are included that help when singularities are encountered. Some computational enhancements include preprocessing (logical inferences to reduce the size and complexity of the problem), a crash procedure to find a good starting basis, and various strategies to overcome degeneracy.

The NLP solver CONOPT [11] is a feasible path solver based on the proven GRG method, especially suitable for highly nonlinear models. It also includes extensions for phase 0, linear mode iterations, a sequential linear programming component, and more recently the use of Hessian information. MINOS [31] solves NLPs with linear constraints using a quasi-Newton, reduced-gradient algorithm. A projected Lagrangian algorithm with a quadratic penalty function is used for the nonlinear constraints. SNOPT [20] applies a sparse sequential quadratic programming (SQP) method, using limited-memory quasi-Newton approximations to the Hessian of the Lagrangian. The merit function for steplength control is an augmented Lagrangian. BARON [42, 45] is a computational system for solving nonconvex optimization problems to global optimality. This *branch and reduce optimization navigator* combines constraint propagation, interval analysis, and duality in its reduce arsenal with enhanced branch and bound concepts.

Although the solvers mentioned above all run locally, it is also possible to solve models on a remote machine. Remote solution is made possible via the Kestrel interface [10] to NEOS [7], the network enabled optimization server. Using Kestrel and NEOS, we have access to many more NLP solvers, in particular the interior point (or barrier) methods KNITRO and LOQO. KNITRO [4] is a trust region method which uses sequential quadratic programming methodology to treat the barrier subproblems. LOQO [49] is a line search algorithm that has much in common with interior algorithms for linear and convex quadratic programming. It is interesting to note that both KNITRO and LOQO use AMPL interfaces; the Kestrel interface

TABLE 4.2. *MCP models*

Name	Variables	Nonzeros	Density (%)
CAMMCP	242	1287	2.20
DUOPOLY	63	252	6.35
EHL_KOST	101	10200	99.99
ELECTRIC	158	539	2.16
FORCEDSA	186	440	1.27
GAMES	16	140	54.69
LINCONT	419	23207	13.22
PGVON105	105	588	5.33
SHUBIK	33	136	12.49
SIMPLE-EX	17	158	54.67
SPILLMCP	110	455	3.76

takes advantage of the convert tool described above to produce an AMPL form of the model in question.

4.4. COMPUTATIONAL RESULTS

4.4.1. Feasibility Problems

We consider a set of 11 test problems that have historically caused difficulties to MCP solvers. All of these are fairly small models; their sizes are given in Table 4.2.

Several models have their origins in the economics literature. The general equilibrium model for Cameroon [6] has been formulated in a number of ways, here in CAMMCP as an MCP. The model DUOPOLY is a dynamic oligopoly model described in [27, 28]. An electricity flow equilibrium model ELECTRIC, a simple exchange model SIMPLE-EX, and a consumption model with spillover effects SPILLMCP were all provided in [41]. A standard n-player Nash equilibrium problem [48] is called GAMES. The von Thünen land use model [14, 44] is implemented in PGVON105, while the Shubik–Quint general equilibrium model with money [43] is used as the basis for SHUBIK. Robinson [36, 37] provides a series of complementarity models used for shadow pricing in red–blue tactical decisions, one of which is called FORCEDSA.

Other examples of complementarity arise in engineering [17]. The remaining two models are examples of these, including a lubrication model EHL_KOST detailed in [25], and a friction-contact problem called LINCONT described in [33].

Table 4.3 gives an indication of which solver/reformulation combinations are most effective in solving the set of MCP models chosen. Effectiveness is measured here only in terms of robustness. In all these feasibility cases, we set up a dummy objective function of 0. Each solver/reformulation combination was tried without options and with one of the option files in Fig. 4.1. The results reported are for the more successful of these runs.

TABLE 4.3. *MCP: Successful solves*

Solver	MCP	ER1 (8)	ER2 (9)	ER9 (17)	ER21 (10)	ER23 (23)
PATH	9					
BARON		5	4	5	7	2
CONOPT		2	3	3	3	1
MINOS		5	6	6	5	3
SNOPT		8	5	9	6	3
FILTER		4	5	6	3	1
KNITRO		1	6	6	0	0
LOQO		5	3	4	5	1

Note: Column headings refer to the reformulation equation number.

Several points are clear from these results. First, as should be expected, a specialized complementarity solver is more robust for solving these feasibility problems, but even on these difficult problems, several nonlinear programming algorithms perform well on certain reformulations. Second, somewhat unexpectedly, the reformulations using the Fischer function (ER23) seem to cause the nonlinear programming solvers distinct difficulty for these models. Finally, although Table 4.3 does not exhibit this fact, for the cases where PATH fails, we can solve the problem by one or more of these reformulations. From a modeler's perspective this is very useful, because during the development cycle many of the deficiencies of the model are best identified from a solution. Unfortunately, the models that are typically hardest to solve are those with errors in their formulation.

Comparison of solution times is quite important, but can easily be misleading. In the case of the solvers tested via the remote Kestrel interface, it is difficult to say for certain what machines the solvers ran on. This and other factors make it difficult to use solution times for any Kestrel solvers in a meaningful way. For these reasons we have not included the results in the above table. However, timing comparisons can be found at http://www.gamsworld.org/mpec/nlpectests. These show that in general the nonlinear programming reformulations are slower than the specialized complementarity solvers. In order not to repeat results that are given elsewhere, we note that for large-scale problems, PATH is typically very effective and fast. Detailed results can be found in [30], for example.

It is also clear that by adjusting certain options (for example, feasibility or optimality tolerances) for each of the solvers, a different set of models could have been solved. We limited our computational testing to the default settings of each solver.

4.4.2. Small Optimization Problems

There is a considerable literature on multiplicity of solutions to complementarity problems, arising both from applications of Nash equilibria and from crack propagation in structural mechanics. Determining which of these multiple solutions satisfies some "optimality criteria" is a problem of much practical interest.

Because in many cases the complementary solutions are isolated, nonlinear programming techniques that find local minimizers are extremely prone to failure, in that while they may find feasible points, the value of the objective could be arbitrarily poor. In order to solve these problems reliably, one of two approaches is needed. As usual, the first (and most generally applicable) approach requires the modeler to provide a starting point that is close to the solution required. The second approach is to use a nonlinear programming code that is designed to find global solutions. Because of the enormous difficulties of these problem classes, the second approach is currently severely limited in problem size, but we will outline its use on two small examples to exhibit the potential for further research in this area.

The first problem comes from the mathematical programming literature [24] and is a four-variable nonlinear complementarity problem with exactly two isolated solutions, namely, $(1.2247, 0, 0, 0.5)$ and $(1, 0, 3, 0)$. We set up two MPECs; the first, KOJSHIN3, minimizes x_3, whereas the second, KOJSHIN4, minimizes x_4. Both of these problems have feasible sets consisting of two points, and each has an optimal value of 0. As is to be expected, the nonlinear programming algorithms applied to the formulations outlined above either fail to find a feasible point, or have a tendency to terminate at the nonoptimal solution.

However, applying the BARON solver (a global method) to reformulation 1 with $\mu = 0$ solves both problems to optimality in under 0.2 seconds. In fact, all the feasible points that lie in some compact set can be enumerated for this example if desired using the "numsol -1" option of BARON. There are some potential difficulties in discriminating among solutions that are subject to rounding error, but in general all solutions will be found.

The second example of this nature is a Nash equilibrium example given in [23]. In this example, three distinct equilibria are known; the models KEHOE1, KEHOE2, and KEHOE3 have objectives set up that respectively minimize or maximize the price variables or find a solution closest to the starting point. In order to enumerate the distinct equilibria, we found it easiest to use BARON on a modification of KEHOE1; we first found the equilibrium that minimized the sum of the prices and then added an extra constraint on the price sum to exclude that solution. Thus, with three solves under BARON, we were able to enumerate all the equilibria, without special knowledge of starting points. A fourth solve confirmed that no more equilibria existed within the (large) compact set used for the problem variables. The example file given in Appendix A was used for this purpose. Note that the complementarity problem is defined using the "." notation and that the income definitions can be treated as general nonlinear constraints. The restriction equation removes any solutions for which the sum of the prices is less than 3.64.

These techniques are unlikely to work for large-scale problems. In these cases, it is likely that multistart or sampling methods will be needed to improve the likelihood of generating a global solution. Some promising approaches that can be used from within GAMS are given in [34, 47].

4.4.3. Feasibility Tests

Computational tests of the sort discussed in this chapter underscore the need for a separate utility to verify the correctness of the solutions obtained and create uniform reports of their accuracy. The GAMS "solver" Examiner is such a utility. GAMS/Examiner is currently under development and was extended to allow checks for feasibility of the MPEC solutions. It performs three separate checks on MPEC models.

The first check is for feasibility in the primal variables x and y with respect to the variable bounds. The error reported is the maximum violation found. GAMS solvers typically maintain primal variable feasibility with zero tolerance, so there is usually nothing to report here.

The second check is for feasibility with respect to the NLP constraints (2) and the equilibrium constraints (3). For the NLP constraints (2), the residual error in the ith row is computed in the obvious way. For the equilibrium constraints (3), however, we assign a nonzero residual to row i only if

1. the matching variable is in $\mathcal{L}$ and h_i is negative, or
2. the matching variable is in $\mathcal{U}$ and h_i is positive, or
3. the matching variable is in $\mathcal{F}$ and h_i is nonzero.

Note that if the matching variable is in $\mathcal{B}$ the residual is set to zero. The error reported is the maximum residual taken over both sets of constraints.

The third check is for complementarity; this check involves only the equilibrium constraints (3) and the variables y. Again, the error reported is the maximum violation found, taken now over all the equilibrium constraints. For each such constraint, we compute errors with respect to the lower and upper variable bounds; the maximum of these two is the residual error r_i. We describe this computation below:

1. $c = \max(0, a_i - y_i), d = \min(1, \max(0, y_i - a_i))$.
2. $r_i = \max(c, d \max(h_i, 0))$
3. $c = \max(0, y_i - b_i), d = \min(1, \max(0, b_i - y_i))$.
4. $r_i = \max(r_i, \max(c, d \max(-h_i, 0)))$.

Unless the variable y is outside of its bounds (a *very* unusual case for any of the NLP solvers tested), the deviation c will always be zero, and the effect is to assign zero error for the lower bound if h_i is negative, and otherwise to scale the error h_i by $\min(y_i - a_i, 1)$. Similarly, we assign zero error for the upper bound if h_i is positive, and otherwise scale the error by $\min(b_i - y_i, 1)$. This definition of the residual error is taken from the GAMS MCP solvers, where it has proven to be very useful in identifying the constraints of interest in unsolvable, poorly formulated, and

TABLE 4.4. *Percentage of successful solves resulting in feasible solutions of MPEC using the NLP reformulations of Section 4.3 with GAMS solver links*

	CONOPT	MINOS	SNOPT	BARON	anysolv
er1 .0	73	39	76	46	85
er1 .1	82	58	78	50	90
er2 .0	72	40	80	46	88
er2 .1	75	73	71	70	90
er3 .1	82	58	79	51	90
er4 .0	71	64	71	66	87
er4 .1	72	84	65	75	89
er5 .0	61	60	70	64	86
er5 .1	68	52	55	71	87
er6 .0	58	59	68	63	85
er7 .0	53	64	75	67	86
er8 .0	62	37	60	53	84
er9 .3	63	54	63	47	79
er10 .4	51	48	54	34	72
er11 .1	79	49	65	59	88
er12 .0	41	60	73	63	85
er12 .5	72	58	64	66	89
er13 .0	37	60	68	64	85
er13 .5	71	61	68	66	89
er16 .0	4	8	8	13	15
er17 .0	9	9	8	16	17
er18 .0	59	67	77	72	89
er19 .0	70	32	76	57	85
er20 .0	73	66	76	72	89
er20 .1	78	86	71	79	91
er21 .0	71	64	74	70	87
er21 .1	76	83	67	77	89
er21 .5	76	84	64	77	89
er22 .5	71	47	63	43	90
er23 .5	75	67	63	64	90
er*.any	96	91	91	85	96

partially completed models. For the purposes of this paper we declare a solution to be feasible if the maximum residual is less than 10^{-5}.

4.4.4. Larger Optimization Problems

Techniques for solving larger problems cannot rely on the sampling techniques or enumerative/branch and reduce techniques that work well on small problems. Instead, currently, much more emphasis is placed on the modeler to provide problems for which the complementarity problems have nice properties (i.e., stability

TABLE 4.5. *Percentage of solves resulting in solutions of MPEC (within 1% of the best found) using GAMS solver links*

	CONOPT	MINOS	SNOPT	BARON	anysolv
er1 .0	43	20	49	41	63
er1 .1	64	43	61	41	80
er2 .0	43	18	45	41	63
er2 .1	47	55	51	55	76
er3 .1	64	43	60	42	82
er4 .0	39	35	39	52	66
er4 .1	41	53	40	58	72
er5 .0	26	23	36	47	62
er5 .1	43	38	40	59	76
er6 .0	24	22	35	46	61
er7 .0	26	21	35	49	62
er8 .0	35	22	32	37	61
er9 .3	45	42	41	41	62
er10 .4	37	37	42	32	57
er11 .1	59	36	40	40	71
er12 .0	26	35	46	32	57
er12 .5	61	33	49	46	78
er13 .0	22	35	41	33	57
er13 .5	61	36	53	45	77
er16 .0	4	7	7	8	10
er17 .0	8	7	7	10	10
er18 .0	30	25	38	53	65
er19 .0	36	21	40	34	60
er20 .0	43	38	45	55	71
er20 .1	49	57	45	64	76
er21 .0	41	35	42	54	68
er21 .5	54	60	49	63	80
er22 .5	64	28	41	37	78
er23 .5	64	48	52	51	75
er*.any	95	75	85	83	96

under perturbations, local uniqueness, etc.), and for which good starting points are known or can be effectively generated.

We have taken as our test bed for MPECs the MPEClib problems. Details on problem size and characteristics can be found in Appendix B. MPEClib currently contains 92 problems. For each of these problems we attempted solution with each of 40 different reformulation/option file combinations and each of the four NLP solvers BARON, CONOPT, MINOS, and SNOPT, for a total of 14,720 solves.

The solution results for the different formulations we outlined in Section 4.3 are given in Table 4.4. For brevity, we report only the percentage of times that the solvers terminated in less than 10 s of CPU time with a feasible solution of the MPEC. If a particular option file significantly outperforms an alternate, we have not reported the poorer results. We have not reported any results for er14 and er15, because the reformulations are nonsmooth. The reformulations er16 and er17 perform poorly due to evaluation errors that occur in the exponential. The row er*.any reports the percentage of successes of each solver on any reformulation with any option file. The column anysolv indicates the percentage of models solved with each reformulation/option combination and at least one of the four solvers.

Table 4.5 show how well the objectives were minimized compared to the best solution that any solver found over all reformulations. We believe this table shows that the approaches postulated here are extremely promising and allow both small and medium scale MPECs to be solved with a variety of algorithms. More details on our testing strategy, coupled with more detailed results of all the tests we performed, are available at http://www.gamsworld.org/mpec/nlpectests.

It is clear that on this test set, a variety of the reformulations are very effective ways to find both feasible solutions and good locally optimal solutions of the MPEC. In particular, it seems that (ordered by increasing solution times) er3 (28), er21 (10), er1 (8), er22 (19), and er13 (27) (coupled with an appropriate option file) are very promising solution approaches.

In a recent paper [46], a suite of MPEC examples were described, along with a variety of techniques for solving them. The results reported there seem to broadly agree with the results described herein. In particular, for large, hard examples, the formulations involving the Fischer function (especially formulation er22) were found to be most effective in terms of solution time and objective value.

4.5. CONCLUSIONS

This paper has described the notion of a mathematical program with equilibrium constraints and given several reformulations of such problems as standard non-linear programming problems. It has outlined several tools to facilitate the automatic generation of these formulations from a GAMS specification of the original problem.

A number of algorithms have been applied to solve a suite of MPEC models that have been collected from a variety of application domains. All the examples cited in this paper are available from the gamsworld website at http://www.gamsworld.org/mpec/.

Several conclusions can be drawn. First, the ability to formulate problems with complementarity constraints as nonlinear programs enhances the ability of a modeler to use complementarity as a technique for answering important economic questions. We have demonstrated both improvements in overall robustness, and several new techniques for exploring more thoroughly the solution space. Second, tools for reformulation provide a variety of solution techniques for MPECs. While this paper does not show definitively what solver or which formulation is to be preferred, it does give a modeler a suite of tools that allow him/her to generate solutions of these problems. In particular, a modeler is able to write down an explicit formulation of the problem as an MPEC and use these tools to generated the required equations to treat complementarity, as opposed to having to generated different model description for each specific way of processing complementarity. Third, the ability to solve large and complex models with complementarity constraints reliably should enable applications (such as optimal tariff determination) to be processed by modelers more readily in the very near future.

It is hoped that the techniques outlined here will provide a basis for future application work in this area and will generate more of the interactions between modelers and algorithmic developers that have proven so successful in the complementarity field. One area of particular interest in applying MPEC models is the choice of optimal tariffs. There is a need for large-scale algorithms in this case due to the size and detail of the underlying datasets. Such problems are regarded as extremely difficult.

APPENDIX A: EXAMPLE OF GAMS MPEC SYNTAX

```
$TITLE   Multiple equilibria in a simple GE model

SET      G        GOODS /G1*G4/
         S        SECTORS /S1,S2/
         C        CONSUMERS /C1*C4/;

TABLE E(G,C) Factor endowments
                  C1        C2        C3        C4
         G1       5
         G2                 5
         G3                           40
         G4                                     40

TABLE ALPHA(G,C)  Budget shares
                  C1        C2        C3        C4
         G1       0.52      0.86      0.50      0.06
         G2       0.40      0.10      0.20      0.25
         G3       0.04      0.02      0.2975    0.0025
         G4       0.04      0.02      0.0025    0.6875

TABLE A(G,S)  Activity analysis matrix
                  S1        S2
         G1       6         -1
         G2       -1        3
         G3       -4        -1
         G4       -1        -1
```

```
POSITIVE
VARIABLES      Y(s)      Activity level
               P(g)      Relative price;
VARIABLES      OBJ
               H(c)      Income level;

EQUATIONS      PROFIT, MARKET, INCOME, OBJDEF;

OBJDEF..       OBJ =E= SUM(G,P(G));

* The following constraint removes one equilibrium
RESTRICT..     SUM(G,P(G)) =G= 3.64;

PROFIT(S)..    SUM(G, -A(G,S)*P(G)) =G= 0;

MARKET(G)..    SUM(C, E(G,C)) + SUM(S, A(G,S)*Y(S))
               =G= SUM(C, ALPHA(G,C) * H(C)/P(G));

INCOME(C)..    H(C) =E= SUM(G, P(G) * E(G,C));

P.L(G) = 1;
* Protect against domain violations
P.LO(G) = 1e-4;
* Fix a numeraire
P.FX("G1") = 1;

MODEL KEHOE /OBJDEF, PROFIT.Y, MARKET.P, INCOME/;

Solve KEHOE using MPEC min obj;
```

APPENDIX B: MODEL STATISTICS FOR TEST PROBLEMS

Name	m	n	nz	n1nz
AAMPEC_1	70	72	430	247
AAMPEC_2	70	72	430	247
AAMPEC_3	70	72	430	247
AAMPEC_4	70	72	430	247
AAMPEC_5	70	72	430	247
AAMPEC_6	70	72	430	247
BARD1	5	6	14	2
BARD2	10	13	33	4
BARD3	6	7	19	5
BARTRUSS3_0	29	36	96	38
BARTRUSS3_1	29	36	96	38
BARTRUSS3_2	29	36	96	38
BARTRUSS3_3	27	34	90	38
BARTRUSS3_4	27	34	90	38
BARTRUSS3_5	27	34	90	38
DEMPE	4	5	9	5
DEMPE2	3	4	7	5
DESILVA	5	7	13	10
EX9_1_1M	8	9	23	0
EX9_1_2M	6	7	14	0
EX9_1_3M	7	9	23	0
EX9_1_4M	5	6	12	0
FINDA10L	229	211	877	200
FINDA10S	229	211	877	200
FINDA10T	229	211	877	200
FINDA15L	229	211	877	200
FINDA15S	229	211	877	200
FINDA15T	229	211	877	200
FINDA30S	229	211	877	200
FINDA30T	229	211	877	200
FINDA35L	229	211	877	200
FINDA35S	229	211	877	200
FINDA35T	229	211	877	200
FINDB10L	203	198	812	200
FINDB10S	203	198	812	200
FINDB10T	203	198	812	200
FINDB15L	203	198	812	200
FINDB15S	203	198	812	200
FINDB15T	203	198	812	200
FINDB30L	203	198	812	200
FINDB30S	203	198	812	200
FINDB30T	203	198	812	200
FINDB35L	203	198	812	200
FINDB35S	203	198	812	200

(continued)

Name	m	n	nz	n1nz
FINDB35T	203	198	812	200
FINDC10L	187	190	772	200
FINDC10S	187	190	772	200
FINDC10T	187	190	772	200
FINDC15L	187	190	772	200
FINDC15S	187	190	772	200
FINDC15T	187	190	772	200
FINDC30L	187	190	772	200
FINDC30S	187	190	772	200
FINDC30T	187	190	772	200
FINDC35L	187	190	772	200
FINDC35S	187	190	772	200
FINDC35T	187	190	772	200
FJQ1	7	8	21	10
FRICTIONALBLOCK_1	682	682	2690	0
FRICTIONALBLOCK_2	1154	1154	4618	0
FRICTIONALBLOCK_3	854	854	3338	0
FRICTIONALBLOCK_4	979	979	3776	0
FRICTIONALBLOCK_5	1025	1025	3924	0
FRICTIONALBLOCK_6	2855	2855	11364	0
GAUVIN	3	4	8	2
HQ1	2	3	5	2
KEHOE1	11	11	49	20
KEHOE2	11	11	49	20
KEHOE3	11	11	49	24
KOJSHIN3	5	5	18	8
KOJSHIN4	5	5	18	8
MSS	5	6	26	25
NAPPI_A	98	116	330	88
NAPPI_B	98	116	330	88
NAPPI_C	98	116	330	88
NAPPI_D	98	116	330	88
OUTRATA31	5	6	17	10
OUTRATA32	5	6	18	11
OUTRATA33	5	6	18	11
OUTRATA34	5	6	20	13
OZ3	6	7	19	0
QVI	3	5	9	4
THREE	4	3	8	6
TINLOI	101	105	10201	100
TINQUE_DHS2	4834	4805	65315	13024
TINQUE_DNS2	4834	4805	65315	13024
TINQUE_MIS2	4066	4037	48803	10912
TINQUE_PSS2	4578	4549	59555	12320
TINQUE_SWS2	4578	4549	59555	12320
TINQUE_SWS3	5699	5671	67397	17920
TOLLMPEC	2377	2380	10488	1754

REFERENCES

[1] K. Arrow and G. Debreu, "Existence of Equilibrium for a Competitive Economy," *Econometrica* 22 (1954): 265–90.

[2] S. C. Billups, *Algorithms for Complementarity Problems and Generalized Equations*, Ph.D. thesis, University of Wisconsin, Madison, Wisconsin, August 1995.

[3] A. Brooke, D. Kendrick, and A. Meeraus, *GAMS: A User's Guide*, The Scientific Press, South San Francisco, CA, 1988.

[4] R. H. Byrd, M. E. Hribar, and J. Nocedal, "An Interior Point Algorithm for Large Scale Nonlinear Programming," *SIAM Journal on Optimization* 9(4) (1999): 877–900.

[5] Chunhui Chen and O. L. Mangasarian, "A Class of Smoothing Functions for Nonlinear and Mixed Complementarity Problems," *Computational Optimization and Applications* 5 (1996): 97–138.

[6] T. Condon, H. Dahl, and S. Devarajan, "Implementing a Computable General Equilibrium Model on GAMS – The Cameroon Model," DRD Discussion Paper 290, The World Bank, Washington, DC, 1987.

[7] J. Czyzyk, M. P. Mesnier, and J. J. Moré, "The NEOS Server," *IEEE Journal on Computational Science and Engineering* 5 (1998): 68–75.

[8] S. P. Dirkse and M. C. Ferris, "The PATH Solver: A Non-monotone Stabilization Scheme for Mixed Complementarity Problems," *Optimization Methods and Software* 5 (1995): 123–56.

[9] ——— "Modeling and Solution Environments for MPEC: GAMS & MATLAB," in *Reformulation: Nonsmooth, Piecewise Smooth, Semismooth and Smoothing Methods*, edited by M. Fukushima and L. Qi, Kluwer Academic, Dordrecht, 1999, pp. 127–48.

[10] E. D. Dolan and T. S. Munson, "The Kestrel Interface to the NEOS Server," Technical Memorandum ANL/MCS-TM-248, Argonne National Laboratory, Argonne, IL, 2001.

[11] A. Drud, "CONOPT: A GRG Code for Large Sparse Dynamic Nonlinear Optimization Problems," *Mathematical Programming* 31 (1985): 153–91.

[12] F. Facchinei, H. Jiang, and L. Qi, "A Smoothing Method for Mathematical Programs with Equilibrium Constraints," *Mathematical Programming* 85 (1999): 107–34.

[13] M. C. Ferris, R. Fourer, and D. M. Gay, "Expressing Complementarity Problems and Communicating Them to Solvers," *SIAM Journal on Optimization* 9 (1999): 991–1009.

[14] M. C. Ferris and T. S. Munson, "Case Studies in Complementarity: Improving Model Formulation," in *Ill–Posed Variational Problems and Regularization Techniques*, edited by M. Théra and R. Tichatschke, Lecture Notes in Economics and Mathematical Systems, No. 477, Springer-Verlag, Berlin, 1999, pp. 79–98.

[15] ——— "Complementarity Problems in GAMS and the PATH Solver," *Journal of Economic Dynamics and Control* 24 (2000): 165–88.

[16] ——— "Preprocessing Complementarity Problems," in *Complementarity: Applications, Algorithms and Extensions*, edited by M. C. Ferris, O. L. Mangasarian, and J. S. Pang, *Applied Optimization*, Vol. 50. Kluwer Academic, Dordrecht, 2001, pp. 143–64.

[17] M. C. Ferris and J. S. Pang, "Engineering and Economic Applications of Complementarity Problems," *SIAM Review* 39 (1997): 669–713.

[18] M. C. Ferris and F. Tin-Loi, "Limit Analysis of Frictional Block Assemblies as a Mathematical Program with Complementarity Constraints," *International Journal of Mechanical Sciences* 43 (2001): 209–24.

[19] A. Fischer, "A Special Newton-Type Optimization Method," *Optimization* 24 (1992): 269–284.

[20] P. E. Gill, W. Murray, and M. A. Saunders, "SNOPT: An SQP Algorithm for Large-Scale Constrained Optimization," *SIAM Journal on Optimization* 12 (2002): 979–1006.

[21] P. E. Gill, W. Murray, M. A. Saunders, and M. H. Wright, "A Practical Anti-cycling Procedure for Linearly Constrained Optimization," *Mathematical Programming* 45 (1989): 437–474.

[22] P. T. Harker and J. S. Pang, "Existence of Optimal Solutions to Mathematical Programs with Equilibrium Constraints," *Operations Research Letters* 7 (1988): 61–4.

[23] T. Kehoe, "A Numerical Investigation of the Multiplicity of Equilibria," *Mathematical Programming Study* 23 (1985): 240–58.

[24] M. Kojima and S. Shindo, "Extensions of Newton and Quasi-Newton Methods to Systems of PC^1 Equations," *Journal of Operations Research Society of Japan* 29 (1986): 352–74.

[25] M. M. Kostreva, "Elasto-hydrodynamic Lubrication: A Non-linear Complementarity Problem," *International Journal for Numerical Methods in Fluids*, 4 (1984): 377–97.

[26] Z.-Q. Luo, J. S. Pang, and D. Ralph, *Mathematical Programs with Equilibrium Constraints*, Cambridge University Press, Cambridge, 1996.

[27] E. Maskin and J. Tirole, "A Theory of Dynamic Oligopoly. I. Overview and Quantity Competition with Large Fixed Costs," *Econometrica* 56 (1988): 549–69.

[28] ———— "A Theory of Dynamic Oligopoly. II. Price Competition, Kinked Demand Curves, and Edgeworth Cycles," *Econometrica* 56 (1988): 571–79.

[29] L. Mathiesen, "Computation of Economic Equilibria by a Sequence of Linear Complementarity Problems," *Mathematical Programming Study* 23 (1985): 144–62.

[30] T. S. Munson, F. Facchinei, M. C. Ferris, A. Fischer, and C. Kanzow, "The Semismooth Algorithm for Large Scale Complementarity Problems," *INFORMS Journal on Computing* 13 (2001): 294–311.

[31] B. A. Murtagh and M. A. Saunders. "MINOS 5.0 User's Guide," Technical Report SOL 83.20, Stanford University, Stanford, CA, 1983.

[32] J. Outrata, M. Kočvara, and J. Zowe. *Nonsmooth Approach to Optimization Problems with Equilibrium Constraints*, Kluwer Academic Publishers, Dordrecht, 1998.

[33] J. S. Pang and J. C. Trinkle, "Complementarity Formulations and Existence of Solutions of Multi-rigid-body Contact Problems with Coulomb Friction," *Mathematical Programming* 73 (1996): 199–226.

[34] J. P. Pinter, *Global Optimization in Action*, Kluwer Academic, Dordrecht, 1996.

[35] D. Ralph, "Global Convergence of Damped Newton's Method for Nonsmooth Equations, via the Path Search," *Mathematics of Operations Research* 19 (1994): 352–89.

[36] S. M. Robinson, "Shadow Prices for Measures of Effectiveness. I. Linear Model," *Operations Research* 41 (1993): 518–35.

[37] S. M. Robinson, "Shadow Prices for Measures of Effectiveness. II. General Model," *Operations Research* 41 (1993): 536–48.

[38] T. F. Rutherford, "MILES: A Mixed Inequality and Nonlinear Equation Solver," Working Paper, Department of Economics, University of Colorado, Boulder, 1993.

[39] T. F. Rutherford, "Extensions of GAMS for Complementarity Problems Arising in Applied Economic Analysis," *Journal of Economic Dynamics and Control* 19 (1995): 1299–324.

[40] T. F. Rutherford, "Applied General Equilibrium Modeling with MPSGE as a GAMS Subsystem: An Overview of the Modeling Framework and Syntax," *Computational Economics* 14 (1999): 1–46.

[41] T. F. Rutherford. Private communication, January 2002. Models available at http://www.gamsworld.org/mpec/mpeclib.htm

[42] N. V. Sahinidis, "BARON: A General Purpose Global Optimization Software Package," *Journal of Global Optimization* 8 (1996): 201–5.

[43] M. Shubik, *Game Theory, Money and the Price System: The Selected Essays of Martin Shubik*, Vol. 2, Edward Elgar, Cheltenham, UK, 1999.

[44] B. H. Stevens, "Location Theory and Programming Models: The von Thünen Case," *Papers of the Regional Science Association* 21 (1968): 19–34.

[45] M. Tawarmalani and N. V. Sahinidis, "Global Optimization of Mixed Integer Nonlinear Programs: A Theoretical and Computational Study," *Mathematical Programming*, in press.

[46] F. Tin-Loi and N. S. Que, "Nonlinear Programming Approaches for an Inverse Problem in Quasibrittle Fracture," *International Journal of Mechanical Sciences* 44 (2002): 843–58.

[47] Z. Ugray, L. Lasdon, J. Plummer, F. Glover, J. Kelly, and R. Marti, "A Multistart Scatter Search Heuristic for Smooth NLP and MINLP Problems," Technical Report, University of Texas at Austin, 2002.

[48] G. van der Laan, A. J. J. Talman, and L. Van der Heyden, "Simplicial Variable Dimension Algorithms for Solving the Nonlinear Complementarity Problem on a Product of Unit Simplices Using a General Labelling," *Mathematics of Operations Research* 12 (1987): 377–97.

[49] R. J. Vanderbei and D. F. Shanno, "An Interior–Point Algorithm for Nonconvex Nonlinear Programming," *Computational Optimization and Applications* 13 (1999): 231–52.

[50] S. J. Wright, *Primal–Dual Interior–Point Methods*, SIAM, Philadelphia, 1997.

5 Nonconvexities in Quantitative General Equilibrium Studies of Business Cycles

Edward C. Prescott

ABSTRACT: This paper reviews the role of micro nonconvexities in the study of business cycles. One important nonconvexity arises because an individual can work only one workweek in a given week. The implication of this nonconvexity is that the aggregate intertemporal elasticity of labor supply is large and the principal margin of adjustment is in the number employed – not in the hours per person employed – as observed. The paper also reviews a business cycle model with an occasionally binding capacity constraint. This model better mimics business cycle fluctuations than the standard real business cycle model. Aggregation in the presence of micro nonconvexities is key in the model.

INTRODUCTION

The tool now used to study business cycles is the discipline of quantitative dynamic general equilibrium. In this discipline, given the question or issue at hand, an explicit model economy is written down and the answer to the question determined for that model economy. Theory, the question, and the available statistics dictate the choice of model economy used in the application. The pioneers in applying the discipline of quantitative general equilibrium are Herbert E. Scarf's students Shoven and Whalley (1972).[1] They applied these tools to problems in public finance. Their models are rich in sector detail, but not truly dynamic. Subsequently Auerbach and Kotlikoff (1987), Jorgenson and Yun (1990), and others have made these public finance models dynamic.

A convenient feature of these early structures is a parametric set of excess demand functions that can be easily calibrated using input–output tables and the

[1] The works of Johansen (1960) and Harberger (1968) were very much in this tradition, but were bascially static.

The author acknowledges financial support of the National Science Foundation. The author thanks Sami Alpanda, Andreas Hornstein, and Alexander Ueberfeldt for comments and discussions. The views expressed herein are those of the author and not necessarily those of the Federal Reserve Bank of Minneapolis or the Federal Reserve System.

equilibrium computed using Scarf's algorithm or other solution methods. Kydland and Prescott (1982) took a different approach in their study of business cycles. We constructed a linear–quadratic economy with the same steady state and local behavior as those of a deterministic growth model.[2] A feature of our approach is that uncertainty is easily introduced. With linear–quadratic economies, the equilibrium stochastic processes are linear, which matches well, but not perfectly, with observations.

The discipline of quantitative dynamic general equilibrium theory, in conjunction with growth theory, now dominates the study of business cycles and the evaluation of tax policies. Recently there have been two important additional successful applications of quantitative dynamic general equilibrium methods using growth theory, along with national income account statistics, to address other macro problems.[3] One success is in determining what the value of the stock market should be when it is reasonable to assume agents expect current tax and regulatory policies to persist into the future,[4] and the other is in studying great depressions of the twentieth century.[5] As in business cycle theory and in public finance, almost surely, the discipline of applied general equilibrium will come to dominate the study of these fields. Of this I am certain.

The consistency of the underlying assumptions concerning preferences and technologies across these diverse applications leads to great confidence in the findings. The fact, for example, that business cycles are what this theory predicts adds confidence to the public finance findings that use the same theory. This never would have happened absent the discipline of quantitative general equilibrium. In this paper I will restrict attention to an important class of issues in business cycle theory, namely, the importance, or in some cases lack of importance, of nonconvexities at the household and production unit levels for business cycle behavior.

In this paper I will abstract from money for three reasons. First, so much work has been done in this area using the discipline of quantitative general equilibrium that reviewing these developments in this paper is not feasible. Second, the findings concerning the role of monetary factors in business cycles are mostly negative, with the correlations of monetary factors with real factors arising for spurious reasons (see Freeman and Kydland 2000). Third, there is not a tested theory for incorporating money into quantitative general equilibrium analysis. One candidate, or maybe the leading candidate, for incorporating money (see Alvarez, Atkeson, and Kehoe 2002) incorporates the Baumol–Tobin inventory theoretical role for money, which introduces a nonconvexity in individual decisions. Even though a tested theory for

---

[2] Technically there is not a steady state for a growing economy. The economy can be made stationary by dividing the date values of each variable by its constant growth value.

[3] Recently there have been a plethora of interesting quantitative general equilibrium analyses using heterogeneous agent economies to evaluate insurance scheme⁻ and labor market policies.

[4] See McGrattan and Prescott (2000, 2001).

[5] The volume edited by Kehoe and Prescott (2002) contains many of these studies as well as references to earlier ones.

introducing money into quantitative GE models does not now exist, almost surely in the not too distant future there will be such a theory and the tools of quantitative general equilibrium will have played a crucial role in its development.

A variety of interesting business cycle questions have been addressed using this discipline of quantiative general equilibrium. The question that Kydland and Prescott (1982, 1991) focused on is, How volatile would the U.S. economy have been in the post–Korean War period if productivity shocks had been the only shocks to the economy? The economy that Kydland and Prescott (1991) use has an important nonconvexity in the stand-in household's consumption set. Workweeks of different lengths are different commodities, and a person is constrained to work one of this continuum of workweek lengths or not at all. This nonconvexity turns out to be important in answering the posed question. Once this feature of reality is introduced, an implication of theory is that the principal margin of labor supply adjustment will be in the number of people working in a given week as opposed to the length of the workweek. This prediction conforms to observation. Previously Gary D. Hansen (1985) had shown that if the only margin of adjustment permitted is the number employed, then the intertemporal elasticity of labor supply is high, something that is needed if the growth model is to generate business cycles.

For many years prior to World War II, many leading economists were concerned with business cycles, namely, the recurrent fluctuations of output and employment about trend. During this period, not surprisingly, economists developed a plethora of stories attempting to explain why these fluctuations occurred. One reason for their failure to develop a successful theory of business cycles was that dynamic economic theory had not yet been sufficiently developed, much less the discipline of quantitative dynamic general equilibrium. It is true that in the 1920s Irving Fisher on this side of the Atlantic and Erik R. Lindahl on the other side recognized that static general equilibrium theory could be made dynamic by adding a date index to commodities. It is also true that in the early 1950s Kenneth J. Arrow and Gerard Debreu recognized that by indexing commodities by events, general equilibrium theory could be extended to uncertainty. But by then, the business cycle was a dormant subject.

Another reason for the failure to develop a theory of business cycles was the lack of good aggregate economic statistics. The modern U.S. quarterly system of national accounts only begins in 1947. Reasonably accurate measures of labor input were not available until about the same time. Still another reason was that modern growth theory, which was developed to account for the secular movements in aggregate outputs and inputs, had not been developed.

In fact, the view in the profession in the 1950s and 1960s was that these fluctuations were not equilibrium phenomena and therefore that general equilibrium language was not useful in their study. Even if this view were not totally dominant in the 1950s and 1960s, there were not the recursive language and computing power needed to compute the equilibrium stochastic laws of motion governing the evolution of model economies.

Equilibrium elements of business cycle model economies are stochastic processes, typically Markov with a stationary transition probability measure. This permits comparison between the statistical properties of the model economies and the corresponding statistical properties of the actual economy. In the 1970s, the prevailing view of the profession was that changes in real factors, such as taxes and total factor productivity, gave rise to the secular movement in the aggregate data and that changes in monetary factors gave rise to business cycle fluctuations.

The use of the discipline of quantitative dynamic general equilibrium to derive the implications of growth theory surprised the profession and forced it to change its views. The result that surprised the profession, including those who first carried out the analysis, is that random persistent changes in the factors that determined the constant growth level (not the growth rate) of the growth model give rise to business cycle fluctuations of the nature observed. It turned out that Eugen Slutsky was right – business cycles are the sum of random causes and not the realization of a damped oscillatory system such as Knut Wicksell's rocking horse randomly being bumped.[6]

Kydland and Prescott (1982) determined how big the variance of the persistent component of technology shock had to be to generate fluctuations of the magnitude observed in the United States in the 1954–1980 period. Subsequent estimates of this variance (Prescott 1986) found that the variance was of this magnitude. This is a success for the discipline of quantiative general equilibrium and for growth theory, a theory that was developed to account for the secular movements in the aggregate time series and not to account for business cycles. Quantitative dynamic general equilibrium methods are needed to show that growth theory implies business cycle fluctuations. This is not something that one can derive without the use of quantitative general equilibrium analysis.

Kydland and Prescott (1982) found that the growth model displays business cycle fluctuations if and only if the aggregate intertemporal elasticity of labor supply is high, a fact that was not then accepted by most labor economists.[7] The labor economists ignored the consequences of aggregation in the face of nonconvexities in coming to their incorrect conclusion that the aggregate elasticity of labor supply is small. Nonconvexities at the household level imply high intertemporal elasticity of labor supply even if the intertemporal elasticity of labor supply of the households being aggregated is small.

This paper considers nonconvexities in quantitative GE business cycle analyses. Nonconvexities at the micro level abound and can be measured. Consistency between micro observations and macro theory is crucial. Only with this consistency can economists evaluate public policies with any confidence. One notable success of

---

[6]   Adelman and Adelman (1959), at the suggestion of Arrow, found that time series models, namely, the Klein–Goldberger Model, displayed damped oscillation, as the dominant eigenvalue of the model was 0.74. This empirical result is consistent with the sum-of-random-causes construct and not with the damped oscillation construct.

[7]   Lucas and Rapping (1969) estimated the intertemporal elasticity of labor supply and found it large.

theory was the recognition that an aggregation result underlies the stand-in household in the aggregate theory. This result is analogous to the aggregation result that justifies the concave, constant-returns-to-scale, aggregate production function. In spite of nonconvexities at the firm or household level, the aggregate economy is convex if the micro units are infinitesimal. A very important implication of this aggregation is that the substitution elasticities of the stand-in household or stand-in firm are very different from the elasticities of the micro units being aggregated.

There is a fundamental and important nonconvexity associated with the work-week length. Rosen (1986) pointed out that workweeks of different lengths are different commodities and that these commodities are indivisible. Rogerson (1988) formalized this concept in a static setting where people either worked a standard workweek in the market or did not work in the market sector. Hansen (1985) introduced this feature into business cycle theory and found that it resulted in a much higher intertemporal elasticity of labor supply for the stand-in household than for individual households and therefore in larger fluctuations in output and employment resulting from any set of shocks.

On the technology side, Herbert E. Scarf's fixed cost associated with lumpiness of investment, which leads to an (S, s) policy, has little consequence for aggregate behavior in the economies of Fisher and Hornstein (2000) and Thomas (2002). These economies are calibrated so that the amounts of micro and aggregate fluctuations are in line with observations.

The findings are dramatic. The paper that makes this clear is Thomas (2002). As she points out, the lumpiness of investment at the plant level is a well-established fact. She carries out an applied general equilibrium analysis with nonconvex adjustment costs at the plant level and (S, s) adjustment rules as equilibrium behavior. In contrast to conclusions based on partial equilibrium analyses, such as those of Abel and Eberly (1996), Bertola and Caballero (1994), Caballero and Engel (1991, 1999), and Cooper, Haltiwanger, and Power (1999), she finds that the aggregate effects of these micro nonconvexities have negligible consequences for aggregate behavior. Partial equilibrium reasoning addressing an inherently general equilibrium question cannot be trusted.

An exception to micro nonconvexities not mattering for business cycle fluctuations is Hansen and Prescott (in press). Hansen and I find that capacity constraints lead to nonlinearities of the type observed in the aggregate time series. This analysis is reviewed in this paper. The resulting aggregate production function is not Cobb–Douglas, yet for secular growth its implications are the same as those of the Cobb–Douglas production function. The second exception is Kahn and Thomas (in press), who introduce nonconvex capital adjustment. In both cases, the consequences of the nonconvexities are small.

There are a number of other interesting quantitative business cycle analyses with nonconvexities. Fitzgerald (1998) endogenizes the workweek length, with skilled and unskilled labor being required to operate a production unit, in order to evaluate laws that restrict workweek length. He finds that the highly paid skilled workers benefit from these laws and the low-paid unskilled workers lose. In his economy, at a given plant in a given period both the skilled and the unskilled must work the same workweek length. Another innovative analysis is that of Hornstein (2002), who introduces the option of varying the number of shifts. His objective was to come up with a better definition of capacity utilization. He was not very successful in achieving this objective, but did show that existing measures of capacity utilization are seriously flawed.

This chapter is organized as follows. Section 5.1 briefly reviews what business cycles are, why they are puzzling, and what the principal findings are to date. Section 5.2 presents the class of economies used in most business cycle research. These economies have a finite number of household types, typically one, and each type has convex preferences. The aggregate technology is a convex cone, typically with a single composite output good that can be used for consumption or investment purposes. This technology is typically represented by an aggregate production function with all the standard properties. Justifications based on aggregation theory are provided for these assumptions in Section 5.3. Section 5.4 presents the case where the workweek length is endogenous. Here there is not an aggregate production function with capital and labor services as the factor inputs. Following Alpanda and Ueberfeldt's (2002) generalization and simplification of Hornstein and Prescott (1993), it is shown that the margin of labor adjustment used is the number employed up to the point where all are employed. The workweek length margin is not used unless all are employed. Section 5.5 presents an economy with a sometimes binding capacity constraint. This micro nonconvexity in technology leads to an interesting nonlinearity in the equilibrium process governing output and employment.

5.1. BUSINESS CYCLES

Robert E. Lucas, Jr. (1977), defines business cycles as being recurrent fluctuations of output and employment about trends with the key regularities being the statistical properties of the comovements of the time series. An issue is, What is the trend? Robert J. Hodrick and I (1997) concluded that theory fails to provide a concept of trend and that it was necessary to come up with an operational definition that mimics the smooth curve that students of business cycles draw through the data. Our particular representation turned out to be a useful way to decompose the data into a trend and a cyclical component. There was a lot of theory behind the representation, which made clear some puzzling behavior of the time series from the perspective of production and utility maximization theory.

Why were business cycles puzzling?

On the household side the puzzling feature of the behavior of the cyclical components was that consumption and the labor input moved strongly procyclically, yet the real wage moved little. Here the real wage is defined to be aggregate labor compensation divided by aggregate market hours. This is puzzling because it requires the intertemporal elasticity of substitution to be high, far higher than what labor economists had estimated at the time.

On the production side, two-thirds of the variation in cyclical output is accounted for by variation in the labor input, and the remainder by total factor productivity, while contemporaneously, the capital stock is orthogonal to output. Labor productivity and hours are positively correlated with output, but they are roughly orthogonal to each other. Increases in the labor input, holding the capital input steady, should lead to declines in labor productivity and a negative association between output and labor productivity by standard production theory.

5.2. CONVEX ECONOMIES

In this paper I will be using the language of Arrow, Debreu, and McKenzie and will be dealing with economies that have the following properties. The aggreagate technology set is a convex cone. An implication of this is that payments to the factors of production exhaust product. There are a finite number of household types with an atomless measure of each type. A consequence of this is that all agents are small, and the no-market-power assumption is literally true in the model economies studied. Preferences of households are not convex, but preferences of the stand-in household for each type will turn out to be convex. Similarly, technologies of individual production units are not convex. Given the assumptions, however, the aggregate technology set will be a convex cone.

We assume that preferences are such that households maximize expected utility and the utility function is continuous. The expected utility assumption is standard in applied analyses and has survived many efforts to replace it with something better. With expected utility maximization and an appropriate commodity vector, preferences of the stand-in households for the types are convex if randomization is permitted.[8] De facto, the model economies are convex and have a finite number of households.

Preferences of the type i stand-in households are ordered by

$$u_i(x) = \max_z \int U_i(c)z(dc)$$

subject to $\int cz(dc) \leq x, z \geq 0,$ and $\int z(dc) = 1.$

In the above maximization problem, the probability measure z is defined on the Borel σ-algebra of the underlying consumption set of a type i, which is denoted by C_i. I emphasize that the problem facing an individual of type i is not convex, or there would be no need for a stand-in household. Thus either U_i is not concave or

---

[8] Prescott and Townsend (1984a, 1984b) introduce lotteries into the Arrow–Debreu–McKenzie general equilibrium framework. They were needed to fully realize all the gains from trade and had the consequence of making preferences convex.

C_i is not convex or both. The set C_i is a compact separable metric space and the function U_i is continuous. Given these conditions, the program has a solution for a given x, provided the constraint set is nonempty. The set X_i is the set for x for which the constraint set is nonempty. This set is convex, given that the program's constraint set is jointly convex in $\{x, z\}$. The set X_i is the *consumption set* of the type i stand-in household. The function $u_i : X_i \rightarrow \Re$ is continuous and concave given the linearity of the constraint correspondence and the linearity of the objective function. The function $u_i : X_i \rightarrow \Re$ is that *utility function* of the type i stand-in household.

Thus preferences of the stand-in households are convex. The advantage of introducing a stand-in household in applied analysis is that the traded commodities are the ones reported in the accounts. This facilitates the interaction between theory and measurement that is central in applied general equilibrium analysis. This is in contrast to the Prescott and Townsend (1984a, 1984b) approach, which treated commodities as probabilities from the perspective of the household.[9]

The commodity space is a normed linear space S. An economy is specified by the set of elements $\{\{\lambda_i, X_i \subset S, u_i\}_{i=1,\dots,I}, Y \subset S\}$. Here $\lambda_i > 0$ is the measure of type i. X_i is the type i stand-in consumption set, and the utility functions $u_i : X_i \rightarrow \Re$ are continuous and concave. The aggregate technology set Y is a convex cone.

An allocation $\{\{x_i\}_{i\in I}, y\}$ is feasible if $x_i \in X_i$ for all i, $y \in Y$, and the resource balance constraint

$$\sum_i \lambda_i \, x_i = y$$

is satisfied. A competitive equilibrium is a feasible allocation and continuous linear function on S such that the stand-in households maximize utility subject to their budget constraint and operators of technologies maximize value given their technology.

As shown by Debreu and Scarf (1963) in their core equivalence paper, with convex preferences, restricting attention to type-identical allocations is not an important restriction, in the following sense. If a non-type-identical equilibrium exists, a type-identical equilibrium exists with the same equilibrium price systems, the same commodity vector for the aggregate technology, the same type-average consumption vector, and the same utilities.

In *theoretical* general equilibrium theory, the household sector demands the commodities and the business sector supplies the commodities. A disadvantage of this approach is that it results in the household sector demanding negative quantities of factors of productions rather than the household supplying factors of production such as labor services and capital services. In *applied* general equilibrium theory, the household sector supplies factors of production and demands other commodities subject to its budget constraint, where the budget constraint constrains expenditures to be less than or equal to income. Income is the value of the factors of production

---

[9]   Here I am following Hansen (1985) and Kehoe, Levine, and Prescott (2002).

that the household supplies. The firm maximizes profit, that is, revenue less costs. Costs are the value of inputs while revenue is the value of output. In theoretical work, the concepts of income, revenue, expenditures, and costs are not needed, but these accounting concepts are useful in applied work. There is no concept of gross national income and product within the more parsimonious theoretical general equilibrium language. When discussing applications, I will use the applied general equilibrium language.

5.3. THE AGGREGATE PRODUCTION FUNCTION

The aggregate production function is used to characterize the aggregate production set. Here I briefly review the aggregation theory underlying aggregate production functions, why they are continuous, increasing, and concave, and why they display constant returns to scale. This aggregation theory will prove useful in endogenizing the workweek length, something that is central in business cycle theory.

The plant technologies underlying the aggregate production function are the following (note that x and y now denote different things than they did in Section 5.2):

(i) There are n factor inputs and a composite output good.[10]
(ii) The vector of inputs is $x \in \Re_+^n$ and the output good is y.
(iii) A plant technology is indexed by $x \in T$, with $f(x)$ being the output of a plant of type x.
(iv) $X \in \Re_+^n$ is the vector of aggregate inputs, and Y is aggregate output.

Definition: An aggregate production function $F(X)$ is the maximum output that can be produced given the input vector X.

Assumption 5.1: Any measure of technologies of type $x \in T$ can be operated.

Assumption 5.2: $T \subset \Re_{++}^n$ and T is compact.

Assumption 5.3: $f : T \to \Re$ is continuous.

The aggregate production function is the solution to the following program, where $M_+(T)$ is the set of measures on the Borel σ-algebra of T:

$$F(X) = \max_{z \in M_+(T)} \int f(x) \, z(dx)$$

$$\text{subject to} \int_T x_i z(dx) \leq X_i \quad i = 1, 2, \ldots, n.$$

---

[10] In this exposition the number of factors is finite. There are important business cycle applications where there is a continuum of factors and the input vector is a measure on the Borel σ-algebra of a subset of a Euclidean space.

Proposition 5.1: $F(X)$ *exists and is weakly increasing, continuous, weakly concave, and homogenous of degree one.*

Proof: Given the assumptions, the constraint set is compact and nonempty and the objective function is continuous in the weak-star topology. Therefore the program has a solution. The function being increasing is immediate, given that larger X increases the constraint set. Continuity follows from the Theorem of the Maximum. Concavity follows from the convexity of the constraint set and the concavity of the objective in (X, z). Because scaling z and X by a common factor is feasible and scales the objective function by the same factor, the function F must be homogenous of degree one. ∎

The function F summarizes the relevant aspects of the aggregate technology set and therefore is the element about which empirical knowledge can be organized. Multi-industry generalizations with intermediate goods are straightforward. However, in macro analyses the single-sector version almost always suffices and is therefore used.

Example: The Cobb–Douglas production function has come to dominate in aggregate quantitative GE analysis. The reason is that both over time and across countries, labor's share of product is surprisingly constant at a little below 70%.[11] The Cobb–Douglas production function, with its unit elasticity of substitution, is the only aggregate production function with the property that factor cost shares are the same for all relative factor prices.

An example of an underlying set of plant technologies for the Cobb–Douglas production function is the following. Suppose that the factor inputs to a production unit are k units of capital and e workers and that the plant technologies are $g(e)k^\theta$, where $0 < \theta < 1$. In addition, the function g is such that the function $g(e)e^{\theta-1}$ has a unique maximum. This maximum is denoted by A and the maximizing e by e^*.

Proposition 5.2: *For this example, the aggregate production function is*

$$F(K, E) = A K^\theta E^{1-\theta},$$

where E is aggregate employment and K aggregate capital.

Proof: The linear program has two constraints. Therefore, there is an optimum that places mass on at most two points. Let (e_i, k_i) be one of these points and (E_i, K_i) be the aggregate quantities of the inputs allocated to this point. As much or more output is produced by (E_i, K_i) if they are allocated to E_i/e^* production units of type $(e^*, K_i/(E_i/e^*))$. Thus, all operated production units have the same number

---

[11]   See Gollin (2002) for the cross-country numbers. He uses the Kravis (1959) economywide assumption
      for assigning proprietors' income and indirect business taxes to capital and labor.

of workers. All operated units have the same quantity of capital as well, because this is necessary to equate marginal products of capital across these units given that employment e is equated across operated units. This implies that it is optimal to assign e^* workers and $k^* = K/(E/e^*)$ to E/e^* operated production units. ∎

5.4. LABOR INDIVISIBILITY

Richard Rogerson, in his dissertation (1984), analyzed an artificial economy where people are confronted with the choice of either working or not working. On first blush this appears to be a nonconvexity. If a point in the commodity space specifies the quantity of the consumption good and the measure of workweek lengths, the economy becomes convex. From the perspective of the aggregate stand-in firm, the measure of workweek lengths specifies the number of people employed that work $h \in B$ for any Borel measurable $B \subseteq H$, where H is the set of possible workweek lengths. From the perspective of a household, the measure of workweek lengths is a probability measure of workweek lengths that the household must supply.

By an appropriate law of large numbers, the total measure of workweek length supplied is the measure of people times the probability that each person works. There are many ways that the firm can pick the set of identical, but not independent, 0–1 random variables specifying whether or not each person works. This is the Prescott–Townsend (1984a, 1984b) lottery equilibrium approach. Another equivalent approach is to construct a stand-in household with all the randomization being done within the group of type-identical individuals. This is the Hansen (1985) approach, which has been generalized by Kehoe, Levine, and Prescott (2002).

The Rogerson economy has measure one of type-identical people. They all maximize expected utility and have identical utility functions. Their utility is $u(c) - v(\bar{h})$ if they work and $u(c)$ if they do not. The function $u : \Re_+ \to \Re$ is continuous, strictly increasing, and concave. The number $v(\bar{h})$ is positive, indicating that people prefer not working to working.

Here we take the stand-in household approach. Let E be the fraction or measure of the group that work. Maximizing the expected utility of group members, the stand-in household's utility function, $U : \Re_+ \times [0, 1] \to \Re$, is

$$U(C, E) = u(C) - Ev(\bar{h}). \tag{1}$$

As shown by Hansen, a simple unemployment insurance scheme works in this environment, where those that do not work receive benefits. Alternatively, having members of the group enter into wealth gambles is another way to support this within-group allocation. Still another way is to index individual allocations by some random variable with a continuous density, which Shell and Wright (1993) call the sunspot approach. The advantage of using lotteries over this sunspot approach is that the economy is convex and all standard general equilibrium theory is easily applied.

The principle is to deal with the simplest commodity space for which preferences are convex. This is sufficient to ensure that there are no gains from introducing randomness. Given that the technology exists for gambling, ruling out trades that are feasible and mutually beneficial is inconsistent with equilibrium. To summarize, once a group exploits all gains from randomization, a type-identical group has a stand-in that behaves as if it is maximizing (1).

5.5. WHY A FIXED WORKWEEK LENGTH?

Hansen (1985) established that the intertemporal elasticity of labor supply is infinite up to the point where all are working if the workweek length is fixed. This fits well with observation, as the principal margin of adjustment is the number employed and not the hours that offices and factories are operated. A question, however, is why the number working and not the length of the workweek is the principal margin of adjustment. In this section this question is addressed.

The model economy used is as follows. There is measure one of identical individuals. Each household's preferences are ordered by the expected value of

$$\sum_{t=0}^{\infty} \beta^t U(c_t, h_t)$$

for $c_t \in C = \Re_+$ and $h_t \in H = [0, 1]$. The maximum amount of time that a given individual can physically work is 1. The utility function is strictly increasing in both its arguments and strictly concave, as well as being continuously differentiable. Each person has $\bar{k} > 0$ units of capital at the beginning of period zero.

The technology is described by the plant production functions

$$c + i \leq g(h)k^\theta.$$

Here consumption is c and investment i. A technology is described by the 4-tuple $s = (c, i, h, k)$. The set of s satisfying the plant technology set is S. A firm's production plan a is a measure on the Borel σ-algebra of S.

Capital depreciates at a rate δ, so $k_{t+1} = (1 - \delta)k_t + i_t$. The function $g(h)$ is concave and increasing. If an individual works h and uses k units of capital, his output is $z \leq Ag(h)^{1-\theta}k^\theta$. Hornstein and Prescott (1993) dealt with the special case where $g(h)^{1/(1-\theta)} = h$. Osuna and Rios-Rull (2001) dealt with the generalization $g(h)^{1/(1-\theta)} = h^\zeta$, where $\zeta > 1 - \theta$. The argument followed here is due to Alpanda and Ueberfeldt (2002). Their argument is more general and simpler than the one Hornstein and I developed.

The period commodity space is $L = M(\Re^2 \times H \times K)$. A point in this space is a measurable set of (c, i, h, k) vectors. Here M denotes a space of signed measures on the Borel σ-algebra of the space in question. The interpretation of h is the amount of workweeks of length h.

The period consumption set is

$$X = \{x \in L \,|\, x \text{ is a probability measure and } k \leq \bar{k} \text{ with probability one}\}.$$

The period utility function is

$$u(x) = \int U(c, h) \, dx.$$

Proposition 5.3: *Preferences are convex.*

This result is immediate given that u is linear and X convex. The convexity of preferences permits attention to be restricted to type-identical allocations. Further, the utility function is continuous.

The period aggregate production set is

$$Y = \{y \in L_+ | \exists \text{ measure of production units such that}$$

(i) $\int (c + i) \, dy - \int A g(h) k^\theta \, da \le 0$
(ii) for all measurable $B \subseteq H$, $\int dy(z|h \in B) = \int da(s|h \in B)$
(iii) $-\int k \, dy + \int k \, da \le 0\}$.

Constraint (i) is that enough is produced to supply the quantity of output specified by commodity vector y. Constraints (ii) are that enough of the types of workweeks are acquired by the firm to carry out its production plan. Constraint (iii) is that the firm acquires a sufficient quantity of capital services to carry out its plan.

Proposition 5.4: *The set Y is convex.*

Proposition 5.5: *A type-identical optimum exists.*

The existence of a type-identical competitive equilibrium is straightforward even if there is uncertainty for this economy. See Stokey and Lucas (1989, ch. 15).

I now show that the workweek is constant up to the point where all are employed if preferences and technology are consistent with constant growth. I deal first with technology. The aggregate production set is characterized by an aggregate production function $F(K, x)$, where x is a measure on the Borel σ-algebra of H. This function has all the standard properties of an aggregate production function, but is difficult to deal with given that x is a signed measure. For this reason, here I restrict the technology in a nonbinding way to one in which only one type of plant is being operated. This greatly simplifies notation. With this restriction, the aggregate production function is

$$c + i \le A h^\zeta k^\theta e^{1-\theta}, \quad \text{where } \zeta > 1 - \theta.$$

Here employment e is the measure of people working a workweek length h.

The utility function is

$$U(c, h) = \frac{[c^\gamma (1 - h)^{1-\gamma}]^\varepsilon - 1}{\varepsilon},$$

where $\varepsilon < 0$. Here we deal only with the case where there is more curvature than the log. The argument simplifies in the case in which the utility function is $U(c, h) = \gamma \log c + (1 - \gamma) \log(1 - h)$.

Proposition 5.6: *In this class of economies, $e < 1$ and $h = \bar{h}$ or $e = 1$ and $h \geq \bar{h}$.*

Proof: I denote the supply reservation price schedule for workweeks of different lengths in units of the consumption good by $w(h)$ for a particular period t given the event-history $(A_1, A_2, \ldots, A_t)$. Throughout this proof the event history argument will be implicit because it plays no role in the argument. Similarly, r is the rental price of capital. These prices are in terms of the period t consumption good.

First I show that if all work, all work the same number of hours. Next I show that if $e < 1$, then some work $h = \bar{h}$ and others work $h = 0$. This $\bar{h}$ depends only on the parameters of preferences and technology and not on the event history or the initial capital stock. Finally I show that if $e = 1$, then $h \geq \bar{h}$.

The first step in showing that if all work, they work the same length workweek is to show that the supply reservation wage is strictly convex in h. This is immediate because

$$w(h) = Bh^{\zeta/(1-\theta)} = \max_k \{Ah^\zeta k^\theta - rk\} \tag{2}$$

given that $\zeta > 1 - \theta$. B is a constant that depends on k and A, which are event-history dependent. In the case $\zeta = 1 - \theta$, function $w(h)$ is proportional to h.

The period problem facing a household is

$$\max_{x \geq 0} \int U(c, h)x(dc \times dh)$$

$$\text{s.t.} \int dx = 1$$

$$\text{s.t.} \int c\,dx - \int w(h)\,dx = \int c\,dx - \int Bh^{\zeta/(1-\theta)}\,dx \leq RB.$$

Here R is a constant that depends upon the event history and the initial capital stock. The first-order conditions for this linear program are

$$U(c, h) - \lambda c + \lambda w(h) + \phi \leq 0. \tag{3}$$

Here ϕ and λ are the Lagrange multipliers associated with the two constraints. Multiplier λ is the marginal utility of consumption and is strictly positive.

Equating the marginal utility of consumption to λ yields

$$c(h, \lambda) = \left(\frac{\gamma}{\lambda}\right)^{1/(1-\gamma\varepsilon)} (1 - h)^{(1-\gamma)\varepsilon/(1-\gamma\varepsilon)}. \tag{4}$$

Using (1) and (3) to substitute for c and $w(h)$, the first-order conditions (2) can be written as a function of h and the Lagrange multipliers only,

$$f(h, \lambda, \phi) \leq 0.$$

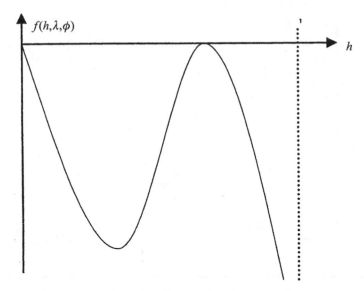

Figure 5.1. The not-all-work case.

Equality must hold at h in the support of the marginal measure on h of the optimal measure.

Function f has a single inflection point, $f_1(h, \lambda, \phi) < 0$, and $f_1(1, \lambda, \phi) = -\infty$. This implies that the shape of the function is as in Fig. 5.1 or Fig. 5.2. Thus the optimum either puts all its measure on a single point or splits the measure between $h = 0$ and some other point. This establishes the first part of the proof.

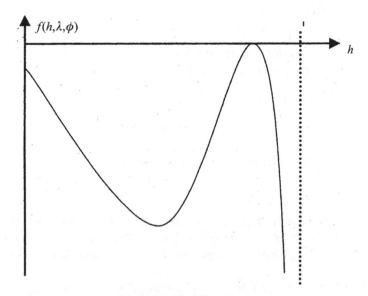

Figure 5.2. The all-work case.

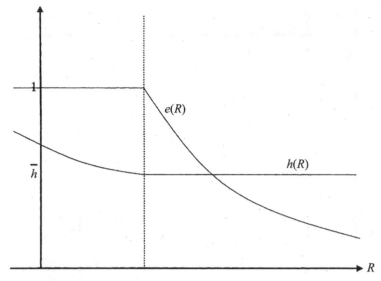

Figure 5.3. Behavior of employment and workweek as R varies.

Consider now the case in which measure is placed on $h = 0$. In this case the program facing the household can be written as

$$\max_{e,c_0,c_1,h_1} \{eU(c_1, h_1) + (1 - e)U(c_0, 0)\}$$

$$\text{s.t. } ec_1 + (1 - e)c_0 - ew(h_1) \le RB.$$

The first-order conditions for this program are

$$U_1(c_1, h_1) = \lambda$$
$$U_1(c_0, 0) = \lambda$$
$$U(c_1, h_1) - U(c_0, 0) + \lambda w(h_1) - \lambda(c_1 - c_0) = 0$$
$$U_2(c_1, h) + \lambda w'(h_1) = 0.$$

Using (2), (4), and the fact that

$$\frac{U_1(c, h)}{\gamma \varepsilon} = \frac{c\lambda}{\gamma \varepsilon} = U(c, h), \tag{5}$$

an implication of these first-order conditions is that

$$(\varepsilon^{-1} - \gamma)(\gamma - 1)^{-1} \left(1 - h - (1 - h)^{\frac{1-\varepsilon}{1-\varepsilon\gamma}}\right) = \frac{w(h)}{w'(h)} = \frac{(1 - \theta)}{\zeta} h. \tag{6}$$

The important result is that Eq. (6) is a function of h and parameters of the model. Let this solution to (6) be $\bar{h}$. What differs if B and R are different is e and not h, unless, of course, the change is so large that $e = 1$. This completes the second part of the proof.

The best h, if all work, is a decreasing function of R as shown in Fig. 5.3. When the function decreases to $\bar{h}$, it is optimal to shift to the e margin of adjustment. At this point, the optimal $e(R)$ becomes strictly decreasing and optimal consumptions remain constant. All increase in "wealth" is taken in the form of a lower fraction of the population that work in the market sector. This completes the proof. ∎

5.6. CAPACITY CONSTRAINTS AND NONLINEARITIES

A problem with the Cobb–Douglas production function is that it implies constant factor shares for both the smooth secular movements in output and the nonsmooth business cycle fluctuations. Cyclically, capital share is procyclical, being particularly high at cyclical peaks. Another problem is that there is nonsymmetry in the economic time series. Business cycle peaks are smaller than troughs and are flatter. This suggests that an alternative aggregate production function is needed to better model business cycle fluctuations. In particular, the abstraction must capture the fact that the economy is hitting capacity constraints at many production units when the economy is at the peak.

The problem is to develop an alternative production technology that is tractable and captures these features. This technology must generate both the growth facts and the business cycle facts. Hansen and Prescott (in press) developed such a technology. We started at the micro level and did the aggregation. The micro foundations are no more realistic than those for the Cobb–Douglas production function, but are important because they led us to this alternative aggregate production function for the study of business cycle fluctuations.

The economy Hansen and I studied is a one-sector stochastic growth model in which output is produced from three factors of production: labor and two types of capital. One type of capital, identified with long-run capacity, for want of a better term, will be referred to as the location at which production can potentially take place. Examples include office buildings, factories, and large ships. The second type of capital is called equipment. It can be assigned, along with labor, to a location to form an operating plant.[12] The production function of a plant is given by

$$y = \begin{cases} zk^\theta n^\phi & \text{if } n \geq \bar{n} \\ 0 & \text{otherwise.} \end{cases} \tag{7}$$

In this expression, k is the quantity of equipment and n is the quantity of labor employed at the plant in a given period. The variable z, where $z \in \{z_1, \ldots, z_{n_z}\}$, is the realization of an aggregate technology shock that follows an n_z-state Markov chain with transition probabilities $\pi_{z,z'}$. We assume eventual decreasing returns to scale at the plant level, so $\theta + \phi < 1$. This assumption guarantees that it is profitable

---

[12] We will refer to this second type of capital as equipment for lack of a better term. The distinction between the two types of capital does not correspond to the distinction between structures and equipment used by the U.S. Department of Commerce. For example, a Boeing 747 is a "location at which production can potentially take place," and is therefore long-run capacity in our model. Similarly, a storage shed used by a manufacturing firm is formally a structure, but is not a location where production takes place and should probably be classified as the second type of capital.

to operate many small plants rather than one large one and that all operating plants will employ the same amount of equipment and labor. In addition, the requirement $n \geq \bar{n}$, along with a limited population of potential workers, implies an upper bound on the total number of plants that can be operated.

In any period there is a fixed number, M, of available locations that can be potentially operated. Equipment and labor (k and n) can be costlessly moved across locations, so these factor inputs will be placed only at operating plants. This assumption, along with the minimum labor requirement ($n \geq \bar{n}$), implies that there may be idle locations in some states, although equipment will never be left idle.

Suppose that in a given period, there are K units of equipment and M locations. In addition, suppose that N units of labor are employed. The aggregate production function is defined by the expression

$$F(K, N, M) \equiv \max_{x \geq 0} \int z k^{\theta} n^{\phi} dx$$

$$\text{subject to} \int k \, dx \leq K \tag{8}$$

$$\int n \, dx \leq N$$

$$\int dx \leq M,$$

where x is the measure of plant types (k, n) that are operated. The measure x is defined on the Borel σ-algebra of the set $\mathfrak{R}_{+} \times [\bar{n}, \infty]$.

A solution to this problem will equate marginal products across operating plants. It can be shown that there will be just one type of plant operated in any particular period, $x_{\hat{k}\hat{n}}$. That is, all operating plants employ the same quantity of equipment and labor. If $m \leq M$ is the number of locations operated, then $\hat{k} = K/m$, $\hat{n} = N/m$, and $m = x_{\hat{k}\hat{n}}$. With this change of variables, Eq. (8) can be rewritten as

$$F(K, N, M) = \max_{m \leq \min\{M, \frac{N}{\bar{n}}\}} z \left(\frac{K}{m}\right)^{\theta} \left(\frac{N}{m}\right)^{\phi} m. \tag{9}$$

The constraint $m \leq N/\bar{n}$ in this problem follows from the requirement that the amount of labor employed at each plant, N/m, must be greater than $\bar{n}$.

The assumption that $\theta + \phi < 1$ implies that the constraint $m \leq \min\{M, N/\bar{n}\}$ will always bind in Problem (9). Hence, two possibilities can arise: $M < N/\bar{n}$, in which case $m = M$ in Eq. (9), or $M > N/\bar{n}$, in which case $m = N/\bar{n}$. Hence, solving Problem (9), we obtain

$$F(K, N, M) = \begin{cases} z K^{\theta} N^{\phi} M^{1-\theta-\phi} & \text{if } N > M\bar{n} \\ z K^{\theta} N^{1-\theta} \bar{n}^{\theta+\phi-1} & \text{if } N < M\bar{n}. \end{cases} \tag{10}$$

The aggregate production function in Eq. (10) can be understood as follows. In the first case, all M locations are assigned equipment and at least $\bar{n}$ units of labor. Hence, the economy is operating at "full capacity" in that all locations are operated and the shadow value of additional locations is positive. As a result, in a decentralized version of this economy with competitive markets, locations earn a share of total income equal to $1 - \theta - \phi$. In the second case, an insufficient amount of labor is employed to operate all M locations, so the economy is operating at less than full capacity. Location capital, because it is not a scarce input, earns no rent. Instead, in this "excess capacity" case, labor earns a larger share, $1 - \theta$, of income. Notice that labor's share under full capacity can be as large as ϕ, which is smaller than $1 - \theta$ given our assumption that $\theta + \phi < 1$.

5.6.1. Resource Constraint and the Evolution of Capital

Output can be used to provide a perishable consumption good C_t, to provide an investment good X_t, and to establish new locations $M_{t+1} - M_t$.

The evolution of the equipment component of the capital stock over time is standard. One unit of investment today produces one unit of equipment, K_{t+1}, available for use in the following period. The depreciation rate is denoted by δ, where $0 < \delta < 1$, so the law of motion of the stock of equipment is given by

$$K_{t+1} = (1 - \delta)K_t + X_t. \tag{11}$$

In comparison, each additional unit of location captial $M_{t+1} - M_t$, which also requires one period to produce, requires that ω units of output be invested today.[13] Location capital does not depreciate, and location investments are irreversible. Hence, the resource constraint can be written

$$C_t + X_t + \omega(M_{t+1} - M_t) \leq z_t F(K_t, N_t, M_t), \tag{12}$$

where $M_{t+1} \geq M_t$.

5.6.2. Preferences

The economy has a measure one continuum of identical individuals, each endowed with one unit of time each period. Preferences are ordered by the expected value of $\sum_{t=0}^{\infty} \beta'[\log c_t + v(l_t)]$, where v is an increasing function of leisure. Labor is indivisible, meaning that individuals work a given workweek length or not at all. In addition, given a lottery mechanism for allocating time use, a stand-in household exists with preferences ordered by the expected value of

$$\sum_{t=0}^{\infty} B^t (\log C_t - \gamma N_t), \quad 0 < \beta < 1, \gamma > 0, \tag{13}$$

where N_t is the fraction of available household time employed in market production.

---

[13] A reasonable assumption would be that more time is required to produce location capital than equipment. Although this is likely to be true in actual economies, we have chosen to make the minimum number of assumptions to guarantee that location capital is not varied over the business cycle in the invariant distribution implied by our theory.

5.6.3. Computing Equilibrium Allocations

Given that there are no distortions in this economy, equilibrium allocations are equivalent to those that would be chosen by a social planner who maximizes (13) subject to (10)–(12). This problem has the property that, once a sufficient amount of location capital has been accumulated, no further investments will be made in M. This follows from the fact that M does not depreciate, that the technology shock z has bounded support, and the fact that we have abstracted from population growth. We assume that this economy has been operating for a long time, so we restrict ourselves to computing equilibrium allocations that are relevant once this sufficient quantity of M has been accumulated.

The result that, in the limit, investment in location capital is zero in all states generalizes to a constant-growth version of this economy with exogenous technological progress. In particular, if we were to replace Eq. (7) with the same technology premultiplied by $\rho^{(1-\theta)t}$, where $\rho > 1$, the balanced growth path would involve output, C_t, X_t, and k_t all growing at the rate $\rho - 1$. The variables M_t and N_t are constant along this balanced growth path. Intuitively, N_t is constant because the population is fixed and M earns rents only if $N_t > M_t \bar{n}$, where $\bar{n}$ is a constant. Hence, M cannot, in the limit, grow at a rate higher than N. Of course, if there is population growth, M does grow and ongoing investment in location capital will be undertaken.

This can be done in two steps. First, optimal decision rules for the social planner's problem given an arbitrary fixed value of M are computed. Second, given these decision rules, one can compute the constant value of M that would hold in a stationary solution to the planner's problems.[14]

The following is the dynamic program solved by a social planner given a fixed value of M:

$$v(z, K; M) = \max_{N, K'} \left\{ \log C - \gamma N + \beta \sum_{z'} \pi_{z,z'} v(z', K'; M) \right\}$$

subject to   (14)

$$C + K' = (1 - \delta)K + \begin{cases} z K^\theta N^\phi M^{1-\theta-\phi} & \text{if } N > M\bar{n} \\ z K^\theta N^{1-\theta} \bar{n}^{\theta+\phi-1} & \text{if } N < M\bar{n} \end{cases}$$

$$0 \leq N \leq 1.$$

The solution to this problem is a set of decision rules of the form $N = N(z, K; M)$, $K' = G(z, K; M)$, and $C = C(z, K; M)$.

The value of M in a stationary solution to the planner's problem is determined by setting the maximal marginal value of an additional location across all possible states equal to the cost of establishing the location, ω. The marginal value of an additional location given the current state, $v_M(z, K, M)$, is the present discounted

---

[14] Alternatively, we can back out the fixed cost ω that would induce the value of M used when computing the decision rules.

marginal product of the location over its infinite lifetime. This can be found by solving the following functional equation:

$$v_M(z, K, M) = \sum_{z'} \pi_{z,z'}[z' F_3(K', N(z', K'; M), M) + v_M(z', K', M)].$$

In this expression, $K' = G(z, K; M)$ and F_3 is the partial derivative with respect to M of the function F in Eq. (10). The stochastic discount factor employed by the social planner, Q, is given by

$$Q(z, z') = \beta \pi_{z,z'} \frac{C(z, K; M)}{C(z', G(z, K; M); M)}.$$

The value of M in a stationary solution to the planner's problem is determined as follows, where E_M is the ergodic subset of the state space implied by the solution to problem (14):

$$\omega = \sup_{\{z,K\}\in E_m} v_M(z, K, M). \tag{15}$$

5.6.4. Computing Equilibrium Factor Shares

Although most of the variables we are interested in are quantities, we are also interested in computing factor shares for this economy. This requires that we compute factor prices. In a decentralized growth model, the wage rate is normally equal to the marginal product of labor evaluated at the values for capital and labor that solve the planner's problem. In this model, however, the presence of a kink in the aggregate production function (at $N = M\bar{n}$) means that the marginal product of labor is not uniquely defined at this point. Hence, given that N will often equal $M\bar{n}$ in our simulations, the wage cannot be computed from the first-order conditions of the firm's problem as is usually done.

This does not mean that the wage is not uniquely determined at the kink point, but instead implies that we must compute it from the first-order conditions of the household's problem rather than the firm's problem. The first-order condition associated with the labor supply decision of the stand-in household, given a period utility function $U(C, N)$, implies that $w = U_2(C, N)/U_1(C, N)$. Given our choice of preferences, this implies that $w = \gamma C$, and, hence, labor's share is equal to $\gamma CN/Y$, where Y is aggregate output.

5.6.5. Solution Method

To solve the planner's problem (14), we use a variation on value interation to compute piecewise linear approximations to the optimal decision rules.[15] In particular, a set

---

[15] Our solution procedure is similar to the Howard improvement algorithm described in Ljungqvist and Sargent (2000).

of values for the stock of equipment with n_K elements is chosen, and we let Ω be the set $\{z_1, \ldots, z_{n_2}\} \times \{K_1, \ldots, K_{n_K}\}$.[16] We then choose initial guesses for the values of the decision rules, $N_0(z, K)$ and $G_0(z, K)$, at each point in Ω that satisfy the constraints in problem (14). We also chose a function $v_0(z, K)$ that assigns a real number to each element of Ω. Setting $\tilde{v}_0(z, K) = v_0(z, K)$, we iterate on the following, mapping a large number (100) of times,

$$\tilde{v}_{i+1}(z, K) = \log C - \gamma N + \beta \sum_{z'} \pi_{z,z'} \tilde{v}_i(z', K'), \quad \text{for all } (z, K) \in \Omega, \quad (16)$$

where $K' = G_0(z, K)$, $N = N_0(z, K)$, $C = zF(K, N, M) + (1 - \delta)K - K'$, and M is taken as a parameter.

The next step is to compute functions $N_1(z, K)$ and $G_1(z, K)$, for each $(z, K) \in \Omega$, as follows:

$$\{N_1(z, K), G_1(z, K)\} = \arg \max\{\log(zF(K, N, M) \quad (17)$$
$$+ (1 - \delta)K - K') - \gamma N + \beta \sum_{z'} \pi_{zz'} \tilde{v}_N(z', K')\}.$$

We use linear interpolation to evaluate $\tilde{v}_N$ at values of K' not in Ω. In addition, we define $v_1(z, K)$ to be the maximized value of the function on the right side of (17).

Using the functions N_1, G_1, and v_1 in place of N_0, G_0, and v_0, these steps are repeated to obtain N_2, G_2, and v_2. We continue in this manner until successive iterations converge. For each $z \in \{z_1, \ldots, z_{n_z}\}$, we form piecewise linear decision rules by linearly interpolating between points on the grid $\{K_1, \ldots, K_{n_k}\}$.

5.7. CONCLUDING COMMENTS

The discipline of applied general equilibrium has provided an understanding of business cycles. Partial equilibrium reasoning led to a conclusion that could stand the test of applied general equilibrium discipline. In this paper, I focused on aggregation when there are nonconvexities at the micro level. Nonconvexities at the firm level give rise to lumpy investment at the production level, but not at the aggregate level. Nonconvexities at the household level give rise to high intertemporal elasticity of supply. The analyses reviewed here use the classical competitive equilibrium theory of Arrow, Debreu, and McKenzie, a theory that abstracts from financial factors. The aggregate economy is convex. This aggregation is important in making connections between the micro observations and the stand-in firm(s) and the stand-in household(s) used in business cycle and other aggregate analyses.

---

[16] We experiment to ensure that the upper and lower bounds of the capital stock grid are chosen so that the interval $[K_1, K_{n_K}]$ includes all points that have positive probability in the invariant distribution implied by the solution to the dynamic program.

REFERENCES

A. B. Abel and J. C. Eberly (1996), "Optimal Investment with Costly Reversibility," *Review of Economic Studies* 63: 581–93.

I. Adelman and F. L. Adelman (1959), "The Dynamic Properties of the Klein–Goldberger Model," *Econometrica* 27: 596–625.

S. Alpanda and A. Ueberfeldt (2002), "A Note on Workweek Variation in Real Business Cycle Models," mimeo, University of Minnesota.

F. Alvarez, A. Atkeson, and P. J. Kehoe (2002), "Money, Interest Rates, and Exchange Rates in Endogenously Segmented Markets," *Journal of Political Economy*, 110: 73–112.

A. J. Auerbach and L. Kotlikoff (1987), *Dynamic Fiscal Policy*, Cambridge: Cambridge University Press.

G. Bertola and R. J. Caballero (1994), "Irreversibility and Aggregate Investment," *Review of Economic Studies* 61: 223–46.

R. J. Caballero and E. Engel (1991), "Dynamic (S,s) Economies," *Econometrica* 59: 1659–86.
(1999), "Explaining Investment Dynamics in U.S. Manufacturing: A Generalized (S,s) Approach," *Econometrica* 67: 783–826.

R. W. Cooper, J. C. Haltiwanger, and L. Power (1999), "Machine Replacement and the Business Cycle: Lumps and Bumps," *American Economic Review* 89: 921–46.

G. Debreu and H. Scarf (1963), "A Limit Theorem on the Core of an Economy," *International Economic Review* 4: 235–46.

J. D. M. Fisher and A. Hornstein (2000), "(S, s) Inventory Policies in General Equilibrium," *Review of Economic Studies* 67: 117–45.

T. J. Fitzgerald (1988), "Work Schedules, Wages, and Employment in a General Equilibrium Model with Team Production," *Journal of Economic Dynamics and Control* 1: 809–30.

S. Freeman and F. E. Kydland (2000), "Monetary Aggregates and Output," *American Economic Review* 90: 1125–35.

D. Gollin (2002), "Getting Income Shares Right," *Journal of Political Economy* 110: 458–74.

G. D. Hansen (1985), "Indivisible Labor and the Business Cycle," *Journal of Monetary Economics* 16: 309–28.

G. D. Hansen and E. C. Prescott (in press), "Capacity Constraints, Asymmetries, and the Business Cycle," *Review of Economic Dynamics*.

A. C. Harberger (1968), "A Landmark in the Annals of Taxation," *Canadian Journal of Economics* 1 [Supplement]: 183–94.

R. J. Hodrick and E. C. Prescott (1977), "Post-War U.S. Business Cycles: A Descriptive Empirical Investigation," *Journal of Money, Credit, and Banking* 29: 1–16.

A. Hornstein (2002), "Towards a Theory of Capacity Utilization: Shiftwork and the Workweek of Capital," *Federal Reserve Bank of Richmond Economic Quarterly* 88: 65–86.

A. Hornstein and E. C. Prescott (1993), "The Firm and the Plant in General Equilibrium Theory," in *General Equilibrium, Growth, and Trade. II. The Legacy of Lionel McKenzie*, edited by R. Becker, M. Boldrin, R. Jones, and W. Thomson, San Diego: Academic Press, pp. 393–410.

L. Johansen (1960), *A Multisector Study of Economic Growth*, Amsterdam: North-Holland.

D. Jorgenson and K. Y. Yun (1990), "Tax Reform and U.S. Economic Growth," *Journal of Political Economy* 98: 151–93.

A. Kahn and J. K. Thomas (in press), "Nonconvex Factor Adjustments in Equilibrium Business Cycle Models: Do Nonlinearities Matter?" *Journal of Monetary Economics*.

T. J. Kehoe, D. K. Levine, and E. C. Prescott (2002), "Lotteries, Sunspots, and Incentive Constraints," *Journal of Economic Theory* 107: 36–9.

T. J. Kehoe and E. C. Prescott (2002), "Great Depressions of the Twentieth Century," *Review of Economic Dynamics* 5: 1–18.

I. Kravis (1959), "Relative Income Shares in Fact and Theory," *American Economic Review* 49: 917–49.

F. E. Kydland and E. C. Prescott (1982), "Time to Build and Aggregate Fluctuations," *Econometrica* 50: 1345–70.

(1991), "Hours and Employment Variation in Business Cycle Theory," *Economic Theory* 1: 63–82.

L. Ljungqvist and T. Sargent (2000), *Recursive Macroeconomic Theory*, Cambridge, MA: MIT Press.

R. E. Lucas, Jr. (1977), "Understanding Business Cycles," in *Stabilization of the Domestic and International Economy*, edited by K. Brunner and A.H. Meltzer, New York: North–Holland.

R. E. Lucas, Jr. and L. A. Rapping (1969), "Real Wages, Employment, and Inflation," *Journal of Political Economy* 77: 721–54.

E. R. McGrattan and E. C. Prescott (2000), "Is the Stock Market Overvalued?" *Federal Reserve Bank of Minneapolis Quarterly Review* (Fall): 20–40.

(2001), "Taxes, Regulation, and Asset Prices," Federal Reserve Bank of Minneapolis Working Paper 610.

V. Osuna and J. V. Rios-Rull (2001), "Implementing the 35 Hour Workweek by Means of Overtime Taxation," mimeo, University of Pennsylvania.

E. C. Prescott (1986), "Theory Ahead of Business Cycle Measurement," *Federal Reserve Bank of Minneapolis Quarterly Review* (Fall): 9–22.

E. C. Prescott and R. Townsend (1984a), "General Competitive Analysis in an Economy with Private Information," *International Economic Review* 25: 1–20.

(1984b), "Pareto Optima and Competitive Equilibria with Adverse Selection and Moral Hazard," *Econometrica* 52: 21–45.

R. Rogerson (1984), *Topics in the Theory of Labor Markets*, Ph.D. Thesis, University of Minnesota.

(1988), "Indivisible Labor, Lotteries, and Equilibrium," *Journal of Monetary Economics* 21: 3–16.

S. Rosen (1986), "The Supply of Work Schedules and Employment," in *Work Time and Employment*, edited by O. Ashenfelter and R. Layard, Amsterdam: Elsevier Science, pp. 641–92.

K. Shell and R. Wright (1993), "Indivisibilities, Lotteries, and Sunspot Equilibria," *Economic Theory* 3: 1–17.

J. B. Shoven and J. Whalley (1972), "A General Equilibrium Calculation of the Effects of Differential Taxation of Income and Capital in the U.S.," *Journal of Public Economics* 1: 281–321.

N. L. Stokey and R. E. Lucas, Jr. (1989), *Recursive Methods in Economic Dynamics*, Cambridge, MA: Harvard University Press.

J. K. Thomas (2002), "Is Lumpy Investment Relevant for the Business Cycle?" *Journal of Political Economy* 110: 508–34.

6 Lotteries for Consumers versus Lotteries for Firms

Lars Ljungqvist and Thomas J. Sargent

ABSTRACT: Edward C. Prescott emphasizes similarities between lotteries that smooth nonconvexities for firms and for consumers–workers. We emphasize their differences. We also argue that models with employment lotteries that are used to generate unemployed individuals in a frictionless framework can have implications very different from those of models embodying frictional unemployment. As an illustration, models with employment lotteries predict effects from job destruction taxes that are the opposite of those in search models.

6.1. INTRODUCTION

James Tobin said that good macroeconomic analysis ignores distribution effects. But in general equilibrium theory, distribution effects usually can't be ignored. Edward Prescott's paper is an elegant summary of a very successful research agenda that manages to apply general equilibrium theory to macroeconomics by carefully setting up redistribution arrangements to smooth the nonconvexities that are confronted by both firms and households, which thereby deliver both a stand-in household and a stand-in firm. Prescott's work continues the Tobin tradition not by ignoring distribution effects but by designing them to facilitate aggregate analysis.

There is much to admire and to copy in Prescott's work in general and in this paper in particular. This is a perfect paper to assign to graduate students. A beautiful aspect of the paper is that because it adheres to the rules for describing competitive equilibria, everything is in the open. We take advantage of this openness to emphasize and challenge an important aspect of Prescott's analysis. Prescott focuses on how nonconvexities at the level of individual households and production units affect outcomes in quantitative general equilibrium models of business cycles. His message is that

One notable success of theory was the recognition that an aggregation result underlies the stand-in household in the aggregate theory. This result is analogous to the aggregation result that justifies the concave, constant-returns-to-scale, aggregate production function.

Prescott (2002, p. 4) has pointed out that while the aggregation theory behind the aggregate production function is well known, there is also "some not-so-well known aggregation theory behind the stand-in household utility function." Prescott emphasizes the formal similarities associated with smoothing out nonconvexities by aggregating over firms, on the one hand, and aggregating over consumers, on the other. We shall argue that the different economic interpretations that attach to these two types of aggregation make the two aggregation theories very different. Perhaps this difference explains why this aggregation method has been applied more to firms than to consumers.[1]

An important distinction between firms and households in general equilibrium theory is that firms have no independent preferences. They serve only as vehicles for generating rental payments for employed factors and profits for their owners. When a firm becomes inactive, that can be bad news for its stakeholders, but the "firm" itself does not care whether it continues or ceases to exist. In contrast, individual consumers do have preferences and care about alternative states of the world. Although the aggregation theory that Prescott likes can be applied both to firms and to consumers to smooth out lumpy behavior at the micro level, the aggregation theory behind the stand-in household has an additional aspect that is not present in the theory that aggregates over firms; namely, it says how consumption and leisure are smoothed across people.

On the household side, Prescott emphasizes the nonconvexity that arises when it is imposed that an individual is allowed only one workweek length. A stand-in household emerges when all individuals participate in an employment lottery that is supplemented with the exchange of state-contingent claims over lottery outcomes, as proposed by Hansen (1985) and Rogerson (1988). Aggregating the work-week length nonconvexity with lotteries divides ex ante identical people into employed and nonemployed individuals and creates a setting in which, despite the absence of search and information frictions, real shocks can give rise to fluctuations in the number of employed individuals. This creates the possibility of emulating fluctuations in employment over the business cycle and is the basis for the notable success that Prescott praises.

This comment points out that despite these possibly appealing implications, Prescott's aggregation strategy also has unattractive implications. We use a particular policy experiment to emphasize the consequences of following Prescott in modeling employment variations as being driven by a high intertemporal elasticity of labor supply that emerges because the economy is effectively pooling all labor income and designing enforceable gambles over who gets to work. In particular, it matters very much that the framework embodies no frictional unemployment in the sense of Friedman and Stigler.

---

[1] Sherwin Rosen often used a lottery model for the household. Instead of analyzing why a particular individual chooses higher education, Rosen modeled a family with a continuum of members that allocates fractions of its members to distinct educational choices that involve different numbers of years of schooling. See Ryoo and Rosen (2003).

For our laboratory, we follow the lead of Prescott's Footnote 3, which refers to interesting quantitative general equilibrium analyses of labor-market policies. In particular, we will contrast the ways that layoff taxes affect employment in a no-frictional-unemployment lotteries model and in a frictional-unemployment island-search model. The effects are very different. In the equilibrium of the lotteries model, unemployment *rises* in response to the introduction of a layoff tax because the private economy perceives higher layoff costs as equivalent to a less productive technology, prompting the stand-in household to substitute away from consumption toward leisure. The market outcome sets the employment lottery to give a lower probability of working. In the island-search model, introducing a layoff tax *reduces* unemployment through its effects on frictional unemployment, an avenue that is not present in the lotteries model.

We make the same assumptions that appear in most analyses of layoff taxes in the literature. The productivity of a job evolves according to a Markov process, and sufficiently poor realization triggers a layoff. The government imposes a layoff tax τ on each layoff. The tax revenues are handed back as equal lump-sum transfers to all agents, denoted by T per capita. Here we assume the simplest possible Markov process for productivity. A new job has productivity p_0. In all future periods, with probability $\xi \in [0, 1)$, the worker keeps the productivity from last period, and with probability $1 - \xi$, the worker draws a new productivity from a distribution $G(p)$.

6.2. LAYOFF TAXES IN AN EMPLOYMENT LOTTERIES MODEL

This section shows analytically that introducing a layoff tax raises unemployment in an employment lotteries model.[2] A market-clearing wage w equates the demand and supply of labor. A constant-returns-to-scale technology implies that an equilibrium wage is determined by the supply side as follows. At the beginning of a period, let the value to a firm of a worker with productivity p be $V(p)$, which satisfies the Bellman equation

$$V(p) = \max\left\{ p - w + \beta\left[\xi V(p) + (1 - \xi) \int V(p')\,dG(p')\right], -\tau \right\}. \quad (2.1)$$

Given a value of w, this Bellman equation determines a reservation productivity $\bar{p}$. If there exists an equilibrium with strictly positive employment, the equilibrium wage must be such that the firm breaks even on new hires; that is,

$$V(p_0) = p_0 - w + \beta\left[\xi V(p_0) + (1 - \xi) \int V(p')\,dG(p')\right] = 0$$

$$\Rightarrow w = p_0 + \beta(1 - \xi)\tilde{V}, \quad (2.2)$$

[2] Our result is the same as in Hopenhayn and Rogerson's (1993) numerical analysis of layoff taxes in a more elaborate employment lotteries framework with firm-size dynamics.

where

$$\tilde{V} \equiv \int V(p')\,dG\,(p').$$

To compute $\tilde{V}$, we first look at the value of $V(p)$ when $p \geq \bar{p}$,

$$\begin{aligned} V(p)\Big|_{p \geq \bar{p}} &= p - w + \beta\left[\xi V(p) + (1-\xi)\tilde{V}\right] \\ &= \frac{p - w + \beta(1-\xi)\tilde{V}}{1 - \beta\xi} = \frac{p - p_0}{1 - \beta\xi}, \end{aligned} \tag{2.3}$$

where we have successively substituted out for $V(p)$ and the last equality incorporates Eq. (2.2). We can then use Eq. (2.3) to find an expression for $\tilde{V}$,

$$\begin{aligned} \tilde{V} &= \int_{-\infty}^{\bar{p}} -\tau\,dG\,(p) + \int_{\bar{p}}^{\infty} V(p)\,dG\,(p) \\ &= -\tau G(\bar{p}) + \int_{\bar{p}}^{\infty} \frac{p - p_0}{1 - \beta\xi}\,dG\,(p). \end{aligned} \tag{2.4}$$

From the Bellman equation (2.1), the reservation productivity $\bar{p}$ satisfies

$$\bar{p} - w + \beta\left[\xi V(\bar{p}) + (1-\xi)\tilde{V}\right] = -\tau.$$

After imposing Eq. (2.2) and $V(\bar{p}) = -\tau$, we find that

$$\bar{p} = p_0 - (1 - \beta\xi)\tau \equiv \bar{p}(\tau). \tag{2.5}$$

The equations (2.2), (2.4), and (2.5) can be used to solve for the equilibrium wage $w = w(\tau)$.

In a stationary equilibrium, let μ be the mass of new jobs created in every period. The mass of jobs with productivity p_0 that have not yet experienced a new productivity draw can then be expressed as

$$\mu \sum_{i=0}^{\infty} \xi^i = \frac{\mu}{1 - \xi}, \tag{2.6}$$

and the mass of jobs that have experienced a new productivity draw and are still operating is given by

$$\begin{aligned} \sum_{i=0}^{\infty} \xi^i \mu(1-\xi)\,[1 - G(\bar{p})] \sum_{j=0}^{\infty} &\{\xi + (1-\xi)\,[1 - G(\bar{p})]\}^j \\ &= \frac{\mu}{1 - \xi}\frac{1 - G(\bar{p})}{G(\bar{p})}. \end{aligned} \tag{2.7}$$

After equating the sum of these two kinds of jobs to N (which we use to denote the total mass of all jobs), we get the following steady-state relationship:

$$\mu = NG(\bar{p})(1 - \xi). \tag{2.8}$$

By letting the continuum of agents be indexed on the unit interval, the total mass of jobs $N \in [0, 1]$ is equal to the fraction of all employed agents, which also equals the probability that an individual agent works. This probability is a utility-maximizing choice of the representative agent. We adopt Prescott's log-linear preference specification, $\sum_{t=0}^{\infty} \beta^t (\log(C_t) - \gamma N_t)$. In a stationary equilibrium with wage w and a gross interest rate $1/\beta$, the representative agent's optimization problem reduces to a static problem of the form

$$\max_{C,N} \log C - \gamma N,$$

subject to

$$C \leq N_w + \Pi + T, C \geq 0, N \in [0, 1], \tag{2.9}$$

where the profits from firms, Π, and the lump-sum transfer of layoff-tax revenues from the government, T, are taken as given by the agents. The optimal choice of the probability of working is then

$$N = \frac{1}{\gamma} - \frac{T + \Pi}{w}. \tag{2.10}$$

The sum of aggregate profits and lump-sum transfers can be computed using the masses of jobs in expressions (2.6) and (2.7),

$$\Pi + T = \frac{\mu}{1 - \xi}(p_0 - w) + \frac{\mu}{1 - \xi}\frac{1 - G(\bar{p})}{G(\bar{p})} \int_{\bar{p}}^{\infty} \frac{p - w}{1 - G(\bar{p})} dG(p)$$

$$= N \left[G(\bar{p})(p_0 - w) + \int_{\bar{p}}^{\infty} (p - w) dG(p) \right], \tag{2.11}$$

where the last equality invokes relationship (2.8).

We now adopt the special assumption that $G(p)$ is a uniform distribution on the unit interval $[0, 1]$, and the initial productivity of a new job is $p_0 = 1$. Expressions (2.4) and (2.11) can then be evaluated as follows:

$$\tilde{V} = -\tau \bar{p} + \left[\frac{1 + \bar{p}}{2} - 1 \right] \frac{1 - \bar{p}}{1 - \beta \xi} \tag{2.12}$$

and

$$\Pi + T = N \left[\bar{p} + (1 - \bar{p}) \frac{1 + \bar{p}}{2} - w \right]. \tag{2.13}$$

From Eq. (2.2) and (2.12),

$$w = 1 + \beta(1 - \xi) \left[-\tau \bar{p} - \frac{(1 - \bar{p})^2}{2(1 - \beta \xi)} \right],$$

and after substitution for $\bar{p}$ from (2.5)

$$w = 1 - \beta(1 - \xi)\tau \left[1 - \frac{(1 - \beta \xi)\tau}{2} \right] \equiv w(\tau). \tag{2.14}$$

By substituting (2.13) into (2.10) and using expressions (2.5) and (2.14), we arrive at an equilibrium expression for N,

$$N(\tau) = \frac{2w(\tau)}{\gamma \left[2\bar{p}(\tau) + 1 - \bar{p}(\tau)^2\right]},$$

with its derivative

$$\frac{d\,N(\tau)}{d\,\tau} = \frac{-2\beta(1 - \xi)\bar{p}(\tau)\left[2\bar{p}(\tau) + 1 - \bar{p}(\tau)^2\right] + 4(1 - \beta\xi)[1 - \bar{p}(\tau)]w(\tau)}{\gamma\left[2\bar{p}(\tau) + 1 - \bar{p}(\tau)^2\right]^2}.$$

Evaluating the derivative at $\tau = 0$, where $\bar{p}(0) = p_0 = 1$, we have

$$\left.\frac{d\,N(\tau)}{d\,\tau}\right|_{\tau=0} = \frac{-\beta(1 - \xi)}{\gamma} < 0.$$

This states that in general equilibrium, employment falls in response to the introduction of a layoff tax. This happens because agents respond to higher layoff costs in the same way that they would to a less productive technology. Thus, the stand-in household substitutes away from consumption toward leisure and so chooses a lower probability of working in the lottery over employment.[3]

6.3. LAYOFF TAXES IN AN ISLAND MODEL

The employment effects of introducing a layoff tax in an island framework are the opposite of those for the lotteries model. Thus, Lucas and Prescott (1974, p. 205) analyzed such effects in an island model and found that

The result is a decrease in unemployment and a decrease in the equilibrium present value of wages. (This example shows that lower average unemployment is not, in general, associated with higher welfare for workers.) It may well be, though one could hardly demonstrate it at this level of abstraction, that differences of this sort in the actual or perceived costs of changing jobs can help to account for the observed differences in average unemployment across occupations and among countries.

Why does the island model yield the opposite outcome from the employment lottery model? Both models have reservation productivity falling and job tenures lengthening in response to an increase in the layoff tax. The difference is that in the island model there is no aggregate mechanism that allows individuals to substitute away from working so individual workers have to fend for themselves: those who want to consume must also work. Layoff taxes in an island model reduce unemployment because there are fewer transitions between jobs/islands and therefore there is less frictional unemployment.

---

[3] The substitution effect prevails over the income effect because to a first-order approximation the latter effect is neutralized when layoff costs are assumed to be a layoff tax, and the tax revenues are handed back to the agents as a lump sum.

6.4. CONCLUDING REMARKS

Rogerson and Hansen's lottery-based model of a stand-in household is elegant and analytically tractable. The lotteries smooth out nonconvexities arising from work-week restrictions and make the stand-in household "one big happy family" that is very willing to reallocate its labor supply over time. Nevertheless, it gives us pause for thought that the theoretical consequences of an important public policy such as employment protection differ so completely between a model with employment lotteries and an island model.[4] The negative employment effects of layoff taxes in an employment lottery model stem directly from the property of that framework that Prescott characterizes as being so important.

Kydland and Prescott (1982) found that the growth model displays business cycle fluctuations if and only if the aggregate intertemporal elasticity of labor supply is high, a fact that was not then accepted by most labor economists. The labor economists ignored the consequences of aggregation in the face of nonconvexities in coming to their incorrect conclusion that the aggregate elasticity of labor supply is small. Nonconvexities at the household level imply high intertemporal elasticity of labor supply even if the intertemporal elasticity of labor supply of the households being aggregated is small.

For the sake of argument, let us set aside the question of frictional unemployment and focus on the substitution effect that is the driving force in the employment lottery model. If labor economists were asked about the substitution effects associated with layoff taxes, they would probably direct their attention to the joint employment decisions of spouses within a family. For an environment that offers families the limited options of sending one or two persons to the labor market either full or part time, labor economists would estimate a low substitution effect in response to layoff taxes. Prescott would presumably argue that those estimates are mistaken because they fail to recognize that it would be possible for a large group of families to join together to randomize over who should be sent to work and who should stay home, while also trading state-contingent claims that would provide consumption for the people who do not work.

This market arrangement and randomization device stand at the center of the employment lottery model. To us, it seems that they make the aggregation theory behind the stand-in household fundamentally different from the well-known aggregation theory for the firm side. Prescott's example of a nonconvex production technology in Section 6 illustrates this point very well. The plants that do not find any workers stay idle; that is just as well for those idle plants, because the plants in operation earn zero rents. In short, whether individual production units operate or exit (or remain idle) is the end of the story in the aggregation theory behind the aggregate production function. But in the aggregation theory behind the stand-in household's utility function, it is really just the beginning.

---

[4] For a detailed discussion of the employment implications of layoff taxes in different frameworks, including the matching model, see Ljungqvist (2001).

REFERENCES

Gary D. Hansen (1985), "Indivisible Labor and the Business Cycle," *Journal of Monetary Economics* 16: 309–27.

Hugo Hopenhayn, and Richard Rogerson (1993), "Job Turnover and Policy Evaluation: A General Equilibrium Analysis," *Journal of Political Economy* 101: 915–38.

Lars Ljungqvist (2001), "How Do Layoff Costs Affect Employment?" *Economic Journal* 112: 829–53.

Robert E. Lucas, Jr., and Edward C. Prescott (1974), "Equilibrium Search and Unemployment," *Journal of Economic Theory* 7(2): 188–209.

Edward C. Prescott (2002), "Richard T. Ely Lecture: Prosperity and Depression," *American Economic Review* 92(2): 1–15.

Richard Rogerson (1988), "Indivisible Labor, Lotteries, and Equilibrium," *Journal of Monetary Economics* 21: 3–16.

Jaewoo Ryoo, and Sherwin Rosen (2003), "The Engineering Labor Market," mimeo, Hong Kong University of Science and Technology.

7 Default and Aggregate Fluctuations in Storage Economies

Makoto Nakajima and José-Víctor Ríos-Rull

ABSTRACT: In this paper we extend the work of Chatterjee, Corbae, Nakajima, and Ríos-Rull (unpublished manuscript, University of Pennsylvania, 2002) to include aggregate real shocks to economic activity. The model, which includes agents that borrow and lend and a competitive credit industry, and which has endogenous default and credit limits, allows us to explore the extent to which aggregate events are amplified or smoothed via the mechanism of household bankruptcy filings. In the model agents are subject to shocks to earnings opportunities, to preferences, and to their asset position and borrow and lend to smooth consumption. On occasion, the realization of the shocks is bad enough so that agents take advantage of the opportunities provided by the U.S. Bankruptcy Code and file for bankruptcy, which wipes out their debt at the expense both of being banned from borrowing for a certain amount of time and of incurring transaction costs. The incentives to default are time-varying and depend on the individual state and general economic conditions. The model is quantitative in the sense that its fundamental parameters are estimated using U.S. data, and the model can replicate the aggregate conditions of the U.S. economy. Especially, the model accounts for the very high number of bankruptcies in the past few years. We report statistics produced by experiments with model economies with various aggregate shocks. Based on these experiments, we analyze the reaction of households to various aggregate real shocks and the interaction between households and the credit industry, and we discuss the aggregate implications of these actions and the direction in which the model might be further extended.

7.1. INTRODUCTION

In this chapter we study a model economy where agents file for bankruptcy that is mapped quantitatively to the U.S. economy and that is subject to aggregate real shocks. We extend the work of Chatterjee et al. (2002) (who studied the steady state of economies with bankruptcy where equilibrium interest rates are indexed by a set of individual characteristics) to study aggregate uncertainty. The aggregate shocks that we study generate expansions and recessions in a variety of ways: (i) a good

Ríos-Rull thanks the National Science Foundation, the University of Pennsylvania Research Foundation, the Spanish Ministry of Education, and the Centro de Altísimos Estudios Ríos Pérez. We thank the organizers of the conference to honor Herbert Scarf.

realization shifts the distribution of efficiency units of labor to the right, and a bad realization shifts it to the left; (ii) shocks increase or decrease the risk-free interest rate; (iii) shocks affect the number of people who suffer asset destruction; or (iv) all of the shocks above occur in combination.

The current chapter is part of an ongoing investigation into the role of bankruptcy filings and general credit disruptions in shaping business cycles. In general the study of these issues is very difficult: not only does it include many agents differing in asset holdings, shocks, and credit ratings, implying that the state of the economy is a probability measure over these characteristics, but also solving the individual problem requires the forecasting of prices, which in turn requires the whole state vector to be part of the individual state. To get around this problem we follow the approach used in Diaz-Gimenez et al. (1992), which specifies the model in a certain way, so that prices are essentially exogenous and hence do not depend on the distribution of agents over states. We are able to do so by (i) assuming a storage technology with exogenous rate of return and by (ii) effectively preventing loans from being held at the time of the resolution of aggregate variables. Only idiosyncratic shocks are realized while loans are outstanding, which guarantees that the law of large numbers applies and that firms' profits coincide with the expected profits (which are zero) in all states of nature, guaranteeing that prices can be forecast based solely on aggregate exogenous variables.

Although the timing that we choose guarantees that the distribution of agents does not affect prices and hence that the model can be solved with relative ease,[1] it also takes away part of the properties that we are interested in: the possible transmission of credit crunches throughout the economy as surprise increases in default will in turn induce more defaults. To address this issue, a different approach is needed, summarizing the distribution of household types by some of its statistics as in Krusell and Smith (1998) and especially Krusell and Smith (1997) (this is the subject of our research agenda starting with Nakajima and Ríos-Rull (2003)).

We estimate the fundamental parameters of the model using U.S. data so that the model can replicate the aggregate conditions of the U.S. economy. Especially, the model accounts for the very high number of bankruptcies in the past few years. Using the calibrated model, we analyze the interaction between various aggregate real shocks and household behavior on bankruptcy filings.

Section 7.2 lays out the model. Section 7.3 specifies a parameterization of the model that has a steady state that can be mapped to the U.S. data. Section 7.4 discusses the experiments that we run. They involve different specifications of what business cycles are but they are all chosen to generate aggregate business cycles statistics like those in the data. Section 7.5 describes the business cycle properties of the baseline model economy, and Section 7.6 studies those properties in the rest of the model economies that we are interested in. Section 7.7 concludes.

---

[1]   The estimation stage of the model still requires us to use a Beowulf cluster.

7.2. THE MODEL ECONOMY

The model is a version of Chatterjee et al. (2002) with aggregate shocks. In the model, agents are subject to idiosyncratic and aggregate shocks, which affect their assessment of consumption and their availability of resources. There are no markets to insure against these contingencies. Moreover, the market structure resembles that of the U.S., where households can borrow and save. They save according to a given storage technology or world interest rate, whereas they can borrow at market interest rates that reflect the fact that households can file for bankruptcy, which condones their debts. This option, which households may use unilaterally, inflicts minimal transaction costs on them and prevents them from having access to future credit for a certain number of years. Aggregate shocks affect the properties of the idiosyncratic earnings shocks.

As we stated above, in this project we specify the aggregate shocks in such a way that they do not generate uncertainty in the realized profits of firms, ensuring that prices of loans, although depending on both the aggregate shocks and the specific circumstances of the borrower, do not depend on the whole distribution of agents. We achieve this by posing a particular timing in the model so that aggregate uncertainty does not affect the default decisions of households. Only idiosyncratic shocks occur while agents hold loans, but the rate of return of these loans is perfectly forecastable. We now proceed to describe the timing of the model.

7.2.1. The Timing

At the beginning of each period, the economy is in an aggregate exogenous state $z \in Z$ that follows a Markov process with transition $\Pi_{z,z'}$, (we use the standard notation of using z, z' to refer to the current and the following periods' value of the variable). Individual households are characterized by a vector of exogenous stochastic characteristics that take only finitely many values and by a value of earnings. These characteristics include a shock that governs the evolution of earnings, $\varepsilon \in \{\varepsilon_1, \ldots, \varepsilon_{n_\varepsilon}\} = \mathcal{E}$, a shock that affects the utility of consumption, which we denote as $\theta \in \{\theta_1, \ldots, \theta_{n_\theta}\} = \Theta$, and a shock that affects asset destruction, $\lambda \in \{\lambda_1, \ldots, \lambda_{n_\lambda}\} = \Lambda$. The shock that affects earnings, ε, has the property of affecting the probability distribution from which households draw their actual earnings. Earnings e has a continuous domain, i.e., $0 < e \in [\underline{e}, \bar{e}] = E$ and has a continuous c.d.f. given by $F(e, \varepsilon, z)$, where ε and z are affecting the actual probability that earnings are less than or equal to e. We denote the vector of individual shocks by $s = \{\varepsilon, \theta, \lambda, e\} \in S$. The timing of the realizations of the shocks is given by Fig. 7.1, which also includes the timing of the decisions that households make.

The individual shocks $\{\varepsilon, \theta, \lambda\}$ follow Markov processes that are also conditional on the aggregate state. In this fashion, we write the transition matrices of the Markov processes as $\pi^\theta_{\theta'|z,\theta,z'}$, $\pi^\varepsilon_{\varepsilon'|z,\varepsilon,z'}$, and $\pi^\lambda_{\lambda'|z,\lambda,z'}$. We write the joint Markov chain that

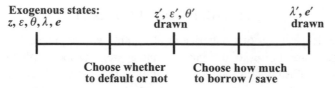

Figure 7.1. Timing of events within a period.

yields the evolution of the individual state variables by $\pi_{s'|z,s,z'}$, although they are not updated simultaneously. We denote the joint transition matrix of individual and aggregate shocks by $\Gamma_{z,s,z's'}$. Note that we allow the individual transitions to depend on the aggregate shocks of two consecutive periods. This is to give ourselves the possibility of having the aggregate measure of people depend only on the aggregate shock and not on the whole history (see Castañeda, Díaz-Giménez, and Ríos-Rull (1998) for details).

We also use the notation $\tilde{s} = \{\varepsilon', \theta', \lambda\} \in \tilde{S}$ to denote the individual state at the time of the saving and borrowing decision, excluding current earnings e (note that e carries no predictive power over tomorrow's earnings, which depend only on z' and ε'), and having the value of the shock to asset holdings, λ, at its previous period value. Associated with this notation we have $\tilde{\Gamma}_{z,s,z',\tilde{s}}$.

A crucial step in the development of the model is the identification of which variables index prices. We proceed by guessing which variables these are and then establishing that indeed these variables are sufficient to characterize prices.

7.2.2. The Default Option and Market Arrangement

We model the default option to be like a filing for bankruptcy under the U.S. Bankruptcy Code. Let $h \in \{0, 1\}$ denote the "bankruptcy flag" for a household, where $h = 1$ indicates a record of a bankruptcy filing in the household's credit history and $h = 0$ denotes the absence of any such record. We can interpret h as the household's credit rating, which is either good ($h = 0$, not having filed for bankruptcy recently) or bad ($h = 1$, having filed for bankruptcy recently and U.S. law allowing this information to be public). Consider a household that starts the current period with a good credit rating and some unsecured debt. If the household files for bankruptcy (and we permit a household to do so irrespective of its current income or past consumption level), the following things happen:

1. The household's liabilities are set to zero (i.e., its debts are discharged) and the household is not permitted to save in the current period. The latter assumption is a simple way to recognize that a household's attempt to accumulate assets during the filing period will result in those assets being seized by creditors.
2. The household begins the next period with a bad credit rating (i.e., $h' = 1$).

3. A household whose beginning-of-period credit rating is bad (i.e., $h = 1$) cannot get any new loans.[2] Also, a household with a bad credit rating experiences a loss equal to a fraction $0 < \gamma < 1$ of earnings, a loss intended to capture the pecuniary costs of a bad credit rating.

4. A household with a bad credit rating will keep its bad credit rating in the following period with exogenous positive probability η and will recover a good credit rating with probability $(1 - \eta)$. This is a simple, albeit idealized, way of modeling the fact that a bankruptcy flag remains on an individual's credit history for only a finite number of years.

The addition of the default option implies that profit-maximizing lenders take into consideration the probabilities of default of the borrowers. Different types of borrowers have different default probabilities, which will imply that the loans are indexed by whatever characteristics of the borrower may affect those probabilities.

We restrict households to choosing from a menu of loans, which we model as a single one-period pure discount bond with a face value in a finite set L^- that has only elements with negative values.[3] A purchase of a discount bond with a negative face value ℓ' means that the household has entered into a contract where it promises to deliver, conditional on not declaring bankruptcy, $-\ell' > 0$ units of the consumption good next period; if it declares bankruptcy, the household delivers nothing.

We conjecture that the price of a loan of size ℓ', which is the per-unit amount of goods that a type $\tilde{s}$ in aggregate state z' gets in exchange for a liability next period of size ℓ', is a function of only these variables and not of any distributional variable or of any time subscript. We denote this price by $q_{z',\tilde{s},\ell'} \geq 0$. Note that the borrower has a commitment, contingent on not filing for bankruptcy, to repay ℓ' next period.

The household can also save, in which case it commands an interest rate $\hat{q}_{z'}$. Note that the exogenous aggregate state that affects the interest rates on savings does so only in a predetermined way. In other words, the interest rate commanded is known at the time of the savings.

Households can save or borrow any amount that they want, but there are endogenously determined upper and lower bounds to their asset holdings. We assume this for now and discuss its verification later. The set of possible asset holdings for the household is $L = L^- \cup L^+$. L^+ contains a finite number of positive values, where

---

[2] This feature requires some discussion. Filing for bankruptcy implies giving up the right to file again for seven years. Then why does a bad credit rating imply that households cannot borrow anymore? We can rationalize the inability to borrow in two ways. One is by modeling the environment as a game and showing that there exists an equilibrium with the characteristic that nobody borrows or lends. This type of equilibrium arises because this game is a coordination game. The other rationalization, which we prefer, is via regulation. Public overseers of private lenders do not approve of loans to people with a bad credit rating. This is just a matter of policy. Note also that private lenders, once they have outstanding loans, want this regulation in place because it gives a rationale for borrowers to try to avoid defaulting by imposing a penalty when they do so.

[3] The finiteness of the set of possible loans is assumed just to have a finite set of prices that simplifies the analysis. Quantitatively, this poses no real restrictions, because the step between consecutive loan sizes can be made arbitrarily small.

0 is the smallest element and ℓ_{max} is the nonbinding upper bound. The smallest element of L is $\ell_{min} < 0$. We also denote the entire set of prices by $q \in I\!R_+^N$, where $N = N_Z \times N_{\tilde{s}} \times N_L$, and where N_Z, $N_{\tilde{s}}$, and N_L refer respectively to the cardinality of the sets Z, $\tilde{S}$ ($= \mathcal{E} \times \Theta \times \Lambda$), and L. In this compact notation we include both the interest rates for borrowers (which depend on $\{z', \tilde{s}, \ell'\}$) and for lenders (notice that interest rates for the lenders depend only on z'). Prices are bounded below by 0 (nobody will acquire a liability in exchange for nothing) and above by $\hat{q}_{z'}$, the state-dependent risk-free rates of return. We denote the set of possible prices by $Q = \{q \in I\!R^N : 0 \le q_{z',\tilde{s},\ell'} \le \hat{q}_{z'}\}$.

7.2.3. Households

The preferences of a household are given by the expected value of a discounted sum of instantaneous utility functions,

$$E_0 \left\{ \sum_{t=0}^{\infty} \beta^t \ u(c_t, \theta_t) \right\}, \tag{1}$$

where $0 < \beta < 1$ is the discount factor, $u : I\!R_+ \to I\!R$ is a continuous, strictly increasing, and strictly concave function, c_t is consumption in period t, and θ_t is the realization of an idiosyncratic shock that affects the marginal utilities of the current period. To be consistent with our description of the timing of events in Fig. 7.1, θ_t corresponds to θ'.

We look at the household decision in two stages. In the first stage the household decides whether to default (if such a choice is an option) and in the second stage the household chooses how much to borrow or save. In the second stage, the household is in one of four situations: (i) having a good credit rating ($h = 0$) and not having defaulted in this period ($d = 0$), (ii) having a good credit rating ($h = 0$) and having defaulted in this period ($d = 1$), (iii) having a bad credit rating ($h = 1$) and not recovering its credit rating ($d = 1$), and (iv) having a bad credit rating ($h = 1$) but recovering its credit rating ($d = 0$).[4]

The household's characteristics at the time of the savings decision are $\{\tilde{s}, e, \ell, h, d\}$, which are the exogenous shocks and earnings, the asset position, the credit history, and the change of the credit status in the current period. The budget set of the household is affected by these characteristics plus the aggregate exogenous state and the loan prices, and we denote it by $B(z', \tilde{s}, e, \ell, h, d, q)$. The budget set takes the following form:

1. If the household has a good credit rating ($h = 0$) and has chosen not to default ($d = 0$), then

$$B(z', \tilde{s}, e, \ell, 0, 0, q) = \{c \in I\!R_+, \ell' \in L : c + q_{z',\tilde{s},\ell'} \ \ell' \le e + \ell - \lambda\}. \tag{2}$$

---

[4] Note that d is a choice variable for households with a good credit rating ($h = 0$) but is a stochastic variable for households with a bad credit rating ($h = 1$).

This is the standard case where the household chooses how much to consume and how much to save given that its resources are its inherited assets and its current earnings. Note that on occasion the budget set may be empty, which requires that a combination of bad things have happened to some extent (the household was deep in debt, earnings were low, new loans are expensive, there is large asset destruction).

2. If the household had debt (and hence a good credit history) and did choose to default ($d = 1$), then

$$B(z', \tilde{s}, e, \ell, 0, 1, q) = \{c \in I\!R_+, \ell' = 0 : c \leq (1 - \gamma)e\}. \tag{3}$$

In this case, inherited debts (including assets destroyed) did disappear from the budget constraint, saving is not possible, and transaction cost associated with a bad credit history is incurred.

3. If the household had a bad credit rating ($h = 1$) (it did not have an option to default) and its credit rating did not improve ($d = 1$), then

$$B(z', \tilde{s}, \ell, 1, 1, e, q)$$
$$= \{c \in I\!R_+, \ell' \geq 0 : c + q_{z', \tilde{s}, \ell'}\ell' \leq (1 - \gamma)e + \max\{\ell - \lambda, 0\}\}. \tag{4}$$

With a sustained bad credit rating, the household cannot borrow and is subject to transaction costs and to some assets destruction.[5]

4. If the household had a bad credit rating ($h = 1$) (it did not have an option to default) and its credit rating improved ($d = 0$) then the budget constraint is the same as in case 1,

$$B(z', \tilde{s}, e, \ell, 1, 0, q) = \{c \in I\!R_+, \ell' \in L : c + q_{z', \tilde{s}, \ell'} \ell' \leq e + \ell - \lambda\}. \tag{5}$$

Before we analyze the decision process, it is convenient to describe the situation of the household on the eve of a period, after consumption and saving (or borrowing) have taken place but before the new shocks are realized (those that determine earnings level and asset destruction). The individual state is $\{z', \tilde{s}, \ell', h'\}$, where $h' = d$. We now define the value of this state for a household by means of the function $w(z', \tilde{s}, \ell', h'; q)\colon Q \to I\!R$, which assigns a utility value, given prices q. We obtain function w as the unknown in a Bellman-type functional equation that we describe, avoiding most technicalities.[6]

We start by defining an operator that yields the maximum lifetime utility achievable when the household's current earnings draw is e and its future lifetime utility is

---

[5] Note that we are assuming that asset destruction cannot result in households with bad credit histories getting indebted. This assumption excludes the situation where a household that is unable to default is borrowing.

[6] For details see Chatterjee et al. (2002).

assessed according to a given function $w(z', \tilde{s}, \ell', h'; q)$. Define $T_1(w)(z, s, \ell, h; q)$ as follows:

1. For $(\ell - \lambda) < 0$, $h = 0$, and $B(z', \tilde{s}, e, \ell, 0, 0, q) = \emptyset$, for some $\{z', \tilde{s}\}$ consistent with $\{z, s\}$:

$$T_1(w)(z, s, \ell, 0, q) = \sum_{z', \tilde{s}} \tilde{\Gamma}_{z,s,z',\tilde{s}} \left\{ u(e, \tilde{s}) + \beta w(z', \tilde{s}, 0, 1; q) \right\}. \qquad (6)$$

2. For $(\ell - \lambda) < 0$, $h = 0$, and $B(z', \tilde{s}, \ell, 0, 0, q) \neq \emptyset$, for all $\{z', \tilde{s}\}$ consistent with $\{z, s\}$:

$$T_1(w)(z, s, \ell, 0, q)$$
$$= \max \left\{ \sum_{z', \tilde{s}} \tilde{\Gamma}_{z,s,z',\tilde{s}} \left\{ u(e, \tilde{s}) + \beta w(z', \tilde{s}, 0, 1; q) \right\}, \right.$$
$$\left. \sum_{z', \tilde{s}} \tilde{\Gamma}_{z,s,z',\tilde{s}} \left\{ \max_{c, \ell' \in B(z', \tilde{s}, e, \ell, 0, 0, q)} u(c, \tilde{s}) + \beta w(z', \tilde{s}, \ell', 0; q) \right\} \right\}. \qquad (7)$$

3. For $(\ell - \lambda) \geq 0$, $h = 0$:

$$T_1(w)(z, s, \ell, 0, q)$$
$$= \sum_{z', \tilde{s}} \tilde{\Gamma}_{z,s,z',\tilde{s}} \left\{ \max_{c, \ell' \in B(z', \tilde{s}, e, \ell, 0, 0, q)} u(c, \tilde{s}) + \beta w(z', \tilde{s}, \ell', 0; q) \right\}. \qquad (8)$$

4. For $(\ell - \lambda) \geq 0$, $h = 1$:

$$T_1(w)(z, s, \ell, 1, q)$$
$$= \eta \left\{ \sum_{z', \tilde{s}} \tilde{\Gamma}_{z,s,z',\tilde{s}} \left\{ \max_{c, \ell' \in B(z, \tilde{s}, e, \ell, 1, 1, q)} u(c, \tilde{s}) + \beta w(z', \tilde{s}, \ell', 1; q) \right\} \right\}$$
$$+ (1 - \eta) \left\{ \sum_{z', \tilde{s}} \tilde{\Gamma}_{z,s,z,\tilde{s}} \left\{ \max_{c, \ell' \in B(z, \tilde{s}, e, \ell, 1, 0, q)} u(c, \tilde{s}) + \beta w(z', \tilde{s}, \ell', 0; q) \right\} \right\}. \qquad (9)$$

The first part of this definition says that if the household has debt and the budget set conditional on not defaulting may be empty, then the household must default. In this case, the expected lifetime utility of the household is simply the sum of the utility from consuming the current endowment and the discounted expected utility of starting the next period with no assets and a bad credit rating. The second part says that if the household has debt and the budget set conditional on not defaulting is not empty, the household chooses whichever default option yields higher lifetime utility. In the case where both options yield the same utility the household may choose either. The distinction between default under part 1 and default under part 2 is the distinction between "involuntary" and "voluntary" default. In the first case, default is the *only* option, whereas in the second case, it's the *best* option. The last two parts apply when the household has no debt (so default is not an option), but distinguish between a good and bad credit rating. Note that when the household's credit rating is bad, there is some probability η that it will continue in that state in the following period. This way of writing the problem is convenient also from the point of view of describing what is known at the time of each decision.

Note that the image of w under T_1 has current earnings as an argument, so it is not the same class of function as w. We denote such an image by $v(z, s, \ell, h, q; w)$. To obtain an updated function w from function v we have to integrate over earnings both with respect to the c.d.f. $F(e', \varepsilon', z')$ and with respect to λ', using transition function $\pi^{\lambda}_{\lambda'|z,\lambda,z'}$. Chaterjee et al. (2002) show that an operator constructed this way is well defined and that it is a contraction. This finding allows us to solve the household problem given prices by successive approximations.

7.2.4. Unsecured Credit Industry and Equilibrium

The competitive firms serving the consumer credit industry have access to a credit market in which they can borrow or lend as much as is needed at a risk-free rate $\hat{q}_{z'}$. In this environment, firms in the consumer credit industry lend to households at the rate that will yield zero profit, and this is no other than the risk-free rate times the probability that the household does not default. Let $p_{z',\bar{s},\ell'}(q)$ be the probability of default for a household with current shock $\bar{s}$ in aggregate state z' that borrows (or lends) ℓ', when the set of prices of loans is $q = \{q_{z',\bar{s},\ell'}\}$. Then competitive equilibrium is defined as follows:

Definition 1: A competitive equilibrium is a set of prices $q^* = \{q^*_{z',\bar{s},\ell'}\}$ such that when agents optimize, taking q^* as given, the probability of default, $p_{z',\bar{s},\ell'}(q^*)$ satisfies

$$q^*_{z',\bar{s},\ell'} = [1 - p_{z',\bar{s},\ell'}(q^*)] \, \hat{q}_{z'}, \qquad \forall \; z', \bar{s}, \ell'. \tag{10}$$

Chatterjee et al. (2002) show that equilibria for economies such as these exist. A version of their characterization of equilibria for this economy indicates that in any competitive equilibrium (i) $q^*_{z',\bar{s},\ell'} = \hat{q}_{z'}$ for $\ell' \geq 0$; (ii) if the grid for L is sufficiently fine, for all z', there exist $\bar{s}$ and $\ell^0 < 0$ such that $q^*_{z',\bar{s},\ell^0} = \hat{q}_{z'}$; (iii) $q^*_{z',\bar{s},\ell^1} \geq q^*_{z',\bar{s},\ell^2}$ for $0 > \ell^1 > \ell^2$; and (iv) $q^*_{\ell_{z',\bar{s},\ell_{\min}}} = 0$.[7] The first property says that the interest rate applied to saving is the risk-free rate, because the consumer credit industry is competitive. The second property says that if the grid is taken to be fine enough, there is always a level of debt for which it is never optimal for households to default. As a result, competition leads firms to charge the risk-free rate on these loans as well. The third property says that the price on loans falls with the size of the loans;

---

[7]   While stating the properties of equilibria we abstract from assets destruction. To account for it is trivial but tedious, except for the case where the mass of agents hit by these shocks varies.

i.e., the implied interest rate on loans rises with the size of the loan. The fourth property says that the prices of loans eventually become zero; in particular, the price of a loan of size ℓ_{min} is always zero in every equilibrium, if we set ℓ_{min} sufficiently small.

Now we are ready to discuss the assumption that there exist endogenous lower and upper bounds of asset holdings. The existence of the lower bound is guaranteed by the third and fourth properties above. Because households will never borrow up to the amount where the price of loans is zero (because households do not gain anything by borrowing up to that amount), the debt level where the price of loans is zero works as a lower bound of asset holdings. The upper bound in assets has a different origin. In models with precautionary savings (and our model is one of them), the existence of an upper bound of asset holdings is implied by the fact that the interest rate is too low in all possible states relative to the rate of time preference. As households increase their wealth, eventually the role of earnings in their income becomes arbitrarily small, whereas this is not the case for the sacrifice that agents have to make to keep saving, and this guarantees the existence of such an upper bound of assets. See Huggett (1993) or Aiyagari (1994) for details.

As we assumed above, prices do not depend on either time or on the distribution of agents: no aggregate uncertainty is revealed in between the instant that loans are issued and the instant in which default is chosen. This means that probabilities of default are not random variables, and that expected profits of firms (zero) coincide with realized profits. Note also that the rates of return of the storage technology are determined exogenously and are not affected by the distribution of agents, and that probabilities of default depend only on individual variables. This feature also guarantees that prices do not depend on time.

7.3. CALIBRATION

We now turn to mapping the model into U.S. data. To do so properly we have to extend the model in two dimensions: the inclusion of depreciation (which affects only accounting) and the explicit consideration of demographics. The latter is more involved and makes it necessary to generate a large number of agents with low assets.[8] We describe those extensions in Section 7.3.1. Section 7.3.2 maps the statistics of a version of the model without aggregate shocks to the U.S. economy and discusses the extent to which the model achieves those targets. Section 7.4 describes the set of economies with aggregate shocks that we explore.

The actual process by which we map the model to data consists in specifying a set of functional forms and parameter values for which we solve the problem of the agents obtaining decision rules that depend only on exogenous shocks and

---

[8]   Again, see details in Chatterjee et al. (2002).

individual state variables. Then we construct a Markov process with the decision rules and the process for the shocks. We then simulate a large number of individual households histories (up to 1,000,000 to avoid sampling error), which we aggregate to get the whole economy from which we compute statistics. We then compare these statistics to those of the U.S. economy (see Ríos-Rull, 1998, for details).

7.3.1. Model Extensions for Calibrating Purposes

We extend the model in two ways that are mostly cosmetic. The first extension is to introduce the depreciation of capital stock. This addition just changes the accounting for the output of the model. It helps to have the appropriate share of consumption and investment out of production.

The second extension is to include population turnover. In this version, households face a constant probability of dying, which generates a constant outflow of households of each type. This is matched by an equal measure of households born every period with zero assets and a good credit history. The initial values of the initial idiosyncratic shocks of the newborns are the same as those of the respective stationary probability distributions. The key difference introduced by this feature of the model is that there are now many agents with a low level of wealth, whereas in a version of the model without population turnover, agents for the most part have large amounts of assets for self-insurance purposes. A large number of households with low wealth implies that some of them will be willing to borrow and then default despite the costly events triggered by these actions.

7.3.2. Calibrating the Deterministic Version of the Model to U.S. Data

We now turn to the map between the model and the data. We start describing our targets and their values in the data, and then we describe the extent to which the model matches them and how it does it.

7.3.2.1. The Targets from the Data

The set of statistics that we choose as targets is depicted in the first column of Table 7.1. The second column depicts the long-run averages of these statistics in the U.S. economy. We divide the statistics into four groups. The first group contains the standard aggregate statistics such as wealth-to-output ratio, consumption and investment shares of output, and labor and capital shares of incomes. Those statistics are based on the standard interpretations of NIPA. The risk-free rate of return is chosen to match the average interest rate applied to the checking accounts of commercial banks, because it is the risk-free interest rate for the majority of people who might file bankruptcy.

The second group contains distributional statistics of earnings. We pick four targets related to earnings because we want the earnings process to produce an

TABLE 7.1. *Statistics of the deterministic economy*

Statistic	Target	Model
Basic aggregate targets		
Wealth-to-output ratio	3.32	3.35
Labor share	0.64	0.64
Risk-free rate of return	0.5%	0.5%
Earnings distribution related targets		
Earnings Gini	0.61	0.61
Bottom 40% earnings	3.8%	7.6%
Fourth quintile earnings	22.9%	19.4%
Top quintile earnings	60.2%	63.4%
Other distributional targets		
Population turnover rate	2.5%	2.5%
Income Gini	0.55	0.56
Wealth Gini	0.80	0.80
Default related targets		
Households filing bankruptcy	1.0%	1.0%
Average length of punishment	10 years	10 years
Households with negative assets	9.9%	10.0%

Source: The source for the distributional data is Budría et al. (2002).

earnings distribution which is similar to that of the United States. In order to achieve these criteria, we employ an earnings process with five parameters.

The third group of statistics contains the distributional targets, except for earnings. It includes the demographic turnover rate and statistics on the distribution of income and wealth. The demographic turnover rate is set to 2.5%. This implies that the average length of adult life is 40 years, as a compromise for an economy without population growth. We use Gini indices of income and wealth as statistics representing the distribution.

The fourth group of statistics are default-related. According to the Administrative Office of the U.S. Courts, the proportion of the households that filed consumer bankruptcy to the total number of households is around 1.3% in recent years. Among them, Chapter 7 bankruptcy, which the model is intended to capture, makes up more than 70%.[9] Therefore we decided to use 1.0% as our target for the proportion of households declaring bankruptcy. The average length of punishment is chosen to be 10 years because the U.S. Bankruptcy Code states this as the length of time for which having filed for bankruptcy stays in the credit rating. In the model we report the average length of bad-credit-rating spells.

---

[9] For a more detailed description of U.S. bankruptcy law and data on bankruptcies, see Chatterjee et al. (2002).

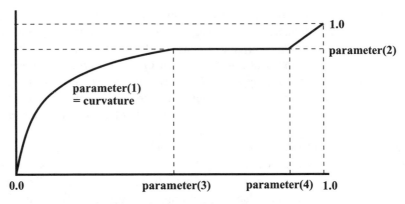

Figure 7.2. Nature of the earnings process.

7.3.2.2. The Targets in the Model

To get the model economy to achieve these targets, we essentially follow the procedures described in Chatterjee et al. (2002), adjusted for the fact that this model economy does not exclude any subset of the population. There are four types of individual shocks to be specified, namely the shock governing the earnings process (ε), the earnings shock (e), the preference shock (θ), and the asset destruction shock (λ). We choose earnings to be independent and independently distributed (i.i.d.) (meaning that the shock ε is irrelevant) with the shape given by Fig. 7.2. This is a four-parameter distribution. In addition there are two more parameters, the upper and lower bounds for earnings. Of these two, one should not matter, as the model is unit independent. This gives a total of five parameters for the distribution of earnings.

As for the preference shock, we assume that it is i.i.d., so it is characterized by two parameters (magnitude and probability of the bad shock). To calibrate our baseline model we abstract from the asset-destruction shock. We will evaluate the effect of the asset-destruction shock later.

In total, there are 14 parameters that have to be pinned down. They are (i) five parameters characterizing the earnings process, (ii) two parameters characterizing the preference-shock process (magnitude and probability of the bad shock), (iii) two preference parameters (time-discount factor and degree of risk aversion[10]), (iv) two parameters specifying bankruptcy law (average length of punishment and cost of having a bad credit history), (v) one demographic transition parameter (population turnover rate), and (vi) two parameters specifying technology (risk-free interest rate and depreciation rate). As there are 13 target statistics in Table 7.1, we set the degree of risk aversion and fix its value to 2.0 to have 13 parameters, and we check the robustness of our results to a change in the value of the risk-aversion parameter later.

---

[10] We use the standard constant relative risk aversion (CRRA) period utility function.

The last column of Table 7.1 shows the values of target statistics in the steady-state version (i.e., without aggregate shocks) in the model economy. A comparison between the last two columns gives us a sense of the fit of the model to data. We immediately see that the statistics of the model economy match their counterparts in the U.S. economy surprisingly well. Especially, the model is successful in replicating the very large number of bankruptcies and the large number of households in debt that are observed in recent years. It is very hard to get simultaneously a high amount of saving (the capital–output ratio is 3.3), a large number of households in debt (around 10% of total number of households), and a large number of defaults simultaneously, even though we add a demographic turnover. As Castañeda et al. (2003) show, simple models with agents differing only in the realizations of uninsurable shocks to earnings have a hard time matching the U.S. wealth distribution. They also show that a large wealth dispersion is achieved by posing very skewed earnings and by modeling households not as purely life-cycle agents but as members of a dynasty. We basically follow their strategy in finding the set of parameters that yields statistics that are closest to the data. It is well worth mentioning that the inequality of earnings, income, and wealth in terms of the Gini index in the model is very similar to the data. Income is less concentrated than earnings, whereas wealth is more concentrated than earnings both in the model and in the data.

7.4. MODEL ECONOMIES WITH AGGREGATE SHOCKS

We now turn to exploring the business-cycle behavior of the stochastic model economies. There are various ways of introducing business cycles via aggregate shocks and we explore many of them. We start by looking at an economy where the business-cycle variation affects only the level of earnings, which we denote as the baseline model economy (i). In the economy, earnings of all households are uniformly higher in an expansion than in a recession. At the same time, we keep the long-run average of aggregate earnings at the same level as in the deterministic economy. We do so by multiplying the earnings of all the households by a number which is a function of the aggregate state of the economy. We use two aggregate states, which is the simplest way to represent expansions and recessions. This implies that we need to pin down three parameters: one for the amplitude of the aggregate shock and two for its persistence. We set the following three targets to calibrate this economy: (i) the volatility of this economy is like that of the U.S. economy, measured in terms of the standard deviations of the logs of HP residuals with parameter 100, (ii) the average duration of recessions is 2 years, and (iii) the average duration of expansions is 10 years. This is in a sense a model of the business cycle that completely ignores one of its important properties: that not all households fare the same in recessions and in expansions. Section 7.5 reports and discusses the properties of the baseline model economy. We then explore the business-cycle behavior of other model economies that have different mechanisms to generate fluctuations in economic activity. Especially, our emphasis is on to what extent these model economies can fix the defects of the baseline economy.

These other economies that we run in addition to those of the baseline model are (ii) an economy with small interest-rate shocks, (iii) an economy with large interest-rate shocks, (iv) an economy with a small asset-destruction shock, (v) an economy with a large asset-destruction shock, and (vi) an economy with all the above (small) shocks. We also explore the properties of (vii) an economy with symmetric i.i.d. aggregate shocks and (viii) an economy with smaller risk aversion.

The next economy we explore, economy (ii), has interest-rate shocks. We want to know how the economy responds to interest-rate hikes and we want to see if in any way they tend to reduce economic activity (which, here, is savings). This economy is like the baseline economy but with the additional feature of interest-rate fluctuations. Its risk-free interest rates are 0.75% in expansions and 0.25% in recessions, making interest rates procyclical.[11] We retain the same transition matrix for the aggregate shocks as the baseline. Still, we have to specify the magnitude of the variations in earnings. We adjust it so that the implied volatility of output is the same as in the baseline model economy.

The next economy, economy (iii), is identical to economy (ii) except for the values for interest rates: its interest rates are 1.0% in expansions and 0.0% in recessions. All the other features are the same as in economy (ii), implying that in the economy (ii) earnings are less volatile than in the baseline but more volatile than in the economy (iii).

Next, in economy (iv) we add to the baseline an asset-destruction shock to some households, of the magnitude of 100% of mean earnings, with i.i.d. probability of 0.1% in expansions and 1.0% in recessions. Economy (v) pumps up these shocks to be 300% of mean earnings. Again, we retain the transition matrix of the earning-level shock in the baseline model and adjust the magnitude of the shock in order to match the volatility of the output. We do this because we interpret these shocks as business losses, not as natural disasters.

Economy (vi) has both small interest-rate shocks and small asset-destruction shocks as above. Again, we adjust the magnitude of the earnings shock to match the volatility of output.

Economies (vii) and (viii) are used to check the robustness of our results from the baseline model economy. The economy (vii) is used to show the importance of our assumption on the persistence of expansions and recessions for our main results. Outputs from the economy (viii) tell how robust the properties of the baseline model are to a change of the risk-aversion parameter, which we set to 2.0 in our baseline economy.

---

[11]   The correlation between HP-filtered output and the 1-month Treasury bill rate is 0.40 according to Cooley and Hansen (1995).

TABLE 7.2. *U.S. economy: Deviation from trend, 1948–1986*

Variable	SD%	Rel to SD% Y	cross				
			\multicolumn{5}{c}{Cross-correlations of output with}				
			$x(-2)$	$x(-1)$	x	$x(+1)$	$x(+2)$
Output	2.63	1.00	0.02	0.56	1.00	0.56	0.02
Consumption	1.27	0.48	−0.16	0.39	0.78	0.53	−0.19
Investment	7.86	2.98	0.07	0.48	0.70	−0.01	−0.33
Labor share	0.66	0.25	−0.42	−0.41	−0.10	0.39	0.30

Source: Castañeda et al. (1998).

In the economy (vii), the aggregate shock is set to i.i.d. The three parameters that govern the aggregate shocks are set by letting $\Gamma_{zz'} = 0.5$ for all z and all z', and we choose the difference between the two values of z to set the volatility of output equal to that in the data, keeping the mean earnings at the same level as the baseline economy.

Finally, economy (viii) is like the baseline, but its risk-aversion parameter is set to 1.2 (almost log) instead of the value of 2.0 used in all the other experiments. Again we adjust the magnitude of the earnings shocks so that the mean and the volatility of earnings are at the same level as in the baseline economy.

7.5. THE BUSINESS CYCLE BEHAVIOR OF THE BASIC MODEL ECONOMY: AGGREGATE SHOCKS TO THE LEVEL OF EARNINGS

7.5.1. Business Cycle Statistics

To compare with the properties of the model economies, Table 7.2 shows the properties of the aggregate fluctuations at a yearly frequency in the U.S. economy. These properties are well known and need not be repeated here.[12] We now describe the business-cycle properties of the basic model with the business cycle affecting earnings of all households in the same proportion.

Table 7.3 reports the main statistics regarding the volatility of the baseline model economy. This table shows the value of the statistics and the standard deviations of those statistics (in parentheses) over nine samples. Each sample has a length of 200 periods (after the first 100 periods are dropped).[13] We see that, in this model economy, some of the standard features of the real-business-cycle model remain the

[12] Both the data and the series from the various model economies have been detrended using the HP filter with parameter 100.
[13] We choose this large length instead of the 40 periods or so of available data because we are exploiting the behavior of the model economies and we do not want a lot of sampling error. This makes the model and the data not strictly comparable.

TABLE 7.3. *Cyclical behavior of the baseline model*

Variable	SD%	Rel to SD% Y	Auto-corr	Cross-correlations of output with				
				$x(-2)$	$x(-1)$	x	$x(+1)$	$x(+2)$
Output	2.64	1.00	0.24	−0.12	0.24	1.00	0.24	−0.12
	(0.33)			(0.07)	(0.07)	(0.07)	(0.00)	(0.07)	(0.07)
Consumption	0.74	0.28	0.64	−0.17	0.47	0.87	0.42	0.08
	(0.08)			(0.04)	(0.06)	(0.02)	(0.01)	(0.07)	(0.09)
Investment	6.63	2.51	0.13	−0.10	0.18	0.99	0.19	−0.16
	(0.86)			(0.07)	(0.07)	(0.07)	(0.00)	(0.06)	(0.06)
Asset holding	1.39	0.53	0.36	−0.24	−0.44	−0.67	0.33	0.57
	(0.19)			(0.07)	(0.09)	(0.05)	(0.04)	(0.03)	(0.03)
Earnings	4.35	1.65	0.21	−0.07	0.28	1.00	0.17	−0.18
	(0.54)			(0.07)	(0.07)	(0.07)	(0.00)	(0.06)	(0.06)
Capital income	0.80	0.30	0.64	−0.41	−0.44	−0.26	0.57	0.66
	(0.10)			(0.05)	(0.06)	(0.04)	(0.04)	(0.01)	(0.03)
Labor share	1.74	0.66	0.20	0.01	0.33	0.97	0.06	−0.28
	(0.21)			(0.07)	(0.08)	(0.07)	(0.01)	(0.05)	(0.04)
Defaulting pop	10.28	3.89	0.27	0.02	0.33	0.93	0.10	−0.41
	(1.30)			(0.06)	(0.09)	(0.07)	(0.01)	(0.03)	(0.05)
Delinquent pop	1.60	0.61	0.66	−0.23	0.05	0.75	0.72	0.30
	(0.19)			(0.04)	(0.05)	(0.07)	(0.01)	(0.03)	(0.08)
Pop in debt	1.80	0.69	0.59	0.24	0.44	0.67	−0.06	−0.52
	(0.20)			(0.05)	(0.09)	(0.05)	(0.04)	(0.03)	(0.01)
Debt stock	22.38	8.47	0.18	−0.01	0.31	0.96	0.06	−0.31
	(2.88)			(0.06)	(0.08)	(0.07)	(0.01)	(0.05)	(0.05)

same, while others are somehow different. Our summary of the findings on basic aggregate statistics of the baseline model economy is as follows:

1. Investment is very volatile, more so than output. Consumption is not very volatile, less so than output. Both are strongly procyclical. These properties are common to most real-business-cycle models and to the data.
2. The volatility of consumption is substantially smaller than in the data.
3. Both the correlation between output and consumption and the correlation between output and investment are close to one, much higher than in the data. This is not surprising given that output in the model has only these two components and in the data there are public expenditures and net exports.
4. Earnings are quite volatile, as they are the main engine of business cycles.
5. Capital income is surprisingly volatile given that the interest rates of savings are constant. This is entirely due to the high volatility of aggregate asset holdings.
6. Labor share is quite volatile, more so than in the data. It is strongly procyclical, whereas it is slightly countercyclical in data. This is an artifact of the definition of the cycle based on earnings variations whereas rates of return are constant.

Table 7.3 also reports the business-cycle properties of the bankruptcy-related statistics. Although these statistics do not have a U.S. economy counterpart because of the availability of data, nor are there outputs from other models to compare with, the output can tell us the mechanism of the model and suggest the direction in which the model should be extended. We list the findings below and discuss them in the next section.

1. The volatility of the number of defaulters is quite large. The standard deviation of the log of the proportion of households declaring bankruptcy is almost four times that of the log of output. The corresponding ratio for the proportion of delinquent households is 60%.
2. The number of borrowers is two-thirds as volatile as the output.
3. The stock of debt is extremely volatile, more than twice as volatile as the proportion of defaulters, which is the next most volatile variable.
4. The number of bankruptcy filings is procyclical. The aggregate amount of debt, as well as the number of households in debt, is also procyclical.

7.5.2. Discussion of the Bankruptcy-Related Statistics

The volatilities of the bankruptcy-related statistics are high, which indicates that they are likely to be an important element characterizing business cycles. Unfortunately bankruptcy filings are *procyclical*, a highly counterfactual feature, and indeed a counterintuitive one, at least at first glance. However, note that an expansion may be a good time to default, because the aggregate state is persistent, and hence the future looks better and the likelihood of needing the option to borrow is small. In addition, loans are very volatile and strongly positively correlated with output.[14] So we have that expansions bring not only good economic conditions, but also more debt and a good outlook, a recipe for a hike in the number of defaulters. We have to ask, then, why a forthcoming expansion induces an increase in loans, at a time when they are perhaps less needed. The reason is that the price of loans goes down dramatically. Although the average borrowing interest rate weighted by the number of borrowers is 22% in expansions and 16% in recessions, the interest rates applied to the same types of loans are moving in opposite directions. For example, the interest rate applied to a loan whose amount is about one-eighth of average income is 7% in expansions and 17% in recessions. Fluctuations of interest rates applied to various sizes of loans are displayed in Fig. 7.3. It shows the interest rate schedule of loans offered to the same types of households in expansions and recessions, and in the deterministic economy.

Given that expansions and recessions are perfectly forecast, the probabilities of default are perfectly known and interest rates adjust accordingly. For example, interest rates for loans go down in expansions, as the decrease in the number of

---

[14] The correlation between initial debt and output is 0.96. Note that loans were taken the period before, but the current period's state of the economy was known at the time.

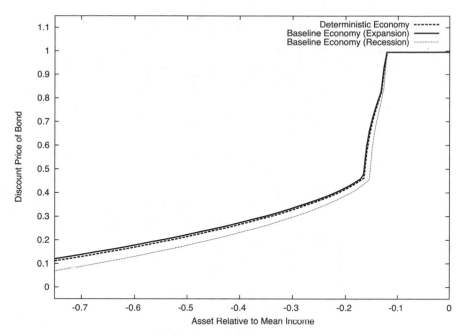

Figure 7.3. Price of loans for the baseline economy.

defaults in the next period is forecast by the loan industry. In equilibrium, then, an expansion induces an enormous increase in debt and a smaller increase in default. In fact, defaults at each loan size go down, allowing interest-rate reductions that are responsible for the increase in debt.

We conjecture that this type of behavior is an artifact of the timing of events in the model. Perfectly forecastable changes in the aggregate state translate into huge movements in interest rates and in debt volumes that override any negative effect of recessions on bankruptcy filings. We think that there are two possible mechanisms to change this counterfactual behavior of bankruptcy filings. One of these mechanisms is the introduction of aggregate shocks that surprise agents, making interest rates much more smooth and hence debt much less volatile. This is part of our ongoing research agenda. The other mechanism that might work is to consider a type of shock that pushes households into debt and that is larger or more frequent in recessions. In this sense, we presume that domino effects in the economy might play an important role in producing the countercyclical nature of the number of bankruptcies. For simplicity, we take shocks to the asset position as a proxy for domino effects in this paper and leave a more careful treatment of domino effects for future research.

7.6. THE BUSINESS-CYCLE BEHAVIOR OF THE OTHER MODEL ECONOMIES

In this section we explore the business-cycle properties of the other model economies that were described in Section 7.4. Table 7.4 summarizes the business-cycle statistics

TABLE 7.4. *Results of experiments 1: Aggregate fluctuations*

Economy	SD relative to SD of Y						Correlation with $Y(t)$					
	Cons	Inv	Asset	Ear	rK	LSh	Cons	Inv	Asset	Ear	rK	LSh
U.S.	0.48	2.98	–	–	–	0.25	0.78	0.70	–	–	–	−0.10
Baseline	0.28	2.51	0.53	1.65	0.30	0.66	0.87	0.99	−0.67	1.00	−0.26	0.97
Interest-rate shock (±0.25%)	0.22	2.66	0.44	1.27	0.61	0.30	0.79	1.00	−0.49	0.99	0.92	0.88
Interest-rate shock (±0.5%)	0.24	2.61	0.37	0.89	1.21	0.16	0.81	0.99	−0.33	0.99	0.99	−0.74
Asset-dest shock (100%)	0.25	2.56	0.51	1.67	0.32	0.69	0.74	0.99	−0.58	0.99	−0.22	0.96
Asset-dest shock (300%)	0.21	2.76	0.46	1.62	0.35	0.64	0.69	0.99	−0.46	0.99	−0.17	0.95
All shocks	0.25	2.49	0.42	1.27	0.62	0.30	0.83	0.99	−0.45	0.99	0.93	0.88
I.i.d. aggregate shock	0.23	2.50	0.53	1.64	0.24	0.65	0.90	1.00	−0.77	1.00	−0.44	0.98
Low risk aversion ($\sigma = 1.2$)	0.27	3.01	0.70	1.50	0.35	0.52	0.84	0.99	−0.72	1.00	−0.26	0.96

Note: rK and LSh denote capital income and labor share of output, respectively.

TABLE 7.5. *Results of experiments 2: Business-cycle statistics of bankruptcy behavior*

Economy	SD relative to SD of Y				Correlation with Y(t)			
	Default	Delinq	Pop debt	Debt	Default	Delinq	Pop debt	Debt
Baseline	3.89	0.61	0.69	8.47	0.93	0.75	0.67	0.96
Interest-rate shock (±0.25%)	2.63	0.41	0.58	5.99	0.90	0.79	0.63	0.92
Interest-rate shock (±0.5%)	2.52	0.37	0.41	5.40	0.87	0.84	0.41	0.89
Asset-dest shock (100%)	1.05	0.25	0.66	6.80	0.24	0.48	0.20	0.93
Asset-dest shock (300%)	3.84	0.67	0.90	3.94	−0.97	−0.57	−0.38	0.93
All shocks	0.93	0.22	0.58	5.71	0.01	0.39	0.03	0.92
I.i.d. agg shock	3.54	0.40	0.41	8.52	0.92	0.86	0.52	0.91
Low risk aversion ($\sigma = 1.2$)	1.76	0.32	0.72	3.67	0.86	0.65	0.76	0.96

Note: Default, Delinq, and Pop debt in the table denote the proportion of households that declare bankruptcy, the proportion of delinquent households, and the proportion of households with negative asset level, respectively. Debt denotes the aggregate debt level of the economy.

of the standard aggregates. Table 7.5 shows the business-cycle statistics related to default and debt. We proceed by comparing these model economies both with the data and with the baseline model economy. Recall that all those experiments are designed to have the same output volatility.

7.6.1. The Business-Cycle Behavior of Economies with Interest-Rate Fluctuations

The third and fourth rows of Table 7.4 show that the business-cycle properties of models with interest-rate shocks are quite similar to those of the baseline model. Interest-rate movements increase the volatility of investment and reduce that of consumption. Capital income becomes more volatile, which reduces the volatility of the labor share to a level that is close to the data, and makes labor share countercyclical, as in the data. This is simply because capital income is now strongly procyclical due to the procyclical nature of interest-rate movement.

As for the cyclical behavior of bankruptcy-related statistics, Table 7.5 shows that the effect of additional interest-rate shocks relative to the baseline is to scale down the volatility and the correlations of all the statistics, while keeping all the qualitative characteristics the same. This result is expected because the exogenous procyclical interest-rate shocks reduce the movements of the interest rates faced by borrowers, counteracting the countercyclicality of the interest rates faced by borrowers in the baseline.

7.6.2. The Business-Cycle Behavior of Economies with Asset-Destruction Shock

According to the fifth and sixth rows of Table 7.4, adding asset-destruction shock does not induce any significant changes in the business-cycle statistics of the main macroeconomic aggregates relative to the baseline model economy. As in the models with interest-rate shocks, the correlation between consumption and output and the volatility of investment become a little closer to the data. The cyclical properties of labor share are virtually the same as in the baseline.

On the other hand, shocks to asset level drastically change the business-cycle properties of bankruptcy-related statistics. We immediately see from Table 7.5 that the correlations between output and the numbers of defaulters, delinquents, and households in debt are lowered by the introduction of asset-destruction shock. They are strongly countercyclical in the case of the economy with large asset-destruction shocks. The property of the model that households face higher interest rates and thus can borrow less in recessions remains, as we can see from the fact that the aggregate level of debt is still procyclical in models with asset-destruction shocks. But because the shock hits more households in debt and they are more likely to default in recessions, the numbers of households that are indebted, declaring bankruptcy, and delinquent increase in recessions, making them countercyclical.

However, the volatility of debt is still quite high and procyclical, the reason again being the perfect predictability of the default rates. The bottom line is that although the models with asset-destruction shocks show more intuitive relations between output and the number of defaulters, they do so only with very high aggregate shocks and simultaneously with large procyclicality of debt.

7.6.3. The Business-Cycle Behavior of Other Economies

The model with both small interest-rate shocks and small asset-destruction shocks shows a result that is a mixture of the two models with one of the two shocks (see the seventh row of Table 7.4 and the sixth row of Table 7.5), which implies that some (the correlation between consumption and output, the volatility of labor share) move a little closer to the data, while others (the volatility of investment, the volatility of consumption) do not change much compared with the baseline model. The correlation between the number of defaulters and the output is almost zero, due to the effect of the asset-destruction shocks, but all four default-related statistics are procyclical, as in the baseline.

The properties of the models that we study in this paper are robust to the changes in two of our assumptions, that the risk aversion parameter is 2.0 and that the average durations of expansions and recessions are 10 and 2 years, respectively. Both in a model with symmetric i.i.d. aggregate shocks and in a model with lower risk aversion the volatility of debt is very high compared to that of other bankruptcy-related variables, which are strongly procyclical, as they are in the baseline economy. These are shown in the last two rows of Tables 7.4 and 7.5. The only noticeable difference is that in the economy with lower risk aversion (and hence higher intertemporal elasticity of substitution), both debt and filings move less than in the baseline.

7.7. CONCLUDING REMARKS

In this paper we have extended the work of Chatterjee et al. (2002) to include aggregate real shocks to economic activity in economies with storage technology. We have shown that the results from the economies studied here lack some interesting aspects regarding bankruptcy. This is because there is no uncertainty in the number of bankruptcies, and hence interest rates on loans completely bear the cyclical changes. This feature also prevents the existence of domino effects. The sources of the shortcomings of the present paper are technical: we have manipulated the timing in the model to prevent the distribution of agents from being important in forecasting economic conditions relevant for the agents (see Ríos-Rull (1998), Krusell and Smith (1997), or Krusell and Smith (1998) in a way similar to that of Diaz-Gimenez et al. (1992)).

In this sense, we see this paper as a progress report toward exploring economies that can be more seriously compared to the U.S. economy. The economy must have a production sector. Aggregate uncertainty should be somewhat unpredictable to generate surprising changes in the volume of default. We are currently working in using modern techniques to overcome these shortcomings and address economies with a more relevant production structure and with the possibility of a domino effect, in which the default of some agents is what triggers the default of others.

We have shown in this paper how the model economies account for the very high number of bankruptcies in recent years, while at the same time they replicate many other main statistics of the macroeconomic aggregates of the U.S. economy. We have analyzed the business-cycle properties of a variety of calibrated models that differ in how we generate business cycles. We have found that the numbers of defaulters, delinquents, and borrowers are quite volatile relative to output fluctuations. We have also found that the existence of negative shocks to wealth during recessions is an important mechanism in generating a more intuitive (i.e., negative) correlation between number of bankruptcies and output. We are excited about the prospect of our research telling us how important this mechanism may be when we look at economies with production and with uncertainty in the profits of lenders as well as other economic activities.

REFERENCES

S. R. Aiyagari (1994), "Uninsured Idiosyncratic Risk, and Aggregate Saving," *Quarterly Journal of Economics* 109: 659–84.

S. Budría, J. Díaz-Gimenez, V. Quadrini, and J.-V. Ríos-Rull (2002), "Updated Facts on the U.S. Distributions of Earnings, Income and Wealth," *Federal Reserve Bank of Minneapolis Quarterly Review* 26 (3): 2–35.

A. Castañeda, J. Díaz-Giménez, and J.-V. Ríos-Rull (1998), "Exploring the Income Distribution Business Cycle Dynamics," *Journal of Monetary Economics* 42 (1): 93–130.

(2003), "Accounting for the U.S. Earnings and Wealth Inequality," *Journal of Political Economy* 111 (4): 818–57.

S. Chatterjee, D. Corbae, M. Nakajima, and J.-V. Ríos-Rull (2002), "A Quantitative Theory of Unsecured Consumer Credit with Risk of Default," unpublished manuscript, University of Pennsylvania.

T. F. Cooley and G. D. Hansen (1995), Money and the Business Cycle, in T. F. Cooley (Ed.), *Frontiers of Business Cycle Research*, Chapter 7. Princeton, NJ: Princeton University Press.

J. Diaz-Gimenez, E. C. Prescott, T. Fitzgerald, and F. Alvarez (1992), "Banking in Computable General Equilibrium Economies," *Journal of Economic Dynamics and Control* 16: 533–59.

M. Huggett (1993), "The Risk Free Rate in Heterogeneous-Agents, Incomplete Insurance Economies," *Journal of Economic Dynamics and Control* 17 (5/6), 953–70.

P. Krusell and A. Smith (1997), "Income and Wealth Heterogeneity, Portfolio Choice, and Equilibrium Asset Returns," *Macroeconomic Dynamics* 1 (2): 387–422.

(1998), "Income and Wealth Heterogeneity in the Macroeconomy," *Journal of Political Economy* 106 (5), 867–96.

M. Nakajima and J.-V. Ríos-Rull (2003), "Defaults and Aggregate Fluctuations in Growth Economies," unpublished manuscript, University of Pennsylvania.

J.-V. Ríos-Rull (1998), "Computing Equilibria in Models with Heterogenous Agents," in R. Marimon and A. Scott (Eds.), *Computational Methods for the Study of Dynamic Economics*, Chapter 9. Oxford: Oxford University Press.

8 New Applications of General Equilibrium to Finance: Default and Collateral

Aloisio Araujo and Mário Páscoa

ABSTRACT: The applications of general equilibrium to finance can be grouped into three waves. The first started with the application of the Arrow–Debreu concept of state-contingent prices developed in the fifties to a better understanding of the Black–Scholes formula and the pricing of derivatives, in general. The second wave studied the abstract incomplete markets model in its several aspects: existence, determinacy, suboptimality, and infinite horizon properties. Market incompleteness was used to understand stochastic volatility of security prices and also to explain the risk premium puzzle. We can consider as a third wave the development of general equilibrium models with default to understand credit risk and institutional arrangements that can deal with it. This third wave was made possible by the incomplete markets theory and motivated by understanding how incompleteness can be mitigated by default or bankruptcy. More specifically, this chapter addresses in its second section the finite-horizon case, covering default and penalties, collateral, and consumers' bankruptcy. The third section deals with the infinite-horizon case, where Ponzi schemes may occur.

8.1. INTRODUCTION

The goal of this chapter is to study credit risk in the context of general equilibrium in incomplete markets. Default and bankruptcy are important real-life phenomena: firms, consumers, exchange houses, and governments fail to honor their commitments or go bankrupt. It is therefore important to incorporate these phenomena into equilibrium models as particular configurations of equilibrium outcomes.

Default can be Pareto-improving. In fact, allowing default increases the set of trading possibilities, because agents can take financial positions that make them insolvent in some states of nature, therefore breaking the Walrasian discipline, which requires agents to have enough income to pay for their expenses and previously committed financial decisions.

Araujo acknowledges support from FAPERJ and CNPq and Páscoa from Project POCTI 36525/2000 (Portuguese Ministry of Science). The authors acknowledge permission of the Econometric Society to quote the results in Section 8.3.1 and also the permission of Springer-Verlag to quote the results in Sections 8.2.1 and 8.2.2.

Default has already been discussed in general equilibrium models by Arrow and Hahn (1971), Shubik and Wilson (1977), and Wilson (1977); see also Araujo and Sandroni (1991, 1999) for a default model where we have convergence to rational expectations.

The first fully specified general equilibrium model with default is due to Dubey, Geanakoplos, and Shubik (1989). There is a literature whose goal is to incorporate adverse selection and moral hazard into the general equilibrium model (see Prescott and Townsend (1984) and Bisin and Gottardi (1999)). The work by Dubey et al. (1989) also has this goal. We make no any contributions in this regard.

In the next section we study default and bankruptcy in finite-horizon economies. We examine first a continuum-of-states model (by Araujo, Monteiro, and Páscoa, 1996, 1998) where default is allowed and utility penalties are imposed on defaulters, as in the pioneering work by Dubey et al. (1989). In this context, existence of equilibrium can be established without requiring any special assumptions. In continuum-of-states models without default, existence of equilibrium required the indispensable assumption that ex post endowments (accrued endowments of real returns from assets) were always nonnegative; that is, the financial sector was assumed to be relatively weak, in comparison with agents' nonfinancial wealth. In the case of debt, initial endowments would always cover negative portfolio returns. When default is allowed, there is no need to make this strongly restrictive assumption. In fact, marginal utilities of endowment income are bounded from above: by the marginal penalty, when the consumer pays, or by the fact that endowments are bounded away from zero, in the case of default. Thus, all equilibrium variables of truncated (finitely many states) economies become uniformly bounded and Fatou's lemma can be used to establish the existence of equilibrium.

We next examine a bankruptcy model (by Araujo and Páscoa (2002)) where agents are liable only up to some fraction of their future endowments. By bankruptcy we mean a situation where the consumer's liable estate does not cover his overall financial debt. When creditors are reimbursed proportionally to the value of their claims, equilibrium exists under bounded short sales. For nonproportional reimbursement rules favoring smaller claims, equilibrium exists provided that Inada's condition holds and liability approaches total garnishment as debts tend to infinity. The extensive cooperative-games literature on bankruptcy has many examples of nonproportional-reimbursement shemes. Our scheme is a parametric method (see Moulin, 1987 and Young, 1988) for which the marginal rate of reimbursement tends to zero as the claim goes to infinity. The constrained-equal-award method is an extreme example of such regressive rules. The constrained-equal-loss method is the extreme opposite progressive rule, and the solution proposed by Aumann and Maschler (1985) is neither regressive nor progressive.

The other finite-horizon model studied here is a model of endogenous collateral (by Araujo, Fajardo, and Páscoa, 2001). Dubey, Geanakoplos, and Zame (1995) had already modeled loans backed by exogenous collateral and discussed how these collaterals might turn out to be endogenously determined, within a menu of finitely many possible values. Here, we allow borrowers to choose their collateral and sell short at a price that reflects this choice. Equilibrium sale prices consist of a base price (a discounted expectation of promised returns) minus a spread (a discounted expectation of future default). As in the collateralized mortgage obligation (CMO) market, households purchase a derivative whose return is the weighted average of the individual repayments, which may be either the promised payment or the depreciated value of individual collateral choices. The model is close to that of Araujo, Orrillo, and Páscoa (2000), but we dispense with the assumption that collateral margin requirements are uniformly bounded away from one.

The section on infinite-horizon models deals with Ponzi schemes in collateral-ized economies. We address a model of short-lived assets backed by durable goods (by Araujo, Páscoa, and Torres-Martinez, 2002). Existence of equilibrium can be established without imposing a priori transversality or debt constraints. Collateral requirements are sufficient to prevent the explosion of the debt.

In the last section we refer to some extensions of the default model to study bubbles. We also mention several recent numerical works.

8.2. DEFAULT AND BANKRUPTCY

8.2.1. Default and Penalties with a Continuum of States

The set of states is $S = [0, 1]$. There are I consumers, J assets, and G goods. The economy has two periods. In the first period there is no consumption, only buying and selling of assets at prices $\pi \in \mathbb{R}^j$. In the second period the state of nature $s \in S$ occurs, and there are consumption $x_s \in \mathbb{R}_+^G$ and delivery of real assets returns $R_{sj} \in \mathbb{R}^G$, $1 \leq j \leq J$.

If y is the portfolio we write $y = \theta - \varphi$, where $\theta_j \geq 0$ is the number of units of asset j the consumer bought and $\varphi_j \geq 0$ is the number of units he sold.

Suppose the prices at state s are $p_s \in \Delta$. The consumer debt will be $p_s R_{sj} \varphi_j$. Of this debt, he pays D_{sj} such that $0 \leq D_{sj} \leq p_s R_{sj} \varphi_j$.

For each state s and asset j there is a market payment rate $k_s^j \in [0, 1]$.

Consumer i's utility function U^i is composed of two parts: his pleasure, $\int u_s^i(x_s) \, ds$, derived from consumption of goods $x : X \to \mathbb{R}_+^G$, and a penalty propor-tional to default, for given penalty coefficients λ_s^j, $\sum_{j=1}^{J} \int \lambda_s^j (p_s R_{sj} \varphi_j - D_{sj})^+ \, ds$. Consumers' endowments are denoted by $W_s^h \in \mathbb{R}_+^G$.

There is a lower bound on asset short sales, $v_i \in -\mathbb{R}_{++}^J$. An economy is char-acterized by a vector (u, λ, W, A) and an equilibrium is a vector $(\bar{p}, \bar{\pi}, \bar{k}, \bar{\theta}^i, \bar{\varphi}^i, \bar{D}^i, \bar{x}^i)_{i \leq I}$ such that

$$\sum_i (\bar{\theta}^i - \bar{\varphi}^i) = 0, \quad \sum_i (\bar{x}^i - W^i) = 0$$

$$k_s^j \cdot \sum_i \bar{p}_s R_{sj} \bar{\theta}_j^i = \sum_i \bar{D}_{sj}^i, \quad 1 \leq j \leq J, \text{ almost every (a.e.)}$$

$(\bar{x}^i, \bar{\theta}^i, \bar{\varphi}^i, \bar{D}^i)$ maximize $U^i(x, \varphi, \bar{p}, D)$ subject to

$$x \in (L_+^\infty)^G, \theta, \varphi \in \mathbb{R}_+^J, v_i \leq -\varphi$$

$$p_s(x_s - W_s^i) \leq \sum_j k_s^j \bar{p}_s R_{sj} \theta_j - \sum_j D_{sj}, \text{ a.e. } s$$

$$\bar{\pi}(\theta - \varphi) \leq 0.$$

Theorem 8.1 (Araujo et al., 1998): *Suppose that*

(i) *$u_s^i : \mathbb{R}_+^G \to \mathbb{R}$ is concave, continuous, monotone and that $u_s^i(0) = 0$; for every $r, s \mapsto u_s^i(r)$ is bounded.*

(ii) *There is a $\delta > 0$ such that $W_s^i \geq (\delta, \ldots, \delta)$ for every i, a.e. s; A^j, W^i are bounded.*

Then there exists an equilibrium.

The existence of equilibria in models with a continuum of states and incomplete markets was first studied by Mas-Colell and Monteiro (1996), Hellwig (1996), Mas-Colell and Zame (1996), and Monteiro (1996). All these authors assumed that portfolio returns can be covered by the initial endowments, i.e., $W_s^i + \sum_j y_j R_{sj} \geq 0$ for almost every s and all admissible portfolios y. A counterexample in Mas-Colell and Zame (1996) shows that without this assumption (but still with a bound on uncovered sales) an equilibrium may not exist. We eliminate this assumption with the introduction of default. Our context is close to that of Dubey et al. (1989), which shows the advantage of the introduction of default in many situations with finitely many states.

The existence argument uses a finite-dimensional approximation and applies Fatou's lemma to a uniformly bounded sequence of equilibrium variables of the truncated economies. This sequence includes prices, allocations, portfolios, and marginal utilities of income, as required to establish market clearing and optimality conditions in the limit economy.

Allowing default and assuming that endowments are bounded away from zero implies that, in each state, marginal utility of income will be bounded from above. In fact, when we allow default, income will be the sum of the value of the endowments plus the positive value of the returns from the assets bought minus the part of the debt that the consumer chooses to pay. When the consumer decides not to pay, income will be bounded from below by the value of the endowment and, hence, bounded away from zero; when the consumer decides to pay it must be the case that the marginal penalty for default exceeds the marginal utility of income. In either case, marginal utility of income is bounded from above. This property is crucial for the application of Fatou's lemma to the sequence of equilibrium variables of the truncated finite-dimensional economies.

Notice that, in the model without default, an assumption imposing an upper bound on marginal utility of consumption would not suffice to guarantee that marginal utility of income was bounded from above, because the multiplier of the nonnegativity constraint might be arbitrarily large in the continuum set up. In fact, relaxing the nonnegativity constraints in a set of arbitrarily small measure would allow new portfolio choices that might generate advantageous income transfers across states and significant utility gains.

Remark 8.1: An equilibrium will be called nontrivial if there is trade in assets or if it is a nontrade equilibrium with $k^j \equiv 1$ for every j. To guarantee the existence of a nontrivial equilibrium we need the penalty rate to be sufficiently large: $\lambda_s^j > \delta^{-1} \max_{1 \le i \le I} \sup_t u_t^i (\sup_g \sum_\ell W_g^\ell)$ for almost every $s \in S, 1 \le j \le J$.

Remark 8.2: The nominal-returns case allows us to dispense with the lower bound on short sales. Suppose $r^j : S \to \mathbb{R}_+$ is the nominal return of asset j, $1 \le j \le J$. Then the economy E with nominal returns $\{r^j\}_{1 \le j \le J}$ has an equilibrium with unrestricted short sales if $\{r^j; 1 \le j \le J\}$ is a linearly independent set.

8.2.2. Bankruptcy

In the present section we address bankruptcy, instead of default, in the context also of the general equilibrium incomplete markets model. By bankruptcy we mean a situation where an agent has no means to pay back his debt, or more precisely, where his garnishable wealth and income do not cover his debt. Bankruptcy is a very important institutional arrangement that offers protection to agents on the basis of the concept of limited liability. When agents are liable only up to some fraction of their wealth and income, it is in their interest to go bankrupt when the debt exceeds that fraction of their estates. Creditors will then be reimbursed using the garnished estates. This procedure should not be confused with default, which is a situation where debtors fail to honor their commitments, even when they could afford to do it.

To simplify the analysis we will concentrate here on a model where all claims are unsecured. A more complex version could be worked out, taking into account the priority of secured claims in the partition of the garnished estate of a bankrupt agent. We assume also that bankrupt agents do not suffer any penalties entering directly into the utility function.

We develop a two-periods model where uncertainty may affect endowments and preferences in the second period, through the realization of S states of nature. For each state of nature, an agent goes bankrupt when his or her financial surplus is negative and its absolute value exceeds the value of the garnishable endowments. This structure for second-period budget constraints introduces a nonconvexity into the consumer's budget set of bundles and portfolios (actually, into the latter). This difficulty is overcome by considering a continuum of consumers and appealing to Liapunov's theorem.

We address two cases: first, a proportional reimbursement rule under bounded short sales and limited liability, and second, a nonproportional reimbursement rule, favoring smaller claims, without bounds on short sales, but assuming that liability approaches total garnishment as debt goes to infinity.

8.2.2.1. *Proportional Reimbursement*

In the first period A nominal assets and L physical goods are traded. The set of consumers is $I = [0, 1]$ (due to nonconvexity). There are $S < +\infty$ possible states in the second period. Preferences are time- and state-separable. Consumers have limited liability in the sense that, in the case of bankruptcy, only some share $\gamma_{s\ell} \in [0, 1]$ of the endowment of good ℓ in state s may be confiscated by the creditors. Bankruptcy by others is anticipated according to a proportional reimbursement rule. Denote consumer h's portfolio by $y^h \in \mathbb{R}^A$ and assume that the returns matrix has nonnegative elements r_{sa}. Let k_{sa} be the mean reimbursement rate. Effective returns $G_{sa}(r_{sa} y_a)$ are given by

$$G_{sa}(r_{sa} y_a) = \begin{cases} r_{sa} y_a, & \text{if } y_a < 0 \\ k_{sa} r_{sa} y_a, & \text{otherwise.} \end{cases}$$

We can now write down the budget constraints in the first period and in each state s, respetively, as:

$$p_0 \cdot (x_0^h - w_0^h) + \pi \cdot y^h = 0 \tag{1}$$

$$p_s \cdot (x_s^h - \omega_s^h) = \max\left(\sum_{a=1}^{A} G_{sa}(r_{sa} y_a^h), -\sum_{\ell=1}^{L} p_{s\ell} \gamma_{s\ell} \omega_{s\ell}^h\right) \equiv f_s^h(y_a^h). \tag{2}$$

When consumer h goes bankrupt, the total amount available to partially reimburse creditors will be $\sum_\ell p_{s\ell} \gamma_{s\ell} \omega_{s\ell}^h + \sum_a (G_{sa}^h)^+$ where $G_{sa}^h \equiv G_{sa}(r_{sa}, y^h)$. This amount will be allocated across assets sold by agent h according to the weights $\tau_{sa}^h = r_{sa}(y_a^h)^- / \sum_b r_{sa}(y_b^h)^-$.

Bankruptcy is correctly anticipated in each asset market provided that

$$k_{sa} = 1 - \frac{\int_I (f_s^h - \sum_{b \leq A} G_{sb}^h) \tau_{sa}^h \, d\lambda(h)}{r_{sa} \int_I (y_a^h)^+ \, d\lambda(h)}. \tag{3}$$

An equilibrium is a vector (x, y, p, q, k) such that

- $(\bar{x}^h, \bar{y}^h)$ maximizes u^h subject to (1) and (2), for a.e. $h \in I$
- markets clear, i.e., $\int_I (x^h - \omega^h) d\lambda(h) = 0$ and $\int_I y^h \, d\lambda(h) = 0$
- Equation (3) holds, for any (s, a).

Theorem 8.2 (Araujo and Páscoa, 2002): *Suppose the endowment allocation w is uniformly bounded, from above and from below, and asset short sales are required to be bounded from below, by $v \in \mathbb{R}_{++}^A$, say. Then an equilibrium exists.*

8.2.2.2. *Nonproportional Reimbursement*

We assume now that reimbursement ratios decrease with the size of the claim. Discounted returns are given by $G_{sa}(r_{sa} y_a)$. The function G_{sa} coincides with the identity map on $(-\infty, 0]$ and is strictly concave on $[0, +\infty)$ when other agents default on asset a in state s.

We appeal to the extensive literature on bankruptcy found in cooperative game theory to rationalize the above nonproportional-reimbursement rule. In this literature, the bankruptcy problem can be formally described as a pair (x, T), where x denotes the vector of n claims on an estate having total value $T \le \sum_i x_i$. A solution is a vector $t \in R^n$ such that $\sum_i t_i = T$ and $0 \le t_i \le x_i$ for all i.

The class of solution methods that has received most attention is the parametric class (see Moulin, 1987, and Young, 1988). Here the solution t_i assigned to each agent is given by a function f that depends on the pair (x, T) only through the individual claim x_i of the agent and a parameter μ chosen so that $\sum_i t_i = T$. Clearly, these parametric methods are compatible with a general equilibrium framework, where each agent should not be concerned with other agents' claims and should take the parameter μ as given. Young (1987) showed that a continuous solution method $F : (x, T) \mapsto t$ is representable by a continuous parametric function f if and only if it is anonymous and pairwise consistent.

Examples of parametric methods include the proportional method (given by $t_i = \mu x_i$), the constained-equal-award (CEA) method (given by $t_i = \min\{\mu, x_i\}$), and the constrained-equal-loss (CEL) method (given by $t_i = \max\{0, x_i - \mu\}$). The CEA rule makes awards as equal as possible, subject to the condition that no agent receives more than his claim, whereas the CEL rule makes losses as close as possible, subject to the condition that no creditor ends up with a negative award (see Herrero and Villar, 1998, on the properties of these two rules).

We will require the reimbursement rule G_{sa} to be parametric and continuous of the form $G_{sa}(r_{sa}y_a, \mu_{sa})$, where μ_{sa} is such that Eq. (3) holds, which is the equation requiring the garnished estates to be equal to the reimbursements to creditors. Furthermore, we will assume regressiveness of returns: the marginal rate of reimbursement should tend to zero as the claim goes to infinity. To simplify, let us assume that G_{sa} is differentiable in the first argument, at least beyond a certain level, and require that

$$\lim_{y_a \to \infty} \partial G_{sa}(r_{sa}y_a, \mu_{sa})/\partial y_a = 0.$$

Clearly, in the case of CEA, the partial derivative is identically zero for $y_a > \mu_{sa}/r_{sa}$. Actually, for bankruptcy to be correctly anticipated, it suffices that μ_{sa} is such that

$$\int (G_{sa}^h)^+ \, d\lambda(h) \ge k_{sa}r_{sa} \int (y_a^h)^+ \, d\lambda(h),$$

where k_{sa} is the mean reimbursement rate (see Eq. (3)).

The CEL rule is not regressive and neither is the solution proposed by Aumann and Maschler (1985). These authors recalled the Talmudic solution to the problem of sharing an estate among the three wives of a deceased man and showed that this function is $v(J) = \max(0, T - \sum_{i \notin J} x_i)$, for any subset J of agents. The solution contemplated by Aumann and Maschler is consistent but may be a concave or a convex function of the individual claim, depending on the relative magnitude of the estate and the claims. It remains unknown whether the solution proposed by Aumann and Maschler is compatible with the existence of equilibria without bounded short sales.

We also assume that the liability coefficients $\gamma_{s\ell}$ tend to one as the debt goes to $-\infty$. More precisely, suppose that there are minimal liability coefficients $\bar{\gamma}_{s\ell}$ and that the actual liability ratios are given by $\gamma_{s\ell} = \bar{\gamma}_{s\ell} + (1 - \bar{\gamma}_{s\ell})\rho(\sum_a G_{sa})$, where $\rho(z) = 0$ for $z \geq -\sum_\ell p_{s\ell}\, \bar{\gamma}_{s\ell}\, \omega_{s\ell}^h$ and $\rho(z) \to 1$ as $z \to -\infty$. This specification for the liability structure, together with Inada's condition on utility, will imply the existence of a lower bound on $\sum_a G_{\Delta a}$.

The second-period budget constraints are given as before, where G_{sa} has this new specification.

In the first period, we add to the linear cost of the portfolio $q \cdot y^h$ a spread that is a discounted expected value of the difference between the bankruptcy given by agent h and the bankruptcy suffered by this agent. Formally, the first period constraint is written as

$$q \cdot y^h + t \sum_{s=1}^{S} \eta_s(f_s^h - r_s y^h) + p_0 \cdot (x_0^h - \omega_0^h) = 0. \tag{4}$$

Here $f_s^h - r_s y^h = f_s^h - \sum_a G_{sa} - (r_s y^h - \sum_a G_{sa})$ is the difference between the default given by agent h in state s and the default suffered by this agent in this state. The discount factor $t \in \mathbb{R}_+$ and the probability measure $\eta \in \Delta^{S-1}$ are to be determined endogenously.

A vector $(\bar{x}, \bar{y}, p, q, t, \eta, \theta)$ is an equilibrium if

- $(\bar{x}^h, \bar{y}^h)$ maximizes u^h subject to (1') and (2), for a.e. $h \in I$
- markets clear, i.e., $\int_I (x^h - \omega^h)\, d\lambda(h) = 0$ and $\int_I y^h\, d\lambda(h) = 0$.

Theorem 8.3 (Araujo and Páscoa, 2002): *Suppose*

(A1) u_s^h *is* C^1 *on* $\mathbb{R}_{++}^L$ *and* $\|\nabla u_s^h(x_s^h)\| \to \infty$ *as* $x_s^h \to 0$;

(A2) $\{u^h\}_h$ *and* $\{Du^h\}_h$ *are equicontinuous;*

(A3) *the endowment allocation* $\omega \in L(I, \mathbb{R}^{L(S+1)})$ *is continuous and uniformly bounded from above and from below;*

(A4) *for* (x^{hn}, y^{hn}) *satisfying the budget constraints, at* $(p^n, q^n, \theta^n, t^n, \eta^n, c^n)$, *we have* $\|\nabla u_s^h(x_s^{hn})\| Df_s^h(\sum_j G_{sj}(r_{sj} y_j^{hn})) \to +\infty$ *when* $\sum_j G_{sj}(r_{sj} y^{hn}) \to -\infty$ *(and therefore* $x_s^{hn} \to 0$), *for any* h.

Then an equilibrium exists.

Assumptions (A2) and (A3) introduce compactness on the set of consumers' characteristics. Assumption (A4) says that, as the debt becomes unbounded in some state, and therefore consumers' income and consumption tend to zero (since the liability coefficients approach one), the marginal utility of income will go to $+\infty$

faster than the derivative of the alienable endowment (with respect to the debt) tends to zero. We knew already that marginal utility of income would go to $+\infty$ as income approaches zero, as the endowment of a defaulter is eventually totally confiscated. We knew also that this endowment is being confiscated at a decreasing rate as the debt increases. We now assume the former dominates the latter, so that the indirect marginal utility, with respect to portfolio returns, explodes as the debt becomes unbounded.

Let us give an example of a liability rule and an utility function satisfying assumption (A4). To simplify, assume there is a single physical good. The liability coefficients γ_s are given by $\overline{\gamma_s} + (1 - \overline{\gamma_s})\rho(\sum_a G_{sa})$, where $\rho(z) = 1 - \exp\{-(z + \overline{\gamma_s}\omega_s)^2\}$ for $z \leq -\overline{\gamma_s}\omega_s$ and $\rho(z) = 0$ otherwise.

Outline of the Proof of the Theorem:

(Step 1) Consider a sequence of truncated economies, where portfolio sets are now $K_n = [-n, n]$. By Liapunov's theorem, equilibria exist for truncated economies.

(Step 2) For each vector $(p, \pi, t, \rho, \eta, c)$ and each state s, ess $\inf_h \sum_j G^h_{sj} > -\infty$ on the set of portfolios that are admissible and undominated in consumers' problem.

(Step 3) Nonarbitrage conditions: $q \in \mathbb{R}^A$, $\theta \in [0, 1]^{SA}$, $t \in \mathbb{R}_+$, and $\eta \in \Delta^{S-1}$ do not allow for arbitrage only if

  (i) $\pi_j \geq t \sum_{s:\theta_{sj}<1} \eta_s r_{sj}$, when $k_j \neq 1$;

  (ii) $\pi_j > 0$, when $k_j = 1$;

  (iii) for each pair (J^+, J^-) of subsets of assets, such that $k_j \neq 1$ for some $j \in J^+$, when

$$\left(\sum_{j \in J^+} r_{sj}\delta_{sj} - \sum_{j \in J^-} r_{sj}\right)^S_{s=1} \geq 0, \text{ we have}$$

$$\sum_{j \in J^+}\left(\pi_j - t\sum_{s:\theta_{sj}<1} \eta_s r_{sj}\right) - \sum_{j \in J^-} \pi_j \geq 0;$$

  (iv) for each pair (J^+, J^-) of subsets of assets, such that $k_j = 1$, $\forall j \in J^+$, when

$$\left(\sum_{j \in J^+} r_{sj}\delta_{sj} - \sum_{j \in J^-} r_{sj}\right)^S_{s=1} \geq 0, \text{ we have } \sum_{j \in J^+} \pi_j - \sum_{j \in J^-} \pi_j > 0.$$

(Step 4) A cluster point (π, t, ρ, η) of the equilibrium sequence $(\pi^n, t^n, \rho^n, \eta^n)$ of the truncated economies is still a nonarbitrage vector.

(Step 5) If $(p^n, \pi^n, t^n, \rho^n, \eta^n, c^n)$ converges to $(p, \pi, t, \rho, \eta, c)$ and both the sequence $(\pi^n, t^n, \rho^n, \eta^n)$ and its limit point are contained in the set of nonarbitrage vectors, then the sequence of demanded bundles and port-folios (x^{hn}, y^{hn}) is uniformly bounded.

We can therefore apply Fatou's lemma: there exists an integrable function (x, y) such that $\int_I x^h \, d\lambda(h) = \int_I w^h \, d\lambda(h)$, $\int_I y^h \, d\lambda(h) = 0$, (x^h, y^h) is a cluster point of (x^{hn}, y^{hn}) for a.e. h, and (3) holds.

Remark 8.3: Without assumption (A4), the default barrier established in Step 2 would not exist and one of the nonarbitrage conditions would be as follows. For any pair (J^+, J^-) of subsets of assets, such that (i) $\sum_{j \in J^+} r_{sj} \delta_{sj} - \sum_{j \in J^-} r_{sj} \equiv r_s$ is negative for $s \in S_1 \neq \emptyset$, positive for $s \in S_3 \neq \emptyset$, and possibly zero for $s \in S_2$, but (ii) $k_{sj} = 1$, $\forall j \in J^+$, $s \in S_2 \cup S_3$, we must have $\sum_{j \in J^+} \pi_j - \sum_{j \in J^-} \pi_j > t(\sum_{s \in S_2 \cup S_2} \eta_s \sum_{j \in J^+} r_{sj} - \sum_s \eta_s \sum_{j \in J^-} r_{sj})$. This strict inequality condition would create a problem when we tried to redo Step 4. In fact, at a cluster point, only the weak inequality is guaranteed to hold, but we might not find a Cramer subsystem of budget constraints to solve for (y_{J^+}, y_{J^-}).

Remark 8.4: If the returns function G_{sj} were piecewise linear (that is, if G_{sj} were given by $t_{sj} r_{sj} y_j$, for $y_j > 0$, as in the proportional reimbursement scheme) the nonarbitrage conditions would be as follows. For any pair (J^+, J^-) of subsets of assets, such that $\sum_{j \in J^+} r_{sj} k_{sj} - \sum_{j \in J^-} r_{sj} \equiv r_s \geq 0$, for any s, and $r_s > 0$, for some s, we must have $\sum_{j \in J^+} (q_j - t \sum_{s:k_{sj}<1} \eta_s(1 - k_{sj})) > \sum_{j \in J^-} \pi_j$. This strict inequality would create a problem when we tried to redo Step 4. In fact, at a cluster point only the weak inequality is guaranteed to hold, but we might not find a Cramer subsystem of budget constraints to solve for (y_{J^+}, y_{J^-}), if k_{sj} were less than one for some $j \in J^+$. This is a case of ex post redundancy of assets, due to default.

8.2.3. Collateral and CMO Markets

Collateralized loans were first addressed in a general equilibrium setting by Dubey et al. (1995). Clearly, in the absence of other default penalties, in each state of nature, a debtor will honor commitments only when the debt does not exceed the value of the collateral. Similarly, each creditor should expect to receive the minimum between his claim and the value of the collateral. This pioneering work studied a two-period incomplete-markets model with default and exogenous collateral coefficients and also discussed the endogenization of these coefficients, within a menu of finitely many strictly positive possible values.

Housing mortgages stand out as the most clear and most common case of collateralized loans. In the past, these mortages were entirely financed by commercial banks that had to face a serious adverse selection problem in addition to the risks associated with concentrating investiments in the housing sector. More recently, banks have managed to pass these risks to other investors. The collateralized mortgage obligation (CMO) market developed in the eighties and nineties constitute the most elaborate mechanism for spreading the risks of investing in the housing market.

These obligations are derivatives backed by a big pool of mortgages that was split into different contingent flows.

Araújo et al. (2000) made the first attempt at modeling CMO markets and established the existence of an equilibrium where the borrowers' choice of collateral is restricted only by the requirement that the loan can finance only up to some certain fraction of the value of the house. Here we present a revised version of Araujo et al.

As in Araújo et al. (2000), equilibrium asset prices received by borrowers include a personalized spread that is a discounted expected value of future default, with respect to some endogenously determined measure on states, common to all borrowers. Debtors more prone to default are penalized by selling assets at lower prices. Similarly, the CMO price consists of the primitive asset base price reduced by subtracting the discounted expected value of the default suffered, with respect to the same endogenously determined measure. This pricing formula may be actually motivated by the nonarbitrage conditions (see Araujo et al., 2001).

8.2.3.1. The Model

We consider an economy with two periods and a finite number S of states of nature in the second period. There are L physical durable commodities and J real assets returns are represented by a random variable $R : S \mapsto \mathbb{R}_+^{JL}$. Let Y_s be the $L \times L$ depreciation matrix in state s.

Each seller of assets chooses also the collateral coefficients for the different assets that he sells. Denote by $M_j \in \mathbb{R}_+^L$ the choice of collateral coefficients. The anonymous collateral coefficients will be denoted by $C \in \mathbb{R}_+^{JL}$ and will be taken as given by creditors. Let π_1 and π_2 be the purchase and sale prices of assets, respectively. Then the budget constraints of each agent will be the following:

$$p_0 x_0 + p_0 M \varphi + \pi_1 \theta \leq p_0 w_0 + \pi_2 \varphi$$

$$p_s x_s + \sum_{j=1}^{J} D_{sj} \varphi_j \leq p_s w_s + \sum_{j=1}^{J} N_{sj} \theta_j + \sum_{j=1}^{J} p_s Y_s M_j \varphi_j + p_s Y_s x_0, \ \forall s \in S.$$

Here $D_{sj} = \min\{p_s R_s^j, p_s Y_s M_j\}$ and N_{sj} is the endogenously determined payoff of the derivative.

8.2.3.2. Equilibria

We assume that there is a continuum of agents $H = [0, 1]$ whose preferences are represented by utility functions $u^h, h \in H$.

Asset prices are assumed to consist of a base price and also a default spread. Let

$$\pi_2 = q - \sum_s \gamma_s g_s,$$

where $g_s = (p_s R_s - p_s Y_s M)^+$ and γ is a vector of deflators taken as given by the consumers.

Definition 8.1: An equilibrium is a vector $((p, \pi_1, \pi_2, C), (x^h, \theta^h, \varphi^h, M^h)_{h \in H})$ such that

$$(x^h, \theta^h, \varphi^h, M^h)$$

maximizes u^h subject to the above budget constraints at (p, π_1, π_2, C);

$$\int_H \left(x_o^h + \sum_{j \in J} M_j^h \varphi_j^h \right) dh = \int_H w_o^h dh;$$

$$\int_H x^h(s) \, dh = \int_H \left(w^h(s) + \sum_{j \in J} (Y_s M_j^h \varphi_j^h + Y_s x_o^h) \right) dh;$$

$$\int_H (\theta_j^h - \varphi_j^h) \, dh = 0;$$

$$\int_H M_j^h \varphi_j^h \, dh = C_j \int \varphi_j^h \, dh; \tag{5}$$

$$N_{sj} \int \theta_j^h dh = \int D_{sj}^h \varphi_j^h dh;$$

$$\pi_{1j} \int \theta_j^h dh = \int \pi_{2j}^h \varphi_j^h dh;$$

Remark 8.5: The above equilibrium concept assumes implicitly the existence of one or several financial institutions that buy the pool of mortgages from the consumers at prices π_2^h and issue the CMOs, selling them back to the consumers at prices π_1. These financial institutions make zero profits in equilibrium since $\int \pi_2^h \varphi^h \, dh = \int \pi_1 \theta^h \, dh$.

Remark 8.6: In equilibrium, when asset j is traded, $\pi_{1j} = \sum_s \gamma_s N_{sj} = q_j - \sum_s \gamma_s (p_s R_{sj} - N_{sj})^+$ and $q_j = \sum_s \gamma_s p_s R_{sj}$.

We will now fix our assumptions on preferences.

Assumption: Preferences are time- and state-separable, monotonic, and representable by a smooth strictly concave utility function, u^h.

Theorem 8.4: *If consumers' preferences satisfy the assumption above and the endowments allocation w belongs to $L^\infty(H, \mathbb{R}_{++}^{(S+1)L})$, then there exists an equilibrium where borrowers choose their respective collateral coefficients subject to the minimum margin requirement $p_0 M_j - \pi_{2j} \geq \varepsilon$.*

Outline of the Proof: We consider a sequence of truncated economies with increasing bounds on portfolios and consumption bundles. For each truncated economy we construct a generalized game played by the continuum of consumers, auctioners maximizing the value of aggregate excess demand in first-period commodity and spot markets (choosing the respective commodity price vectors in the simplex Δ^{L-1}), and another fictitious agent choosing $\pi_{1j} \in [0, 1]$, $q_j \in [0, \overline{\gamma} \max_{s,k} R_{sjk}]$, $N_{sj} \in [0, n]$, and $\gamma_s \in [0, \overline{\gamma}]$ for every j and s in order to minimize

$$\sum_j \left(\left(\pi_{1j} \int_H \theta_j^h dh - \int_H \pi_{2j}^h \varphi_j^h dh \right)^2 + \left(q_j - \sum_s \gamma_s p_s R_{sj} \right)^2 \int_H \theta_j^h dh \right.$$

$$\left. + \sum_s \left(N_{sj} \int_H \theta_j^h dh - \int_H \min\{p_s R_{sj}, p_s Y_s M_j^h\} \varphi_j^h dh \right)^2 \right).$$

This game has an equilibrium in mixed strategies and, by an argument appealing to Liapunov's theorem, there exists a pure strategies equilibrium. Then we use the margin requirement $p_0 M_j - \pi_j \geq \varepsilon$ to show that the sequence of truncated equilibrium short sales is uniformly bounded. Existence of equilibrium can be established using the multidimensional Fatous lemma and the lower hemicontinuity of consumers' budget correspondences (for $p_s \in \Delta^{L-1}$, $s = 0, 1, \ldots, S$).

8.2.3.3. Extensions: Arbitrage and Equilibrium without Minimum Margin Requirements

Recent work by Araujo, Fajardo, and Páscoa (still in progress) removed the minimum margin requirement $p_0 M_j - \pi_{2j} \geq \varepsilon$ and studied the nonarbitrage conditions in this model. If the minimum margin requirement is dropped, then budget-feasible portfolios are no longer bounded (by $\max_l \varpi_{0l}^h / \varepsilon$ as in the above model) and, for this reason, there are now opportunities for unbounded arbitrage gains at some price vectors. Nonarbitrage prices of primitive assets π_{2j} are shown to include the discounted promised payments, a default spread, a term that reflects the depreciation of the collateral, and also a negative tail due to the nonpecuniary utility returns from consumption of the collateral. Kuhn–Tucker conditions suggest the same submartingale pricing formula.

More precisely, the net price of the joint operation of constituting collateral and short selling becomes a strict supermartingale in the pecuniary returns from this operation, because of the additional nonpecuniary utility returns from consumption of the collateral (given by $\nabla u_0^h \cdot M_j$ in marginal terms); that is, $p_0 M_j - \pi_{2j} > \sum_{s=1}^{S} \mu_s (p_s Y_s M_j - \min\{p_s Y_s M_j, p_s R_{sj}\})$, where μ_s are deflators compatible with the nonarbitrage conditions (namely the Lagrange multipliers of the budget constraints). Hence, prices of primitive assets follow a strict submartingale with regard to pecuniary returns: $\pi_{2j} < \sum_{s=1}^{S} \mu_s \min\{p_s Y_s M_j, p_s R_{sj}\} + (p_0 - \sum_{s=1}^{S} \mu_s p_s Y_s) M_j$.

In the absence of a minimum margin requirement, the existence argument becomes harder, because the sequence of short sales equilibrium allocation of truncated economies (as the respective bounds become larger) must be shown to be uniformly bounded in order to apply the multidimensional Fatou lemma. This recent work deals with this difficulty by showing that it is never in borrowers' interest to default in all states and, therefore, collateral coefficients become uniformly bounded from below (so that the depreciated value of the collateral matches the promised payment in at least one state).

8.3. DEFAULT AND COLLATERAL IN INFINITE HORIZON

8.3.1. A General Model with Short-Lived Assets: Collateral Avoids Ponzi Schemes

When consumers have an infinite life span, the existence of equilibria requires some mechanism that prevents the explosion of consumers' debts by restricting the possibility of asking for successively higher loans in order to pay back previous debts. These Ponzi schemes have been avoided in the incomplete markets literature through the imposition of debt constraints or transversality conditions (see Magill and Quinzzi, 1994, 1996; Hernandez and Santos, 1996; Levine and Zame, 1996; and Florenzano and Gourdel, 1996 for trees with countably many nodes, and Araujo et al., 1996 for trees with a continuum of successors at each node). However, debt or transversality constraints are hard to justify because they are not implied by budgetary or rationality reasons and, furthermore, it is not clear which deflator should be used in a transversality constraint. In fact, under market incompleteness, there is a continuum of state price deflators compatible with nonarbitrage conditions period by period.

Araujo, Páscoa, and Torres-Martinez (2002) showed that collateralized economies dispense with any debt or transversality constraints. For short-lived assets collateralized by durable goods, short sales become bounded at each node (because aggregate endowments of durable goods are bounded and the collateral coefficients are exogenous) and, moreover, nonarbitrage conditions imply that the real value of borrowing becomes uniformly bounded along the infinite tree. In fact, the joint operation of purchasing collateral and selling short has nonnegative returns (because the debtors never reimburse more than the depreciated collateral) and, therefore, by nonarbitrage, borrowing can never exceed collateral costs. This implies that the real value of a loan is bounded by the aggregate resourses of durables (current endowments plus depreciated consumption).

More precisely, denote by $\xi = (t, \sigma)$ the node at time t when state $\sigma \in \{1, \ldots, S\}$ occurs and denote by ξ^+ the set of its immediate successors. Let D^∞ be the node set. There are finitely many, H, infinite-lived consumers whose endowments $\varpi_\xi^h \in \Re_{++}^L$ and utility functions U^h satisfy

(1) $\sum_{l=1}^L \varpi_{\xi l}^h \le \overline{\varpi}, \forall_\xi$, and
(2) $U^h(x) = \sum_{\xi \in D^\infty} u^h(\xi, x_\xi) < \infty$ for any $x \in l_+^\infty(D^\infty \times L)$ and $u^h(\xi, .)$ is continuous, strictly increasing, concave and $u^h(\xi, 0) = 0$.

It is also assumed that

(3) each asset $j \in J$ has real returns $R_{\xi j} \in \Re^L$ and collateral coefficients $C_{\xi j} \in \Re_+^{L'} \{0\}$, and
(4) the durability of commodities is described by $L \times L$ positive diagonal matrices Y_ξ whose elements are uniformly bounded by $k \in (0, 1)$.

It is important to notice that endowments ϖ_ξ^h and collateral coefficients $C_{\xi j}$ are not required to be uniformly bounded away from zero.

Given $p \in \Re_+^{D^\infty \times L}$, a spot price process, and $\pi \in \Re_+^{D^\infty \times (J)}$, an asset price process, the agent h can choose a vector $(x^h, \theta^h, \varphi^h)$ in the state space $\Re_+^{D^\infty \times L} \times \Re_+^{D^\infty \times 2J}$, subject to the budgetary restrictions

$$p_{\xi_0} x_{\xi_0}^h + p_{\xi_0} C_{\xi_0} \varphi_{\xi_0}^h + \pi_{\xi_0}(\theta_{\xi_0}^h - \varphi_{\xi_0}^h) \le p_{\xi_0} \varpi_{\xi_0}^h \qquad (6)$$

$$p_\xi x_\xi^h + p_\xi C_\xi \varphi_\xi^h + \pi_\xi (\theta_\xi^h - \varphi_\xi^h) \le p_\xi \varpi_\xi^h + p_\xi Y_\xi (x_{\xi^-}^h + C_{\xi^-} \varphi_{\xi^-}^h) \qquad (7)$$
$$+ \min \left\{ p_\xi Y_\xi C_{\xi^-}, p_\xi R_{\xi j} \right\} (\theta_{\xi^-}^h - \varphi_{\xi^-}^h), \qquad \forall \xi \in D^\infty : \xi > \xi_0.$$

Define an economy $\mathcal{E}$ as a vector $((U^h, \varpi^h)_{h \in H}, R, C, Y)$ describing consumers' preferences and endowments, assets' returns and collateral coefficients, and also the durability of commodities.

Definition 8.2: An *equilibrium* for the economy $\mathcal{E}$ is a vector $((\bar{x}, \bar{\theta}, \bar{\varphi}); (\bar{p}, \bar{\pi}))$ in $(\Re_+^{D^\infty \times L} \times \Re_+^{D^\infty \times 2J})^H \times (\Delta^{L+J-1})^{D^\infty}$ such that

- $(\bar{x}^h, \bar{\theta}^h, \bar{\varphi}^h)$ maximizes U^h subject to the above budget constraints.
- The following feasibility conditions are satisfied for all $\xi > \xi_0$:

$$\sum_{h \le H} (\bar{x}_{\xi_0}^h + C_{\xi_0} \bar{\varphi}_{\xi_0}^h) = \sum_{h \le H} \varpi_{\xi_0}^h; \qquad (8)$$

$$\sum_{h \le H} (\bar{x}_\xi^h + C_\xi \bar{\varphi}_\xi^h) = \sum_{h \le H} (\varpi_\xi^h + Y_\xi \bar{x}_{\xi^-}^h + Y_\xi C_{\xi^-} \bar{\varphi}_{\xi^-}^h). \qquad (9)$$

- The pair $(\bar{\theta}, \bar{\varphi})$ satisfies

$$\sum_{h \le H} \bar{\theta}^i = \sum_{h \le H} \bar{\varphi}^i. \qquad (10)$$

Theorem 8.5 (Araujo, Páscoa and Torres-Martinez 2002): *Under assumptions (1)–(4) there is an equilibrium for the economy $\mathcal{E}$.*

Outline of the Proof:

(i) Consider a sequence of economies with increasing finite horizon T. For each of these truncated economies feasible allocations are bounded (due to the collateral requirement on short sales) and an equilibrim exists.

(ii) The nonarbitrage condition $p_\xi C_{\xi j} - \pi_{\xi j} \geq 0$ must hold at any equilibrium for the infinite or a finite horizon economy. This condition implies that $\sum_{l \leq L} p_{\xi l} \geq (1 + \max_l \sum_{j \leq J} C_{\xi jl})^{-1}$ for a nonarbitrage vector $(p, \pi) \in (\Delta^{L+J-1})^{D^\infty}$.

(iii) Take a sequence $((\overline{x}^T, \overline{\theta}^T, \overline{\varphi}^T); (\overline{p}^T, \overline{\pi}^T))$ of truncated equilibria and also associated sequences $\{\mu^{Th}\}_T$ of Lagrange multipliers for the budget constraints. For each node ξ, the sequence $\{\mu_\xi^{Th}\}_T$ is bounded, because (1), (2), and (4) imply that $\mu_\xi^{Th} \sum_{l \leq L} \overline{p}_{\xi l}^T \min_l \varpi_{\xi l}^h \leq \sum_{\xi' \geq \xi} u^h(\xi', b)$, where b is the bundle whose L components are all equal to the bound $H\overline{\varpi}/(1 - k)$ on resources (currect endowments plus depreciated previous consumption bundles).

(iv) Countability of D^∞ implies that there is an order of the nodes. Starting with the first node, we find cluster points for the equilibrium variables of this node (including Lagrange multipliers); then we take the convergent subsequence of economies for which this cluster point is a limit and apply the same procedure to the second node. Repeating and passing to the diagonal sequence, we find a vector $((\overline{x}, \overline{\theta}, \overline{\varphi}); (\overline{p}, \overline{\pi}))$ for which all feasibility and budget conditions of the economy E hold.

(v) To establish individual optimality, take pointwise limits in the Kuhn–Tucker conditions of truncated economies and then check if there are budget-feasible vectors for $(\overline{p}, \overline{\pi})$ yielding higher utility than $(\overline{x}^T, \overline{\theta}^T, \overline{\varphi}^T)$. This last step consists in ruling out Ponzi schemes and here the nonarbitrage condition in step (ii) plays a crucial role, because it implies that the real value of borrowing $(\overline{\pi}_{\xi j} \varphi_{\xi j}/\sum_{l \leq L} \overline{p}_{\xi l}, \forall_{\varphi_j})$ becomes uniformly bounded (by b, defined in (iii) above) along the infinite tree.

It is interesting to see that the collateral structure dispenses with a priori transversality conditions or debt constraints, but one may ask whether transversality conditions, analogous to the conditions imposed in models without default, still hold endogenously in equilibrium. Some transversality conditions that follow from individual optimality do hold but the controversial one, requiring no one to be a net borrower as time goes to infinity, does not always hold. In fact, we have:

(i) The discounted value at a node ξ of the total loans given by the agent i at the period T converges to zero as T goes to infinity:

$$\lim_{T \to \infty} \sum_{\{\xi' \geq \xi; \bar{t}(\xi') = T\}} \overline{\mu}_{\xi'}^i \overline{\pi}_{\xi'} \overline{\theta}_{\xi'}^i = 0.$$

(ii)   The discounted value node ξ of the net cost of borrowing (known to be non-negative) tends to zero as T goes to infinity:

$$\lim_{T\to\infty} \sum_{(\xi'\geq\xi;\bar{t}(\xi')=T)} \bar{\mu}^i_{\xi'}(\bar{p}_{\xi'}C_{\xi'} - \bar{\pi}_{\xi'})\bar{\varphi}^i_{\xi'} = 0.$$

Condition (i) says that no agent wants to be a lender at infinity. As Magill and Quinzii (1994) remarked, this is an uncontroversial condition. In our context, the analogous transversality condition on borrowing holds under an assumption on endowments which is not necessary for the existence of equilibria.

If we had assumed that there is a positive scalar $\underline{w}$ such that $w^i(\xi, l) \geq \underline{w}$, for all (ξ, l, i), then the discounted value at ξ of the total resources borrowed by agent $i \in \bar{I}$ at period T goes to zero as T tends to infinity:

$$\lim_{T\to\infty} \sum_{(\xi'\geq\xi;\bar{t}(\xi')=T)} \bar{\mu}^i_{\xi'} \bar{\pi}_{\xi'}\bar{\varphi}^i_{\xi'} = 0.$$

Recall that, at equilibrium, the sequence of debt values is bounded, but the personalized state prices $(\bar{\mu}_\xi)$ (which can be interpreted as marginal utilities of endowment income) may explode if agent i's endowments went to zero fast enough.

8.3.2. Extensions: Markov Equilibria and Computational Algorithms, Bubbles, and International Bankrupty

In a recent paper (still in progress) Araujo, Páscoa and Torres-Martinez extend the model of Section 8.3.1 to the case of infinite-lived assets, allow physical collateral coeffients to be endogenously adjusted in order to meet certain fixed margin requirements in value, and study the fundamental value of assets. The goal of this work is to identify conditions that rule out speculative bubbles in asset prices when short sales are backed by physical collateral (directly or indirectly, through other assets secured by durable goods) and default is allowed. Examples of bubbles are also presented and a comparison is made with results established by Santos and Woodford (1997) and Magill and Quinzii (1996) for default-free assets.

Magill and Quinzii (1996) and Santos and Woodford (1997) had shown that (1) if endowments are uniformly bounded away from zero and (2) if an asset j is in positive net supply, then the difference between an asset price and its fundamental value, $\lim_{T\to\infty} \sum_{t(\xi)=T} \mu_\xi \pi_{\xi j}$, is zero; that is, bubbles are ruled out (using as deflators the Lagrange multipliers μ_ξ). In fact, (1) implies that $(\mu_\xi \sum_{l\leq L} p_{\xi l})_\xi \in l^1$ and (2) implies that $(\pi_{\xi j}/\sum_{l\leq L} p_{\xi l})_\xi \in l^\infty$ and therefore $(\mu_\xi \pi_{\xi j}) \in l^1$. This proposition still holds when assets are collateralized and subject to default but the recent work by Araujo, Páscoa, and Torres-Martinez (2003) dispenses with (1) as an assumption for the existence of equilibria (just as in the case of short-lived assets presented in Section 3.1). Now, bubbles may occur in equilibrium when (1) is violated and never occur when (1) holds, even for assets in zero net supply, provided that collateral coefficients are uniformly bounded: the nonarbitrage condition $p_\xi C_{\xi j} - \pi_{\xi j} \geq 0$

implies already that $(\pi_{\xi j}/\sum_{l \le L} p_{\xi l})_\xi \in l^\infty$. The recent results by Araujo, Páscoa, and Torres-Martinez (2003) actually contain milder sufficient conditions for the absence of bubbles, involving not just the paths of endowments but also assumptions on depreciation and consumers' impatience.

In a recent paper, Kubler and Schmedders (2003) consider a collateral model computationally tractable. The authors prove the existence of a Markov equilibrium and show how one can approximate this equilibrium numerically. For the special case where approximate equilibria can be described by a single-valued policy correspondence, they develop an algorithm to approximate Markov equilibria numerically. The algorithm searches for a continuous policy function that describes prices and allocations such that markets clear and agents make small optimization errors. The authors compute approximate equilibria for a stylized example that illustrates the impact of collateral requirements on equilibrium welfare and show that agents may disagree on the optimal margin requirements. Agents who own most of the financial wealth in the economy prefer low collateral requirements, although they lead to frequent default in equilibrium, whereas poor households prefer high requirements that lead to no default. In the Kubler and Schmedders model it is also shown how equilibrium default may be welfare-improving. This result differs from Lustig's (2001), where a complete set of Arrow securities is traded in each period of the infinite-horizon economy subject to aggregate uncertainty. In this model default is never optimal, and margin requirements ensure that it never happens in equilibrium. For models that share this property see Alvarez and Jerman (2000) and Levine and Zame (1996). For another class of model as well as numerical examples see Sabarwal (2003a, b).

In a series of very interesting papers Cole and Kehoe (1996, 1998, 2000) developed a model of international general equilibrium and bankrupty to explain the Mexican international debt crisis of the eighties. The penalty in this model is the loss of output of the country in the case of default. They compute a numerical equilibrium for the case of Mexico. Araujo and Leon (2002a, b) modify the model to study the question of best monetary regimes – dollarization, monetary unions, or own currency – and apply it to Brazil.

REFERENCES

F. Alvarez and Jerman (2000), "Efficiency, Equilibrium, and Asset Pricing with Risk of Default," *Econometrica* 68 (4): 775–98.

A. Araujo, J. F. Fajardo, and M. Páscoa (2001), "Endogenous Collateral: Arbitrage and Equilibrium Without Bounded Short Sales," IMPA Working Paper.

A. Araujo and M. S. León (2002a), "Speculative Attacks on Debts and Dollarization," *Revista Brasileira de Economia* 56 (1): 7–46.

A. Araujo and M. S. León (2002b), "Speculative Attacks on Debts, Dollarization and Optimum Currency Area," Working Paper, Banco Central do Brasil.

A. Araujo, P. Monteiro, and M. Páscoa (1996), "Infinite Horizon Incomplete Markets with a Continuum of States," *Mathematical Finance* 6: 119–32.

A. Araujo, P. Monteiro, and M. Páscoa (1998), "Incomplete Markets, Continuum of States and Default," *Economic Theory* 11: 205–13.

A. Araujo, J. Orrillo, and M. Páscoa (2000), "Equilibrium with Default and Endogenous Collateral," *Mathematical Finance* 10 (1): 1–22.

A. Araujo and M. Páscoa (2002), "Bankruptcy in a Model of Unsecured Claims," *Economic Theory* 20 (3): 455–81.

A. Araujo, M. Páscoa, and J. P. Torres-Martinez (2002), "Collateral Avoids Ponzi Schemes in Incomplete Markets," *Econometrica*, in press.

A. Araujo, M. Pascoa, and J. P. Torres-Martínez (2003), "Infinite Horizon Incomplete Markets: Long-Lived Assets, Default and Bubbles," mimeo, IMPA.

A. Araujo and A. Sandroni (1991), "Convergence to Rational Expectation," annals SBE.

A. Araujo and A. Sandroni (1999), "On the Convergence to Homogeneous Expectations When Markets are Complete," *Econometrica* 67: 663–72.

K. Arrow and F. Hahn (1971), *General Competitive Analysis*, North-Holland, Amsterdam.

R. J. Aumann and M. Maschler (1985), "Game Theoretic Analysis of a Bankruptcy Problem from the Talmud," *Journal of Economic Theory* 36: 195–213.

A. Bisin and P. Gottardi (1999), "Competitive Equilibria with Asymmetric Information," *Journal of Economic Theory* 87: 1–48.

M. Braun and B. Larrain (2003), "Finance and Business Cycle: International, Interindustry Evidence," Harvard University Department of Economics.

H. Cole and T. Kehoe (1996), "A Self-Fulfilling Model of Mexico's 1994–1995 Debt Crisis," *Journal of International Economics* 41: 309–30.

H. Cole and T. Kehoe (1998), "Self-Fulfilling Debt Crises," Federal Reserve Bank of Minneapolis, Research Department Staff Report 211.

H. Cole and T. Kehoe (2000), "Self-Fulfilling Debt Crises." *Review of Economic Studies* 67: 91–116.

J. Cvitanić and I. Karatzas (1993), "Hedging Contingent Claims with Constrained Portfolios," *Annals of Applied Probability* 3: 652–81.

J. Danielsson and Jean-Pierre Zigrand (2003), "What Happens When You Regulate Risk? Evidence from a Simple Equilibrium Model," London School of Economics.

J. Danielsson, H. S. Shin, and Jean-Pierre Zigrand (2002), "The Impact of Risk Regulation on Price Dynamics," Financial Markets Group, London School of Economics.

P. Dubey, J. Geanakoplos, and M. Shubik (1989), "Liquidity and Bankruptcy with Incomplete Markets: Pure Exchange," Cowles Foundation Discussion Paper 900.

P. Dubey, J. Geanakoplos, and W. Zame (1995), "Default, Collateral, and Derivatives," mimeo, Yale University.

D. Duffie, J. Geanakoplos, A. Mas-Colell, and A. McLennan (1994), "Stationary Markov Equilibria," *Econometrica* 62: 745–81.

D. Duffie and K. Singleton (2003), *Credit Risk: Pricing, Management and Measurement*, Princeton University Press, Princeton, NJ.

N. El Kaoui and M. Quenez (1995), "Dynamic Programming and Pricing of Contingent Claims in an Incomplete Market," *SIAM Journal of Control and Optimization* 33: 29–66.

M. Florenzano and P. Grourdel (1996), "Incomplete Markets in Infinite Horizon: Debt Constraints Versus Node Prices," *Mathematical Finance* 6: 157–96.

J. Geanakoplos (1996), "Promises Promises," mimeo, Yale University.

J. Geanakoplos and W. Zame (2002), "Collateral and the Enforcement of Intertemporal Contracts," discussion paper, Yale University.

J. Geanakoplos and H. Polemarchakis (1986), "Existence, Regularity and Constrained Sub-optimality of Competitive Allocations When the Asset Market is Incomplete," in W. Heller, R. Starr, and D. Starrett (Eds.), *Essays in Honor of K. Arrow*, Cambridge University Press, Cambridge, UK.

O. Hart (1975), "On the Optimality of Equilibrium When the Market Structure Is Incomplete," *Journal of Economic Theory* 11: 418–30.

M. Hellwig (1996), "Rational Expectations Equilibria in Sequence Economies with Symmetric Information: Two-Periods Case," *Journal of Mathematical Economics* 26: 9–50.

A. Hernandez and M. Santos (1996), "Competitive Equilibria for Infinite Horizon Economies with Incomplete Markets," *Journal of Economic Theory* 71: 102–30.

C. Herrero and A. Villar (1998), "Preeminence and Sustainability in Bankruptcy Problems," working paper 98-17, Universidad de Alicante.

E. Jouini and H. Kallal (1995), "Arbitrage in Security Markets with Short-Sales Constraints," *Mathematical Finance* 5 (3): 197–232.

T. Kehoe and D. Levine (1993), "Debt Constrained Asset Markets," *Review of Economic Studies* 63: 597–609.

F. Kubler and K. Schmedders (2003), "Stationary Equilibria in Asset-Pricing Models with Incomplete Markets and Collateral," *Econometrica* 71 (6): 1767–1993.

D. Levine and W. Zame (1996), "Debt Constraint and Equilibrium in Infinite Horizon Economies with Incomplete Markets," *Journal of Mathematical Economics* 126: 103–31.

H. Lustig (2000), "Secured Lending and Asset Prices," mimeo, Stanford University.

H. Lustig (2001), "Bankruptcy and Asset Prices," mimeo, University of Chicago.

H. Lustig (2003), "The Market Price of Aggregate Risk and the Wealth Distribution," mimeo, University of Chicago.

M. Magill and M. Quinzii (1994), "Infinite Horizon Incomplete Markets," *Econometrica* 62: 853–80.

M. Magill and M. Quinzii (1996), "Incomplete Markets over an Infinite Horizon: Long Lived Securities and Speculative Bubbles," *Journal of Mathematical Economics* 26: 133–70.

M. Magill and M. Quinzii (1998), "The Theory of Incomplete Markets," Vol. 1. Cambridge, MA: MIT Press.

M. Magill and W. Shaffer (1991), "Incomplete Markets," in W. Hildenbrand and H. Sonnenschein (Eds.), *Handbook of Mathematical Economics*, Vol. IV, North-Holland, Amsterdam.

A. Mas-Colell and P. Monteiro (1996), "Self-fulfilling Equilibria: An Existence Theorem for General State Space," *Journal of Mathematical Economics* 26: 51–62.

A. Mas-Colell and W. Zame (1996), "The Existence of Security Market Equilibrium with a Non-atomic State Space," *Journal of Mathematical Economics* 16: 63–84.

S. Modica, A. Rustichini, and J. M. Tallon (1995), "Unawareness and Bankruptcy: A General Equilibrium Model," *Economic Theory*, forthcoming; revised version of the CORE discussion paper 9573 "A Model of General Equilibrium with Unforeseen Contingencies."

P. Monteiro (1996), "A New Proof of the Existence of Equilibrium in Incomplete Markets Economies," *Journal of Mathematical Economics* 26: 85–102.

H. Moulin (1987), "Equal or Proportional Division of a Surplus, and Other Methods," *International Journal of Game Theory* 16: 161–86.

E. Prescott and R. Townsend (1984), "Pareto Optima and Competitive Equilibrium with Adverse Selection and Moral Hazard," *Econometrica* 52: 21–45.

T. Sabarwal (2003a), "Competitive Equilibria With Incomplete Markets and Endogenous Bankruptcy," *Contributions to Theoretical Economics* 3 (1): Article 1.

T. Sabarwal (2003), "On the Allocative Efficiency of Competitive Prices in Economies with Incomplete Markets," working paper.

M. Santos and M. Woodford (1997), "Rational Asset Pricing Bubbles," *Econometrica* 65 (1): 19–58.

M. Shubik and C. Wilson (1977), "The Optimal Bankruptcy Rule in a Trading Economy Using Fiat Money," *Zeitschrift für Nationalökonomie* 37: 3–4.

C. Wilson (1977), "A Model of Insurance Markets with Incomplete Information," *Journal of Economic Theory* 16: 167–207.

H. P. Young (1987), "On Dividing an Amount According to Individual Claims or Liabilities," *Mathematics of Operations Research* 12: 398–414.

H. P. Young (1988), "Distributive Justice in Taxation," *Journal of Economic Theory* 44: 321–335.

W. Zame (1993), "Efficiency and the Role of Default When Security Markets are Incomplete," *American Economic Review* 83: 1142–64.

9 Efficient Taxation of Income

Dale W. Jorgenson and Kun-Young Yun

9.1. INTRODUCTION

In June 2001 President George W. Bush signed the Economic Growth and Tax Relief and Reconciliation Act into law, initiating a ten-year program of tax reductions. In January 2003 the President proposed a second round of tax cuts, leaving open the possibility, suggested by former Secretary of the Treasury Paul O'Neill, that the Bush Administration would propose a thoroughgoing reform of our tax system. Tax reforms must be carefully distinguished from tax reductions. Former Secretary O'Neill emphasized that any Bush Administration proposals for tax reform would be revenue-neutral, so that the federal deficit would be unaffected.

Pamela Olson, Treasury's top tax official, reiterated the goal of revenue neutrality in a Washington Post interview in October 2002. This was an important objective of the last major tax reform in 1986 and insulated the two-year debate over reform from the contentious issue of the federal deficit. Olson has divided the Treasury's tax reform programs between short-run measures to simplify the tax code and long-run proposals to reform the tax system. It is important to emphasize that there is no conflict between these goals. Somewhat paradoxically, tax simplification is necessarily complex, because it would eliminate many, but not all, of the myriad special provisions of tax law affecting particular transactions. By contrast, tax reform is relatively straightforward.

A major objective of tax reform is to remove barriers to efficient allocation of capital that arise from disparities in the tax treatment of different forms of income. The centerpiece of the Bush Administration's new round of tax cuts is the elimination of taxes on dividend income at the individual level. This would help to remedy one of the most glaring deficiencies in the existing U.S. tax system, namely, discriminatory taxation of corporate income. In the United States, as in most other countries, corporate income is taxed twice, first through the corporate income tax and second through taxes paid by individuals on corporate dividends. Noncorporate income is taxed only at the individual level. Eliminating individual taxes on dividends would move toward parity between corporate and noncorporate income.

To achieve revenue neutrality the dividend tax would have to be replaced by another source of revenue. One possibility would be to introduce a value-added tax levied on business revenues less expenses, including investment outlays on buildings and equipment. Purchases by individuals and governments are all that remain of business income after business expenses are excluded. As a consequence, substitution of a value-added tax for the tax on dividends would have the effect of shifting the tax burden from corporate income to consumption. With Australia's adoption of a value-added tax in 1999, the U.S. remains the only industrialized country without such a tax. During the 1990s the Committee on Ways and Means of the U.S. House of Representatives held extensive hearings on consumption tax proposals, including the value-added tax, the Hall–Rabushka flat tax, and a national retail sales tax. These differ primarily in methods for tax collection.

Substitution of a value-added tax for the tax on dividends would reduce one of the two main barriers to efficient capital allocation in our existing system. Exclusion of owner-occupied housing from the tax base is a second and more substantial deficiency. Shifting a dollar of investment from owner-occupied housing to rental housing in the corporate sector would double the rate of return to society, as measured by the return before taxes. Any proposal that leaves housing unaffected would sacrifice most of the gains from tax reform.

One advantage of a consumption tax is a low marginal tax rate, the rate that applies to the last dollar of consumption. This would provide powerful new incentives for work and saving. The U.S. corporate income tax rate is currently 40%, combining federal, state, and local taxes. This does not include taxes on corporate dividends and interest through the individual income tax. One popular proposal for replacing the existing income tax system by a consumption tax, the Hall–Rabushka flat tax, would reduce the marginal rate to 19%. However, a revenue-neutral flat tax that included state and local as well as federal taxes would require a rate of 29%.

The Achilles heel of proposals to shift the tax base from income to consumption, at least so far, is the redistribution of tax burden. Recipients of income from property, including corporate bonds and shares, are generally much more affluent that recipients of income from work. Excluding property-type income from the tax base would shift the burden of taxation from the rich to the poor. Attempts to make a consumption tax progressive would drastically raise the marginal rate. Because of the redistribution of tax burdens under a consumption tax, the second phase of the tax reform debate is likely to focus on improvement of our existing income tax system. The objectives would remain the same, namely, treating income sources symmetrically, reducing marginal rates, and retaining progressivity. While this may sound suspiciously like trisecting an angle, these three objectives can be accomplished simultaneously by efficient taxation of income.

Efficient taxation of income is a new approach to tax reform based on taxation of income rather than consumption. This would avoid a drastic shift in tax burdens by introducing different tax rates for property-type income and earned income from work. Earned income would be taxed at a flat rate of 10.9%, while property-type income would be taxed at 30.8%. Precisely the same distinction between earned and property-type income existed in the U.S. tax code between 1969 and 1982, so that no new tax loopholes would be created. Another important advantage of efficient taxation of income is that adjusted gross income for individuals and corporate income would be defined exactly as in the existing tax code. Individuals would continue to file the familiar form 1040 for individual income, and corporations would file corporate income tax retuns. Because the definitions of individual and corporate income would be unchanged, no cumbersome transition rules would be required. Efficient taxation of income could be enacted today and implemented tomorrow.

Deductions from taxable income, as well as tax credits and exemptions, would be unaffected by efficient taxation of income. Businesses would continue to claim depreciation on past investments, as well as tax deductions for interest paid on debt. Mortgage interest and property taxes would be deductible from individual income for tax purposes. The tax treatment of Social Security and Medicare, as well as private pension funds, would be unchanged. The pension-fund industry would not be eviscerated and pension plans would be unaffected. In short, efficient taxation of income would preserve all the features of the existing tax code that have been carefully crafted by generations of lawmakers since adoption of the federal income tax in 1913. At the same time, this new approach to tax reform would remedy the glaring deficiencies in our tax system. These arise from differential taxation of corporate income and exclusion of owner-occupied housing and consumer durables from the income tax base.

Another major concern is the impact of efficient taxation of income on states and localities. Most states use the same tax bases as the federal corporate and individual taxes. Since these tax bases would not change, state and local income taxes would be unaffected and would continue to generate the tax revenues that support schools, law enforcement, and other services provided by state and local governments. Finally, it is important to emphasize that there is no conflict between efficient taxation of income and tax simplification.

Efficient taxation of income also involves a system of investment tax credits that would equalize tax burdens on all sources of business income. Each dollar of new investment would generate a credit against taxes on business income. The rates for these tax credits would be chosen to equalize burdens. The average tax credits for corporations would be 4% on equipment and 19% on structures. Noncorporate businesses would receive smaller credits of 0.5% on equipment and 8% on structures. In order to equalize tax burdens on business and household assets, including housing and consumers' durables such as automobiles, taxes on new investments by households would be collected by car dealers, real estate developers, and other providers. The rates would be 7% on new durables and 32% on new housing. This new source of revenue would precisely offset the new tax credits for business investment, preserving revenue neutrality. (See also Table 9.5(5)).

Owners of existing homes would be deemed to have prepaid all taxes at the time of their original purchase, so that no new taxes would be imposed on housing already in place. The new taxes and tax credits would apply only to new investments. Taxes on new housing would protect property values from collapsing after tax reform was enacted. This is essential for enactment, because 68% of households own their homes and homeowners are also voters who can express concerns about preserving property values at the ballot box. The tax credits for new investments in structures by corporations and noncorporate businesses would apply to new rental housing. These credits would provide incentives for real estate developers to expand the construction of rental housing. The added supply of housing would provide existing renters with more attractive and affordable options. It would also substantially reduce housing costs for newly formed households.

What are the gains from tax reform? This requires an answer to the question: How much additional wealth would be required to purchase the additions to consumption of goods and services, as well as leisure, made possible by the reform? Because consumption, not investment, is the goal of economic activity, this is the most appropriate yardstick for comparing alternative tax reform proposals. We estimate that gains from efficient taxation of income would be equivalent to 19 cents for every dollar of U.S. national wealth. The total gains would be a whopping $4.9 trillion. By comparison GDP was $8.1 trillion and national wealth was $25.4 trillion in 1997, the base year for this comparison. These gains encapsulate the benefits of shifting investment to higher yielding assets. They also reflect greater investment and faster economic growth.

Instituting the new investment tax credits would stimulate investment, especially in the corporate sector. The revival of economic activity would raise both earned income from work and property-type income and also would stimulate consumption. Efficient taxation of income would have a much greater impact than a revenue-neutral version of the flat tax. We estimate that the flat tax would yield $2.1 trillion, by comparison with gains from efficient taxation of income of $4.9 trillion. Tax reform proposals, like cherry blossoms, are hardy perennials of the Washington scene. Occasionaly, a new approach to tax reform appears and changes the course of the debate. President Reagan's proposal of May 1985 is the most recent example of a new approach to tax reform. Like efficient taxation of income, this retained the income tax rather than shifting to a consumption tax. This is still the most fruitful direction for reform.

9.2. INCOME TAX REFORM

The effects of taxation on the allocation of resources depend not only on the size of tax wedges imposed on transactions but also on elasticities of substitution along the relevant margins. Moreover, tax distortion of resource allocation at one margin has further impacts at other margins. The analysis of taxation in terms of effective tax rates and tax wedges may be suggestive but incomplete as an economic analysis of the tax distortion of resource allocation; in certain contexts, it may even be inappropriate, due to limitations of the typically static and partial-equilibrium nature of the analysis.

To evaluate the economic impact of alternative tax-reform proposals, we employ a dynamic general-equilibrium model.[1] Equilibrium is characterized by an intertemporal price system that clears markets for labor and capital services and consumption and investment goods. This equilibrium links the past and the future through markets for investment goods and capital services. Assets are accumulated through investments, while asset prices equal the present values of future services. Consumption must satisfy conditions for intertemporal optimality of the household sector under perfect foresight. Similarly, investment must satisfy requirements for asset accumulation.

We employ our dynamic general-equilibrium model to simulate the economic impact of alternative policies for reforming the taxation of capital income. For this purpose we have designed a computational algorithm for determining the time path of the U.S. economy following the reform. This algorithm is composed of two parts. We first solve for the unique steady state of the economy corresponding to the tax policy of 1996, our reference tax policy. We then determine the unique transition path for the U.S. economy, consistent with the initial conditions and the steady state. This is the base case for our analysis of changes in tax policy.

The second part of our algorithm is to solve our model for the unique transition path of the U.S. economy following tax reform. We first consider the elimination of differences in marginal effective tax rates among different classes of assets and different sectors – ten alternative programs for reforming the taxation of capital income in the U.S. We also consider the cost of progressivity in the taxation of labor income by comparing the existing labor-income tax with a flat labor-income tax These are the alternative cases for our tax-policy analysis.

We compare the level of social welfare associated with each policy with the welfare level in the base case. We translate these welfare comparisons into monetary terms by introducing an intertemporal expenditure function, giving the wealth required to achieve a given level of welfare for the representative consumer in our model of the U.S. economy. Using this expenditure function, we translate the differences in welfare into differences in wealth.

In evaluating the welfare effects of various tax policies we require a reference economy with which the resource allocation and welfare under alternative tax policies can be compared. We take the U.S. economy under the tax laws effective in 1996 as the reference economy. The simulated dynamic path of the reference economy with an annual inflation rate of 4% is the "base case" for our

---

[1] This model updates the dynamic general equilibrium model presented in Jorgenson and Yun (1990). Additional details are given by Jorgenson and Yun (2001).

Dale W. Jorgenson and Kun-Young Yun

TABLE 9.1. *Inflation and tax rates (1996)*

Inflation Rate	0.0	0.04	0.08
1. Marginal tax rates on individual capital income			
t_q^e	0.20166	0.20203	0.20228
t_m^e	0.28786	0.28786	0.28786
t_h^e	0.28786	0.28786	0.28786
t_q^g	0.05589	0.05589	0.05589
t_m^g	0.07196	0.07196	0.07196
t_h^g	0.00000	0.00000	0.00000
t_q^d	0.17096	0.18228	0.18971
t_m^d	0.22480	0.23003	0.23346
t_h^d	0.26910	0.26917	0.26921
t_g^d	0.19893	0.20252	0.20488

2. Corporate income tax rate

t_q	0.38799

3. Marginal tax rate on labor income

t_L^m	0.26447

4. Average tax rate on personal income

t_L^a	0.12657
t_e^a	0.18304
t_d^a	0.18304

5. Sales tax

t_C	0.05800
t_I	0.05800

6. Property tax

t_q^p	0.01201
t_m^p	0.01137
t_h^p	0.00912

7. Others

t_t	0.00675
t_w	0.00083

Note: We set $t_h^e = t_m^e$ and $t_h^g = 0$. t_q^e, t_m^e, t_h^e: Average marginal tax rates of individual income accruing to corporate, noncorporate, and household equities, respectively. t_q^g, t_m^g, t_h^g: Average marginal tax rates of capital gains accruing to corporate, noncorporate, and household equities, respectively. t_q^d, t_m^d, t_h^d, t_g^d: Average marginal tax rats of interest income accruing to corporate, noncorporate, household, and government debts, respectively. t_q: Corporate income tax rate (federal + state and local). t_L^m: Average marginal tax rate of labor income. t_L^a: Average tax rate of labor income. t_e^a, t_d^a: Average tax rates of personal capital income from equity and debt. t_c, t_I: Sales tax rates of consumption and investment goods. t_q^p, t_m^p, t_h^p: Property tax rates of corporate, noncorporate, and household assets, respectively. t_t: Rate of personal nontaxes. t_w: Effective rate of wealth taxation.

simulation analysis. Because the base case serves as the reference for the evaluation of the performance of the economy under alternative tax policies, it is useful to describe its main characteristics. We describe the construction of the base case by presenting the exogenous variables that are common to all the simulations we consider.

We take January 1, 1997, as the starting point for all the simulations we consider. The main role of the initial year of the simulation is to determine the initial values of the stock variables and the scale of the economy. The stock variables determined by the starting year are the total time endowment (LH), the capital stock (KL), and the claims of the government and the rest of the world (GL and RL). In our simulations, the starting values of LH, KL, GL, and RL are set in their historical values. Specifically, in 1997, $LH = \$17,571$ billion, $KL = \$25,847$ billion, and $GL = \$3,784$ billion. Because inflation is assumed to be 4% per year in the base case, we set PKL, PGL, and PRL at $(1 + 0.04)^{-1} = 0.96154$ dollar per unit. After 1997, we assume that the distribution of individuals among categories distinguished by age, sex, and level of education will stabilize and hence the quality of time endowment, the leisure, and the labor employed in the various sectors of the economy will not change. This implies that the growth rate of the total effective time endowment will be the same as the growth rate of population. We assume that population will grow at an annual rate of 1% per year and the efficiency of labor improves at the rate of productivity growth we estimated by pooling the entire producer model.

In Table 9.1 we present the tax rates that describe the U.S. tax system in 1996. These include the marginal tax rates on individual capital income, the corporate income tax rate, the marginal tax rate on labor income, and the average tax rate on personal income. The tax rates also include sales and property taxes, personal nontaxes, and wealth taxes. Capital consumption allowances are allowed only for corporate and noncorporate business sectors.

To estimate the average tax rates on labor and capital income of individuals, we use Tables 9.2 and 9.3 based on Internal Revenue Service, *Statistics of Income–1996, Individual Income Tax Returns*. First, we reconcile the total adjusted gross income (AGI) in the two tables by creating a zero tax rate bracket in Table 9.3 and allocating the excess of total positive AGI in Table 9.2 over that of Table 9.3 ($\$4,536.0 - \$4,439.7 + \$54.6 = \$150.9$ billions) to the zero tax rate bracket.

Second, assuming that the marginal tax rate increases with the AGI bracket in Table 9.2, we allocate the tax revenue of Table 9.3 across the positive AGI brackets of Table 9.3. We then allocate the tax revenue in each AGI bracket of Table A.2 between labor and nonlabor income, using the share of labor income in each AGI bracket (see column 3 of Table 9.2). Third, we calculate the average federal labor income tax rate t_L^{af} by dividing the total tax revenue allocated to wages and salaries with the total wages and salaries in AGI. Similarly, we calculate the average federal

TABLE 9.2. *Adjusted gross income and wages and salaries*

Size of AGI (1,000 dollars)	AGI (billions of dollars)	W	S
No AGI	−54.6	7.2	−
under 5	38.3	33.8	0.88045
5−10	102.1	75.4	0.73816
10−15	165.2	122.0	0.73874
15−20	202.3	154.1	0.76212
20−25	217.9	176.0	0.80738
25−30	221.1	181.2	0.81975
30−40	436.4	362.3	0.83017
40−50	426.8	353.8	0.82907
50−75	871.8	715.5	0.82074
75−100	498.4	394.9	0.79240
100−200	603.7	433.7	0.71840
200−500	347.4	204.7	0.58926
500−1000	144.8	70.5	0.48675
1000 or more	314.4	91.7	0.29181
ALL RETURNS, TOTAL	4536.0	3376.9	0.74446

Note: (1) AGI is net of deficit. (2) All figures are estimates based on samples. AGI: adjusted gross income. W: wages and salaries. S: share of wages and salaries in AGI (W/AGI).
Source: Internal Revenue Service, *Statistics of Income – 1996, Individual Income Tax Returns.*

TABLE 9.3. *Tax generated at all rates by marginal tax rate (units: %, billions of dollars)*

Marginal tax rate	AGI	Tax generated at all rates, after credit
0.0	(150.9)	0.0
15.0	1681.8	128.9
28.0	1625.7	235.7
31.0	355.0	70.0
36.0	249.2	59.0
39.6	527.9	161.8
TOTAL	4439.7	655.4

Source: Internal Revenue Service, *Statistics of Income – 1996, Individual Income Tax Returns.*

TABLE 9.4. *Present value of capital consumption allowances (1996)*

Inflation rate	Corporate		Noncorporate	
	Short	Long	Short	Long
0.00	0.9299	0.5418	0.9347	0.4962
0.04	0.8801	0.4574	0.8878	0.3909
0.08	0.8360	0.3982	0.8460	0.3197

nonlabor income tax rate and interpret it as the average federal income tax rate on individual capital income t_K^{af}. The results are $t_L^{af} = 0.12970$ and $t_K^{af} = 0.18757$.

We note that our approach has a number of shortcomings. For example, AGI does not include income not reported in the tax returns; AGI excludes tax-exempt income; labor income of the self-employed is included in nonlabor income; and nonlabor income includes income other than capital income such as alimony, social security benefits, unemployment compensation, and gambling earnings. To offset some the biases that may be caused by these factors, we calculate the federal and state and local average tax rates on labor and capital income as

$$t_L^a = \frac{t_P^a \cdot t_L^{af}}{t_P^{af}}$$

$$t_K^a = \frac{t_P^a \cdot t_K^{af}}{t_P^{af}},$$

where t_P^{af} is the average federal tax rate, defined as the total tax revenue divided by the total positive AGI, and t_P^a is the federal and state and local average personal income tax rates estimated from the National Income and Product Accounts. We estimate that $t_P^{af} = 0.14449$ and $t_P^a = 0.141$ for 1996. We assume that the average tax rates are the same for dividends and interest income. The results are $t_L^a = 0.12657$ and $t_e^a = t_d^a = 0.18304$, as shown in Table 9.1.

Capital consumption allowances are allowed only for the corporate and noncorporate business sectors. In Table 9.4 we present the present value of these allowances for short-lived and long-lived assets under three alternative rates of inflation. We begin the calculation of the capital consumption allowances with the statutory depreciation schedules. We employ the after-tax nominal interest rate for discounting depreciation allowances. The nominal interest rate is the sum of the real interest rate and the inflation rate. The real interest rate is set equal to the average of the Baa corporate bond rate for our sample period 1970–1996, 0.048604. The rate of inflation varies with the simulation scenario and takes the values of 0, 4, and 8% per year. The after-tax nominal interest rate is calculated as $i \cdot (1 - t_q)$, where t_q is the corporate tax rate given in Table 9.1.

TABLE 9.5. *Welfare effects of inflation under the law*
(billions of 1997 dollars)

Rate of inflation	Revenue adjustment	Welfare effect
0%	Lump-sum tax	482.4
	Labor-income tax	−89.5
	Sales tax	−96.8
	Individual income tax	−89.2
4%	Lump-sum tax	0.0
	Labor-income tax	0.0
	Sales tax	0.0
	Individual income tax	0.0
8%	Lump-sum tax	−407.0
	Labor-income tax	15.6
	Sales tax	31.6
	Individual income tax	19.0

Note: In 1997, the national wealth (beginning of the year) and GDP
were $25,378 and $8,111 billion, respectively.

In our model, the time horizon of the consumer is infinite and the model is consistent with a wide range of steady-state configurations of the economy. From a practical point of view, this implies that the steady-state configuration of the economy can be very different from the initial conditions of the economy. We estimate the welfare effects of the alternative tax-reform proposals under three alternative assumptions on the rate of inflation and four alternative methods of adjusting tax revenues. The adjustment of tax revenues is necessary to keep the government's real budgetary position on the same path as in the base case economy. This approach ensures that the government budget does not affect the measured differential welfare effects either through expenditures or through budget deficits/surpluses. However, it should be noted that when the revenue adjustment involves changes in the marginal rate of the adjusted tax, there will be substitution effects.

Under the 1996 tax law, inflation increases the tax burden of corporate assets faster than that of noncorporate assets and the burden of noncorporate assets faster than that of household assets. But inflation has mixed effects on the absolute size of the intersectoral tax wedges where the tax wedges have negative sign. Table 9.5 shows the impact of inflation on the performance of the U.S. economy under the 1996 tax law. An increase in the rate of inflation reduces welfare under a lump-sum tax adjustment, but enhances welfare under labor income tax, sales tax, and individual income tax adjustments. The welfare cost of the distortion of resource allocation by taxes can be measured as the improvement in the economic welfare of the economy when the tax wedges are eliminated. We first analyze the impact of distortions resulting from the taxation of income from capital. We consider

TABLE 9.6. *Steady state of the base case (rate of inflation: 4%)*

	Corporate		Noncorporate		Household	
	Short	Long	Short	Long	Short	Long
w	0.0868	0.2430	0.0178	0.2076	0.0968	0.3480
z	0.8801	0.4574	0.8878	0.3909	0.0000	0.0000
δ	0.1367	0.0175	0.1533	0.0112	0.1918	0.0107
PKS	0.2211	0.1066	0.2276	0.0849	0.2486	0.0602

Note: w: share of capital stock. z: present value of consumption allowances. δ: economic depreciation rate. *PKS*: price of capital services.

the elimination of interasset, intersector, and intertemporal tax wedges. Specifically, we measure the efficiency gains from the following changes in the 1996 tax system:

1. Eliminate intrasectoral tax wedges between short-lived and long-lived assets.
2. Eliminate intersectoral tax wedges for short-lived and long-lived assets in the business sector – corporate and noncorporate.
3. Eliminate intersectoral tax wedges among all private sectors – corporate, noncorporate, and household.
4. Eliminate intersectoral and intrasectoral tax wedges in the business sector.
5. Eliminate intersectoral and intrasectoral tax wedges in the private sector.
6. Corporate tax integration.
7. Eliminate taxation of income from capital.
8. Eliminate capital income taxes and the sales tax on investment goods.
9. Eliminate capital income taxes and property taxes.
10. Eliminate capital income taxes, the sales tax on investment goods, and property taxes.

In order to eliminate tax wedges between a set of asset categories, we set their social rates of return to be equal. We achieve this objective by assigning an appropriate investment tax credit for each category. Note that equalizing social rates of return across sectors is not equivalent to equalizing effective tax rates, because the private rate of return varies with the capital structure of each sector. However, equalizing the social rates of return to short-lived and long-lived assets within a given sector is equivalent to equalizing their effective tax rates. Table 9.6 shows the present value of capital consumption allowances z and the rates of economic depreciation δ. It also shows the allocation of capital stock w and the prices of capital services *PKS* in the steady state of the base case corresponding to the 1996 tax system.

The tax credits required for the first six sets of changes in the 1996 tax system given above are presented in panel 2 of Table 9.7, along with the corresponding

TABLE 9.7. *Elimination of interasset and intersectoral tax wedges (rate of inflation: 4%)*

	Corporate		Noncorporate		Household	
	Short	Long	Short	Long	Short	Long
1. Base Case						
$\sigma - \pi$	0.0789	0.0884	0.0681	0.0733	0.0491	0.0491
e	0.3983	0.4625	0.3240	0.3715	0.1223	0.1223
k	0.0000	0.0000	0.0000	0.0000	0.0000	0.0000
2. Alternative Policies						
(1) No interasset wedges: corporate and noncorporate sectors						
$\sigma - \pi$	0.0859	0.0859	0.0729	0.0729	0.0491	0.0491
e	0.4470	0.4470	0.3680	0.3680	0.1223	0.1223
k	−0.0219	0.0216	−0.0163	0.0049	0.0000	0.0000
(2) No intersector wedges: corporate and noncorporate sectors						
$\sigma - \pi$	0.0771	0.0814	0.0771	0.0814	0.0491	0.0491
e	0.3840	0.4167	0.4025	0.4342	0.1223	0.1223
k	0.0058	0.0604	−0.0308	−0.0981	0.0000	0.0000
(3) No intersector wedges: all sectors						
$\sigma - \pi$	0.0636	0.0673	0.0636	0.0673	0.0636	0.0673
e	0.2538	0.2947	0.2762	0.3159	0.3227	0.3599
k	0.0481	0.1829	0.0155	0.0718	−0.0600	−0.3392
(4) No interasset and intersector wedges: all assets, corporate and noncorporate sectors						
$\sigma - \pi$	0.0806	0.0806	0.0806	0.0806	0.0491	0.0491
e	0.4108	0.4108	0.4285	0.4285	0.1223	0.1223
k	−0.0053	0.0675	−0.0429	−0.0883	0.0000	0.0000
(5) No interasset and intersector wedges: all assets, all sectors						
$\sigma - \pi$	0.0666	0.0666	0.0666	0.0666	0.0666	0.0666
e	0.2868	0.2868	0.3083	0.3083	0.3528	0.3528
k	0.0388	0.1893	0.0053	0.0808	−0.0722	−0.3253
(6) Corporate tax integration						
$\sigma - \pi$	0.0681	0.0733	0.0681	0.0733	0.0491	0.0491
e	0.3030	0.3520	0.3240	0.3715	0.1223	0.1223
k	0.0340	0.1311	0.0000	0.0000	0.0000	0.0000

Notes: $\sigma - \pi$: social rate of return. e: effective tax rate. k: investment tax credit. π: rate of inflation.

social rates of return and effective tax rates. Base case figures are presented in panel 1 for comparison. In the first tax change we equalize the social rates of return to short-lived and long-lived assets within each sector, by setting the social rates of return for short-lived and long-lived assets at their sectoral average in the steady state of base case, where the composition of capital stock in the steady state of base case in Table 9.6 is used as the weight. Once the social rate of return for an asset is determined, the required rate of investment tax credit can be solved from the cost of capital formula.

There is, of course, no interasset tax wedge within the household sector, since no tax is levied on the income of the household sector and property tax rates are the same for short-lived and long-lived assets. In this tax change the intersectoral tax wedges among corporate, noncorporate, and household sectors are maintained. In the second tax change, we follow the same procedure and equalize social rates of return of short-lived assets in the corporate and noncorporate sectors and similarly for long-lived assets, but the interasset wedges remain the same. The third tax change extends this analysis to the household sector. In the fourth tax change, both interasset and intersectoral tax wedges in the business sectors are eliminated, and the fifth extends the analysis to the household sector. We eliminate tax wedges in the first five tax changes given above by setting the relevant social rates of return at the average value in the steady state of the base case corresponding to the 1996 tax law. This ensures that the resulting tax change will be approximately revenue neutral. We implement corporate tax integration, the sixth tax change given above, by setting the social rates of return for short-lived and long-lived assets in the corporate sector equal to their values in the noncorporate sector. This is not, of course, revenue neutral.

In the seventh through tenth tax changes we evaluate the potential welfare gains from the elimination of intertemporal tax wedges. These are determined by capital income taxes, sales taxes on investment goods, and property taxes. The seventh tax change measures the welfare gain from elimination of the taxation of capital income for both individuals and corporations. We then move step by step to eliminate intertemporal tax wedges. In the eighth tax change, we eliminate the sales tax on investment goods, as well as capital income taxes. In the ninth tax change, we also eliminate property taxes. Finally, in the tenth change, we eliminate capital income taxes, sales taxes on investment goods, and property taxes.

The welfare effects of the ten simulations are summarized in Table 9.8. Beginning with the simulations with a lump-sum tax adjustment, we find that the welfare gain from the elimination of the interasset tax wedges within sectors are $182.1 billion under the 1996 Tax Law. Under the lump-sum tax adjustment, elimination of intersectoral wedges between corporate and noncorporate assets yields a welfare gain of $45.1 billion.

The result of the third simulation suggests that there is potentially a very large welfare gain to be realized from eliminating the intersectoral wedges between the business and household sectors. The estimated gains are $1,616.8 billion under the 1996 Tax Law. This result is not surprising, given the large tax wedges between business and household assets. The welfare gains from eliminating the interasset and intersectoral wedges between business assets are estimated to be $127.6 billion under the 1996 Tax Law. The welfare gain from eliminating all the atemporal tax wedges in the entire private economy is estimated to be $1,692.7 billion under the

TABLE 9.8. *Welfare effects of tax distortion: 1996 tax law*
(billions of 1997 dollars)

Eliminated wedges and method of revenue adjustment	Welfare effect	
	Additive	Proportional
(1) *Within-sector interasset distortion*		
Lump-sum tax adjustment	182.1	182.1
Labor-income tax adjustment	193.4	266.5
Sales tax adjustment	185.5	185.5
Individual income tax adjustment	184.6	252.0
(2) *Intersector distortion: corporate and noncorporate sectors*		
Lump-sum tax adjustment	45.1	45.1
Labor-income tax adjustment	−25.3	−59.0
Sales tax adjustment	−31.4	−31.4
Individual income tax adjustment	−32.2	−48.4
(3) *Intersector distortion: all sectors*		
Lump-sum tax adjustment	1616.8	1616.8
Labor-income tax adjustment	1716.8	1906.8
Sales tax adjustment	1709.5	1709.5
Individual income tax adjustment	1701.5	1849.6
(4) *Interasset and intersector distortion: corporate and noncorporate sectors, all assets*		
Lump-sum tax adjustment	127.6	127.6
Labor-income tax adjustment	80.4	67.0
Sales tax adjustment	70.5	70.5
Individual income tax adjustment	70.1	72.3
(5) *Interasset and intersector distortion: all sectors, all assets*		
Lump-sum tax adjustment	1692.7	1692.7
Labor-income tax adjustment	1810.2	2015.0
Sales tax adjustment	1800.3	1800.3
Individual income tax adjustment	1789.6	1949.9
(6) *Corporate tax integration (set $\sigma^q = \sigma^m$)*		
Lump-sum tax adjustment	1067.4	1067.4
Labor-income tax adjustment	282.8	−976.2
Sales tax adjustment	250.3	250.3
Individual income tax adjustment	280.4	−595.2
(7) *Capital income taxes (business and personal)*		
Lump-sum tax adjustment	2691.5	2691.4
Labor-income tax adjustment	362.9	−5480.2
Sales tax adjustment	493.0	493.0
Individual income tax adjustment	362.9	−5480.2
(8) *Capital income taxes and sales tax on investment goods*		
Lump-sum tax adjustment	3367.4	3367.4
Labor-income tax adjustment	383.6	−8957.9
Sales tax adjustment	710.2	710.3
Individual income tax adjustment	383.6	−8957.9

| Eliminated wedges and | Welfare effect | |
method of revenue adjustment	Additive	Proportional
(9) *Capital income taxes and property taxes*		
Lump-sum tax adjustment	3723.2	3723.3
Labor-income tax adjustment	−1085.0	–
Sales tax adjustment	−554.0	−554.0
Individual income tax adjustment	−1085.0	–
(10) *Capital income taxes, sales tax on investment goods, and property taxes*		
Lump-sum tax adjustment	4309.5	4309.3
Labor-income tax adjustment	−1101.0	–
Sales tax adjustment	−237.8	−237.9
Individual income tax adjustment	−1101.0	–

Notes: 1. Inflation is fixed at 4% per year. 2. Under the additive tax adjustment, the average and marginal tax rates of labor income and the average tax rates of individual capital income are adjusted in the same percentage points. The marginal tax rates of individual capital income are adjusted in the same proportion as the marginal tax rate of labor income. 3. Under the proportional tax adjustment, average and marginal tax rates are adjusted in the same proportion.

1996 Tax Law. Most of this welfare gain can be attributed to the elimination of the tax wedges between business and household sectors.

In the sixth simulation we eliminate the intersectoral tax wedges between the assets in the corporate and noncorporate assets by setting the social rates of return of corporate assets to be equal to the corresponding rates of return of the noncorporate assets in the reference case. The tax burdens on the corporate assets are unambiguously reduced without an offsetting increase in other marginal tax rates. The estimated welfare gains from this experiment are $1,067.4 billion under the 1996 Tax Law. These welfare gains are more than half of those attainable by eliminating all the atemporal tax wedges.

In the first six simulations we focused on the distortionary effects of atemporal tax wedges. However, in the following four simulations, we estimate the welfare cost of intertemporal tax distortions. For this purpose we measure the welfare gains from eliminating the distortions caused by the taxes on capital income, including property taxes and sales taxes on investment goods. In the seventh simulation we set the effective tax rates on all forms of capital equal to zero. Social rates of return are not equalized across sectors, due to the differences in the debt/asset ratios and the property tax rates.

We find that elimination of capital income taxes at both individual and corporate levels generates a welfare gain of $2,691.5 billion under the 1996 Tax Law. Eliminating sales taxes on investment goods as well increases this gain to $3,367.4 billion. Eliminating capital income taxes and property taxes produces a gain of $3,723.2, while eliminating taxes on investments goods as well generates a gain of $4,309.0 billion. If we start with the 1996 Tax Law and eliminate all intertemporal tax wedges, the welfare gain is as large 53.1% of the U.S. GDP and 16.8% of the private national wealth in 1997.

Table 9.8 shows that the magnitudes of welfare gains under the distortionary tax adjustments are substantially different from those under the lump sum tax adjustment. Because the elimination of the tax wedges is not calibrated to be revenue neutral, the changes in the marginal tax rates due to the revenue adjustments can generate significant substitution effects. We find that the welfare effects from the elimination of tax wedges are very sensitive to the choice of the revenue-adjustment method. The welfare effects are most sensitive to the choice between the lump-sum tax adjustment and the distortionary tax adjustments. The results are also somewhat sensitive to the choice among the distortionary tax adjustments, especially when the size of the required revenue is large.

Note that when elimination of tax wedges implies tax cuts at the relevant margins, the welfare gains under the distortionary tax adjustments are substantially smaller than the corresponding gains under the lump-sum tax adjustment. The logic underlying this observation is straightforward. The excess burden tends to increase more than proportionally with the required revenue increase. When elimination of tax wedges involves tax cuts with substantial revenue impacts, the welfare measures under the lump-sum tax adjustment are best interpreted as the upper bounds of the welfare gains. Lowering marginal tax rates coupled with broadening the tax base is a successful strategy for improving the efficiency of resource allocation.

The fact that the estimated welfare gains from the elimination of the intertemporal tax wedges is in the range of $2,691.5–4,309.0 billion suggests that the potential welfare gain from replacing the current income taxes with consumption-based individual taxes is potentially very large. At the same time, welfare gains under the distortionary tax adjustments are much smaller, indicating that improvements in the efficiency of resource allocation can be best achieved by reducing distortions at the atemporal margins of resource allocation.

Our final simulation is intended to measure the distortions associated with progressivity of the tax on labor income. This produces marginal tax rates far in excess of average tax rates. Our point of departure is the elimination of all intersectoral and interasset tax distortions in Panel (5) of Table 9.8. In Table 9.9, we replace the progressive labor-income tax by a flat labor-income tax with the same average tax rate. Under a lump-sum tax adjustment this generates a welfare gain of $4,585.9 billion, relative to the 1996 Tax Law. We conclude that elimination of the progressive labor-income tax, together with elimination of all intersectoral and interasset tax distortions, would produce the largest welfare gains of all the tax changes we have considered. These gains are even larger with distortionary tax adjustments because the lower marginal tax rate on labor income improves resource allocation and allows the marginal tax rates of the adjusted taxes to be lowered.

TABLE 9.9. *Welfare cost of labor tax progressivity under efficient capital allocation (billions of 1997 dollars)*

	Progressive		Proportional
Revenue adjustment	Additive	Proportional	Additive
Lump-sum tax	1692.7	1692.7	4585.9
Labor-income tax	1810.2	2015.0	4823.0
Sales tax	1800.3	1800.3	4899.9
Individual income tax	1789.6	1949.9	4857.8

Notes: 1. Inflation is fixed at 4% per year. 2. Under the additive tax adjustment, the average and marginal tax rates of labor income and the average tax rates of individual capital income are adjusted in the same percentage points. The marginal tax rates of individual capital income are adjusted in the same proportion as the marginal tax rate of labor income. 3. Under the proportional tax adjustment, average and marginal tax rates are adjusted in the same proportion. 4. The figures for the progressive labor income tax are the same as in Panel (5) of Table 9.8. 5. Under the proportional labor income tax, additive and proportional tax adjustments are equivalent.

9.3. CONSUMPTION TAX PROPOSALS

In the United States proposals to replace income by consumption as a tax base have been revived during the 1990s. These include the Hall–Rabushka (1983, 1995) flat tax proposal, a European-style consumption-based value-added tax, and a comprehensive retail sales tax on consumption. We compare the economic impact of these proposals, taking the 1996 Tax Law as our base case. In particular, we consider the impact of the Hall–Rabushka proposal and the closely related Armey–Shelby proposal. We also consider the economic impact of replacing the existing tax system by a national retail sales tax, levied on personal consumption expenditures at the retail level.

From the economic point of view, the definition of consumption is straightforward. A useful starting point is personal consumption expenditures (PCE) as defined in the U.S. National Income and Product Accounts (NIPA). However, the taxation of services poses important administrative problems, reviewed in the U.S. Treasury (1984) monograph on the value-added tax. First, PCE includes the rental equivalent value of owner-occupied housing, but does not include the services of consumers' durables. Both are substantial in magnitude, but could be taxed by the "prepayment method" described by Bradford (1986). In this approach, taxes on the consumption of services would be prepaid by including investment rather than consumption in the tax base.

The prepayment of taxes on services of owner-occupied housing would remove an important political obstacle to substitution of a consumption tax for existing income taxes. At the time the substitution takes place, all owner-occupiers would be treated as having prepaid all future taxes on the services of their dwellings. This is equivalent to excluding not only mortgage interest from the tax base, but also returns to equity, which might be taxed upon the sale of a residence with no corresponding purchase of residential property of equal or greater value. Of course, this argument is vulnerable to the specious criticism that homeowners should be allowed to take the mortgage deduction twice – when they are deemed to have paid all future taxes and, again, when tax liabilities are actually assessed on the services of household capital.

Under the prepayment method, purchases of consumers' durables by households for their own use would be subject to tax. This would include automobiles, appliances, home furnishings, and the like. In addition, new construction of owner-occupied housing would be subject to tax, as would sales of existing renter-occupied housing to owner-occupiers. These are politically sensitive issues and it is important to be clear about the implications of prepayment as the debate proceeds. Housing and consumers' durables must be included in the tax base in order to reap the substantial economic benefits of substituting consumption for income as a basis for taxation.

Other purchases of services that are especially problematical under a consumption tax would include services provided by nonprofit institutions, such as schools and colleges, hospitals, and religious and eleemosynary institutions. The traditional, tax-favored status of these forms of consumption would be tenaciously defended by recipients of the services and, even more tenaciously, by the providers. For example, elegant, and sometimes persuasive, arguments can be made that schools and colleges provide services that represent investment in human capital rather than consumption. However, consumption of the resulting enhancements in human capital often takes the form of leisure time, which would remain the principal untaxed form of consumption. Taxes could be prepaid by including educational services in the tax base.

Finally, any definition of a consumption tax base must distinguish between consumption for personal and business purposes. Ongoing disputes over exclusion of home offices, business-provided automobiles, equipment, and clothing, as well as business-related lodging, entertainment, and meals, would continue to plague tax officials, the entertainment and hospitality industries, and users of expense accounts. In short, substitution of a consumption tax for the existing income tax system would not eliminate the practical issues that arise from the necessity of distinguishing between business and personal activities in defining consumption. However, these issues are common to the two tax bases.

The first issue that will surface in the tax reform debate is *progressivity* or use of the tax system to redistribute economic resources. We consider alternative tax reform proposals that differ in their impact on the distribution of resources. However, our simulations are limited to the efficiency impacts of these proposals.[2] One of our

---

[2] For distributional effects of fundamental tax reform, see Hall (1996, 1997), Fullerton and Rogers (1996), Feenberg, Mitrusi, and Poterba (1997), Gravelle (1995), and Gentry and Hubbard (1997). On transition and other issues, see McLure (1993), Sakar and Zodrow (1993), Poddar and English (1997), Fullerton and Rogers (1997), Engen and Gale (1997), Fox and Murray (1997), Hellerstein (1997), and Bradford (2000).

most important findings is that redistribution through tax policy is very costly in terms of efficiency. Unfortunately, there is no agreed-upon economic methodology for trading off efficiency and equity. It is, nonetheless, important to quantify the impact of alternative tax policies on the efficiency of resource allocation.

The second issue to be debated is *fiscal federalism*, or the role of state and local governments. Because state and local income taxes usually employ the same tax bases as the corresponding federal taxes, it is reasonable to assume that the substitution of a consumption tax for income taxes at the federal level would be followed by similar substitutions at the state and local level. For simplicity, we consider the economic effect of substitutions at all levels simultaneously. Because an important advantage of fundamental tax reform is the possibility, at least at the outset, of radically simplifying tax rules, it makes little sense to assume that these rules would continue to govern state and local income taxes, even if federal income taxes were abolished.

The third issue in the debate will be the impact of the *federal deficit*. Nearly two decades of economic disputation over this issue have failed to produce a clear resolution. No doubt this dispute will continue to occupy the next generation of fiscal economists, as it has the previous generation. An effective device for insulating the discussion of fundamental tax reform from the budget debate is to limit consideration to revenue neutral proposals. This device was critical to the eventual enactment of the Tax Reform Act of 1986 and is, we believe, essential to progress in the debate over fundamental tax reform.

9.3.1. Tax Reform Proposals

The subtraction method for implementing a consumption tax is the basis for the ingenious flat tax proposed by Hall and Rabushka (1995). The Hall–Rabushka (HR) proposal divides tax collections between firms and households. Firms would expense the cost of all purchases from other businesses, including purchases of investment goods, as in the subtraction method for implementing a consumption tax. However, firms would also deduct all purchases of labor services, so that labor compensation – wages and salaries, health insurance, pension contributions, and other supplements – would be taxed at the individual level. This would permit the introduction of allowances for low-income taxpayers in order to redistribute economic resources through the flat tax.

Taxation of business firms under the HR proposal is different from the current income tax system in three ways. First, a flat rate is applied to the tax base; hence the identification of this proposal as the flat tax. Second, interest paid by the firm is treated as part of property income and is no longer deducted from the tax base. Third, investment spending is recovered through immediate writeoffs rather than depreciation over time, so that the effective tax rate on capital is zero. The inclusion of interest payments in the tax base eliminates the differential tax treatment of debt and equity, ensuring the financial neutrality of the tax system.

The federal tax rate proposed by HR is 19% for both businesses and individuals. However, if unused depreciation from capital accumulation predating the tax reform is allowed as a deduction from the tax base, the tax rate will rise to 20.1%. Personal allowances under the Hall–Rabushka proposal for 1995 are $16,500 for married taxpayers filing jointly, $14,000 for head of household, and $9,500 for single taxpayer. The allowance for each dependent is $4,500. A family of four with two adults filing jointly, for example, is entitled to a deduction of $25,500. Personal allowances are indexed to the Consumer Price Index (Hall–Rabushka, 1995, p. 144).

The Armey–Shelby (AS) proposal, introduced in the 104th Congress by Representative Richard Armey and Senator Dick Shelby, is best considered as a variant of the HR flat tax proposal. The principal differences between HR and AS are the flat tax rate and the level of personal allowances. The AS flat tax rate is 20% for the first two years and 17% thereafter. Compared with the HR tax rate of 19%, the AS rate is higher during the first two years by one percentage point, but lower by two percentage points thereafter. Personal allowances under AS are $21,400 for married taxpayers filing jointly, $14,000 for head of household, and $10,700 for single taxpayers. The allowance for each dependent is $5,000, so that a family of four with two adults filing jointly would be entitled to a deduction of $31,400.

The AS proposal is more generous to the taxpayer than the HR proposal in the sense that the flat tax rate is lower after the first two years and the family allowances are higher. The natural question is, would the AS proposal raise sufficient tax revenue to replace the income tax system? Since Hall and Rabushka have calibrated their proposal to the National Income and Product Accounts of 1993 and set the flat tax rate to make the HR proposal revenue-neutral, it is clear that tax revenue under the AS would fall short of the level required for neutrality. We will show, however, that revenues raised under either flat tax proposal would be substantially below this level.

A proposal for replacing the income tax system with a national retail sales tax has been introduced by Representatives Dan Schaefer, Bill Tauzin (ST), and others.[3] The ST proposal replaces personal and corporate income taxes, estate and gift taxes, and some excise taxes with a 15% national retail sales tax on a tax-inclusive consumption base. On this definition the tax base would include sales tax revenues as well as the value of retail sales to consumers. The tax rate would be lower on a tax-inclusive basis than a tax-exclusive basis, that is, where the sales tax base excluded the tax revenues. The tax rate under the ST proposal would be 17.6% on a tax-exclusive base. The ST proposal allows a family consumption refund for qualified family units in order to redistribute economic resources.[4]

Americans for Fair Taxation (AFT) have advanced an alternative proposal for a national retail sales tax. The AFT proposal replaces personal and corporate income

---

[3] The ST proposal was first introduced in the 104th Congress of 1996, and again in the 105th Congress in 1997. See Schaefer et al. (1997).

[4] The refund is equal to the tax-inclusive tax rate times the lesser of the poverty level and the wage and salary income of the family unit.

taxes, estate and gift taxes, and the payroll tax with a 23% national retail sales tax on a tax-inclusive base similar to that of the ST proposal (29.9% on a tax-exclusive base). The AFT proposal is more ambitious than the ST proposal in that it replaces the payroll tax, used to fund entitlements such as Social Security and Medicare, as well as the income tax system. This has two important implications. The first is that the unfunded liabilities of the entitlement systems would ultimately have to be funded through the sales tax. The second is that a revenue-neutral tax rate would be very high.

Gale (1999) estimates that, assuming perfect compliance and no politically motivated erosion of the statutory tax base, the tax-exclusive sales tax rate has to be as high as 31.6% for the ST proposal and 53.6% for the AFT proposal to achieve revenue neutrality.[5] Comparison of these tax rates with the proposed rates of 17.6% and 29.9% reveals the dimensions of the potential revenue shortfall. Furthermore, if state and local income taxes are replaced along with the federal taxes, the tax rates have to be about 30% higher for the AFT proposal and 50% higher for the ST proposal.

The very high tax rate of the national retail sales tax provides powerful incentives for tax evasion and renders effective tax administration difficult. Although it is possible to mitigate compliance problems, controlling the erosion of the tax base within a tolerable limit appears to be more problematic.[6] To achieve revenue neutrality through a national retail sales tax, we consider a number of alternatives to the ST and AFT proposals. In all of these alternatives, the capital income tax would be eliminated. We construct a prototype NRST and then develop alternative proposals by varying the degree of progressivity and the division of revenues between a labor income tax and a sales tax. Both the sales tax and the labor income tax may be flat, that is, proportional to the tax base, or may be made progressive by introducing a system of family allowances.

9.3.2. Modeling the Tax Reform Proposals

We maintain the role of the property tax in the existing U.S. tax system in all of our simulations. However, we consider alternative treatments of existing sales taxes on consumption and investment goods. The key tax parameter of the HR and AS proposals is the flat tax rate. If investment is expensed, the effective tax rate on capital income is equal to zero, whatever the flat tax rate, so that the choice of this rate does not affect intertemporal resource allocation. On the other hand, the flat tax

---

[5]   See also discussions in Aaron, Gale, and Sly (1999).
[6]   On tax evasion of the consumption tax, see Murray (1997) and Mikesell (1997). To deal with the complicance problem Zodrow (1999) proposes withholding at the manufacturing and wholesale level, bringing the NRST closer to a VAT. To reduce the administative burden and ensure the deduction of investment spending, he proposes a "business tax rebate" for inputs that can be used for both business and personal purposes. The purchaser of such an input would pay the tax at the time of the purchase, but business purchasers would be eligible for a tax rebate.

rate plays a very important role in the labor–leisure choice of households. It also affects the tax burden on capital assets already accumulated at the time of the tax reform

Provided that the value added by a business firm is greater than its compensation for labor input, the marginal and average tax rates are the same as the statutory flat rate. However, a large number of households are exempt from taxation due to personal allowances. For tax-exempt households, the average tax rate is zero, and for most of them, the marginal tax rate is zero as well. We represent the distribution of marginal tax rates between zero and the flat tax rate by the average marginal tax rate for labor income. At the same time, we measure the average tax burden on labor income by the average tax rate.

Under the HR proposal the statutory flat tax rate is 19%. Under the AS proposal a flat tax rate of 20% applies in the first two years after the tax reform, followed by a lower rate of 17% thereafter. These rates are chosen in order to replace federal tax revenues. In our model all three levels of government – federal, state, and local – are combined into a single government sector. If the federal income tax is replaced by a flat tax, we assume that the state and local income taxes are also replaced by a flat tax. In addition, we assume that the state and local flat tax is deductible at the federal level. We then calibrate the flat tax system to the 1996 federal, state, and local income tax revenues.

Specifically, we assume that the federal, state, and local flat tax revenues are generated according to the equations

$$R_F^f = (B - R_F^s) \cdot t_F^f \tag{1}$$

$$R_F^s = B \cdot t_F^s, \tag{2}$$

where B is the state and local flat tax base, t_F^f and t_F^s are the federal and the state and local flat tax rates, and R_F^f and R_F^s are the corresponding tax revenues. The flat tax rate for the government sector, t_F, is defined as

$$t_F = t_F^s + t_F^f(1 - t_F^s), \tag{3}$$

where the expression in the parentheses reflects the deduction of state and local taxes at the federal level.

Because the federal flat tax rate, t_F^f, is known, we first set federal and state and local revenues, R_F^f and R_F^s, equal to the federal and the state and local corporate income tax revenues of 1996, \$194.5 and \$34.5 billion, respectively. We then solve Eqs. (1) and (2) for the state and local flat tax rate, t_F^s, and obtain the overall flat tax rate, t_F, from Eq. (3). The resulting flat tax rates are $t_F = 0.2164$ for the HR proposal and $t_F = 0.1943$ for the AS proposal. These rates may be compared with the corporate income tax rate $t_q = 0.3880$ at federal, state, and local levels, corresponding to the federal corporate income tax rate of 0.35 under the 1996 Tax Law.

The average marginal tax rate for labor income is defined as a weighted average of the marginal tax rates of individual taxpayers, where the share of labor income for each taxpayer in total labor income is used as the weight. The average tax rate is simply the total tax revenue divided by the total labor income. Using the same National Income and Product Accounts for 1993 as Hall and Rabushka (1995, p. 57; Table 9.10), we estimate that the average labor income tax rate is 0.0855 for the HR flat tax proposal.

In order to determine the average marginal tax rates for the HR and AS proposals on a consistent basis, we require the distribution of labor income by the marginal tax rate of the individual taxpayer. We use the 1996 Current Population Survey to estimate the average and the average marginal tax rates on labor income for both the HR and AS Flat Tax proposals.[7] We find that the average tax rates on labor income at the federal level, t_L^{af}, are 0.1232 for HR and 0.0961 for AS, and the corresponding average marginal tax rates, t_L^{mf}, are 0.1797 and 0.1551, respectively.

In order to determine the average marginal tax rate on labor income for the government sector as a whole, we follow the same procedure as in calculating the marginal rate t_F. In place of the corporate income tax revenues, we use the individual income tax revenues for 1996. The results are that the average marginal tax rate, t_L^m, is 0.2114 for HR and 0.1834 for AS. The corresponding figure for the Tax Law of 1996 is 0.2645. We could have used a similar approach for estimating the average tax rates for the government sector. However, in order to reflect the realities of tax administration, we estimate the average tax rate, t_L^a, as

$$t_L^a = \frac{t_L^{af} \cdot t_{P96}^a}{t_{P96}^{af}},$$

where t_{P96}^a is the average tax rate of individual income in 1996 and t_{P96}^{af} is the average federal tax rate on individual income in the same year.[8] Our estimate of t_L^a is 0.1202 for HR and 0.0938 for AS. These figures may be compared with the corresponding figure of 0.1266 for the 1996 Tax Law, or with the federal tax rate of 0.0855 estimated by Hall and Rabushka.

---

[7] Suppose there are H taxable units indexed by h, $h = 1, \ldots, H$. Let W_k and A_k be the labor income and personal exemptions of taxable unit h. Then the average tax rate at the federal level, t_L^{af}, and the corresponding average marginal tax rate, t_L^{mf}, are defined as

$$t_L^{af} = \frac{\sum_{W_h - A_h > 0}(W_h - A_h)t_F^f}{\sum_{j=1}^{H} W_h}, \quad t_L^{mf} = \frac{\sum_{W_h - A_h > 0} W_h \cdot t_F^f}{\sum_{h=1}^{H} W_h},$$

where t_F^f is the statutory federal flat tax rate applicable to labor. We assume that married couples file jointly. We are indebted to M.S. Ho for these calculations. For more details, see Ho and Stiroh (1998).

[8] Note that t_{P96}^{af} is estimated from a sample of tax returns in the Statistics of Income and t_L^{af} is based on the data from the Current Population Survey for 1996. We estimate that $t_{P96}^a = 0.1411$ and $t_{P96}^{af} = 0.1445$, based on the U.S. National Income and Product Accounts. This procedure adjusts the average tax rate of labor income for less than perfect tax compliance and administration.

We can summarize the tax rates as follows:

Hall–Rabushka
    Business tax rate, average and marginal: $t_F = 0.2164$
    Labor income tax rate, marginal: $t_L^m = 0.2114$
    Labor income tax rate, average: $t_L^a = 0.1201$
Armey–Shelby
    Business tax rate, average and marginal: $t_F = 0.1943$
    Labor income tax rate, marginal: $t_L^m = 0.1834$
    Labor income tax rate, average: $t_L^a = 0.0938$
Tax Law of 1996
    Corporate income tax rate: $t_q = 0.3880$
    Labor income tax rate, marginal: $t_L^m = 0.2645$
    Labor income tax rate, average: $t_L^a = 0.1266$.

We develop a number of alternative plans for the NRST by combining a sales tax on consumption and a labor-income tax. In all of the alternative plans the capital income tax is eliminated. Although the existing sales taxes on investment spending may or may not be abolished, we prefer the policies with no sales tax on investment. As before, property taxes are left unchanged in our simulations. The alternative proposals differ in progressivity. They also differ in the division of revenue-raising roles between the sales tax and the labor income tax. This division has the effect of altering the relative tax burden between labor income and capital accumulated prior to the tax reform.

In order to develop alternative plans, we first construct a prototype sales tax and a prototype labor-income tax. The labor-income tax is based on the HR flat tax proposal. The sales tax is a flat tax rate with personal exemptions. We set the proportion of total exemptions in retail sales equal to the proportion of total exemptions in HR, which is 0.3516. Assuming that the federal sales tax rate is 17%, as in Aaron and Gale (1996), Table 1.1, we estimate that the corresponding average tax rate is 11.02%. In order to represent the current sales taxes, used mainly by the state and local governments, we add a flat tax of 5.8% to the progressive tax system we have derived. At this point, we have a progressive NRST with a marginal tax rate of 22.80% and an average tax rate of 16.82%.

We construct eight alternative NRST plans. Each plan consists of two parts – a sales tax and a labor-income tax. The first two plans are limited to a sales tax, whereas the last two consist of a labor-income tax alone. Although these two plans are not sales taxes in the usual sense, they provide benchmarks for analyzing the effects of the NRST plans on resource allocation and economic welfare. We evaluate the efficiency of resource allocation under all eight plans. However, we consider plans involving a sales tax as the most interesting proposals for implementing the NRST.

In Plan 1, a progressive NRST replaces the capital and labor income taxes. Since the revenue requirement is very large in relation to the sales tax base, we start with tax rates twice as high as those of the prototype, that is

$$t_C = 2^*(0.17 + 0.058) = 0.4560$$

and

$$t_C^a = 2^*(0.1102 + 0.058) = 0.3365,$$

$$t_L^m = t_L^a = 0,$$

where t_C is the average marginal tax rate and t_C^a is the average tax rate. These sales tax rates serve as the starting values for our simulations and will be adjusted to meet the budget constraints of the government sector.

In Plan 2, we remove the progressivity from the sales tax of Plan 1 and set the marginal tax rate equal to the average tax rate, so that

$$t_C = t_C^a = 0.3365,$$

$$t_L^m = t_L^a = 0.$$

In Plan 3, we introduce the prototype labor-income tax from the HR flat tax proposal and combine it with the prototype sales tax with the progressivity removed. As a consequence, the sales tax is flat, whereas the labor income tax has the same progressivity as IIR. Compared with Plan 1, the role of the sales tax as an instrument for tax collection and redistribution is substantially reduced. Specifically, we set

$$t_C = t_L^a = 0.1682,$$

$$t_L^m = 0.2114,$$

$$t_L^a = 0.1202.$$

In Plan 4, we replace the current income tax system with the combination of a flat sales tax and a flat labor-income tax. Since no attempt is made to redistribute economic resources through the tax system, this plan may be politically unpopular. On the other hand, the efficiency loss is minimal. In this sense, Plan 4 provides a useful benchmark for the possible trade-offs between equity and efficiency. The sales tax rate is set at the average tax rate of the prototype NRST and the labor-income tax rate is set at the average tax rate of the HR proposal, so that

$$t_C = t_C^a = 0.1682,$$

$$t_L^m = t_L^a = 0.1202.$$

Plan 5 combines a progressive sales tax with a flat labor-income tax. Although the sales tax redistributes economic resources, the revenue-raising function is shared with the flat labor tax and there is less redistribution than in Plan 1. The sales tax is the same as in the prototype sales tax plan and the rate of the labor-income tax is set at the average tax rate of the HR proposal, so that

$$t_C = 0.2280,$$

$$t_C^a = 0.1682,$$

$$t_L^m = t_L^a = 0.1202.$$

Plan 6 combines the prototype sales tax with the labor income tax of the HR proposal. Because both segments of the plan are progressive, the sacrifice of efficiency may be substantial. The tax parameters are

$$t_C = 0.2280,$$

$$t_C^a = 0.1682,$$

$$t_L^m = 0.2114,$$

$$t_L^a = 0.1202.$$

In Plan 7, the labor income tax is flat and there is no sales tax. The average and the average marginal tax rates of labor income are equal. Since all the replacement tax revenue is raised by the tax on labor, we start with a labor income tax rate twice that of the HR flat tax proposal,

$$t_C = t_C^a = 0,$$

$$t_L^m = t_L^a = 0.2404.$$

Finally, in Plan 8, we introduce an element of progressivity into Plan 7 by setting the average marginal tax rate of labor income at twice the level in the HR proposal:

$$t_C = t_C^a = 0,$$

$$t_L^m = 0.4228,$$

$$t_L^a = 0.2404.$$

Business investment is expensed in the HR and AS flat tax proposals. In the NRST proposals household investment is taxed as consumption, which may be interpreted as a prepayment of taxes on the services of household capital. To represent the flat tax proposals of HR and AS and the various NRST plans, we must determine the allocation of gross private investment among the three private sectors – corporate, noncorporate, and household. To determine the investment in each of these sectors, we first allocate the total value of investment among the six asset categories in proportion to the capital stock. This is equivalent to assuming that the capital stocks in the three private sectors grow at the same rate.

Next we add the current value of economic depreciation to obtain the gross investment, VIG_i, in asset category i, so that

$$VIG_i = \left(\delta_i + \frac{VIN}{VK} \right) VK_i$$

where δ_i is the economic depreciation rate, VIN is the total value of net private investment, VK is the total current value of lagged private capital stock, and VK_i is the current value of lagged capital stock in asset category i. In this expression VIN and VK are defined as

$$VIN = (IS - IG - IR) \cdot PI - D$$

$$VK = VKL(1 + \pi),$$

where IS is the total supply of investment goods, IG is the government demand for investment goods, IR is the demand from the rest of the world, PI is the price of investment goods, and D is economic depreciation on private capital. In a steady state the allocation of gross investment across the asset categories takes a simpler form,

$$VIG_i = [(1 - \alpha_T)(1 + n) - (1 - \delta_i)]VK_i,$$

where $-\alpha_T$ is the rate of technical change, and n is the growth rate of time endowment.

We preserve revenue neutrality by requiring the government sector to follow the same time paths of real spending and government debt under all the tax reform proposals. We also fix the time path of the claims on the rest of the world. These assumptions are necessary to separate the economic impacts of alternative tax policies from the effects of changes in the government budget and the balance of payments. Government revenues must be adjusted through changes in the tax policy instruments to satisfy the government budget constraints in every period along the transition path to a steady state.

In some simulations we take the flat tax rate in the HR and AS proposals or the sales tax or labor income tax rates in the NRST plans to be fixed and vary other taxes in order to meet the government budget constraints. In other simulations we vary the tax rates themselves to meet these constraints, so that the rates we have derived serve only as starting values. For example, in the case of the HR and AS proposals, the simulation with adjustment of the flat tax rate, where t_F, t_L^m, and t_L^a are adjusted simultaneously and in the same proportion, will generate a configuration of the U.S. tax system that is revenue-neutral. Similarly, in the analysis of an NRST plan, adjustment of the sales tax and the labor-income tax rates achieves revenue neutrality. In the sales tax adjustment, t_C and t_C^a are adjusted in the same proportion; in the labor-income tax adjustment, t_L^m and t_L^a are adjusted similarly.

In the HR and AS proposals the effective tax rate on investment is zero, reducing the tax wedge between returns to investors and earnings of savers. The remaining distortion at the intertemporal margin of resource allocation is due to the property tax and the sales tax on investment goods. In the NRST all taxes on capital income are abolished and the sales tax on investment goods is abolished as well in some of the alternatives we consider. The only remaining source of intertemporal distortions is the property tax. In our model the sales tax on investment goods affects the producer price of investment goods. Therefore, formulas for the cost of capital are not affected by the tax.

The price of capital services from one unit of capital, P_j, is

$$P_j = \left[RD_j + \frac{1 - D \cdot t_F}{1 - t_F} \cdot t_s^P \right] \cdot q_j, \quad j = QS, QL, MS, ML \tag{4}$$

$$P_j = [RD_j + (1 - D \cdot t_L^m)t_j^P] \cdot q_j, \quad j = HS, HL, \tag{5}$$

where RD is the gross discount rate, t_F is the flat tax rate, t_j^P is the property tax rate, q_j is the lagged price of a capital asset, the subscript j stands for the short-lived and long-lived assets in the corporate, noncorporate, and household sectors, and s stands for the three private sectors. Thus $s = q$ if $j = QS, QL$; $s = m$ if $j = MS, ML$; and $s = h$ if $j = HS, HL$. $D = 1$ if property tax is deductible and $D = 0$ otherwise.

In the HR and AS flat tax proposals, the labor income tax is the only tax, other than property tax, that is collected directly from the household sector. Hence, we allow the property tax as a deduction from labor income. The gross discount rate, RD_j, is defined as the sum of the after-tax real discount rate and the economic depreciation rate adjusted for inflation,

$$RD_j = (1 - \beta_s)(\rho^e - \pi) + \beta_s(i - \pi) + (1 + \pi)\delta_j,$$
$$j = QS, QL, MS, ML, HS, HL, \quad \text{and} \quad s = q, m, h \tag{6}$$

where ρ^e is the after-tax nominal rate of return to equity, i is the nominal interest rate, β_s is the debt/asset ratio, π is inflation rate, and δ_j is the rate of economic depreciation.

Equations (4)–(6) apply to the HR and AS proposals, as well as the NRST. However, Eq. (5) must be interpreted with some care. Investment spending on household assets is included in the sales tax base under the NRST. The most important type of investment spending is the purchase of owner-occupied housing. We model the sales tax on household investment by imposing taxes on sales to the household sector. At the same time we increase the price of capital services by the amount of the sales tax. This treatment of the sales tax on household investment is equivalent to prepayment of the consumption tax on household capital services. Thus, we may interpret (5) as the "producer" price of household capital services, while the corresponding "consumer" price is defined as

$$P_j^C = (1 + t_C)[RD_j + t_h^P] \cdot q_j, \quad j = HS, HL, \tag{7}$$

where we set $D = 0$.

TABLE 9.10. *Tax parameters of fundamental tax reform proposals – Lump sum tax adjustment, central cases*

Tax reform proposal and welfare effect	t_q or t_F	t_L^m	t_L^a	t_C	t_C^a	t_I
1. Base Case						
(1) Tax Law of 1996	0.3880	0.2645	0.1265	0.0580	0.0580	0.0580
2. Flat Tax						
(1) Hall–Rabushka	0.2164	0.2114	0.1202	0.0580	0.0580	0.0580
(2) Armey–Shelby	0.1943	0.1834	0.0938	0.0580	0.0580	0.0580
3. National Retail Sales Tax						
(1) Progressive sales tax and no labor income tax	0.0 0.0	0.0	0.4560	0.3365	0.0	
(2) Proportional sales tax and no labor income tax	0.0 0.0	0.0	0.3365	0.3365	0.0	
(3) Proportional sales tax and progressive labor income tax	0.2114	0.1202	0.1682	0.1682	0.0	0.0
(4) Proportional sales tax and proportional labor income tax	0.0	0.1202	0.1202	0.1682	0.1682	0.0
(5) Progressive sales tax and proportional labor income tax	0.0	0.1202	0.1202	0.2280	0.1682	0.0
(6) Progressive sales tax and progressive labor income tax	0.0	0.2114	0.1202	0.2280	0.1682	0.0
(7) No sales tax, proportional and labor income tax	0.0	0.2404	0.2404	0.0	0.0	0.0
(8) No sales tax, progressive labor income tax	0.0	0.4228	0.2404	0.0	0.0	0.0

Notes: 1. In the central case, $t_C = t_C^a = t_I = 0.058$ for the flat tax (HR and AS), and $t_I = 0$ for the NRST. 2. In the cases of flat tax adjustment, the values of t_F, t_L^m, and t_L^a in the table are used as the starting values for iteration. Similarly for sales tax and labor income tax adjustment. Parameters: t_F: flat tax rate; t_L^m: average marginal tax rate of labor income; t_L^a: average tax rate of labor income; t_C: average marginal tax rate of retail sales; t_C^a: average tax rate of retail sales; t_I: sales tax rate of investment spending.

9.3.3. Welfare Impacts of Fundamental Tax Reform

Table 9.10 summarizes the key tax parameters of the fundamental tax reform proposals and Tables 9.11 and 9.12 report the estimated welfare effects. In Table 9.11, we present two sets of results. In the first set of simulations the corporate and individual income taxes of 1996 are replaced by the HR or AS flat tax, whereas sales

TABLE 9.11. *Welfare effects of fundamental tax reform – Flat tax*
(billions of 1997 dollars)

Tax reform proposal and revenue adjustment	Welfare effect	
	$t_C = t_C^a = t_I = 0.058$	$t_C = t_C^a = t_I = 0$
1. Hall–Rabushka		
Lump-sum tax	3637.3	4991.6
Flat tax	2056.2	814.9
Sales taxes	2582.2	–
Flat tax and sales taxes	2240.1	–
2. Armey–Shelby		
Lump-sum tax	4173.0	5392.2
Flat tax	1229.3	−756.0
Sales taxes	2476.2	–
Flat tax and sales taxes	1772.7	–

Note: Inflation is fixed at 4% per year. t_C: marginal sales tax rate of consumption goods. t_C^a: average sales tax rate of consumption goods. t_I: flat sales tax rate of investment goods.

taxes on consumption and investment goods remain unchanged (column 2). In the second set of simulations we replace the sales taxes as well, so that $t_C = t_C^a = 0$ and $t_I = 0$ (column 3). In the second set of simulations, all the intertemporal distortions, except for the property tax, are eliminated because $t_I = 0$.

With the initial flat tax rates both the HR and the AS proposals fall short of revenue neutrality. The welfare impact of these proposals depends on the tax instrument chosen to raise the necessary revenue. If sales taxes on consumption goods and investment goods are maintained, the welfare gains are in the ranges of $2.06–3.64 trillion for HR and $1.23–4.17 trillion for AS, measured in 1996 dollars. Converted into annual flows at the long-run real private rate of return of 4.45%, the welfare gains are in the range of $92–162 billion for HR and $55–186 billion for AS. The largest welfare gains are obtained when a lump-sum tax is used to compensate for the revenue shortfall. Because the lump-sum tax is not available in practice, the welfare gains for the lump-sum tax adjustment may be interpreted as the potential gains in welfare from a flat tax proposal.

If both income taxes and sales taxes are replaced by a flat tax and a lump-sum tax is used to compensate for the revenue shortfall, the welfare gains are very substantial, $3.64 trillion for HR and $4.17 trillion for AS. If sales taxes, as well as corporate and individual income taxes, are replaced with a flat tax and a lump-sum tax is used to raise the additional revenue, the gains are even larger, almost $5 trillion for HR and $5.39 trillion for AS. The welfare gains from the flat tax proposals are lower when distorting taxes are increased to meet the revenue requirement. The actual welfare gain depends critically on the taxes that are replaced and the tax distortions introduced to meet the revenue requirement. If the flat tax rate is adjusted to make

TABLE 9.12. *Welfare effects of fundamental tax reform – National retail sales tax (billions of 1997 dollars)*

Tax reform proposal and revenue adjustment	Welfare effect	
	$t_I = 0.058$	$t_I = 0$
1. Grad Sales, No Labor-Income Tax		
Lump-sum tax	1830.1	2583.9
Labor-income tax	–	–
Sales taxes	3268.5	3323.6
Labor-income tax and sales taxes	–	–
2. Flat Sales, No Labor-Income Tax		
Lump-sum tax	3500.8	4115.6
Labor-income tax	–	–
Sales taxes	4540.8	4686.8
Labor-income tax and sales taxes	–	–
3. Flat Sales Tax, Graduated Labor-Income Tax		
Lump-sum tax	1924.0	2678.3
Labor-income tax	3413.0	3086.9
Sales taxes	2686.1	2871.3
Labor-income tax and sales taxes	2992.9	2965.8
4. Flat Sales, Flat Labor-Income Tax		
Lump-sum tax	3838.3	4427.8
Labor-income tax	4504.9	4697.3
Sales taxes	4545.5	4696.5
Labor-income tax and sales taxes	4530.3	4697.3
5. Graduated Sales Tax, Flat Labor-Income Tax		
Lump-sum tax	2965.1	3633.8
Labor-income tax	3666.8	3868.9
Sales taxes	3888.8	3946.0
Labor-income tax and sales taxes	3796.9	3910.1
6. Graduated Sales Tax, Graduated Labor-Income Tax		
Lump-sum tax	769.3	1609.3
Labor-income tax	2233.3	1802.7
Sales taxes	1694.0	1737.5
Labor-income tax and sales taxes	1921.3	1766.5
7. No Sales, Flat Labor-Income Tax		
Lump-sum tax	4106.1	4664.3
Labor-income tax	4354.6	4527.8
Sales taxes	–	–
Labor-income tax and sales taxes	–	–
8. No Sales, Graduated Labor Tax		
Lump-sum tax	−1806.8	−818.2
Labor-income tax	−2869.3	−4447.9
Sales taxes	–	–
Labor-income tax and sales taxes	–	

Note: 1. Inflation is fixed at 4% per year. t_I: Rate on investment goods.

up the revenue shortfall, substitution of the HR flat tax for corporate and individual income taxes would produce a welfare gain of only $2.06 trillion. If sales taxes are also replaced the gain falls to $0.81 trillion. The corresponding welfare gains for the AS flat tax are $1.23 trillion for replacement of income taxes and a negative $0.76 trillion for replacement of sales taxes as well. These results imply that the distortions resulting from the flat tax are worse than those from the sales tax at the margin.

The most interesting cases in Tables 9.11 and 9.12 are the simulations where personal allowances are held fixed and the flat tax rate is adjusted to make up lost revenue. The welfare gains are $2.06 trillion for the HR proposal and $1.23 trillion for the AS proposal. The reason for the relatively poor performance of the AS proposal is the higher marginal tax rate on labor.[9] Recall that the HR proposal has a higher tax rate than the AS proposal. However, given the constraint imposed by fixed time paths of government debt and real government spending, the more generous personal allowances in the AS proposal imply a higher tax rate. Table 9.12 reports the welfare effects of the six plans for replacing the corporate and individual income taxes with an NRST and the two additional plans for replacing income taxes with a labor income tax. We present two sets of simulations – one with the sales tax on investment goods and the other without. First, note that the case without a sales tax on investment goods is more in the spirit of the NRST, which exempts sales of investment goods from taxation. Unsurprisingly, the cases with sales taxes on investment removed are generally more efficient than those with sales taxes unchanged ($t_I = 0.058$).

Second, in Plans 1 through 6, a sales tax is included as a part of the replacement tax policy; the tax parameters in Panel 3 of Table 9.10, together with sales taxes on investment goods ($t_I = 0.058$ or $t_I = 0$), generate revenue surpluses and require either a negative lump sum tax or a decrease in tax rates. This explains the fact that welfare gains under the lump-sum tax adjustment are lower than under other tax adjustments.[10] Third, except for Plan 8 and possibly for Plan 6, the welfare gains are impressive. Plan 4, with flat sales and labor-income taxes and no tax on investment goods ($t_I = 0$), attains a welfare gain of $4.70 trillion, more than five times the corresponding gain for the HR flat tax proposal. However, Plan 2 and Plan 7 are not far behind in terms of gains in welfare. Finally, the welfare gains attainable with the progressive Plans 1, 3, and 5 are also much higher than those of the HR and AS flat tax proposals.

A second set of comparisons that is highly relevant to deliberations about tax reform is the cost of progressivity. One of the most attractive features of the HR and AS flat tax proposals is the possibility of introducing a system of family allowances in order to preserve the important function of the existing U.S. tax system

---

[9]   A high flat tax rate implies a heavy lump-sum tax on "old" capital, offsetting the distorting effects of the tax on labor.

[10] Revenue shortfalls occur in Plan 7 with $t_I = 0$ and Plan 8 with either $t_I = 0.058$ or $t_I = 0$.

in redistributing economic resources. Plan 1 for the NRST also retains this feature of the tax system, but generates welfare gains of $3.32 trillion, exceeding those of the HR flat tax proposal by more than 50%. Of course, a sales tax can be employed to compensate for the revenue shortfall of the HR flat tax, reducing the difference between the welfare gains. However, the NRST is clearly superior to the flat tax as an approach to tax reform when both retain an element of progressivity.

The costs of progressivity can be ascertained by comparing the welfare gains between Plan 1, a progressive sales tax, and Plan 2, a flat sales tax. With no sales tax on investment goods and adjustment of the sales tax on consumption goods to achieve revenue neutrality, the gain in welfare from eliminating progressivity is $1.36 trillion, added to the welfare gain of a progressive sales tax of $3.32 trillion for an overall gain of $4.69 trillion. Similar comparisons can be made between Plan 3 with a flat sales tax and a progressive labor-income tax and Plan 4 with flat sales and labor-income taxes. The welfare gains from eliminating progressivity are $1.61 trillion when the labor income tax is used to achieve revenue neutrality and $1.83 trillion when the sales tax is used for this purpose. Other comparisons between progressive and flat versions of the NRST given in Tables 9.11 and 9.12 generate estimates of the cost of progressivity that are similar in magnitude.

Because taxes distort resource allocation, a critical requirement for a fair comparison among alternative tax reform proposals is that all proposals must raise the same amount of revenue. It is well known that the ST and AFT sales tax proposals fail to achieve revenue neutrality and tax rates must be increased substantially above the levels proposed by the authors of the plans.[11] The authors of the HR flat tax proposal have calibrated their tax rates to the National Income and Product Account for 1993 in such a way that the resulting tax regime is revenue neutral. It is clear that the AS proposal falls short of revenue neutrality because it is more generous in personal allowances and applies a lower tax rate than the HR proposal. As it turns out, however, the HR proposal also raises too little revenue to be neutral.

Based on the federal flat tax rate proposed by Hall and Rabushka, we have estimated three tax rates under the assumption that the state and local income taxes are also replaced by a flat tax. Specifically, we start with the flat tax rate $t_F = 0.2164$, the marginal tax rate on labor income $t_L^m = 0.2114$, and the average tax rate on labor income $t_L^a = 0.1202$. In order to meet the government sector revenue requirement, these tax rates must be increased by a factor of 1.27–1.33. It follows that the statutory federal flat tax rate must be increased from 19% to 24–25%. The problem is even more severe with the AS proposal, where the tax rates must be increased by a factor of 1.60–1.67, implying that the proposed federal flat tax rate must be increased from 17% to 27–28%.

The need for a major upward adjustment in the flat tax rate conflicts with the fact that HR is originally designed to be revenue-neutral. The explanation is that the data

---

[11] For example, see Aaron and Gale (1996) and Gale (1999).

set employed by Hall and Rabushka, the U.S. National Income and Product Accounts of 1993, was generated under a tax system with a significant tax burden on capital.[12] Unsurprisingly, they found a large tax base in the business sector. Although the flat tax imposes a lump-sum tax on "old" capital accumulated before the tax reform, the flat tax does not impose any tax burden on "new" capital accumulated through investment after the reform. The tax base of the business portion of the tax shrinks dramatically and a large revenue shortfall emerges, requiring an increase in the flat tax rate.

From the point of view of efficiency the most attractive approach to tax reform we have considered is Plan 4 for the NRST, which combines a flat sales tax with a flat labor-income tax and eliminates sales taxes on investment goods. In Panel 3 of Table 9.10 we see that this requires an initial sales-tax rate of 15.9% and a labor-income-tax rate of 11.3% with both rates gradually declining over time. The welfare gain would be diminished relatively little by shifting the burden toward the labor income tax, as in Plan 7. The combination of an NRST collected at the retail level and a labor-income tax collected as at present would be administratively attractive and would generate welfare gains amounting to more than half of the gross domestic product in 1997, the benchmark year for our simulations.

9.4. CONCLUSIONS

Our final objective is to evaluate the cost of capital as a practical guide to reform of taxation and government spending. Our primary focus is U.S. tax policy, because the cost of capital has been used much more extensively in the U.S. than other countries. Auerbach and Jorgenson (1980) introduced the key concept, the marginal effective tax rate, early in the debate over the U.S. Economic Recovery Tax Act of 1981. They showed that the tax policy changes of the early 1980s, especially the 1981 Tax Act, increased barriers to efficient allocation of capital.

By contrast, we showed that the Tax Reform Act of 1986 substantially reduced barriers to efficiency.[13] The erosion of the income-tax base to provide incentives for investment and saving was arrested through vigorous and far-reaching reforms. Incentives were sharply curtailed and efforts were made to equalize marginal effective tax rates among assets. The shift toward expenditure and away from income as a tax base was reversed. Jorgenson's international comparisons of 1993 showed that these reforms had important parallels in other industrialized countries.

The cost-of-capital approach has also proved its usefulness in pointing the direction for future tax reforms. For this purpose information about the cost of capital

---

[12] In 1993, the corporate income taxes were $138.3 billion for the Federal Government and $26.9 billion for the state and local governments. In the same year, the Federal Government collected $508.1 billion of income tax from individuals and the state and local governments collected $124.2 billion.

[13] Jorgenson and Yun (1990) and Yun (2000).

must be combined with estimates of the substitutability among different types of outputs and inputs by businesses and households. The most substantial gains from tax reform are associated with equalizing tax burdens on all assets and all sectors. These gains produce a better balance of the tax burden between household assets, especially owner-occupied residential real estate, and business assets, especially plant and equipment in the corporate sector. Combining this with a proportional tax on labor income, efficient taxation of income produces the largest welfare gains of any tax reform proposal that we consider.

During the 1990s, tax reformers have renewed their interest in replacing income by consumption as the basis for taxation. We have shown that the most popular flat tax proposals for achieving this objective would generate substantial welfare benefits. However, a national retail sales tax would produce benefits that are 50% higher. The cost of maintaining a progressive rate structure within the framework of the national retail sales tax is very large. The benefits of a national retail sales tax with a flat rate structure are double those of a flat tax and almost comparable with those of the largest welfare gains from efficient taxation of income.

Our overall conclusion is that the cost of capital and the closely related concept of the marginal effective tax rate have provided an important intellectual impetus for tax reform. The new frontier for analysis of tax and spending programs is to combine the cost of capital and the marginal effective tax rate with estimates of substitution possibilities by businesses and households. This combination makes it possible to evaluate alternative tax reforms programs in terms of economic welfare. We have illustrated this approach for a variety of fundamental tax reforms. Our hope is that these illustrations will serve as an inspiration and a guide for policy makers who share our goal of making the allocation of capital within a market economy more efficient.

APPENDIX: ELASTICITIES AND NONTAX PARAMETERS

The estimated values of the parameters in our models of consumer and producer behavior provide important information on the responses of consumers and producers to changes in tax policy. In this section we supplement this information by deriving price elasticities of demand and supply implied by our parameter estimates, including the compensated price elasticity of supply for labor services. We also provide elasticities of substitution in consumption and production, including the intertemporal elasticity of substitution, a constant parameter in our model of consumer behavior.

A.1. Consumer Behavior

In our model for consumer behavior the quantity index of full consumption is an index of consumer welfare. The compensated demand functions for the three components of full consumption are obtained by solving the share equations

$$v_D = \alpha_{PD} + B_{PD} \ln PD$$
$$v_H = \alpha_{PH} + B_{PH} \ln PH$$

for the quantities demanded as functions of full consumption and the prices. As an illustration, we consider the compensated demand for consumption goods,

$$C = F \cdot \frac{PF}{PC} v_C,$$

where v_C is the share of consumption goods in full consumption. We obtain the compensated own-price elasticity of demand for consumption goods, say ϵ_{CC}:

$$\epsilon_{CC} = v_C + \frac{\beta_{CC}}{v_C} - 1. \tag{8}$$

Similarly, we obtain the cross-price elasticities of demand,

$$\epsilon_{CL} = v_{LJ} + \frac{\beta_{CL}}{v_C},$$

$$\epsilon_{CH} = v_{HD} + \frac{\beta_{CH}}{v_C},$$

where ϵ_{CL} is the elasticity of demand for consumption goods with respect to the price of leisure and ϵ_{CH} is the elasticity of demand with respect to the price of household capital services. We calculate similar own-price and cross-price elasticities of demand for leisure and household capital services, using pooled estimates for our model of consumer behavior and average shares for the period 1970–1996. The results are presented in panel 2 of Table A.1.

The average share of leisure is more than 68% of full consumption, the share of consumption goods and services is slightly more than 24%, and the share of household capital services is around 7.5%. The own-price elasticity of demand for consumption goods and services is around a third, whereas the own-price elasticity of demand for leisure is only 0.10 and the elasticity of demand for capital services is 0.17. Cross-elasticities of demand are substantial, especially the cross-elasticity of demand for goods with respect to the price of leisure of 0.28; the three commodity groups are substitutes rather than complements.

The compensated elasticity of labor supply is, perhaps, a more familiar parameter than the elasticity of demand for leisure. To derive the compensated elasticity of labor supply, we first consider the following identity for the value of the time endowment $PLH \cdot LH$:

$$PLH \cdot LH - PLJ \cdot LJ = (1 - t_L^m)(PLD \cdot LD + PLG \cdot LG$$
$$+ PLE \cdot LE + PLR \cdot LR).$$

Defining the value of labor supply $PL \cdot L$ as follows,

$$PL \cdot L = PLD \cdot LD + PLG \cdot LG + PLE \cdot LE + PLR \cdot LR,$$

TABLE A.1. *Elasticities of consumer behavior*

1. Basic information

A. *Average shares 1970–1996*

$$v_C = 0.24120$$
$$v_{LJ} = 0.68263$$
$$v_{HD} = 0.07617$$
$$v_{HS} = 0.56948$$

B. *Second-order coefficients*

$$\beta_{CC} = 0.10580$$
$$\beta_{CL} = -0.097349$$
$$\beta_{CH} = -0.0084549$$
$$\beta_{LL} = 0.14657$$
$$\beta_{LH} = -0.049217$$
$$\beta_{HH} = 0.057672$$
$$\beta_{SS}^{H} = 0.161082$$

2. Compensated elasticities (with constant full consumption)

A. *Elasticities of demand*

$$\epsilon_{CC} = -0.32015$$
$$\epsilon_{CL} = 0.27904$$
$$\epsilon_{CH} = 0.041112$$
$$\epsilon_{LC} = 0.098596$$
$$\epsilon_{LL} = -0.10266$$
$$\epsilon_{LH} = 0.0040659$$
$$\epsilon_{HC} = 0.13020$$
$$\epsilon_{HL} = 0.036441$$
$$\epsilon_{HH} = -0.16664$$

B. *Elasticity of labor supply*

$$\epsilon_{LL}^{S} = 0.31653$$

3. Elasticity of intertemporal substitution

$$\sigma^{-1} = 0.39145$$

4. Elasticities of intratemporal substitution

$$e_{CL} = -0.40907$$
$$e_{CH} = -0.26597$$
$$e_{LH} = -0.16753$$
$$e_{HD} = -0.34299$$

we obtain

$$PLH \cdot LH - PLJ \cdot LJ = (1 - t_L^m)PL \cdot L.$$

Under the assumption that relative prices of the time endowment, leisure, labor supply, and the components of labor demand are fixed, we obtain the following expression for the compensated elasticity of labor supply, say ϵ_{LL}^{S}:

$$\epsilon_{LL}^{S} = -\epsilon_{LL} \frac{PLJ \cdot LJ}{PLH \cdot LH - PLJ \cdot LJ}. \tag{9}$$

We employ the average ratio of the values of leisure and labor supply for the period 1970–1996 in estimating this elasticity; the result, given at the bottom of panel 2, Table A.1, is 0.31653. The elasticity of intertemporal substitution in consumption is the inverse of σ, estimated from the transition equation for full consumption,

$$\ln \frac{F_t}{F_{t-1}} = \frac{1}{\sigma}[\ln(1 + r_t) - \ln(1 + \bar{r})] + \epsilon_{F_t}, \quad t = 1, 2, \ldots, T.$$

The estimate of this elasticity, reported in panel 3 of Table A.1, is 0.39145. This parameter describes the rate of adjustment of full consumption to the difference between the real private rate of return and its long-run equilibrium value.

The elasticity of substitution between two consumption goods is defined as the ratio of the proportional change in the ratio of the quantities consumed relative to the proportional change in the corresponding price ratio. The prices of other components are held constant, while the quantities are allowed to adjust to relative price changes. Our estimates of elasticities of substitution are based on parameter values from the pooled estimation of the model of consumer behavior, using average shares for the period 1970–1996.

We first consider substitution between consumption goods and leisure. Using the share equation for consumption goods we can express the elasticity of substitution, say e_{CL}, as follows:

$$e_{CL} = -1 + \frac{\partial \ln v_C}{\partial \ln \left(\frac{PC}{PLJ}\right)} - \frac{\partial \ln v_{LJ}}{\partial \ln \left(\frac{PC}{PLJ}\right)}.$$

Since we are holding the price of household capital services *PHD* constant, we can rewrite this elasticity in the form

$$e_{CL} = -1 + \frac{\beta_{CC}}{v_C} - \frac{\beta_{CL}}{v_{LJ}} - \left(\frac{\beta_{CH}}{v_C} - \frac{\beta_{LH}}{v_{LJ}}\right)\left(\frac{\partial \ln PLJ}{\partial \ln \frac{PC}{PLJ}}\right).$$

Differentiating $\ln \left(\frac{PF}{PLJ}\right)$ with respect to $\partial \ln \left(\frac{PC}{PLJ}\right)$ while holding *PF* and *PHD* constant, we obtain

$$\frac{\partial \ln PLJ}{\partial \ln \left(\frac{PC}{PLJ}\right)} = \frac{v_C}{v_{HD} - 1}.$$

Substituting this expression into our formula for the elasticity of substitution, we obtain

$$e_{CL} = (\epsilon_{CC} - \epsilon_{LC}) - (\epsilon_{CH} - \epsilon_{LH})\frac{v_C}{v_{HD} - 1}. \tag{10}$$

Similarly

$$e_{CH} = (\epsilon_{CC} - \epsilon_{HC}) - (\epsilon_{CL} - \epsilon_{HL})\frac{v_C}{v_{LJ} - 1}$$

and

$$e_{LH} = (\epsilon_{LL} - \epsilon_{HL}) - (\epsilon_{LC} - \epsilon_{HC})\frac{v_{LJ}}{v_C - 1}.$$

We report estimates of the elasticities of substitution in panel 4 of Table A.1. By definition these elasticities are symmetric. The elasticity of substitution between the services of the long-lived and short-lived household assets e_{HD} can be derived along similar lines and estimates are presented at the bottom of panel 4, Table A.1. All of these elasticities are considerably less than one, so that the corresponding value shares rise with an increase in price.

A.2. Producer Behavior

As in our model of consumer behavior, we can define elasticities of substitution in production by allowing the relative quantities to adjust to changes in relative prices, while holding the prices of other inputs and outputs constant. We derive the formulas for the elasticities of substitution in production and estimate these elasticities, based on parameter values from the pooled estimation of our model of producer behavior and the average value shares for the period 1970–1996.

We first consider the elasticity of substitution between labor input and consumption goods output, defined as[14]

$$e_{CL} = -1 + \frac{\partial \ln v_{CS}}{\partial \ln(PCS/PLD)},$$

where the other prices – PIS, PQD, PMD – are held constant. Making use of the share equation for the output of consumption goods, this elasticity of substitution can be rewritten as

$$e_{CL} = -1 + \frac{1}{v_{CS}} \beta_{CC} \frac{\partial \ln PCS}{\partial \ln(PCS/PLD)},$$

where

$$\frac{\partial \ln PCS}{\partial \ln(PCS/PLD)} = \frac{1}{1 - v_{CS}},$$

so that

$$e_{CL} = -1 + \frac{\beta_{CC}}{v_{CS}(1 - v_{CS})}. \tag{11}$$

Similarly, we can derive elasticities of substitution between labor input and investment goods output and between labor and capital services inputs from corporate and

---

[14] We treat inputs and outputs symmetrically and do not distinguish between substitution between outputs and transformation from inputs to outputs.

noncorporate assets:

$$e_{IL} = -1 + \frac{\beta_{II}}{v_{IS}(1 - v_{IS})},$$

$$e_{QL} = -1 + \frac{\beta_{QQ}}{v_{QD}(1 - v_{QD})},$$

$$e_{ML} = -1 + \frac{\beta_{MM}}{v_{MD}(1 - v_{MD})}.$$

The formulas for the elasticities of substitution between outputs and inputs other than labor can be derived along the same lines as for substitution in consumption. It is convenient at this point to introduce symbols for price elasticities of factor demand and product; supply; for example,

$$\epsilon_{II} = v_{IS} + \frac{\beta_{II}}{v_{IS}} - 1, \tag{12}$$

and

$$\epsilon_{IC} = v_{CS} + \frac{\beta_{IC}}{v_{IS}}.$$

As an illustration, the elasticity of substitution between consumption and investment goods outputs is defined by

$$e_{CI} = -1 + \frac{\partial \ln v_{CS}}{\partial \ln(PCS/PIS)} - \frac{\partial \ln v_{IS}}{\partial \ln(PCS/PIS)}.$$

Holding the prices PQD and PMD constant, we can rewrite this elasticity as

$$e_{CI} = (\epsilon_{CC} - \epsilon_{IC}) - (\epsilon_{CQ} + \epsilon_{CM} - \epsilon_{IQ} - \epsilon_{IM})\frac{\partial \ln PIS}{\partial \ln(PCS/PIS)},$$

where

$$\frac{\partial \ln PIS}{\partial \ln(PCS/PIS)} = -\frac{v_{CS}}{v_{CS} + v_{IS}}.$$

We report the results in panel 2 of Table A.2. We also give the elasticities of substitution between the capital services from the short-lived and long-lived assets in the corporate and noncorporate sectors, e_{QD} and e_{MD}. The relative value shares of labor and the two capital inputs rise with a price increase if these elasticities of substitution are less than unity and fall with a price increase if the elasticities are greater than unity. The elasticities of substitution among inputs are less than unity; for example, the elasticities of substitution between labor and corporate capital and between the two types of capital are around one-half, while the elasticity of substitution between labor and noncorporate capital is about 0.7.

TABLE A.2. *Elasticities of producer behavior*

1. Basic information

A. *Average shares*

$v_{CS} = 0.94256$

$v_{IS} = 0.50597$

$v_{QD} = -0.30931$

$v_{MD} = -0.13897$

$v_{QS} = 0.41891$

$v_{MS} = 0.20617$

B. *Second-order coefficients*

$\beta_{CC} = 0.67559$

$\beta_{CI} = -0.58758$

$\beta_{CQ} = -0.035933$

$\beta_{CM} = -0.052074$

$\beta_{II} = 0.28858$

$\beta_{IQ} = 0.21940$

$\beta_{IM} = 0.079597$

$\beta_{QQ} = -0.20393$

$\beta_{QM} = 0.020463$

$\beta_{MM} = -0.047986$

$\beta_{SS}^{Q} = -0.081301$

$\beta_{SS}^{M} = 0.11168$

2. Elasticities of substitution

$e_{CL} = 11.47882$

$e_{IL} = 0.15449$

$e_{QL} = -0.49644$

$e_{ML} = -0.69683$

$e_{CI} = 0.43277$

$e_{CQ} = -0.25525$

$e_{CM} = -0.58933$

$e_{IQ} = -2.43209$

$e_{IM} = -1.17369$

$e_{QM} = -0.46605$

$e_{QD} = -1.33399$

$e_{MD} = -0.31762$

A.3. Nontax Parameters

We conclude this appendix by assigning values to the parameters of our dynamic general equilibrium model of the U.S. economy that cannot be estimated from our econometric models of consumer and producer behavior. These include the ratio of government expenditures to gross domestic product, *SGOV*, the share of unemployed labor time in total labor supply, *SLU*, and the shares of government expenditures, net of interest payments on government debt – *SCG, SIG, SLG, SEL, SER*. These parameters are given in the first three panels of Table A.3.

TABLE A.3. Nontax parameters

1. Size of government

$SGOV = 0.2132$ Government expenditure including debt service/gross domestic product

2. Unemployment

$SLU = 0.0$ Share of unemployed time in total labor supply

3. Allocation of government expenditure, net of interest payments
(1970–1996 averages)

$SCG = 0.1738$	Share of consumption goods
$SIG = 0.1837$	Share of investment goods
$SLG = 0.4889$	Share of labor services
$SEL = 0.1450$	Share of transfer payments
$SER = 0.0085$	Share of transfer to foreigners

4. Government enterprises (1970–1996 averages)

$SLE = 0.0198$	Share of labor used by government enterprises
$SCE = 0.0298$	Ratio of consumption goods produced by government enterprises and the private sector

5. Export–Import

$SCR = -0.0103$	Net export of consumption goods as a fraction of total domestic demand for consumption goods
$SIR = 70.0128$	Net export of investment goods as a fraction of total domestic production of investment goods
$SLR = -0.0001$	Share of exported labor

6. Financial variables (1970–1996 averages)

$\alpha = 0.42620$	Dividend payout ratio
$\beta_q = 0.16524$	Debt/capital ratio in the corporate sector
$\beta_m = 0.19798$	Debt/capital ratio in the noncorporate sector
$\beta_h = 0.28647$	Debt/capital ratio in the household sector
$i_0 = 0.048604$	Real interest rate

7. Other parameters

$LH = 17571$	Total time endowment in efficiency units of 1997
$n = 0.01$	Growth rate of time endowment

8. Wealth composition (steady state)

Government debt/GDP $= 0.20$

Claims on the rest of the world/GDP $= 0.10$

9. Rates of economic depreciation (1996 values)

$\delta_q^S = 0.1367$	Short-lived corporate asset
$\delta_q^L = 0.0175$	Long-lived corporate asset
$\delta_m^S = 0.1533$	Short-lived noncorporate asset
$\delta_m^L = 0.0112$	Long-lived noncorporate asset
$\delta_h^S = 0.1918$	Short-lived household asset
$\delta_h^L = 0.0107$	Long-lived household asset

10. Prices of assets and investment goods (1997 values)

$PK_{QS} = 4.8798$	Short-lived corporate asset
$PK_{QL} = 10.5343$	Long-lived corporate asset
$PK_{MS} = 4.8316$	Short-lived noncorporate asset
$PK_{ML} = 12.5564$	Long-lived noncorporate asset
$PK_{HS} = 4.3224$	Short-lived household asset
$PK_{HL} = 15.6756$	Long-lived household asset
$PI = 1.0683$	Investment goods

11. Relative prices of labor (1980–1996 averages, relative to PLD)

$A_{LH} = 1.0101$	Time endowment (before tax)
$A_{LJ} = 1.0044$	Leisure (before tax)
$A_{LG} = 1.0049$	Labor employed in general government
$A_{LE} = 0.9824$	Labor employed in government enterprises
$A_{LR} = 1.0$	Exported labor (assumption)
$A_{LU} = 1.0$	Unemployed time (assumption)

The next group of parameters includes the proportions of labor employed by government enterprises and net exports of labor services to the total labor supply – *SLE* and *SLR*. It also includes the production of consumption goods by government enterprises as a proportion of the total consumption goods produced by the business sector, *SCE*. Finally, it includes net exports of consumption goods as a proportion of the total domestic demand for consumption goods, *SCR*, and net exports of investment goods as a proportion of the total domestic production of investment goods, *SIR*. This group of parameters is given in the fourth and fifth panels of Table A.3.

The third group of parameters includes the dividend payout ratio of the corporate sector, α, the debt/asset ratios of the corporate, noncorporate, and household sectors, β_q, β_m, and β_h, and the real interest rate. This group of parameters is given in the sixth panel of Table A.3. The parameters – *SGOV*, *SCR*, *SIR* – are used to calibrate the size of government debt and claims on the rest of the world in the steady state of our model of the U.S. economy. All other parameter values are set at the averages for the sample period, 1970–1996.

The fourth group of parameters is given in panels 7 and 8 of Table A.3. These are important determinants of the size and rate of growth of the U.S. economy. These include the time endowment, *LH*, and its growth rate, *n*. They also include steady-state values of government debt and claims on the rest of the world, relative to the U.S. gross domestic product. The time endowment is set at the historical value in 1997; the growth of the time endowment reflects the growth of population as well as changes in the quality of labor.[15]

---

[15] Changes in the quality of the time endowment are due to changes in the composition in the population by age, sex, education, and class of employment. We define separate quality indexes for the time endowment, leisure, and labor employed in the business, government, government enterprises, and rest-of-the-world sectors. Further details are given by Jorgenson, Gollop, and Fraumeni (1987).

During our sample period, 1970–1996, the average annual growth rate of the U.S. time endowment was 1.72% per year. However, we assume that population growth and changes in labor quality will decline in the future and set the growth rate, n, at 1% per year. The initial values of the quantity indices of the capital stock, government debt, and claims on the rest of the world are set at their historical values in 1997. This procedure guarantees that the size of our simulated economy is equal to that of the U.S. economy in 1997.

The ratio of government debt to the U.S. gross domestic product has shown a distinct downward trend after the two world wars. The recent increase in this ratio may be seen as an aberration from the longer-term perspective. Accordingly, we set the steady-state ratio of government debt to gross domestic product at 0.2, close to the postwar low. On similar grounds we set the steady-state ratio of U.S. claims on the rest of the world to the gross domestic product at 0.10. We treat the paths of government debt and claims on the rest of the world as exogenous.

Our fifth group of parameters includes the rates of economic depreciation. We distinguish among corporate, noncorporate, and household sectors and two types of assets, short-lived and long-lived, within each sector. For the corporate and noncorporate sectors the short-lived asset includes producers' durable equipment, while the long-lived asset includes structures, inventories, and land. For the household sector the short-lived asset includes thirteen types of consumers' durables, whereas the long-lived asset includes structures and land.

The rates of economic depreciation of the six classes of assets, two classes within each of the three sectors, are weighted averages of their components with capital stocks at the end of 1996 as weights. For example, the rate of economic depreciation of the long-lived corporate asset is the average depreciation rate of twenty-three categories of nonresidential structures, residential structures, nonfarm inventories, and land employed in the corporate sector. Economic depreciation rates for the six categories of assets are shown in panel 9 of Table A.3.

Finally, we present two sets of relative prices in panels 10 and 11 of Table A.3. The relative prices of the six categories of assets in the corporate, noncorporate, and household sectors and the price of investment goods are the first of these. We set the relative prices of the six categories of assets and investment goods at their 1996 values, adjusted for the inflation of 1997. The relative prices of the time endowment, leisure, and labor employed in the various sectors of the economy and the rest of the world are set at historical averages for the period 1980–1996.

REFERENCES

Henry J. Aaron and William B. Gale (Eds.) (1996), *Economic Effects of Fundamental Tax Reform*, Washington, DC: Brookings Institution.

Henry J. Aaron, William B. Gale, and James Sly (1999), The Rocky Road to Tax Reform, in Henry J. Aaron and Robert D. Reischauer (Eds.), *Setting National Priorities – The 2000 Election and Beyond*, Washington, DC: Brookings Institution, pp. 211–66.

Alan J. Auerbach and Dale W. Jorgenson (1980), "Inflation-Proof Depreciation of Assets," *Harvard Business Review* 58(5): 113–18.

David F. Bradford (1986), *Untangling the Income Tax*. Cambridge, MA: Harvard University Press.

(2000), *Taxation, Wealth, and Saving*. Cambridge, MA: MIT Press.

David F. Bradford and Don Fullerton (1981), "Pitfalls in the Construction and Use of Effective Tax Rates," in Charles R. Hulten (Ed.), *Depreciation, Inflation, and the Taxation of Income from Capital*, Washington, DC: Urban Institute Press, pp. 251–278.

Bureau of Economic Analysis (1977), *The National Income and Product Accounts of the United States, 1929–1974: Statistical Tables, A Supplement to the Survey of Current Business*. Washington, DC: U.S. Department of Commerce.

(1986), *The National Income and Product Accounts of the United States, 1929–1982: Statistical Tables*. Washington, DC: U.S. Department of Commerce.

(1987), *Fixed Reproducible Tangible Wealth in the United States, 1925–1985*. Washington, DC: U.S. Government Printing Office.

Congressional Budget Office (1997), *The Economic Effects of Comprehensive Tax Reform*. Washington, DC: Congress of the United States.

Eric Engen and William Gale (1997), "Macroeconomic Effects of Fundamental Tax Reform: Simulations with a Stochastic Life-Cycle, Overlapping Generations, General Equilibrium Model," In Joint Committee on Taxation, *Joint Committee on Taxation Tax Modeling Project and 1997 Tax Symposium Papers*. Washington, DC: U.S. Government Printing Office, pp. 101–129.

Daniel R. Feenberg, Andrew W. Mitrusi, and James M. Poterba (1997), "Distributional Effects of Adopting a National Retail Sales Tax," in James M. Poterba (Ed.), *Tax Policy and the Economy*, Vol. 11. Cambridge, MA: MIT Press, pp. 49–89.

William F. Fox and Matthew N. Murray (1997), "The Sales Tax and Electronic Commerce: So What's New?" *National Tax Journal* 50(3): 573–92.

Don Fullerton and Diane Lim Rogers (1996), "Lifetime Effects of Fundamental Tax Reform," in Henry Aaron and William B. Gale (Eds.), *Economic Effects of Fundamental Tax Reform*. Washington, DC: Brookings Institution, pp. 321–352.

(1997), "Neglected Effects on the Uses Side: Even a Uniform Tax Would Change Relative Goods Prices," *American Economic Review* 87(2): 120–5.

William G. Gale (1999), "The Required Tax Rate in a National Retail Sales Tax," *National Tax Journal* 52(3): 443–57.

William M. Gentry and R. Glenn Hubbard (1997), "Distributional Implications of Introducing a Broad-Based Consumption Tax," in James M. Poterba (Ed.), *Tax Policy and the Economy*, Vol. 11. Cambridge, MA: MIT Press, pp. 1–47.

Jane G. Gravelle (1995), "The Flat Tax and Other Proposals: Who Will bear the Tax Burden?" CRS Report for Congress. Washington, DC: Congressional Research Service.

Robert E. Hall (1996), "The Effects of Tax Reform on Prices and Assets," in James M. Poterba (Ed.), *Tax Policy and the Economy*, Vol. 10. Cambridge, MA: MIT Press, pp. 71–88.

(1997), "Potential Disruption from the Move to a Consumption Tax," *American Economic Review* 87(2): 147–50.

Robert E. Hall and Alvin Rabushka (1983), *Low Tax, Simple Tax, Fair Tax*. New York: McGraw–Hill.

(1995), *The Flat Tax*, 2nd ed. Stanford, CA: Hoover Institution Press.

Walter Hellerstein (1997), "Transaction Taxes and Electronic Commerce: Designing State Taxes that Works in an Interstate Environment?" *National Tax Journal* 50(3): 593–606.

Mun S. Ho and Kevin J. Stiroh (1998), "Revenue, Progressivity, and the Flat Tax," *Contemporary Economic Policy* 45(1): 85–97.

Joint Committee on Taxation (1987), *General Explanation of the Tax Reform Act of 1986*. Washington, DC: Government Printing Office.

   (1997), *Joint Committee on Taxation Tax Modeling Project and 1997 Tax Symposium Papers*. Washington, DC: Government Printing Office.

Dale W. Jorgenson (1993), "Introduction and Summary," in Dale W. Jorgenson and Ralph Landau (Eds.), *Tax Reform and the Cost of Capital: An International Comparison*. Washington, DC: Brookings Institution, pp. 1–56.

Dale W. Jorgenson, Frank M. Gollop, and Barbara M. Fraumeni (1987), *Productivity and U.S. Economic Growth*. Cambridge, MA: Harvard University Press.

Dale W. Jorgenson and Kun-Young Yun (1990), "Tax Reform and U.S. Economic Growth," *Journal of Political Economy* 98(5, part 2): S151–93.

   (2001), *Lifting the Burden: Tax Reform, the Cost of Capital, and U.S. Economic Growth*. Cambridge, MA: MIT Press.

Charles E. McLure Jr. (1993), "Economic, Administrative, and Political Factors in Choosing a General Consumption Tax," *National Tax Journal* 46(3): 345–58.

Charles E. McLure Jr. and George R. Zodrow (1987), "Treasury I and the Tax Reform Act of 1986: The Economics and Politics of Tax Reform," *Journal of Economic Perspectives* 1: 37–58.

John L. Mikesell (1997), "The American Retail Sales Tax: Considerations on their Structure, Operations and Potential as a Foundation for a Federal Sales Tax," *National Tax Journal* 50(1): 149–65.

Matthew N. Murray (1997), "Would Tax Evasion and Tax Avoidance Undermine a National Sales Tax?" *National Tax Journal* 50(1): 167–82.

Office of Tax Analysis (1990), *Depreciation of Scientific Instruments*. Washington, DC: U.S. Department of the Treasury.

   (1991a), *Depreciation of Business-Use Passenger Cars*. Washington, DC: U.S. Department of the Treasury.

   (1991b), *Depreciation of Business-Use Light Trucks*. Washington, DC: U.S. Department of the Treasury.

Satya Poddar and Morley English (1997), "Taxation of Financial Service Under a Value-Added Tax: Applying the Cash-Flow Approach," *National Tax Journal* 50(1): 89–111.

Shounak Sakar and George R. Zodrow (1993), "Transitional Issues in Moving to a Direct Consumption Tax," *National Tax Journal* 46(3): 359–76.

Dan Schaefer and Billy Tauzin (1997), "National Retail Sales Tax Act of 1996," H.R.3039, introduced in the 104th Congress, March 6, 1996; also "National Retail Sales Tax Act of 1997," H.R.2001, introduced in the 105th Congress, June 19, 1997.

U.S. Department of the Treasury (1987), *Compendium of Tax Research 1987*. Washington, DC: Office of Tax Analysis.

   (1984), *Tax Reform for Simplicity, Fairness, and Economic Growth*, three vols. Washington, DC: U.S. Government Printing Office.

Kun-Young Yun (2000), "The Cost of Capital and Intertemporal General Equilibrium Modeling of Tax Policy Effects," in Lawrence J. Lau (Ed.), *Econometrics and the Cost of Capita*. Cambridge, MA: MIT Press, pp. 227–72.

George R. Zodrow (1995), "Taxation, Uncertainty, and the Choice of a Consumption Tax Base," *Journal of Public Economics* 58(2): 257–65.

   (1999), "The Sales Tax, the VAT, and Taxes in Between – Or, is the Only Good NRST a VAT in Drag?" *National Tax Journal* 52: 429–42.

10 Representative versus Real Households in the Macroeconomic Modeling of Inequality

François Bourguignon, Anne-Sophie Robilliard, and Sherman Robinson

ABSTRACT: To analyze issues of income distribution, most disaggregated macroeconomic models of the computable general equilibrium (CGE) type specify a few representative household groups (RHG) differentiated by their endowments of factors of production. To capture "within-group" inequality, it is often assumed, in addition, that each RHG represents an aggregation of households in which the distribution of relative income within each group follows an exogenously fixed statistical law. Analysis of changes in economic inequality in these models focuses on changes in inequality between RHGs. Empirically, however, analysis of household surveys indicates that changes in overall inequality are usually due at least as much to changes in within-group inequality as to changes in the between-group component. One way to overcome this weakness in the RHG specification is to use real households, as they are observed in standard household surveys, in CGE models designed to analyze distributional issues. In this integrated approach, the full heterogeneity of households, reflecting differences in factor endowments, labor supply, and consumption behavior, can be taken into account. With such a model, one could explore how household heterogeneity combines with market equilibrium mechanisms to produce more or less inequality in economic welfare as a consequence of shocks or policy changes. An integrated microsimulation–CGE model must be quite large and raises many issues of model specification and data reconciliation. This paper presents an alternative, top-down method for integrating microeconomic data on real households into modeling. It relies on a set of assumptions that yield a degree of separability between the macro, or CGE, part of the model and the micro-econometric modeling of income generation at the household level. This method is used to analyze the impact of a change in the foreign trade balance, and the resulting change in the equilibrium real exchange rate, in Indonesia (before the Asian financial crisis). A comparison with the standard RHG approach is provided.

10.1. INTRODUCTION

There are various ways in which distributional issues might be analyzed within the framework of economy-wide models. The most common method relies on defining

This paper was presented in various conferences and seminars. Comments by participants in those seminars are gratefully acknowledged. We thank T. N. Srinivasan for very detailed comments that led to substantial rewriting of the paper. However, we remain responsible for any remaining errors.

219

representative household groups (RHG) characterized by different combinations of factor endowments and possibly different labor supply, saving, and consumption behavior. The heterogeneity of the population of households is integrated into economy-wide or macro modeling through a two-way channel. In one direction, heterogeneity affects aggregate demand and labor supply and their structure in terms of goods and labor types. In the other direction, household income heterogeneity depends on the remuneration rates of the various factors of production, which are determined at the aggregate level.

The amount of heterogeneity that can be accounted for with this approach depends on the number of RHGs specified in the model. It is easier to work with a small number of groups because they can be more easily differentiated and the number of equations to deal with is smaller. To get closer to observed heterogeneity, it is then often assumed that each group results from the aggregation of households that are heterogeneous with respect to their preferences or the productivity of the factors they own. Practically, however, it is assumed that the distribution of relative income *within* a RHG follows some law that is completely exogenous. In general, this law is estimated on the basis of household surveys where the same groups as in the macro model may be identified.[1] This specification permits making the distribution of income "predicted" or simulated with the model closer to actual distribution data. It remains true, however, that the inequality being modeled in counterfactual analyses essentially is the inequality "between" representative groups.

From a conceptual point of view, the difficulty with this approach is that the assumption of exogenous within-group income heterogeneity is essentially ad hoc. If households within a group are different, why would their differences be independent of macroeconomic events? From an empirical point of view, the problem is that observed changes in income distribution are such that changes in within-group inequality generally are at least as important as changes in between-group inequality.[2]

An example may help to understand the nature of the difficulty. Suppose that a sizable proportion of households in a country obtain income from various sources – wage work in the formal or informal sector, farm income, other self-employment income – as is common in many developing countries, especially in Asia. If RHGs are defined, as is usually done, by the sector of activity and the employment status of the head (small farmers, urban unskilled workers in the formal sector, etc.), it does not seem difficult to take into account this multiplicity of income sources. In

---

[1] For early applications of this type of model, see Adelman and Robinson (1978) and Dervis, de Melo, and Robinson (1982), who specified lognormal within-group distributions with exogenous variances. The tradition is now well established – as may be seen in the surveys of CGE models for developing countries by Decaluwe and Martens (1988) and Robinson (1989). This approach may also distinguish among various income sources, in which case within-group variances and covariances must be exogenously specified – see Narayana, Parikh, and Srinivasan (1991).

[2] Starting with Mookherjee and Shorrocks's (1982) study of UK, there are now numerous examples of "within/between" decomposition analysis of changes in inequality leading to the same conclusion. Ahuja et al. (1997) illustrate this point very well for several Asian countries in the 1980s and 1990s.

generating counterfactuals, however, two difficulties arise. First, imagine that the counterfactual drastically modifies the number of unskilled urban workers employed in the formal sector. What should be done with the number of households whose head is in that occupation? Should it be modified? If so, from which groups must new households in that RHG be taken or to which groups should they be allocated? Would it then be reasonable to assume that the distribution of income within each of these RHGs remains the same despite movements from one to the other? Second, assume that changes in occupation affect only other members and not household heads, so that weights of RHGs within the population are unchanged. Is it reasonable then to assume that all households in a group are affected in the same way by this change in the activity of some of their members? That a member other than the head moves out of the formal sector back into family self-employment may happen only in a subgroup of households belonging to a given representative group. Yet it may seriously affect the distribution within this group. Although this kind of phenomenon may be behind the importance of the within-group component in decomposition of changes in inequality, it is practically ignored in multisector, multihousehold RHG models.

What may be wrong in the preceding example is that RHGs are defined too precisely. Why look at urban unskilled workers in the formal sector, and not at urban unskilled workers in general? But if one looks at a broader group, despite the fact that wage differentials are observed between the formal and informal urban sectors, then the assumption of constant within-group distributions becomes untenable for any counterfactual that modifies the relative weights of the two sectors. An obvious alternative approach, and a more direct way of dealing with distributional issues in macro modeling, would be to specify as many representative household groups as there are households in the population or in any available representative sample from the population. Computable general equilibrium (CGE) models based on observed rather than representative households do exist. But they usually concern a specific sector, a specific market, or a community – for example, CGE models of village economies.[3] Dealing with the whole economy and a representative sample of the whole population raises more difficulties.[4] The issue is not so much computational – computing simultaneous equilibrium in markets with thousands of independent agents is no longer very difficult. The real problem is that of identifying the heterogeneity of factor endowments or preferences at the level of a single household or individual.

Calibrating the consumption and labor-supply behavior of a representative household is generally done by assuming some functional form for preferences and

---

[3]   See for instance Taylor and Adelman (1996) for village models and Heckman (2001) for labor market applications.

[4]   For attempts at the full integration of micro data and household income-generation modeling within multisectoral general frameworks, see Cogneau (2001) and Cogneau and Robilliard (2001). A general discussion of the link between CGE modeling and micro-unit household data is provided by Plumb (2001).

ignoring the underlying individual heterogeneity. Operating at the individual level requires dealing explicitly with that heterogeneity and introducing "fixed effects" to represent it. This is generally done by estimating a structural model on the observed cross section of households and interpreting residuals as fixed individual effects. This estimation usually involves identification assumptions, which may be debatable. For instance, the estimation of the price elasticity of labor supply often calls for exclusion restrictions, and fixed effects behind the residuals of wage or labor-supply equations are likely to reflect a very specific kind of preference or labor skill heterogeneity, together with measurement errors and other disturbances. Another difficulty is the complexity of structural models meant to represent household income-generation behavior satisfactorily. This is true in particular when the modeling of the labor market requires accounting explicitly, as in the example above, for the joint labor supply behavior of individual household members. These two difficulties explain why micro-data-based applied general equilibrium models often rely on relatively simple structural models focusing on only one or two dimensions of household or individual behavior – see for instance Browning, Hansen and Heckman (1999), Townsend and Ueda (2001), or Heckman (2001). Yet it is not clear that this type of model may be convincingly used to describe the full complexity of household income inequality and the way it may be affected by macroeconomic policies.

In this paper, we propose an alternative approach to quantifying the effects of macroeconomic shocks on poverty and inequality, which tries to bypass the preceding difficulties. It combines a standard multisector CGE model with a microsimulation model that describes real income-generation behavior among a representative sample of households. This microsimulation model is based on econometric reduced-form equations for individual earnings, household income from self-employment, and the occupational choices of all household members of working age. Such an integrated set of equations has proved useful in analyzing observed changes in the distribution of income over some period of time in various countries – see Bourguignon, Fournier, and Gurgand (2001) and the various papers in the MIDD project run by Bourguignon, Ferreira, and Lustig.[5] It is used here to study changes between two hypothetical states of the economy as described by an economy-wide CGE model.

What makes the method proposed in this paper simpler than a fully integrated model with as many RHGs as actual households in a representative sample is that the two parts of the modeling structure are treated separately, in a top-down fashion. The macro or CGE model is solved first and communicates with the microsimulation model through a vector of prices, wages, and aggregate employment variables. Then the microsimulation model is used to generate changes in individual wages, self-employment incomes, and employment status in a way that is consistent with the

---

[5]   These papers are currently being edited into a volume. They may be obtained at http://www.iadb.org/sds/pov/publication/gen_21_2349_e.htm. For the original proposal, see Bourguignon, Ferreira, and Lustig (1998).

set of macro variables generated by the macro model. When this is done, the full distribution of real household income corresponding to the shock or policy change initially simulated in the macro model may be evaluated.

For illustrative purposes, this framework is used to estimate the effects on the distribution of household income of various scenarios of real devaluation in Indonesia. The CGE part of this framework is fairly standard and could be replaced by any other macro model that could provide satisfactory counterfactuals for the variables that ensure the link with the microsimulation model. For this reason, the presentation focuses more on the microsimulation model than on the CGE model or the nature of the macro shock driving the simulations.

The paper is organized as follows. Section 10.2 shows the structure of the microsimulation model and how it is linked to the CGE model. Section 10.3 describes the general features of the CGE model. The devaluation scenario and its implications for the distribution of household income are presented in Section 10.4. Finally, Section 10.5 discusses the differences between the micro/macro framework proposed in this paper and the standard representative household group (RHG) approach.

10.2. THE MICROSIMULATION MODEL

This section describes the specification of the household income model used for microsimulation and then focuses on the way consistency between the microsimulation model and the predictions of the CGE model is achieved. A detailed discussion of the specification and econometric estimates of the various equations of the household income generation model and simulation methodology may be found in Alatas and Bourguignon (2000).[6]

10.2.1. The Household Income Generation Model

With the notation used in the rest of this paper, the household income generation model for household m and working age household members $i = 1, \ldots, k_m$ consists of the following set of equations:

$$\text{Log } w_{mi} = \alpha_{g(mi)} + x_{mi} \beta_{g(mi)} + v_{mi} \qquad i = 1, .. k_m \qquad (1)$$

$$\text{Log } y_m = \gamma_{f(m)} + Z_m \delta_{f(m)} + \lambda_{f(m)} N_m + \eta_m \qquad (2)$$

$$Y_m = \frac{1}{P_m} \left(\sum_{i=1}^{k_m} w_{mi} I W_{mi} + y_m \text{ Ind}(N_m > 0) + y_{0m} \right) \qquad (3)$$

$$P_m = \sum_{k=1}^{K} s_{mk} p_k \qquad (4)$$

---

[6] A more general discussion of the model may be found in Bourguignon et al. (1998) and Bourguignon et al. (2001).

$$IW_{mi} = \text{Ind}[a_{h(mi)}^w + z_{mi}b_{h(mi)}^w + u_{mi}^w > \text{Sup}(0, a_{h(mi)}^s + z_{mi}b_{h(mi)}^s + u_{mi}^s)] \quad (5)$$

$$N_m = \sum_{i=1}^{k_m} \text{Ind}[a_{h(mi)}^s + z_{mi}b_{h(mi)}^s + u_{mi}^s > \text{Sup}(0, a_{h(mi)}^w + z_{mi}b_{h(mi)}^w + u_{mi}^w)].$$

$$(6)$$

The first equation expresses the logarithm of the (full-time) wage of member i of household m as a function of his/her personal characteristics, x. The residual term, v_{mi}, describes the effects of unobserved earning determinants and possibly measurement errors. This earning function is defined independently on various "segments" of the labor market defined by gender, skill (less than secondary or more than primary), and area (urban/rural). The function $g()$ is an index function that indicates the labor market segment to which member i in household m belongs. Individual characteristics, x, thus permit representing the heterogeneity of earnings within wage-earner groups due to differences in age, educational attainment within primary or secondary school, and region. The second equation is the (net) income function associated with self-employment, or small entrepreneurial activity, which includes both the opportunity cost of household labor and profit. This function is defined at the household level. It depends on the number N_m of household members actually involved in that activity and on some household characteristics, Z_m. The latter include area of residence, the age and schooling of the household head, and land size for farmers. The residual term, η_m, summarizes the effects of unobserved determinants of self-employment income. A different function is used depending on whether the household is involved in farm or nonfarm activity. This is exogenous and defined by whether the household has access to land or not, as represented by the index function $f(m)$.

The third equation is an accounting identity that defines total household real income, Y_m, as the sum of the wage income of its members, profit from self-employment, and (exogenous) nonlabor income, y_{0m}. In this equation, the notation IW_{mi} stands for a dummy variable that is equal to unity if member i is a wage worker and zero otherwise. Thus wages are summed over only those members actually engaged in wage work. Note that it is implicitly assumed here that all wage workers are employed full-time. This assumption will be weakened later. Income from self-employment has to be taken into account only if there is at least one member of the household engaged in self-employment activity, that is, if the indicator function, Ind, defined on the logical expression ($N_m > 0$) is equal to unity. Total income is then deflated by a household specific consumer price index, P_m, which is derived from the observed budget shares, s_{mk}, of household m and the price, p_k, of the various consumption goods, k, in the model (Eq. (4)).

The last two equations represent the occupational choice made by household members. This choice is discrete. Each individual has to choose from three alternatives: being inactive, being a wage worker, or being self-employed. A fourth alternative consisting of being both self-employed and a wage worker is also taken into account but, for the sake of simplicity, it is ignored in what follows. Individuals choose among alternatives according to some criterion the value of which is specific to the alternative. The alternative with the highest criterion value is selected.

The criterion value associated with being inactive is arbitrarily set to zero, whereas the values of being a wage worker or self-employed are linear functions of a set of individual and household characteristics, z_{mi}. The intercept of these functions has a component, a^w or a^s, that is common to all individuals and an idiosyncratic term, u_{mi}, that stands for unobserved determinants of occupational choices. The coefficients of individual characteristics z_{mi}, b^w or b^s, are common to all individuals. However, they may differ across demographic groups indexed by $h(mi)$. For instance, occupational choice behavior, as described by coefficients a^w, a^s, b^w, and b^s and the variables in z_{mi}, may be different for household heads, spouses, and male or female children. The intercepts may also be demography-specific.

Given this specification, an individual will prefer wage work if the value of the criterion associated with that activity is higher than that associated with the two other activities. This is the meaning of Eq. (5). Likewise, the number of self-employed workers in a household is the number of individuals for whom self-employment yields a criterion value higher than that of the two alternatives, as represented in (6).[7]

The model is now complete. Overall, it defines the total real income of a household as a nonlinear function of the observed characteristics of household members (x_{mi} and z_{mi}), some characteristics of the household (Z_m), its budget shares (s_m), and unobserved characteristics of the household (η_m) or household members (v_{mi}, u_{mi}^w, and u_{mi}^s). This function depends on five sets of parameters : the parameters in the earning functions (α_g and β_g) for each labor market segment, g; the parameters of the self-employment income functions (γ_f, δ_f, and λ_f) for the farm or nonfarm sector, f; the parameters of the occupational choice model (a_h^w, b_h^w, a_h^s and b_h^s), for the various demographic groups, h, and the vector of prices, p. It will be seen below that it is through a subset of these parameters that the results of the CGE part of the model may be transmitted to the microsimulation module.

The microsimulation model gives a complete description of household income generation mechanisms by focusing on both earning and occupational choice determinants. However, a number of assumptions about the functioning of the labor market are incorporated into this specification. The fact that labor supply is considered as a discrete choice between inactivity and full-time work for wages or for self-employment income within the household calls for two sets of remarks. First, the assumption that individuals either are inactive or work full time is justified essentially by the fact that no information on working time is available in the micro

---

[7] As mentioned above, the possibility that a person is involved simultaneously in wage work and self-employment is also considered. This is taken as an additional alternative in the discrete-choice model (5). A dummy variable controls for this in the earning equation (1) and this person is assumed to count for half a worker in the definition of N_m. See details in Alatas and Bourguignon (2000).

data source used to estimate the model coefficients. Practically, this implies that estimated individual earning functions (1) and profit functions (2) may incorporate some labor-supply dimension. Second, distinguishing between wage work and self-employment is implicitly equivalent to assuming that the Indonesian labor market is imperfectly competitive. If this were not the case, then returns to labor would be the same in both types of occupations and self-employment income would be different from outside wage income only because it would incorporate the returns to nonlabor assets being used. The specification that has been selected is partly justified by the fact that assets used in self-employment are not observed, so that one cannot distinguish between self-employment income due to labor and that due to other assets. But it is also justified by the fact that the labor market may be segmented, in the sense that labor returns are not equalized across wage work and self-employment. There may be various reasons for this segmentation. On the one hand, there may be rationing in the wage labor market. People unable to find jobs as wage workers move into self-employment, which thus appears as a kind of shelter. On the other hand, there may be externalities that make working within and outside the household imperfect substitutes. All these interpretations are fully consistent with the way in which the labor market is represented in the CGE part of the model – see below.[8]

10.2.2. Estimation of the Model for the Benchmark Simulation

The benchmark simulation of the model requires previous econometric estimation work. This is necessary to have an initial set of coefficients (α_g, β_g, γ_f, δ_f, λ_f, a_h^w, b_h^w, a_h^s, b_h^s) as well as an estimate of the unobserved characteristics, or fixed effects, that enter the earning and profit functions, or the utility of the various occupational alternatives, through the residual terms (v_{mi}, η_m, u_{mi}^w, u_{mi}^s).

The data base consists of the sample of 9,800 households surveyed in the "income and saving" module of Indonesia's 1996 SUSENAS household survey. This sample is itself a subsample of the original 1996 SUSENAS. The coefficients of earning and self-employment income functions and the corresponding residual terms are obtained by ordinary-least-squares estimation on wage earners and households with some self-employment activity.[9] This estimation also yields estimates of the residual terms, v_{mi} and η_m. For individuals at working age (i.e., 15 years and older) who are not observed as wage earners in the survey, unobserved characteristics, v_{mi}, are generated by drawing random numbers from the distribution that is observed for actual wage earners. The same is done with η_m for those households that are not

---

[8]   This "rationing" view at the labor market explains why we refrain from calling "utility" the criteria that describe occupational choices, as is usually done. Actually, the functions defined in (5) and (6) combine both utility aspects and the way in which the rationing scheme may depend on individual characteristics.

[9]   Correction for selection biases did not lead to significant changes in the coefficients of these equations and was thus dropped.

observed as self-employed in the survey but might get involved in that activity in a subsequent simulation.[10]

Parameters of the occupational choice model were obtained through the estimation of a multilogit model, thus assuming that the residual terms (u_{mi}^w, u_{mi}^s) are distributed according to a double exponential law. The estimation was conducted on all individuals of working age, but separately for three demographic groups (h): household heads, spouses, and other family members. The set of explanatory variables, z_{mi}, includes not only the sociodemographic characteristics of the individual, but also the average characteristics of the other members in the household and the size and composition of the household. In addition, it includes the occupational status of the head, and possibly his/her individual earnings, for spouses and other household members. For all individuals, values of the residual terms (u_{mi}^w, u_{mi}^s) were drawn randomly in a way consistent with observed occupational choices.[11] For instance, residual terms for a wage earner should be such that

$$\hat{a}_{h(mi)}^w + z_{mi}\hat{b}_{h(mi)}^w + u_{mi}^w > \text{Sup}(0, \hat{a}_{h(mi)}^s + z_{mi}\hat{b}_{h(mi)}^s + u_{mi}^s),$$

where the ^ notation corresponds to multilogit coefficient estimates.[12]

To save space, the results of this estimation work are not reported in this paper. Interested readers may find a presentation and a discussion of a similar household income model in Alatas and Bourguignon (2000). Note that the CPI equation (4) does not call for any estimation since it is directly defined on observed household budget shares.

10.2.3. Link with the CGE Model

In principle, the link between the microsimulation model that has just been described and the CGE model is extremely simple. It consists of associating macroeconomic shocks and changes in policies simulated in the CGE model with changes in the set of coefficients of the household income generation model, (1)–(6). With a new set of coefficients $(\alpha_g, \beta_g, \gamma_f, \delta_f, \lambda_f, a_h^w, b_h^w, a_h^s, b_h^s)$ and the observed and unobserved individual and household characteristics $(x_{mi}, z_{mi}, Z_m, s_m, v_{mi}, \eta_m, u_{mi}^w, u_{mi}^s)$, these equations permit computing the occupational status of all household members, their earnings, their self-employment income, and finally the total real income of the household. But this association has to be done in a consistent way. Consistency with the equilibrium of aggregate markets in the CGE model requires that (1) changes

---

[10] Actually, homoskedastic normal distributions were assumed in both cases. No attempt has been made to incorporate heteroskedasticity.

[11] In general, the residual terms in the occupational functions (u_{mi}^w, u_{mi}^s) should be assumed to be correlated with the residual terms of the earning and self-employment income functions (v_{mi}, η_m). Failure to find significant self-selection correction terms in the latter equations suggests that this correlation is negligible, however.

[12] This may be done by drawing (u_{mi}^w, u_{mi}^s) independently in double-exponential laws until they satisfy the preceding condition. A more direct technique is given in Bourguignon et al. (2001).

in average earnings with respect to the benchmark in the microsimulation must be equal to changes in wage rates obtained in the CGE model for each segment of the wage labor market; (2) changes in self-employment income in the microsimulation must be equal to changes in informal sector income per worker in the CGE model; (3) changes in the number of wage workers and self-employed by labor-market segment in the microsimulation model must match the same changes in the CGE model: and (4) changes in the consumption price vector, p, must be consistent with the CGE model.

The calibration of the CGE model, or of the social accounting matrix behind it, is done in such a way that the preceding four sets of consistency requirements are satisfied in the benchmark simulation. Let E_G be the employment level in the G segment of the wage labor market, w_G the corresponding wage rate, S_G the number of self-employed in the same segment, and I_F the total self-employment household income in informal sector F (farm and nonfarm). Finally, let q be the vector of prices for consumption goods in the CGE model. Consistency between the micro database and the benchmark run of the CGE model is described by the set of constraints

$$\sum_{m} \sum_{i,g\ (mi)=G} \mathrm{Ind}[\hat{a}^{w}_{h(mi)} + z_{mi} \cdot \hat{b}^{w}_{h(mi)} + \hat{u}^{w}_{mi} > \mathrm{Sup}(0, \hat{a}^{s}_{h(mi)}$$

$$+ z_{mi} \cdot \hat{b}^{s}_{h(mi)} + \hat{u}^{s}_{mi})] = E_G$$

$$\sum_{m} \sum_{i,g\ (mi)=G} \mathrm{Ind}[\hat{a}^{S}_{h(mi)} + z_{mi} \cdot \hat{b}^{S}_{h(mi)} + \hat{u}^{S}_{mi} > \mathrm{Sup}(0, \hat{a}^{w}_{h(mi)}$$

$$+ z_{mi} \cdot \hat{b}^{w}_{h(mi)} + \hat{u}^{w}_{mi})] = S_G$$

$$\sum_{m} \sum_{i,g\ (mi)=G} \mathrm{Exp}(\hat{\alpha}_G + x_{mi} \cdot \hat{\beta}_G + \hat{v}_{mi}) \cdot \mathrm{Ind}[\hat{a}^{w}_{h(mi)} + z_{mi} \cdot \hat{b}^{w}_{h(mi)}$$

$$+ \hat{u}^{w}_{mi} > \mathrm{Sup}(0, \hat{a}^{s}_{h(mi)} + z_{mi} \cdot \hat{b}^{s}_{h(mi)} + \hat{u}^{s}_{mi})] = w_G$$

$$\sum_{m, f(m)=F} \mathrm{Exp}(\hat{\gamma}_F + Z_m \cdot \hat{\delta}_F + \hat{\lambda}_F \cdot \hat{N}_m + \hat{\eta}_m) \cdot \mathrm{Ind}(N_m > 0) = I_F$$

$$\mathrm{with} \quad \hat{N}_m = \sum_{i} \mathrm{Ind}[\hat{a}^{S}_{h(mi)} + z_{mi} \cdot \hat{b}^{S}_{h(mi)} + \hat{u}^{S}_{mi} > \mathrm{Sup}(0, \hat{a}^{w}_{h(mi)}$$

$$+ z_{mi} \cdot \hat{b}^{w}_{h(mi)} + \hat{u}^{w}_{mi})]$$

for all labor-market segments, G, and both self-employment sectors, F.

In these equations, the ˆnotation refers to the results of the estimation procedure described above. Given the way in which the unobserved characteristics or fixed effects ($v_{mi}, \eta_m, u^{w}_{mi}, u^{s}_{mi}$) have been generated, predicted occupational choices, earnings, and self-employment income that appear in these equations are identical to those actually observed in the micro database for all households and individuals.

Consider now a shock or a policy measure in the CGE model, which changes the vector (E_G, S_G, w_G, I_F, q) into ($E^{*}_G, S^{*}_G, w^{*}_G, I^{*}_F, q^{*}$). The consistency problem is to find a new set of parameters $C = (\alpha_g, \beta_g, \gamma_f, \delta_f, \lambda_f, a^{w}_h, b^{w}_h, a^{s}_h, b^{s}_h, p)$ of the microsimulation model such that the preceding set of constraints will continue to hold for the new set of right-hand macro variables $(E_G^*, S_G^*, w_G^*, I_F^*, q^*)$. This is trivial for consumption prices, p, which must be equal to their CGE counterpart. For the other parameters, there are many such sets of coefficients, so that additional restrictions are necessary. The choice made in this paper is to restrict the changes in C to changes in the *intercepts* of all earning, self-employment income, and occupational criterion functions – that is changes in α^g, γ^f, a_h^w, and a_h^s.

The justification for that choice is that it implies a *neutrality* of the changes being made with respect to individual or household characteristics. For example, changing the intercepts of the log earnings equations generates a proportional change of all earnings in a labor-market segment, irrespective of individual characteristics – outside those that define the labor-market segments, that is skill, gender, and area. The same is true of the change in the intercept of the log self-employment income functions. It turns out that a similar argument applies to the criteria associated with the various occupational choices. Indeed, it is easily shown that changing the intercepts of the multilogit model implies the following neutrality property. The relative change in the ex ante probability that an individual has some occupation depends only on the initial ex ante probabilities of the various occupational choices, rather than on individual characteristics.

More precisely, let P_{mi}^w, P_{mi}^s, and P_{mi}^0 be the a priori probabilities of wage work, self-employment, and no employment for individual mi. According to the multilogit model, these probabilities have the expression[13]

$$
P_{mi}^w = \frac{\text{Exp}(a^w + z_{mi}b^w)}{1 + \text{Exp}(a^w + z_{mi}b^w) + \text{Exp}(a^s + z_{mi}b^s)},
$$

$$
P_{mi}^s = \frac{\text{Exp}(a + z_{mi}b^s)}{1 + \text{Exp}(a^w + z_{mi}b^w) + \text{Exp}(a^s + z_{mi}b^s)}
$$

$$(7)$$

and $P_{mi}^0 = 1 - P_{mi}^w - P_{mi}^s$. Thus, differentiating with respect to the intercepts yields the preceding property, namely,

$$
\frac{dP_{mi}^w}{P_{mi}^w \cdot da^w} = (1 - P_{mi}^w), \quad \frac{dP_{mi}^s}{P_{mi}^s \cdot da^w} = \frac{dP_{mi}^0}{P_{mi}^0 \cdot da^w} = -P_{mi}^w,
$$

$$(8)$$

and symmetrically for a^s.

There are as many intercepts as there are constraints in the preceding system. Thus, the linkage between the CGE part of the model and the microsimulation part

---

[13] The following argument is cast in terms of ex ante probabilities of the various occupations rather than the actual occupational choices that appear in the preceding system of equations. This is for the sake of simplicity. Note that ex ante probabilities given by the multilogit model correspond to the observed frequency of occupations among individuals with the same observed characteristics. Also note that, for simplicity, we ignore demographic group heterogeneity $h(mi)$ in what follows.

is obtained through the resolution of the following system(s) of equations

$$\sum_{m\,i,g\,(mi)=G} \text{Ind}[a^{w^*}_{h(mi)} + z_{mi}\hat{b}^w_{h(mi)} + \hat{u}^w_{mi} > \text{Sup}(0, a^{s^*}_{h(mi)} + z_{mi}\hat{b}^s_{h(mi)} + \hat{u}^s_{mi})] = E^*_G$$

$$\sum_{m\,i,g\,(mi)=G} \text{Ind}[a^{s^*}_{h(mi)} + z_{mi}\hat{b}^s_{h(mi)} + \hat{u}^s_{mi} > \text{Sup}(0, a^{w^*}_{h(mi)} + z_{mi}\hat{b}^w_{h(mi)} + \hat{u}^w_{mi})] = S^*_G$$

$$\sum_{m\,i,g\,(mi)=G} \text{Exp}(\alpha^*_G + x_{mi}\hat{\beta}_G + \hat{v}_{mi})\text{Ind}[a^{w^*}_{h(mi)} + z_{mi}\hat{b}^w_{h(mi)} + \hat{u}^w_{mi}$$

$$> \text{Sup}(0, a^{s^*}_{h(mi)} + z_{mi}\hat{b}^s_{h(mi)} + \hat{u}^s_{mi})] = w^*_G\ (S)$$

$$\sum_{m,f(m)=F} \text{Exp}(\gamma^*_F + Z_m\hat{\delta}_F + \hat{\lambda}_F\hat{N}_m + \hat{\eta}_m)\text{Ind}(N_m > 0) = I^*_F$$

$$\text{with} \qquad \hat{N}_m = \sum_i \text{Ind}[\,a^{s^*}_{h(mi)} + z_{mi}\hat{b}^{s^*}_{h(mi)} + \hat{u}^s_{mi}$$

$$> \text{Sup}(0, a^{w^*}_{h(mi)} + z_{mi}\hat{b}^w_{h(mi)} + \hat{u}^w_{mi})]$$

for all labor-market segments, G, and both self-employment sectors, F. The unknowns of this system are $\alpha_g{}^*$, γ_f^*, $a_h^{w^*}$, and $a_h^{s^*}$. There are as many equations as unknowns.[14] No formal proof of existence or uniqueness has yet been established. But there is a strong presumption that these properties hold. Indeed, the last two sets of equations in α_g^*, γ_f^* are independent of the first two sets and clearly have a unique solution for given values of $a_h^{w^*}$ and $a_h^{s^*}$, because left-hand sides are monotone functions that vary between zero and infinity. Things are more difficult for the first two sets of equations, in particular because of the discreteness of the Ind( ) functions. If there are enough observations, these functions may be replaced by the probability of being in wage work or self-employed, as given by the well-known multilogit model. This would make the problem continuous. It can then be checked that local concavity properties make standard Gauss–Newton techniques convergent. However, the minimum number of observations necessary for the multilogit probability approximation to be satisfactory is not clear.[15]

Once the solution is obtained, it is a simple matter to compute the new income of each household in the sample, according to model (1)–(6), with the new set of coefficients α_g^*, γ_f^*, $a_h^{w^*}$, and $a_h^{s^*}$, and then to analyze the modification that this implies for the overall distribution of income.

In the Indonesian case, the number of variables that allow the micro and macro parts of the overall model to communicate, that is, the vector $(E^*_G, S^*_G, w^*_G, I^*_F, q^*)$, is equal to 26 plus the number of consumption goods used in defining the household-specific CPI deflator. There are eight segments in the labor market. The employment requirements for each segment in the formal (wage work) and the informal (self-employment) sectors (E^*_G and S^*_G) lead to 16 restrictions. In addition, there are eight

---

[14] Of course, this requires some particular relationship between the number of demographic groups, h, and the number of labor-market segments, G.

[15] In the event, we were able to solve the model using a standard Newton method (programmed in STATA).

wage rates in the formal sector (w_G^*) and two levels of self-employment income (I_F^*) in the farm and nonfarm sectors. Thus, simulated changes in the distribution of income implied by the CGE part of the model are obtained through a procedure that comprises a rather sizable number of degrees of freedom.

10.2.4. Interpretation of the Consistency System of Equations

The micro–macro linkage described by the preceding system of equations may be seen as a generalization of familiar grossing-up operations aimed at correcting a household survey to make it consistent with other data sources – for example, another survey, a census, or national accounts. The first type of operation consists of simply rescaling the various household income sources, with a scaling factor that varies across the income sources and labor-market segments. This corresponds to the last two set of equations in the consistency system (S). However, because households may derive income from many different sources, this operation is more complex and has more subtle effects on the overall distribution than simply multiplying the total income of households whose heads belong to different groups by different proportionality factors, as is often done. It is also worth stressing that, because various labor segments are distinguished by gender, area, and skill, changing the intercepts of the various wage equations is actually equivalent to making the coefficients of education, gender, or area of residence in a single wage-earning function endogenous and consistent with the CGE model. The second operation would consist of reweighting households depending on the occupations of their members.[16] This approach loosely corresponds to the first two sets of restrictions in system (S). Here again, however, this procedure is considerably different from reweighting households on the basis of a simple criterion such as the occupation of the household head, his/her education, or his/her area of residence. There are two reasons for this. First, reweighting takes place on individuals rather than households, so that the composition of households and the occupations of their members matter. Second, the reweighting being implemented is highly selective. For instance, if the CGE model results require that many individuals move from wage work to self-employment and inactivity, individuals whose occupational status will change in the microsimulation model will not be drawn randomly from the initial population of individuals in the formal sector. On the contrary, they will be drawn in a selective way, essentially based on cross-sectional estimates of their a priori probability of being formal wage workers or self-employed. Standard reweighting would consist of modifying these ex ante probabilities of being a formal wage worker, P_{mi}^w, in the same proportion. The selective reweighting used here is such that this proportion depends itself on the ex ante probabilities of being a wage worker, as shown by Eq. (8). For instance, the youngest employees in a household with many employees, but with self-employed parents, might be more likely to move than an older person in a small

---

[16] For simulation techniques for income or earnings distributions based on straight reweighting of a benchmark sample see DiNardo, Fortin, and Lemieux (1996).

household. As the earnings or the income of the former may be different from those of the latter, this selectivity of the reweighting procedure has a direct effect on the distribution of earnings *within* the group of formal wage workers.

10.2.5. Interpreting the Intercepts of Occupational Choice Criteria

There is another way of interpreting this reweighting procedure, or the changes in the multilogit intercepts that it relies on, that can be made consistent with standard utility maximizing behavior and with the CGE part of the whole model.

Consider that each occupation yields some utility that can be measured by the log of the money income it yields, net of working disutility. To simplify, ignore momentarily the distinction between individuals and households and write the utility of the three occupations with obvious notations as

$$
\begin{aligned}
U_i^w &= \text{Log } w_i - \text{Log } CPI_i(p) - (\varphi_w z_i + \mu_i^w) \\
U_i^s &= \text{Log } y_i - \text{Log } CPI_i(p) - (\phi_s z_i + \mu_i^s) \\
U_i^0 &= \text{Log } Y_i - \text{Log } CPI_i(p) - (\phi_0 z_i + \mu_i^0),
\end{aligned}
\tag{9}
$$

where Y_i is the monetary equivalent of domestic production in the case of no employment. In all these cases, the first two terms on the RHS correspond to the (log) of the real (or real equivalent) return to each occupation, and the third term to the disutility of that occupation. This disutility is itself expressed as a linear function of individual or household characteristics, z_i, and a random term, μ_i. Of course, such a specification of the indirect utility function presupposes some separability between consumption and the disutility of occupations in the direct utility function.[17]

This specification permits putting more economic structure into the initial specification of the multilogit model for occupational choices. In particular, it is possible to replace $\text{Log}(w_i)$ and $\text{Log}(y_i)$ by their expressions in (1) and (2). In addition, we know that the intercept of the earnings function depends on the earnings of the labor-market segment an individual belongs to, as given by the CGE model. Likewise, the intercept of the self-employment income function depends on the value-added price of the output of self-employment activity, and therefore on the whole price vector as given by the CGE model. Of course, the same can be said of the unobserved domestic output, Y_i, in the case of inactivity. Thus the income terms in (9) may be rewritten as

$$
\begin{aligned}
\text{Log } w_i &= \alpha(w_{G(i)}) + z_i \cdot \beta_{G(i)} + v_i \\
\text{Log } y_i &= \gamma_{f(i)}(p) + z_i \cdot \delta_{f(i)} + \eta_i \\
\text{Log } Y_i &= \chi(p) + z_i \cdot \lambda + \zeta_i,
\end{aligned}
\tag{10}
$$

---

[17]   A direct utility function of the type $U_i(c, l; z_i) = \text{Log}[a_i(c)] - b(l, z_i)$, where $a_i(c, z)$ is a linearly homogeneous function of the consumption vector, c, and $b(l, z)$ is the disutility of labor, would be consistent with this model.

where w_G and p are earnings and prices given by the CGE model. Combining (7) and (10) finally leads to the equivalent of the formulation of occupational choice in (5) and (6). Using inactivity as the default choice permits eliminating the heterogeneity in consumption preferences associated with specific CPI indices, $CPI_i(p)$. The preferred occupational choice of individual i, C_i, belonging to labor market segment G, which is wage work, W, self-employment, S, or inactivity, I, is then given by a conditional system with the following structure:

$$C_i = W \text{ if } A_w(w_{G(i)}, p) + z_i \cdot B_w^{G(i)} + \omega_i^w \geq \text{Sup} \left[0, A_s(p) + z_i \cdot B_s^{G(i)} + \omega_i^s \right]$$

$$C_i = S \text{ if } A_s(p) + z_i \cdot B_s + \omega_i^s \geq \text{Sup} \left[0, A_w(w_{G(i)}, p) + z_i \cdot B_w^{G(i)} + \omega_i^w \right]$$

$$C_i = I \text{ if } \text{Sup} \left[A_s(p) + z_i \cdot B_s + \omega_i^s, \, A_w(w_{G(i)}, p) + z_i \cdot B_w^{G(i)} + \omega_i^w \right] < 0.$$

If the functions $A_w(w_{G(i)}, p)$ and $A_s(p)$ were known, we would have a complete microeconomic structural labor supply model that could nicely fit into the CGE model. Given a wage–price vector *(w, p)*, this model would give the occupational choice of every individual in the sample and therefore the labor supply in the CGE. It would then be possible to have the whole microsimulation structure integrated into the CGE model. The fundamental point, however, is that *there is no way we can get an estimate of these functions on a microeconomic cross-sectional basis*, for there is no variation of the price vector, p, in the data. If we do not want to import the functions $A_w(w_{G(i)}, p)$ and $A_s(p)$ arbitrarily from outside the microsimulation framework and household survey data, the only way to achieve consistency with the CGE part of the model is to assume that these functions are such that the equilibrium values of wages and prices coming from the CGE model ensure the equilibrium of markets for both goods and labor. This is equivalent to looking for the *intercepts* that ensure supply–demand equilibrium of the labor markets behind the last two sets of equations of system (S). Solving system (S) for those intercepts thus is consistent, under the preceding assumptions above, with the full general equilibrium of the economy and full utility-maximizing behavior at the micro level. It is a solution that permits avoiding the arbitrary assumptions necessary to get a structural representation of individual labor choices that and explicitly consistent with the CGE model.

It must be kept in mind that the preceding argument has been conducted in terms of the textbook consumption unit, rather than individuals belonging to the same household, as explicitly stated in the microsimulation model (1)–(6). Interpreting the occupational status equations in terms of rational individual behavior would thus require specifying some intrahousehold task/consumption allocation model. Because of the cross-wage elasticities of occupational choices, it is not clear, in particular, that the standard unitary model is consistent with the idea that all price and wage effects in the microsimulation model are included in the intercepts of the multilogit criterion functions. Justifying that assumption may require invoking some nonunitary model of household decisions, but this point was not investigated further. All the preceding discussion is based on a purely competitive view of the labor market. But the occupational model represented by Eqs. (5) and (6) may be justified by other arguments, for instance, by the existence of selective rationing. This would seem natural in view of the imperfection assumed for the labor markets in the CGE – see below. Most of the preceding conclusions would still hold, however. Maintaining the maximum dichotomy between the micro and the macro parts of the model requires avoiding the import of structural assumptions from outside the microeconomic model. At the same time, ensuring consistency through the intercepts simplifies things but also imposes implicit assumptions that one would like to identify more precisely.

The lack of communication between the macro and the micro parts of the model is also concerned with the nonlabor income variable, y_{0m}. It is taken as exogenous (in nominal terms) in all simulations. Yet it includes housing and land rents, dividends, royalties, imputed rents from self-occupied housing, and transfers from other households and institutions. It could have been possible to endogenize some of these items in the CGE model, but this was not done.

10.3. THE CGE MODEL

The macro model used in this paper is a conventional, trade-focused CGE model.[18] It is based on a social accounting matrix (SAM) for the year 1995. The SAM has been disaggregated using cross-entropy estimation methods (Robinson, Cattaneo, and El-Said, 2001) and includes 38 sectors ("activities"), 14 goods ("commodities"), 14 factors of production (8 labor categories and 6 types of capital), and 10 household types, as well as the usual accounts for aggregate agents (firms, government, rest of the world, and savings–investment). The CGE model starts from the standard neoclassical specification in Dervis, de Melo, and Robinson (1982), but it also incorporates disaggregation of production sectors into formal and informal activities and associated labor-market imperfections, as well as working capital. The SAM, including the sector and agent breakdown, is given in Appendix A.

The model is Walrasian in the sense that it determines only relative prices and other endogenous real variables in the economy. Financial mechanisms are modeled implicitly and only their real effects are taken into account in a simplified way. Sectoral product prices and factor prices are defined relative to the producer price index of goods for domestic use, which serves as the numeraire.

In common with many trade-focused CGE models, the model includes an explicit exchange-rate variable. Because world prices are measured in U.S. dollars and domestic prices in Indonesian currency, the exchange-rate variable has units of domestic currency per unit of foreign exchange – it is used to convert world prices of imports and exports to prices in domestic currency units, and also to convert foreign-exchange flows measured in dollars (e.g., foreign savings). Given the

---

[18] For a detailed exposition of this type of model, and for the implementation of the "standard" model in the GAMS modeling language, see Lofgren, Harris, and Robinson (2001).

choice of numeraire, the exchange rate variable can be interpreted as the real price-level-deflated (PLD) exchange rate, deflating by the domestic (producer) price of nontraded goods.[19] Because world prices are assumed to be fixed, the exchange-rate variable corresponds to the real exchange rate, measuring the relative price of traded goods (both exports and imports) and nontraded goods.

Following Armington (1969), the model assumes imperfect substitutability for each good between the domestic commodity – which itself results from a combination of formal and informal activities – and imports. What is demanded is a composite good, which is a CES aggregation of imports and domestically produced goods. For export commodities, the allocation of domestic output between exports and domestic sales is determined on the assumption that domestic producers maximize profits subject to imperfect transformability between these two alternatives. The composite production good is a CET (constant-elasticity-of-transformation) aggregation of sectoral exports and domestically consumed products.[20]

Indonesia's economy is dualistic, which the model captures by distinguishing between formal and informal "activities" in each sector. Both subsectors produce the same "commodity" but differ in the types of factors they use.[21] This distinction allows treating formal and informal factor markets differently. On the demand side, imperfect substitutability is assumed between formal and informal products of the same commodity classification.

For all activities, the production technology is represented by a set of nested CES (constant-elasticity-of-substitution) value-added functions and fixed (Leontief) intermediate input coefficients. Domestic prices of commodities are flexible, varying to clear markets in a competitive setting where individual suppliers and demanders are price-takers.

10.3.1. Factors of Production

There are eight labor categories: Urban Male Unskilled, Urban Male Skilled, Urban Female Unskilled, Urban Female Skilled, Rural Male Unskilled, Rural Male Skilled, Rural Female Unskilled, and Rural Female Skilled. Male and female, as well as skilled and unskilled labor, are assumed to be imperfect substitutes in the production activities.

In addition, labor markets are assumed to be segmented between formal and informal sectors. In the formal sectors, a degree of imperfect competition is assumed

---

[19] This terminology was standardized in a series of NBER studies in the 1970s in a project led by Jagdish Bhagwati and Anne Krueger.

[20] The appropriate definition of the real exchange rate in this class of model, with a continuum of substitutability between domestically produced and foreign goods, is discussed in Devarajan, Lewis, and Robinson (1993).

[21] Typically, CGE models assume a one-to-one correspondance between activities and commodities. This model allows many activities producing the same commodity or one activity producing many commodities. See Lofgren et al. (2001).

to result in there being an increasing wage–employment curve, and real wages are defined by the intersection of that curve with competitive labor demand. Informal sector labor is equivalent to self-employment. Wages in that sector are set so as to absorb all the labor not employed in the formal sectors. Non-wage income results from the other factors operated by self-employed.

Land appears as a factor of production in all agricultural sectors. Only one type of land is considered in the model. It is competitively allocated among the different crops and sectors so that its marginal revenue product is equated across all uses. Capital is broken down into six categories, but, given the short-run nature of the model, it is assumed to be fixed in each activity.

10.3.2. Households

The disaggregation of households in the CGE model is not central for our purpose, because changes in factor prices are passed on directly to the microsimulation model, without use of the representative household groups (RHG) used in the original SAM and in the CGE model. Yet this feature will later permit comparing the methodology developed in this paper with the standard CGE/RHG approach. Thus RHGs are endowed with some specific combination of factors (labor and capital) and derive income from the remuneration of these factors, which they supply in fixed quantities to the rest of the economy. Consumption demand by households is specified as a linear expenditure system (LES), with fixed marginal budget shares and a minimum consumption (subsistence) level for each commodity.

10.3.3. Macro Closure Rules

Aside from the supply–demand balances in product and factor markets, three macroeconomic balances must hold in the model: (i) the external trade balance (in goods and nonfactor services), which implicitly equates the supply and demand for foreign exchange flows; (ii) the savings–investment balance; and (iii) the fiscal balance, with government savings equal to the difference between government revenue and spending. As far as foreign exchange is concerned, foreign savings are taken as exogenous and the exchange rate is assumed to clear the market – the model solves for an equilibrium real exchange rate given the fixed trade balance. Concerning the last two constraints, three alternative closures will be considered in what follows. The objective behind these three macroeconomic closures is to see whether they may affect the nature of the results obtained with the microsimulation model and how they compare with those obtained with the RHG method.

The first macro closure assumes that aggregate investment and government spending are in fixed proportions to total absorption. Any shock affecting total absorption is thus assumed to be shared evenly among government spending, aggregate investment, and aggregate private consumption. Although simple, this "balanced" closure effectively assumes a "successful" structural adjustment program whereby a

TABLE 10.1. *Simulations*

Terms of trade shock (50% decrease in price of petroleum and chemicals)	
SIMTOT1	BALANCED CLOSURE (all elements of absorption adjust)
SIMTOT2	SAVING-DRIVEN INVESTMENT & FLEXIBLE GOVERNMENT SPENDING
SIMTOT3	SAVING-DRIVEN INVESTMENT & FLEXIBLE VAT RATE
Devaluation (30% decrease in foreign savings)	
SIMDEV1	BALANCED CLOSURE (all elements of absorption adjust)
SIMDEV2	SAVING-DRIVEN INVESTMENT & FLEXIBLE GOVERNMENT SPENDING
SIMDEV3	SAVING-DRIVEN INVESTMENT & FLEXIBLE VAT RATE

macro shock is assumed not to cause particular actors – government, consumers, and industry – to bear a disproportionate share of the adjustment burden. This closure implies that the fiscal balance is endogenous.

In the second macro closure, investment is savings-driven and government spending adjusts to maintain the fiscal balance at the same level as in the benchmark simulation, which fits the economic situation observed in 1997. Note, however, that government employment remains constant. The third macro closure achieves the same fiscal balance through a uniform increase in indirect (VAT) tax rates.[22]

10.4. SCENARIOS AND SIMULATION RESULTS

As the purpose of this section is essentially to illustrate empirically the way the microsimulation model is linked with the CGE model, the nature of the shock being simulated does not matter very much. A companion paper uses an extended version of the model to describe the dramatic crisis that hit Indonesia in 1998.[23] Two simpler scenarios are considered here – see Table 10.1. They allow some foreign-sector parameters to vary under the three alternative macroeconomic closures listed above.

The first scenario consists of a major terms-of-trade shock that reduces the foreign price of both crude oil and exports of processed oil products – amounting altogether to approximately 40% of total Indonesian exports – by 50%. The corresponding drop in foreign exchange receipts results in a devaluation of the equilibrium exchange rate (in order to increase exports and reduce imports) to maintain the fixed trade balance, under the three macroeconomic adjustment scenarios described above.

---

[22] The Indonesian CGE model includes other features, including demand for working capital in all sectors. These features have not been discussed here because no use is made of them in the experiments we report. See Robilliard et al. (2001) for a discussion of how the model was extended to capture the impact of the Asian financial crisis. See also Aziz and Thorbecke (2001).

[23] See Robilliard et al. (2001).

The corresponding simulations appear respectively under the headings SIMTOT1 to SIMTOT3 in the tables below.

The second scenario consists of a 30% drop in exogenous foreign savings. This shock also results in a devaluation, under the same three macroeconomic adjustment scenarios as above. The corresponding simulations are referred to as SIMDEV1 to SIMDEV3. The main difference from the first set of simulations is that there is no change in relative prices before the devaluation, whereas the terms-of-trade shock in SIMTOT first reduces the relative prices of oil and oil products on both the export and import sides, with spillover to the structure of domestic prices.

Table 10.2 shows the effects of these shocks on some macroeconomic indicators. Results are unsurprising. GDP is little affected because both capital and the various types of labor are assumed to be fully employed. The small drop that is observed corresponds to sectoral shifts and price index effects. The effect of SIMTOT on the exchange rate and the volume of foreign trade is much less pronounced than that of SIMDEV. This result reflects the relative sizes of both shocks. In both cases, the resulting change in relative prices leads to an increase in the relative price of food products, which are largely untraded. In turn, this causes an absolute increase in the real income of farmers that contrasts with the drop in the real income of self-employed persons in the urban sector and of all workers. With no change in the wage curve and a drop in labor demand coming from traded good sectors, which are the main employers of wage labor, wages fall. The drop is more pronounced for unskilled workers, reflecting more exposure to foreign competition by the sectors employing them. All these effects depend on the size of the devaluation, and are bigger in SIMDEV.

As far as the three macroeconomic closures are concerned, it may be seen in Table 10.2 that they make a difference only in the case of the foreign saving shock, SIMDEV. The last two closures lead to more intense sectoral reallocations due to the change in the structure of absorption and the composition of aggregate demand. This effect is slightly bigger with the last closure, where the fiscal balance is reestablished through a uniform change in VAT rates. Because the VAT affects the various sectors in different proportions, with exemptions for informal sectors, the sectoral shift in aggregate demand is more important. Changes in the relative remuneration of the various types of labor are also more pronounced under the last two closures in the pure devaluation scenario. These effects are practically absent in the terms-of-trade scenario because all sectoral shifts are dominated by the initial change in foreign prices.

Table 10.3 shows the effect of the simulated shocks on the distribution of income after the microsimulation model is fed with values for the linkage variables provided by the CGE counterfactuals. Overall, the distributional effects of the terms-of-trade shock as reflected in standard summary inequality and poverty measures are limited. Inequality tends to go down, but the change in inequality measures shown in the table barely exceeds 1%. The change is slightly more pronounced for poverty, reflecting the general drop in per capita income. It remains small, though. The only substantial

TABLE 10.2. *Macroeconomic simulation results*

	BASE	SIMTOT1	SIMTOT2	SIMTOT3	SIMDEV1	SIMDEV2	SIMDEV3
GDP at factor costs (Rp thousands of billions)	535.6	-0.4	-0.5	-0.4	-0.9	-1.6	-1.6
Exports (Rp thousands of billions)	122.7	4.4	3.5	4.2	28.5	25.2	25.5
Imports (Rp thousands of billions)	126.8	-10.0	-10.9	-10.3	-19.5	-22.7	-22.5
Exchange rate	1.0	15.0	14.5	15.1	31.6	25.7	25.8
Food/nonfood terms of trade	1.0	7.1	9.0	7.6	15.2	16.8	16.2
Incorporated capital income	1.0	-13.1	-15.1	-18.0	6.5	0.2	-0.6
Agricultural self-employment income	1.6	7.3	9.3	6.1	8.0	9.0	8.0
Nonagricultural self-employment income	4.5	-6.0	-7.0	-6.5	-4.9	-7.4	-7.2
Skilled labor wage	4.9	-5.4	-4.8	-8.2	-8.4	-11.0	-12.0
Unskilled labor wage	2.7	-6.6	-6.0	-9.8	-12.6	-25.0	-26.1

Notes: 1. Incorporated capital income includes private, public, and foreign capital income. 2. Self-employment incomes are equal to value added divided by the number of labor units. 3. Wage incomes are equal to value added divided by the number of labor units. 4. Simulation results are expressed as percentage derivations from base values.

Source: CGE model simulation results.

TABLE 10.3. *Microeconomic simulation results with full microsimulation model (FULL)*

	BASE	SIMTOT1	SIMTOT2	SIMTOT3	SIMDEV1	SIMDEV2	SIMDEV3
All							
Per capita income	121.1	-2.6	-2.4	-3.8	-4.3	-6.4	-6.8
Entropy index (0)	35.5	-1.4	-1.5	-0.6	1.7	4.9	5.2
Entropy index (1)	49.3	-0.8	-1.0	-0.1	2.2	4.4	4.7
Gini index	45.6	-0.8	-0.9	-0.4	0.6	2.0	2.1
Head-count index (P0)	9.2	5.3	4.4	9.8	15.5	36.9	39.6
Poverty gap index (P1)	2.2	4.1	3.1	11.8	22.6	49.9	53.1
Poverty severity index (P2)	0.9	5.4	3.9	14.2	27.9	60.6	63.8
Urban							
Per capita income	170.9	-5.1	-5.3	-6.5	-6.8	-9.7	-10.0
Entropy index (0)	38.7	2.6	3.0	3.6	6.0	9.2	9.5
Entropy index (1)	53.9	2.7	3.0	3.5	5.8	8.5	8.6
Gini index	47.5	1.2	1.3	1.6	2.7	4.1	4.2
Head-count index (P0)	4.0	29.1	31.1	37.8	40.8	74.9	77.5
Poverty gap index (P1)	1.1	29.8	34.3	41.7	50.8	90.5	94.0
Poverty severity index (P2)	0.4	37.3	42.8	51.0	60.8	111.3	115.3
Rural							
Per capita income	90.6	0.3	1.0	-0.7	-1.5	-2.6	-3.1
Entropy index (0)	25.5	-0.4	-0.1	1.1	3.4	9.4	9.8
Entropy index (1)	33.1	0.0	-0.2	1.2	3.4	8.2	8.7
Gini index	38.7	-0.3	-0.3	0.3	1.3	4.0	4.2
Head-count index (P0)	12.4	0.6	-0.9	4.3	10.5	29.4	32.2
Poverty gap index (P1)	2.9	-1.6	-3.8	5.3	16.4	40.9	44.1
Poverty severity index (P2)	1.2	-1.5	-4.6	6.2	20.7	49.5	52.6

Notes: Simulation results are expressed as percentage deviations from base values.

effect occurs for SIMTOT3, when the poverty gap (P1) or the mean poverty gap squared (P2) is used, suggesting a worsening of the distribution at the very bottom.

As could be expected from the discussion above, distribution effects are more pronounced with the pure devaluation simulation, SIMDEV, and still more so with the last two macroeconomic closures. The two entropy inequality measures increase by approximately 5% and the Gini coefficient gains 2%. As the drop in per capita income is bigger in this scenario, so is the increase in poverty. The same worsening at the very bottom of the income distribution as in SIMTOT3 is reflected in the larger increase of the P1 and P2 poverty measures.

The last two panels of Table 10.3 reflect the asymmetry stressed above between the urban and the rural sectors. With the terms-of-trade scenario, inequality increases in the urban sector, but falls in the rural sector, the same being true with poverty in the first two macroeconomic closures. With the pure devaluation scenario, the distribution worsens quite substantially – that is, practically two percentage points of the Gini – in both sectors, and poverty increases. The reason these changes are larger than observed for the overall distribution is that per capita income falls less in the countryside. Thus, the increase in inequality within both sectors is compensated by a fall in the inequality existing between sectors. Relative changes in poverty measures in both sectors match that evolution. They are smaller in the rural sector.

Microsimulation techniques allow a much more detailed description of distribution effects than may be seen from looking at a few summary inequality and poverty measures. For the terms-of-trade shock, the solid curves in Figs. 10.1 and 10.2 show the full change in the distribution of income by picturing the percentage change in the mean income of each percentile of the population – using smoothed curves (cubic splines). These curves will be referred to as "income change curves" below.

Percentiles on the horizontal axis in Fig. 10.1 correspond to the initial ranking of households in the benchmark simulation. In that graph, the terms-of-trade shock appears to be equalizing. The income change curve decreases with the household rank, except for the highest ranks, where lower food budget shares dampen the negative effect of increasing relative food prices on real income. This result corresponds to what might be expected from the macro results in Table 10.2. Rural agricultural self-employment incomes, which go to households that are located at the bottom of the distribution, decline less (in effect they increase) than the wage of skilled workers, who tend to be in the upper part. In turn, those households tend to lose less than households depending on self-employment nonagricultural income, many of which are located at the top of the distribution. On the other hand, it is striking that the three macroeconomic closures lead to practically the same curve.

Percentiles on the horizontal axis in Fig. 10.2 are obtained after reranking households by increasing per capita income in the counterfactual, as for standard inequality measurement. Again, the solid line represents changes in mean incomes. The difference from Fig. 10.1 is that households for which these mean changes are computed are not the same. Reranking may imply, for instance, that a household that was

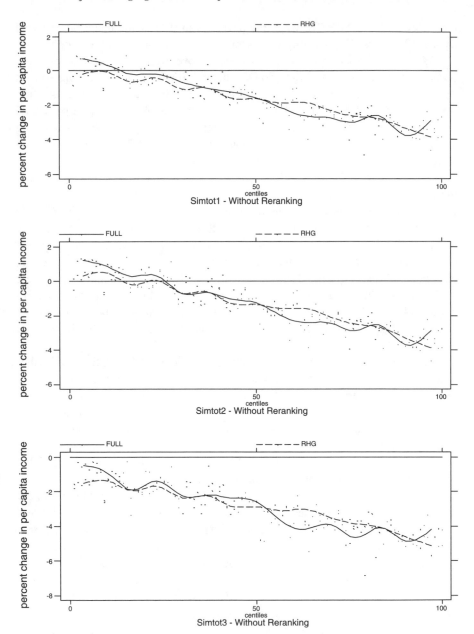

Figure 10.1. Terms-of-trade simulation results without reranking.

in the 15th percentile in the benchmark distribution ends up in the first percentile after the terms-of-trade shock because somebody in the household lost his/her job. Indeed, such an event would produce a relatively large relative loss in the income of the household. Yet this kind of phenomenon would not show up in Fig. 10.1 unless

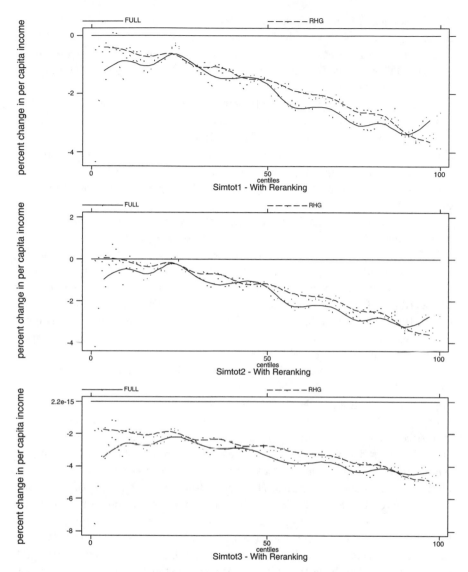

Figure 10.2. Terms-of-trade simulation results with reranking.

households facing this situation were concentrated in some specific percentiles. If this is not the case, income changes due to occupational switches caused by the shock are simply averaged out. They appear more clearly in Fig. 10.2 after reranking. In particular, they are responsible for the fact that the poorest percentiles, which do not necessarily comprise only those households that were initially the poorest, are more affected by the crisis than percentiles in the lower middle income range in SIMTOT1. The comparison with the other macroeconomic closures shows that the preceding effect may be more or less accentuated. The income change curve is increasing rather steeply over the first quartile of the distribution for SIMTOT1, but it is much flatter for SIMTOT2. That the curve is the steepest at the very bottom for SIMTOT3 is due to the bigger increase in extreme poverty shown by P1 and P2 in Table 10.3 for that closure.

The upper part of the income change curves is still decreasing, except at the very top. The shape is much closer to what was obtained in Fig. 10.1 with no reranking. That part of the curve is responsible for the drop in summary inequality measures shown in Table 10.3. Yet it is clear from Fig. 10.2 that this drop in inequality is ambiguous. An inequality measure with enough weight on the bottom of the distribution would show an unequalizing, rather than equalizing, effect of the terms-of-trade shock.

The difference between income change curves without and with reranking is still more striking with the scenario of a devaluation caused by a drop in foreign savings (SIMDEV in Figs. 10.3 and 10.4). Without reranking, the same downward-sloping shape as with SIMTOT is obtained for the first three quartiles. In the upper quartile, income losses tend to decrease as one moves further up in the distribution. With SIMTOT, this effect was limited to the top decile. The explanation of that difference comes from the fact that the change in the relative price of food products is much bigger with SIMDEV. Thus the dampening effect of decreasing food shares starts at a level of income lower than for SIMTOT.

Reranking in Fig. 10.4 modifies the shape of the income change curves more radically than in the previous scenario. First, the same steeply increasing segment appears at the bottom of the distribution, which may be interpreted in the same way as for SIMTOT. Differences in steepness are also noticeable when the first macroeconomic closure and the others are compared. Second, the middle of the curve becomes flat, whereas it was decreasing before reranking. As a result, the whole income change curve now looks upward-sloping everywhere, and is so under all three macroeconomic closures. The explanation for this flattening of the income change curve after reranking is the same as that for the change of slope at the bottom. It is essentially due to changes in occupations producing bigger changes in household income than changes in wage rates or self-employment incomes. Because the shock is bigger in SIMDEV, this phenomenon is stronger than with SIMTOT. Closer scrutiny also shows that it is more frequent in the third quartile, where most workers in the formal sector are located. Reranking sends these households further down in the distribution and moves up those households in the second quartile that had the least negative income change. This switch contributes to flattening the income-change curve.

10.5. MICROSIMULATION VERSUS REPRESENTATIVE HOUSEHOLD GROUPS (RHG)

A key question is whether this microsimulation approach adds very much to the standard RHG approach to modeling distribution issues within a macroeconomic

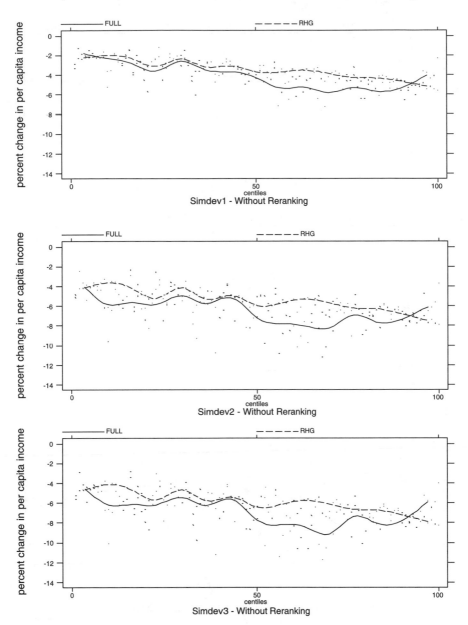

Figure 10.3. Devaluation simulation results without reranking.

framework. To answer this question, this section compares the preceding results obtained with the help of the microsimulation model with results that would have been obtained using RHGs and assuming that the within-group distributions do not change. This comparison suggests that the differences may be quite substantial, in one case even reversing the sign of the effect of the shock on inequality.

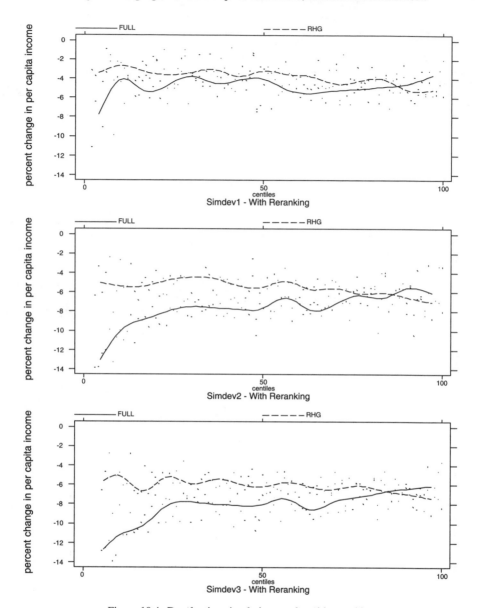

Figure 10.4. Devaluation simulation results with reranking.

Rather than using the prediction of the CGE model for the mean income of the RHGs incorporated in it, and accordingly combining the income distribution observed within those groups, a shortcut was used. We classified households in the original microsimulation sample into groups corresponding to the RHGs in the CGE model – see Appendix A – and then multiplied their incomes by the average income change predicted for that group in the simulation under study. The average income change found in the microsimulation, rather than the change found in the CGE model, was used. Thus, the result does not really correspond to what would have been obtained directly with a CGE/RHG approach. The bias implied by this simplification is to make the two approaches more similar. Simulated changes in summary inequality and poverty measures obtained with the RHG approach appear in Table 10.4. Dotted curves in Figs. 10.1–10.4 show the mean income change by percentile of the distribution simulated with the RHG approach before and after reranking – note that the reranking generally is not the same with the microsimulation and the RHG approaches.

Differences in summary inequality and poverty measures between microsimulation (FULL) in Table 10.3 and the RHG approach in Table 10.4 are readily apparent. Because the overall effect of the terms-of-trade shock on summary aggregate inequality measures is low, the comparison of these aggregate measures is not meaningful. For the urban sector, however, the difference is substantial. The microsimulation model results show an increase in inequality, whereas the RHG approach shows practically no change. Likewise, the increase in all poverty measures is much bigger with the microsimulation model.

Because distribution effects are bigger, the SIMDEV simulation leads to much larger differences between the two approaches. Some results are even contradictory. Thus, the microsimulation shows a clear increase in inequality for the whole distribution as well as for both its urban and rural components, whereas the RHG approach shows a drop in inequality for the whole distribution and practically no change in the urban and rural distributions. Likewise, the microsimulation model leads to much bigger estimates of the effect of the shock on poverty.

The comparison of the dotted and solid curves in Figs. 10.1–10.4 leads to a simple interpretation of the preceding differences. As all effects are more prominent with the SIMDEV simulation, it is convenient to focus on this scenario first. Three observations come immediately to mind when Figs. 10.3 and 10.4 are examined: (a) The dotted and solid income-change curves are very close to each other when no reranking of households takes place. Both sets of curves are downward-sloping overall, although the microsimulation (solid) curves change slope at the very top of the distribution. (b) The dotted curves are very similar across macroeconomic closures, whereas this is much less the case for the solid curves. (c) Reranking drastically modifies the income-change curves for the microsimulation approach, which then slope upward. In contrast, minor changes take place for the dotted RHG curves. Overall, the difference between the income-change curves associated with the two approaches in Fig. 10.4 is striking: a slight equalizing of real incomes for the RHG approach and an unambiguous worsening of the distribution for the microsimulation approach.

Two features of the microsimulation approach are responsible for these three differences. The first has to do with the role of occupational changes in the microsimulation approach. As long as there is no reranking, these occupational changes are interpreted in the same way as changes in earnings or self-employed incomes, and

TABLE 10.4. *Microeconomic simulation results with representative household groups (RHG)*

	BASE	SIMTOT1	SIMTOT2	SIMTOT3	SIMDEV1	SIMDEV2	SIMDEV3
			All				
Per capita income	121.1	−2.5	−2.3	−3.8	−4.3	−6.4	−6.8
Entropy index (0)	35.5	−2.6	−3.0	−2.6	−2.1	−2.1	−2.0
Entropy index (1)	49.3	−2.5	−2.9	−2.6	−2.1	−2.3	−2.2
Gini index	45.6	−1.3	−1.5	−1.3	−1.1	−1.1	−1.0
Head-count index (P0)	9.2	0.8	−0.8	4.0	8.1	16.2	17.2
Poverty gap index (P1)	2.2	0.8	−0.8	5.1	8.4	17.5	19.5
Poverty severity index (P2)	0.9	0.9	−0.5	4.9	8.1	16.8	18.6
			Urban				
Per capita income	170.9	−4.9	−5.1	−6.4	−6.6	−9.5	−9.8
Entropy index (0)	38.7	−0.4	−0.4	−0.3	0.3	1.0	1.1
Entropy index (1)	53.9	−0.4	−0.5	−0.4	0.0	0.2	0.3
Gini index	47.5	−0.2	−0.2	−0.1	0.2	0.4	0.5
Head-count index (P0)	4.0	17.7	18.3	22.5	26.6	39.1	39.3
Poverty gap index (P1)	1.1	14.6	15.1	20.2	25.5	43.2	45.3
Poverty severity index (P2)	0.4	13.4	13.8	19.1	24.4	42.6	44.9
			Rural				
Per capita income	90.6	0.2	0.9	−0.8	−1.7	−2.8	−3.3
Entropy index (0)	25.5	−0.5	−0.6	−0.2	−0.2	0.9	1.0
Entropy index (1)	33.1	−0.3	−0.3	0.0	0.1	1.3	1.3
Gini index	38.7	−0.3	−0.3	−0.1	−0.1	0.4	0.4
Head-count index (P0)	12.4	−2.5	−4.6	0.4	4.4	11.7	12.8
Poverty gap index (P1)	2.9	−2.2	−4.3	1.7	4.6	11.8	13.8
Poverty severity index (P2)	1.2	−1.8	−3.6	1.8	4.5	11.1	12.9

the two approaches yield similar income change curves. On closer scrutiny, however, it is found that these occupational changes tend to concentrate in those percentiles where the distance between the two curves in Fig. 10.3 is the largest. This result is to be expected. If occupational changes leading to big changes in household income were uniformly distributed within each representative group, there would be no difference between the two approaches from that point of view. The same argument also explains why reranking substantially modifies the income-change curve with the microsimulation approach, but has limited effects in the case of the RHG approach.

The second feature responsible for the differences outlined above is the heterogeneity of consumption behavior – that is, budget shares – in the microsimulation approach. The distribution of real income within each household group in the RHG approach is assumed to be constant and could not be affected by a change in relative consumer prices. Things are different in the microsimulation approach. Even though the relative nominal incomes within each group might not be affected by the shock being simulated, a change in relative consumption prices would be responsible for changes in the distribution of real income. As noted above, this phenomenon is responsible for the upward sloping of the income change curve at the right end of the distribution even before reranking. It is not present in the dotted curves of Fig. 10.3.

10.6. CONCLUSION

The top-down, micro–macro framework discussed in this paper generates income changes in a sample of actual households drawn from a household survey that are consistent, once they have been aggregated, with the predictions of a multisector CGE macro model. At the micro level, income changes are obtained through an explicit representation of the actual combination of different income sources within households, the way in which these income sources are affected by macro phenomena, and the way their combination may change through desired or undesired modifications in the occupational status of household members. This method for estimating the distributional impact of macro shocks and policies contrasts with the usual approach, which consists of modeling the behavior of various representative household groups at the macro level and then assuming that the distribution of income within those groups is exogenous and independent of the macro phenomena being studied.

The results from the experiments reported in this paper suggests that the microsimulation and RHG approaches may lead to quite different estimates of the distributional effects of macroeconomic shocks and policy changes. In some cases, the results have different signs – the microsimulation approach points to a strongly unequalizing effect of a devaluation due to a reduction in foreign savings, whereas the RHG approach predicts a slight improvement in the distribution of real household income. There are two main reasons for this difference. First, the fact that the microsimulation approach takes into account changes in occupations allows for an important source of actual changes in the distribution of income that is absent from the RHG approach. Second, the microsimulation approach explicitly accounts for heterogeneous consumption behavior.

The fact that the microsimulation approach proves to be more sensitive than the RHG approach in terms of income distribution is not necessarily a test of whether it is superior. Ultimately, its superiority lies in the fact that it accounts for phenomena that are known to be important in explaining distributional changes – that is, changes in types of occupation or combination of income sources and heterogeneous consumption behavior. But then the problem is to know whether the representation of these phenomena is satisfactory. The ad hoc nature of some of the assumptions that permit linking in a simple top-down way a macro model and a household-income model based on a full sample of households has been explicitly stressed. The same is true for the fact that the representation of the income generation behavior of households is based on reduced form rather than structural econometric modeling. More work is needed in order to integrate satisfactorily micro and macro approaches to distributional issues. The method proposed in this paper may be a useful practical step in that direction.

APPENDIX A: STRUCTURE OF THE SOCIAL ACCOUNTING MATRIX

Activities

AA-AGFOO	Farm Food Crops
AA-AGCAS	Farm Nonfood Crops
AA-AGLIV	Livestock Products
AA-AGFOR	Forestry and Hunting
AA-AGFIS	Fishery and Drying and Salting of Fish
AF-COGAP	Coal and Metal Ore and Petroleum and Natural Gas
AI-OTHMI	Other Mining and Quarrying – Informal
AF-OTHMI	Other Mining and Quarrying – Formal
AI-FOODB	Food, Beverages, and Tobacco Manufacturing – Informal
AF-FOODB	Food, Beverages, and Tobacco Manufacturing – Formal
AI-TEXTI	Spinning and Textile and Leather and Wearing Apparel Manufacturing Industry – Informal
AF-TEXTI	Spinning and Textile and Leather and Wearing Apparel Manufacturing Industry – Formal
AI-WOODI	Wood and Wood Products Industries – Informal
AF-WOODI	Wood and Wood Products Industries – Formal
AI-PAPER	Paper Printing, Transport Equipment, Metal Products, and Other Manufacturing Industries – Informal

AF-PAPER	Paper Printing, Transport Equipment, Metal Products, and Other Manufacturing Industries – Formal
AI-CHEMF	Chemical Fertilization and Clay Products and Cement and Basic Metal Manufacturing Industries – Informal
AF-CHEMF	Chemical Fertilization and Clay Products and Cement and Basic Metal Manufacturing Industries – Formal
AF-ELECW	Electricity and Gas and Water Supply
AI-CONST	Construction Sector – Informal
AF-CONST	Construction Sector – Formal
AI-TRADE	Whole Sale and Retail Trade and Transport – Storage – Warehousing – Informal
AF-TRADE	Whole Sale and Retail Trade and Transport – Storage – Warehousing – Formal
AI-RESTA	Restaurants – Informal
AF-RESTA	Restaurants – Formal
AI-HOTEL	Hotel and Lodging Places – Informal
AF-HOTEL	Hotel and Lodging Places – Formal
AI-TRANS	Road Transport and Railways – Informal
AF-TRANS	Road Transport and Railways – Formal
AI-AIRTR	Air and Water Transport and Communications – Informal
AF-AIRTR	Air and Water Transport and Communications – Formal
AI-BANKI	Banking and Insurance – Informal
AF-BANKI	Banking and Insurance – Formal
AI-REALE	Real Estate and Business Services – Informal
AF-REALE	Real Estate and Business Services – Formal
AF-PUBLI	Public Administration, Defense, Social, Recreational and Cultural Services
AI-OTHSE	Personal Household and Other Services – Informal
AF-OTHSE	Personal Household and Other Services – Formal

Commodities

C-AGFOOD	Farm Food Crops
C-AGCASH	Farm Nonfood Crops
C-AGLIVE	Livestock and Products
C-AGFORE	Forestry and Hunting
C-AGFISH	Fishery and Drying and Salting of Fish
C-COGAPE	Coal and Metal Ore and Petroleum and Natural Gas
C-OTHMIN	Other Mining and Quarrying
C-FOODBE	Food and Beverages and Tobacco Manufacturing
C-TEXTIL	Spinning and Textile and Leather and Wearing Apparel Manufacturing Products
C-WOODIN	Wood and Wood Products

C-PAPERP	Paper Printing, Transport Equipment, Metal Products, and Other Manufacturing Products
C-CHEMFE	Chemical Fertilization and Clay Products and Cement and Basic Metal Manufacturing Products
C-ELECWA	Electricity and Gas and Water Supply
C-CONSTR	Construction Sector
C-TRADES	Wholesale and Retail Trade and Transport – Storage – Warehousing
C-RESTAU	Restaurants
C-HOTELS	Hotel and Lodging Places
C-TRANSP	Road Transport and Railways
C-AIRTRN	Air and Water Transport and Communications
C-BANKIN	Banking and Insurance
C-REALES	Real Estate and Business Services
C-PUBLIC	Public Administration, Defense, Social, Recreational and Cultural Services
C-OTHSER	Personal Household and Other Services

Labor

LAB-UMU	Urban Male Unskilled Labor
LAB-UMS	Urban Male Skilled Labor
LAB-UFU	Urban Female Unskilled Labor
LAB-UFS	Urban Female Skilled Labor
LAB-RMU	Rural Male Unskilled Labor
LAB-RMS	Rural Male Skilled Labor
LAB-RFU	Rural Female Unskilled Labor
LAB-RFS	Rural Female Skilled Labor

Capital

CAP-LAND	Land
CAP-HOUS	Owner Occupied Housing
CAP-ORUR	Unincorporated Rural Capital
CAP-OURB	Unincorporated Urban Capital
CAP-PRIV	Incorporated Domestic Private Capital
CAP-PUBL	Incorporated Domestic Public Capital
CAP-FORE	Incorporated Foreign Capital

Institutions

HH-AGEMP	Agricultural Households – Employees
HH-AGL05	Agricultural Households – Operators 0.0 to 0.5 ha
HH-AGL10	Agricultural Households – Operators 0.5 to 1.0 ha
HH-AGLBG	Agricultural Households – Operators more than 1.0 ha
HH-LORUR	Nonagricultural Households – Lower Level Rural
HH-NLRUR	Nonagricultural Households – Non Labor Force Rural

HH-HIRUR   Nonagricultural Households – Higher Level Rural
HH-LOURB   Nonagricultural Households – Lower Level Urban
HH-NLURB   Nonagricultural Households – Non Labor Force Urban
HH-HIURB   Nonagricultural Households – Higher Level Urban
ENT   Companies
GOV   Government
VATAX   Value Added Tax
STAX   Sales Tax
IMPTAX   Import Tax
DIRTAX   Direct Tax
ROW   Rest of the World
SAVINV   Savings–Investment Account

REFERENCES

I. Adelman and S. Robinson (1978), *Income Distribution Policy in Developing Countries: A Case Study of Korea*. New York: Oxford University Press.

V. Ahuja, B. Bidani, F. Ferreira, and K. Walton (1997), *Everyone's Miracle? Revisiting Poverty and Inequality in East Asia*. Washington, DC: World Bank.

V. Alatas and F. Bourguignon (2000), "The Evolution of the Distribution of Income During Indonesian Fast Growth: 1980–1996," mimeo, Princeton University.

P. Armington (1969), "The Geographic Pattern of Trade and the Effects of Price Changes," *International Monetary Fund Staff Papers* 16(2): 179–201.

I. Aziz and E. Thorbecke (2001), "Modeling the Socio-Economic Impact of the Financial Crisis: The Case of Indonesia," mimeo, Cornell University.

F. Bourguignon, F. Ferreira, and N. Lustig (1998), "The Microeconomics of Income Distribution Dynamics, a Research Proposal." Washington, DC: The Inter-American Development Bank and the World Bank.

F. Bourguignon, M. Fournier, and M. Gurgand (2001), "Fast Development with a Stable Income Distribution: Taiwan, 1979–1994." *Review of Income and Wealth*, 47(2): 139–63.

M. Browning, L. Hansen, and J. Heckman (1999), "Microdata and General Equilibrium models," in John B. Taylor and Michael Woodford (Eds.), *Handbook of Macroeconomics*, Vol. 1A. Amsterdam: North-Holland.

Central Bureau of Statistics (CBS) (1998), "Perhitungan Jumlah Penduduk Miskin dengan GNP Per Kapita Riil," mimeo. Jakarta.

D. Cogneau (2001), "Formation du revenu, segmentation et discrimination sur le marché du travail d'une ville en développement: Antananarivo fin de siècle," DIAL DT/2001/18.

D. Cogneau and A-S. Robilliard (2001), "Growth, Distribution and Poverty in Madagascar: Learning from a Microsimulation Model in a General Equilibrium Framework," IFPRI TMD Discussion Paper No. 61 and DIAL DT/2001/19.

B. Decaluwe and A. Martens (1988), "CGE Modeling and Developing Economies: A Concise Empirical Survey of 73 Applications to 26 Countries," *Journal of Policy Modeling* 10(4): 529–68.

K. Dervis, J. de Melo, and S. Robinson (1982), *General Equilibrium Models for Development Policy*. New York: Cambridge University Press.

S. Devarajan, J. D. Lewis, and S. Robinson (1993), "External Shocks, Purchasing Power Parity, and the Equilibrium Real Exchange Rate," *World Bank Economic Review* 7(1): 45–63.

J. DiNardo, N. Fortin, and T. Lemieux (1996), "Labor Market Institutions and the Distribution of Wages, 1973–1992: A Semiparametric Approach," *Econometrica* 64(5): 1001–44.

J. Heckman (2001), "Accounting for Heterogeneity, Diversity and General Equilibrium in Evaluating Social Programmes," *Economic Journal*, v111, n475, 654–99

H. Lofgren, R. L. Harris, and S. Robinson (2001), "A Standard Computable General Equilibrium (CGE) Model in GAMS," IFPRI, Trade and Macroeconomics Division, Discussion Paper No. 75.

D. Mookherjee and A. Shorrocks (1982), "A Decomposition Analysis of the Trend in UK Income Inequality," *Economic Journal* 92(368): 886–902.

N. S. S. Narayana, K. S. Parikh, and T. N. Srinivasan (1991), *Agriculture, Growth and Redistribution of Income: Policy Analysis with a General Equilibrium Model of India*, Contributions to Economic Analysis, no. 190. Amsterdam, Oxford, Tokyo: North-Holland, distributed in the U.S. and Canada by Elsevier Science, New York/New Delhi: Allied.

M. Plumb (2001), *"Empirical Tax Modeling: An Applied General Equilibrium Model for the UK Incorporating Micro-unit Household Data and Imperfect Competition*, D.Phil. Thesis, Nuffield College, University of Oxford.

A.-S. Robilliard, F. Bourguignon, and S. Robinson (2001), "Crisis and Income Distribution: A Micro–Macro Model for Indonesia," mimeo.

S. Robinson (1989), "Multisectoral Models," in H. Chenery and T. N. Srinivasan (Eds.), *Handbook of Development Economics*. Amsterdam: North–Holland, Chap. 18.

S. Robinson, A. Cattaneo, and M. El-Said (2001), "Updating and Estimating a Social Accounting Matrix Using Cross Entropy Methods," *Economic Systems Research* 13(1): 47–64.

E. Taylor and I. Adelman (1996), *Village Economies: The Design, Estimation and Use of Villagewide Economic Models*. Cambridge: Cambridge University Press.

R. M. Townsend and K. Ueda (2001), "Transitional Growth and Increasing Inequality with Financial Deepening," paper presented at IMF Conference on Macro Economics and Poverty Reduction."

11 General Equilibrium Modeling for Global Climate Change

Alan S. Manne

ABSTRACT: The economic analysis of climate policy measures has evolved in response to the United Nations Framework Convention on Climate Change, and then the Kyoto Protocol. The original book by William Nordhaus led to a large and growing literature on the economics of climate change. Rather than attempt to describe all these papers in detail, I cover some of their principal findings through results reported by the Energy Modeling Forum. I also summarize portions of my own joint work with Richard Richels. Despite its simplicity, our model illustrates some of the most controversial issues in this debate. It provides a perspective on emissions and on taxes to restrain these emissions. It illustrates the implications of alternative discount rates. It also illustrates some conditions under which we can separate equity from efficiency issues.

11.1. INTRODUCTION

Global climate change is a multidisciplinary topic. The work was begun by physical scientists and then taken up by ecologists. Economists were latecomers, but they have been highly articulate. It was easy for everyone to agree on "win–win" strategies, for example, energy conservation measures that would reduce carbon emissions and also reduce costs. The economists made it clear, however, that it would be much more difficult to reach agreement on "cost–benefit" strategies – international protocols in which near-term costs are incurred by one group of nations so that future benefits can be obtained by others. Discounting and equity–efficiency tradeoffs are an essential feature of this problem. They are a central issue in integrated assessment modeling, and this is why it is useful to apply the framework of general equilibrium analysis.

The economic analysis of climate policy measures has evolved in response to the United Nations Framework Convention on Climate Change, and then the Kyoto Protocol. The original book by William Nordhaus (1994) led to a large and growing

Presented at the conference "Frontiers in Applied General Equilibrium Modeling" held at the Cowles Foundation, Yale University, on April 5–6, 2002. Helpful comments have been received from Kirit Parikh, Richard Richels, Thomas Rutherford, T. N. Srinivasan, and John Weyant. For research assistance, the author is indebted to Charles Ng.

literature on the economics of climate change. Rather than attempt to describe all these papers in detail, I cover a few of their findings through results reported by the Energy Modeling Forum. I also summarize portions of my own joint work with Richard Richels. Despite its simplicity, our model illustrates some of the most controversial issues in this debate. It provides a perspective on emissions and on taxes to restrain these emissions. It illustrates the implications of alternative discount rates. It also illustrates some conditions under which we can separate equity from efficiency issues.

11.2. THE FRAMEWORK CONVENTION ON CLIMATE CHANGE AND THE KYOTO PROTOCOL ON CLIMATE CHANGE

The United Nations Framework Convention on Climate Change (FCCC) was adopted on May 9, 1992, and it was opened for signature at the UN Conference on Environment and Development in June 1992. No binding quantitative measures were adopted at that time, but the FCCC's purpose was stated clearly: "to achieve... stabilization of greenhouse gas concentrations in the atmosphere at a level that would prevent dangerous anthropogenic interference with the climate system" [Article 2].

In December 1997, the Third Conference of the Parties (COP-3) to the FCCC deliberated in Kyoto, Japan. At that point, there were extensive negotiations and hard bargaining. Little or no emphasis was placed on economic efficiency. The earlier general goal was translated into specific numerical targets for the first "budget period," 2008–2012. The greenhouse gas reductions were to apply solely to the "Annex 1" group of industrialized countries. In the aggregate, these limits were designed to lead to greenhouse gas emissions about 5% below the 1990 level. No specific rationale was produced for the 5% reduction – in terms of either costs or benefits of abatement. And no emissions reductions were imposed on the developing countries – those outside Annex 1.

Subsequent meetings have attempted to clarify various ambiguities in the Kyoto Protocol: the scope for emissions trading, incentives for the developing countries to join in a "clean development mechanism," carbon sinks, and the role of noncarbon greenhouse gases. The international negotiating process has been anything but smooth. It received a severe blow in March 2001, when President Bush announced that he opposed the Protocol. It is still an open issue whether the United States will eventually participate in any international agreement of this type.

11.3. A MULTIMODEL EVALUATION BY THE ENERGY MODELING FORUM

The Kyoto Protocol stimulated a good deal of controversy. Some of this was polemic, but some was analytic and lent itself to model comparisons of the type for which the Energy Modeling Forum (GMF) is internationally known. John Weyant, the director

TABLE 11.1. *Models analyzing post-Kyoto EMF scenarios*

Model acronym (name)	Home institution(s)
ABARE-GTEM (Global Trade and Environmental Model)	Australian Bureau of Agriculture and Resource Economics (ABARE, Australia)
AIM (Asian–Pacific Integrated Model)	National Institute for Environmental Studies (NIES-Japan) Kyoto University
CETA (Carbon Emissions Trajectory Assessment)	Electric Power Research Institute Teisberg Associates
FUND (Climate Framework for Uncertainty, Negotiation, and Distribution)	Vrije Universiteit Amsterdam (Netherlands)
G-Cubed (Global General Equilibrium Growth Model)	Australian National University University of Texas U.S. Environmental Protection Agency
GRAPE (Global Relationship Assessment to Protect the Environment)	Institute for Applied Energy (Japan) Research Institute of Innovative Technology for Earth (Japan) University of Tokyo
MERGE 3.0 (Model for Evaluating Regional and Global Effects of GHG Reduction Policies)	Stanford University Electric Power Research Institute
MIT-EPPA (Emissions Projection and Policy Analysis Model)	Massachusetts Institute of Technology
MS-MRT (Multi-Sector-Multi-Region Trade Model)	Charles River Associates University of Colorado
Oxford Model (Oxford Economic Forecasting	Oxford Economic Foreasting
RICE (Regional Integrated Climate and Economy Model)	Yale University
SGM (Second Generation Model)	Battelle Pacific Northwest National Laboratory
WorldScan	Central Planning Bureau/Rijksinstituut voor Volksgezondheid en Milieuhygiene (RIVM) (Netherlands)

of the EMF, edited a special issue of *The Energy Journal.* The following charts and tables are reproduced from the summary paper by Weyant and Hill (1999).

The EMF study was based upon work undertaken jointly by 13 modeling groups. (See Table 11.1.) Half of them originated in the United States, and half were from other nations. All these papers report carbon emissions, and they all report the carbon taxes implied by the Kyoto Protocol for 2010. Beyond that, there is a wide diversity in their nature. Some have a multisector, general equilibrium structure, and some provide energy-sector technology details. Some are intertemporal, and others are recursive. All are multiregional. Only one of these models is designed to report short-run unemployment and financial effects such as exchange-rate movements. For additional general equilibrium models related to trade and environmental policies, see the following Web site: http://www.ksg.harvard.edu/tep/enveclink.htm.

The EMF asked its participants to report detailed results for fifteen scenarios. Of these, perhaps the most instructive is the very first one – a "modelers' reference" case, with the modelers free to make their own projections of each region's GDP, population, energy prices, and so forth. This scenario was to be based on no new policies other than those effective prior to the Kyoto accord. Figure 11.1 shows the carbon emissions reported by the EMF models for the Annex I countries. It is not altogether surprising that there are three-to-one differences for the distant future, the year 2100. This could well be the result of differences in estimates of GDP growth, carbon-saving technology developments, and so forth.

It is far more surprising, however, that the modeling teams reported an almost two-to-one difference in their carbon projections for the year 2000. Figure 11.1 suggests that the baseline statistics differed significantly between these models. Moreover, the geographical definition of "Annex I" could well have differed from one model to another. To the extent that the Kyoto negotiators faced this type of uncertainty, their task would have been even more difficult than it seemed at the time.

Given the year 2000 emission differences in the "reference case," it is little wonder that the individual models report wide differences in the costs of meeting the Kyoto targets. The higher the reference case emissions projection, the greater is the percentage cutback effort that has to be made in order to meet a 1990-based target. It then becomes much easier to understand the range of carbon tax results that are reported by the EMF modelers. A "carbon tax" may be interpreted literally, but also serves as shorthand for a variety of policy measures that might be undertaken in order to meet Kyoto commitments. Examples of such measures might include tax rebates, public transport subsidies, and efficiency standards. To a political leader, these would have the advantage of lower visibility than direct tax measures.

Now consider Fig. 11.2, the "carbon tax" results for the United States in 2010. For each model, up to four EMF scenarios are reported: (1) one in which there is no international trading of emission rights, (2) one in which trading is limited to the Annex I nations, (3) one in which there is a "double bubble" (that is, there is internal trading within the European Union, and there is trading within the balance of Annex I countries), and (4) one in which there is full global trading, with the non-Annex I countries constrained to their reference scenario emissions. These scenarios can be interpreted in terms of the gains from trade – for short, "where" flexibility. Depending on *where* the mitigation takes place, there are different economic impacts on different regions.

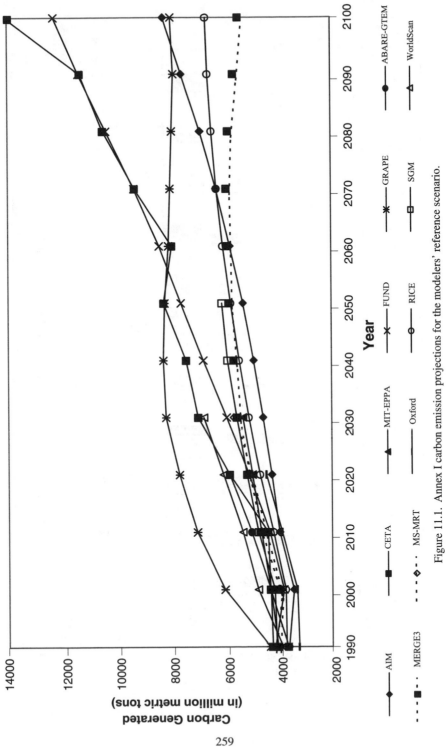

Figure 11.1. Annex I carbon emission projections for the modelers' reference scenario.

AIM   CETA   FUND   MIT-EPPA   GRAPE   ABARE-GTEM

MERGE3   MS-MRT   Oxford   RICE   SGM   WorldScan

259

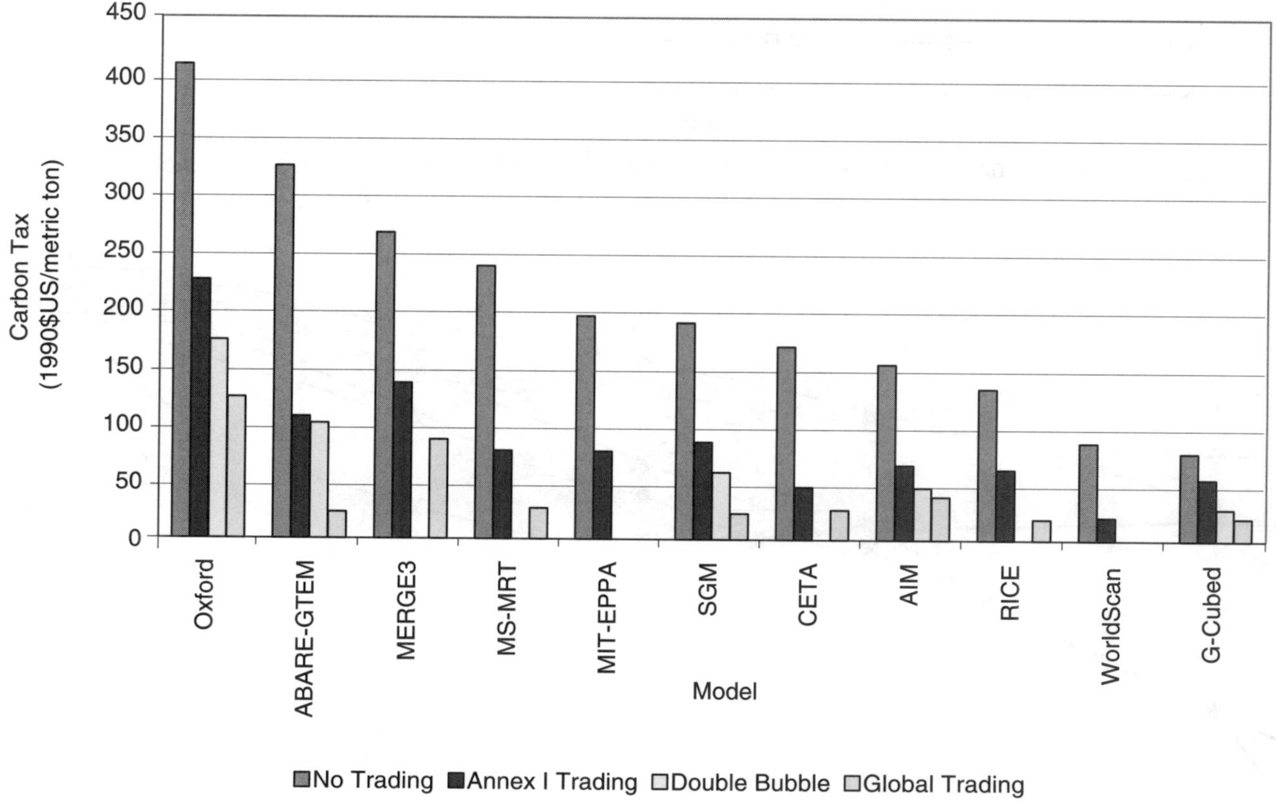

Figure 11.2. Year 2010 carbon tax comparisons for the the United States.

■No Trading ■Annex I Trading □Double Bubble □Global Trading

Each reader is free to make an independent assessment of the likelihood of acceptability of any of these trading scenarios. Each scenario makes it painfully clear who might be the gainers and who might be the losers from the Kyoto round of emission restrictions. In this respect, climate change policy resembles other forms of world trade negotiations.

Figure 11.2 contains both good news and bad news. The bad news is that there is a more than ten-to-one range between the carbon taxes implied by the different models. How can a parliament be asked to endorse a carbon tax if it does not know whether this tax is going to be $20 per ton or $200? This range is a consequence of the very different assumptions made by these models with respect to price elasticities, adjustment lags, and underlying growth.

The good news is that the models uniformly report that there can be substantial reductions in the emissions tax if there is trade between nations. In particular, the collapse of the former Soviet Union led to a drastic cut in its GDP and carbon emissions between 1990 and 1997, but the Kyoto Protocol provided it with sufficient emission rights to serve as a major exporter of these rights to the remainder of the Annex I countries. This is sometimes termed "Russian hot air." The greater the possibilities for trade in "hot air," the lower are the direct economic losses associated with the Kyoto Protocol in 2010.

In order to make a quantitative estimate of these losses, it is clear that we need some sort of general equilibrium model of international trade. At a minimum, such a model will include carbon emission rights. Many of the EMF models also allow trade in oil, gas, and coal. Several of them allow trade in energy-intensive commodities such as iron, steel, and other primary metals. The greater the variety of goods and services considered, the greater are the possibilities for "carbon leakage" – adaptation to inefficient carbon constraints by changing the region-of-origin patterns of international trade.

11.4. STRUCTURE OF MERGE

We will now turn to a specific model named MERGE (model for evaluating regional and global effects of greenhouse gas reductions). In referring to this model, I refer to a more recent version than that included in EMF16. See the Web site www.stanford.edu/group/MERGE. Perhaps the most significant revision is one involving the base year for "benchmarking" the model's parameters. For the EMF 16 study, we used 1990 as the base year. Since then, we have shifted to 2000. From a theoretical perspective, this is a trivial modification. From a practical perspective, it is a major change. With less time for adjustment, this leads to a drastic lowering of the supply and demand elasticities in 2010, and it becomes more expensive to reach the abatement goals of the Kyoto Protocol.

Much of the theoretical structure of MERGE has remained unchanged since the model was first formulated. Throughout its development, the energy sector has been described in much greater detail than the nonenergy sector. Within each region, there are two submodels. ETA is a "bottom-up" model of energy technology assessment, and MACRO is a "top-down" model of energy demands. That is, there is a nested economy-wide production function with inputs of capital, labor, and electrical and nonelectrical energy. This allows directly for price-induced energy conservation – and also for autonomous energy efficiency improvements. The aggregate output is the numéraire of the system. It is employed for consumption, investment, international trade, and energy costs.

For each point in time, the population, the labor force, and the *potential* GDP are taken as input assumptions. It is assumed that the world's population will nearly double by the end of the twenty-first century, but that it will stabilize thereafter. The overall GDP growth is broadly consistent with IPCC (International Panel on Climate Change) scenarios. Productivity gains are expressed in terms of the potential for per capita GDP growth.

Through 2020, these GDP estimates are taken directly from the U.S. Energy Information Administration (2002). Thereafter, they are projected by means of region-specific logistic functions. These are specified through three points: the EIA value in 2020, an asymptotic convergence of all regions to a GDP of $200,000 per capita, and a value in 2100 that is chosen to avoid a sharp discontinuity in the growth rate immediately after 2020. With these logistic functions, the OECD regions continue to grow at a modest pace during the twenty-first century, but the developing countries grow more rapidly. This is an optimistic scenario – one in which there is growth and eventual convergence between the technologies and living standards in all regions.

Each region's labor force is expressed in terms of "efficiency units" and is taken as an index number proportional to the potential GDP. The marginal productivity of capital may change over time, but – with an open international capital market – it must be uniform between regions at a single point in time. Through a Ramsey-type model of savings and investment, we endogenously deduce the quantity of capital supplied and demanded.

Initially, international trade was modeled in terms of five geopolitical regions. Today the model is disaggregated into nine regions: the USA, Western Europe, Japan, CANZ (Canada + Australia + New Zealand), EEFSU (Eastern Europe + former Soviet Union), China, India, MOPEC (Mexico + OPEC), and ROW (rest of world). This provides a handy way to enter into the climate debate through distinctions between Annex 1 countries, the 1990 membership of the OECD, the oil-exporting nations, and so forth. This geographical structure is, however, too aggregated to provide the kind of detailed picture that is needed, say, for a pipeline and tanker network of crude oil and natural gas movements. The internationally tradeable goods include the numéraire, oil, gas, carbon emission rights, and EIS (an aggregate of the goods originating in the energy-intensive sectors of manufacturing).

The MACRO model's parameters are derived from the *potential* GDP – together with the base year prices and quantities of energy, capital, and labor. The *realized* GDP is endogenously derived from the MACRO model, and the general equilibrium structure automatically allows for changes in the prices of each of the production inputs. In almost all scenarios that have been explored with MERGE, it turns out that the maximum difference between the potential and the realized GDP is only a few percentage points. Why this small difference? Because the value of energy constitutes only a small share of the total value of the inputs.

At first, the solution of our model was based upon an informal price-guided decomposition procedure. Fortunately, it was at about this time that Rutherford devised his variant of the Negishi weight algorithm. He showed that when production sets are convex, each agent (here each region) has homothetic preferences, and each agent has fixed endowments of goods, it is possible to convert the standard economic equilibrium problem into a sequence of "joint maximization" problems. In equilibrium, it turns out that the Negishi weights are equal to each agent's share of the present value of global endowments. See Rutherford (1999).

To initiate the algorithm, an arbitrary Negishi weight is associated with each agent's utility. A joint maximization problem is solved – with constraints to ensure a balance between the supplies and demands of each good. The Negishi weights are then revised so that each agent comes closer to satisfying its budget constraint. Each of the budget constraints is expressed in terms of present-value prices (based on the international productivity of capital), and the cumulative present value of each region's current account deficit must add up to zero.

There is no theoretical proof that Rutherford's algorithm will converge, and some numerical counterexamples have been developed. In practice, however, the procedure works well. Not many iterations are required to obtain good numerical convergence. Currently, it is routine for us to solve problems with nine Negishi agents (one for each region) and 50,000 prices plus activity levels. Using GAMS in conjunction with Drud's CONOPT3 solver on a 1000-mHz machine and a "hot start," the run times seldom exceed an hour.

One detail arises in connection with models of global climate change. In addition to private goods (e.g., capital and labor resources), there are *public* goods. In some climate change models, the public good may be described as "carbon concentrations." In others, it may be "mean global temperature change" or an "economic loss factor" associated with climate change. In any case, we all inhabit a world in which greenhouse gases are thoroughly mixed in the atmosphere. At each point in time, all nations are confronted with the identical quantity of this public good. For price-guided decentralization, one must then assign ownership rights. If, for example, the analysis represents an extension of the Kyoto Protocol, one can imagine an assignment of greenhouse gas emission rights to each region in each future time period. One can then examine the region-by-region costs of abatement and also the implications for global temperature change.

To obtain some idea of the structure that is currently included, see the constraints listed in Table 11.2. These are grouped under four main headings: MACRO, ETA, CLIMATE, and IMPACTS. Three sets of indices appear in most of the constraints: one each for regions (rg), time periods (tp), and states-of-world (sw) for decisions under uncertainty. Other indices play a more specialized role, for example, expansion and decline limits. Not all of the constraints are imposed in all applications.

TABLE 11.2. *Equations of the MERGE model*

Index definitions	
rg	Regions
tp	Time periods (usually decades)
sw	States of world (for analysis of decisions under uncertainty)
trd	Tradeables
dle	Electricity technologies subject to decline limits
dln	Nonelectric technologies subject to decline limits
xle	Electricity technologies subject to expansion limits
xlg	Gas-fired technologies subject to expansion limits
xln	Nonelectric technologies subject to expansion limits
x	Exhaustible fossil fuel resources (oil, gas and coal)
box	Carbon dioxide decay boxes
ghg	Greenhouse gases

MACRO submodel	
nweldf	Negishi welfare definition
newcap(rg,tp,sw)	New capital
newprod(rg,tp,sw)	New production
newelec(rg,tp,sw)	New electric energy
newnon(rg,tp,sw)	New nonelectric energy
totalcap(rg,tp,sw)	Total capital stock
totalprod(rg,tp,sw)	Total production
tc(rg,tp,sw)	Terminal condition on investment and capital stock

ETA submodel	
supelec(*,*,sw)	Supply of electricity
supnon(*,*,sw)	Supply of nonelectric energy
supgas(*,*,sw)	Supply of gas
supoil(*,*,sw)	Supply of oil
supcoal(*,*,sw)	Supply of coal
supeis(*,*,sw)	Supply of eis (energy-intensive sectors)
gfrac(rg,tp,sw)	Gas fraction of nonelectric energy
rscav(rg,tp,x,sw)	Undiscovered resources available
rsvav(rg,tp,x,sw)	Proven reserves available
rdflim(rg,tp,x,sw)	Resource depletion limit
prvlim(rg,tp,x,sw)	Production-reserve limit
expe(rg,tp,xle,sw)	Expansion rate of xle technologies
expg(rg,tp,sw)	Expansion rate of xlg technologies
expn(rg,tp,xln,sw)	Expansion rate of xln technologies
dece(rg,tp,dle,sw)	Decline rate of dle technologies
decn(rg,tp,dln,sw)	Decline rate of dln technologies
deco(rg,tp,sw)	Decline rate of oilnon
decg(rg,tp,sw)	Decline rate of gasnon

cpedf(tp,sw)	Cumulative global production of learning by doing – electric energy
cpndf(tp,sw)	Cumulative global production of learning by doing – nonelectric energy
costnrg(rg,tp,sw)	Cost of energy
cc(rg,tp,sw)	Capacity constraint
trdbal(tp,trd,sw)	Global trade balance
ntdef(trd,tp,rg,sw)	Triggers definition of positive exports
carlev(rg,tp,sw)	Carbon emissions level – billion tons
clevbd(tp,rg,sw)	Upper bound on annual carbon-equivalent emissionsq
shares(rg,tp,sw)	Shares in global carbon emissions

CLIMATE submodel

co2abt(tp,rg,sw)	Upper bound on regional CO_2 abatement (sinks)
ch4abt(tp,rg,sw)	Upper bound on regional methane abatement
n2oabt(tp,rg,sw)	Upper bound on regional N_2O abatement
wcardf(tp,sw)	Definition of world energy-related CO_2 emissions
wch4df(tp,sw)	Definition of world energy-related CH_4 emissions
co2box(box,tpsw)	CO_2 accumulation in each box
co2stock(tp,sw)	Atmospheric CO_2 stock accumulation
ostock(ghg,tp,sw)	Other greenhouse gases stock accumulation
ptdf(tp,sw)	Potential temperature definition
atdf(tp,sw)	Actual temperature definition
atin(tp,sw)	Decadal increment in actual temperature

IMPACTS submodel

marketd(rg,tp,sw)	Market damages from temperature increase
elfdf(rg,tp,sw)	Nonmarket damages from temperature increase

For example, in most case studies with MERGE, uncertainty is handled through sensitivity analysis. It is only in special applications that we define several states of world and then assign explicit probabilities and dates for the resolution of these uncertainties. For an EMF study applying this type of decision analysis, see Manne (1996).

By taking a close look at Table 11.2, the reader can get some idea of the modeling details. For example, there are exhaustible oil and gas resources in each of several different cost categories. The model allows for technical progress so that the price of these resources does not inevitably rise over time. Technical progress is introduced in two forms – autonomous (time-dependent) and learning-by-doing. Learning may be important, but it leads to nonconvexities. One idea might be to follow the approach taken by Van der Zwaan et al. (1999) and by Kypreos and Bahn (2001), and apply mixed integer programming. Another approach might be to rely upon the work of Sahinidis (2000) and incorporate nonconvexities directly into a nonlinear programming model by "branch-and-reduce" methods. At this point, MERGE relies on a heuristic for ruling out local optima. Nonconvexities may be important, but they also create difficulties for the standard general equilibrium concept of price-guided decentralization. Even though the Rutherford algorithm is based on the absence of nonconvexities, in practice we have experienced no difficulties arising from their presence through learning-by-doing.

The logic of the model is set up so that carbon and other greenhouse gas emissions are translated directly into concentrations. In turn, concentrations may be translated into radiative forcing, then into potential mean temperature change, actual temperature change, and into both market and nonmarket impacts. Each of these steps involves even more guesswork than is usual in economics. Some of us are reluctant to go beyond the analysis of alternative concentration targets. Others proceed to temperature targets, and others go all the way to translating the impacts into economic loss factors. None of these approaches is altogether satisfactory. No one model is ideally designed to handle all of these features simultaneously.

Space does not permit us to consider the case of decisions under uncertainty. The state-of-world index (sw) will therefore be omitted in the following exposition. Rather than write down all the MERGE equations explicitly, it will be instructive to examine just two classes of them. One is perhaps the most speculative relationship in the entire model – the definition of $ELF_{rg,tp}$, the economic loss factor associated with nonmarket damages in region rg, time period tp. These damages might include species losses anywhere in the world, and they might also include the risks of disrupting ocean circulation processes. There is little consensus about the nature of these damages – or about our willingness to pay to avoid them. Here, the economic loss factor (a fraction between zero and unity) is taken to be the following modified quadratic function of ATP_{tp}, the actual change in mean global temperature from its initial level in the year 2000:

$$ELF_{rg,tp} = \left[1 - \left(\frac{ATP_{tp}}{catt_{rg}} \right)^2 \right]^{\lambda_{rg,tp}}$$

For consistency with other studies, the economic loss factor is calibrated around the impact of a 2.5°C rise in mean global temperature. Under business as usual, this is a level that might be reached in the middle or late twenty-first century. Our definition of $ELF_{rg,tp}$ implies that nonmarket damages are negligible at the year 2000 level of global temperature. The parameters are chosen so that at high income levels, we would be willing to give up 2% of our consumption to avoid a temperature rise of 2.5°, and therefore would be willing to give up 8% of our consumption to avoid a temperature rise of 5.0°. The value of the world's entire economic product would be wiped out at a catastrophic level of temperature increase labeled $catt_{rg}$.

The quadratic loss function is modified by the exponent $\lambda_{rg,tp}$. The values of this parameter are defined by a logistic function of potential per capita income. In this way, $\lambda_{rg,tp}$ allows for differences in willingness to pay to avoid climate change costs between regions at different income levels and different points of time. For high-income regions and time periods, the exponent $\lambda_{rg,tp}$ is close to unity. For low-income regions, it is close to zero. This allows for the idea that in the low-income regions, it is a much more immediate priority to overcome poverty, malnutrition, and ill health than to be concerned about the more distant threat of global climate change.

The economic loss factor interacts with the Negishi weights nwt_{rg}, the utility discount factors $udf_{tp,rg}$, and the utility (the logarithm) of the aggregate consumption in each region and time period $C_{rg,tp}$. The maximand is the following Negishi welfare function:

$$\sum_{rg} nwt_{rg} \sum_{tp} udf_{tp,rg} \cdot \log \left(ELF_{rg,tp} \cdot C_{rg,tp} \right)$$

11.5. DISCOUNTING IN MERGE

Not surprisingly, it turns out that discounting is one of the more contentious issues in the climate debate. The discount rate is directly related to "when" flexibility – that is, *when* to undertake abatement. Much depends upon whether one adopts a "descriptive" or a "prescriptive" approach. With a descriptive approach, one relies upon market-oriented criteria such as the long-run rate of return on capital – not upon subjective criteria such as the utility discount rate.

Why have we adopted a descriptive approach to discounting? In my opinion, there are both short-term and long-term reasons for rejecting the prescriptive approach. Typically, this approach leads to a zero or low rate of discount. In the short term – with a low rate of discount – it is optimal to undertake an implausibly rapid immediate stepup in the formation of physical capital. This goes along directly with reducing the rate of depletion of environmental capital. In turn, this implies that one will have to cut back drastically on aggregate consumption. There are also difficulties in the long run – at a zero or a low rate of discount. Present-day decisions will then be dominated by environmental and technology developments that will not materialize for a century or more. Is it plausible that this generation's abatement decisions are to be governed almost entirely by one's beliefs in the feasibility of, say, carbon-free thermonuclear fusion that might be developed a hundred years from now? Discounting automatically dampens the effect of distant future uncertainties upon today's investment decisions.

So, in an applied general equilibrium model like MERGE, how do we handle discounting? First, we make an estimate of the current global marginal productivity of capital – and how this might change over time. Following much the same reasoning as Nordhaus (1994, pp. 122–135), we estimate that the current rate of return to capital is 5% per year (in real terms, net of depreciation – including taxes). Moreover, we assume that this rate of return will decline gradually along with the decline in potential GDP growth in the twenty-first century. (In our reference cases, world GDP begins the century at a growth rate of 3%, and it declines to 2% by the end of the century.) This is why the mpk (marginal productivity of capital) drops to 4% in the year 2100.

In MERGE, we assume that interregional capital flows will wipe out any regional differences in the rate of return. It is true that there can be large differences in the anticipated rates of return, but it would be a formidable task to establish that the real rate in country X will consistently exceed that in country Y by, say, 3% per year. If one heeds the advice of optimistic specialists in country X, one must also then allow for differences in the probabilities of unfavorable exchange rate movements – and in the risk of expropriation of domestic and foreign investors.

Each region is viewed as a long-lived agent maximizing the discounted utility (the logarithm) of its aggregate consumption over time. No adjustment is made to this welfare function for differences in rates of population growth. It is assumed that both consumption and GDP grow at the same rate as the labor force, measured in "efficiency units." It is then straightforward to establish that at each point along an optimal growth path,

$$\text{marginal productivity of capital} = \text{utility discount rate}$$
$$+ \text{consumption growth rate}$$

That is,

$$\text{mpk} = \text{udr} + \text{grow}$$

The next steps are admittedly ad hoc, but they do not appear inferior to other ideas that have been proposed for numerical models of this type. MERGE is based upon the proposition that mpk and grow are observable parameters, but not udr. Mpk and grow are therefore taken as inputs to the model, and udr is derived from these inputs through the optimal growth equation shown above. If the GDP growth rate is unchanged, a reduction in the mpk will therefore reduce the udr by the same amount.

With unlimited capital transfers, market forces will work so that the mpk is identical among regions at a given point of time. Each region, however, may have a different GDP growth rate, and this rate may change over time. For some regions, for example, China during the next few decades, the domestic GDP growth rate will almost surely exceed the world mpk of 5%. This implies a negative udr for China during these decades. Nonetheless, the MERGE solution remains plausible. Interregional capital flows remain reasonably low throughout the planning horizon. If we had postulated very different initial rates of return between regions, a free trade model would have produced unreasonably large flows of capital to equalize these rates of return in the short term. Alternatively, we could have imposed limits on international capital transfers, but this in turn would lead to arbitrary foreign exchange premia.

11.6. EQUITY AND EFFICIENCY

It will come as no surprise that the productivity of capital can have a major influence on both the prices and quantities of greenhouse gas abatement. But if there is free trade in emission rights, these prices and quantities are virtually independent of how emission shares are allocated between regions. Why? With trade, emission rights have only a minor effect on the total value of each region's endowments, and that is why this is a case in which there is no significant conflict between equity and efficiency goals.

First, consider the goal of economic efficiency. We will compare two Pareto-optimal scenarios of MERGE. Both employ the same assumptions with respect to mitigation costs, and also with respect to market and nonmarket damages. Both are based upon the optimal growth equation relating the udr to the mpk and the aggregate growth rate. The only difference is that one is based on the conventional MERGE mpk assumptions employed by Manne and Richels (a 5% mpk rate beginning in 2000, and declining to 4% in 2100), and the other is based on the random walk model proposed by Newell and Pizer (2001) for dealing with climate change under uncertainty with respect to the productivity of capital. (This is a 4% mpk rate beginning in 2000, and declining to 1.7% by 2100.)[1] Hereafter, we will refer to this as the "low-mpk" case. Each of these mpk scenarios leads to a different set of utility discount rates in each region.

The two mpk scenarios both lead to efficient allocations of resources, but they lead to very different amounts of carbon abatement. (See Fig. 11.3.) Beginning in 2030, there is at least a two-billion-ton difference in the Pareto-optimal emissions that result from the two different mpk paths. There is also a big difference between the two series of efficiency prices of carbon. Figure 11.4 indicates that the carbon price differs by a factor of 4 during most of the twenty-first century. These price differences are significant – even though not quite as large as those reported by the individual EMF models for the Kyoto Protocol in 2010.

For the regional implications of the two mpk scenarios, see Figs. 11.5 and 11.6. These figures show the share of each region in the global total of carbon emissions. During the early decades of the twenty-first century, both show that nearly half of these emissions are produced by the four wealthy OECD regions: the USA, Western Europe, Japan, and CANZ. By 2030, however, these nations contribute less than 40% of the global total. If there is to be a global abatement effort, abatement efforts in the high-income regions must be supplemented by emission reductions in the low-income, coal-based regions such as China and India.

---

[1] The post-2000 values are based upon the present-value factors reported on p. 21 of the Newell–Pizer paper. Throughout the later portion of the planning horizon, the Newell–Pizer mpk values are somewhat lower than the rate of growth assumed here for gross world product. This can lead to technical difficulties such as "horizon effects." The MERGE horizon extends to 2150, but we do not report results after 2100.

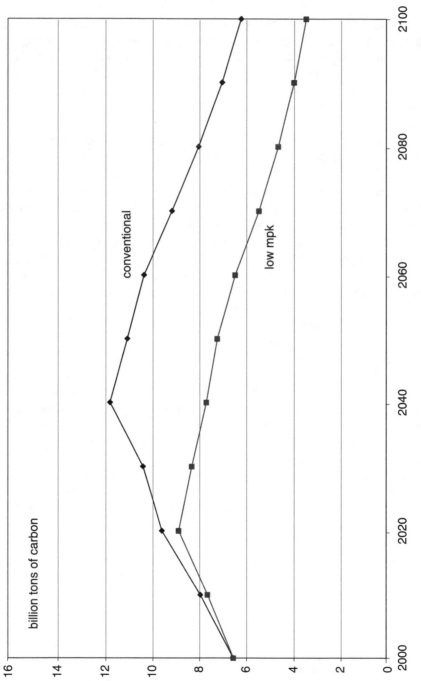

Figure 11.3. Global carbon emissions – alternative mpk and udr scenarios.

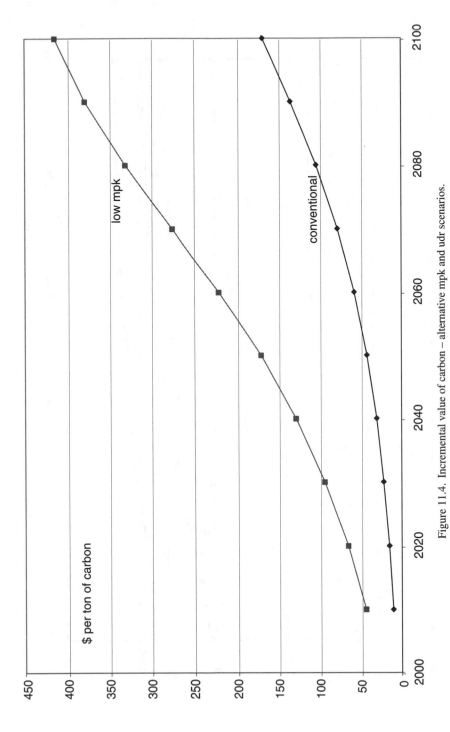

Figure 11.4. Incremental value of carbon – alternative mpk and udr scenarios.

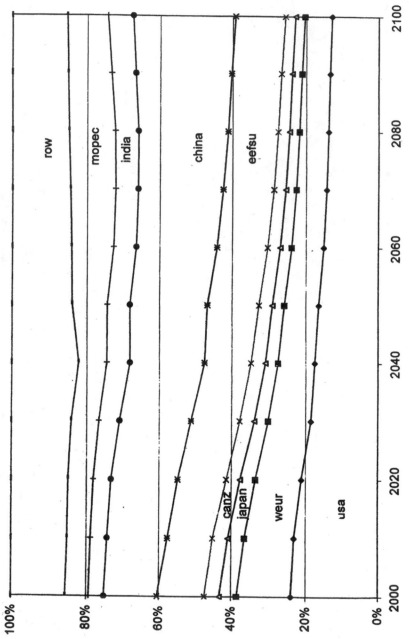

Figure 11.5. Shares in global carbon emissions – conventional mpk.

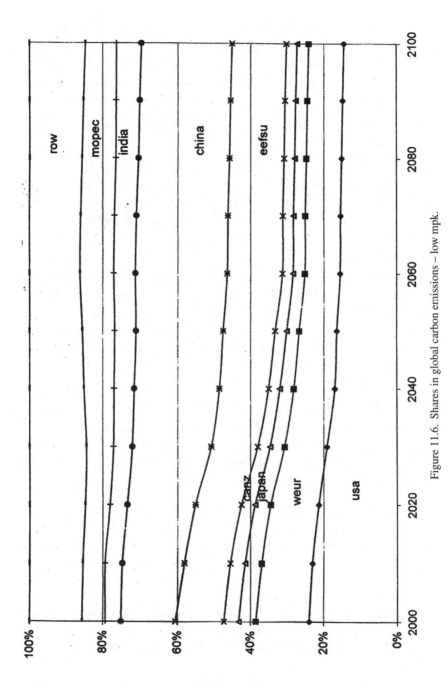

Figure 11.6. Shares in global carbon emissions – low mpk.

273

TABLE 11.3. *Negishi weights under alternative mpk and sharing rule scenarios*

Scenario: Sharing rule:	Conventional mpk			Low mpk		
	Egalitarian	Pragmatic	Egalitarian/ pragmatic	Egalitarian	Pragmatic	Egalitarian/ pragmatic
USA	0.224516	0.224759	0.999	0.162068	0.162547	0.997
OECDE	0.225625	0.225738	0.999	0.168281	0.168517	0.999
JAPAN	0.089233	0.089272	1.000	0.064270	0.064352	0.999
CANZ	0.032243	0.032280	0.999	0.026128	0.026200	0.997
EEFSU	0.044120	0.044191	0.998	0.046288	0.046422	0.997
CHINA	0.094155	0.094065	1.001	0.139007	0.138819	1.001
INDIA	0.044032	0.043879	1.003	0.083866	0.083557	1.004
MOPEC	0.047114	0.047117	1.000	0.053269	0.053274	1.000
ROW	0.198962	0.198700	1.001	0.256824	0.256312	1.002
TOTAL	1.000000	1.000001		1.000001	1.000000	

What conclusions can be drawn from this numerical exercise? The experiment does not tell us what is the "right" and what the "wrong" rate of return on capital to adopt for long-term models of global climate change. Perhaps it does serve as a reminder, however, of the wisdom of Tjalling Koopmans. He observed that:

the problem of optimal growth is too complicated, or at least too unfamiliar, for one to feel comfortable in making an *entirely* a priori choice of an optimality criterion before one knows the implications of alternative choices. One may wish to choose between principles on the basis of the results of their applications. In order to do so, one first needs to know what these results are. This is an economic question logically prior to the ethical or political choice of a criterion. [Koopmans, 1965, p. 226]

This is a piece of advice that is just as pertinent today as it was when first enunciated.

Now consider the goal of equity. What about equity–efficiency conflicts? Up to this point, we have not spelled out the emission rights sharing rule that lies behind these scenarios. Consider two very different rules. The first is an egalitarian criterion, and the second is a more pragmatic one:

Egalitarian: emission rights are allocated at all times in proportion to each region's initial population;

Pragmatic: emission rights are initially allocated in proportion to year 2000 emissions, but there is a gradual transition (by 2050) to shares based on each region's initial population.

These two different sharing rules lead to virtually identical global and regional emission paths. This is because they have only a minor impact upon the value of each region's endowments. As a summary measure, it is convenient to compare the aggregate value of each region's endowments through its Negishi weight: the share of each region in the global value of endowments.

Table 11.3 shows the consequences of the two different sharing rules under the two mpk scenarios already described in Figs. 11.3–11.6. It can be seen that the mpk scenarios have a major impact upon the Negishi weights, but the sharing rules have only a minor impact. With the low-mpk assumption, there are higher present-value prices placed on future endowments. That is why higher Negishi weights are assigned to the rapidly growing developing nations – and lower weights to the slowly growing nations of the OECD. For example, the United States drops from a Negishi weight of 0.225 to one of 0.162, and China's weight rises from 0.094 to 0.139.

In order to observe the effects of the sharing rule upon the Negishi weights, one must move from three to six decimal digits. Table 11.3 explains why the two radically different sharing rules lead to virtually no differences between the price of emissions and the amounts of abatement in each region. The sharing rule makes a noticeable difference in the exports and imports of emission rights between the regions. But in turn, this leads to only small differences in the values of regional endowments. This can be seen in the two columns labeled "egalitarian/pragmatic," the ratio of the Negishi weights under the two different sharing rules. According to Table 11.3, the egalitarian rule leads to slightly higher Negishi weights for the high-population regions China, India, and ROW, and to slightly lower weights for the United States with its high propensity to emit carbon. But these Negishi weights differ by small fractions of a percent. For both the "conventional" and "low-mpk" scenarios, the value of carbon emission rights is a virtually negligible proportion of total resource endowments in each region.

This same type of result has been observed repeatedly in MERGE scenarios that provide for universal participation in global abatement – plus free trade in emission rights. It can be described as equity–efficiency *separability*. We do *not* find separability when there are inefficient sharing rules – that is, when specific regions are exempted from abatement, or when there are constraints on trade in emission rights. The Kyoto Protocol is an example of this type of inefficient sharing rule. By contrast, universal participation and the reassignment of tradeable emission rights could make all parties better off. Computable general equilibrium models cannot solve all the dilemmas that are faced by today's policymakers, but they can at least identify some of the difficulties that arise in constructing a reasonably equitable and efficient global abatement agreement.

REFERENCES

Energy Information Administration (2002), *International Energy Outlook 2002*. Washington, DC: U.S. Department of Energy.

T. C. Koopmans (1965), "On the Concept of Optimal Economic Growth," in *Econometric Approach to Development Planning*, Pontificiae Academiae Scientiarum Scripta Varia 28. Amsterdam: North-Holland, Chicago: Rand McNally.

S. Kypreos and O. Bahn (2001), "MERGE-ETL: An Optimisation Equilibrium Model with Endogenous Technological Learning," working paper, Paul Scherrer Institute, Switzerland.

A. S. Manne (1996), "Hedging Strategies for Global Carbon Dioxide Abatement: A Summary of Poll Results – EMF 14 Subgroup – Analysis for Decisions under Uncertainty," pp. 207–228, in N. Nakicenovic W. D. Nordhaus, R. Richels, and F. L. Toth (Eds.), *Climate Change: Integrating Science, Economics, and Policy*. Laxenburg, Austria: International Institute for Applied Systems Analysis, CP-96-1.

R. Newell and W. Pizer (2001), "Discounting the Benefits of Climate Change Mitigation – How Much Do Uncertain Rates Increase Valuations?" Washington, DC: Pew Center for Global Climate Change.

W. D. Nordhaus (1994), *Managing the Global Commons: The Economics of Climate Change*. Cambridge, MA: MIT Press.

T. Rutherford (1999), "Sequential Joint Maximization," J. P. Weyant (Ed.), *Energy and Environmental Policy Modeling*. Norwell, MA: Kluwer Academic Publishers.

N. Sahinidis (2000), "BARON: Branch and Reduce Optimization Navigator," User's Manual Version 4.0. Department of Chemical Engineering, University of Illinois at Urbana-Champaign.

B. C. Van der Zwaan, R. Gerlagh, G. Klaassen, and L. Schrattenholzer (1999), "Endogenous Technological Change in Climate Change Modelling," Report D-99/15. Amsterdam: Institute for Environmental Studies.

J. P. Weyant and J. N. Hill (1999), "Introduction and Overview" and "The Costs of the Kyoto Protocol: A Multi-model Evaluation," *The Energy Journal* (Special Issue).

12 Simulation and Estimation of Hedonic Models

James Heckman, Rosa Matzkin, and Lars Nesheim

ABSTRACT: Making use of restrictions imposed by equilibrium, theoretical progress has been made on the nonparametric and semiparametric estimation and identification of scalar additive hedonic models and scalar nonadditive hedonic models. However, little is known about the practical aspects of estimating such models or of the characteristics of equilibrium in such models. This paper presents computational and analytical results that fill some of these gaps. We simulate and estimate examples of equilibrium in the additive hedonic models and provide evidence on the performance of a maximum likelihood estimation technique. We also simulate examples of equilibria in nonadditive models and provide evidence on the performance of the nonadditive estimation techniques developed by Heckman, Matzkin, and Nesheim (unpublished working paper, 2002).

12.1. INTRODUCTION

Hedonic models are general equilibrium frameworks that characterize the pricing of differentiated goods, viewed as bundles of attributes, and the demand and supply of those goods (attributes) under different assumptions about preferences and technology. They allow a systematic economic analysis of the demand and supply of quality. Quality includes enhancement of the attributes of a good embodied in a unit of the good (such as the attributes of a house or a car, as in Rosen, 1974), characteristics of a job (risk or unpleasantness as in Tinbergen, 1956; Sattinger, 1975, 1980, 1993; Thaler and Rosen, 1975) or the amenities offered by an environmental or recreational improvement (as in Smith and Huang, 1995; Banzhaf et al., 2000). Understanding the structure of demand in markets for differentiated products is a crucial ingredient of models of monopoly pricing (Wilson, 1993; Rochet and Stole, 2001; Armstrong, 1996). The hedonic model underlies general equilibrium analyses of local public goods (Epple, 1987; Epple and Sieg, 1999; Bayer, 2000) and models in which social interactions are priced (Nesheim, 2001). The promise of the

This research was supported by NSF Grant SES-0241858 to James Heckman and NSF Grant SES-0099195 to James Heckman, Rosa Matzkin, and Lars Nesheim. We thank Andrew Chesher, Hidehiko Ichimura, and Simon Lee for helpful comments.

hedonic approach is great. It offers insight into the economics of variety and heterogeneity in product quality and worker skill, which are hallmark features of modern economies. It offers a consistent approach to adjusting price indices for quality and valuing new goods (or environmental offerings) that can be viewed as new packages of old attributes (Lancaster, 1966, 1975; Triplett, 2000; or the essays in Bresnahan and Gordon, 1997). With hedonic models, it is possible to interpret wage data on heterogeneous labor, to evaluate alternative policy proposals for workplace safety (as in Kniesner and Leeth, 1988, 1995), to evaluate proposals to subsidize education and job training (Teulings and van Rens, 2002; Tinbergen, 1956), and to examine their consequences for worker and firm welfare and for wage inequality.

The potential applications of hedonic models are myriad but their application and development, except in certain special cases, have been hindered by computational difficulties, approximations that ignore the implications of equilibrium in the hedonic model, and the widely held belief that identification of the structural parameters in a hedonic model is not possible using data from a single market. Recent theoretical progress has been made in understanding these issues, making, use of restrictions imposed by equilibrium. Ekeland, Heckman, and Nesheim (2004) and Heckman, Matzkin, and Nesheim (2002) have shown that contrary to the widely held belief that identification is impossible in a single market, nonparametric and semiparametric estimation and identification of scalar additive hedonic models and scalar nonadditive hedonic models are possible.

However, little is known about the practical aspects of estimating such models or the characteristics of equilibria in these two classes of models. This paper presents computational and analytical results that fill these gaps. We simulate and estimate examples of equilibrium in these classes of hedonic models and provide evidence on the performance of several estimation techniques. The simulations show the shapes of the pricing function that result from various assumptions about the underlying structural parameters in the economy. The estimation results demonstrate that structural parameters in an additive economy can be precisely estimated. In addition, these results demonstrate that in a nonadditive economy, nonparametric techniques can be used to recover estimates of the structural parameters.

In Section 12.2 we present the general hedonic model. In Section 12.3 we discuss Tinbergen's (1956) pioneering model, which was the first formulation of an equilibrium hedonic model. In Section 12.4 we discuss identification of the model and conditions sufficient for identification in the additive and nonadditive cases. In Section 12.5 we discuss estimation of the model based on the preceding analysis. In Section 12.6 we present simulation and estimation results before concluding in Section 12.7.

12.2. GENERAL HEDONIC MODEL

We first present a general statement of the classical hedonic model. For specificity, consider a labor market setting. Our analysis applies more generally, but it is useful to have a specific example in hand. Assume a static model. Consumers (workers) match to single worker firms. Workers are heterogeneous. They have characteristics (x, ε), where $x \in X \subseteq R^{n_x}$ and $\varepsilon \in E \subseteq R^{n_\varepsilon}$ are observable and unobservable (to the econometrician) characteristics that affect their utility from different job types. Firms are also heterogeneous. They have characteristics (y, η), where $y \in Y \subseteq R^{n_y}$ and $\eta \in H \subseteq R^{n_\eta}$ are observable and unobservable characteristics that affect the output and profits they obtain from different job types. Job types have attributes $z \in Z$, where $Z \subseteq R^{n_z}$. Z is the set of feasible job types. For example, z could be a (possibly multidimensional) measure of the riskiness of the job. Alternatively, in a housing market setting, z could be a vector of attributes of a neighborhood or a house. We focus attention on the classical case where $n_z = n_\varepsilon = n_\eta$, assuming a smooth equilibrium pricing function. This is the hedonic model analyzed by Tinbergen (1956), Rosen (1974), Epple (1987), and Kniesner and Leeth (1988, 1995). It is also the example that has dominated much of the literature on hedonic models. The theoretical analysis, the simulation models, and the empirical results to follow in Sections 12.4 and 12.6 restrict the analysis further and focus on the scalar hedonic model in which $n_z = 1$.

The distribution of consumer characteristics in the population is characterized by the density functions f_x and f_ε, both strictly greater than zero in the interiors of X and E, respectively. We assume that x is independent of ε. Similarly, the distribution of firm characteristics is characterized by the density functions f_y and f_η, also strictly positive in the interiors of their respective supports. y is independent of ε and ε and η are mutually independent.

Workers of type (x, ε) choose jobs of type z to maximize utility. $P(z)$ is the earnings of workers supplying attribute vector z, which is a disamenity. To focus on the main ideas, we study the quasilinear utility model (also known as the transferable utility model in the assignment literature and in the theoretical public economics literature; see Gretsky, Ostroy, and Zame, 1999, and Wooders, 1994). Define $U^*(c, z, x, \varepsilon) = c - U(z, x, \varepsilon)$, where x and ε are as defined above and c is consumption. For simplicity assume $c = P(z)$, so workers consume their earnings. More generally, $c = P(z) + R$, where R is nonlabor income, but for ease of exposition, assume $R = 0$. Workers who do not work get reservation utility V_0. We initially restrict our analysis to economies for which the equilibrium price function is smooth. Similar analyses can be done for economies in which the equilibrium price function is not smooth. Smoothness is not a generic property of hedonic models, even when the underlying preferences are smooth.[1] Given $P(z)$, a twice continuously differentiable price function, and assuming that the utility function is twice differentiable, for those who choose to work we obtain the following first-order conditions for a maximum:

$$P_z(z) - U_z(z, x, \varepsilon) = 0. \tag{1}$$

---

[1] For examples of sorting problems with nonsmooth pricing functions see Wilson (1993), Nesheim (2001), and Heckman et al. (2002).

The second-order conditions (SOC) require that $P_{zz'} - U_{zz'}$ be negative definite. Assuming that the SOC are satisfied and using the implicit function theorem, (1) determines $z = s(x, \varepsilon)$, the quality of the good supplied by each worker (x, ε). Assuming $U_{z\varepsilon'}$ is invertible, it also determines the inverse mapping $\varepsilon = \widetilde{s}(z, x)$. Further assuming that $U_{z\varepsilon'}$ is negative definite implies that $\frac{\partial \widetilde{s}(z,x)}{\partial z}$ is positive definite. Note that $\widetilde{s}(z, x)$ implicitly depends on the marginal price function $P_z(z)$. The two mappings $s(x, \varepsilon)$ and $\widetilde{s}(z, x)$ are the focus of both our theoretical and empirical study of the classical hedonic model.

Firms of type (y, η) demand attribute z and maximize profits, which are equal to output $\Gamma(z, y, \eta)$ minus production costs $P(z)$, where y and η are defined above. We assume that the production function is twice differentiable. If the firm hires no workers, reservation profits are Π_0. Otherwise, profits are $\Pi(z, y, \eta, P(z)) = \Gamma(z, y, \eta) - P(z)$ and the first-order conditions at a maximum for each firm that enters the market are

$$\Gamma_z(z, y, \eta) - P_z(z) = 0. \tag{2}$$

The second-order conditions require that $\Gamma_{zz'} - P_{zz'}$ be negative definite. Assuming the SOC are satisfied and using the implicit function theorem, (2) defines $z = d(y, \eta)$, the type of job demanded by each firm (y, η). Assuming $\Gamma_{z\varepsilon'}$ is invertible, it also determines the inverse mapping $\eta = \widetilde{d}(z, y)$. Further assuming that $\Gamma_{z\eta'}$ is positive definite implies that $\frac{\partial \widetilde{d}(z,y)}{\partial z}$ is positive definite. As on the supply side, $\widetilde{d}(z, y)$ implicitly depends on the marginal price function $P_z(z)$.

At equilibrium, the density of the demanded z must equal the density of the supplied z for all values of z. To express this condition in terms of the primitive functions, consider the transformation defined by the consumer first-order conditions $\varepsilon = \widetilde{s}(z, x)$ and $x = x$. The Jacobian of this transformation is

$$\det \begin{pmatrix} \dfrac{\partial \widetilde{s}(z, x)}{\partial z} & \dfrac{\partial \widetilde{s}(z, x)}{\partial x} \\ 0 & 1 \end{pmatrix} = \det \left(\dfrac{\partial \widetilde{s}(z, x)}{\partial z} \right).$$

Assuming that all potential workers actually work, this transformation induces a density of consumers supplying each type of job z. Thus, the *supply density* is

$$\int_X f_\varepsilon (\widetilde{s}(z, x)) f_x(x) \det \left(\dfrac{\partial \widetilde{s}(z, x)}{\partial z} \right) dx.$$

Analogous arguments yield the density of z demanded. Consider the transformation derived from the firms' FOC, $\eta = \widetilde{d}(z, y)$ and $y = y$, with Jacobian

$$\det \begin{pmatrix} \dfrac{\partial \widetilde{d}(z, y)}{\partial z} & \dfrac{\partial \widetilde{d}(z, y)}{\partial y} \\ 0 & 1 \end{pmatrix} = \det \left(\dfrac{\partial \widetilde{d}(z, y)}{\partial z} \right).$$

Assuming that all firms enter the market, this transformation induces a density of demand for every job type z. The *demand density* is

$$\int_Y f_\eta\left(\tilde{d}(z, y)\right) f_y(y) \det\left(\frac{\partial \tilde{d}(z, y)}{\partial z}\right) dy.$$

Equilibrium in hedonic markets requires that demand and supply be equated at each point of the support of z. So equilibrium prices must satisfy the following second-order differential equation in $P(z)$:

$$\int_X f_\varepsilon\left(\tilde{s}(z, x)\right) f_x(x) \det\left(\frac{\partial \tilde{s}(z, x)}{\partial z}\right) dx \tag{3}$$

$$= \int_Y f_\eta(\tilde{d}(z, y)) f_y(y) \det\left(\frac{\partial \tilde{d}(z, y)}{\partial z}\right) dy.$$

Observe that $\tilde{s}(z, x)$ and $\tilde{d}(z, y)$ implicitly depend on P_z and $P_{zz'}$. In addition, the solution depends on the structural parameters of the model: the technology of the firms Γ, the utility function of the workers, U, and the distributions of firms and workers in the population $(f_x, f_\varepsilon, f_y, f_\eta)$. Economic theory implies that marginal products and marginal utilities are nonnegative in most cases. In order for agents to participate in the market, firms and workers must receive wages and profits above reservation levels. If not, Eq. (3) must be suitably adjusted. These criteria generate the boundary conditions that determine the solution of the differential equation for equilibrium prices.

Equations (1), (2), and (3) and the data generated by them are the focus of our analysis. They determine all the theoretical and statistical properties of the model. In general, equations such as (3) have no closed-form solution except in special cases such as the Tinbergen model. Although progress has been made in understanding such equations in the mathematics and numerical analysis literature, little is known about their solutions in economics.[2] The inability to compute or even characterize the equilibria from this model even in the cases of scalar attributes has inhibited application of the hedonic model to economic problems. It has also hindered understanding of the statistical properties of hedonic models relevant to identification and estimation. Our simulations, presented in Section 12.6, help remedy this problem. We first present the Tinbergen model, which implicitly or explicitly has been the point of departure for all empirical work on hedonics.

12.3. TINBERGEN'S LINEAR–QUADRATIC MODEL

Assume that preferences are quadratic in z and linear in c, that unearned income $R = 0$, and that individual heterogeneity (x, ε) affects utility only through the single

---

[2] Notable exceptions include Kniesner and Leeth (1995), Teulings and van Rens (1995), and Nesheim (2001).

index $\theta = \mu_\theta(x) + \varepsilon$, where $\dim(\theta) = \dim(z)$ and "dim" stands for dimension.[3] Consumers maximize

$$U(c, z, \theta, A) = P(z) + \theta' z - \frac{1}{2} z' A z.$$

The conditions determining a consumer maximum are

$$P_z + \theta - Az = 0,$$

where $P_{zz'} - A$ is negative definite. On the firm side, assume that the production function is quadratic in z and that firm heterogeneity affects profits only through the single index $v = \mu_v(y) + \eta$, where $\dim(v) = \dim(z)$. Profits are

$$\Pi(z, v, B, P(z)) = v'z - \frac{1}{2} z' B z - P(z)$$

and the conditions determining a firm's optimum are

$$v - Bz - P_z = 0,$$

where $-(B + P_{zz'})$ is negative definite. The distributions of θ and v in the population are normal. The distribution of θ is $\theta \sim N(\mu_\theta, \Sigma_\theta)$, and the distribution of v is $v \sim N(\mu_v, \Sigma_v)$.

An arbitrary price function induces a density of demand and a density of supply at every location z. The equilibrium price function can be found by equating these densities at every point z and solving the differential equation (3). However, in the linear–quadratic–normal case one can correctly guess that the solution to the problem is quadratic in z,

$$P(z) = \pi_0 + \pi_1' z + \frac{1}{2} z' \pi_2 z,$$

and then find the coefficients (π_0, π_1, π_2) that satisfy the equilibrium equation. Assuming that the price function is quadratic, the first-order condition for a consumer is

$$\pi_1 + \pi_2 z + \theta - Az = 0. \tag{4}$$

For a firm, it is

$$v - Bz - \pi_1 - \pi_2 z = 0. \tag{5}$$

The second-order conditions require that both $A - \pi_2$ and $B + \pi_2$ be positive definite. Thus we may solve for z from (4) to obtain

$$z = (A - \pi_2)^{-1}(\theta + \pi_1) \tag{6}$$

and from (5) to obtain

$$z = (B + \pi_2)^{-1}(v - \pi_1). \tag{7}$$

---

[3]   The model in this example was first analyzed by Tinbergen (1956) and has been used by Epple (1987) and Tauchen and Witte (2001), among others.

These equations define mappings from workers θ and firms v to job types z. These mappings determine the density of supply and demand at every location and the types of workers and firms at every location. Equilibrium is characterized by a vector π_1 and a matrix π_2 that equate demand and supply at all z. However, because both θ and v are normally distributed, this only requires equating the mean and variance of supply and demand.

The mean supply $E^S(z)$ is obtained from Eq. (6):

$$\text{(Average Supply)} \quad E^S(z) = (A - \pi_2)^{-1} E(\theta + \pi_1).$$

The mean demand is obtained from Eq. (7):

$$\text{(Average Demand)} \quad E^D(z) = (B + \pi_2)^{-1} E(v - \pi_1).$$

Because $\mu_\theta = E(\theta)$ and $\mu_v = E(v)$, the condition $E^S(z) = E^D(z)$ implies that

$$\text{(Equality of means)} \quad (A - \pi_2)^{-1} (\mu_\theta + \pi_1) = (B + \pi_2)^{-1} (\mu_v - \pi_1).$$

Rearranging terms, we obtain an explicit expression for π_1 in terms of A, B, μ_θ, μ_v and π_2:

$$\pi_1 = [(A - \pi_2)^{-1} + (B + \pi_2)^{-1}]^{-1}[-(A - \pi_2)^{-1}\mu_\theta + (B + \pi_2)^{-1}\mu_v].$$

To determine π_2, compute the variances of supply and demand from Eqs. (6) and (7), respectively, to obtain

$$\Sigma_z^S = (A - \pi_2)^{-1}\Sigma_\theta(A - \pi_2)^{-1}$$

$$\Sigma_z^D = (B + \pi_2)^{-1}\Sigma_v(B + \pi_2)^{-1},$$

where Σ_z^S is the variance of supply and Σ_z^D is the variance of demand. From equality of variances of the demand and supply distributions we obtain an implicit equation for π_2:

$$\text{(Equality of variances)} \quad (A - \pi_2)^{-1}\Sigma_\theta(A - \pi_2)^{-1} = (B + \pi_2)^{-1}\Sigma_v(B + \pi_2)^{-1}.$$

We pin down initial conditions using the restrictions that $U \geq \bar{U}$, a reservation value, and that profits are positive ($\Pi \geq 0$). Equilibrium profits as a function of location are $\frac{1}{2}z'(B + \pi_2)z - \pi_0$. Hence nonnegativity of profits implies that $-\pi_0 \geq 0$, because $(B + \pi_2)$ is positive definite by the second-order conditions. Setting reservation utility equal to zero, a similar argument on the worker side implies that $\pi_0 \geq 0$. Hence $\pi_0 = 0$.

Once we have solved for π_1 and π_2, Eqs. (6) and (7) also define the equilibrium matching function linking the characteristics of suppliers (θ) to those of demanders (v). For each z, this function is

$$(A - \pi_2)^{-1}(\theta + \pi_1) = (B + \pi_2)^{-1}(v - \pi_1).$$

Thus, the equilibrium relationship between θ and v is

$$\theta = (A - \pi_2)(B + \pi_2)^{-1}(v - \pi_1) - \pi_1. \tag{8}$$

This relationship has important empirical implications, as noted by Epple (1987) and Kahn and Lang (1988). Conditional on location choice, worker and firm characteristics are not statistically independent in equilibrium. There is a functional relationship between them.

In the separable case where Σ_θ, Σ_v, A, and B are diagonal, π_2 is diagonal. Effectively, this is a scalar case. In the scalar case, equality of variances implies that $(A - \pi_2)^2 \Sigma_v = (B + \pi_2)^2 \Sigma_\theta$. When we use the notation $\sigma_\theta = (\Sigma_\theta)^{\frac{1}{2}}$ and $\sigma_v = (\Sigma_v)^{\frac{1}{2}}$ and note that the second-order conditions imply $A - \pi_2 > 0$ and $B + \pi_2 > 0$, this means that

$$\pi_2 = \frac{A\sigma_v - B\sigma_\theta}{\sigma_\theta + \sigma_v},$$

$$\pi_1 = \frac{-\mu_\theta \sigma_v + \mu_v \sigma_\theta}{\sigma_\theta + \sigma_v}.$$

π_2, the curvature of the price function, is a weighted average of the curvatures of workers' and firms' preference and technology functions. π_1 is a weighted average of the means of worker and firm distributions of heterogenity. In both cases, the weights depend on the relative variances of worker and firm heterogeneity. If workers are much more heterogeneous than firms, so that $\sigma_\theta \gg \sigma_v$, π_2 will approximately equal B, the curvature of firms' technology, and π_1 will approximately equal μ_v, the mean of the firm technology distribution.

If $\sigma_\theta = \sigma_v$ and $A = B$, $\pi_2 = 0$ is a solution and the equilibrium price function is linear in z. If $\sigma_\theta = \sigma_v$, but $A \neq B$, then $\pi_2 = \frac{A-B}{2}$. In the polar cases where $\sigma_\theta = 0$ or $\sigma_v = 0$, there is effectively only one type of consumer or one type of firm, respectively. If $\sigma_\theta = 0$ and $\sigma_v > 0$, then $\pi_2 = A$ and $\pi_1 = -\mu_\theta$. Thus, prices reveal the parameters of consumer preferences. If $\sigma_v = 0$ and $\sigma_\theta > 0$, $\pi_2 = B$ and $\pi_1 = \mu_v$. These two polar cases are discussed in Rosen (1974) and featured in the applied literature generated by his paper. Only in these two polar cases do prices directly reveal consumer preferences or firm productivities, respectively. Similar results hold when z, θ, and v are vectors. We next turn to an analysis of identification in the general hedonic model.

12.4. IDENTIFICATION

The most direct approach to estimating hedonic models is to solve the second-order differential equation (3) implied by equilibrium for $P(z)$ in terms of the parameters of preferences, technology, and the distributions of tastes and productivity and to jointly estimate the demand function corresponding to (2), the supply function corresponding to (1), and the distributions of unobservable preference and technology heterogeneity (f_η and f_ε), exploiting all of the information in the equilibrium conditions, including data on demand, supply and the pricing function.

Rosen (1974) suggested an intuitively plausible and computationally simpler two-step estimation procedure that has been widely criticized. In step 1 of his procedure, the analyst estimates $P(z)$ from market data. In step 2, the analyst uses first-order conditions in conjunction with the marginal prices obtained from step 1 to recover preferences and technology, respectively. Suppose that consumer and firm first-order conditions (1) and (2) are linear and z is a scalar. These are exactly the first-order conditions (4) and (5) of the Tinbergen model. (The scalar assumption is made only to simplify the argument and is not essential.) In this case, for the consumers, Eq. (1) would be of the form

$$P_z(z) - Az + \theta_0 + \theta_1' x + \varepsilon = 0. \tag{9}$$

For the firms, Eq. (2) would be of the form

$$-Bz + v_0 + v_1' y + \eta - P_z(z) = 0. \tag{10}$$

Suppose further that the pricing function is quadratic, as in Tinbergen (1956). Then the first stage of Rosen's procedure would be to estimate the pricing function $P(z) = \pi_0 + \pi_1 z + \frac{1}{2}\pi_2 z^2$ and recover estimates of $\widehat{\pi}_1$ and $\widehat{\pi}_2$ ("^" denotes an estimate) and the marginal prices $\widehat{P_z}(z) = \widehat{\pi}_1 + \widehat{\pi}_2 z$. The second stage substitutes the estimated prices into Eqs. (9) and (10) and estimates the curvature parameters. Thus, Rosen proposed to estimate B and v_1 from the least-squares regression

$$\widehat{P_z}(z) = \widehat{\pi}_1 + \widehat{\pi}_2 z = v_0 + v_1' y - Bz + \eta. \tag{11}$$

A parallel proposal for preferences estimates A and θ_1 from the regression

$$\widehat{P_z}(z) = \widehat{\pi}_1 + \widehat{\pi}_2 z = -\theta_0 - \theta_1' x + Az - \varepsilon. \tag{12}$$

James Brown and Harvey Rosen (1982) analyze this method. They interpret (11) and (12) as linearized *approximations* to the general first-order conditions for the model. The linear–quadratic–normal model of Tinbergen (1956) is the framework in which these approximations are exact.

In this approximation interpretation, the distributions of η and ε are kept in the background. Standard linear econometric methods are applied to identify the parameters of (11) and (12), and connections among the parameters of preferences, technology, and the distributions of tastes and productivity are not made explicit. Issues of identification are confused with issues of estimation. Common to an entire genre of empirical economics, this literature focuses on finding "good instruments" and misses basic sources of identification in hedonic models.

Starting from (11) and (12), Brown and Rosen (1982) make three points that have been reiterated in the subsequent empirical literature.

Point One: Identification can be obtained only through arbitrary functional form assumptions. Because z is on both sides of Eqs. (11) and (12), by a property of least squares, a regression using the constructed price $\widehat{P_z}(z) = \widehat{\pi}_1 + \widehat{\pi}_2 z$ as the dependent variable in Eqs. (11) or (12) identifies only π_2. In general, π_2 does not identify any technology or preference parameter. In the special cases where there is no variation in preference parameters ε or where there is no dispersion in η, π_2 identifies preference

(A) or production parameters (B), respectively (see Rosen, 1974, or Ekeland et al., 2004).

However, if the constructed price is a nonlinear function of z, this argument no longer holds. The nonlinear variation in $\widehat{P}_z(z)$ gives an added piece of information that can help to identify technology and preference parameters. This identification strategy works because it rules out collinearity between z and $\widehat{P}_z(z)$, but such nonlinearity is widely viewed as an artificial source of identification that is thought to be "arbitrary." Theorem 1 of Ekeland, et al. (2004) proves that this nonlinearity is a generic property of equilibrium in the hedonic model. In a parametric framework, Nesheim (2001) shows that nonlinearity is a robust feature of hedonic economy with social interactions. In the context of the Tinbergen economy, this nonlinearity is generic.

Point Two: Endogeneity. Even if such "arbitrary" assumptions are made, so that one can use the nonlinearity in $\widehat{P}_z(z)$ to help identify the parameters and circumvent Point One, one still faces standard endogeneity problems. z is correlated with η and ε in Eqs. (11) and (12), respectively. Moreover, exclusion restrictions from the other side of the market cannot be justified. The equilibrium matching condition requires that $\eta = -\varepsilon - (A + B)z - \theta_0 - \theta_1'x + \nu_0 + \nu_1'y$, so that conditional on z there is a functional and statistical dependence connecting ε, η, z, and the regressors. Conditional on z, η, and ε, x and y become stochastically dependent, even if initially in the underlying population they are mutually independent.

With data from a single market, one is forced to hunt for "clever" instruments with a questionable economic basis. Thus, even if "arbitrary" nonlinearities are invoked, standard instruments may be lacking. Ekeland et al. (2004) show that the economics of the model guarantees valid instruments even though there are no exclusion restrictions. In the particular case of Eq. (10), when $P_z(z)$ is nonlinear, $E(z|y)$ is not a linear function of y and so can be used as an instrument for z in this equation. Hence, generically, $E(z|y)$ is a valid instrument for z. This is discussed at more length below and holds in more general settings.

Point Three: Use of Multimarket Data. Rosen (1974), Brown and Rosen (1982), Epple (1987), and Kahn and Lang (1988) consider estimation of first-order conditions using multimarket data either across regions or across time in the same region. In this case, if we assume that preference parameters common across agents remain constant across markets, whereas distributions of individual heterogeneity vary across markets, we can use cross-market variation in prices and location choices to estimate the common preference parameters. However, this identification strategy relies on assumptions that can be tested if hedonic models can be identified in a single market. Using the techniques we discuss later in this paper, the structure of hedonic models can be estimated and identified using data from a single market for a class of additive parametric structures that includes the linear model as a special case.

Our results invalidate the interpretation that has been given to Brown and Rosen's criticism. What has been interpreted as an identification failure is in fact the failure of an estimation procedure, coupled with an approach that disregards basic sources of identification and mainly focuses on finding exclusion restrictions. Ekeland et al. (2004) and Heckman et al. (2002) show that when attributes are observed and some structure is put on preferences and technologies, everything can be identified up to normalizations using single-market data. In particular, Ekeland et al. (2004) show that putting an additive structure on preferences is sufficient for identification. We describe these results in the next section. Alternatively, if the additive structure is too restrictive or is rejected by the data, Heckman et al. (2002) show that in the nonadditive case alternative assumptions on preferences can lead to identification. We describe these results in Section 12.4.2. Both sets of results consider the case where z is unidimensional.

12.4.1. Identification of the Additive Model

To show that the preferences and technologies generating a hedonic equilibrium price function can be identified up to normalizations, using single-market data and without any exclusion restrictions, suppose that z is one-dimensional. Assume further that for unknown functions M_f and n_f, the production function, $\Gamma(z, y, \eta)$, of a typical firm is $\Gamma(z, y, \eta) = M_f(z) + z n_f(y) + z\eta$. The firms' first-order condition for profit maximization, Eq. (2), becomes

$$P_z(z) = m_f(z) + n_f(y) + \eta, \tag{13}$$

where $m_f(z) = \partial M_f(z)/\partial z$, and the second-order condition is $\partial m_f(z)/\partial z - P_{zz}(z) < 0$. This is a special case of Eq. (2) and is a significant generalization of Eq. (10); it reduces to Eq. (10) when m_f and n_f are linear functions.

In a parallel manner, we may assume that the marginal utility is also of an additive form. The first-order condition (1) of the worker becomes

$$P_z(z) = m_w(z) + n_w(x) + \varepsilon$$

for some unknown functions m_w and n_w. These equations are the empirical equations we seek to estimate and the equations that generate the equilibrium of the model through Eq. (3).

In the empirical analysis, we focus on the firms' equation. The analysis is analogous for the worker side of the market. We have a dataset with observations on N firms drawn at random from a single market. For each firm, we observe the vector $(P_z(z), z, y)$. These data are generated from the equilibrium of a single hedonic market. This implies that for each firm, Eq. (13) holds where η is unobservable to the econometrician, and $m_f(z)$, $n_f(y)$, and F_η, the distribution of η, are to be estimated. We assume $P_z(z)$ is known to focus on the issue of identification and estimation of the structural parameters. In all cases, if $P_z(z)$ is unknown because there is measurement error in prices, then a two-stage procedure can be implemented à la Rosen (1974). First, estimate $P_z(z)$; then proceed to estimate Eq. (13), replacing the true price slope with the estimated slope. Alternatively, Eq. (13) and the equilibrium price equation (3) can be estimated simultaneously.

Much of the identification analysis is conducted without using equilibrium equation (3); it studies the conditional cumulative distribution function (CDF) of z implied by Eq. (13) and in particular makes use of the transformation function[4]

$$T(z) = P_z(z) - m_f(z).$$

In terms of this function, the CDF of z is

$$F_{z|y}(z, y) = F_\eta\left(T(z) - n_f(y)\right), \tag{14}$$

where $F_{z|y}(z, y)$ is the CDF of z conditional on y evaluated at the point (z, y) and F_η is the CDF of η. Differentiating (14) with respect to z and y_i, the ith component of the vector y, we have

$$\frac{\partial F_{z|y}(z, y)}{\partial z} = f_\eta\left(T(z) - n_f(y)\right) \frac{\partial T(z)}{\partial z}$$
$$\frac{\partial F_{z|y}(z, y)}{\partial y_i} = -f_\eta\left(T(z) - n_f(y)\right) \frac{\partial n_f(y)}{\partial y_i}.$$

Taking the ratio of the derivatives, we have

$$-\frac{\dfrac{\partial F_{z|y}(z, y)}{\partial z}}{\dfrac{\partial F_{z|y}(z, y)}{\partial y_i}} = \frac{\dfrac{\partial T(z)}{\partial z}}{\dfrac{\partial n_f(y)}{\partial y_i}}.$$

Defining $h_i(z, y) = \ln\left(-\dfrac{\frac{\partial F_{z|y}(z,y)}{\partial z}}{\frac{\partial F_{z|y}(z,y)}{\partial y_i}}\right)$, we can write this equation as

$$h_i(z, y) = \ln\left(\frac{\partial T(z)}{\partial z}\right) - \ln \frac{\partial n_f(y)}{\partial y_i}. \tag{15}$$

This implies that $h_i(z, y) = h_{0i} + h_1(z) + h_{2i}(y)$, as shown in Ekeland et al. (2004), and further that

$$T(z) = R_1 + K_1 \int_0^z \exp\left(h_1(s)\right) ds. \tag{16}$$

This solution enables us to solve for $n_f(y)$. Using Eqs. (16) and (15), we have

$$\frac{\partial n_f(y)}{\partial y_i} = K_1 \exp(-h_{0i} - h_{2i}(y)), \quad i = 1, \ldots, n_y. \tag{17}$$

---

[4]   See Horowitz (1996).

This defines $n_f(y)$ as the solution of a set of partial differential equations. The solution of this set of equations is

$$n_f(y) = C_1 + K_1 \tilde{n}_f(y),$$

where C_1 is a constant of integration and

$$\tilde{n}_f(y) = \sum_{i=1}^{n_y} \int_0^{y_i} \exp(-h_{0i} - h_{2i}(y_1, \ldots, y_i', \ldots, y_{n_y})) \, dy_i' \qquad (18)$$

$$+ \sum_{k=2}^{n_y} (-1)^{k-1} H_k(y_1, \ldots, y_n),$$

where

$$H_k(y) = \left(\sum_{i_1=1}^{(1+n_y-k)} \sum_{i_2=i_1+1}^{(2+n_y-k)} \cdots \sum_{i_k=i_{k-1}+1}^{n_y} \right.$$

$$\times \left(\int_0^{y_{i_1}} \cdots \int_0^{y_{i_k}} \frac{\partial \exp\left(-h_{0i_1} - h_{2i_1}\left(y_1, \ldots, y_{i_1}', \ldots, y_{i_k}', \ldots, y_n\right)\right)}{\partial y_{i_2} \cdots \partial y_{i_k}} \right.$$

$$\left. \left. \times \, dy_{i_1}' \cdots dy_{i_k}' \right) \right).$$

For the case where $n_y = \dim(y) = 1$, this implies that

$$n_f(y) = C_1 + K_1 \exp(-h_0) \int_0^y \exp(-h_2(y')) \, dy' \qquad (19)$$

for some R_1, K_1, and C_1. Because h_{0i}, h_1, and h_{2i} can be derived from the CDF $F_{z|y}$ the functions $T(z)$ and $n_f(y)$ are known up to the three unknown constants. This in turn determines $m_f(z) = P_z(z) - T(z)$. Finally, after fixing the constants and fixing y, the CDF of η can be calculated as

$$F_\eta(e) = F_{z|y}(z(e), y), \qquad (20)$$

where $z(e)$ satisfies

$$e = T(z(e)) - n_f(y).$$

Thus, the parameters $m_f(z)$, $n_f(y)$, and $F_\eta(\eta)$ are identified up to the constants R_1, K_1, and C_1. This derivation suggests an estimation procedure. First, estimate $F_{z|y}$ and calculate $h_i(z, y)$. Then, using $P_z(z)$ and the definition of $T(z)$, recover m_f, n_y, and F_η from (16), (19), and (20). We develop this procedure further in the next section.

The above procedure leaves the three constants undetermined. Additionally, we can recover the parameter K_1 if more information is available. If, for example, total output of the firm is observable, this information can be used to recover an estimate of K_1. This is developed further in Ekeland et al. (2004). Alternatively, if it is known that $m_f(z)$ belongs to a known finite-dimensional vector space V such that $m_f(z) = \sum_{j=1}^{M} \theta_j \xi_j(z)$, where ξ_j are the basis functions of the vector space, then we can go one step further and recover the unknown parameter K_1.

To see this, define $\widetilde{T}(z) = \int_0^z \exp(h_1(s)) ds$. Then using Eq. (16) and the definition of $T(z)$,

$$\widetilde{T}(z) = \frac{P_z(z) - \sum_{j=1}^{M} \theta_j \xi_j(z) - R_1}{K_1}. \tag{21}$$

Theorem 2 in Ekeland et al. (2004) proves that generically $P_z(z)$ does not belong to V. That is, generically $P_z(z)$ is linearly independent of $m_f(z)$. As a result, a regression of $\widetilde{T}(z)$ on $P_z(z)$, a constant, and the functions ξ_j for $j = 1, \ldots, M$ will recover K_1 from the coefficient on $P_z(z)$.

This procedure suggests a two-step estimator for K_1. First estimate $\widetilde{T}(z)$, and then run the regression of $\widetilde{T}(z)$ on $P_z(z)$, ξ_j, and a constant. $\widehat{K}_1$ is the inverse of the coefficient on $P_z(z)$. Our experience to date with this estimator is unfavorable. We develop an alternative estimator in Section 12.5.1 that estimates a semiparametric version of the model using semiparametric maximum likelihood, where the Monte Carlo results are much better.

12.4.2. Identification of the Nonadditive Model

Heckman et al. (2002) have shown that for identification of the preferences and technologies generating a hedonic equilibrium price function, it is not necessary that the marginal utility and marginal product functions be additive functions of the types specified in Section 12.4.1. Under certain conditions, one can identify nonadditive marginal utilities and nonadditive marginal product functions, using single-market data and no exclusion restrictions. Nonadditive specifications for either of these marginal functions allow us to model environments in which the curvatures of technologies or preferences vary across agents. It is important to be able to allow these more flexible types of specifications when estimating preferences and technologies.

Because the arguments for the identification and estimation of the marginal product function are analogous to those used to establish the identification of the marginal utility function, we will discuss only the latter. From the analysis in Section 12.2, it follows that from the first- and second-order conditions of utility maximization by a worker, we can establish the existence of a supply function $z = s(x, \varepsilon)$, where z denotes the quality or type of labor supplied by a worker with observable characteristic x and unobservable characteristic ε. The function s is strictly increasing in ε if $U_{z\varepsilon} < 0$. Assume, as in the previous sections, that ε is distributed independently of x; then by the arguments introduced in Matzkin (1999), and further developed in Matzkin (2003), it follows that, subject to some normalizations, the function s and the distribution of ε can be nonparametrically identified from the conditional distribution of z given x. Knowledge of the function s and of the distribution of ε, together with knowledge of P_z, allows one to identify the marginal utility function from the first-order conditions of utility maximization. This last step requires a separability restriction on the marginal utility function, of the type studied by Matzkin (2002, 2003).

To present one such set of separability restrictions and normalizations, suppose that for some unknown function m, which is strictly increasing in its first argument and strictly decreasing in its second argument,

$$U_z(z, x, \varepsilon) = m(q(z, x), \varepsilon),$$

where q is a known function, which is strictly increasing in each argument. Normalize the values of the unknown function m by requiring that for some value $\bar{x}$ of x, and for all t,

$$m(q(t, \bar{x}), t) = P_z(t).$$

Then, as shown by Heckman et al. (2002), under these restrictions and normalizations, both the distribution of ε and the function m are nonparametrically identified from the conditional distribution of z given x. We now sketch the proof.

The weak separability restriction in U_z allows one to recover the marginal utility when the supply function is given. The normalization that fixes the value of the function m at one point of x allows one to recover the supply function $s(x, \varepsilon)$ and the distribution of ε from the conditional distribution of z given x. To see this last point, note that the normalization restriction, together with the first-order conditions, implies that for all ε,

$$s(\bar{x}, \varepsilon) = \varepsilon,$$

because, when $x = \bar{x}$ and $z = \varepsilon$,

$$U_z(\varepsilon, \bar{x}, \varepsilon) = m(q(\varepsilon, \bar{x}), \varepsilon) = P_z(\varepsilon).$$

The strict monotonicity of s in ε and the statistical independence between x and ε, imply that, for all values of x and ε,

$$F_\varepsilon(e) = \Pr(\varepsilon \le e) = \Pr(\varepsilon \le e|x) = \Pr(s(x, \varepsilon) \le s(x, e)),$$

and that

$$\Pr(s(x, \varepsilon) \le s(x, e)) = \Pr(z \le s(x, e)|x) = F_{z|x}(s(x, e)).$$

Letting $x = \bar{x}$, this implies that

$$F_\varepsilon(e) = F_{z|\bar{x}}(s(\bar{x}, e)) = F_{z|\bar{x}}(e).$$

Hence, we can recover the distribution of ε from the conditional distribution of z given $x = \bar{x}$. Next, because for all x and e, $F_\varepsilon(e) = F_{z|x}(s(x, e))$, it follows that, under conditions guaranteeing that $F_{z|x}$ is strictly increasing,

$$s(x, e) = F_{z|x}^{-1}(F_\varepsilon(e)) = F_{z|x}^{-1}\left(F_{z|\bar{x}}(e)\right). \tag{22}$$

Hence, we can recover the function s from the conditional distribution of z given x. (See Matzkin 2003 for details.)

To see that under the separability restriction, the function m is identified, let (t_1, t_2) denote a vector on the domain of m. Find x^* such that

$$q(s(x^*, t_2), x^*) = t_1. \tag{23}$$

Then, $x^*(t_1, t_2)$ is a function of (t_1, t_2). From the definition of m and the first-order conditions of utility maximization,

$$m(t_1, t_2) = U_z(s(x^*(t_1, t_2), t_2), x^*(t_1, t_2), t_2) \tag{24}$$
$$= P_z(s(x^*(t_1, t_2), t_2)).$$

It follows that, from knowledge of the function q, s, and P_z, we can recover the function m, which gives the values of the marginal utility function (See Heckman et al., 2002, for details). Estimation of the function m and the distribution of ε follows the steps described above and is detailed in section 12.5.2.

12.5. ESTIMATION

Several estimation techniques are available to implement the analysis presented in Sections 12.4.1 and 12.4.2. All make use of the structure that the additive and nonadditive models impose on $F_{z|y}$. In the case of the nonadditive model, a fully nonparametric estimator is described in Section 12.5.2. In the case of the additive model, this information is sufficient to identify the structural parameters up to location and scale. Additionally, if parametric restrictions are placed on $m_f(z)$ in the additive model, the generic nonlinearity of the hedonic model can be exploited to estimate the scale. For ease of exposition in developing an estimator and presenting the estimation results for the additive model, we focus on a semiparametric estimator that exploits knowledge of the functional forms of $m_f(z)$ and $n_f(y)$ but that makes no further assumptions on the distribution of η. This estimator is semiparametric in that m_f and n_f are known up to a finite-dimensional parameter set, whereas the distribution of η is unknown. We also restrict the exposition to the case where the dimension of y is 1. We develop this estimator for the additive model in the next section.

12.5.1. Estimation of the Additive Model

In our limited Monte Carlo investigations, we generate data from and develop an estimator for specifications of $m_f(z)$ and $n_f(y)$ in Eq. (13) that are linear in the parameters. The first-order condition (1) may then be written

$$P_z(z) = \sum_{i=0}^{N_{zf}} \beta_i z^i + \sum_{j=0}^{N_v} v_j y^j + \eta. \tag{25}$$

We assume that a random sample of data on $(P_z(z_n), P_{zz}(z_n), z_n, y_n)$ for $n = 1, \ldots, N$ are available for a single market. To focus on the estimation of preferences or technology, we assume that $P_z(z)$ and $P_{zz}(z)$ are known. If instead prices were measured with error, the technique described below would need to be augmented to adjust standard errors for estimation of the pricing function. The technique exploits all the information in the model and uses the generic nonlinearity in the model to identify not only the shape of the marginal product function but also the scale.

Using $m_f(z) = \sum_{i=0}^{N_{zf}} \beta_i z^i$ and $n_f(y) = \sum_{j=0}^{N_v} v_j y^j$, the density of the nth observation z_n conditional on y_n is

$$f_{z|y}(z_n, y_n) = \widehat{f_\eta}\left(P_z(z_n) - \sum_{i=0}^{N_{zf}} \beta_i z_n^i - \sum_{j=0}^{N_v} v_j y_n^j\right) \cdot \left|P_{zz}(z_n) - \sum_{i=1}^{N_{zf}} i\beta_i z_n^{i-1}\right|,$$

where

$$\widehat{f_\eta}(\eta) = (Nh)^{-1}\sum_{k=1}^{N} K\left(\frac{\eta_k - \eta}{h}\right)$$

is the kernel density estimator of f_η. We propose to estimate the parameters by maximizing the likelihood function for the sample.

Let β and v be the vectors of parameters, excluding β_0 and v_0. The log likelihood function for the sample is

$$l(\beta, v, \beta_0, v_0) = \sum_{n=1}^{N} \ln \widehat{f_\eta}\left(P_z(z_n) - \beta_0 - \sum_{i=1}^{N_{zf}} \beta_i z_n^i - v_0 - \sum_{j=1}^{N_v} v_j y_n^j\right)$$
$$+ \sum_{n=1}^{N} \ln\left(P_{zz}(z_n) - \sum_{i=1}^{N_{zf}} i\beta_i z_n^{i-1}\right),$$

which simplifies to

$$l(\beta, v) = \sum_{n=1}^{N} \ln\left((Nh)^{-1}\sum_{k=1}^{N} K(\xi_{kn})\right) + \sum_{n=1}^{N} \ln\left(P_{zz}(z_n) - \sum_{i=1}^{N_{zf}} i\beta_i z_n^{i-1}\right),$$

where

$$\xi_{kn} = \frac{P_z(z_k) - P_z(z_n) - \sum_{i=1}^{N_{zf}} \beta_i\left(z_k^i - z_n^i\right) - \sum_{j=1}^{N_v} v_j\left(y_k^j - y_n^j\right)}{h}.$$

It is immediately obvious that $E(\eta)$ and $\beta_0 + v_0$ are not independently identified.

For ease of computation, we make the normalization that $\beta_0 = v_0 = 0$. It is also immediate that the parameters β are identified if and only if $P_z(z)$ is not a polynomial of degree less than or equal to N_{zf}. Theorem (1) of Ekeland et al. (2004) guarantees that generically the slope parameters in β are identified. The maximum likelihood estimators of β and ν are found by maximizing the log likelihood subject to $P_{zz}(z_n) - \sum_{i=1}^{N_{zf}} i\beta_i z_n^{i-1} > 0$ for all n. An estimator of f_η is

$$\widehat{f_\eta}(\eta) = (Nh)^{-1} \sum_{k=1}^{N} K\left(\frac{\widehat{\eta}_k - \eta}{h}\right),$$

where $\widehat{\eta}_k = P_z(z_k) - \sum_{i=1}^{N_{zf}} \widehat{\beta}_i z_k^i - \sum_{j=1}^{N_\nu} \widehat{\nu}_j y_k^j$.

12.5.2. Estimation of the Nonadditive Model

The most direct procedure to estimate the function m and the distribution of ε in the nonadditive model follows the steps described in Section 12.4.2. First, $F_{z|x}$ is estimated nonparametrically using data on the joint distribution of (z, x). This nonparametric estimator is $\widehat{F}_{z|x}$. Then this estimator is substituted into Eq. (22). This defines an estimator of $s(x, \varepsilon)$, $\widehat{s}(x, e) = \widehat{F}_{z|x}^{-1}\left(\widehat{F}_{z|\bar{x}}(\varepsilon)\right)$. Heckman et al. (2002) have shown that when $\widehat{F}_{z|x}$ is a kernel estimator for $F_{z|x}$, defined by

$$\widehat{F}_{z|x}(t) = \frac{\sum_{i=1}^{N} \widetilde{K}\left(\frac{t-z_i}{\sigma}\right) K\left(\frac{x-x_i}{\sigma}\right)}{\sum_{i=1}^{N} K\left(\frac{x-x_i}{\sigma}\right)},$$

where K is a kernel function, $\widetilde{K}$ is the integral of a kernel function, and σ is a bandwidth, the estimators for the distribution of ε and for the function m are consistent and asymptotically normally distributed. Finally, using this estimator $\widehat{s}(x, \varepsilon)$, data on the marginal price $P_z(z)$, and Eq. (23) and (24), m is estimated as

$$m(t_1, t_2) = P_z\left(\widehat{s}\left(x^*, t_2\right)\right), \tag{26}$$

where x^* solves $q\left(\widehat{s}(x^*, t_2), x^*\right) = t_1$.

12.6. SIMULATION AND ESTIMATION RESULTS

In this section, we present simulation results from a range of specifications of three basic hedonic models. In each case, these simulations show the shape of the equilibrium pricing function, the population density at each point z, and the generic nonlinearity of the hedonic model. The accompanying estimation results demonstrate the performance of the estimation techniques described in Sections 12.5.1 and 12.5.2.

Models 1 and 2 are examples of additive hedonic models. For these models we study the equilibria for several sets of parameter values and study how the shape of the equilibrium price varies with alternate parameter values. Then we simulate data from these sample hedonic economies and test the performance of the maximum likelihood estimation technique on the simulated data. For each model we simulate data from fifteen parameter specifications. For each specification, we generate 100 independent samples, each with 1000 observations. Using these simulated data, we estimate the parameters using the technique described in Section 12.5.1. The mean and the variance of the parameter estimates are compared with the true parameter values used to generate the simulated data.

Model 3 is an example of a nonadditive hedonic model. The estimation technique that is used to estimate the parameters of the additive models is not applicable to data generated from the nonadditive economy. Instead, the technique from Section 12.5.2 must be used. For Model 3, we simulate data from a sample economy and study the performance of the nonadditive model estimator described in Section 12.5.2.

All models are completely specified by the firms' technology $\Gamma(z, y, \eta)$, the workers' utility $U(z, x, \varepsilon)$, and the distributions of firm and worker heterogeneity f_y, f_η, f_x, and f_ε. For each model, these objects are specified, and then standard numerical methods are used to approximate $P_z(z)$, the solution to the equilibrium differential equation (3). Throughout the exposition below, $\phi(x, \mu, \Sigma)$ denotes the density function of a normal random variable with mean μ and covariance Σ. Model 1 is a quadratic model with nonnormal heterogeneity. Model 2 is an additive model in which m_f, n_f, m_w, and n_w are low-degree polynomials. For both models we discuss features of the equilibrium price function, simulate data, and estimate the structural parameters that describe firm technologies. Model 3 is a nonadditive model in which firms are homogeneous and workers have Cobb–Douglas utility. It is described further below.

12.6.1. Model 1: Specification and Simulation Results

The simplest generalization of the normal–quadratic Tinbergen model is the quadratic hedonic model with nonnormal heterogeneity. This model specification imposes $N_{zf} = 1$ and $N_v = 1$ in Eq. (25) and in the analogous equation for workers. However, in contrast to the classical Tinbergen model, this model allows the heterogeneity parameters to be distributed as a mixture of normals. Details of Model 1 are given in Table A1 in the Appendix. This table details the exact functional forms that describe the model.

For this model, in a preliminary analysis we simulate pricing functions for a large number of specifications. In all of these specifications, parameters were restricted to cases where worker and firm heterogeneity were distributed as mixtures of normals, each with two components in the mixture. The extreme cases of these specifications include the Tinbergen–normal case when the weights on the two components of the mixture are 0 and 1 or 1 and 0. In this set of specifications the parameters that most affected the shape of the pricing function were the mean and variance of worker and firm heterogeneity and the weights on the components of the mixture-of-normals distribution. In all cases the curvature of the pricing function is a linear combination of the curvatures of worker preferences and firm technologies. (See Ekeland et al., 2004 and Heckman et al., 2002.)

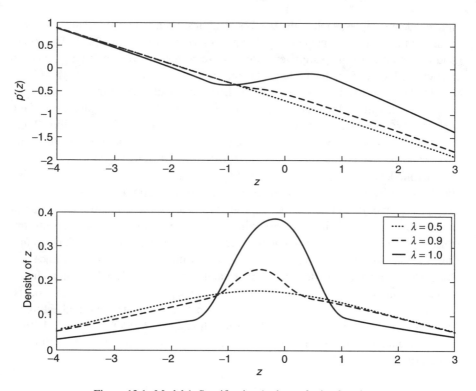

Figure 12.1. Model 1, Specification 1: slope of price function.

From among the specifications investigated we selected fifteen to report here. The specifications are detailed in Tables A2 and A3. The tables list five specifications. For each of these specifications we allowed the parameter $\lambda_{\eta 1} = \lambda_{\varepsilon 1} = \lambda$ to vary from 0.1, to 0.5, to 0.9.[5] Thus there are three variations of each of five specifications. Specifications 1 and 5 represent two extreme cases and specifications 2–4 represent linear combinations of those cases.

The price functions associated with each specification are depicted in Figures 12.1–12.20. For each economy, we display the slope of the price function, the population density at each location z, and the curvature of the price function. Figures 12.1–12.10 show how the slope, the curvature, and the density vary as λ varies from 0.5 to 0.9 to 1.0. Figures 12.11–12.20 show how the slope, the curvature, and the density vary as λ varies from 0.0 to 0.1 to 0.5. The figures largely tell the same story. When $\lambda = 0.0$ or 1.0, the slope is a straight line, the curvature is constant, and the density is a normal density. However, when $\lambda = 0.1$ or 0.9, the slope is not a straight line, the curvature is not constant, and the density is not a

---

[5] The cases in which $\lambda = 0$ or $\lambda = 1$, the Tinbergen normal–quadratic cases, are displayed in the figures for comparison.

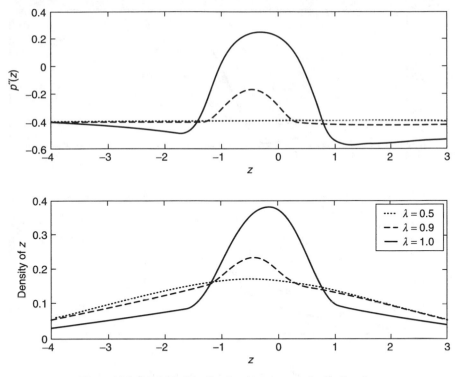

Figure 12.2. Model 1, Specification 1: curvature of price function.

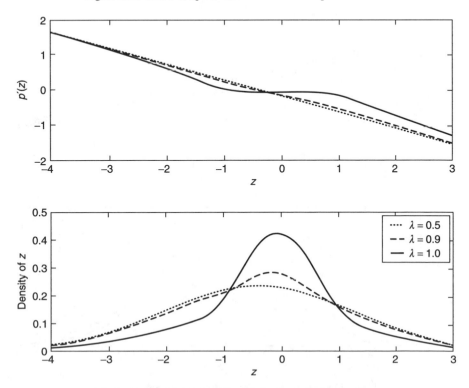

Figure 12.3. Model 1, Specification 2: slope of price function.

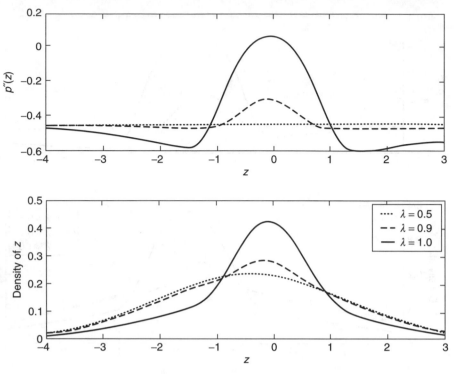

Figure 12.4. Model 1, Specification 2: curvature of price function.

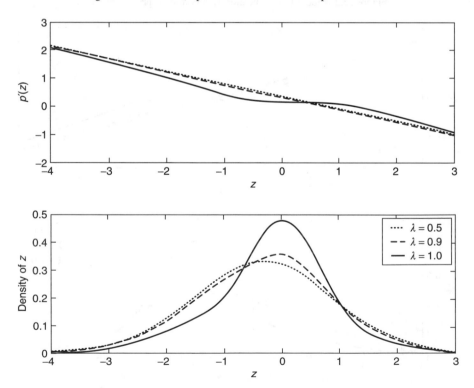

Figure 12.5. Model 1, Specification 3: slope of price function.

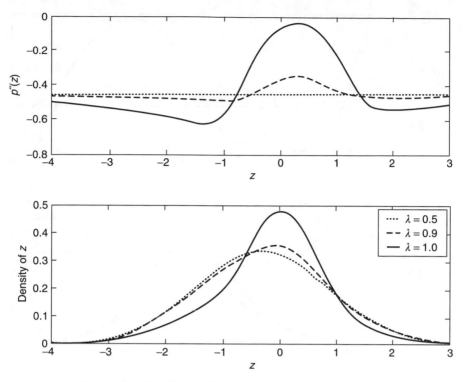

Figure 12.6. Model 1, Specification 3: curvature of price function.

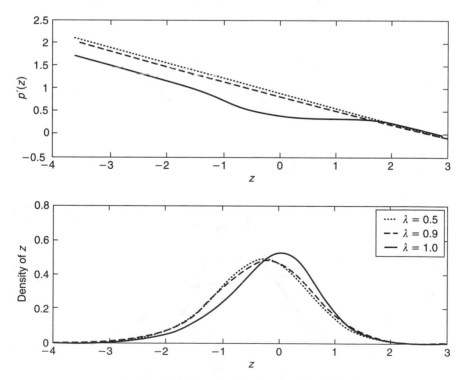

Figure 12.7. Model 1, Specification 4: slope of price function.

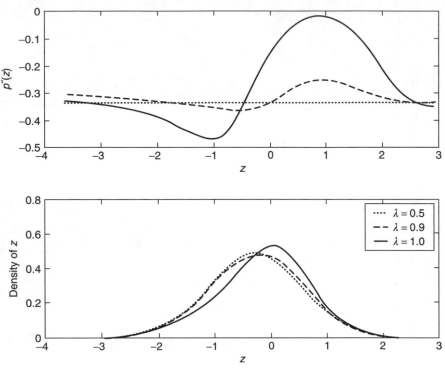

Figure 12.8. Model 1, Specification 4: curvature of price function.

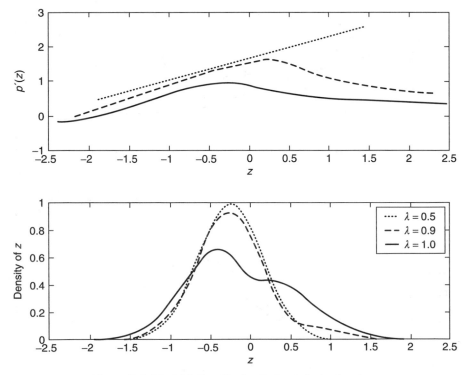

Figure 12.9. Model 1, Specification 5: slope of price function.

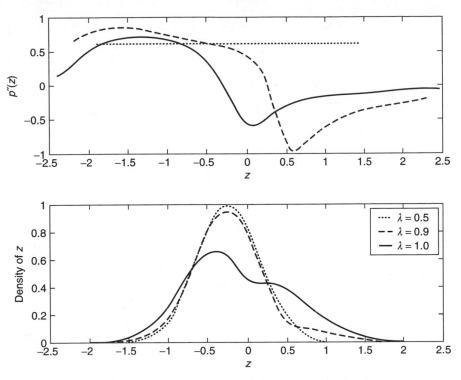

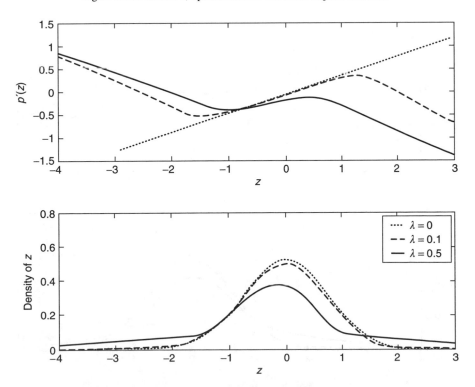

Figure 12.10. Model 1, Specification 5: curvature of price function.

Figure 12.11. Model 1, Specification 1: slope of price function.

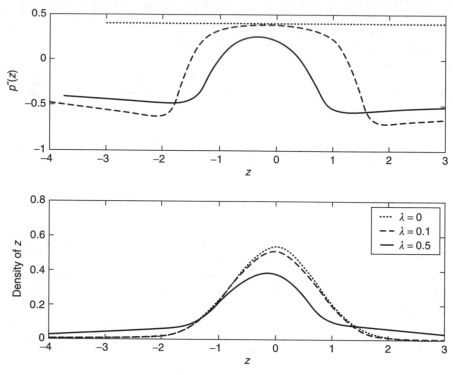

Figure 12.12. Model 1, Specification 1: curvature of price function.

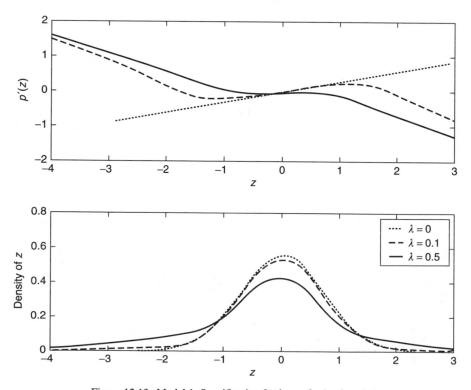

Figure 12.13. Model 1, Specification 2: slope of price function.

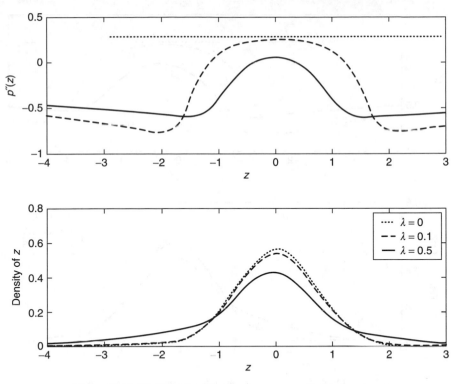

Figure 12.14. Model 1, Specification 2: curvature of price function.

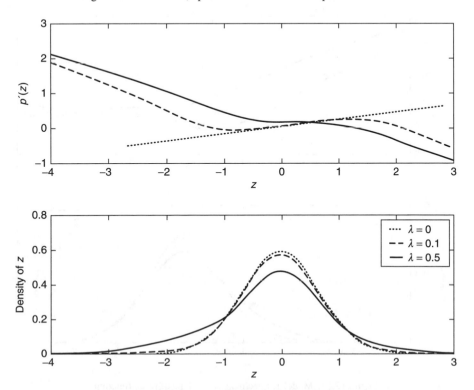

Figure 12.15. Model 1, Specification 3: slope of price function.

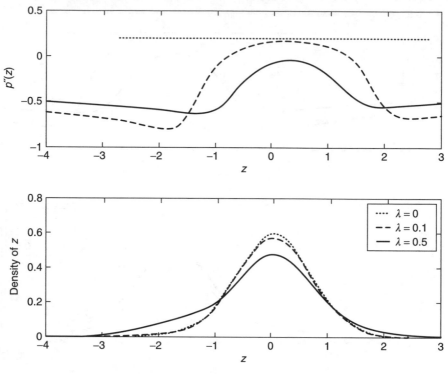

Figure 12.16. Model 1, Specification 3: curvature of price function.

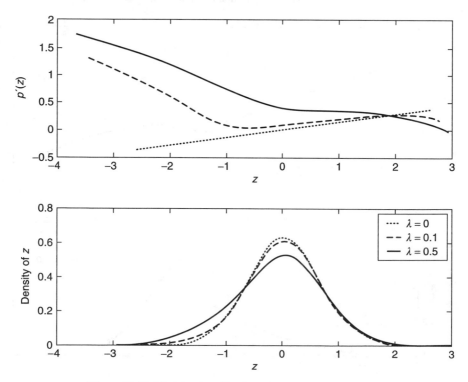

Figure 12.17. Model 1, Specification 4: slope of price function.

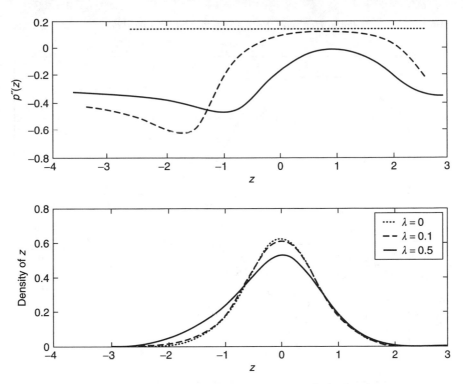

Figure 12.18. Model 1, Specification 4: curvature of price function.

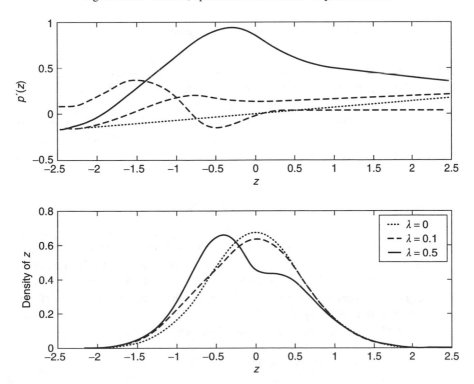

Figure 12.19. Model 1, Specification 5: slope of price function.

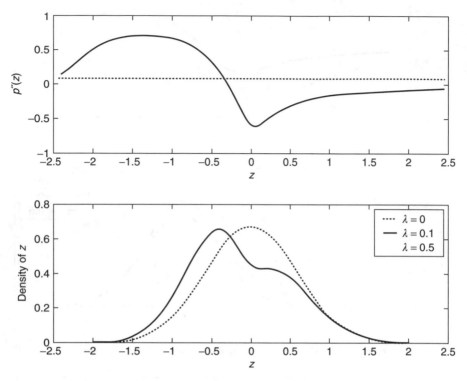

Figure 12.20. Model 1, Specification 5: curvature of price function.

normal density. These deviations from the Tinberger case are even stronger when $\lambda = 0.5$. The figures also show that the slope of the price function deviates most sharply from a straight line in the two extreme cases, specification 1 and specification 5. All the figures show, however, that the curvature deviates strongly from a constant when heterogeneity is not normal. The closer the distribution of heterogeneity is to normal, the closer the curvature is to a constant.

12.6.2. Model 1: Estimation Results

The figures described in the previous section show that there is nonlinearity in the marginal price function and nonconstancy in the curvature of the price function when heterogeneity is not normally distributed in the population in this quadratic model. The question remains: Is that nonlinearity sufficient to estimate the structural parameters in the model with precision? To shed light on this question, we generated data from the fifteen specifications described in the previous section and in Tables A2 and A3 and estimated the Model 1 version of Eq. (25),

$$P_z(z) = -Bz + v_0 + v_1'y + \eta.$$

We generated 100 datasets, each of sample size 1000, for each specification and then estimated the parameters B and ν_1 using the technique discussed in Section 12.5.1. The results are displayed in Tables A4, A5, and A6. Table A4 displays results for each of the five specifications listed when $\lambda_{\eta 1} = \lambda_{\varepsilon 1} = \lambda = 0.5$. Table A5 displays results for each specification when $\lambda = 0.9$ and Table A6 displays results for each specification when $\lambda = 0.1$. The contrast between Table A4 and Tables A5 and A6 gives some indication of how much the precision of the results deteriorates when the economy is closer to the normal–quadratic Tinbergen economy, which is not identified.

First consider the results in Table A4. The bias of the maximum likelihood (ML) estimator is never larger than 3%. The standard errors range from 0.0349 in specification 1 to 0.287 in specification 4. Specifications 3 and 4 have the largest standard errors. Looking at Tables A2 and A3, we see that these are the specifications in which the two components of the mixtures of normals distribution are most similar. That is, these are the two specifications that are closest to being not identified.

Tables A5 and A6 investigate how the results in Table A4 change when $\lambda = 0.9$ and 0.1. In these cases, the distributions of worker and firm heterogeneity are closer to being normally distributed and the price function is closer to being linear. In these cases, the ML results are essentially unchanged from the case with $\lambda = 0.5$. The bias of the ML estimator is of the same order of magnitude. The biggest increase is for specification 4, when λ decreases from 0.5 to 0.1. In this case, the bias of the ML estimator increases from 0.02 to 0.12. This is still less than 7% of the parameter value. The standard errors of the estimates increase slightly. The biggest increase when λ increases from 0.5 to 0.9 is in specification 1, for which the standard errors increase from 0.0349 and 0.0518 to 0.12 and 0.194. The standard errors after the increase are still only 12% and 20% of the parameter values.

The results indicate that the ML estimator produces very good parameter estimates in a range of specifications. These results apply to the linear–quadratic model of Tinbergen with nonnormal heterogeneity and to the linear approximations of Brown and Rosen (1982). Far from not being identified, the parameters are estimated with a high degree of precision.

12.6.3. Nonlinear Additively Separable Specifications, Model 2: Simulation Results

The results of Ekeland et al. (2004) apply to additive models more general than the quadratic model. Model 2 generalizes Model 1 by replacing the linear–quadratic terms in the production and utility functions with nonlinear terms. Model 2 is detailed in Table A7. The specification was chosen so that every function is a polynomial, $v(y)$ is strictly increasing ($v_1 > 0$), $\theta(x)$ is strictly increasing ($\theta_1 > 0$), and $m_f(z) < m_w(z)$. This last restriction rules out bunching (see Heckman et al., 2002). The specification allows the curvatures of utility and preferences to be flexible and vary with z. It also allows a flexible relation between preference heterogeneity $v(y)$ and

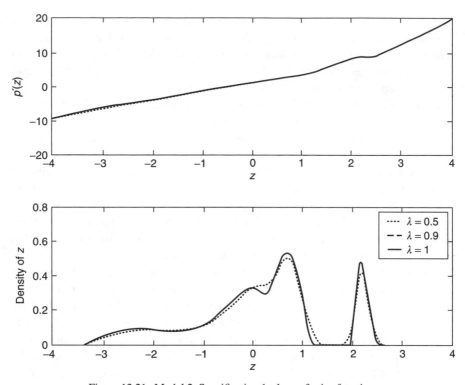

Figure 12.21. Model 2, Specification 1: slope of price function.

observable firm traits y. Power-series representations detailed in Table A7 could be replaced with orthogonal polynomial representations or representations based on other basis functions. The power-series representations were chosen for ease of exposition.

It was more costly in terms of computer time to simulate equilibria and generate data from Model 2. We studied a more limited set of specifications. In particular, five specifications were chosen at random from a compact parameter space. The five chosen are detailed in Tables A8 and A9. The parameters that were allowed to vary across specifications include β, v_1, μ_η, σ_η, α_0, α_1, μ_ε, and σ_ε. These parameters govern the curvature of the firms' technology, the minimum slope of $v(y)$, the mean and variance of unobservable firm heterogeneity, the curvature of worker preferences, and the mean and variance of worker heterogeneity.

Figures 12.21–12.30 display the slope of the price function, the curvature of the price function, and the density of z for specifications 1 through 5. For each specification, three variations are plotted; one with $\lambda = 0.5$, one with $\lambda = 0.9$, and one with $\lambda = 1.0$. Similar graphs depicting the cases in which $\lambda = 0.0$ and 0.1 are available from the authors upon request. Clearly a wide variety of shapes of the price function are possible. In all cases, it appears as if the price function might be well approximated by a quadratic or a cubic, but there are sharp deviations from these

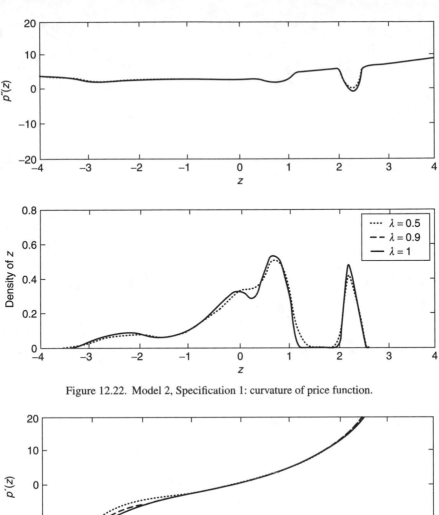

Figure 12.22. Model 2, Specification 1: curvature of price function.

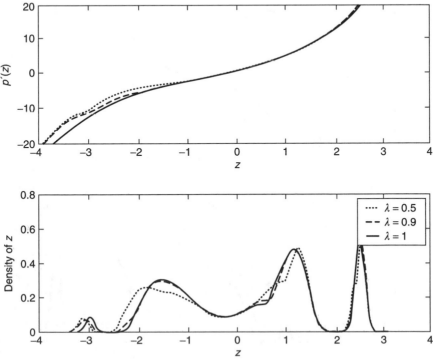

Figure 12.23. Model 2, Specification 2: slope of price function.

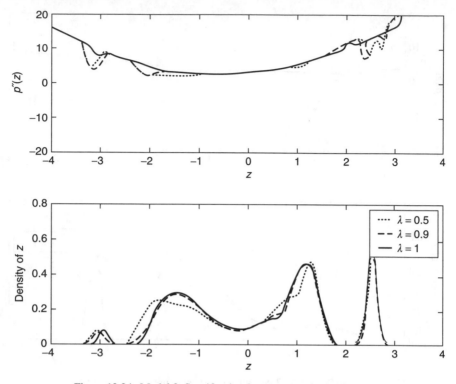

Figure 12.24. Model 2, Specification 2: curvature of price function.

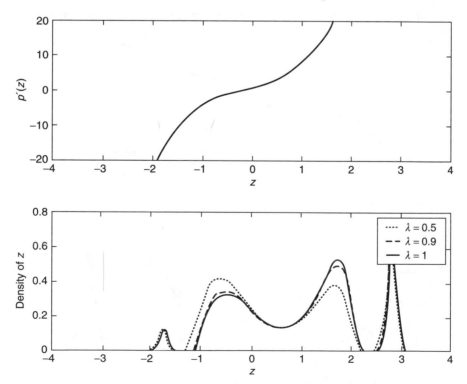

Figure 12.25. Model 2, Specification 3: slope of price function.

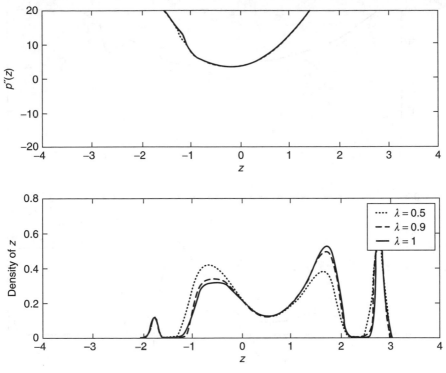

Figure 12.26. Model 2, Specification 3: curvature of price function.

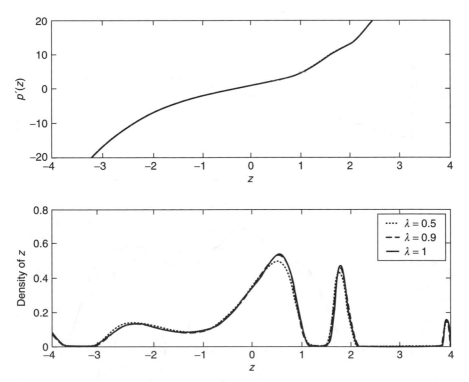

Figure 12.27. Model 2, Specification 4: slope of price function.

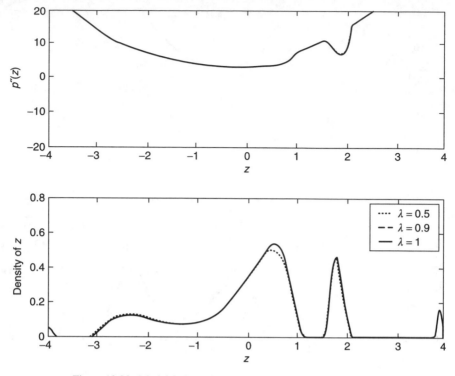

Figure 12.28. Model 2, Specification 4: curvature of price function.

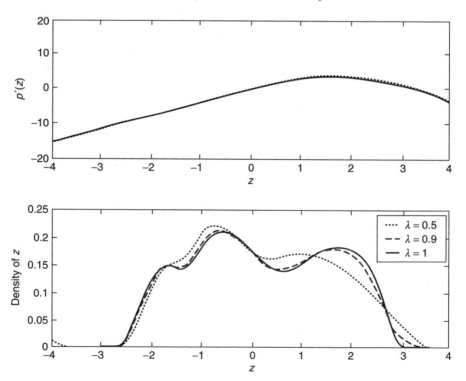

Figure 12.29. Model 2, Specification 5: slope of price function.

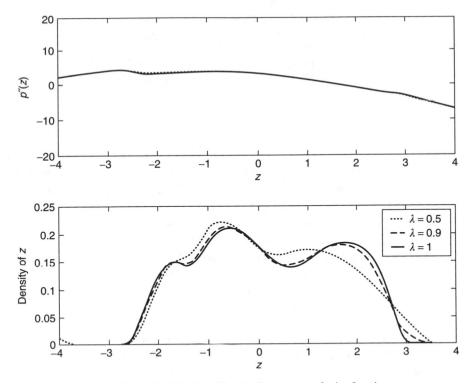

Figure 12.30. Model 2, Specification 5: curvature of price function.

shapes. Simple quadratic or cubic approximations to the price function would miss these important deviations. Also noteworthy is the shape of the equilibrium density of z. In all the cases displayed, this density has many modes and is far from being a normal density. In particular, this model is capable of generating equilibria in which there are nearly gaps in the range of products marketed. In Fig. 12.21, the fraction of firms demanding $z < 1$ is positive and large, the fraction demanding $z \in (1, 2)$ is nearly zero (though positive), and the fraction demanding $z > 2$ is positive and large. This gap in the product range reflects two factors, the distribution of heterogeneity in the population, and the curvature of preferences and technology.

The value of λ does not appear to have large impacts on the slope, the price, or the density. It does cause deviations in the shapes of these objects, but not large ones. This lack of impact is likely to be an artifact of the set of specifications investigated. In all specifications, the distribution of firm heterogeneity is determined by both the distribution of $v(y)$ and the distribution of η. Because $v(y)$ is a fifth-order polynomial in y, the variance of $v(y)$ dominates the variance of η in all specifications. Hence, η only has small local effects on the equilibrium and does not have large nonlocal impacts. Nevertheless, the model is far from the normal model because $v(y)$ is far from being normal.

TABLE 12.1. *Model 3 functional forms*

Firm	technology	$\Gamma(z)$	Az^α
worker	utility	$U(z, x, \varepsilon)$	$Bz^\beta x^{\beta-1}\varepsilon^\delta$
	Density of x	$f_x(x)$	$U[0.5, 1.5]$
	Density of ε	$f_\varepsilon(\varepsilon)$	$U[3.0, 4.0]$

12.6.4. Model 2: Estimation Results

Tables A10–A19 present the estimation results for Model 2. Tables A10–A14 present results for specifications 1 through 5 when $\lambda = 0.5$. Tables A15–A19 present results for the same specifications when $\lambda = 0.9$. Results for the cases where $\lambda = 0.1$ are omitted to economize on space. They are available from the authors upon request; they are qualitatively similar to those presented here.

In all the specifications estimated the ML estimator again performs very well. In Table A10, for instance, the true value of β_1 is 0.623. The average estimate is 0.637. The bias is 2%. This degree of bias is typical of all parameter estimates across all specifications. In all cases the bias has an order of magnitude never larger than 0.03, in the range of 2–3% of the parameter values. The standard error of the estimates of β_1 in Table A10 is 0.243 or 39% of the parameter value. In percentage terms this standard error is the fourth largest standard error for any parameter in any of the specifications. The other large standard errors are β_1 in Table A15 and β_1 in Tables A13 and A18. The largest standard error obtained is the standard error of the estimate of β_1 in Table A18, which is 0.405 or 63% of the true parameter value. Standard errors for all other parameter estimates in all specifications are much lower than this. In Table A10 the second largest standard error in percentage terms is the standard error on ν_{c1}, which is 0.256 or 13.8% of the parameter value. Most of the standard errors in Tables A10 through A19 range between 5% and 20%.

Thus, the ML estimator performs very well. Despite the high degree of non-linearity in these additive models, the technique recovers parameter estimates with small bias and reasonable standard errors.

12.6.5. Model 3: Simulation and Estimation Results

When the data reject the additive specifications above, alternative techniques are required. Some techniques for estimating nonadditive models are developed in Sections 12.4.2 and 12.5.2. To evaluate the small-sample properties of these estimators for economies where the marginal utility function, the marginal product function, or both are nonadditive in the unobservable characteristics, we consider an economy where workers differ in the value of the observable characteristic x and the unobservable characteristic ε. To focus analysis on estimation of the utility functions we generate observations from an economy with homogeneous production technologies. The marginal price function is given by the marginal product function. The specification that we use is described in Table 12.1.

In this economy, profit maximization by each of the homogenous firms implies that the first-order condition

$$A\alpha z^{\alpha-1} - P_z(z) = 0$$

and the second-order condition

$$A\alpha(\alpha - 1)z^{\alpha-2} - P_{zz}(z) \leq 0$$

are satisfied. Since all the firms have the same production technology, the only possible equilibrium price function for this economy is given by

$$P_z(z) = A\alpha z^{\alpha-1}.$$

This is an instance of Rosen's 1974 argument that when one side of the market is homogenous, the price function directly reveals parameters of that side of the market.

The first-order condition for utility maximization of a worker with characteristics (x, ε) is

$$P_z(z) - B\beta z^{\beta-1}x^{\beta-1}\varepsilon^\delta = 0 \tag{27}$$

and the second-order condition is

$$P_{zz}(z) - B\beta(\beta - 1)z^{\beta-2}x^{\beta-1}\varepsilon^\delta < 0.$$

Using the equilibrium price function, we get that the supply function of the worker, describing the quality of labor supplied, is

$$z = \left(\frac{A\alpha}{B\beta}x^{1-\beta}\varepsilon^{-\delta}\right)^{\frac{1}{\beta-\alpha}}$$

as long as

$$A\alpha(\alpha - 1)z^{\alpha-2} - B\beta(\beta - 1)z^{\beta-2}x^{\beta-1}\varepsilon^\delta < 0.$$

The latter inequality is satisfied as long as

$$A\alpha(\alpha - 1)\left(\frac{A\alpha}{B\beta}x^{1-\beta}\varepsilon^{-\delta}\right)^{\frac{\alpha-2}{\beta-\alpha}} - B\beta(\beta - 1)\left(\frac{A\alpha}{B\beta}x^{1-\beta}\varepsilon^{-\delta}\right)^{\frac{\beta-2}{\beta-\alpha}} x^{\beta-1}\varepsilon^\delta < 0$$

or

$$(A\alpha)^{\frac{\beta-2}{\beta-\alpha}} (B\beta)^{\frac{\alpha-2}{\beta-\alpha}} \left(x^{1-\beta}\varepsilon^{-\delta}\right)^{\frac{\alpha-2}{\beta-\alpha}} [\alpha - \beta] < 0.$$

Hence, when $A > 0$, $B > 0$, $\varepsilon > 0$, and $x > 0$, if $0 < \alpha < \beta$, the equilibrium price function is

$$P_z(z) = A\alpha z^{\alpha-1}$$

and the supply function of a worker with characteristics (x, ε) is

$$z = \left(\frac{A\alpha}{B\beta}\right)^{\frac{1}{\beta-\alpha}} x^{\frac{1-\beta}{\beta-\alpha}} \varepsilon^{\frac{-\delta}{\beta-\alpha}}. \tag{28}$$

To evaluate the estimators for the marginal utility of the workers obtained using the estimators developed by Heckman et al. (2002), we simulate observations for pairs (x, z) generated by this supply function and the specifications described above for the distributions of x and ε. We will require that for some strictly increasing function m

$$U_z(z, x, \varepsilon) = m(zx, \varepsilon).$$

The utility function described in Table 12.1 satisfies this restriction. The true function m is $m(zx, \varepsilon) = \beta B (zx)^{\beta-1} \varepsilon^\delta$. Assuming that the true function is unknown and that the true distribution of ε is unknown, we impose the normalization that, for all t within the relevant domain,

$$m(t\bar{x}, t) = P_z(t).$$

Because the equilibrium marginal price function satisfies $P_z(z) = A\alpha z^{\alpha-1}$, the normalization implies that

$$m(t\bar{x}, t) = A\alpha t^{\alpha-1}.$$

We could choose any value for $\bar{x}$ and use a transformation to modify the true marginal utility function m and the true distribution of ε to lie within the set of marginal utilities and distributions that are consistent with the normalization imposed by our particular choice of $\bar{x}$. However, for simplicity, we choose the value of $\bar{x}$ and of the other parameters to be such that the true function m and the distribution of ε are consistent with the normalization generated by that $\bar{x}$. Our choices for the parameters are

A	α	B	β	δ	$\bar{x}$
0.55	0.3	0.15	-1.1	-0.8	1.

The equilibrium marginal price function for this economy is depicted with a solid line in Fig. 12.31. The dotted lines represent bounds on feasible marginal prices produced by the restriction that an equilibrium marginal price must satisfy Eq. (27) for some (x, ε), and (x, ε) must be elements of a compact set.

Using these parameters and the derivations already given, we generated 100 independent samples, each with 100 observations of (z, x) pairs. Using these samples, we estimated the distribution of ε, the workers' supply function $z = s(x, \varepsilon)$, and the marginal utility function m. To estimate the conditional distribution of z given x, bandwidths were chosen by cross validation.

Figure 12.32 displays estimates of the distribution function of ε. In both panels of the figure, the solid line displays the true distribution function. The dashed line displays an estimate. The dashed lines in the lower panel display the median and average of the 100 estimates of the distribution function. These track the true distribution function quite closely. The maximum gap in the tails of the distribution is about 0.05. The maximum gap outside the tails is negligible. The dotted lines in the panel plot the 5th and 95th percentiles of the estimates. The maximum gap

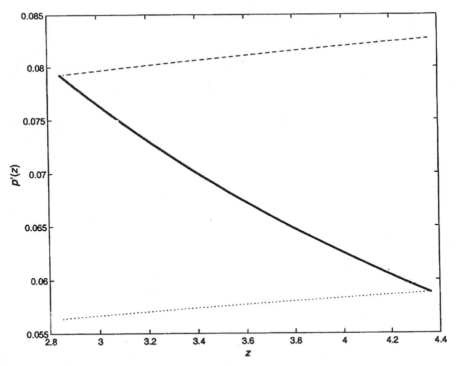

Figure 12.31. Model 3: slope of price function. The solid line depicts the marginal price function. The dashed and dotted lines depict the upper and lower bounds of feasible values for the marginal price.

between these two quantiles and the true distribution function is about 0.2 . This graph shows that the nonparametric estimate of the distribution function tracks the true distribution function very well.

Figures 12.33 and 12.34 plot the estimates of the supply function (28). The upper panels display three-dimensional graphs of this function. The lower panels display cross sections of the function at particular values of x and ε. Figure 12.33 illustrates how well a single of the supply function can do. Figure 12.34 illustrates the median and average of the 100 independent estimates. The dashed lines in the lower panels show that when $\varepsilon = 3.45$ or when $x = 0.62$, the median and average estimates track the true supply function with negligible error. The dotted lines depict the 5th and 95th percentiles of these estimates.

Finally, Figs. 12.35 and 12.36 portray estimates of the marginal utility function. Figure 12.35 shows how well a single estimate can do, showing the three-dimensional $m(zx, \varepsilon)$ in the upper panels and the marginal utility $m(zx, \varepsilon)$ for fixed values of ε and zx, respectively, in the lower two panels. Figure 12.36 illustrates the average and median estimates, as well as the 5th and 95th percentiles. When ε is fixed at $\varepsilon = 3.45$, the median and average estimates of $m(zx, 3.45)$, plotted with dashed lines, track the true function with negligible error. Similarly, when zx is fixed at

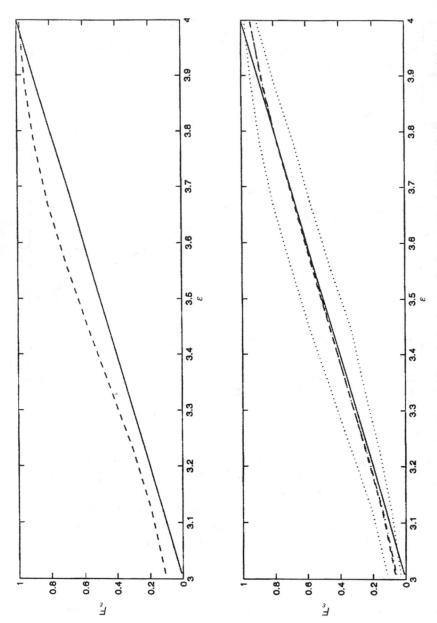

Figure 12.32. Model 3: distribution of ε. The solid lines depict the true distribution. The dashed line in the upper panel depicts a single estimate of the distribution. The dashed lines in the lower panel depict the average and median estimates of the distribution. The dotted lines plot the 5th and 95th percentile estimates.

318

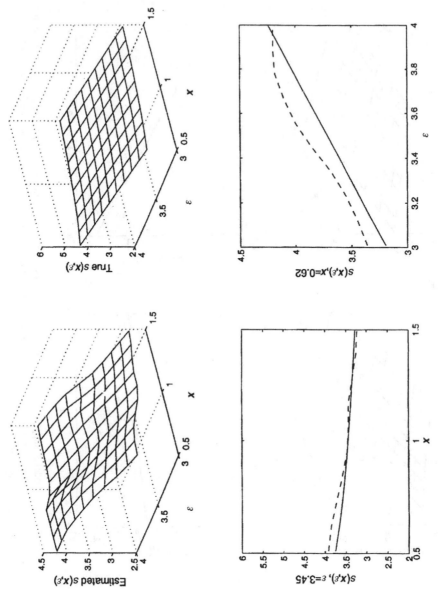

Figure 12.33. Model 3: supply function, single estimate. The solid lines in the lower panels depict the true function s. The dashed lines depict a single estimate of s.

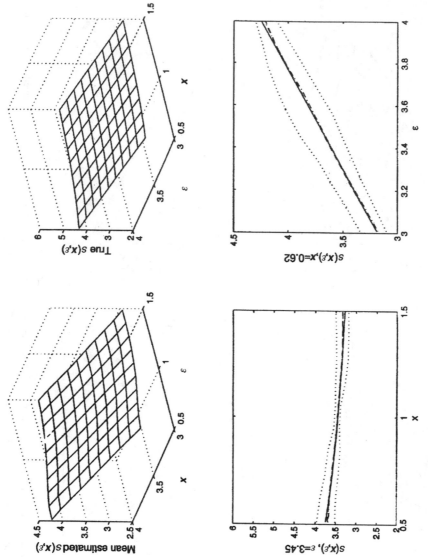

Figure 12.34. Model 3: supply function, median and average estimates. The solid lines in the lower panels depict the true function s. The dashed lines depict the average and median estimates of the function s and the dotted lines depict the 5th and 95th percentile estimates.

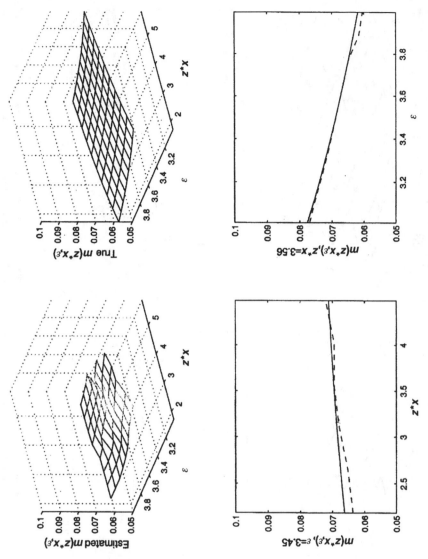

Figure 12.35. Model 3: marginal utility function, single estimate. The solid lines in the lower panels depict the true function m. The dashed lines depict a single estimate of the function.

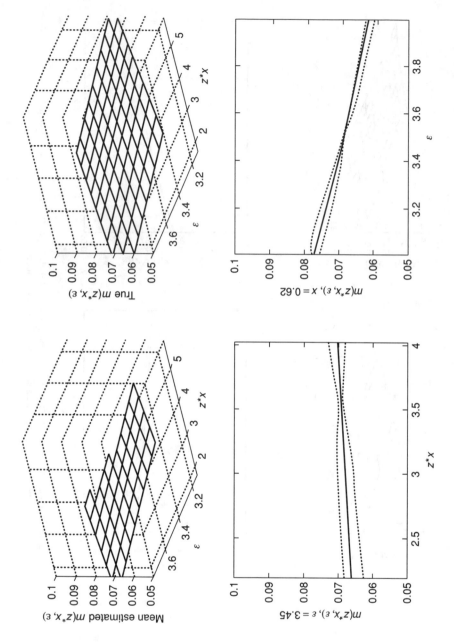

Figure 12.36. Model 3: marginal utility function, median and average estimates. The solid lines depict the true function m. The dashed lines depict the average and median estimates of m and the dotted lines plot the 5th and 95th percentile estimates.

$zx = 3.56$, the median and average estimates are indistinguishable from the true function. Again, the dotted lines show the 5th and 95th percentile estimates.

12.7. CONCLUSIONS

Much of the previous analysis of hedonic models has neglected to consider the strong implications imposed by equilibrium on the data generated from an hedonic model. In particular, strong restrictions on preferences and technologies such as additive separability impose a great deal of structure on the joint distribution of observable random variables. In this paper, we have developed these points in our discussion and illustrated them with three computational examples. The graphical displays of equilibrium prices in the array of models we consider demonstrate the strong non-linearities that are generic features of hedonic models. Nonlinearity in these models is not arbitrary, but emerges quite naturally. This nonlinearity, in conjunction with restrictions such as additivity, allows identification and estimation of the hedonic model. In finite samples of size 1000, the semiparametric maximum likelihood technique performs well in recovering estimates of structural parameters both in the linear–quadratic model and in Model 2, where the nonlinearities in the structure of the economy are more severe. Finally, in Model 3, with sample sizes of only 100, the nonparametric techniques developed for nonadditive models work very well.

The structural parameter estimates obtained in these exercises are crucial for any general equilibrium analysis that seeks to address the welfare consequences of policy changes in hedonic markets. They are also crucial for employing hedonic methods to correct cost-of-living indices for changes in the characteristics of marketed goods. Without estimation of the structural parameters underlying a hedonic market, changes in the hedonic pricing relationship are uninterpretable.

APPENDIX: TABLES

TABLE A1: *Model 1 functional forms*

Firm	Technology	$\Gamma(z, y, \eta)$	$(v_0 + v_1 y + \eta)z - \frac{Bz^2}{2}$
	Density of y	$f_y(y)$	$\sum_{i=1}^{M_y} \lambda_{yi}\phi(y, \mu_{yi}, \Sigma_{yi})$
	Density of η	$f_\eta(\eta)$	$\sum_{i=1}^{M_\eta} \lambda_{\eta i}\phi(\eta, \mu_{\eta i}, \Sigma_{\eta i})$
Worker	Utility	$U(z, x, \varepsilon)$	$(\theta_0 + \theta_1 x + \varepsilon)z - \frac{Az^2}{2}$
	Density of x	$f_x(x)$	$\sum_{i=1}^{M_x} \lambda_{xi}\phi(x, \mu_{xi}, \Sigma_{xi})$
	Density of ε	$f_\varepsilon(\varepsilon)$	$\sum_{i=1}^{M_\varepsilon} \lambda_{\varepsilon i}\phi(\varepsilon, \mu_{\varepsilon i}, \Sigma_{\varepsilon i})$

Note: (z, η, ε) are all scalars. y is of dimension n_y and x is of dimension n_x. The parameters (B, v_0, v_1) and (A, θ_0, θ_1) are common across all firms and workers, respectively.

TABLE A2: *Model 1 parameter values for firms*

Parameter	Specification 1	Specification 2	Specification 3	Specification 4	Specification 5
B	1.0	1.25	1.5	1.75	2.0
ν_0	0.0	0.0	0.0	0.0	0.0
ν_1	1.0	1.0	1.0	1.0	1.0
n_y	1	1	1	1	1
M_y	2	2	2	2	2
λ_y	$(1.0, 0.0)'$	$(1.0, 0.0)'$	$(1.0, 0.0)'$	$(1.0, 0.0)'$	$(1.0, 0.0)'$
μ_{y1}	0.0	0.0	0.0	0.0	0.0
μ_{y2}	0.0	0.0	0.0	0.0	0.0
Σ_{y1}	$\begin{bmatrix} 1.0 & 0.0 \\ 0.0 & 0.1 \end{bmatrix}$	$\begin{bmatrix} 1.0 & 0.0 \\ 0.0 & 0.1 \end{bmatrix}$	$\begin{bmatrix} 1.0 & 0.0 \\ 0.0 & 0.1 \end{bmatrix}$	$\begin{bmatrix} 1.0 & 0.0 \\ 0.0 & 0.1 \end{bmatrix}$	$\begin{bmatrix} 1.0 & 0.0 \\ 0.0 & 1.0 \end{bmatrix}$
Σ_{y2}	$\begin{bmatrix} 0.5 & 0.0 \\ 0.0 & 0.5 \end{bmatrix}$	$\begin{bmatrix} 0.45 & 0.0 \\ 0.0 & 0.45 \end{bmatrix}$	$\begin{bmatrix} 0.4 & 0.0 \\ 0.0 & 0.4 \end{bmatrix}$	$\begin{bmatrix} 0.35 & 0.0 \\ 0.0 & 0.35 \end{bmatrix}$	$\begin{bmatrix} 0.3 & 0.0 \\ 0.0 & 0.3 \end{bmatrix}$
M_η	2	2	2	2	2
$\lambda_{\eta1}$	λ	λ	λ	λ	λ
$\mu_{\eta1}$	−1.0	−0.5	0.0	0.5	1.0
$\mu_{\eta2}$	0.0	0.0	0.0	0.0	0.0
$\sigma^2_{\eta1}$	1.0	0.775	0.55	0.325	0.1
$\sigma^2_{\eta2}$	0.1	0.2	0.3	0.4	0.5

Note: In all specifications both η and ε are distributed as mixtures of normals with two components. $\lambda_{\eta1} = \lambda_{\varepsilon1} = \lambda$ are the weights on the first components of these mixtures. $\lambda_{\eta1}$ and $\lambda_{\varepsilon1}$ are constrained to be equal for economy of presentation. Each of the specifications above was simulated five times with five different values of λ. The five different values were $\lambda = 0.0, 0.1, 0.5, 0.9,$ and 1.0. The two extreme cases represent cases where the model reduces to the linear–quadratic normal model. Figures showing the shape of the pricing function in all cases are displayed below. Estimation results are presented for the cases $\lambda = 0.1, 0.5,$ and 0.9.

TABLE A3: *Model 1 parameter values for workers*

Parameter	Set 1	Set 2	Set 3	Set 4	Set 5
A	1.0	1.25	1.5	1.75	2.0
θ_0	0.0	0.0	0.0	0.0	0.0
θ_1	1.0	1.0	1.0	1.0	1.0
M_x	2	2	2	2	2
n_x	1	1	1	1	1
λ_x	$(1.0, 0.0)'$	$(1.0, 0.0)'$	$(1.0, 0.0)'$	$(1.0, 0.0)'$	$(1.0, 0.0)'$
μ_{x1}	0.0	0.0	0.0	0.0	0.0
μ_{x2}	0.0	0.0	0.0	0.0	0.0
Σ_{x1}	$\begin{bmatrix} 0.1 & 0.0 \\ 0.0 & 0.1 \end{bmatrix}$	$\begin{bmatrix} 0.15 & 0.0 \\ 0.0 & 0.15 \end{bmatrix}$	$\begin{bmatrix} 0.2 & 0.0 \\ 0.0 & 0.2 \end{bmatrix}$	$\begin{bmatrix} 0.25 & 0.0 \\ 0.0 & 0.25 \end{bmatrix}$	$\begin{bmatrix} 0.3 & 0.0 \\ 0.0 & 0.3 \end{bmatrix}$
Σ_{x2}	$\begin{bmatrix} 0.1 & 0.0 \\ 0.0 & 0.1 \end{bmatrix}$	$\begin{bmatrix} 0.15 & 0.0 \\ 0.0 & 0.15 \end{bmatrix}$	$\begin{bmatrix} 0.2 & 0.0 \\ 0.0 & 0.2 \end{bmatrix}$	$\begin{bmatrix} 0.25 & 0.0 \\ 0.0 & 0.25 \end{bmatrix}$	$\begin{bmatrix} 0.3 & 0.0 \\ 0.0 & 0.3 \end{bmatrix}$
M_ε	2	2	2	2	2
λ_ε	λ	λ	λ	λ	λ
$\mu_{\varepsilon1}$	0.0	-0.5	-1.0	-1.5	-2.0
$\mu_{\varepsilon2}$	0.0	0.0	0.0	0.0	0.0
$\sigma_{\varepsilon1}^2$	10.5	7.9775	5.255	2.7325	0.01
$\sigma_{\varepsilon2}^2$	0.1	0.325	0.55	0.775	1.0

Note: In all specifications both η and ε are distributed as mixtures of normals with two components. $\lambda_{\eta1} = \lambda_{\varepsilon1} = \lambda$ are the weights on the first components of these mixtures. $\lambda_{\eta1}$ and $\lambda_{\varepsilon1}$ are constrained to be equal for economy of presentation. Each of the specifications above was simulated five times with five different values of λ. The five different values were $\lambda = 0.0, 0.1, 0.5, 0.9,$ and 1.0. The two extreme cases represent cases where the model reduces to the linear–quadratic normal model. Figures showing the shape of the pricing function in all cases are displayed below. Estimation results are presented for the cases $\lambda = 0.1, 0.5,$ and 0.9.

TABLE A4: *Model 1 parameter estimates for* $\lambda = 0.5$

	Specification 1		Specification 2		Specification 3		Specification 4		Specification 5	
	B	ν_1	B	ν_1	B	ν_1	B	ν_1	B	ν_1
True value	1.0	1.0	1.25	1.0	1.5	1.0	1.75	1.0	2.0	1.0
ML	1.01	1.01	1.28	1.03	1.54	1.03	1.77	1.01	1.99	0.996
	(0.0349)	(0.0518)	(0.0983)	(0.102)	(0.138)	(0.116)	(0.287)	(0.193)	(0.144)	(0.0788)

Note: Data were simulated for each specification listed in Tables A2 and A3. $\lambda_{\eta 1} = \lambda_{\varepsilon 1} = \lambda = 0.5$ in all specifications. One hundred independent samples each with sample size 1000 were generated. Then the parameters B and ν_1 were estimated using the semiparametric maximum likelihood technique described in Section 12.5.1. Row 1, labeled "True value," lists the true parameter values for each specification. For each specification, 100 independent estimates were generated, one from each sample. Row 2, labeled "ML," reports the averages and standard errors of these maximum likelihood estimates.

326

TABLE A7: *Model 2 functional forms*

Firm	Technology	$\Gamma(z, y, \eta)$	$(v(y) + \eta)z + \int\limits_0^z m_f(s)ds$
		$v(y)$	$v_0 + v_1 y + \int\limits_0^y \left(\sum\limits_{i=0}^{N_v} v_{2ai} s^i \right)^2 ds$
		$m_f(z)$	$\sum\limits_{i=0}^{N_{zf}} \beta_i z^i$
	Density of y	$f_y(y)$	$\sum\limits_{i=1}^{M_y} \lambda_{yi} \phi(y, \mu_{yi}, \Sigma_{yi})$
	Density of η	$f_\eta(\eta)$	$\sum\limits_{i=1}^{M_\eta} \lambda_{\eta i} \phi(\eta, \mu_{\eta i}, \Sigma_{\eta i})$
Worker	Utility	$U(z, x, \varepsilon)$	$(\theta(x) + \varepsilon)z - \int\limits_0^z m_w(s)ds$
		$\theta(x)$	$\theta_0 + \theta_1 x + \int\limits_0^x \left(\sum\limits_{i=1}^{N_\theta} \theta_{2ai} s^i \right)^2 ds$
		$m_w(z)$	$m_f(z) + \alpha_{0Z} + \int\limits_0^z \left(\sum\limits_{i=0}^{N_{zw}} \alpha_{1ai} s^i \right)^2 ds$
	Density of x	$f_x(x)$	$\sum\limits_{i=1}^{M_x} \lambda_{xi} \phi(x, \mu_{xi}, \Sigma_{xi})$
	Density of ε	$f_\varepsilon(\varepsilon)$	$\sum\limits_{i=1}^{M_\varepsilon} \lambda_{\varepsilon i} \phi(\varepsilon, \mu_{\varepsilon i}, \Sigma_{\varepsilon i})$

Note: (z, η, ε) are all scalars. y is of dimension N_y and x is of dimension N_x. The parameters in Table A7 are common across all firms and workers, respectively.

TABLE A8: *Model 2 parameter values for firms*

Parameter	Specification 1	Specification 2	Specification 3	Specification 4	Specification 5
N_{zf}	3	3	3	3	3
β	$\begin{bmatrix} 1.0 \\ 0.6228 \\ -0.7684 \\ -0.1889 \end{bmatrix}$	$\begin{bmatrix} 1.0 \\ 2.7419 \\ 0.4115 \\ -0.2051 \end{bmatrix}$	$\begin{bmatrix} 1.0 \\ 2.6676 \\ 2.2527 \\ 1.4152 \end{bmatrix}$	$\begin{bmatrix} 1.0 \\ 0.6411 \\ -0.9606 \\ 0.0888 \end{bmatrix}$	$\begin{bmatrix} 1.0 \\ 2.5746 \\ -0.4444 \\ -0.2047 \end{bmatrix}$
v_0	0.0	0.0	0.0	0.0	0.0
v_1	0.8632	0.9712	0.6817	0.9201	0.4486
N_v	2	2	2	2	2
v_{2a}	$(1.0, 1.0, 1.0)'$	$(1.0, 1.0, 1.0)'$	$(1.0, 1.0, 1.0)'$	$(1.0, 1.0, 1.0)'$	$(1.0, 1.0, 1.0)'$
n_y	1	1	1	1	1
M_y	2	2	2	2	2
λ_y	$(1.0, 0.0)'$	$(1.0, 0.0)'$	$(1.0, 0.0)'$	$(1.0, 0.0)'$	$(1.0, 0.0)'$
μ_{y1}	0.0	0.0	0.0	0.0	0.0
μ_{y2}	0.0	0.0	0.0	0.0	0.0
Σ_{y1}	$\begin{bmatrix} 1.0 & 0.0 \\ 0.0 & 0.1 \end{bmatrix}$	$\begin{bmatrix} 1.0 & 0.0 \\ 0.0 & 0.1 \end{bmatrix}$	$\begin{bmatrix} 1.0 & 0.0 \\ 0.0 & 0.1 \end{bmatrix}$	$\begin{bmatrix} 1.0 & 0.0 \\ 0.0 & 0.1 \end{bmatrix}$	$\begin{bmatrix} 1.0 & 0.0 \\ 0.0 & 0.1 \end{bmatrix}$
Σ_{y2}	$\begin{bmatrix} 0.5 & 0.0 \\ 0.0 & 0.5 \end{bmatrix}$	$\begin{bmatrix} 0.5 & 0.0 \\ 0.0 & 0.5 \end{bmatrix}$	$\begin{bmatrix} 0.5 & 0.0 \\ 0.0 & 0.5 \end{bmatrix}$	$\begin{bmatrix} 0.5 & 0.0 \\ 0.0 & 0.5 \end{bmatrix}$	$\begin{bmatrix} 0.5 & 0.0 \\ 0.0 & 0.5 \end{bmatrix}$
M_η	2	2	2	2	2
$\lambda_{\eta1}$	λ	λ	λ	λ	λ
$\mu_{\eta1}$	0.4542	-0.3814	0.6770	0.1361	-0.2592
$\mu_{\eta2}$	0.4055	0.0931	-0.1102	0.3891	0.2426
$\sigma_{\eta1}^2$	0.3869	1.3644	0.6055	1.0833	0.3017
$\sigma_{\eta2}^2$	1.3958	0.7567	1.7200	1.7073	1.1871

Note: In all specifications, $\lambda_{\eta1} = \lambda_{\varepsilon1} = \lambda$. Simulation results are presented for $\lambda = 0.0, 0.1, 0.5, 0.9,$ and 1.0. Estimation results are presented for $\lambda = 0.1, 0.5,$ and 0.9.

TABLE A9: *Model 2 parameter values for workers*

Parameter	Specification 1	Specification 2	Specification 3	Specification 4	Specification 5
N_{zw}	1	1	1	1	1
α_0	1.4501	0.7311	1.1068	0.9860	1.3913
α_1	$\begin{bmatrix} 1.2863 \\ 0.8463 \end{bmatrix}$	$\begin{bmatrix} 0.3694 \\ 1.3758 \end{bmatrix}$	$\begin{bmatrix} -0.9445 \\ 1.7654 \end{bmatrix}$	$\begin{bmatrix} 1.4642 \\ 1.2146 \end{bmatrix}$	$\begin{bmatrix} 0.3341 \\ -0.4712 \end{bmatrix}$
θ_0	0.0	0.0	0.0	0.0	0.0
θ_1	0.5	0.5	0.5	0.5	0.5
N_θ	1	1	1	1	1
θ_{2a}	$(1.0, 1.0)'$	$(1.0, 1.0)'$	$(1.0, 1.0)'$	$(1.0, 1.0)'$	$(1.0, 1.0)'$
n_x	2	2	2	2	2
M_x	2	2	2	2	2
λ_x	$(1.0, 0.0)'$	$(1.0, 0.0)'$	$(1.0, 0.0)'$	$(1.0, 0.0)'$	$(1.0, 0.0)'$
u_{x1}	0.0	0.0	0.0	0.0	0.0
u_{x2}	0.0	0.0	0.0	0.0	0.0
Σ_{x1}	$\begin{bmatrix} 0.3 & 0.0 \\ 0.0 & 0.3 \end{bmatrix}$	$\begin{bmatrix} 0.3 & 0.0 \\ 0.0 & 0.3 \end{bmatrix}$	$\begin{bmatrix} 0.3 & 0.0 \\ 0.0 & 0.3 \end{bmatrix}$	$\begin{bmatrix} 0.3 & 0.0 \\ 0.0 & 0.3 \end{bmatrix}$	$\begin{bmatrix} 0.3 & 0.0 \\ 0.0 & 0.3 \end{bmatrix}$
Σ_{x2}	$\begin{bmatrix} 0.3 & 0.0 \\ 0.0 & 0.3 \end{bmatrix}$	$\begin{bmatrix} 0.3 & 0.0 \\ 0.0 & 0.3 \end{bmatrix}$	$\begin{bmatrix} 0.3 & 0.0 \\ 0.0 & 0.3 \end{bmatrix}$	$\begin{bmatrix} 0.3 & 0.0 \\ 0.0 & 0.3 \end{bmatrix}$	$\begin{bmatrix} 0.3 & 0.0 \\ 0.0 & 0.3 \end{bmatrix}$
M_ε	2	2	2	2	2
$\lambda_{\varepsilon1}$	λ	λ	λ	λ	λ
$\mu_{\varepsilon1}$	−0.0069	0.7995	0.6433	0.2898	0.6359
$\mu_{\varepsilon2}$	0.3205	−0.3161	−0.4205	−0.3176	0.0682
$\sigma_{\varepsilon1}^2$	1.6762	0.0393	1.3626	0.7590	1.6636
$\sigma_{\varepsilon2}^2$	1.0056	1.4189	0.8578	0.6092	0.3793

Note: In all specifications, $\lambda_{\eta 1} = \lambda_{\varepsilon 1} = \lambda$. Simulation results are presented for $\lambda = 0.0$, 0.1, 0.5, 0.9, and 1.0. Estimation results are presented for $\lambda = 0.1$, 0.5, and 0.9.

331

TABLE A10: *Model 2, specification 1*
parameter estimates for $\lambda = 0.5$

	True value	ML
β_1	0.623	0.637
		(0.243)
β_2	−0.768	−0.767
		(0.0902)
β_3	−0.189	−0.192
		(0.0231)
v_{c1}	1.86	1.86
		(0.256)
v_{c2}	1.00	0.992
		(0.113)
v_{c3}	1.00	1.00
		(0.0978)
v_{c4}	0.500	0.501
		(0.0426)
v_{c5}	0.200	0.203
		(0.0202)

Note: In Tables A10–A14, $\beta_i, i = 1, \ldots, 3$, and v_{cj}, $j = 1, \ldots, 5$, are the subset of structural parameters of firm technologies in Model 2 that are identified. β_0, which equals 1.0 in all specifications, is not identified. The parameters v_{cj} satisfy $\sum_{j=1}^{5} v_{cj} y^{j-1} = v_1 + (\sum_{i=0}^{2} v_{2ai} y^i)^2$. One hundred independent samples each of size 1000 were generated using the parameter values in Tables A8 and A9. In all specifications, $\lambda_{\eta 1} = \lambda_{\varepsilon 1} = 0.5$. Column 2 reports the true values of the parameters used to simulate the data. One hundred independent estimates were obtained using the maximum likelihood technique described in Section 12.5.1. Column 3, labeled "ML," reports the averages and standard errors of these estimates.

TABLE A11: *Model 2, specification 2*
parameter estimates for $\lambda = 0.5$

	True value	ML
β_1	2.74	2.75
		(0.0744)
β_2	0.412	0.408
		(0.0629)
β_3	−0.205	−0.210
		(0.0570)
ν_1	1.97	1.98
		(0.246)
ν_2	1.00	1.00
		(0.131)
ν_3	1.00	1.00
		(0.123)
ν_4	0.500	0.504
		(0.0480)
ν_5	0.200	0.202
		(0.0175)

TABLE A12: *Model 2, specification 3*
parameter estimates for $\lambda = 0.5$

	True value	ML
β_1	2.67	2.67
		(0.200)
β_2	2.25	2.27
		(0.206)
β_3	1.42	1.40
		(0.120)
ν_1	1.68	1.69
		(0.275)
ν_2	1.00	1.01
		(0.146)
ν_3	1.00	1.01
		(0.145)
ν_4	0.500	0.507
		(0.0593)
ν_5	0.200	0.202
		(0.0225)

TABLE A13: *Model 2, specification 4*
parameter estimates for $\lambda = 0.5$

	True value	ML
β_1	0.641	0.627
		(0.337)
β_2	−0.961	−0.984
		(0.216)
β_3	0.0888	0.0781
		(0.0651)
ν_1	1.92	1.95
		(0.330)
ν_2	1.00	1.00
		(0.167)
ν_3	1.00	1.01
		(0.151)
ν_4	0.500	0.509
		(0.0636)
ν_5	0.200	0.204
		(0.0259)

TABLE A14: *Model 2, specification 5*
parameter estimates for $\lambda = 0.5$

	True value	ML
β_1	2.5746	2.58
		(0.103)
β_2	−0.4444	−0.440
		(0.0251)
β_3	−0.2047	−0.206
		(0.0072)
ν_1	1.4486	1.44
		(0.193)
ν_2	1.00	0.988
		(0.141)
ν_3	1.00	1.01
		(0.111)
ν_4	0.500	0.512
		(0.0513)
ν_5	0.200	0.205
		(0.0203)

TABLE A15: *Model 2, specification 1*
parameter estimates for $\lambda = 0.9$

	True value	ML
β_1	0.623	0.619
		(0.291)
β_2	-0.768	-0.776
		(0.115)
β_3	-0.189	-0.194
		(0.0302)
ν_1	1.86	1.88
		(0.283)
ν_2	1.00	1.00
		(0.149)
ν_3	1.00	1.01
		(0.132)
ν_4	0.500	0.505
		(0.0551)
ν_5	0.200	0.204
		(0.0252)

Note: In Tables A15–A19, β_i, $i = 1, \ldots, 3$, and ν_{cj}, $j = 1, \ldots, 5$, are the subset of structural parameters of firm technologies in Model 2 that are identified. β_0, which equals 1.0 in all specifications, is not identified. The parameters ν_{cj} satisfy $\sum_{j=1}^{5} \nu_{cj} y^{j-1} = \nu_1 + (\sum_{i=0}^{2} \nu_{2ai} y^i)^2$. One hundred independent samples each of size 1000 were generated using the parameter values in Tables A8 and A9. In all specifications, $\lambda_{\eta 1} = \lambda_{\varepsilon 1} = 0.9$. Column 2 reports the true values of the parameters used to simulate the data. One hundred independent estimates were obtained using the maximum likelihood technique described in Section 12.5.1. Column 3, labeled "ML," reports the averages and standard errors of these estimates.

TABLE A16: *Model 2, specification 2
parameter estimates for* $\lambda = 0.9$

	True value	ML
β_1	2.74	2.75
		(0.0705)
β_2	0.412	0.403
		(0.0553)
β_3	−0.205	−0.216
		(0.0506)
ν_1	1.97	2.00
		(0.228)
ν_2	1.00	1.01
		(0.122)
ν_3	1.00	1.02
		(0.108)
ν_4	0.500	0.510
		(0.0422)
ν_5	0.200	0.203
		(0.0154)

TABLE A17: *Model 2, specification 3
parameter estimates for* $\lambda = 0.9$

	True value	ML
β_1	2.67	2.66
		(0.218)
β_2	2.25	2.27
		(0.230)
β_3	1.42	1.40
		(0.149)
ν_1	1.68	1.72
		(0.322)
ν_2	1.00	1.02
		(0.191)
ν_3	1.00	1.02
		(0.183)
ν_4	0.500	0.512
		(0.0766)
ν_5	0.200	0.203
		(0.0284)

TABLE A18: *Model 2, specification 4*
parameter estimates for $\lambda = 0.9$

	True value	ML
β_1	0.641	0.640
		(0.405)
β_2	−0.961	−0.980
		(0.266)
β_3	0.0888	0.079
		(0.0809)
ν_1	1.92	1.933
		(0.366)
ν_2	1.00	0.998
		(0.196)
ν_3	1.00	1.01
		(0.190)
ν_4	0.500	0.508
		(0.0785)
ν_5	0.200	0.204
		(0.0316)

TABLE A19: *Model 2, specification 5*
parameter estimates for $\lambda = 0.9$

	True value	ML
β_1	2.57	2.58
		(0.137)
β_2	−0.444	−0.440
		(0.0271)
β_3	−0.205	−0.206
		(0.0101)
ν_1	1.45	1.44
		(0.217)
ν_2	1.00	0.987
		(0.165)
ν_3	1.00	1.01
		(0.152)
ν_4	0.500	0.514
		(0.0746)
ν_5	0.200	0.205
		(0.0279)

REFERENCES

M. Armstrong (1996), "Multiproduct Nonlinear Pricing," *Econometrica* 64 (1): 51–75.

H. Banzhaf, H. Sieg, V. K. Smith, and R. Walsh (2000), "Estimating the General Equilibrium Benefits of Large Changes in Spatially Delineated Public Goods," NBER Working Paper No. 7744.

P. Bayer (2000), "Tiebout Sorting and Discrete Choices: A New Explanation for Socioeconomic Differences in the Consumption of School Quality," mimeo, Yale University.

T. Bresnahan and R. Gordon (1997), *The Economics of New Goods.* Chicago: University of Chicago Press.

J. Brown and H. Rosen (1982), "On the Estimation of Structural Hedonic Price Models," *Econometrica* 50 (3): 765–69.

I. Ekeland, J. Heckman, and L. Nesheim (2004), "Identification and Estimation of Hedonic Models," *Journal of Political Economy*, 112 (1): S60–S109.

D. Epple (1987), "Hedonic Prices and Implicit Markets: Estimating Demand and Supply Functions for Differentiated Products," *Journal of Political Economy* 95: 59–80.

D. Epple and H. Sieg (1999), "Estimating Equilibrium Models of Local Jurisdictions," *Journal of Political Economy* 107: 645–81.

N. Gretsky, J. Ostroy, and W. R. Zame (1999), "Perfect Competition in the Continuous Assignment Model," *Journal of Economic Theory* 88: 60–118.

J. Heckman, R. Matzkin, and L. Nesheim (2002), "Non-parametric Estimation of Nonadditive Hedonic Models," working paper, University of Chicago.

J. Horowitz (1996), "Semiparametric Estimation of a Regression Model with an Unknown Transformation of the Dependent Variable," *Econometrica* 64: 103–37.

S. Kahn and K. Lang (1988), "Efficient Estimation of Structural Hedonic Systems," *International Economic Review* 29: 157–66.

T. Kniesner and J. Leeth (1988), "Simulating Hedonic Labor Market Models: Computational Issues and Policy Applications," *International Economic Review* 29 (4): 755–89.

——— (1995). *Simulating Workplace Safety Policy*, Boston: Kluwer Academic.

K. Lancaster (1966), "A New Approach to Consumer Theory," *Journal of Political Economy* 74 (2): 132–57.

——— (1975), "Socially Optimal Product Differentiation," *American Economic Review* 65 (4): 567–85.

R. Matzkin (1999), "Nonparametric Estimation of Nonadditive Random Functions," first version, working paper, Northwestern University.

——— (2002), "Estimation of Nonadditive Functions Using Functional Restrictions," working paper, Northwestern University.

——— (2003), "Nonparametric Estimation of Nonadditive Random Functions," *Econometrica*, 71 (5): 1339–75.

L. Nesheim (2001), "Equilibrium Sorting of Heterogeneous Consumers Across Locations: Theory and Empirical Implications," Ph.D. Thesis, University of Chicago.

J.-C. Rochet and L. Stole (2001), "The Economics of Multidimensional Screening," working paper, The University of Chicago.

S. Rosen (1974), "Hedonic Prices and Implicit Markets: Product Differentiation in Pure Competition," *Journal of Political Economy* 82: 34–55.

M. Sattinger (1975), "Comparative Advantage and the Distributions of Earnings and Abilities," *Econometrica* 43 (3): 455–68.

——— (1980), *Capital and the Distribution of Labor Earnings*, New York: North-Holland.

(1993), "Assignment Models of the Distribution of Earnings," *Journal of Economic Literature* 31 (2): 831–80.

V. K. Smith and J. C. Huang (1995), "Can Markets Value Air Quality: A Meta-Analysis of Hedonic Property Value Models," *Journal of Political Economy* 103 (1): 209–27.

H. Tauchen and A. Witte (2001), "Estimating Hedonic Models: Implications of the Theory," unpublished manuscript, University of North Carolina Department of Economics.

C. Teulings (1995), "The Wage Distribution in a Model of the Assignment of Jobs to Skills," *Journal of Political Economy* 103 (2): 280–315.

C. Teulings and T. van Rens (2002), "Education Growth and Income Inequality," Tinbergen Institute Discussion Paper TI 2002-001/3.

R. Thaler and S. Rosen (1975), "The Value of Saving a Life: Evidence from the Labor Market," in Nester Terleckyj (Ed.), *Household Production and Consumption*. National Bureau of Economic Research, New York: Columbia University, pp. 265–98.

J. Tinbergen (1956), "On The Theory of Income Distribution," *Weltwirtschaftliches Archiv* 77: 155–73.

J. Triplett (2000), *Handbook on Quality Adjustment of Price Indexes for Information and Communication Technology Products*. Paris: OECD.

R. Wilson (1993), *Nonlinear Pricing*. Oxford: Oxford University Press.

M. Wooders (1994), "Equivalence of Games and Markets," *Econometrica* 62 (5): 1141–60.

PART SIX. POLICY USES AND PERFORMANCE OF AGE MODELS

13 An Evaluation of the Performance of Applied General Equilibrium Models on the Impact of NAFTA

Timothy J. Kehoe

ABSTRACT: This paper evaluates the performance of three of the most prominent multi-sectoral static applied general equilibrium (GE) models used to predict the impact of the North American Free Trade Agreement (NAFTA). These models drastically underestimated the impact of NAFTA on North American trade. Furthermore, the models failed to capture much of the relative impact on different sectors. Ex post performance evaluations of applied GE models are essential if policymakers are to have confidence in the results produced by these models. Such evaluations also help make applied GE analysis a scientific discipline in which there are well-defined puzzles with clear successes and failures for competing theories. Analyzing sectoral trade data indicates the need for a new theoretical mechanism that generates large increases in trade in product categories with little or no previous trade. To capture changes in macroeconomic aggregates, the models need to be able to capture changes in productivity.

13.1. INTRODUCTION

Herbert Scarf's work on the computation of economic equilibrium has transformed the way economists think about putting general equilibrium (GE) theory to use. Previous economists – notably Leontief (1941), Johansen (1960), and Harberger (1962) – had matched simple GE models to data and used these models to answer important economic questions. Scarf's work (1967, 1973) on computation forged the link between applied GE analysis and the theory of general economic equilibrium developed by researchers such as Arrow and Debreu (1954) and McKenzie (1959). Much of Scarf's influence in this field can be seen in the work of students such as Shoven and Whalley (1973). The work of researchers in the Scarf school of applied GE analysis is characterized by a focus on important economic issues, by a careful

I am grateful to the participants at the Frontiers in Applied General Equilibrium Modeling Conference at the Cowles Foundation, April 2002, especially Sherman Robinson, Jaime and T. N. Srinivasan, for valuable comments. I thank Kim Ruhl for excellent research assistance and the National Science Foundation for financial support. The data used in this paper are available at http://www.econ.umn.edu/~tkehoe/. The views expressed herein are those of the author and not necessarily those of the Federal Reserve Bank of Minneapolis or the Federal Reserve System.

treatment of the data, and – most distinctly – by a rigorous grounding of the model in economic theory.

This chapter stresses the need for a different sort of rigor in applied GE analysis. We need to constantly test our theories by matching the results from our models with the data.

Some tests will confirm our theories. Suppose, for example, that we are interested in building a model of the impact of China's joining the World Trade Organization (WTO). We could take a model with the same theoretical structure, calibrate it to the economies of North America in the early 1990s, and carry out numerical experiments in which we changed policy parameters to simulate Mexico's joining the North American Free Trade Area (NAFTA – also the acronym for the North American Free Trade Agreement, which established this organization). If the model is capable of capturing the impact of this trade liberalization between a developing country and its richer neighbors, we would have some confidence in applying a model with the same theoretical structure to later trade liberalizations. There would always be some uncertainty about predictions, of course, because of uncertainty about choices of parameters or uncertainty about other shocks that might buffet the economy. Furthermore, we probably would want to modify some of this theoretical structure of the Mexico–NAFTA model to fit the institutional details of the China–WTO experience.

Even more importantly, in matching the results from our models with the data, some tests will establish puzzles that can be resolved only by modifications in the theory. If our proposed model of China's joining the WTO failed to capture the impact of previous trade liberalizations, we would want to change its theoretical structure before applying it. To the extent that applied GE analysis is a scientific discipline, failures of the theory can be even more important than confirmations for making progress.

In the early 1990s, the tool of choice for analyzing the impact of NAFTA on the economies of Canada, Mexico, and the United States was the multisectoral applied GE model. In fact, at a U.S. International Trade Commission conference held in February 1992 at the request of the U.S. Congress, to which all economists studying the economy-wide impact of NAFTA had been invited, 10 of the 12 studies presented used applied GE models. These studies were collected in United States International Trade Commission (1992); revised versions of most of the papers were later published in Francois and Shiells (1994).[1]

This paper uses economic data to systematically evaluate the performance of three of the most prominent applied GE models that had been constructed to predict the impact of NAFTA: the Brown–Deardorff–Stern model of all three North

---

[1] The two studies that did not use applied GE models were (1) a macroeconometric forecasting model linked with country-specific input–output models developed by the Interindustry Research Fund and summarized by Shiells and Shelburne (1992) and (2) an outline by Kehoe (1992) of the issues involved in modeling capital flows and productivity growth along with calculations of the relative magnitudes of these sorts of dynamic factors.

American economies (see Brown 1992, 1994 and Brown, Deardorff, and Stern 1992, 1995), the Cox–Harris model of Canada (see Cox 1994, 1995 and Cox and Harris 1992a, 1992b), and the Sobarzo model of Mexico (see Sobarzo 1992a, 1992b, 1994, 1995). Given the importance of the NAFTA policy debate, it is surprising that no one had carried out such a model evaluation exercise previously.

NAFTA presents an important policy experiment that allows economic researchers to test modeling strategies, particularly the specifications of imperfect competition and product differentiation that characterized most of the applied GE trade models used in the early 1990s. Indeed, much is to be learned from the model evaluation exercise: The models drastically underestimated the impact of NAFTA on North American trade, which has exploded over the past decade. Furthermore, the models failed to capture much of the relative impact on different sectors.

After evaluating the performance of the three applied GE models, we speculate about the theoretical features more successful models would need to include. Analysis of sectoral trade data indicates the need for a new theoretical mechanism for generating trade in the models – a mechanism in which large increases in trade can take place in product categories with little or no previous trade. To capture changes in macro aggregates, the models must be able to capture changes in productivity. Although foreign investment is crucial in determining relative prices and the allocation of production across traded and nontraded goods sectors, its impact on macro aggregates is felt mostly through its impact on productivity.

13.2. APPLIED GENERAL EQUILIBRIUM MODELS CAN DO A GOOD JOB: SPAIN 1985–1986

To illustrate the sort of ex post performance evaluation that is possible for an applied GE model, we evaluate the performance of a model constructed by a team at the Universitat Autònoma de Barcelona in 1985–86. This model was used to analyze the impact on the Spanish economy of the reforms implemented in 1986 to accompany Spain's entry into (what was then known as) the European Community (EC). The results obtained in this analysis were issued as working papers or published in a variety of outlets (see Kehoe et al. 1985, 1986a, 1986c; Kehoe et al. 1988; and Kehoe et al. 1989).

Kehoe, Polo, and Sancho (1995) have compared the results generated by the model with the changes that actually occurred in Spain during the period 1985–86. They find that the model performed well in capturing the changes that actually occurred. This is particularly true when they incorporate two major exogenous shocks that hit the Spanish economy in 1986: a decline in productivity in the agricultural sector, due mostly to weather conditions, and a sharp fall in the international price of petroleum. Like a few other applied GE researchers – notably Johansen (1960) and Dervis, de Melo, and Robinson (1982) – Kehoe et al. (1995) investigate how well their model did in tracking the impact of policy changes and external shocks after these changes occurred. Like Adams et al. (1994), they also compare the data with some model results that were pure predictions when they were made.

Spain's 1986 entry into the European Community was accompanied by two major government policy reforms. The first, and most significant, policy reform introduced a consumption value-added tax to replace the previous indirect tax system. The second policy reform reduced trade barriers and investment barriers with other EC countries. In contrast to the fiscal policy reform, which took place immediately, the trade policy reform was scheduled to be phased in gradually over six years. The part of the trade reform that took place in 1986 mostly involved reductions in tariff rates. The various versions of the Spanish model incorporated tax and tariff parameters into the model that corresponded to both these policy reforms. It should be stressed, however, that the parameter changes involved in the tax reform were far larger than those involved in the trade reform. In this section, we confront the results generated by the model with the data that describe the changes that actually took place in the Spanish economy during the period 1985–86. It is changes over a one- or two-year time horizon that Kehoe et al. (1995) argue that this type of model can capture. On one hand, this time horizon is long enough to allow enough gestation and depreciation of capital stocks in each sector to justify assuming mobility of capital, provided changes in capital utilization per sector are less than, say, 10%. On the other hand, this time horizon is short enough to justify ignoring secular trends and the intersectoral impact of changes in productivity and population growth rates. More modern applied GE models would specify a dynamic structure with explicit treatment of gestation, depreciation, productivity growth, and population growth.

In reporting both the simulation results and the actual data, we deflate by an appropriate price or output index. The weights used in the different indices are taken from the 1980 social accounting matrix constructed by Kehoe et al. (1986b) and Kehoe et al. (1988), which provided the data set for the calibration of the model. The precise question that the numerical experiments answered, therefore, was,

Suppose that the tax and tariff changes adopted by the Spanish government in 1986 to accompany the integration into the European Community had been adopted in 1980. What would the impact have been?

Because the model was calibrated to a different year than the year in which the tax reform took place, the choice of weights is somewhat arbitrary. Fortunately, calculations not reported here indicate that the results are not sensitive to this choice. In retrospect, it would have been preferable to use weights that correspond to the base period for the numerical experiments, that is, to the year before the reform took place, in this case 1985. This would have allowed us to compare the results of this model with the results of other models calibrated to different data sets. Even better, the model could have been recalibrated to match aggregates in 1985, even if some micro parameters necessarily would still have depended on 1980 data for their calibration. Such a recalibration would allow us to take more seriously the

TABLE 13.1. *Changes in consumer prices relative to CPI in the Spanish model (percent)*

Sector	Data: 1985–1986	Model: policy only	Model: shocks only	Model: policy and shocks
Food and nonalcoholic beverages	1.8	−2.3	4.0	1.7
Tobacco and alcoholic beverages	3.9	2.5	3.1	5.8
Clothing	2.1	5.6	0.9	6.6
Housing	−3.3	−2.2	−2.7	−4.8
Household articles	0.1	2.2	0.7	2.9
Medical services	−0.7	−4.8	0.6	−4.2
Transportation	−4.0	2.6	−8.8	−6.2
Recreation	−1.4	−1.3	1.5	0.1
Other services	2.9	1.1	1.7	2.8
weighted correlation with data		−0.08	0.87	0.94
variance decomposition of change		0.30	0.77	0.85
regression coefficient *a*		0.00	0.00	0.00
regression coefficient *b*		−0.08	0.54	0.67

comparison between changes in the data over the period 1985–86 with the results of numerical experiments using the model.

Tables 13.1–13.4 present the actual changes that occurred in the Spanish economy over the period 1985–86 in terms of relative prices of consumer goods, composition of output, macroeconomic aggregates, and trade patterns. Comparing the first column in Table 13.1 with the second column, we see that the model did poorly in predicting the changes that actually took place in two large sectors, food and transportation. The reasons for this are readily apparent to observers of the Spanish economy in 1986. In that year, food prices rose sharply because of a poor harvest, and energy prices fell sharply because of both an appreciation of the peseta against the dollar and a fall in the dollar price of petroleum. The third column of Table 13.1 reports the results of a numerical experiment that takes these two exogenous shocks into account in the simplest possible ways. First, we reduce the ratio of output to inputs in the agricultural production sector by 7.7%. This number is the fall in the ratio of an index of output to an index of intermediate inputs in agriculture from 1985 to 1986. We also reduce the foreign price of energy by 47.6%. This number is the fall in the price index of energy imports relative to an overall import price index from 1985 to 1986. (See Kehoe et al. 1995 for details.) The fourth column of Table 13.1 reports the results of a numerical experiment that takes into account both the changes in policy and the two exogenous shocks. Keep in mind that, whereas the second column reports predictions of the model, the third and forth columns report results of numerical experiments that used information that was available only after 1986.

TABLE 13.2. *Changes in value of gross output relative to GDP in the Spanish model (percent)*

Sector	Data: 1985–1986	Model: policy only	Model: shocks only	Model: policy and shocks
Agriculture	−0.4	−1.1	8.3	6.9
Energy	−20.3	−3.5	−29.4	−32.0
Basic industry	−9.0	1.6	−1.8	−0.1
Machinery	3.7	3.8	1.0	5.0
Automobile industry	1.1	3.9	4.7	8.6
Food products	−1.8	−2.4	4.7	2.1
Other manufacturing	0.5	−1.7	2.3	0.5
Construction	5.7	8.5	1.4	10.3
Commerce	6.6	−3.6	4.4	0.4
Transportation	−18.4	−1.5	1.0	−0.7
Services	8.7	−1.1	5.8	4.5
Government services	7.6	3.4	0.9	4.3
weighted correlation with data		0.16	0.80	0.77
variance decomposition of change		0.11	0.73	0.71
regression coefficient *a*		−0.52	−0.52	−0.52
regression coefficient *b*		0.44	0.75	0.67

In comparing the results of the model with the data, we report four statistics that measure the accuracy of prediction.

The first two statistics implicitly compare the match between the model's prediction of change and the actual change with the match between the prediction of no change and the actual change. The first statistic is the weighted correlation coefficient, with weights that correspond to the relative sizes of sectors in the base period, as explained above. The second statistic is a decomposition of the weighted variance of changes in the data that is meant to measure the fraction of this variance accounted for by the predictions of the model. Let

$$\bar{x} = \sum_{i=1}^{n} \alpha_i x_i$$

be the weighted mean of a vector of percentage changes,

$$\text{var}(x) = \sum_{i=1}^{n} \alpha_i^2 (x_i - \bar{x})^2$$

be the weighted variance of this vector of changes, and

$$\text{cov}(x, y) = \sum_{i=1}^{n} \alpha_i^2 (x_i - \bar{x})(y_i - \bar{y})$$

be the covariance of two vectors of changes. The weighted correlation coefficient is

$$\text{corr}(x^{\text{data}}, x^{\text{model}}) = \frac{\text{cov}(x^{\text{data}}, x^{\text{model}})}{\left(\text{var}(x^{\text{data}})\text{var}(x^{\text{model}})\right)^{1/2}}.$$

TABLE 13.3. *Changes in composition of GDP and public finances in the Spanish model (percent of GDP)*

Variable	Data: 1985–1986	Model: policy only	Model: shocks only	Model: policy and shocks
Wages and salaries	−0.53	−0.87	−0.02	−0.91
Business income	−1.27	−1.63	0.45	−1.24
Net indirect taxes and tariffs	1.80	2.50	−0.42	2.15
correlation with data		0.998	−0.94	0.99
variance decomposition of change		0.93	0.04	0.96
regression coefficient *a*		0.00	0.00	0.00
regression coefficient *b*		0.73	−3.45	0.85
Private consumption	−0.81	−1.23	−0.51	−1.78
Private investment	1.09	1.81	−0.58	1.32
Government consumption	−0.02	−0.06	−0.38	−0.44
Government investment	−0.06	−0.06	−0.07	−0.13
Exports	−3.40	−0.42	−0.69	−1.07
Imports	3.20	−0.03	2.23	2.10
correlation with data		0.40	0.77	0.83
variance decomposition of change		0.20	0.35	0.58
regression coefficient *a*		0.00	0.00	0.00
regression coefficient *b*		0.87	1.49	1.24
Indirect taxes and subsidies	2.38	3.32	−0.38	2.98
Tariffs	−0.58	−0.82	−0.04	−0.83
Social security payments	0.04	−0.19	−0.03	−0.22
Direct taxes and transfers	−0.84	−0.66	0.93	0.26
Government capital income	−0.13	−0.06	0.02	−0.04
correlation with data		0.99	−0.70	0.92
variance decomposition of change		0.93	0.08	0.86
regression coefficient *a*		−0.06	0.35	−0.17
regression coefficient *b*		0.74	−1.82	0.80

A high correlation coefficient rewards predictions that have the right signs and relative magnitudes. It does not take into account the absolute magnitudes of changes, however. The decomposition of the weighted variance of the changes in the data is

$$\text{vardec}(x^{\text{data}}, x^{\text{model}}) = \frac{\text{var}(x^{\text{model}})}{\text{var}(x^{\text{model}}) + \text{var}(x^{\text{data}} - x^{\text{model}})}.$$

Although this measure has the advantage of taking into account absolute magnitudes of changes, it only measures well the fraction of variance accounted for by the model

TABLE 13.4. *Changes in trade flows relative to GDP in the Spanish
model (percent)*

Direction of exports	Data: 1985–1986	Model: policy only	Model: shocks only	Model: policy and shocks
Spain to rest of European Community	−6.7	−3.2	−4.9	−7.8
Spain to rest of world	−33.2	−3.6	−6.1	−9.3
Rest of European Community to Spain	14.7	4.4	−3.9	0.6
Rest of world to Spain	−34.1	−1.8	−16.8	−17.7
weighted correlation with data		0.69	0.77	0.90
variance decomposition of change		0.02	0.17	0.24
regression coefficient *a*		−12.46	2.06	5.68
regression coefficient *b*		5.33	2.21	2.37

if the changes in the model are highly correlated with those in the data. Because
variance is not a linear function of vectors of changes,

$$\text{var}(x^{\text{data}}) = \text{var}(x^{\text{model}}) + \text{var}(x^{\text{data}} - x^{\text{model}}) + 2\text{cov}(x^{\text{data}}, x^{\text{data}} - x^{\text{model}})$$
$$\neq \text{var}(x^{\text{model}}) + \text{var}(x^{\text{data}} - x^{\text{model}}),$$

any variance decomposition statistic has to do something with the covariance term.
Our statistic distributes the covariance proportionally.

The second two statistics are derived from running a weighted least-squares
regression of actual changes on predicted changes:

$$x_i^{\text{data}} = a + b x_i^{\text{model}} + e_i.$$

Specifically, we estimate the coefficients a and b by solving the least-squares
problem

$$\text{minimize} \sum_{i=1}^{n} \alpha_i \left(a + b x_i^{\text{model}} - x_i^{\text{data}} \right).$$

The deviation of the estimated coefficient b from 1 indicates how well the model
does in predicting signs and the absolute magnitude of the changes in the data. The
deviation of the estimated coefficient a from 0 indicates how well the model does
in matching the average change in the data. (Notice that, if changes are relative
to an index, where the weighted sum of the changes equals 0, then $a = 0$.) The
deviation of the R^2 statistic of this regression from 1 indicates how well the model
does in predicting the relative magnitudes of the changes in the data, but because
$R^2 = \text{corr}(x^{\text{data}}, x^{\text{model}})^2$ in this simple sort of regression, we do not report this
statistic. To a large extent, the final two statistics are substitutes for the first two, at
least if we are willing to report an R^2 statistic for the regression. As more of these
sorts of ex post performance analyses are carried out, conventions for comparing

model results with data will have to be established. At this point, we report the two different sets of statistics to illustrate different possibilities.

Tables 13.1 and 13.2 show that the model did a good job of capturing the changes in relative prices and production levels that occurred in 1986, at least after we take into account the agricultural productivity shock and the petroleum price shock. The performance of the model in capturing changes in major macroeconomic variables, reported in Table 13.3, is, at first glance, spectacular. Much of the model's success in this direction, however, lies in the fact that the model predicted that the tax reform would result in a substantial increase in indirect taxes paid by consumers. It is worth pointing out that in 1985 this prediction of the model was controversial and was treated with considerable skepticism by a number of policymakers in the Spanish government. That the 1986 fiscal reform would be a substantial tax increase was the central prediction in all versions of the model, including the earliest one (Kehoe et al. 1985), and does not depend on the incorporation of the agricultural productivity shock and the petroleum price shock into the model. Furthermore, this prediction required the full sectoral specification of the model to compare the value-added tax with the previous indirect tax system where intermediate transactions were taxed and in which there were many different tax rates.

The performance of the model in capturing changes in trade patterns, reported in Table 13.4, is less impressive than that for the macroeconomic variables reported in Table 13.3. It is worth noting that the Spanish model was not intended to capture changes in trade patterns, and the theoretical structure of the trade side of the model was extremely simple. This should be kept in mind in the next section, when we evaluate the performance of the models of NAFTA in which trade was the emphasis.

13.3. MODELS OF NAFTA DID NOT DO A GOOD JOB

The typical sort of model used to analyze the impact of the North American Free Trade Agreement was a static applied GE model with a large number of industries, some form of imperfect competition, and a finite number of firms in some industries. Kehoe and Kehoe (1995) explain the theoretical structures of three of the most important models and show how these structures drive the results of the models: the Brown–Deardorff–Stern model of all three North American economies (see Brown et al. 1995), the Cox–Harris model of Canada (see Cox 1995), and the Sobarzo model of Mexico (see Sobarzo 1995).

Like a number of other models of NAFTA, the Brown–Deardorff–Stern model and the Cox–Harris model were extensions of previous models constructed to analyze the Canada–U.S. Free Trade Agreement (FTA) to include Mexico (see Brown and Stern 1989 and Cox and Harris 1985). This fact helps explain the importance of increasing returns and imperfect competition in the structure of the models. The "New Trade Theory" developed by such researchers as Krugman (1979) had adapted the industrial organization theory of monopolistic competition of Dixit and

TABLE 13.5. *Changes in trade flows relative to GDP in Brown–Deardorff–Stern model (percent)*

Variable	Data: 1988–1999	Model
Canadian exports	52.9	4.3
Canadian imports	57.7	4.2
Mexican exports	140.6	50.8
Mexican imports	50.5	34.0
U.S. exports	19.1	2.9
U.S. imports	29.9	2.3
weighted correlation with data		0.64
variance decomposition of change		0.08
regression coefficient a		23.20
regression coefficient b		2.43

Stiglitz (1977) to account for the large volumes of trade observed between such economically similar countries as Canada and the United States. Models in which trade depends on differences across countries – as in the Heckscher–Ohlin form of differences in endowments and/or in the Ricardian form of differences in technologies – have trouble accounting for this trade. Furthermore, Harris (1984) had found that an applied GE model with some form of imperfect competition – in Harris's case a collusive pricing rule called Eastman–Stykolt pricing – predicted far larger impacts of trade liberalization between Canada and the United States than did models in which trade depended on differences in endowments and/or technologies across countries.

Of course, analyzing the integration of Mexico into the Canada–U.S. FTA focused attention on issues that had not been as important in studies of just Canada and the United States. In particular, modelers were concerned with the impact of capital flows into Mexico. The static nature of most of the models of NAFTA limited their ability to predict the size and impact of such capital flows. Typically, capital flows were incorporated into experiments in which new capital owned by consumers in the rest of North America was placed in Mexico. Kehoe (1992) also stressed the importance of differences in the demographic structure of Mexico from those of its North American neighbors, the potential effects of NAFTA on productivity, especially in Mexico, and the potential for large capital flows to put Mexico in danger of a financial crisis. These sorts of dynamic factors were not incorporated into the models, however.

Tables 13.5–13.11 compare the predictions of the three models with changes in the data over the period 1988–99. As with the comparisons of the Spanish model with the data in the previous section, the choice of years is somewhat arbitrary. The models had been calibrated to data from years different from 1993, the year before NAFTA went into force: The Brown–Deardorff–Stern model was calibrated to a 1976 input–output matrix for Canada, a 1980 input–output matrix for Mexico,

TABLE 13.6. *Changes in Canadian exports relative to Canadian GDP in the Brown–Deardorff–Stern model (percent)*

	Exports to Mexico		Exports to United States	
Sector	1988–1999	Model	1988–1999	Model
Agriculture	122.5	3.1	106.1	3.4
Mining and quarrying	−34.0	−0.3	75.8	0.4
Food	89.3	2.2	91.7	8.9
Textiles	268.2	−0.9	97.8	15.3
Clothing	1544.3	1.3	237.1	45.3
Leather products	443.0	1.4	−14.4	11.3
Footwear	517.0	3.7	32.8	28.3
Wood products	232.6	4.7	36.5	0.1
Furniture and fixtures	3801.7	2.7	282.6	12.5
Paper products	240.7	−4.3	113.7	−1.8
Printing and publishing	6187.4	−2.0	37.2	−1.6
Chemicals	37.1	−7.8	109.4	−3.1
Petroleum and products	678.1	−8.5	−42.5	0.5
Rubber products	647.4	−1.0	113.4	9.5
Nonmetal mineral products	333.5	−1.8	20.5	1.2
Glass products	264.4	−2.2	74.5	30.4
Iron and steel	195.2	−15.0	92.1	12.9
Nonferrous metals	38.4	−64.7	34.7	18.5
Metal products	767.0	−10.0	102.2	15.2
Nonelectrical machinery	376.8	−8.9	28.9	3.3
Electrical machinery	633.9	−26.2	88.6	14.5
Transportation equipment	305.8	−4.4	30.7	10.7
Miscellaneous manufactures	1404.5	−12.1	100.0	−2.1
weighted correlation with data		−0.91		−0.43
variance decomposition of change		0.003		0.02
regression coefficient *a*		249.24		79.20
regression coefficient *b*		−15.48		−2.80

and a 1977 input–output matrix for the United States. Sectoral and macroeconomic aggregates were calibrated to 1989 data, but trade barriers were set equal to estimates from before the year in which the Canada–U.S. FTA had gone into force, 1989. The Cox–Harris model had been calibrated to a 1981 data set, but trade barriers were set equal to estimates from 1988. The Sobarzo model had been calibrated to a 1985 input–output matrix, but trade barriers were set equal to estimates from 1989. There are two considerations that determine the choice of the years 1988 and 1999 in our comparisons: First, the Brown–Deardorff–Stern and Cox–Harris models included the changes in trade policies in the Canada–U.S. FTA in their numerical experiments, which makes 1988 the latest year possible for an initial year. Second, NAFTA included changes in trade barriers scheduled to be implemented over a 15-year period, that is, up until 2009, making the latest year available in the data

TABLE 13.7. *Changes in Mexican exports relative to GDP in the Brown–Deardorff–Stern model (percent)*

	Exports to Canada		Exports to United States	
Sector	1988–1999	Model	1988–1999	Model
Agriculture	−20.5	−4.1	−15.0	2.5
Mining and quarrying	−35.5	27.3	−22.9	26.9
Food	70.4	10.8	9.4	7.5
Textiles	939.7	21.6	832.3	11.8
Clothing	1847.0	19.2	829.6	18.6
Leather products	1470.3	36.2	618.3	11.7
Footwear	153.0	38.6	111.1	4.6
Wood products	4387.6	15.0	145.6	−2.7
Furniture and fixtures	4933.2	36.2	181.2	7.6
Paper products	23.9	32.9	70.3	13.9
Printing and publishing	476.3	15.0	122.1	3.9
Chemicals	204.6	36.0	70.4	17.0
Petroleum and products	−10.6	32.9	66.4	34.1
Rubber products	2366.2	−6.7	783.8	−5.3
Nonmetal mineral products	1396.1	5.7	222.3	3.7
Glass products	676.8	13.3	469.8	32.3
Iron and steel	32.5	19.4	40.9	30.8
Nonferrous metals	−35.4	138.1	111.2	156.5
Metal products	610.4	41.9	477.2	26.8
Nonelectrical machinery	570.6	17.3	123.6	18.5
Electrical machinery	1349.2	137.3	744.9	178.0
Transportation equipment	2303.4	3.3	349.0	6.2
Miscellaneous manufactures	379.4	61.1	181.5	43.2
weighted correlation with data		0.19		0.71
variance decomposition of change		0.01		0.04
regression coefficient *a*		120.32		38.13
regression coefficient *b*		2.07		3.87

the most attractive terminal year for our comparisons. The latest year for trade data in the World Bank's Trade and Production Database (Nicita and Olarreaga 2001), which serves as our data source, is 1999. (See the Appendix for details on the data that we use.)

Tables 13.5–13.8 compare changes in the data over the period 1988–99 with the results of a numerical experiment of the Brown–Deardorff–Stern model that incorporated not just estimates of the changes in tariffs and nontariff trade barriers, but also a 10% increase in the capital stock in Mexico owned by consumers in Canada, the United Sates, and the rest of the world. The changes in both the data and the model results are calculated relative to the gross domestic product (GDP) of the country referred to in the change. For example, in the data

TABLE 13.8. *Changes in U.S. exports relative to U.S. GDP in the Brown–Deardorff–Stern model (percent)*

Sector	Exports to Canada		Exports to Mexico	
	1988–1999	Model	1988–1999	Model
Agriculture	−24.1	5.1	6.5	7.9
Mining and quarrying	−23.6	1.0	−19.8	0.5
Food	62.4	12.7	37.7	13.0
Textiles	177.2	44.0	850.5	18.6
Clothing	145.5	56.7	543.0	50.3
Leather products	29.9	7.9	87.7	15.5
Footwear	48.8	45.7	33.1	35.4
Wood products	76.4	6.7	25.7	7.0
Furniture and fixtures	83.8	35.6	224.1	18.6
Paper products	−20.5	18.9	−41.9	−3.9
Printing and publishing	50.8	3.9	507.9	−1.1
Chemicals	49.8	21.8	61.5	−8.4
Petroleum and products	−6.9	0.8	−41.1	−7.4
Rubber products	95.6	19.1	165.6	12.8
Nonmetal mineral products	56.5	11.9	55.9	0.8
Glass products	50.5	4.4	112.9	42.3
Iron and steel	0.6	11.6	144.5	−2.8
Nonferrous metals	−20.7	−6.7	−28.7	−55.1
Metal products	66.7	18.2	301.4	5.4
Nonelectrical machinery	36.2	9.9	350.8	−2.9
Electrical machinery	154.4	14.9	167.8	−10.9
Transportation equipment	36.5	−4.6	290.3	9.9
Miscellaneous manufactures	117.3	11.5	362.3	−9.4
weighted correlation with data		−0.01		0.50
variance decomposition of change		0.14		0.02
regression coefficient a		37.27		190.89
regression coefficient b		−0.02		3.42

in Table 13.5, we calculate that Canadian exports increased by 52.9% relative to GDP as follows: Total Canadian exports increased from 116.418 billion U.S. dollars (USD) in 1988 to 237.337 billion USD in 1999. During the same period, Canadian GDP increased from 492.322 billion USD to 656.420 billion USD. We calculate

$$1.529 = \frac{0.362}{0.236} = \frac{237.337/656.420}{116.418/492.322}.$$

In other words, Canadian exports increased from 23.6% of GDP in 1988 to 36.2% in 1999, and we say that the increase relative to GDP was 52.9%.

We strive to treat the model results the same way that we treat the data. Brown et al. (1995) reported that Canadian exports increased by 5.858 billion USD

TABLE 13.9. *Changes in Canadian trade volumes relative to Canadian GDP in Cox–Harris model (percent)*

Variable	Data: 1988–1989	Model
Total trade	57.2	10.0
Trade with Mexico	280.0	52.2
Trade with United States	76.2	20.0
weighted correlation with data		0.99
variance decomposition of change		0.52
regression coefficient *a*		38.40
regression coefficient *b*		1.93

and that Canadian GDP increased by 0.7% in their numerical experiment. We calculate

$$1.043 = \frac{(116.418 + 5.858)/116.418}{1.007}.$$

TABLE 13.10. *Changes in Canadian trade relative to Canadian GDP in the Cox–Harris model (percent)*

Sector	Total exports		Total imports	
	1988–2000	Model	1988–2000	Model
Agriculture	−13.7	−4.1	4.6	7.2
Forestry	215.5	−11.5	−21.5	7.1
Fishing	81.5	−5.4	107.3	9.5
Mining	21.7	−7.0	32.1	4.0
Food, beverages, and tobacco	50.9	18.6	60.0	3.8
Rubber and plastics	194.4	24.5	87.7	13.8
Textiles and leather	201.1	108.8	24.6	18.2
Wood and paper	31.9	7.3	97.3	7.2
Steel and metal products	30.2	19.5	52.2	10.0
Transportation equipment	66.3	3.5	29.7	3.0
Machinery and appliances	112.9	57.1	65.0	13.3
Nonmetallic minerals	102.7	31.8	3.6	7.3
Refineries	20.3	−2.7	5.1	1.5
Chemicals and misc. manufactures	53.3	28.1	92.5	10.4
weighted correlation with data		0.49		0.85
variance decomposition of change		0.32		0.08
regression coefficient *a*		41.85		22.00
regression coefficient *b*		0.81		3.55

TABLE 13.11. *Changes in Mexican trade relative to Mexican GDP in the Sobarzo model (percent)*

Sector	Exports to North America		Imports from North America	
	1988–2000	Model	1988–2000	Model
Agriculture	−15.3	−11.1	−28.2	3.4
Mining	−23.2	−17.0	−50.7	13.2
Petroleum	−37.6	−19.5	65.9	−6.8
Food	5.2	−6.9	11.8	−5.0
Beverages	42.0	5.2	216.0	−1.8
Tobacco	−42.3	2.8	3957.1	−11.6
Textiles	534.1	1.9	833.2	−1.2
Wearing apparel	2097.3	30.0	832.9	4.5
Leather	264.3	12.4	621.0	−0.4
Wood	415.1	−8.5	168.9	11.7
Paper	12.8	−7.9	68.1	−4.7
Chemicals	41.9	−4.4	71.8	−2.7
Rubber	479.0	12.8	792.0	−0.1
Nonmetallic mineral products	37.5	−6.2	226.5	10.9
Iron and steel	35.9	−4.9	40.3	17.7
Nonferrous metals	−40.3	−9.8	101.2	9.8
Metal products	469.5	−4.4	478.7	9.5
Nonelectrical machinery	521.7	−7.4	129.0	20.7
Electrical machinery	3189.1	1.0	749.1	9.6
Transportation equipment	224.5	−5.0	368.0	11.2
Other manufactures	975.1	−4.5	183.6	4.2
weighted correlation with data		0.61		0.23
variance decomposition of change		0.0004		0.002
regression coefficient *a*		495.08		174.52
regression coefficient *b*		30.77		5.35

In Table 13.5, notice that the Brown–Deardorff–Stern model did a fairly good job of capturing the relative sizes of the increases in overall trade, predicting that the largest impact of NAFTA would be on Mexico, followed by Canada, and then the United States. The reported correlation coefficient, 0.74, is weighted using the sizes of trade in 1988. The model fails badly on magnitudes, however, and accounts for only a small fraction, 0.08, of the variance in changes in trade shares observed in the data. Notice too how much larger than 0 is the coefficient *a* and how much larger than 1 is the coefficient *b*. To match what actually occurred, the best linear adjustment of the predictions for changes in trade patterns of the Brown–Deardorff–Stern model is to take these predictions, multiply them by a factor of 2.43, and then add 23.20% to each.

Tables 13.6, 13.7, and 13.8 report comparisons between the changes in exports by sector for each of the three North American countries in the results of the Brown–Deardorff–Stern model and the changes that actually occurred in the data. Once again, all changes, both in the results of the numerical experiment and in the data, are calculated relative to the GDP of the country. The correlation coefficients are weighted using the size of 1988 exports. Some of the correlations between predictions and changes in the data are fairly high. The correlation between the predictions and the data for Mexican exports to the United States in Table 13.7, for example, is 0.71. This high correlation is driven largely by the prediction that exports of electrical machinery would increase more than the average increase in exports. Similarly, the weighted correlation between the predictions and the data for U.S. exports to Mexico is fairly high, 0.50, because the model predicted that exports of electrical machinery would increase less than average (actually the model predicted a decrease) and that exports of transportation equipment would increase more than average. Electrical machinery and transportation equipment were the largest sectors both in Mexican exports to the United States and in U.S. exports to Mexico in 1988. The model failed badly in predicting relative magnitudes of sectoral changes for some other bilateral trade relationships, however. In the case of Canadian exports to Mexico, the model failed to predict the huge increases in exports of electrical machinery and of transportation equipment. In the case of U.S. exports to Canada, the model failed to predict the drop in exports of paper products. The variance decomposition statistics in Tables 13.6, 13.7, and 13.8 come as no surprise given the results of the predictions of aggregates in Table 13.5. The model missed completely on the magnitude of the changes in trade that occurred after NAFTA.

Tables 13.9 and 13.10 compare changes in the data over the period 1988–99 with the results of a numerical experiment of the Cox–Harris model that incorporated the tariff changes in both NAFTA and the Canada–U.S. FTA. Like the Brown–Deardorff–Stern model, the Cox–Harris model does a good job of predicting the relative sizes of the increases in overall trade, with Canadian trade with Mexico increasing much more than overall trade and Canadian trade with the United States increasing more than that with the rest of the world. The variance decomposition statistic is also fairly high at 0.52. In this case, however, we can see a limitation of decomposition of variance. What is important in our statistic is changes relative to the mean change. Although these magnitudes are fairly close in the data and the model predictions, the mean change of the model predictions is much smaller than that of the changes in the data. An alternative statistic that more accurately reflects the model's failure to predict the huge increase in Canadian trade volumes after the Canada–U.S. FTA and NAFTA is a decomposition of the mean squared error, rather than the variance:

$$\text{msedec}(x^{\text{data}}, x^{\text{model}}) = \frac{\sum_{i=1}^{n} \alpha_i^2 (x_i^{\text{model}})^2}{\sum_{i=1}^{n} \alpha_i^2 (x_i^{\text{model}})^2 + \sum_{i=1}^{n} \alpha_i^2 (x_i^{\text{data}})^2}.$$

This statistic is the same as our variance decomposition statistic except that it uses uncentered – rather than centered – sample moments. Calculating the decomposition of mean squared error, we obtain 0.07 for the prediction of the Cox–Harris model in Table 13.9. It is worth pointing out that the decomposition of squared error usually produces results similar to those of the decomposition of variance; the results in Table 13.9 are the major exception in this chapter.[2] The point, however, is that in interpreting the decomposition of variance we always need to take into account how similar the mean change in the data is to the mean change in the model results. In this case the regression coefficients provide a better indicator of how far off the predictions are: The best that we can do with the small predictions in trade patterns to match the large changes that occurred is to multiply them by 1.93 and then add 39.40% to each.

The predictions of the Cox–Harris model for overall trade by sector in Table 13.10 are fairly accurate in terms of relative magnitudes. The model correctly predicted that exports of machinery and appliances would increase more than average and that imports of transportation equipment would increase less than average. The variance decomposition statistics show that the model did not do as well in predicting the increase in Canadian trade. At first glance, we might be tempted to conclude from comparing Table 13.10 with Tables 13.6, 13.7, and 13.8 that the Cox–Harris model was more successful than the Brown–Deardorff–Stern model in predicting changes in sectoral trade. It is apparently far more difficult to predict changes in bilateral trade patterns than changes in overall trade, however, because bilateral trade by sector seems to be far more volatile.

Table 13.11 compares changes in the data with the results of a numerical experiment of the Sobarzo model that eliminated Mexican tariffs and allowed capital inflows into Mexico. In this experiment, Mexico ran a substantial trade deficit, reflected in the results in Table 13.11, where increases in imports are much larger than increases in exports. The predictions of the model for relative changes in exports are fairly accurate, as reflected in the weighted correlation coefficient of 0.61. In particular, the model predicted the observed increase in exports of electrical machinery relative to GDP and the decrease in mining (which is mostly petroleum in the case of Mexico). The model was able to account for only a minuscule fraction of the variance of changes in exports, however. The model did not do quite as well in predicting relative changes in imports. In particular, the model failed to predict that imports of mining and nonelectrical machinery would increase less than average. The model was successful, however, in predicting that imports of electrical machinery and transportation equipment would increase more than average. The fraction of the variance of changes in imports accounted for by the model is, once again, minuscule, however.

---

[2] For results like those reported in Table 13.1, where the weighted mean of the changes is equal to 0, the two measures are, of course, identical.

13.4. WHAT DO WE LEARN FROM THESE EVALUATIONS?

The Spanish model seems to have been far more successful in predicting the consequences of policy changes than the three models of NAFTA evaluated in the previous section. When comparing the predictions of the model of Spain's entry into the EC with those of the three NAFTA models, however, we need to keep in mind that the evaluation of the Spanish model by Kehoe et al. (1995) was carried out by members of the team that had constructed the original model. This implies at least three major differences between their evaluation and the typical evaluation that could be carried out by an outsider:

1. Kehoe et al. knew the structure of their model well enough to precisely identify the relationships between the variables in their model and those in the data. Specifically, they knew the concordance between sectors in the data and those in the model.[3] They were able to construct variables in the model exactly as the corresponding variables had been constructed in the data. Brown et al. (1995) are to be commended for providing a concordance between the sectors in their model and the sectors in the International Standard Industrial Classification (ISIC). The comparisons of model results and data reported in Tables 13.10 and 13.11 for the Cox–Harris and Sobarzo models, in contrast, are products of concordances produced by the author and reported in the Appendix.
2. Kehoe et al. were able to use the model to carry out numerical exercises to incorporate the impact of exogenous shocks. The importance of being able to do this can be seen by comparing the results in the fourth columns of Tables 13.1–13.4 – where both the agricultural productivity shock and the petroleum price shock are included – with the results in the second columns, where only the policy changes associated with entering the EC are taken into account. Without access to the models of NAFTA, it is impossible to provide the results of new numerical experiments for these models.
3. Kehoe et al. had a natural incentive to show their model in the best possible light. The aspect of the evaluation where this incentive probably had the most impact was on the choice of which exogenous shocks to incorporate. It should be noted, however, that the success of the model in predicting the behavior of macroeconomic variables, particularly indirect tax revenues, in Table 13.3 was not significantly altered by the incorporation of these shocks. The biggest success of the Spanish model was its bottom-line prediction before the policy change took place – that the tax reform was in fact a substantial tax increase. This shows up loud and clear in the data. If we take the bottom-line prediction of the three models of NAFTA to be that there would only be modest increases in trade flows, then these models clearly failed. Because trade flows in North

---

3   A detailed concordance had already been published by Kehoe et al. (1988).

America have exploded over the past decade, it is hard to imagine what sorts of exogenous shocks could be incorporated to rectify this failure of the models.[4]

If applied GE analysis is to make progress as a scientific discipline, researchers have to provide access both to the data and to the computer codes needed to calibrate and run their models. Improvements in computer technology have made it far easier to do this using the Internet, in the form of both Web sites and FTP (file transfer protocol) sites, than it was over a decade ago when the models of NAFTA were being developed. This sort of access would allow other researchers to carry out evaluations that would eliminate at least the first two discrepancies discussed above. Modelers should also feel it incumbent on themselves to carry out this sort of evaluation of their own models. Otherwise, if any evaluations are to be done at all, they will necessarily be done by researchers with less incentive to show their models in a positive light.

Comparing the evaluation of the model of Spain's entry into the EC with those of the models of NAFTA, we can speculate about why the Spanish model was more successful. It may be that we, as economists, understand public finance issues better than we do international trade. It may also be that applied GE models do a better job of making predictions over time horizons of one or two years than they do of making predictions over time horizons as long as a decade. Fox (1999) carries out a performance evaluation of the Brown–Stern (1989) model of the Canada–U.S. FTA using data from the period 1988–92 and obtains somewhat more favorable results than we are able to in the previous section for the models of NAFTA. Fox has the advantage of being able to run numerical experiments on the Brown–Stern model with partial tariff reductions to account for phased-in tariff reductions that had taken place by 1992. Given that NAFTA is scheduled to be phased in over 15 years, that the published results of the models incorporate the complete set of policy changes, and that we cannot run new numerical experiments of the models to incorporate partial changes, we are forced to use a long time horizon. Once again, this is the sort of limitation that would be eliminated by access to the model's data and computer codes. In any case, to test the speculative hypotheses that we have made, far more research comparing model results with data is needed.

13.5. SECTORAL DETAIL: WHAT DRIVES INCREASES IN TRADE?

The evaluation of the performances of the models of NAFTA suggests that we need to reexamine the theoretical mechanisms that drive increases in trade in applied GE models. The Brown–Deardorff–Stern, Cox–Harris, and Sobarzo models all rely

---

[4] It should be noted that Burfisher, Robinson, and Thierfelder (2001) cast a more favorable light on predictions made by applied GE models of NAFTA, although they do not perform the sort of systematic comparison of model results with the data as that reported in the previous section. They focus more on predictions of macroeconomic variables such as unemployment and trade deficits, pointing out that the models predicted little change in these variables.

on "New Trade Theory" mechanisms in which trade is driven by the Dixit–Stiglitz (1977) taste-for-variety specification, either in utility functions or in production functions. Bergoeing and Kehoe (1999) and Yi (2003) argue that these sorts of models cannot account for the large increases in international trade observed since the end of World War II.

The basic problem is that the taste-for-variety specification led the three models of NAFTA to predict that the largest increases in trade would occur in sectors in which there already is significant trade. The Dixit–Stiglitz (1977) specification of taste-for-variety says that inputs of goods, into either consumption or production, from the same sector but from different firms, are close, but not perfect, substitutes. In theoretical models, the typical functional form is

$$x_i = \theta_i \left(\sum_{j=1}^{n_i} x_{i,j}^\rho \right)^{1/\rho},$$

where x_i is the effective input from sector i, n_i is the total number of firms in sector i in the whole world, $x_{i,j}$ is the input from firm j, $\theta_i > 0$, and $1 > \rho > 0$. A problem well understood by trade economists in calibrating models with this sort of taste-for-variety is that of home-country bias. For reasonable values of the substitution parameter ρ, the model predicts far too much trade given observed trade barriers and transportation costs. To get around this problem, calibrated models typically modify the taste-for-variety function. In Mexico, for example, the effective value of inputs from sector i would be

$$x_i^{\text{mex}} = \theta_i \left(\alpha_{i,\text{can}}^{\text{mex}} \sum_{j=1}^{n_{i,\text{can}}} x_{i,j,\text{can}}^\rho + \alpha_{i,\text{mex}}^{\text{mex}} \sum_{j=1}^{n_{i,\text{mex}}} x_{i,j,\text{mex}}^\rho + \alpha_{i,\text{us}}^{\text{mex}} \sum_{j=1}^{n_{i,\text{us}}} x_{i,j,\text{us}}^\rho \right.$$
$$\left. + \alpha_{i,\text{rw}}^{\text{mex}} \sum_{j=1}^{n_{i,\text{rw}}} x_{i,j,\text{rw}}^\rho \right)^{1/\rho},$$

where inputs are differentiated not just by firm but by country of origin – Canada, Mexico, the United States, or the rest of the world. The parameters $\alpha_{i,\text{can}}^{\text{mex}}$, $\alpha_{i,\text{us}}^{\text{mex}}$, and $\alpha_{i,\text{rw}}^{\text{mex}}$ are smaller than $\alpha_{i,\text{mex}}^{\text{mex}}$ and are calibrated to base-year trade flows. (See Kehoe and Kehoe 1995 for details.) This calibration goes a long way toward locking in trade patterns of the model. If base-year Canadian exports of good i to Mexico are very small, for example, then $\alpha_{i,\text{can}}^{\text{mex}}$ is calibrated to be very small, and even large changes in trade barriers would have little effect on these trade flows.

Yi (2003) proposes a model, based on Dornbusch, Fischer, and Samuelson's (1997) Ricardian model with a continuum of goods, in which there are large increases in trade in goods not previously traded. Before studying how a Ricardian model can generate large increases in trade in new categories of goods, we look at data to answer the questions: In which sectors did the large increases in trade associated with NAFTA occur? In those sectors already heavily traded? Or in those sectors with little or no trade before NAFTA?

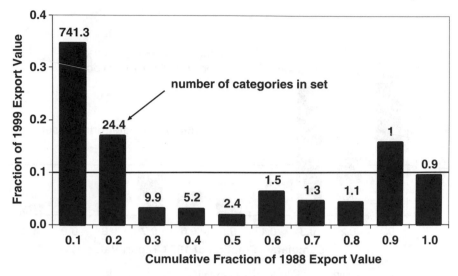

Figure 13.1. Composition of exports: Canada to Mexico.

To answer these questions both for NAFTA and for a large number of other trade liberalization episodes, Kehoe and Ruhl (2002) perform the following data exercise. They take four-digit Standard International Trade Classification (SITC, Revision 2) bilateral trade data obtained from the Organisation for Economic Co-operation and Development (OECD). There are 789 categories of goods in these data. First, they rank categories in order of base-year exports, from categories with the smallest amount of trade to the categories with the largest amount. Second, they form ten sets of categories by cumulating exports – the first 741.3 categories account for 10% of exports, for example; the next 24.4 categories account for 10% of exports; the next 9.9 categories account for 10% of exports; and so on. Third, they calculate the share of exports in subsequent years accounted for by each set of categories. Figures 13.1–13.4 show the results of this exercise for trade between Canada and Mexico over the period 1988–99. What stands out in both Fig. 13.1 and Fig. 13.2 is that the largest increases in the share of exports occur for those sets of categories that accounted for the smallest amount of trade in 1988. The 741.3 smallest categories of exports from Canada to Mexico accounted for 10% of exports in 1988, but in 1999 these same 741.3 categories accounted for 34.6% of exports.

There were some spectacular increases in the shares of exports from Canada to Mexico in some individual categories in the set with the smallest exports in 1988. Exports of Motor Cars for Transport of Passengers and Goods (7810), for example, went from 0.01% of Canada's exports to Mexico in 1988 to 5.06% in 1999; Meat of Bovine Animals, Fresh, Chilled, or Frozen (0111), went from 0.08 to 2.28%; and Aluminum and Aluminum Alloys, Unwrought (6841), went from 0 to 1.33%.

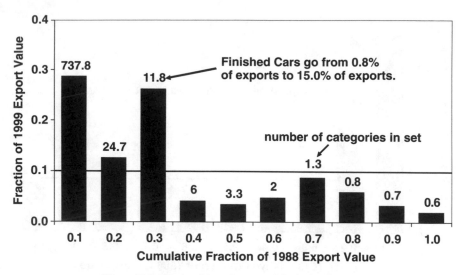

Figure 13.2. Composition of exports: Mexico to Canada.

Focusing only on the categories with these spectacular increases gives a misleading impression, however. If we eliminate the categories with the largest increases, we see that there were a very large number of categories in which Canada went from exporting little or nothing in 1988 to exporting significant amounts in 1999.

Eliminating the 10 categories that accounted for the most trade in 1999 of the 741.3 smallest categories in 1988, we are left with 731.3 categories that accounted for 6.2% of exports in 1988, but 16.6% in 1999. Coated/Impregnated Textile Fabrics

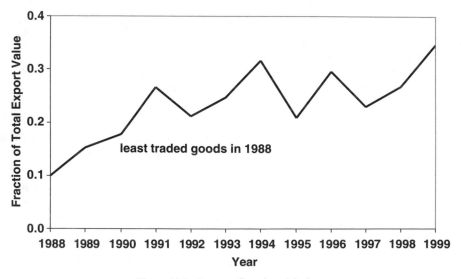

Figure 13.3. Exports: Canada to Mexico.

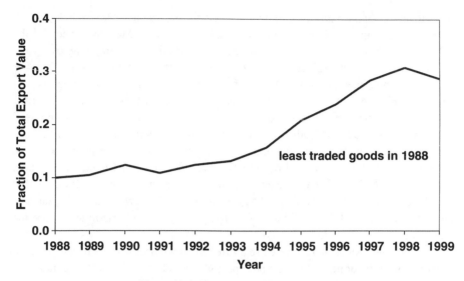

Figure 13.4. Exports: Mexico to Canada.

and Products (6573), for example, went from 0.05% of Canada's exports to Mexico in 1988 to 0.48% in 1999; Polystyrene and Its Copolymers (5833) went from 0% to 0.22%; and Cheese and Curd (0240) went from 0% to 0.09%.

At the other end of the list of categories, some categories that accounted for large shares of exports in 1988 saw their shares increase in 1999. Other Parts and Accessories of Motor Vehicles (7849), for example, increased from 10.25% of exports to 16.85% (accounting for the large increase in the share of the 0.8–0.9 set of categories in 1988 in Fig. 13.1); and Newsprint (6411) increased from 1.35 to 1.55%. On the whole, however, those categories that accounted for the largest shares of exports in 1988 saw their shares decline by 1999. These tendencies help account for the dismal failure of the Brown–Deardorff–Stern model to predict the pattern of changes in sectoral trade in Table 13.6.

Figure 13.2, which depicts the change in composition of Mexican exports to Canada over the period 1988–99, shows much the same pattern as Fig. 13.1. The set of least traded categories in 1988 has the largest increase in export share by 1999. A striking difference between Fig. 13.1 and Fig. 13.2 is the large jump in the share of exports of the 0.2–0.3 set of categories in Fig. 13.3. This increase in share is completely accounted for by one category, Motor Cars for Transport of Passengers and Goods (7810), whose exports went from 0.76% of Mexican exports to Canada in 1988 to 15.02% in 1999.

Figures 13.3 and 13.4 show the evolution over the period 1988–99 of the export shares of the set of categories least traded in 1988. What is worth noting is how these shares increase gradually over time. (Kehoe and Ruhl [2002] show that this sort of pattern of increase does not occur for bilateral trade between countries that have not undergone significant trade liberalization.) It is also interesting to note the more volatile nature of the patterns of trade in exports from Canada to Mexico in Fig. 13.3, perhaps due to more volatile macroeconomic conditions in Mexico, especially the 1995 crisis. That the change in trade patterns should take place gradually over time is partly to be expected given the nature of gradual trade liberalization in Mexico before the implementation of NAFTA and the timed phasing-out of trade barriers under NAFTA. Nonetheless, Figs. 13.3 and 13.4 suggest that the impact of trade liberalization on trade patterns takes place over time. Once again, we see the need for a dynamic model to analyze the impact of trade liberalization. We also have a potential reconciliation of the relatively poor evaluation that we produce for the Brown–Deardorff–Stern model of NAFTA, even for bilateral Canada–U.S. trade, with Fox's (1999) more favorable evaluation of the earlier version of this model that had focused on the Canada–U.S. FTA. It may be that Fox, who only looks at data over the period 1988–1992, did not use a long enough time horizon to capture the full effects of the Canada–U.S. FTA.

To see how a Ricardian model can capture large increases in trade in categories or sectors with little or no trade in the base period, consider a model with a continuum of goods $x \in [0, 1]$. The production technologies in the home and foreign countries are $y(x) = \ell(x)/a(x)$ and $y^*(x) = \ell^*(x)/a^*(x)$, where the unit labor requirement functions $a(x)$ and $a^*(x)$ are continuous. Assume that the two countries impose uniform *ad valorem* tariffs τ, τ^*. Then, if

$$(1 + \tau^*)wa(x) < w^*a^*(x)$$

$$\frac{a(x)}{a^*(x)} < \frac{w^*}{(1 + \tau^*)w},$$

the home country produces good x and exports it to the foreign country, which does not produce the good. Similarly, if

$$\frac{a(x)}{a^*(x)} > \frac{(1 + \tau)w^*}{w},$$

then the foreign country produces good x and exports it to the home country, which does not produce the good. Notice that

$$\frac{w^*}{(1 + \tau^*)w} < \frac{a(x)}{a^*(x)} < \frac{(1 + \tau)w^*}{w}$$

implies that both countries produce good x, which is not traded. Lowering tariffs can generate trade in previously nontraded goods.

In their exposition, Dornbusch et al. (1977) proposed reordering the goods on the interval [0, 1] in order of increasing comparative advantage for the home country, that is, so that the ratio of unit labor requirements $a(x)/a^*(x)$ is a nonincreasing function of the name of the good x. Textbook expositions of the Ricardian model have followed this convention ever since. In contrast, Kehoe and Ruhl (2002) propose leaving the goods on the interval in the same order that the SITC would order them if this classification could be done to an arbitrarily high number of digits. A four-digit SITC category is now an interval on the line as depicted in Fig. 13.5. (Figure 13.5 is

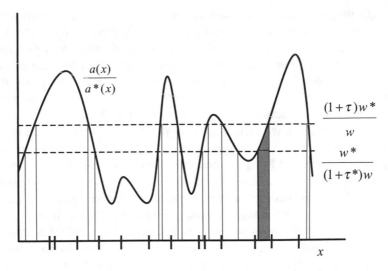

$$\frac{a(x)}{a^*(x)}$$

$$\frac{(1+\tau)w^*}{w}$$

$$\frac{w^*}{(1+\tau^*)w}$$

x

Figure 13.5. Ricardian model with a continuum of goods.

only meant to represent a subset of the interval [0, 1] – remember that we have 789 categories.) The curve that represents the ratio of unit labor requirements $a(x)/a^*(x)$ and determines trade patterns is now more arbitrary. Notice how, for the curve drawn in Fig. 13.5, there are categories such as the shaded one where reducing trade barriers in the form of the tariffs τ, τ^* generates huge increases in trade where there was little or none before.

Kehoe and Ruhl (2002) propose and calibrate a method for generating relative-unit-labor-requirement functions $a(x)/a^*(x)$, and they argue that this sort of model can go a long way in explaining the sorts of changes in trade patterns we see in Figs. 13.1 and 13.2. All of their analysis maintains the assumption of uniform trade barriers across goods. Romalis (2002) demonstrates that differences across sectors in changes in trade barriers were important in determining changes in trade patterns after NAFTA. This point is not necessarily relevant to our argument that we need models that generate large increases in trade in categories or sectors where there had been little or no trade, however: Kehoe and Ruhl (2002) demonstrate that the distribution of reductions in trade barriers within the set of categories with the least trade in 1988 was not noticeably different from the distribution of the reduction in trade barriers for all other categories. Obviously, much work is needed before any conclusions can be drawn.

13.6. BIG QUESTION: WHAT DRIVES CHANGES IN PRODUCTIVITY?

The papers in the volume edited by Kehoe and Prescott (2002) employ a simple applied GE methodology to analyze the causes of large macroeconomic fluctuations, specifically the great depressions that occurred in Europe and North America in the 1920s and 1930s, in Latin America in the 1980s, and in Japan in the 1990s. Using this methodology, we can determine whether economic fluctuations are caused by changes in inputs of labor, by changes in inputs of capital, or by changes in the efficiency with which these factors are used, measured as total factor productivity. Bergoeing et al. (2002) study the great depressions that began in Chile and Mexico in the early 1980s and the radically different recovery paths that these two countries followed afterward, with Chile growing rapidly and Mexico mired in crisis or stagnation until 1995. Bergoeing et al. conclude that the differences in the recovery paths of Chile and Mexico were primarily due to differences in the paths of total factor productivity rather than differences in their rates of employment or investment. They hypothesize that these different productivity paths were due to Chile's earlier reforms in banking and bankruptcy procedures, which encouraged a distribution of firms with higher productivity than that of the distribution of firms in Mexico. In both countries, fiscal reforms in the mid to late 1980s led to an increase in investment rates, but this increased both recovery paths rather than causing the two paths to differ.

The research of Bergoeing et al. has obvious general relevance for applied GE analysis of the impact of NAFTA. In line with the theme of this paper, however, we focus the relevance very tightly as a challenge to modelers of the impact of NAFTA: We use a simple aggregate dynamic GE model to show that, if we can successfully model the determinants of total factor productivity, then we understand the determinants of most of the macroeconomic fluctuations that occurred in Mexico over the period 1988–2002. The changes in trade flows and foreign investment associated with NAFTA are relevant to the extent that they help us determine productivity, not employment or – surprisingly – even investment. To make the point bluntly and perhaps a little too crudely, if NAFTA was not important for total factor productivity in Mexico, then it was not important in determining macroeconomic fluctuations there.

It is worth pointing out that Trefler (2001) finds that a major impact of the Canada–U.S. FTA on Canada was in changing the distribution of firms in terms of size and productivity. Trefler also argues that the change in the distribution of firms that occurred in Canada did not match the predictions of applied GE models – such as the three models of NAFTA that we have examined – that relied on the Dixit–Stiglitz (1977) theory of industrial organization.

We modify the simple, one-sector, closed economy model of Bergoeing et al. (2002) to include fluctuations in the trade balance.[5] The aggregate feasibility constraint in this economy is

$$C_t + K_{t+1} - (1 - \delta)K_t + X_t = A_t K_t^\alpha L_t^{1-\alpha}.$$

---

[5]   See Bergoeing et al. (2002) for details. We also extend their analysis to cover 2001 and 2002 and
      employ improved estimates of hours worked in Mexico.

Here C_t is aggregate consumption, both private and public, measured in constant pesos; K_t is capital; $K_{t+1} - (1 - \delta)K_t$ is gross investment; δK_t is depreciation; X_t is the trade balance; and L_t is the labor input measured in hours worked per year. Following Bergoeing et al., we set $\delta = 0.05$ and cumulate investment to calculate the path for the capital stock,

$$K_{t+1} = I_t + (1 - \delta)K_t,$$

and then set $\alpha = 0.30$ to calculate the path for total factor productivity,

$$A_t = \frac{C_t + K_{t+1} - (1 - \delta)K_t + X_t}{K_t^\alpha L_t^{1-\alpha}} = \frac{Y_t}{K_t^\alpha L_t^{1-\alpha}}.$$

We now consider a simple dynamic model in which we take fluctuations in total factor productivity A_t as exogenous. The point is not that we as applied GE modelers should want to take productivity as exogenous. In fact, the point is exactly the opposite: If a model with A_t treated as exogenous accounts for most macroeconomic fluctuations, then we know that it is changes in A_t that we need to be able to explain!

The stand-in consumer chooses sequences of consumption, capital, and hours worked to maximize

$$\sum_{t=1980}^{\infty} \beta^t \left[\gamma \log C_t + (1 - \gamma) \log(\bar{h}N_t - L_t) \right]$$

subject to the budget constraint in each period,

$$C_t + K_{t+1} - K_t = w_t L_t + (1 - \tau_t)(r_t - \delta)K_t + T_t - X_t,$$

and an initial condition on capital, K_{1988}. Here $\bar{h}$ is the number of hours available, taken to be 100 hrs per week, 52 weeks per year for working-age (15–64) persons; N_t is the population aged 15–64; and $(\bar{h}N_t - L_t)$ is leisure. In addition, r_t and w_t are the marginal products of the production function with respect to K_t and L_t; τ_t is the income tax rate on capital income; and T_t is a lump-sum transfer that at equilibrium is equal to tax revenue $\tau_t(r_t - \delta)K_t$.

Using the first-order condition for the labor–leisure decision from the stand-in consumer's problem, we follow Bergoeing et al. in using 1960–1980 data to estimate $\gamma = 0.30$. Setting $\beta = 0.98$, we use the first-order condition for the consumption–investment decision to estimate a tax distortion $\tau_t = 0.43$.

Figures 13.6–13.9 present the results of numerical experiments in which the sequences of A_t and X_t are treated as exogenous. The panel in the upper left of each figure shows the time paths for output per working aged person Y_t/N_t, the capital–output ratio K_t/Y_t, and the hours worked per working aged person L_t/N_t (measured in hours per week) for the base case numerical experiment. Bergoeing et al. argue that the failure of the model to track the paths of these macroeconomic variables is due to its neglect of fiscal reforms in 1987 and 1989, which lowered the effective tax on capital income. They estimate that these reforms had the effect of lowering the tax distortion to $\tau_t = 0.12$. The panel in the lower right of each figure

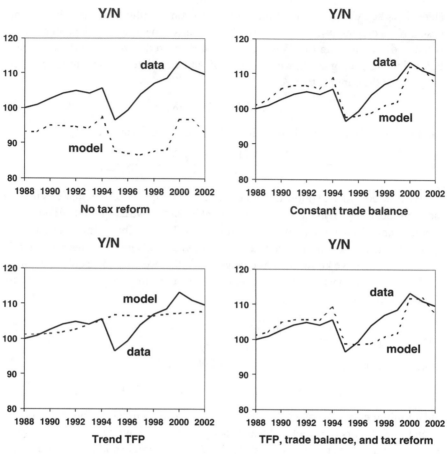

Figure 13.6.

shows the time paths of the variables in the numerical experiment that incorporates this tax reform.

The excellent performance of the model in tracking the macroeconomic variables should not be interpreted as saying that the fiscal reforms were the only major determinants of macroeconomic fluctuations. Remember that we still need to explain the path of total factor productivity! Comparing the results of the numerical experiments in the lower right with the remaining two numerical experiments emphasizes the point that it is productivity that we need to understand if we are to understand macroeconomic fluctuations: The panels in the upper right of each graph present the results of the experiment in which we restrict the trade balance to be constant at its average value over the period 1988–2002. Notice that this restriction has almost no effect at all on the results except for its impact on investment. The fluctuations in foreign capital flows increase investment in Fig. 13.9 during the early 1990s and then lower it sharply in 1995. That foreign capital flows have almost no other

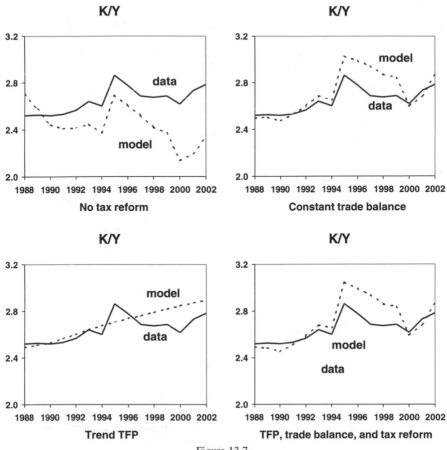

Figure 13.7.

effect in this simple one-sector model does not imply that fluctuations in foreign investment and the trade balance were not important in determining macroeconomic fluctuations in Mexico over the period 1988–2002. As Fernández de Córdoba and Kehoe (2000) show, these sorts of fluctuations have large effects on relative prices and the allocation of resources across traded and nontraded goods sectors. It is just that whatever impact these fluctuations have at a macroeconomic level works through fluctuations in productivity rather than through fluctuations in aggregate employment or investment.

The numerical experiment whose results are depicted in the panels at the lower left of each figure further emphasizes the importance of fluctuations in productivity rather than fluctuations in the trade balance. Here we model total factor productivity as following its trend growth path, and we lose almost all ability to account for fluctuations, even though we still incorporate fluctuations in the trade balance into the model. If we have total factor productivity follow a different growth rate, we

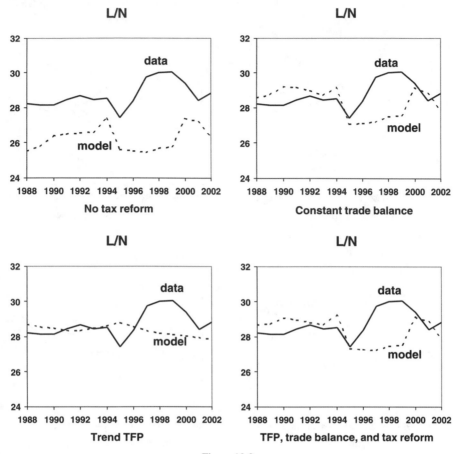

Figure 13.8.

produce time paths for the macroeconomic variables that differ even more from the data. Once again, we are stressing the point that, if capital flows into Mexico are to have important effects on macro aggregates, then these effects have to operate through productivity and not just by loosening the feasibility constraint or altering aggregate employment or investment.

13.7. CHALLENGE

In this article, I have tried to challenge applied GE modelers to do a better job. After a policy change such as NAFTA has taken place, we need to go back and see how well the predictions of our models fared. Making predictions with deterministic models in a world with uncertainty is difficult. An easy way out of this difficulty is to say that predictions are meant to hold *ceteris paribus* and to assert that everything was not equal, especially in Mexico, where a major financial crisis occurred the year

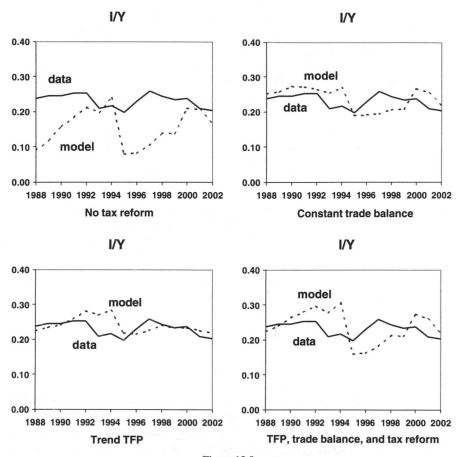

Figure 13.9.

after NAFTA went into effect. What is more difficult is to go back and to identify exactly what exogenous parameter changes need to be imposed on a model so that it can reproduce what actually happened. The less plausible these parameter changes, the less plausible the original predictions.

It is my conjecture that no plausible parameter changes can get the models of NAFTA built on the Dixit–Stiglitz specification to match what actually happened in North America. By simply imposing large elasticities of substitution between different types of goods in a sector, it is possible to generate large increases in trade flows in response to tariff changes, but it is likely to do so in the wrong sectors. Modelers are also likely to find high elasticities of substitutions unattractive and/or implausible for other reasons. High elasticities of substitution imply that trade liberalization has very small welfare consequences, for example. Furthermore, in international real-business-cycle models, such high elasticities imply implausibly large volatilities of the trade balance. In any case, it is the responsibility of modelers to demonstrate that their models are capable of predicting observed changes, at least ex post. If a modeling approach is not capable of reproducing what has happened, then it should be discarded. It may be that we applied GE modelers eventually decide that the biggest effect of liberalization of trade and capital flows is on productivity – through changing the distribution of firms and encouraging technology adoption – rather than the effects emphasized by the models used to analyze the impact of NAFTA.

Much is at stake both in terms of scientific discipline and in terms of policy analysis. During the political debate prior to approval of NAFTA by the U.S. Congress, American businessman and politician Ross Perot criticized the same models of NAFTA that we have analyzed in this paper, saying,

[T]hese studies are based on unrealistic assumptions and flawed mathematical models. . . . Let's be clear about this: these studies certainly do not provide a basis on which Congress can make an informed decision about NAFTA. [Perot with Choate, 1993, pp. 66–67]

We economists can comfort ourselves by observing that his own predictions of the impact of NAFTA on the U.S. economy turned out to be far less accurate than that of the models that he criticized. Nevertheless, as researchers in a scientific discipline, we need to build on our past shortcomings and strive to build better models to use in the future.

APPENDIX

Data on Gross Domestic Product (GDP) and exchange rates are taken from the International Monetary Fund's *International Financial Statistics*. A country's U.S. dollar GDP is calculated by dividing GDP denominated in local currency by the yearly average dollar exchange rate. Data on total trade by country is from the International Monetary Fund's *Direction of Trade Statistics*.

Data on trade in manufactures is taken from the World Bank's *Trade and Production Database*. The database contains bilateral trade flow data reported according to the International Standard Industrial Classification (ISIC) at the three- and four-digit level for manufactured goods. The World Bank created the ISIC data by converting data from the Standard International Trade Classification (SITC) using a concordance created by the OECD and provided by the World Bank (see Nicita and Olarreaga 2001).

Since the World Bank database does not provide data for nonmanufactures, the data for ISIC major divisions 1 and 2 need to be calculated by converting SITC trade data to ISIC. We obtain data on trade classified by SITC from the OECD's *International Trade by Commodity Statistics Database*. We derive a concordance from SITC to ISIC major divisions 1 and 2 from the OECD concordance as follows: After using the OECD concordance to extract the manufacturing data from the SITC trade flows, the residual SITC data contain the trade in agricultural products, fishing, and mining and quarrying. We make the concordance from SITC to ISIC

TABLE A1: *Concordance from SITC to ISIC nonmanufactures*

ISIC code	3-digit SITC Add	4-digit SITC Add	Subtract	5-digit SITC Add	Subtract
11	001, 041, 043, 044, 045, 054, 057, 075, 212, 222, 223, 264, 265, 271, 292	0251, 0421, 0616, 0721, 0742, 1211, 0.5* 2681, 2683, 2685	0546, 0572, 0576, 2223, 2232, 2239	07111, 08111, 08112, 09808, 21199, 26901, 29115, 29191, 29197	05771, 05774, 05775, 05799, 07528, 26512, 26513, 26599, 29291
12	232, 244, 245, 247			23322, 24601	24402, 24502
130		.7* 0036, 0341			
210	322			32313	
220	333, 341				34131
230	281, 286, 287, 289		2814		28722, 28732, 28902
290	273, 274, 277, 278				27324, 27721, 27861

major divisions 1 and 2 by assigning the residual values of SITC sections 0, 1, 2, and 3 to the appropriate divisions and major groups of ISIC major divisions 1 and 2. The resulting concordance is displayed in Table A1.

Tables 13.10 and 13.11 require data mapped from the ISIC aggregation into the aggregates in the Cox–Harris and Sobarzo models. The concordances used are listed in Tables A2 and A3.

TABLE A2: *Concordance between ISIC and Cox–Harris aggregates*

Cox–Harris aggregate	ISIC code
Agriculture	11
Forestry	12
Fishing	13
Mining	2
Food, beverages, and tobacco	311 + 312 + 313 + 314
Rubber and plastics	355 + 356
Textiles and leather	321 + 323
Wood and paper	331 + 332 + 341
Steel and metal products	371 + 372 + 381
Transportation equipment	384
Machinery and appliances	382 + 383
Nonmetallic minerals	361 + 369
Refineries	353 + 354
Chemicals and misc. manufactures	351 + 352 + 385

TABLE A3: *Concordance between ISIC and Sobarzo aggregates*

Sobarzo aggregate	ISIC code
Agriculture	1
Mining	2
Petroleum	354 + 353
Food	311 + 312
Beverages	313
Tobacco	314
Textiles	321
Wearing apparel	322
Leather	323
Wood	331 + 332
Paper	341
Chemicals	351 + 352
Rubber	355 + 356
Nonmetallic mineral products	361 + 369
Iron and steel	371
Nonferrous metals	372
Metal products	381
Nonelectrical machinery	382
Electrical machinery	383
Transportation equipment	384
Other manufactures	385

REFERENCES

P. Adams, P. Dixon, D. McDonald, G. Meagher, and B. Parmenter (1994), "Forecasts for the Australian Economy Using the MONASH Model," *International Journal of Forecasting* 10: 557–71.

K. J. Arrow and G. Debreu (1954), "Existence of Equilibrium for a Competitive Economy," *Econometrica* 22: 265–90.

R. Bergoeing and T. J. Kehoe (1999), "Trade Theory and Trade Facts," Federal Reserve Bank of Minneapolis.

R. Bergoeing, P. J. Kehoe, T. J. Kehoe, and R. Soto (2002), "A Decade Lost and Found: Mexico and Chile in the 1980s," *Review of Economic Dynamics* 5: 166–205.

D. K. Brown (1992), "Properties of Computable General Equilibrium Trade Models with Monopolistic Competition and Foreign Direct Investment," in United States International Trade Commission, *Economy-Wide Modeling of the Economic Implications of a FTA with Mexico and a NAFTA with Canada and Mexico*. Washington, DC: United States International Trade Commission, pp. 95–125.

(1994), "Properties of Computable General Equilibrium Trade Models with Monopolistic Competition and Foreign Direct Investment," in J. F. Francois and C. R. Shiells (Eds.), *Modeling Trade Policy: Applied General Equilibrium Assessments of North American Free Trade*. New York: Cambridge University Press, pp. 124–50.

D. K. Brown, A. V. Deardorff, and R. M. Stern (1992), "A North American Free Trade Agreement: Analytical Issues and a Computational Assessment," *The World Economy* 15: 11–30.

  (1995), "Estimates of a North American Free Trade Agreement," in P. J. Kehoe and T. J. Kehoe (Eds.), *Modeling North American Economic Integration*. Boston: Kluwer Academic, pp. 59–74.

D. K. Brown and R. M. Stern (1989), "Computable General Equilibrium Estimates of the Gains from U.S.-Canadian Trade Liberalization," in R. C. Feenstra (Ed.), *Trade Policies for International Competitiveness*. Chicago: University of Chicago Press, pp. 217–245.

M. E. Burfisher, S. Robinson, and K. Thierfelder (2001), "The Impact of NAFTA on the United States," *Journal of Economic Perspectives* 15: 125–44.

D. J. Cox (1994), "Some Applied General Equilibrium Estimates of the Impact of a North American Free Trade Agreement on Canada," in J. F. Francois and C. R. Shiells (Eds.), *Modeling Trade Policy: Applied General Equilibrium Assessments of North American Free Trade*. New York: Cambridge University Press, pp. 100–23.

  (1995), "An Applied General Equilibrium Analysis of NAFTA's Impact on Canada," in P. J. Kehoe and T. J. Kehoe (Eds.), *Modeling North American Economic Integration*. Boston: Kluwer Academic Publishers, pp. 75–90.

D. J. Cox and R. G. Harris (1985), "Trade Liberalization and Industrial Organization: Some Estimates for Canada," *Journal of Political Economy* 93: 115–45.

  (1992a), "North American Free Trade and its Implications for Canada," in United States International Trade Commission, *Economy-Wide Modeling of the Economic Implications of a FTA with Mexico and a NAFTA with Canada and Mexico*. Washington, DC: United States International Trade Commission, pp. 139–65.

  (1992b), "North American Free Trade and its Implications for Canada: Results from a CGE Model of North American Trade," *The World Economy* 15: 31–44.

K. Dervis, J. de Melo, and S. Robinson (1982), *General Equilibrium Models for Development Policy*. Cambridge: Cambridge University Press.

A. K. Dixit and J. E. Stiglitz (1977), "Monopolistic Competition and Optimum Product Diversity," *American Economic Review* 67: 297–308.

R. Dornbusch, S. Fischer, and P. Samuelson (1977), "Comparative Advantage, Trade and Payments in a Ricardian Model with a Continuum of Goods," *American Economic Review* 67: 823–29.

G. Fernández de Córdoba and T. J. Kehoe (2000), "Capital Flows and Real Exchange Rate Movements Following Spain's Entry into the European Community," *Journal of International Economics* 51: 49–78.

A. K. Fox (1999), "Evaluating the Success of a CGE Model of the Canada–U.S. Free Trade Agreement," University of Michigan.

J. F. Francois and C. R. Shiells (Eds.) (1994), *Modeling Trade Policy: Applied General Equilibrium Assessments of North American Free Trade*. New York: Cambridge University Press.

A. C. Harberger (1962), "The Incidence of the Corporate Income Tax," *Journal of Political Economy* 70: 215–40.

R. Harris (1984), "Applied General Equilibrium Analysis of Small Open Economies with Scale Economies and Imperfect Competition," *American Economic Review* 74: 1016–32.

L. Johansen (1960), *A Multi-Sectoral Study of Economic Growth*. Amsterdam: North-Holland.

T. J. Kehoe (1992), "Modeling the Dynamic Impact of North American Free Trade," in United States International Trade Commission, *Economy-Wide Modeling of the Economic Implications of an FTA with Mexico and a NAFTA with Canada and the United States.* Washington, DC: United States International Trade Commission, pp. 249–76.

P. J. Kehoe and T. J. Kehoe (Eds.) (1995), *Modeling North American Economic Integration.* Boston: Kluwer Academic Publishers.

T. J. Kehoe, A. Manresa, P. J. Noyola, C. Polo, and F. Sancho (1988), "A General Equilibrium Analysis of the 1986 Tax Reform in Spain," *European Economic Review* 32: 334–42.

T. J. Kehoe, A. Manresa, P. J. Noyola, C. Polo, F. Sancho, and J. Serra-Puche (1985), *Modelos de equilibrio general aplicado (MEGA): Un análisis del impacto del impuesto sobre el valor añadido (IVA) sobre la economía española.* Madrid: Instituto de Estudios Fiscales.

(1986a), "A General Equilibrium Analysis of the Indirect Tax Reform in Spain," Working Paper 66.86, Departament d'Economia i d'Història Econòmica, Universitat Autònoma de Barcelona.

(1986b), "A Social Accounting System for Spain: 1980," Working Paper 63.86, Departament d'Economia i d'Història Econòmica, Universitat Autònoma de Barcelona.

(1986c), "Política Econòmica i Equilibri General. Quins són els Efectes de l'IVA?" *Revista Econòmica de Catalunya* 2: 76–81.

T. J. Kehoe, A. Manresa, C. Polo, and F. Sancho (1988), "Una Matriz de Contabilidad Social de la Economía Española," *Estadística Española* 30: 5–33.

T. J. Kehoe, A. Manresa, C. Polo, and F. Sancho (1989), "Un Análisis de Equilibrio General de la Reforma Fiscal de 1986 en España," *Investigaciones Económicas* 13: 337–85.

T. J. Kehoe, C. Polo, F. Sancho (1995), "An Evaluation of the Performance of an Applied General Equilibrium Model of the Spanish Economy," *Economic Theory* 6: 115–41.

T. J. Kehoe and E. C. Prescott (2002), "Great Depressions of the 20th Century," special issue of *Review of Economic Dynamics* 5.

T. J. Kehoe and K. J. Ruhl (2002), "How Important is the New Goods Margin in International Trade?" Federal Reserve Bank of Minneapolis.

P. Krugman (1979), "Increasing Returns, Monopolistic Competition, and International Trade," *Journal of International Economics* 9: 469–79.

W. W. Leontief (1941), *Input–Output Economics.* New York: Oxford University Press.

L. McKenzie (1959), "On the Existence of General Equilibrium for a Competitive Market," *Econometrica* 27: 54–71.

A. Nicita and M. Olarreaga (2001), "Trade and Production, 1976–1999," The World Bank, available at www.worldbank.org/research/trade.

R. Perot, with P. Choate (1993), *Save Your Job, Save Our Country: Why NAFTA Must Be Stopped – Now!* New York: Hyperion.

J. Romalis (2002), "NAFTA's and CUSFTA's Impact on North American Trade," University of Chicago.

H. E. Scarf (1967), "On the Computation of Equilibrium Prices," in W. J. Feller (Ed.), *Ten Economic Studies in the Tradition of Irving Fisher.* New York: Wiley, pp. 207–30.

H. E. Scarf, with the collaboration of T. Hansen (1973), *The Computation of Economic Equilibria.* New Haven: Yale University Press.

C. R. Shiells and R. C. Shelburne (1992), "A Summary of 'Industrial Effects of a Free Trade Agreement Between Mexico and the United States,'" in United States International Trade Commission, *Economy-Wide Modeling of the Economic Implications of a FTA with Mexico and a NAFTA with Canada and Mexico.* Washington, DC: United States International Trade Commission, pp. 5–19.

J. B. Shoven and J. Whalley (1973), "General Equilibrium with Taxes: A Computational Procedure and an Existence Proof," *Review of Economic Studies* 40: 475–89.

H. Sobarzo (1992a), "A General Equilibrium Analysis of the Gains from Trade for the Mexican Economy of a North American Free Trade Agreement," in United States International Trade Commission, *Economy-Wide Modeling of the Economic Implications of a FTA with Mexico and a NAFTA with Canada and Mexico*. Washington, DC: United States International Trade Commission, pp. 599–653.

(1992b), "A General Equilibrium Analysis of the Gains from Trade for the Mexican Economy of a North American Free Trade Agreement," *The World Economy* 15: 83–100.

(1994), "The Gains from Trade for the Mexican Economy of a North American Free Trade Agreement – An Applied General Equilibrium Assessment," in J. F. Francois and C. R. Shiells (Eds.), *Modeling Trade Policy: Applied General Equilibrium Assessments of North American Free Trade*. New York: Cambridge University Press, pp. 83–99.

(1995), "A General Equilibrium Analysis of the Gains from NAFTA for the Mexican Economy," in P. J. Kehoe and T. J. Kehoe (Eds.), *Modeling North American Economic Integration*. Boston: Kluwer Academic Publishers, pp. 91–116.

D. Trefler (2001), "The Long and Short of the Canada–U.S. Free Trade Agreement," University of Toronto.

United States International Trade Commission (1992), *Economy-Wide Modeling of the Economic Implications of a FTA with Mexico and a NAFTA with Canada and Mexico*. Washington, DC: United States International Trade Commission.

K.-M. Yi (2003), "Can Vertical Specialization Explain the Growth of World Trade?" *Journal of Political Economy* 111: 52–102.

14 Decompositional Analysis Using Numerical Equilibrium Models: Illustrations from Trade Literature

Lisandro Abrego and John Whalley

14.1. INTRODUCTION

This chapter discusses recent applications of general equilibrium computational methods in the international trade area which are backwards (ex post) rather than forwards (ex ante) focused. The example chosen is the trade and wages debate, where the issue is disentangling the relative importance of multiple influences on wage inequality change (trade surges from low-wage countries and skill-biased technical change). The relevant literature includes Abrego and Whalley (2000, 2001).

In the past, most applied general equilibrium modelling (AGM) of international trade has been forward focussed, attempting to provide some basis of assessment as to what might happen if particular measures are adopted. This includes assessing the effects of NAFTA in advance of its enactment (Francois and Shiells, 1994) and ex ante assessment of the impacts of the Uruguay Round as agreed in the World Trade Organisation (WTO) (Martin and Winters, 1996; Whalley, 2000).

In such exercises, calibration usually takes place around benchmark equilibrium data set for a reference year; counterfactual computations then shed light on what this reference year equilibrium might have looked like if a policy or other change, not yet enacted, had been in place.

In ex post analysis, it is typically the case that calibration to two or more years is needed. The issue is, given a model consistent with observations in both years X and Y, how its equilibrium might look like were only one (or a subset) of the changes actually occurring between the years actually to occur. In the trade and wages case, what would wage inequality in the terminal year have been without the influence of low-wage import surges (or technical change); or what would wage

This chapter draws heavily on a recent joint paper on decompositional methods for trade and wages issues by Abrego and Whalley (2001). The chapter reflects the personal views of the first author, not necessarily those of the IMF. We are indebted to T. N. Srinivasan for detailed comments on earlier drafts.

inequality in the initial year have been with the low-wage import surge (or technical change) actually in place? The model specification clearly needs to be consistent with data in the two years, rather than one year, and dual calibration is therefore needed.

The chapter first explores how dual calibrations can be performed. One way is to use an assumption that all parameters of the model are free to change across the years, a strong assumption. Economists are usually uncomfortable with specifications in which preferences, for example, change through time (especially where welfare analysis is involved), or prefer to see systematic change over time in some specified form. Such requirements may restrict the dual calibration, and could make it inexact insofar as with such calibration it is no longer possible to reproduce base- or terminal-year data as an explicit model solution from the parameterisation generated by calibration. Some goodness-of-fit measure may need to be developed (implicitly a distance measure between actual and model predicted equilibria) as a reference point for calibration.

Drawing on Abrego and Whalley (2001), we first set out and illustrate the issues posed by ex post decompositional analysis in the trade area. In the process, both exact and inexact calibration are discussed; the techniques are presented for a Ricardo–Viner model used for trade and wages decompositional analysis using U.K. data for 1979 and 1995. Results of decompositions are then discussed.

The general argument of the paper is to argue that much of the literature on micro-based equilibrium simulation has been focussed on ex ante evaluational questions of a type similar to those discussed in pure theory. When applied empirically, this involves calibration to a single base case, and counterfactual equilibrium analysis around this reference point. This is useful for ex ante projections but useless for explaining or rationalising changes that have actually occurred.

Many issues arise and require different procedures and techniques in such an ex post evaluation of policy and other changes. For example, in an ex post analysis of the effects of regional trade agreements (RTAs) from observed data, one has to disentangle the effects of RTAs from those of other changes. More generally, one needs a methodology of isolating the effects of one from several factors underlying a change in observed outcomes. These issues also arise in many other areas. For example, one might ask how important technical change was to the growth surge accompanying the Industrial Revolution (as against population growth); how much railroads contributed to U.S. growth in the nineteenth century (Fogel's (1964) question); how much U.S. tax reform of the 1980s contributed to elevated growth in the 1990s? Growth accounting procedures and econometric techniques, such as analysis of variance and covariance, factor analysis, and principal components analysis, just to mention a few, have been used in answering these questions. The discussion and techniques presented here attempt to answer, if not the same, closely related question, using the AGM methodology.

14.2. BACKGROUND

Economists have long been interested in decomposing observed economic outcomes driven by multiple factors into parts attributable to each. This is the case in both the growth accounting literature (Solow, 1957) and the economic history literature (Fogel, 1964), for instance. The majority of these exercises focus on identifying the separate role played by a few key factors presumed to be the main sources behind the outcome, typically leaving a residual, as attributed to factors not explicitly modelled. How to decompose observed economic outcomes has been little studied in the applied general equilibrium literature (see Shoven and Whalley, 1992). Models have, instead, largely been used for ex ante counterfactual exercises of anticipated policy changes, whose outcome has not been observed.[1]

The motivation for the decomposition analysis discussed here is the extensive literature which tries to attribute portions of recent changes in wage inequality in OECD countries to various contributory factors. Few or none of these decompositions use the explicit equilibrium structures which dominate related trade-theoretic literature; rather, reduced-form econometrics motivated by the theory are used instead.

In recent trade and wages literature, most attention has been paid to two factors behind increased inequality: trade with low-wage countries and factor-biased technical change (e.g., Burtless, 1995; Slaughter, 1999). Some have also looked at the contribution of changes in relative factor supplies (e.g., Bound and Johnson, 1992; Baldwin and Cain, 1997), as well as of changes in labour-market institutions (e.g., Fortin and Thomas, 1997; Card, 1998; Machin and van Reenen, 1998). With only a few exceptions (Wood, 1994; Feenstra and Hanson, 1996), this work has concluded that the contribution of trade to increased OECD wage inequality has been small, with technical change playing the more important role. Empirical evidence on the role of changes in factor supplies is conflicting, and sometimes statistically insignificant.[2] Some studies (Gottschalk and Smeeding, 1997; Card, 1998; Machin and van Reenen, 1998) have also reported a substantial role for changes in labour-market institutions.

Some limitations of the reduced-form econometric methodologies used have been discussed in Abrego and Whalley (2000); they point out the possibility of alternative structural-form specifications, each of which is consistent with observed changes, but provides different decomposition results which cannot be ruled out. Indeed, such a possibility is the analogue of structural specifications that yield the same reduced-form specifications in situations of lack of identification of structural forms in econometrics. Also, technological change has been treated in this literature

---

[1] An exception is Devarajan and Sierra (1994), where multiperiod calibration and ex post decomposition are done in a dynamic framework. Unlike ours, however, Devarajan and Sierra's calibration procedure does not replicate the various observed equilibria.

[2] See, for example, Murphy and Welch (1989); Bound and Johnson (1992); Baldwin and Cain (1997); and Harrigan and Balaban (1999).

in different ways; as a residual in a Solow-type (Solow, 1957) (sectoral) growth-accounting framework (Leamer, 1998; Harrigan and Baliban, 1999); as the change in research and development expenditures (e.g., Machin and van Reenen, 1998; Anderton and Brenton, 1998); as the change in a factor's cost share not explained by the factor price change (e.g., Berman, Bound, and Griliches, 1994; Haskel and Slaughter, 1998); or merely as the factor that is left in determining the wage inequality change after trade is taken into account (Abrego and Whalley, 2000). An advantage of the techniques that are used here is that the measure of technical change determined through such calibration is fully consistent with the model structure being used and the observed equilibria.

In Abrego and Whalley (2001), the ex post general equilibrium calibration methodology is discussed and used to decompose observed economic outcomes generated by multiple sources into components attributed to each source. We apply it to the trade–technology debate on the causes of increased OECD wage inequality (Leamer, 2000; Krugman, 2000). We decompose observed (ex post) economic outcomes into portions attributed to component influences, rather than computing ex ante counterfactual equilibria, recognizing that these influences need not be and typically will not be additive. The analysis is based on multiple-period rather than single-period calibration, since model parameterisations need to be consistent with changes over time, not just a base-year observation. Our calibration to initial- and terminal-year data may be either exact or inexact (see Dawkins, Srinivasan, and Whalley, 2000), depending on the restrictions imposed.

The model structure we use in that paper is a specific-factors (or Ricardo–Viner) trade model, which differs from a more standard Heckscher–Ohlin-type structure through the presence of specific factors that are immobile across sectors, and hence it yields decreasing returns to scale to the mobile factors. The traditional Heckscher–Ohlin model with fully mobile factors and constant returns to scale, when used with conventional functional forms (such as constant elasticity of substitution (CES)), cannot accommodate relative product-price changes of the magnitude observed along with actual increased wage inequality in countries such as the United States or the U.K. (see OECD, 1997; Abrego and Whalley, 2000). This is due to the near linearity of the transformation frontier associated with this model structure and the ensuing problems of full specialisation documented some years ago by Johnson (1966). For the small-open-economy case, the standard Heckscher–Ohlin model is also unable to accommodate factor-biased technical change as a source of relative wage change (Leamer, 1998; Krugman, 2000). This is unsatisfactory because the available empirical evidence seems to support the hypothesis that factor-biased technical change has been a major source of increased OECD wage inequality. A specific-factors model eliminates specialisation problems, produces significant relative wage changes under factor-biased technical change, and hence can be used for decomposing wage inequality change.

The techniques are applied to a component decomposition of increased wage inequality, such as that occurred for a number of OECD countries over the 1980s and 1990s, such as the United States and the U.K. (e.g., Gottschalk and Smeeding, 1997; Slaughter, 1999). The literature on recent increases in wage inequality has concentrated on two main contributing factors – trade with low-wage countries and technological change. Most literature concludes that technological change is the main source of this increased inequality, rather than trade (Bound and Johnson, 1992; Baldwin and Cain, 1997). The model and the techniques used in Abrego and Whalley (2001) suggest that, within a general equilibrium setting, other factors, such as changes in endowments and a wider variety of technical change, also enter the picture and can play a significant role.

Two earlier papers have reported on decomposition-type experiments more limited than those here, also using multisector general equilibrium models (e.g., Abrego and Whalley, 2000; Francois and Nelson, 1998). One weakness of earlier procedures is that if the second counterfactual equilibrium is unconstrained, except for consistency with the wage inequality change (as in Abrego and Whalley, 2000), model solutions will not generally correspond to observed data for both periods. The wage change may be replicated but trade, output, employment, and consumption changes will not. The procedures discussed here remedy these weaknesses and involve changes over time in the relative wages of skilled and unskilled labour. These are accompanied by both trade changes (reflected in changes in the terms of trade) and technology changes (which may be sector- or factor-biased), and the issue is the contribution of each factor.

14.3. A TRADE MODEL FOR DECOMPOSITION ANALYSIS

For the purposes of illustrating decompositional analysis we will discuss the model of a small open, price-taking economy calibrated by Abrego and Whalley (2001) to data for the U.K. for two years (1979 and 1995). In that paper, we used a Ricardo–Viner specific-factors model, in contrast to a Hecksher–Ohlin-type fully-mobile-factors model. During the period we study, a substantial increase in wage inequality occurred. Most of the empirical literature assessing the importance of factors contributing to increased wage inequality notes that OECD countries generally import low-skill-intensive and export high-skill-intensive goods. The issue we pose is what portion of the observed change can be attributed to import surges of low-wage goods and what to technical change.

Decompositional analysis in its general equilibrium form usually employs an analytical structure close to the theoretical literature, which is calibrated to multiple-year observations. Counterfactual analyses focus on the behaviour of the calibrated model, excluding one or more influences on observed behaviour in the terminal year, or including such influences missing in the base year. Several critical factors enter into the design of decomposition experiments. One is the way the decomposition experiments are specified; another is the choice of analytical model; yet another is the choice of data and base and terminal years.

It is common in numerical modelling in the trade area to use structures based on Heckscher–Ohlin trade theory, in which goods are homogeneous and relative factor endowments determine the pattern of trade (see Shoven and Whalley, 1984; Whalley, 1985). Other work, such as that of Francois and Reinert (1997) and Harris (1984), uses structures in which there are product differentiation and scale economies in production, and the market structure is one of Chamberlinian monopolistic competition in the tradition of Dixit and Stiglitz (1977).

The attraction for earlier researchers in the trade area, such as Leamer (1998) and Whalley (1985), of using Heckscher–Ohlin-type models in earlier numerical modelling had been that they provided a simple but widely used analytical framework in which the relationship between relative wages and relative price changes is clearly defined. But for widely used functional forms, the Heckscher–Ohlin model (with homogeneous goods and constant returns to scale) has problems in accommodating relatively large product-price changes (Abrego and Whalley, 2000).

Although Armington (country differentiated product) models have also been widely used in the applied general equilibrium literature (see Shoven and Whalley, 1992), they are harder to work with analytically and, until recently, no general results linking changes in relative prices with relative wages have been available from them.[3] A specific-factors trade model (Ricardo–Viner) with decreasing returns to scale, a structure that has been more widely explored in the analytical literature of international trade (Jones, 1971; Samuelson, 1971; Mussa, 1974), yields decreasing returns in each sector with respect to a composite of mobile skilled and unskilled labour and relative wage variation without specialisation and provides a structure directly usable for trade–wages decompositions.

14.3.1. Production

We treat the U.K. as a small open price-taking economy that produces two goods, M and E, both of which are traded at fixed world prices (P_{it}; $i = M, E$), in period t. We model fixed factors in each of two sectors (skilled- and unskilled-labour-intensive) as well as two fully mobile factors, (skilled and unskilled labour). The production of each good in each period requires the use of two mobile factors, skilled labour, S, and unskilled labour, U, along with a sector-specific fixed factor. Production, consumption, and trade take place in each of the two time periods, 1 and 2, which we refer to as the initial and terminal periods.

Thus, each good in each period is produced according to a decreasing-returns-to-scale technology,

$$Y_{it} = A_{it}L_{it}^{\alpha_{it}}, \quad i = M, E; t = 1, 2 \tag{1}$$

where Y_{it} represents the output of good i in period t, A_{it} denotes a sector-specific efficiency measure of a composite labour-factor input, and L_{it} is use of a composite labour input. α_{it} is the output elasticity with respect to composite labour, assumed

---

[3] Robinson and Thierfelder (1996) have extended the Heckscher–Ohlin framework to include nontraded goods and imperfect substitution between imports and domestically produced goods, and they derive some analytical results.

to be strictly less than one to yield decreasing returns to scale. Consistent with a Ricardo–Viner approach, (1) implicitly defines a fixed factor in production in each sector, with a Cobb–Douglas share $(1 - \alpha_{it})$.

The composite labour input in each sector, L_{it}, is, in turn, a CES aggregate of unskilled and skilled labor, U and S,

$$L_{it} = B_{it}\left[\beta_{it}\left(\delta_t^U U_{it}\right)^{(\rho_{it}-1)/\rho_{it}} + \left(1 - \beta_{it}\right)\left(\delta_t^S S_{it}\right)^{(\rho_{it}-1)/\rho_{it}}\right]^{\frac{\rho_{it}}{\rho_{it}-1,}}$$
$$i = M, E; t = 1, 2 \tag{2}$$

where B_{it} defines units for composite labor used in sector i in period t, and β_{it} is the CES share parameter in the aggregation function. δ_t^U and δ_t^S are factor-augmenting technical change parameters which capture changes in input quality over time. ρ_{it} denotes the elasticity of substitution in sector i in period t between unskilled and skilled labour.[4] Combining (1) and (2) for each sector in each period yields

$$Y_{it} = \gamma_{it}\left[\beta_{it}\left(\delta_t^U U_{it}\right)^{(\rho_{it}-1)/\rho_{it}} + \left(1 - \beta_{it}\right)\left(\delta_t^S S_{it}\right)^{(\rho_{it}-1)/\rho_{it}}\right]^{\frac{\alpha_{it}\rho_{it}}{\rho_{it}-1,}}$$
$$i = M, E; t = 1, 2 \tag{3}$$

where the units parameter $\gamma_{it} = A_{it}B_{it}^{\alpha_{it}}$. In (3), changes in γ_{it} define sector-specific, Hicks-neutral technical change, whereas δ_t^U and δ_t^S reflect factor-biased technical change.[5] In empirical implementation of this model, it is assumed that (as in most OECD economies) production of the importable good, M, is intensive in unskilled labour in both periods; that is, $\beta_{Mt} > \beta_{Et}\forall t$.

14.3.2. Labour Markets

If competitive labour markets are assumed, each type of labour is paid its marginal value product, with full employment of each type of labour in each period. The endowments of unskilled and skilled labour are assumed to be fixed in each time period, but vary across periods at $\overline{U}_t$ and $\overline{S}_t$, respectively.

First-order conditions for factor demands implied by marginal-product pricing are given by

$$W_{Ut} = P_{it}\alpha_{it}\beta_{it}\delta_{it}Y_{it}^{[\rho_{it}(\alpha_{it}-1)+1]/\alpha_{it}\rho_{it}}/U_{it}^{\rho_{it}}\gamma_{it}^{((\rho_{it}-1)/\alpha_{it}\cdot\rho_{it})},$$
$$i = M, E; t = 1, 2 \tag{4}$$
$$W_{St} = P_{it}\alpha_{it}(1 - \beta_{it})\delta_{it}Y_{it}^{[\rho_{it}(\alpha_{it}-1)+1]/\alpha_{it}\rho_{it}}/S_{it}^{\rho_{it}}\gamma_{it}^{((\rho_{it}-1)/\alpha_{it}\cdot\rho_{it})},$$
$$i = M, E; t = 1, 2(5) \tag{5}$$

---

[4] This treatment implies that the marginal rate of substitution between skilled and unskilled labour is independent of the amount of the specific factor used.

[5] Specific-factor-biased technical change is assumed away.

where W_{Ut} and W_{St} denote unskilled and skilled wage rates, respectively, and P_{it} is the (fixed) world price of good i in period t.[6] Given the decreasing-returns technology set out in (1), payments to unskilled and skilled labour do not exhaust the value of production in either sector, and the remaining factor income implied by (1) accrues to the fixed factor in each sector.

14.3.3. Trade

We model trade shocks in this framework as changes in world prices, which, in turn, typically induce increased import volumes. We consider the shock to be a fall in the relative price of unskilled-intensive to skill-intensive goods between the initial and terminal years. These generate larger import volumes in the model, adjustment of labour out of the unskilled-intensive sector, and increases in exports.

When international income transfers, and borrowing and lending, are ruled out in equilibrium a zero-trade-balance condition holds,

$$\sum_{i=M,E} P_{it} T_{ti} = 0 \tag{6}$$

where T_{it} denotes the net trades (i.e., production less consumption) of the country in the two goods, M and E. It follows that if good i is exported, T_i is positive; if good i is imported, T_i is negative. Imports and competitive domestically produced goods are treated as homogeneous, as is also assumed to be the case for exports. This homogeneity assumption implies that trade flows in any good are always one-way and that one of the goods is exported and the other imported.

14.3.4. Equilibrium Conditions

Given the small-open-economy assumption in the model, goods markets do not clear domestically. Imports and exports reflect positive and negative excess demands, which are absorbed or met by world markets subject to trade balance, with the small economy facing perfectly elastic demands for its exports and supplies of its imports at world prices.

In this model, equilibrium in each period is given by unskilled and skilled wage rates such that the two domestic labour markets clear. The value marginal product of each mobile factor in each sector is equal to the corresponding wage rate, as in (4) and (5), and the fixed factor in each sector receives the residual in return, F_{it}, in

---

[6] The implications of the separability assumption can be seen in W_{Ut}/W_{St} being a function only of S_{it}/U_{it} and independent of the amount of the specific factor used.

period t. Market-clearing conditions hold in both periods; i.e.,

$$\sum_i U_{it} = \overline{U}_t, \quad i = M, E; t = 1, 2 \tag{7}$$

$$\sum_i S_{it} = \overline{S}_t, \quad i = M, E; t = 1, 2 \tag{8}$$

The two market-clearing conditions (7) and (8) determine the equilibrium wage rates for skilled and unskilled labour. The fixed factor in each sector receives the difference between the value of production at world prices and payments to mobile factor inputs. This enters incomes which, in turn, finance goods demands.

Consumption of each good in equilibrium is given by the difference between production and net trade; that is,

$$C_{it} = Y_{it} - T_{it}, \quad i = M, E; t = 1, 2 \tag{9}$$

where C_{it} denotes consumption of good i in period t. As long as international income transfers, borrowing, and lending are ruled out, a property of equilibrium in such a model (from the Walras law) is that trade balance (6) will be satisfied.

14.4. CALIBRATING A TRADE MODEL FOR DECOMPOSITIONAL ANALYSIS

Calibration is now a widely used technique for specifying numerical values of parameters in general equilibrium simulation (see Kydland and Prescott, 1982; Mansur and Whalley, 1984; Hansen and Heckman, 1996; and Dawkins et al., 2000). The use of the term calibration differs between micro and macro modellers. For the former, basic data are preadjusted to meet all required equilibrium conditions, and traditional endogenous variables in equilibrium computation (prices and quantities) become exogenous (given by data). What are usually exogenous variables in equilibrium computation (preference and technology parameters and endowments) become endogenous for calibration. Calibration is thus exact in directly generating parameters from adjusted data (characterizing a model equilibrium by assumption) that, when reintroduced into the model, exactly reproduce the adjusted data as a model solution. For real-business-cycle macro models, in contrast, parameters from literature are introduced into parsimonious models with an examination made as to how close the model solution is to the data. No exact calibration appears, even though with sufficient model richness it is possible (see Watson, 1994, for a discussion of goodness-of-fit measures for calibrated macro models).

Usually, in micro-based trade models used to evaluate policy options such as regional or global trade agreements on an ex ante basis, calibration occurs in so-called levels form to a single, model-consistent equilibrium data set constructed from observed outcomes. The sub data sets are built from basic data, which may violate the model equilibrium conditions, but which are adjusted for model compatibility (see Shoven and Whalley, 1992). In decomposition analysis, because of the focus on understanding factors behind ex post changes in key variables (skilled and unskilled wage rates), a different calibration procedure is needed, one which is consistent with data and which also captures the changes in variables over time that are at the heart of the analysis. In its simplest form, it involves two data observations, rather than one, as in more conventional calibration.

For the model structure specified above, calibration consists of choosing values for model parameters such that the model gives equilibrium solutions consistent with data in both periods as far as possible. In the model considered here, with its small-open-economy treatment, equilibrium conditions on the demand and production sides of the model are independent of each other. This allows the decomposition experiment to concentrate only on production-function parameters in calibration, because the focus of the decomposition analysis is on determinants of wage-rate change and does not involve demand-side considerations (as statements about consumer welfare would do). Thus, in the calibration discussed here, the demand side of the model is irrelevant to the outcome of the decomposition of wage inequality change.

In single-period calibration it is usual to assume that the values of elasticities of substitution in production (ρ) are exogenously given, based on separate literature-based estimation of parameters. Abrego and Whalley continue to assume that this is the case, but in their decomposition analysis, now for both periods. This leaves sixteen production-side parameter values to be determined through calibration: the output elasticities with respect to composite labour, the units terms in sector production functions, CES shares in aggregation functions, and factor-biased technological change parameters, that is,

$$\alpha_{it}, \gamma_{it}, \beta_{it}, \delta_t^U, \delta_t^S; \quad i = M, E; t = 1, 2 \tag{10}$$

If these parameters are to be consistent with the model equilibrium conditions in each period, the values determined for them must satisfy the first-order conditions (4) and (5), as well as Eq. (3). These equations yield a system of 12 equations in 16 unknowns.

To determine parameter values additional identifying restrictions are needed. One can first set

$$\delta_1^U = \delta_1^S = 1 \tag{11}$$

This is a normalization rule for factor-biased technological change terms and can be adopted because it is only changes in technology parameters over time that are relevant in the model.

One can then impose further restrictions on the model parameterisation to yield an equation system for calibration across the two time periods in which the remaining endogenous model parameters are exactly identified. We use three alternative sets of restrictions, each of which yields an exactly identified system of equations from which parameter values for the model are determined. These are

$$(1) \ \gamma_{i1} = \gamma_{i2}, \quad i = M, E \tag{12}$$

or

$$(2) \ \delta_2^U = \delta_2^S = 1 \tag{13}$$

or

$$(3) \ \beta_{i1} = \beta_{i2}, \quad i = M, E \tag{14}$$

These three alternatives differ in their implied treatment of technical change, over time. Restriction 1 implies that no Hicks-neutral technical change takes place over time.[7] Restriction 2 implies that no factor-biased technical change occurs over time. Restriction 3 allows technical change to be both Hicks-neutral and factor-biased, but rules out any change in share parameters in the composite CES labour aggregation function over time. Using each of these sets of restrictions, it is possible to calibrate the model and assess the implications for decomposition results. It seems implausible to restrict the α_{it} when implementing calibration, because these parameter values represent the share of the composite labour input in sectoral income and must be consistent with the shares implied by the data assembled for each time period.

With this calibration setup, changes in technology go beyond a simple Hicks-neutral/factor-biased classification, because other technology-related model parameters can also change. Restrictions 1 and 2 leave the β_{it} unconstrained, and therefore subject to variation across time. Under all the calibration restrictions listed above, the assumption that the outcome observed in each period constitutes an equilibrium implies that the elasticity of output with respect to the aggregate labour input (α_{it}) is also varying through time.

For these three sets of calibration restrictions, exact identification of parameter values from model equilibrium conditions will not hold if further restrictions are imposed on parameter values. One can therefore construct a further double-calibration procedure in which calibration is inexact rather than exact, taking such added restrictions into account. One option is to maintain exact calibration for period 1 and allow parameter values to be chosen for period 2 such that the sum of squared deviations of model-predicted values from actual values is minimized for endogenous variables, subject to the full set of general equilibrium conditions holding for the model-predicted equilibrium values. Parameters chosen in this way must be consistent with both optimising behaviour and the model equilibrium conditions. To implement this, one sets factor-biased technological change parameters to one in the first period (making the equation system exactly identified for that period), but allows them to be endogenously determined in the second period. Calibration is

---

[7] In the production function given by Eq. (1) composite labour is the only factor explicitly incorporated, and as γ_{ij}, also contains capital, it is not a pure Hicks-neutral technical change parameter. For simplicity, we will keep referring to it as the Hicks-neutral technical change parameter, although this is not conventional terminology.

exact in one period, but inexact in the other. This units convention can be reversed, allowing exact calibration in the second period and inexact calibration in the first period.

To simplify computations when implementing inexact calibration it is convenient to consider only the case where technical change is factor-biased, a variant on calibration restrictions 1 and 3 above, and one with both β_{it} and γ_{it} held fixed over time. In inexact calibration, the model-generated equilibrium values for period 2 differ from the observed values, and the model parameterisation is determined by minimising a criterion function as above.

The objective function that is minimised when inexact calibration is implemented is the sum of squared deviations of model-predicted values relative to observed values for the second period. We apply this criterion to four variables: output, consumption (and hence trade), and employment of the two labour types. Values for the two factor-biased technological change parameters (δ_2^U, δ_2^S) are chosen to minimise the criterion function when the model equilibrium conditions hold. Other criterion functions can be used (such as adding further variable differences between actual and predicted values), although computational experience indicates that differences in subsequent decomposition results from doing this are small. In the inexact-calibration results reported here, only one additional parameter is restricted relative to exact calibration. Factor endowments and the parameters α_{it} are given by the data, and both vary from period to period as with exact calibration.

More formally, the optimisation problem solved under this form of inexact calibration is given by

$$\min_i \sum_i P_{i2} \left(Y_{i2} - \hat{Y}_{i2} \right)_t^2 + \sum_i P_{i2} \left(C_{i2} - \hat{C}_{i2} \right)^2 + \sum_i W_2^S \left(S_{i2} - \hat{S}_{i2} \right)^2$$
$$+ \sum_i W_2^U \left(U_{i2} - \hat{U}_{i2} \right)^2 \qquad (15)$$

w.r. to δ_2^u, δ_2^s

s.t. (3)–(9)

where $\hat{Y}_{i2}$, $\hat{C}_{i2}$, $\hat{S}_{i2}$, and $\hat{U}_{i2}^2$ are model-predicted values in period 2 for output, consumption, employment of skilled labour, and employment of unskilled labour. The choice variables are the factor-biased technological change parameters, δ_2^u and δ_2^s. The model first-order conditions and equilibrium conditions are given by (3)–(9).

14.5. DECOMPOSITION EXPERIMENTS WITH CALIBRATED TRADE MODELS

The above model, calibrated using each of the three sets of restrictions set out above, can be used to generate estimates of the contributions of increased trade, factor-biased technical change, and factor endowment change (demographics) to increases in wage inequality. We consider the U.K. between 1979 and 1995 and capture trade shocks as changes in world prices (the price of skill-intensive relative to unskilled-intensive goods). These affect trade flows, which are also endogenously determined in the model. We consider a fall in the relative price of unskilled-intensive products (aggregated as M) for the U.K. between 1979 and 1995. Factor-biased technical change over time is modeled as changes in the factor-augmenting technical change parameters δ_t^U and δ_t^S. We also consider other production-function parameter changes generated by the model and calibration restrictions.

Both exact and inexact calibration are used to carry out decomposition experiments using the model. In the process, changes in model technology parameters over time are determined using two-period data along with the various calibration restrictions. The parameter values that are generated change with the restrictions used.

For any model parameterisation generated by calibration, one can thus assess the contribution of each individual component of a package of changes (trade surges and technological changes) to wage inequality change. This can be done by first taking the equilibrium of period 1 as the base model solution and solving the model considering only the trade shock. This allows a calculation of the portion of the total change in wage inequality over the period attributable to this shock. One can then change each of the technology parameters implied by the calibration procedure used and repeat the procedures. One can thus also assess the impact of changes in factor endowments on inequality. These changes taken together are consistent with the observed wage inequality change, as well as other characteristics of the observed period 2 equilibrium. One could alternatively work backwards from the period 2 equilibrium and remove the effects of shocks on a piecewise basis.

The proportions of the total change attributed in this way to individual sources need not (and typically will not) sum to the total change, independent of the base point assumed. Typically, each experiment considers a change in only one of three variables, and these variables have interacting effects which imply that their separate contributions may sum to more or less than the observed wage inequality change. The quantitative significance of this nonadditivity property in results is something which only numerical computation can reveal.

14.6. U.K. DATA FOR TRADE DECOMPOSITION EXPERIMENTS

We perform trade decomposition experiments using U.K. data for the two years 1979 and 1995. As Table 14.1 indicates, this choice of years covers a period during which there was substantial change in wage inequality in the U.K., with a near 25% decline in the ratio of unskilled to skilled wage rates. There was also a significant increase in real U.K. GDP, a rise in trade (imports), a roughly constant composition of employment of unskilled and skilled labour by sector, and a sharp rise in the size of the skilled labour pool.

The model described in the previous section is parameterised and the calibration methods set out above are applied. Using calibration procedures in this way, we fit

TABLE 14.1. *Abrego and Whalley's (2001) U.K. data for 1979 and 1995*

	1979	1995
U.K. GDP in 1979 prices (billion pounds)	198	262
Import to gross output ratio for unskilled-intensive products	0.129	0.173
% employment in skilled-intensive sector	48.0	49.8
Ratio of unskilled to skilled labour employment aggregate	1.04	0.715
Unskilled to skilled labour wage rate ratio	1.0	0.769
(1979 set at 1.0 as a normalization)		

Source: Office for National Statistics (1997a).

the model to both initial and end-of-period observations. Three main issues arise in producing consistent micro data covering each of the two years. One is how to aggregate more detailed and sectorally disaggregated data from original sources into the skilled–unskilled-intensive breakdown in the model. Another is how to define the returns to skilled and unskilled labour by sector and to aggregate these factor returns from information on more detailed sectoral classifications. The third relates to the definition of other variables: production, trade, and broader factor incomes.

Following the model structure, we aggregate U.K. production activities into the two broad sectoral groups of skilled-intensive and unskilled-intensive. Table 14.2 presents a list of those industries from U.K. national accounts classifications, which are included in each of these two groupings. Sectoral employment of skilled and unskilled workers is taken as given by the use of nonmanual and manual workers by industry as reported in the U.K. Office for National Statistics (ONS) *Employment Gazette* and *Labour Market Trends*. Though this measure of skill differentiation is

TABLE 14.2. *U.K. national accounts industries included in the skilled (S)-and unskilled (U)-intensive sectors used by Abrego and Whalley (2001)*

S-intensive sector	U-intensive sector
Mining and quarrying	Agriculture, hunting and forestry
Paper and publishing	Food, beverages and tobacco
Petroleum products and nuclear fuel	Textiles and textile products
Chemicals	Leather and leather products
Machinery and equipment	Wood and wood products
Electrical and optical equipment	Rubber and plastic
Transport equipment	Non-metallic minerals
Electricity, gas and water	Basic metals and metal products
Transport, storage and communication	Other manufacturing
Financial intermediation	Construction
Real estate	Trade, restaurants and hotels
Public administration, defence	Health and social work
and social security services	Education; other

not entirely satisfactory, it has been widely used in other recent wage-inequality literature for both the United States and the United Kingdom (e.g., Sachs and Shatz, 1994; Machin and van Reenen, 1998; Haskel and Slaughter, 1999).

Sectoral production, broad-factor income (labour and capital), and trade data for 1979 come from the U.K. input–output table for that year (OECD, 1995). We separate manual from nonmanual labour income by sector using ONS data on employment and wages for these two groups for the closest available year (1981–82). These data do not split employment and wages by worker type for the sector disaggregation reported in Table 14.1, and only allow disaggregation of employment data into manual and nonmanual categories for the whole economy. From this information, however, one can determine aggregate income for each labour type and combine this with data on wage rates by skill level to determine sectoral employment and wage bill data for each labour category for 1979.

We use information from ONS sources (for 1981–82 and 1996) for the change in relative hourly wage rates for the period 1979–95. These data cover all full-time adult workers in each year and yield a sizeable relative decline of 23.1% in the wage of unskilled workers compared to skilled workers.[8] Drawing on an earlier paper of theirs, Abrego and Whalley (2000) (who, in turn, draw on Neven and Wyplosz, 1999) use the figure of 7.9% as the fall in the relative price of the unskilled-intensive good on international markets faced by the U.K. producers.[9] This is the trade shock experienced by the U.K. in the model over the period 1979–95 and is an input into their calibration procedures.

Data on production, broad-factor income, and trade for 1995 are obtained from the U.K. input–output table for the year (ONS, 1997b). Data on sectoral employment and wages by skill category from ONS (1996) are used to obtain wage bill data for each labour type. Using data on hours worked by sector from the same source, we are able to measure the amount of each labour input used by each sector (in terms of hours).

When the model is calibrated, data are adjusted so that the terminal year (1995) reflects the observed relative price and wage changes (in real terms) relative to the base year. Changes in the value of sector output experienced over the period are similarly adjusted. All this information is used to parameterise the model using each of the sets of calibration restrictions described in the preceding section, including inexact calibration as set out above. We use a base value for the elasticity of substitution between skilled and unskilled labour, ρ_{it}, of 1.25, which is consistent with input substitution elasticity estimates reported in Hamermesh (1993).

Table 14.3 reports the 1979 and 1995 model parameters implied by use of each of the calibration restrictions, as well as the changes between equilibria and other

[8] This differs from the 15% figure used by Abrego and Whalley (2000), because it covers all full-time workers and involves a slightly different time period (Abrego and Whalley's earlier figure is based on male workers only and is for the period 1976–90).

[9] This estimate was based on information in Neven and Wyplosz (1999).

TABLE 14.3. *Production-side parameters, relative prices, and endowments for 1979 and 1995 from the calibrations used by Abrego and Whalley (2001)*

	Calibration restrictions of type 1			Calibration restrictions of type 2			Calibration restrictions of type 3		
	1979	1995	% change in parameter values	1979	1995	% change in parameter values	1979	1995	% change in parameter values
δ^U	1.00	1.17	17.2	1.00	1.00	0.00	1.00	0.23	−76.9
δ^S	1.00	1.95	95.3	1.00	1.00	0.00	1.00	3.81	281.1
β_M	0.53	0.42	−21.4	0.53	0.40	−26.0	0.53	0.53	0.0
β_E	0.38	0.28	−26.7	0.38	0.26	−31.9	0.38	0.38	0.0
γ_M	17.56	17.56	0.0	17.5	24.6	40.2	17.56	24.0	36.5
γ_E	18.58	18.58	0.0	18.5	26.1	40.6	18.58	19.6	5.4
α_M	0.68	0.73	8.3	0.68	0.73	8.3	0.68	0.73	8.3
α_E	0.64	0.64	0.1	0.64	0.64	0.1	0.64	0.64	0.1
P_M/P_E	1.00	0.92	−7.9	1.00	0.92	−7.9	1.00	0.92	−7.9
U	1.00	0.75	−25.0	1.00	0.75	−25.0	1.00	0.75	−25.0
S	1.00	1.09	9.3	1.00	1.09	9.3	1.00	1.09	9.3
ρ_{ltt}	1.25	1.25	0.0	1.25	1.25	0.0	1.25	1.25	0.0

Notes: Type 1 implies no Hicks-neutral technical change; type 2 implies no factor-biased technical change; type 3 implies no changes in CES share parameters.

TABLE 14.4. *Abrego and Whalley's U.K. 1979–1995 wage inequality decomposition experiments under alternative calibration restrictions – % of wage inequality change attributed to each contributing factor*

	Calibration restrictions of type 1	Calibration restrictions of type 2	Calibration restrictions of type 3
Increased trade	17	17	17
Factor-biased technical change	47	0	211
Hicks-neutral technical change	0	1	−49
Factor endowment changes	−144	−144	−144
Changes in β_{it}	157	183	0
Changes in α_{it}	−19	−19	−19

Notes: Type 1 implies no Hicks-neutral technical change; type 2 implies no factor-biased technical change; type 3 implies no changes in CES share parameters.

information used in subsequent decomposition experiments. Some of the changes in technology parameters that these procedures produce (especially procedure 3) are large, and for δ^U changes are of different signs across procedures.

14.7. SOME RESULTS FROM DECOMPOSITION EXPERIMENTS

We perform decomposition experiments with both exact and inexact double calibration. For each of the decomposition experiments we separately evaluate the influences of trade, technology, and endowments on observed relative wage change for the U.K. between 1979 and 1995. In all these experiments substitution elasticities are given, and relative goods prices and factor endowments change over time, as does (through the data and calibration) the output elasticity with respect to the composite labour input, α_{it}. Sensitivity of results for each experiment to different values of production substitution elasticities, ρ_{it}, can be evaluated.

Table 14.4 presents our main decomposition results. The calibration restrictions used in the first experiment imply that no Hicks-neutral technical change occurs over time and that technical change is factor-biased. The calibration restrictions used in experiment 2 remove factor-biased technical change and allow Hicks-neutral change. In both of these experiments, the production function parameter in each sector β_{it} (the share of unskilled labour in composite labour) varies over time. Experiment 3 allows both factor-biased and Hicks-neutral technical change, but in this case β_{it} is constant over time.

These experiments are performed by introducing each of the changes specified in the first column of Table 14.4 into the relevant base-period version of the model and comparing the resulting model solution to the full observed change. The separate effects of changes in exogenous variables between periods from these decomposition results (such as changes in world prices which generate trade surges) are taken to imply the importance of each of the factors involved for the total change. For changes in trade, results are the same under all calibration procedures, because the size of the trade shock is unique and is not generated by calibration. Where calibrated technology parameters change over time (as with factor-biased technical change), results vary with the set of calibration restrictions used, because the size of the change in these parameters depends on the specific restrictions employed (see Table 14.3).

Although results in Table 14.4 vary with the calibration restrictions used, they all show the same relatively small contribution of trade to increased wage inequality (17%) over the period, because the size of the trade shock does not change with calibration. A larger role emerges for factor-biased technical change (calibrations 1 and 3), which, in turn, varies significantly depending upon the restrictions used. Where changes in share parameters, β_{it}, are not allowed for, factor-biased technical change accounts for more than the observed wage-inequality change. Factor endowment changes have large negative effects on wage inequality, but these are offset by the positive effects of changes in share parameters under restrictions 1 and 2 and by factor-biased technical change under restriction 3.

Under restriction 1, factor-biased technical change is responsible for slightly less than half the relative wage change. This is accompanied by larger offsetting positive and negative effects from changes in β_{it} and endowments. Under restriction 3 the contribution of factor-biased technical change is more than twice the observed change in wage inequality, but is offset by an opposite effect generated by both Hicks-neutral technical change and a relative decrease in the endowment of unskilled labour. Changes in the parameters α_{it} act as an offset to factor-biased technical change in all cases, though to a much lesser degree.

Results using restrictions 1 and 3 thus appear to confirm the finding in the trade and wages literature that skilled-biased technical change is a more significant contributory factor to increased wage inequality than trade, although results using calibration 2 produce results in which the effects of factor-biased technical change are absent by construction. Results from using restriction 3, in which the parameter β_{it} is held constant across periods, also emphasize a feature which has figured less prominently in the literature, namely, that changes in factor endowments offset wage inequality associated with trade and factor-biased technical change. Other technology-related factors, importantly sector-specific technical change, are also nontrivial factors. Finally, results using restriction 3 suggest that the impact of skill-biased technical change on wage inequality could be more significant than existing literature suggests.

Results using restriction 2 are similar to those from restriction 1 in that increases in wage inequality are accounted for mainly by changes in β_{it}. Relative to those generated using restriction 3, these results point to a smaller role for Hicks-neutral technical change, although changes in β_{it} cannot themselves be interpreted as technical change in a conventional sense.

The identical contributions of -144% for factor endowment changes and -19% for changes in α_{it} across the three alternative calibration restrictions in Table 14.4

occur because under the calibrations we use the base-year model parameterisation is the same independent of the identifying restriction used. The counterfactuals we perform are all around the same base-year model specification. If the counterfactual is (say) removing technical change, the parameters of the model used vary with the restriction used, and the columns of results in the table will vary. Where it is endowment change, the parameterisation is the same and the effects are the same in the columns of Table 14.4.

These large endowment effects are important for the trade and wages debate. This is because there is an observed increase in the wage of skilled relative to unskilled labour, despite the endowment of skilled relative to unskilled labour increasing substantially. As a result the contribution of technical change to wage change has to be even larger than the literature suggests to offset this endowment effect also.

Sensitivity analyses performed on these results generated by changing the exogenous values set for the elasticity of substitution in production, ρ_{it}, in the central-case model specification for each of the three sets of calibration restrictions are presented in Table 14.5 for cases where $\rho_{it} = 0.5$ and $\rho_{it} = 2.0$.

For $\rho_{it} = 0.5$, the magnitude of the trade effect is double that of the central case, whereas the contribution of factor endowment changes almost trebles. This is because as the elasticities of substitution in production fall, price and wage responses to shocks are larger and quantity responses are smaller. The size of the effects attributed to factor-biased technological change increases substantially and becomes a major factor in offsetting the effects of trade and factor-biased technical change on increased wage inequality.

Increasing ρ_{it} to 2.0 also produces significant differences in results, most notably in the size of the factor-biased technical-change effect – which increases sharply for restriction set 1 – and changes in factor endowments, whose effects are reduced by about half relative to the central case. These results, taken together with those using the central-case model parameterisations, suggest that Hicks-neutral technical change tends to reduce wage inequality, but the magnitude of the effect is small.

Taken as a set, these results seem to indicate that the qualitative pattern of the decomposition result remains unchanged in terms of relative rankings of various factors acting on wage inequality change as one moves across different model parameterisations by the use of alternative identifying restrictions, but there are clearly significant quantitative changes. Factor-biased technological change seems to have played a larger role in generating increased wage inequality than previously suggested in the literature, and changes in factor endowments have been a key offsetting force.

It is also possible to generate decomposition results using inexact calibration. To implement this, the effects of factor-biased technical change can be isolated using a model calibration in which both Hicks-neutral technical change parameters, γ_{it}, and factor shares in production, β_{it}, remain constant across periods.

Results (in Table 14.6) emphasize both the significance of the contribution of factor-biased technical change to wage inequality and the offsetting effects coming

TABLE 14.5. *Sensitivity analyses of Abrego and Whalley's decomposition results to alternating values of elasticities of substitution in production – % of wage inequality change attributed to each contributing factor*

	$\rho_{it} = 0.5$			$\rho_{it} = 2.0$		
	Calibration restrictions of type 1	Calibration restrictions of type 2	Calibration restrictions of type 3	Calibration restrictions of type 1	Calibration restrictions of type 2	Calibration restrictions of type 3
Increased trade	37	37	37	11	11	11
Factor-biased technical change	−22	0	241	164	0	159
Hicks-neutral technical change	0	−16	490	0	2	−3
Factor endowment changes	−385	−385	−385	−88	−88	−88
Change in β_{it}	274	267	0	−9	155	0
Change in α_{it}	−45	−45	−45	−12	−12	−12

Notes: Type 1 implies no Hicks-neutral technical change; type 2 implies no factor-biased technical change, type 3 implies no changes in CES share parameters.

TABLE 14.6. *Wage inequality*
decomposition with inexact calibration – %
of wage inequality change attributed to each
contributing factor

Increased trade	17
Factor-biased technical change	183
Factor endowment changes	−144
Change in α_{it}	−19

from changes in factor endowments as earlier. These are similar to results obtained using calibration restriction 3 earlier in Table 14.4. Inexact calibration in this case corresponds to exact calibration procedure 3 but without Hicks-neutral technical change. Since the effect on Hicks-neutral technical change using calibration restriction 3 is relatively small (Table 14.4), the difference between the two sets of results is not large. Inexact calibration can also be seen as a variant on the use of calibration restriction 1, the difference being that under the former the share parameters β_{it} do not change over time. Because changes in the β_{it} can have a large impact on wage inequality (Table 14.4), the difference between the two sets of results is now substantial.[10]

14.8. CONCLUDING REMARKS

This chapter discusses the use of ex post decomposition techniques in numerical general equilibrium trade models, drawing a contrast with ex ante analyses such as those used to assess the impact of regional and/or global trade agreements. The latter typically involve calibration to data for a single base year followed by computation of a hypothetical counterfactual equilibrium. The former involve fitting a model to two or more data points, and the use of the model to evaluate separately the contribution of each of several factors underlying the observed change in model endogenous variables. Techniques are presented for performing ex post decomposition analysis using such models, and Abrego and Whalley's work (2001) applying them to an analysis of the sources of increases in wage inequality in the U.K. between 1979 and 1995 is discussed. The main novelty in using these techniques lies in calibrating a general equilibrium model to two observations and generating parameter values which allow the model to reflect the influences of various exogenous changes which jointly contribute to the observed outcome being decomposed. Relative to existing

---

[10] Compared to the use of calibration restriction 3, the effects of factor-biased technical change under inexact calibration are moderated because under the former the impact of Hicks-neutral technical change (which the latter now implicitly incorporates) is negative. Compared to the use of calibration restriction 1, however, factor-biased technical change has a larger impact on inequality because under the former the change in β_{it} (now implicitly incorporated in the latter) is inequality-increasing.

trade and wages literature, a full structural-form general equilibrium model rather than an estimated reduced form is used.

The calibrations involved can be performed in ways that are either exact or inexact. These procedures allow direct estimation of the main sources of increased wage inequality discussed in the recent literature (increased trade and factor-biased technical change), as well as of other technology-related factors (including sector-biased technical change) and changes in factor endowments.

Results suggest that between 1979 and 1995 the role of factor-biased technological change in generating increased wage inequality in the U.K. has been even larger than suggested by other literature. Also, changes in factor endowments have played a major role in partially offsetting pressures for increased wage inequality from trade and factor-biased technological change – a feature that has received less attention in the existing literature. Estimates of the contribution of increased trade to U.K. wage inequality from this work are small, and consistent with the thrust of earlier literature for other economies.

In other areas, such as regionalism, little firm evidence is available in the literature on what the effects of trade agreements have actually been, or what factors cause a result from higher trade volumes, and so ex post decomposition analysis seems likely to be a more major part of the empirical trade (and other) modelling literature in the years ahead. This paper seeks to contribute to this work by stressing ex post analysis of data using equilibrium modelling, rather than the more usual ex ante policy evaluation.

REFERENCES

L. Abrego and J. Whalley (2000), "The Choice of Structural Model in Trade-Wages Decompositions," *Review of International Economics* 9 (3): 462–77.

—— (2001), "Decomposing Wage Inequality Change Using General Equilibrium Models," working paper, Centre for the Study of Globalization, University of Warwick.

B. Anderton and P. Brenton (1998), "The Dollar, Trade, Technology and Wage Inequality in the USA," mimeo, CEPS, Brussels.

R. E. Baldwin and G. G. Cain (1997), "Shifts in US Relative Wages: The Role of Trade, Technology and Factor Endowments," NBER Working Paper No. 5934.

E. Berman, J. Bound, and Z. Griliches (1994), "Changes in the Demand for Skilled Labour within US Manufacturing: Evidence from Annual Survey of Manufactures," *Quarterly Journal of Economics* 109: 367–98.

J. Bound and G. Johnson (1992), "Changes in the Structure of Wages in the 1980's: An Evaluation of Alternative Explanations," *American Economic Review* 82: 371–92.

G. Burtless (1995), "International Trade and the Rise in Earnings Inequality," *Journal of Economic Literature* 33: 800–16.

D. Card (1998), "Falling Union Membership and Rising Wage Inequality: What's the Connection?" NBER Working Paper No. 6520.

C. Dawkins, T. N. Srinivasan, and J. Whalley (2000), "Calibration," in E. C. Leamer and J. Heckman (Eds.), *Handbook of Econometrics*. Amsterdam: North-Holland, pp. 3653–3703.

S. Devarajan and H. Sierra (1994), "Growth Without Adjustment: Thailand, 1973–82," in Pradeep K. Meetra (Ed.), *Adjustment in Oil-Importing Developing Countries: A Comparative Economic Analysis*. Cambridge: Cambridge University Press.

A. K. Dixit and J. E. Stiglitz (1977), "Monopolistic Competition and Optimum Product Diversity," *American Economic Review* 67 (3): 297–308.

R. Feenstra and G. Hanson (1996), "Globalization, Outsourcing and Wage Inequality,"*American Economic Review* 86: 240–45.

(1999), "The Impact of Outsourcing and High-Technology Capital on Wages: Estimates for the United States, 1979–90," *Quarterly Journal of Economics* 113: 907–40.

R. Fogel, (1964), *Railways and American Economic Growth*. Baltimore: John Hopkins Press.

M. Fortin and L. Thomas (1997), "Institutional Changes and Rising Wage Inequality," *Journal of Economic Perspectives* 11: 75–96.

F. Francois and D. Nelson (1998), "Trade, Technology and Wages: General Equilibrium Mechanics," *Economic Journal* 108: 1483–99.

F. Francois and K. Reinert (1997), *Applied Methods for Trade Policy Analysis: A Handbook*. Cambridge New York/Melbourne: Cambridge University Press, pp. xv, 560.

J. F. Francois and C. R. Shiells (1994), *Modeling Trade Policy: Applied General Equilibrium Assessments of North American Free Trade*. Cambridge: Cambridge University Press.

P. Gottschalk and T. Smeeding (1997), "Cross National Comparisons of Earnings and Income Inequality," *Journal of Economic Literature* 35: 633–87.

D. Hamermesh (1993), *Labor Demand*. Princeton: Princeton University Press.

L. Hansen and J. Heckman (1996), "The Empirical Foundations of Calibration," *Journal of Economic Perspectives* 10 (1): 87–104.

J. Harrigan and R. Balaban (1999), "US Wages in General Equilibrium: The Effects of Prices, Technology, and Factor Supplies, 1963–1991," NBER Working Paper No. 6981.

R. Harris (1984), "Applied General Equilibrium Analysis of Small Open Economies with Scale Economies and Imperfect Competition," *American Economic Review* 74 (5): 1016–32.

J. Haskel and M. Slaughter (1998), "Does the Sector Bias of Skilled-Biased Technical Change Explains Changing Wage Inequality?" NBER Working Paper No. 6565.

(1999), "Trade Technology and UK Wage Inequality," NBER Working Paper No. 6978.

H. G. Johnson (1966), "Factor Market Distortions and the Shape of the Transformation Frontier," *Econometrica* 34: 686–98.

R. W. Jones (1971), "A Three-Factor Model in Theory, Trade and History," in J. N. Bhagwati, R. A. Mundell, and J. Vanek (Eds.), *Trade Balance of Payments and Growth: Essays in Honor of Charles P. Kindleberger*. Amsterdam: North-Holland.

P. Krugman (2000), "Technology, Trade and Factor Prices," *Journal of International Economics* 50: 51–71.

F. E. Kydland and E. C. Prescott (1982), "Time to Build and Aggregate Fluctuations," *Econometrica* 50 (6): 1345–70.

E. Leamer (1998), "In Search of Stolper–Samuelson Linkages Between International Trade and Lower Wages," in S. M. Collins (Ed.), *Imports, Exports, and the American Worker*. Washington, DC: Brookings Institution.

(2000), "What's the Use of Factor Contents?" *Journal of International Economics* 50: 17–49.

S. Machin and J. van Reenen (1998), "Technology and Changes in Skill Structure: Evidence from Seven OECD Countries," *Quarterly Journal of Economics* 113: 1215–44.

A. Mansur and J. Whalley (1984), "Numerical Specification of Applied General Equilibrium Models: Estimation, Calibration, and Data," in Herbert E. Scarf and John B. Shoven (Eds.), *Applied General Equilibrium Analysis*. Cambridge/New York/Sydney: Cambridge University Press, pp. 69–127.

W. Martin and A. Winters (1996) , *The Uruguay Round and the Developing Countries*. Cambridge: Cambridge University Press.

K. Murphy and F. Welch (1989), "Wage Premiums for College Graduates: Recent Growth and Possible Explanations," *Educational Researcher* 18: 17–26.

M. Mussa (1974), "Tariffs and the Distribution of Income: The Importance of Factor Specificity, Substitutability, and Intensity in the Short and Long Run," *Journal of Political Economy* 82: 1191–1204.

D. Neven and C. Wyplosz (1999), "Relative Prices, Trade and Restructuring in European Industry," in *Trade and Wages in Europe: Much Ado about Nothing*? Oxford: Oxford University Press, pp. 33–59.

OECD (1995), *The OECD Input–Output Database*. OECD: Paris.

   (1997), "Trade, Earnings and Employment: Assessing the Impact of Trade with Emerging Economies on OECD Labour Markets," in OECD, *Employment Outlook, June 1997*, Paris: OECD.

Office for National Statistics (1981–82), *Employment Gazette* (various issues). London: ONS.

   (1996), *Labour Market Trends* (May issue). London: ONS.

   (1997a), *United Kingdom National Accounts*. London: ONS.

   (1997b), *Input–Output Balances for the UK*. London: ONS.

S. Robinson and K. Thierfelder (1996), "The Trade–Wage Debate in a Model with Nontrated Goods: Making Room for Labor Economists in Trade Theory," TMD Discussion Paper No. 9. Washington, DC: IFPRI.

J. Sachs and H. Shatz (1994), "Trade and Jobs in US Manufacturing," *Brookings Papers of Economic Activity* 0: 1–69.

P. A. Samuelson (1971), "Ohlin Was Right," *Swedish Journal of Economics* 73: 365–84.

J. Shoven and J. Whalley (1984), "Applied General Equilibrium Models of Taxation and International Trade: An Introduction and Survey," *Journal of Economic Literature* 22 (3): 1007–51.

   (1992), *Applying General Equilibrium*. Cambridge: Cambridge University Press.

M. Slaughter (1999), "Globalization and Wages: A Tale of Two Perspectives," *World Economy* 22: 609–29.

R. Solow (1957), "Technical Change and the Aggregate Production Function," *Review of Economics and Statistics* 39: 312–20.

M. Watson (1994), "Measures of Fit for Calibrated Models," *Journal of Political Economy* 101 (6): 1011–41.

J. Whalley (1985), *Trade Liberalization among Major World Trading Areas*. Cambridge, MA: MIT Press.

   (2000), "What Can the Developing Countries Infer from the Uruguay Round Models for Future Negotiations," UNCTAD Discussion Paper No. 4.

A. Wood (1994), *North–South Trade, Employment and Inequality*. Oxford: Clarendon Press.

15 The Influence of Computable General Equilibrium Models on Policy

Shantayanan Devarajan and Sherman Robinson

ABSTRACT: This paper reviews experience with the use of computable or applied general equilibrium (CGE or AGE) models to affect public policy. The range of issues on which CGE models have had an influence is quite wide, and includes structural adjustment policies, international trade, public finance, agriculture, income distribution, and energy and environmental policy. In the cases where CGE models have enlightened the policy debate, the reasons have to do with one or more of the following: (i) consistency between results from CGE models and other types of analysis (for instance, in the debate on NAFTA); (ii) the fact that the CGE models captured particular features of the economy, such as some structural rigidities and institutional constraints, that rules of thumb, based on simpler analysis, failed to capture; or (iii) the fact that CGE models provided a consistent framework to assess linkages and trade-offs among different policy packages. We also consider misuses of CGE models in policy debates. Most of these stem from (i) pushing the model beyond its domain of applicability; (ii) violating the principle of Occam's razor – use of the simplest model suited to the task; (iii) the "black box syndrome" – results whose link with the policy change is opaque. In assessing the use of models in policy, it is important to distinguish between stylized and applied models. Both have been used in policy debates, but there are important differences in their uses, particularly in their domain of applicability. Stylized models tend to be small and narrowly focused, and emphasize a particular causal chain or policy. Applied models are usually larger, seek to capture important institutional characteristics of the economy being modeled, and encompass a wider spectrum of issues, but they are vulnerable to the black-box syndrome and violation of Occam's razor. Complementary use of stylized and applied CGE models has enhanced the effectiveness of both in policy debates.

15.1. INTRODUCTION

In the four decades since Johansen's (1960) model of Norway, applied or computable general equilibrium models (AGE or CGE) have grown in importance, as

Revised version of a paper presented at a conference on "Frontiers in Applied General Equilibrium Modeling" sponsored by the Cowles Foundation and held at Yale University, New Haven, CT, April 5-6, 2002. We wish to thank Anne Krueger, Sam Morley, Jim Ryan, and T. N. Srinivasan for helpful comments on earlier drafts.

a tool of both research and policy analysis.[1] Initially confined to universities and research institutions, CGE models today are routinely used by governments in policy formulation and debate. Modeling capacity, either in government agencies or in policy research institutes, can be found in at least twenty countries and in the major multilateral agencies.[2] This paper selectively reviews experience in the use of CGE models to affect public policy.[3] The range of issues on which CGE models have had an influence is quite wide, and includes international trade, public finance, agriculture, structural adjustment policies, and income distribution. We start by describing properties that policy models need to have in order to be useful in policy formulation and debate. We then review experience with CGE models in policy debates in several areas.

In reviewing the experience, we find it useful to distinguish between stylized and applied CGE models.[4] Stylized models stay as close to the underlying analytic model as possible in order to isolate the empirical importance of a linkage that theory identifies as potentially important. Stylized models are not meant to be "realistic" because they are designed to focus on particular causal mechanisms, often ignoring other effects that might be important empirically. Applied models tend to be larger, seek to incorporate more descriptive detail on the economy being modeled, and encompass a wider spectrum of issues. Both stylized and applied models have been used in policy debates, but there are important differences in their uses. Stylized models tend to be narrowly focused, but their simplicity can be a virtue in explaining results to policymakers. When pushed beyond their domain of applicability, however, they can be misused. Although applied models, by design, incorporate more institutional and structural detail, their additional complexity may lead to problems in identifying the main causal mechanisms at work – the "black box syndrome" that critics argue is a common problem with simulation models. In short, to be useful for policy and avoid some of the pitfalls, modelers would do well to be guided by their own version of Occam's razor: "Use the simplest model adequate to the task at hand."

In this review, we start by laying out desirable features for policy models if they are to be used effectively in policy debates. We then discuss uses of CGE models in policy debates in a number of areas: trade policy, public finance, structural adjustment, and income distribution.

---

[1] In this paper, we use CGE and AGE as synonyms.

[2] We made an informal inquiry and found government CGE modeling capability in the United States, Denmark, Norway, the Netherlands, France, Sweden, Switzerland, Australia, Argentina, Brazil, India, Bangladesh, Thailand, Indonesia, China, Vietnam, South Africa, and Mozambique. Many other countries regularly use CGE models in policy analysis, relying on consultants and nongovernmental research institutions.

[3] The term "selectively" is crucial here. Our intent is not to survey the numerous applications of CGE models to policy. Rather, we choose some selected examples to illustrate the lessons learned from this wide-ranging experience.

[4] See Robinson (1989).

15.2. DESIDERATA FOR POLICY MODELS

To be useful for policy analysis, economic models should have a number of features:

1. Policy relevance. The models should link values of policy variables to economic outcomes that are of interest to policy makers and useful in policy debates.
2. Transparency. The links between policy variables and outcomes should be easy to trace and explain.
3. Timeliness. Policy models must be based on relevant data, which implies that they must be implemented with recent data if they are to be used in ongoing policy debates.
4. Validation and estimation. Estimated model parameters and model behavior need to be validated for the "domain of application" of the model. The model must be determined to achieve accurate results for the domain of potential policy choices under consideration in the policy debate – validation involves notions of both goodness of fit and robustness.
5. Diversity of approaches. Validating results from policy models is greatly strengthened by analysis using a variety of models and at different levels of aggregation. Such diversity tests the robustness of the results and the importance of assumptions made in the various approaches.

15.2.1. Model Design

The first two criteria strongly support using models based on micro foundations, that is, structural models explicitly incorporating agents that interact across markets. The model parameters are "deep," describing technology, tastes, and market institutions. Macro-econometric models typically do not incorporate explicit links between policy variables and economic outcomes. Or, if they do, the structure of such models often makes it difficult, if not impossible, to identify the underlying micro behavior, and hence to trace out the links between policy variables and outcomes.

Policy relevance requires modelers to address issues of interest in the policy debate. An academic perspective might lead to a focus on indicators of aggregate welfare, such as equivalent or compensating variation. Policy debates, however, are rarely concerned with such aggregate measures and tend, instead, to focus on identifying the winners and losers from proposed policy changes. Political reality, not to mention good welfare economics, requires us to identify who is affected by policy changes in order to determine if compensation schemes to generate ex post Pareto improvements are feasible and, if not, to understand the trade-offs between distributional and aggregate impacts. For policy analysis, tracing out the impact of shocks on the structure of production, trade, and employment is at least as important as generating aggregate welfare measures – arguing again for micro-based models that identify consumers and producers.

The issue of transparency argues for the use of stylized models, because it is relatively easy to describe the results and the causal chains involved. Policy relevance, however, often requires more sectoral and institutional detail, which mandates the use of applied models that are larger and more complex. We present some examples of the policy use of stylized versus applied CGE models below, but the distinction is more general – for example, between Samuelson's stylized overlapping generations model and Auerbach and Kotlikoff's applied generational accounting framework.[5]

In applying Occam's razor, it is also important to note that a CGE model provides the policy analyst with a simulation laboratory that supports individual, controlled experiments. Any empirical result from an applied model can be explained in terms of parameters, structural data, and behavioral specification. A CGE model can, and often does, generate empirical surprises. In policy analysis, one important lesson is that it is crucial to decompose any policy results through the use of controlled experiments to determine the empirically important causal chains at work.

Timeliness is very important for ongoing debates, but historical analysis may also be useful. One can use a policy model to analyze the impact of past policy choices in order to draw lessons for current debates. The problem is that it is then necessary to show how the historical analysis is applicable to the current debate, which requires showing both that the historical structural model is relevant and that the domain of applicability of the past policy changes is similar enough to offer valid lessons for current policy. Usually, credibility in policy debates requires up-to-date models and data.

15.2.2. Estimation and Validation

For all models, the domain of applicability must be contained within the historical range of the data used to estimate the model. When the historical data used for estimation do not encompass the shock or policy change under consideration, then it is crucial to use a model whose parameters are invariant to these shocks. Models whose parameters describe underlying tastes and technology are likely to be robust for analyzing out-of-sample shocks.

An example can make this discussion more concrete. During the various oil crises of the 1970s, a number of large macroeconometric models were used to analyze the impact on the U.S. economy of large changes in oil prices. These models were estimated over past periods in which oil prices were relatively stable, and turned out not to capture in their (largely reduced-form) specification the relevant links between oil prices and economic performance. Although these models included oil prices, their domain of applicability was too limited to capture the impact of large changes in world oil prices. To capture these links, new structural models were

---

[5]   Auerbach, Kotlikoff, and Leibfritz (1999).

developed that explicitly incorporated behavior of producers and consumers, and whose parameters described technology and tastes. These models were successfully used to analyze the impact of higher oil prices on the economy. A number of CGE models were developed for this purpose.

In model validation, there is a trade-off between using a micro-based structural model, which requires estimation of a large number of parameters, and a macro-econometric model with less explicit micro foundations and, usually, far fewer parameters. Micro-based models such as CGE models are based on data such as input–output tables that are available only for a few periods, with long gaps. Macro-econometric models are usually much sparser in their parameter requirements, and can be estimated with readily available time-series data. On the one hand, structural models such as CGE models use data from a single year (a social accounting matrix or SAM) to estimate input–output coefficients and expenditure shares, and draw on other partial studies for estimates of important behavioral parameters such as elasticities that determine supply and demand behavior of economic actors. On the other hand, many macro-econometric models are so limited in their domains of applicability as to be virtually useless in policy analysis. The experience of the past twenty years seems to demonstrate that it is better to have a good structural model capturing the relevant behavior of economic actors and their links across markets, even if the parameters are imperfectly estimated, because the domain of applicability of such models makes them far more useful for policy analysis.

Furthermore, recent advances in methods of econometric parameter estimation should reduce the trade-offs. The estimation of a micro-based CGE model incorporates a great deal of knowledge from economic theory regarding the values of the structural parameters. For example, both theory and econometric work provide prior information on the likely range of values of various structural elasticity parameters in production and demand. At the other extreme, in reduced-form VAR models, for example, there is little if any prior information even regarding the signs of various parameters available for estimation. The problem is to make effective use of this prior information about the parameters of a structural model in estimation procedures. New methods of "maximum-entropy econometrics" are providing a framework for econometric estimation that supports use of information in many forms, and from many sources, in estimating structural parameters. The approach supports the use of theoretical information about the parameters of structural models, and the use of scattered data from a variety of sources in a unified estimation framework. Recently, these new methods have been used to estimate SAMs for a large number of countries and to estimate crucial elasticity parameters in a single-country model.[6]

---

[6] See, for example, Golan, Judge, and Robinson (1994); Robinson, Cattaneo, and El-Said (2001); and Arndt, Robinson, and Tarp (2002). The general approach is described by Golan, Judge, and Miller (1996).

For CGE models, there are essentially two kinds of parameters that need to be estimated:

1. Share parameters such as intermediate input costs, consumer expenditure shares, average savings rates, import and export shares, government expenditure shares, and average tax rates. These share parameters can be estimated from a recent SAM under the assumption that the base year represented by the SAM is an equilibrium solution of the CGE model.
2. Elasticity parameters describing the curvature of various structural functions (e.g., production functions, utility functions, import demand functions, and export supply functions). These cannot be estimated from a single SAM, but require additional data.

The use of a SAM, coupled with the assumption that the base data represent an equilibrium solution of the model, to estimate share parameters has been described as "benchmark estimation" and has been widely used in CGE models.[7] The assumption of base-year equilibrium is very powerful and imposes a great deal of prior information on parameter estimation. The estimation of elasticities, however, is more difficult. Knowledge of a base-year SAM and the assumption that the base is an equilibrium do not provide any information about the values of elasticities. Additional information and data are required for estimation of these parameters.

Model validation requires both estimation of model parameters and testing of the ability of the model to accurately trace out the impact of policy changes. Validation is necessarily linked to the issues to be analyzed, and should provide an indication of the domain of applicability of the model. One way to validate a policy model is to test it with historical data relevant to its intended domain of applicability. How well does the model explain past events? This sort of heuristic validation can be done with incomplete historical data. The model can be used in simulation mode to map out the model's response function for relevant shocks. These can be compared to the stylized facts for historical experience, or even from experience of comparable countries.

15.2.3. Effective Use of Policy Models

The effectiveness of any one policy model is greatly enhanced by the use of a diversity of model approaches in analyzing a particular issue. For example, a number of trade-focused CGE models were used to analyze the impact of the North American Free Trade Agreement (NAFTA) on U.S. and Mexican agriculture. One common result was that trade liberalization would increase Mexican exports of fruits and vegetables to U.S. markets. These results were obtained under a number of simplifying

---

[7] See Mansur and Whalley (1984). The benchmark approach was used in the earliest CGE models. See, for example, Johansen (1960) and Dixon et al. (1982), who use a solution approach that requires that the model start from an equilibrium data base.

assumptions in the CGE models, such as the use of simple neoclassical production functions (e.g., CES functions) for agriculture; no consideration of marketing costs; no capacity constraints on the rural transportation infrastructure in either country; and no consideration of seasonality. Although the results were suggestive, they became much more persuasive when detailed commodity studies of potential increased production and distribution of fruits and vegetables indicated that such increases were feasible. Also, because the CGE studies were comparative-static, detailed commodity analysis provided indications of how long it would take for the changed incentives from NAFTA to generate supply and demand responses in particular markets.

Policy models are often used to analyze the impact of existing policies and to aid in the design of better or even "optimal" policies. In policy debates, an effective approach is to use the CGE model in simulation mode and do controlled experiments that map out "policy response" relationships. The idea is to look for empirically important effects and indirect general equilibrium links. There is often a lot of synergy between policies, and the model can be used to explore mixes of policies in various second-best environments. From the perspective of the policy maker, the model provides a simulation laboratory – acting like the "real world" for its domain of applicability. The policy maker need not know or understand in detail how the simulation laboratory works – no more than a pilot needs to understand the insides of a flight simulator. Both need only be confident that the simulator works well for the situations they will likely face.

When the results from a CGE model used for policy analysis are explained, the model can effectively disappear. The CGE model produces all price and quantity data resulting from policy experiments. The analyst should be able to explain the causal chains, determining the results by standard, usually simple, economics. If results arise from complex interactions, they can be sorted out by controlled simulation experiments designed to decompose the various effects at work – although "decomposition" can often be done in a variety of ways, complicating interpretation. The use of an explicit model can significantly elevate the policy debate, providing a structure for discussing the validity of results in terms of the strengths of the various forces at work and the links between policy choices and outcomes.

15.3. TRADE POLICY

We turn now to the first of several areas where CGE models have been used to affect policy. It is perhaps fitting to start with trade policy. Most of the effects surrounding trade policy, such as those captured in the Stolper–Samuelson Theorem, are general-equilibrium effects. Not surprisingly, therefore, CGE models have been used extensively to analyze, and in some cases influence, trade policy. The models themselves have been surveyed elsewhere.[8] Rather than review the experience with

---

[8]   See de Melo (1988) and Francois and Shiells (1994a).

all the models applied to policy, we concentrate on a particular episode, namely, the negotiation of the North American Free Trade Agreement in the early 1990s. The extensive use of CGE models in this debate illustrates many of the uses (and some abuses) of this class of models to inform policy.

15.3.1. NAFTA

In 1990, the Mexican government formally asked the U.S. government to negotiate a free trade agreement (FTA) between the two countries. Since the U.S. had recently completed such an agreement with Canada, the negotiations quickly involved all three countries and resulted, in late 1993, in Congressional approval of the North American Free Trade Agreement (NAFTA). Starting with the request to Congress by the first Bush Administration for "fast track" authority to negotiate NAFTA through to its final approval during the Clinton Administration, CGE models were widely and effectively used to inform the policy debate. The models were used both in the negotiating process and in the political debate regarding approval of the final deal.

A number of questions were raised early in the debate, and continued to be the focus of analysis throughout the negotiations:

(1) What would be the benefits and costs to the three countries if NAFTA were implemented? While there was some mild interest in whether the U.S., Canada, and Mexico would gain in terms of some aggregate measures of welfare, most of the concern and policy debate centered on identifying winners and losers.
(2) What would be the impact on labor in the U.S., in terms of both employment and wages? The labor unions argued that there would be, in the words of Ross Perot, a "giant sucking sound" of jobs moving to Mexico as employers took advantage of cheap Mexican labor, resulting in loss of jobs and lower wages in the U.S.[9] Proponents argued that increased U.S. trade in North America would help U.S. exports, resulting in increased employment in relatively high-wage jobs in exporting sectors.
(3) What would be the impact of NAFTA on migration between Mexico and the U.S.? Migration was a contentious issue well before NAFTA was proposed, but the NAFTA debate gave it a new focus, even though NAFTA, as proposed and as finally passed, did not include any provisions concerning migration.[10]
(4) What would be the impact at the sectoral level in the three countries? A few sectors were particularly sensitive and the focus of much debate: agriculture, autos, and textiles. However, in the negotiations and in the political debate in the U.S. Congress, there was an enormous amount of policy attention to detailed analysis of sectoral and commodity impacts.

---

[9] See Perot and Choate (1993).
[10] With the exception of some guarantees that businessmen would be able to travel without restrictions across the three countries.

(5) What would be the impact of NAFTA on the U.S. and Mexican trade balances, particularly the bilateral balance between Mexico and the U.S.? Coupled with this was a concern about the impact of the agreement on flows of private financial capital to Mexico. The labor unions worried about capital flight from the U.S. to Mexico. The financial community wanted more open financial markets. Only a few economists were concerned about the overvaluation of the Mexican peso and whether capital inflows into Mexico were sustainable.[11]

15.3.2. CGE Models in the NAFTA Debate

At the time NAFTA was proposed, a great deal of work was already under way to analyze the impact of the ongoing Uruguay Round of GATT negotiations, which had started in 1987. A number of single-country and multicountry CGE models had been developed to analyze various reform scenarios in the Uruguay Round, and researchers quickly adapted these models to look at the potential effects of NAFTA. There were also many detailed industry and sectoral studies underway, which could be, and were, adapted to look at NAFTA. The result was that, from the beginning and throughout the negotiations, high-quality economic analysis was available on a timely basis to inform the debate.

Most of the analysis in the U.S. was either performed by or done in close collaboration with government agencies, particularly the Economic Research Service of the U.S. Department of Agriculture (ERS/USDA), the International Trade Commission (ITC), the Department of Labor, the Department of Commerce, and the Congressional Budget Office (CBO). All these agencies either produced or used CGE models, as well as detailed partial-equilibrium studies. As Francois and Shiells (1994a) put it (p. 5):

For the first time in the United States, the AGE trade policy-modeling community found itself in the limelight, providing direct input for the government's trade policy process.... Ambassador Hills employed these studies in her frequent statements in favor of the agreement before the Congress and the public.

Policy makers in both Mexico and Canada also had access to CGE models and used them to analyze the impact of NAFTA on their countries. In the case of Mexico, the lead minister responsible for the negotiations, the Secretary of Commerce and Development, was Jaime Serra-Puche, who had done his Ph.D. thesis on a CGE model of Mexico. Various other government officials in Mexico, including officials in the important Ministries of Agriculture and Foreign Affairs, were familiar with these models and effective consumers of the work.

Equally important to the policy debate were the impartial surveys of the economic work, which summarized the areas of agreement and controversy across the various studies. Influential and timely surveys were done by the Brookings

---

[11] See, for example, Manchester and McKibbin (1995) and U.S. Congressional Budget Office (1993).

Institution, the ITC, the CBO, the Congressional Research Service (CRS), the General Accounting Office (GAO), and the Department of Labor.[12] These surveys were influential in the policy debate because they were correctly seen as impartial evaluations of the results of economic analysis of NAFTA, including a lot of work with CGE models. These reviews were highly critical of some of the methodologies used to evaluate NAFTA (e.g., the use of simple macro trade multipliers), and provided balanced, generally approving, evaluations of the CGE work and the various detailed micro studies. The result was that the summaries, especially the first three, helped define the boundaries of "good" analysis, and work outside of this mainstream was discounted in the policy debate.

The surveys also found a great deal of agreement among the various studies, which was surprising considering the wide variety of models and methodologies, at various levels of aggregation, that were employed. The CBO study summarized the results (p. xi):

A thorough review of the myriad changes brought about by NAFTA, and of their interactions, leads to the single resounding conclusion that the net effect on the U.S. economy would be positive and very small. The biggest changes introduced by NAFTA would be those related to Mexico. . . .

These evaluations appear to have been correct, as Burfisher, Robinson, and Thierfelder (2001), in their survey of studies of the actual impact of NAFTA on the U.S. since it was passed, conclude (p. 141):

. . . economists can do a reasonably good job of projecting the gains from trade liberalization agreements. The mainstream forecasts during the NAFTA debate were basically correct: NAFTA has had relatively small positive effects on the U.S. economy and relatively large positive effects on Mexico.

There was also a broad consensus among the studies relying on CGE models, surveyed by Brown (1992) and the ITC (1992) during the debate. Francois and Shiells (1994a) conclude (p. 34):

The main conclusions that can be drawn from the large, multisector AGE models of NAFTA are as follows. First, models that incorporate some form of imperfect competition obtain larger impact effects than models that assume perfect competition. . . . Second, nontariff barriers (NTBs) are potentially as important as tariff barriers . . . Third, international capital mobility induced by NAFTA is potentially more important than trade liberalization contained in NAFTA, especially for Mexico. . . . Finally, real wages in Canada and the United States are expected to rise as a result of NAFTA, in sharp contrast to what would be expected based on the Stolper–Samuelson theorem.

---

[12]   See Lustig, Bosworth, and Lawrence (1992); U.S. International Trade Commission (1992); U.S. Congressional Budget Office (1993); and U.S. Department of Labor (1993). Francois and Shiells (1994b) brought together some of the important CGE work, based largely on the ITC survey.

Burfisher et al. (2001) also surveyed the prospective CGE studies of NAFTA that addressed the issue of whether NAFTA, as a preferential trade agreement, would be net trade-creating or net trade-diverting (p. 140):

The studies of NAFTA, whether in a single or multicountry context, all concluded that NAFTA was net trade creating and would benefit all three countries, with the largest relative gains for Mexico.

They also concluded that the prospective studies were correct. Post-NAFTA studies, at various levels of aggregation, have concluded that NAFTA has been net trade creating, and that actual trade diversion was much smaller than had been feared during the NAFTA debate.

These results, and the consistency of results across many studies, contributed to raising the level of the NAFTA debate, essentially preventing studies based on weak analysis from ever dominating the discussion. For example, the book by Perot and Choate (1993), arguing that NAFTA would devastate the U.S. labor market, was quickly discredited for its weak analytic foundation and baseless conclusions.

The open discussion of the various models also helped increase their credibility. For example, the CGE model by Roland-Holst, Reinert, and Shiells (1994), which was developed at the ITC, generated estimates of the gains from NAFTA that were larger than those from any other static model. Surveys of the CGE work by Brown (1992) and Francois and Shiells (1994a) sorted out why: the model included imperfect competition, economies of scale, large non-tariff barriers, and aggregate employment effects.[13] These outlier results were able to be put in perspective, and were somewhat discounted in the debate.

While the eventual role of computable general equilibrium models was certainly beneficial to the NAFTA debate, there are also lessons concerning how *not* to use CGE models in policy debates.[14] During the early debate concerning whether Congress should grant the Bush Administration fast-track negotiating authority for NAFTA, the ITC published a study in early 1991 that drew on studies of particular industries and also presented results from a highly stylized CGE model, which was developed internally by an ITC staff member. This toy empirical model was designed to explore Stolper–Samuelson effects within a neoclassical two-country trade model, with a large country trading with a small one. Not surprisingly, the model found that the Stolper–Samuelson theorem is correct: with increasing trade, the real wage went up in the small developing country and went down a tiny bit in the large developed country. The ITC did not publish the model and reported only the qualitative result that NAFTA might lead to a "slight" fall in the average wage of unskilled labor in the U.S. The AFL–CIO immediately put out a press release saying that an official U.S. government study showed that NAFTA would cause wages of unskilled labor in the U.S. to fall. The ITC did not define "unskilled labor," so the

---

[13] The version of the model that Brown (1992) surveyed was described in a 1992 working paper.
[14] Francois and Shiells (1994a, p. 5) tell part of this story. See also Hinojosa and Robinson (1992).

AFL-CIO said that it must amount to 60% of the labor force, and that NAFTA was therefore a very bad idea.

For reasons that remain unclear, the initial response of the ITC was to state that it would not release the CGE model, or even describe it in detail – although they eventually released the estimates of the change in the wage, which ranged from −0.002 percent to +0.01 percent! The next day, the AFL–CIO issued a press release stating that a *secret* U.S. government study showed that 60% of workers in the U.S. would be hurt by NAFTA. Fortunately for the reputation of CGE models, results from a series of larger, more realistic, applied models appeared quickly and provided a far better, open, and transparent framework for discussion and debate.[15]

This experience provides a couple of lessons. First, do not use a stylized model when a more realistic, applied model is called for. The issues around employment and wages were obviously controversial and contentious, and any adequate analysis would obviously require serious attention to the modeling of the labor markets. Second, policy models are useful only if they can provide a framework for discussion and debate, which requires that they be publicly available and that their results be "explainable." A "secret" model is worse than useless – it raises suspicions, diverts discussion into fruitless speculation, and generates heat but no light. Fortunately, the ITC redeemed itself by later sponsoring a public symposium on NAFTA models and by doing an excellent job of evaluating and synthesizing the results.

15.3.3. Agriculture, Migration, and Labor Markets

The analysis of the impact of NAFTA on labor markets ranged from micro industry studies to input–output multiplier studies, CGE models, and Keynesian macro trade multiplier models.[16] The macro multiplier models were very influential, especially early in the debate, but were heavily criticized on methodological grounds – they seem to be completely inappropriate for evaluating the long-run impacts of trade liberalization.[17] While the multiplier models were never really fully discredited during the debate, the combination of work by CGE models and sector studies gradually dominated the discussion of the impact of NAFTA on labor, focusing on the extent of labor displacement. The CBO (1993) surveyed the available studies and concluded that the aggregate job losses related to NAFTA would be very small

---

[15] In particular, early CGE models by KPMG Peat Marwick (1991) and Hinojosa-Ojeda and Robinson (1992) found potential gains for labor in the United States. Many other applied models followed.

[16] This work was surveyed by Hinojosa-Ojeda and Robinson (1992), the CBO (1993), and the U.S. Department of Labor (1992).

[17] Hinojosa-Ojeda and Robinson (1992) described them as "striking in their lack of theoretical underpinnings." See also Burfisher et al. (2001), who criticize the use of mercantilist models in evaluating the effects of trade liberalization.

relative to normal labor turnover in the U.S. economy, but also warned (p. xi), "That the net effects for the United States are positive, of course, should not obscure the painful adjustments and losses some U.S. workers, firms, and communities will undoubtedly experience."

In response to the concerns about labor displacement, the Clinton Administration and the Congress agreed to legislation creating a NAFTA Trade Adjustment Assistance Program (NAFTA-TAA). Given the wide agreement among analysts, including those working with CGE models, that the aggregate employment effects of NAFTA would be small, the NAFTA-TAA program was designed as an open-ended commitment to provide assistance to all workers who could show that they had lost their jobs due to NAFTA. This open-ended commitment was quickly enacted by Congress. If the estimates of job displacement had been very large, this legislation would have been much more controversial. In the event, the predictions were correct and the number of applications for NAFTA-TAA assistance has been relatively small, although significant – just under a quarter of a million certified participants as of July 1999.[18]

Although NAFTA did not include any provisions regarding migration, concerns about Mexican–U.S. migration were a major issue in the NAFTA negotiations. This turned out to be an issue in which CGE models played a significant role. Before NAFTA was proposed, Mexico embarked on a program of major reform of its agricultural sector. These reforms were being designed and implemented as the NAFTA negotiations were in progress, and involved politically difficult policy choices by the Mexican government. The concern from the Mexican side was that too rapid reform would displace a large number of small farmers in the Mexican countryside, leading to a major increase in migration to the cities, and also to the United States. The reforms needed to be timed in such a way that the displaced workers could be absorbed in new, labor-intensive agricultural activities (e.g., high-value fruits and vegetables) and in a growing industrial labor market in the cities. NAFTA, which was to include liberalization of agricultural trade between the United States and Mexico, was a potential threat to the Mexican reform process, possibly forcing the pace of reform in Mexico too quickly.

A number of CGE models were developed to analyze the impact on Mexico of agricultural reform combined with trade reform, and the impact of these reforms on rural–urban migration within Mexico and migration to the United States.[19] Complemented by sector and commodity studies, these CGE models were especially influential. All were applied models in which the authors included institutional details of the labor markets in the two countries, trade policies, agricultural policies, and adequate disaggregation of the agricultural sectors to capture

---

[18]   See Burfisher et al. (2001, p. 129).
[19]   Especially important were models by Levy and van Wijnbergen (1994); Hinojosa-Ojeda and Robinson (1991); Burfisher, Robinson, and Thierfelder (1992, 1994, 1997); and Robinson et al. (1993). The model by Levy and van Wijnbergen was of Mexico alone; the others were all multicountry NAFTA models.

the effects of policy changes in both countries. A number of robust conclusions emerged:

- Opening Mexican corn markets to U.S. imports would be good for U.S. farmers. U.S. exports would increase significantly.
- Too rapidly increased corn imports into Mexico would greatly disrupt Mexican agriculture, especially poor corn farmers, and lead to large migration out of the rural sector, with significant increases in migration to the U.S.
- Opening up of U.S. agricultural markets to Mexican exports of high-value agriculture (e.g., fruits and vegetables) would help keep rural employment up in Mexico, ameliorating migration pressures. The effect, however, was not as large as the impact of increased corn imports, especially given the time needed to increase production of high-value crops.
- Given time and successful Mexican growth, the economy could absorb the rural workers displaced by agricultural reforms. In the long run, Mexican growth should reduce migration pressure.

From the U.S. perspective, trade reform represented a stark tradeoff between what would be good for Iowa corn farmers, and bad for California and Texas labor markets. From the Mexican perspective, the problems were how to design and implement the agricultural reforms, and how to prevent NAFTA from complicating the delicate process of reform that they had already initiated.[20]

In the event, the results of the various studies increased sensitivity on both sides of the negotiations. The final NAFTA agreement provided 15 years for implementation of the provisions regarding agriculture, which effectively meant that NAFTA did not constrain Mexican agricultural reform policies.[21] However, the fact that NAFTA set a schedule for trade liberalization in agriculture meant that farmers in Mexico could see that agricultural policy changes had to occur – the government's reform efforts became more credible.

15.4. PUBLIC FINANCE

Harberger's (1964) seminal paper on the distortionary effects of taxation, which used an extremely simple general-equilibrium model for their calculation, set the stage for CGE models' entry into the domain of public finance. And because public finance is the quintessential concern of policymakers, it would be natural for CGE models to enter into the policy arena through this field. Some of the earliest CGE models of the United States, for instance, were designed to examine questions of

---

[20] This process has continued since the passage of NAFTA, and there is a continuing program using CGE models to analyze the impact of changes in agricultural policies on NAFTA countries. See, for example, Burfisher, Robinson, and Thierfelder (2000).

[21] The letter of transmittal that the Bush administration sent to Congress with the completed NAFTA agreement actually stated that the reason they had agreed that agriculture should have a 15-year transition period was that studies had shown the dangers from too-rapid reform.

tax reform.[22] Subsequent versions of their model were installed in the U.S. Treasury to examine tax reform proposals. Similarly, large-scale CGE models have been used to evaluate public-finance issues in other developed countries, such as Canada and Australia (Powell and Snape, 1993). In retrospect, CGE models' influence on public finance policy has been significant, but limited. The reason for their limited application in policymaking is similar to that identified elsewhere in this paper: questions of tax reform or the evaluation of public projects are too important to be decided by one class of models. CGE models have helped shape the debate, and in some cases provided valuable support to the final policies adopted. But their influence has been greatest when model results have coincided with those obtained from other types of analysis, including stylized models, partial-equilibrium models, and microsimulation models.

The two specific areas where CGE models have been used are (i) estimates of the marginal cost of funds and (ii) analyzing tax reform.

15.4.1. Marginal Cost of Funds

At first glance, it would seem that the marginal cost of funds (MCF) was an ideal candidate for estimation by CGE models. The marginal welfare cost of raising taxes in one market depends not just on the distortion in that market, but on the distortions in other markets – something that can only be captured by multisectoral, economywide models. Yet a large number of estimates of the MCF are carried out without using CGE models. One reason is that there are a host of conceptual issues surrounding the calculation, and these are best illustrated using simple, stylized models.[23] For example, Harberger (1964) and Browning (1987) implicitly compare distortionary taxes with equal-revenue lump-sum taxes. Because income effects are equal by construction, their analysis involves only substitution effects and depends upon compensated demand and supply elasticities. Because these substitution effects are distortionary, the MCF is necessarily (weakly) greater than one. By contrast, in Stiglitz and Dasgupta (1971) and Atkinson and Stern (1974) taxes are raised to spend on a public project. Since the taxes generate income effects, their analyses depend upon uncompensated demand and supply elasticities. Because these income effects offset the (distortionary) substitution effects, the MCF is not necessarily greater than one.

Approaches to estimating the MCF empirically have followed one of two routes: formulae based on closed-form solutions to analytical models, and numerical simulations. Browning (1987) uses an analytical, partial-equilibrium formula to estimate the marginal excess burden (MEB) of labor taxes in the United States. Ahmad and Stern (1987) use a simplified analytical formula based on effective taxes (the amount by which government revenue would increase if there were a unit increase in final

---

[22]   Shoven and Whalley (1984).
[23]   These conceptual issues are surveyed in Fullerton (1991) and Ballard and Fullerton (1992).

TABLE 15.1. *Estimates of the marginal cost of funds (with CGE model-based estimates in boldface)*

Country	Tax type	Estimate	Source
United States	surcharge	1.17–1.56	**Ballard, Shoven, and Whalley (1985)**
	labor	1.21–1.24	Stuart (1984)
	labor	1.32–1.47	Browning (1987)
	labor	1.08–1.14	Ahmed and Croushore (1994)
Sweden	surcharge	0.67–4.51	**Hansson and Stuart (1985)**
New Zealand	labor	1.18	Diewert and Lawrence (1994)
India	excise	1.66–2.15	Ahmad and Stern (1987)
	sales	1.59–2.12	
	import	1.54–2.17	
Bangladesh, Cameroon, Indonesia	trade, sales	0.5–2.2	**Devarajan, Suthiwart-Narueput, and Thierfelder (2001)**

demand for a good) to calculate the welfare cost of various taxes in India. Ahmed and Croushore (1994) derive MCF estimates for the United States when public spending is nonseparable in utility. Snow and Warren (1996) derive a more general analytical formula to reconcile a variety of previous MCF estimates.

Among estimates that rely on simulation models, Stuart (1984) and Ballard, Shoven, and Whalley (1985) use computable general equilibrium (CGE) models of the United States to estimate the MCF. Hansson and Stuart (1985) use a CGE model of Sweden to estimate a MCF that is sensitive to both the type of tax and spending. As noted in Fullerton (1991) and Snow and Warren (1996), it should be emphasized that these studies encompass myriad approaches and definitions.

Table 15.1 provides estimates of the MCF from different studies. The range of estimates reported reflects the different costs of raising funds in applications of the particular tax instrument considered. Although a variety of tax instruments are considered, it is worth noting that the majority of the estimates, across countries and using different methods, fall within the range 1.2–2.2.

Despite the considerable care with which the MCF has been estimated, by CGE models or other methods, the use of these estimates in public policy has been varied. In some cases, such as Sweden, the estimates of a high MCF served to reinforce the notion that the tax system in the country was highly distorted. Here it was not the precise magnitude of the MCF estimate, but its broad range that influenced policy. In other cases, the large differences in the MCF across tax instruments opened policymakers' eyes to how distorted the current tax system was, and to potential areas for tax reform (Jorgenson and Yun, 1986; Ahmad and Stern, 1987). Almost never were these estimates used in the evaluation of public projects. But the reasons have more to do with the incentives for undertaking rigorous project analysis in lending institutions rather than with the techniques used to calculate the MCF in a country (Devarajan, Squire, and Suthiwart-Narueput, 1997).

15.4.2. Tax Reform

The use of CGE models in tax reform has followed a similar route. Simple, stylized models have given way to larger, complex models that capture a myriad of effects. Perhaps the most comprehensive effort in this area has been the work of Dale Jorgenson (1997). His co-authors and he demonstrated the overwhelmingly favorable effects of unifying the corporate and personal income tax in the United States, of replacing capital taxation with consumption taxation, and so forth. All of these could have been demonstrated with the use of a simple, stylized model. But Jorgenson and his collaborators showed, using a dynamic, multisectoral, multi-household model, that the welfare gains from undertaking such tax reforms could be substantial indeed. In the past decade, U.S. tax policy did move in this direction, albeit more slowly than the Jorgenson analysis would deem optimal.

A particular area of tax policy that has attracted several CGE applications has been energy and environmental taxation. Energy and environmental issues became hot, both literally and figuratively, in the mid-1980s, just as CGE models were beginning to come on stream as standard tools of policy analysis. Furthermore, especially in the case of energy, the general-equilibrium effects are significant, as almost every industry and household in the economy uses energy (Hudson and Jorgenson, 1974). Similarly, with environmental issues such as climate change, intertemporal aspects, increasingly captured by CGE models, were the reason for using CGE models (Nordhaus, 1990; Manne et al., 1995). The influence of these models on policy has mirrored experience with other public-finance applications. When, as in energy models, other tools exist for corroborating CGE model results, the impact on policy has been substantial. Model results have informed U.S. energy policy, from gasoline taxes to greenhouse gases. In Europe, they have influenced nuclear energy policy (Bergman, 1989) and carbon taxes (Nieuwkoop, personal communication). For example, in Sweden, an environmental CGE model has been used to develop the government's policy on climate change, including calculating the level of carbon taxation required to meet the Kyoto protocols (Nilsson, personal communication).

Even when other tools are not available, CGE models have been influential when they represent a second-generation of a well-established model. For example, in Australia, the ORANI model was first developed in 1977. By the late 1990s, its successor, ORANI/MONASH and derivative models have played an important role in public debates on motor vehicle tariffs, textile tariffs, overall protection and sales taxes (Dixon, 2001).

CGE models have been used in tax policy beyond simply providing welfare calculations. For instance, the introduction of a value-added tax, when (as in most cases) the VAT does not cover the entire economy, requires a CGE model to gauge the effects of the tax. Bovenberg's (1987) analysis of the difference between zero-rating and exemptions in a VAT regime, and its implications for tax incidence, had an effect on tax reforms in numerous countries, including Thailand (the country of Bovenberg's model). In the early 1990s, the Philippine government, despite a looming budget deficit, was reluctant to increase energy taxes because the poor spent a larger fraction of their income on energy than the rich. However, a CGE analysis by Devarajan and Hossain (1998) showed that the rich actually consumed more energy-intensive goods, rendering the overall incidence of energy taxes broadly neutral. In the event, the Philippine government raised energy taxes and proceeded to enjoy an unprecedented period of economic growth. Finally, without relying on a particular empirical estimate, CGE models have played a role in shaping the structure of taxes. Perhaps the most significant has been the debate about whether it is better to have uniform or variegated import tariffs. Although there may be plenty of reasons to adopt uniform import tariffs, including administrative simplicity and resistance to lobbying, welfare maximization is not one of them, as pointed out by several authors, using stylized models (Panagariya, 1994, Hatta, 1994), and confirmed by some CGE models (Dahl et al., 1994).

There are also examples in the public finance literature where CGE models have been misused in policy debates. For example, during a national debate about South Africa's fiscal deficit, Gibson and Seventer (2000) published a column in the newspaper where they described simulations with their CGE model of South Africa that revealed that a slight increase in the fiscal deficit would increase the GDP growth rate. It turned out that this result was achieved by assuming that public spending "crowds in" private spending. However, the critical parameter that determines the extent of crowding in (the effect of pubic spending on private investment) was assumed to be quite large in the Gibson–Seventer model, with almost no empirical evidence to substantiate the assumption. It was not surprising, therefore, that they obtained this unusual result. Inasmuch as there were several models of the South African economy engaged in the debate, and the Gibson–Seventer model was alone in showing a positive GDP growth effect of an increase in the fiscal deficit, it was viewed as an extreme outlier and the newspaper column had little impact on the policy debate.

In sum, despite their natural affinity to analysis of public-finance issues, CGE models have had a modest, but significant, influence on policy in the area. Where particular estimates from CGE models have been influential, they have usually been confirmed by studies from other methods. In other cases, CGE models have played the role of uncovering a particular mechanism that had not been apparent before. In such instances, the benefits of CGE models are enhanced when their application is timely, and when the mechanism being uncovered is simple enough to be communicated to policymakers.

15.5. STRUCTURAL ADJUSTMENT

The oil price shocks of the 1970s caused severe disruptions in developing countries, requiring them to adjust their exchange rate and other macroeconomic policies in response. Many of these countries had distorted structural policies, such as trade restrictions, as well. The realization that the more distorted the structure, the worse the impact of the shock (Balassa, 1983), led some countries, with the support of the World Bank and International Monetary Fund, to undertake structural adjustment programs aimed at restoring macroeconomic balance while reducing distortions in economic structure. In many ways, CGE models were ideally suited for evaluating such programs. They were able to portray the macroeconomic adjustments, such as a depreciation of the real exchange rate, alongside some of the microeconomic policies, such as reduction of trade barriers, in a consistent framework. Furthermore, inasmuch as the economic structure was changing, standard macro-econometric models, where parameters such as the import-demand elasticity were based on historical relationships, were clearly inappropriate.

Accordingly, during the 1980s a reasonably large number of CGE models of developing countries were built, mostly under the sponsorship of the World Bank. Although this effort led to a substantial amount of research only a few of these models actually ended up directly supporting policy makers.[24] One reason was that, at that time, the technology of building and running CGE models was not as developed as it is today, so that a modeling exercise would often take longer than the policy maker's time horizon. Another reason was that the data required to estimate or even calibrate these models were hard to come by, further delaying the process. Nevertheless, on at least three occasions, a second-generation model was used to underpin a structural adjustment program. In Yugoslavia, a CGE model showed the high costs in terms of output and foreign exchange of the country's system of foreign exchange allocation; a few months later the system was abandoned (Dewatripont et al., 1990). The model of Turkey pointed out that the real-exchange-rate depreciation required in response to the combined oil-price and workers' remittance shocks was much greater than what standard methods of calculation, such as the purchasing-power-parity method, would yield (Lewis and Urata, 1984). Although Turkey chose to devalue by a smaller amount, the new exchange rate was short-lived, the regime collapsed, and the lire eventually approached a level close to that predicted by the CGE model. Finally, in the early 1990s, most observers agreed that the CFA franc, the currency of thirteen francophone African countries, was overvalued. Yet the standard PPP estimates yielded only mild degrees of overvaluation, since inflation in these countries was close to French inflation (the CFA franc was pegged to the French franc). However, a simple CGE-model calculation, taking into account the terms-of-trade shocks these countries faced in the late 1980s/early 1990s, showed the CFA franc to be overvalued by almost 50%. On January 14, 1994, the CFA franc was devalued by 50% (Devarajan, 1997).

The experience with structural adjustment demonstrates both the potential and the limits of CGE models in informing policy. The potential lies in their ability to

---

[24] Dervis, de Melo, and Robinson (1982), Gelb (1989), and Mitra (1994). The model of Turkey by Dervis et al. (1982, Chap. 8) was used to support a World Bank mission to Turkey in 1978 to deal with their foreign exchange crisis, which started in late 1977.

integrate the micro and macro elements of a structural adjustment program, especially as it affects the structure of trade and the real exchange rate. They also can provide some simple and easy-to-communicate lessons about adjustment policy, such as the formula for calculating the real-exchange-rate depreciation required to adjust to a terms-of-trade shock (Devarajan, Lewis, and Robinson, 1993), or that trade reform without accompanying tax measures could undermine the intended benefits of that reform.

The limits of CGE models in analyzing issues of structural adjustment arise from the same source; namely, the problems of integrating micro and macro aspects in a single model. The neoclassical CGE framework, specifying simultaneous flow equilibria across many well-functioning markets in a single period and determining only relative prices, is an uneasy host for any analysis of the impact of macro shocks. The sorts of financial crises that typically accompany structural-adjustment problems are inherently dynamic, working through changes in financial markets that, in the short run, throw product and factor markets out of long-run equilibrium. There is still an enormous theoretical gap between neoclassical general equilibrium models and short-run, dynamic macro models.

There is, of course, a vast literature on imposing macro adjustment mechanisms on CGE models in a "top down" manner, working with alternative "macro closures" of the CGE models.[25] A number of applied CGE models in this tradition have been used in policy debates. All these models embody some necessarily ad hoc assumptions about the operation of markets or the behavior of agents in order to impose realistic macro behavior on the neoclassical CGE model. Critics such as Bell and Srinivasan (1984) and Srinivasan (1982) particularly disliked the mixing of macro and Walrasian elements in a CGE model.

However, there is an active and growing literature using CGE models to provide the supply side in dynamic macro models – for example, see Agénor and Montiel (1996) and McKibbin and Sachs (1989).[26] There is also a literature which incorporates financial assets and asset markets in dynamic CGE models – see Bourguignon, de Melo, and Suwa (1991) and the survey of this work by Robinson (1991), who relates it to the literature on macro closure. There is much interesting research under way from both the CGE and macro sides on developing better dynamic models that incorporate expectations, asset markets, financial instruments, and "nominal" variables, and also incorporate elements of the CGE specification of flow equilibria in product and factor markets, but in models that allow for unemployment.

Given the present state of research, however, policy analysis has usually proceeded with care, using separate CGE and macro models. The corroboration of the CGE model results by those from other types of analysis, such as partial-equilibrium

---

[25] Any discussion of macro closure is well beyond the scope of this paper. A survey of the early debate is provided by Rattso (1982) and Robinson (1989).

[26] The McKibbin–Sachs model was used to evaluate the impact of NAFTA. See Manchester and McKibbin (1995) and U.S. Congressional Budget Office (1993).

models or simple macro models, is one way of reassuring policymakers and their advisers that the common lessons coming from these models may be saying something im,·ortant.

15.6. INCOME DISTRIBUTION

The earliest CGE models of developing countries were designed to examine issues of income distribution.[27] Partly because of the complexity of these models, and partly because distributional issues left center stage in the policy arena during the debt crisis and adjustment era of the 1980s, these models had little influence on policy. Nevertheless, the power of CGE models to illuminate distributional questions continues to make them the dominant tool. Beginning in the early 1990s, a series of CGE models examined the distributional consequences of adjustment policies (Sahn, 1996; Bourguignon, de Melo, and Morrison, 1991; Narayana et al., 1990). These models were the first to be able to specify a counterfactual in analyzing structural adjustment: how would the poor, say, have fared in the absence of adjustment policies? The fact that different models of different countries led to similar conclusions – the poor would have fared worse, although adjustment policies could be improved by better cushioning the poor from transitory effects – gave the model results some credence, especially in policy circles. The critics of adjustment policies now had to answer to a set of rigorous, empirically based results that contradicted what they were saying. Although the scale of the debate and rhetoric did not subside, it became more nuanced and refined.

The most recent development in this arena is the introduction of poverty-reduction strategy papers (PRSPs) to underpin foreign aid and concessional lending from multilateral agencies. Because these strategies have to show the effects of all government policies (including macroeconomic and structural policies) on poverty, various CGE models are currently being used to develop these poverty reduction strategies.[28] Although some of these have been used for the macroeconomic framework of these strategies, it is too early to tell whether CGE models' influence on poverty-reduction policy will be significant. There is also a growing literature on incorporating household survey data into an economy-wide framework provided by a CGE model. Although there is not enough evidence of their influence on policy, these microsimulation models appear to have the potential for analyzing the links between macro policy choices and shocks, and the distribution of income at the household level.[29]

---

[27] Adelman and Robinson (1978) and Lysy and Taylor (1979).

[28] Agénor, Izquierdo, and Fofack (2001) and Devarajan and Go (2001).

[29] See Bourguignon, Fournier, and Gurgand (2001), Cogneau and Robilliard (2001), and Bourguignon, Robinson, and Robilliard (2002).

15.7. CONCLUSIONS

Responsible economists who do policy analysis believe in the obverse of Gresham's Law applied to policy debate – good numbers drive out bad numbers. Although not always true, and acknowledging that a significant amount of policy formulation and debate does not rely on any numbers, experience in policy debates covering a variety of issues in a variety of countries supports qualified optimism – good analysis does matter and can affect policy choices. But, to be effective, economists must provide policy analysis that is relevant, transparent, and timely. Their methods and models must meet acceptable standards of validation. And, finally, credibility in policy debates is greatly enhanced when a variety of different approaches and models are applied, and there is a consensus about the results. Robustness is more important than elegance.

It has been about forty years since the first applied or computable general equilibrium model was developed for Norway by Lief Johansen. Active work with these models started up in the 1970s, with continuing advances in theory, data, and computing power. CGE models have now become part of the standard toolkit of economists, and recent advances in software have made them accessible to anyone with undergraduate training in economics. They are widely used in academic research and in policy analysis, whenever it is necessary to consider the empirical implications of simultaneous equilibrium in a number of markets. In policy analysis, they are useful whenever policy changes affect a large share of economic activity or when it is important to consider changes in the sectoral structure of output, trade, demand, employment, and/or prices.

The CGE models used in policy work vary widely in size, complexity, and domain of applicability – but all are designed to analyze the links between policy choices and economic outcomes. The questions driving the policy debate also must drive the models. What an academic researcher considers to be the "relevant" questions may differ greatly from the questions considered important in the political arena. Furthermore, academics and policy analysts may have different time horizons, with the latter having to deliver advice that is timely. Finally, the policymaker is more concerned about getting consensus results from different analytical tools than with polishing and sharpening any one particular tool. Given the overriding need for relevance and timeliness in policy debates, it is hardly surprising that much of the work developing and using CGE models for policy analysis takes place in government agencies or research institutes.

In the past thirty years, there has been a healthy and productive tension between policy applications of CGE models and developments in theory, econometrics, and data. Sometimes the models have been ahead of the theory, incorporating ad hoc specifications to capture what are considered to be empirically important effects, or to achieve realism in applied models – a good example is the work on structural-adjustment models. In many cases, the response of the research community has been to advance the theory, develop new data sources, improve estimation methods, and develop new solvers to meet the needs of modelers. On the other side, theoretical developments in modeling household behavior, dynamics, and the operation of markets are starting to show up in empirical models. With advances in software and computer capacity, the time gap between developing a new theory and implementing it in an empirical model is now quite short, so there is even more scope for productive collaboration between theorists, applied econometricians, and policy modelers. The numbers should get better, the policy debate will be better focused, and the result could be better policies.

REFERENCES

I. Adelman and S. Robinson (1978), *Income Distribution Policy in Developing Countries: A Case Study of Korea.* Stanford, CA: Stanford University Press and Oxford: Oxford University Press.

P.-R. Agénor, A. Izquierdo, and H. Fofack (2001), "IMMPA: A Quantitative Macroeconomic Framework for the Analysis of Poverty-Reduction Strategies." Washington, DC: World Bank Institute.

P.-R. Agénor and P. J. Montiel (1996), *Development Macroeconomics.* Princeton, NJ: Princeton University Press.

E. Ahmad and N. Stern (1987), "Alternative Sources of Government Revenue: Illustrations from India, 1979–80," in D. Newbery and N. Stern (Eds.), *The Theory of Taxation for Developing Countries.* Oxford: Oxford University Press.

S. Ahmed and D. Croushore (1994), "The Marginal Cost of Funds with Nonseparable Public Spending," Working Paper No. 94–5. Federal Reserve Bank of Philadelphia.

C. Arndt, S. Robinson, and F. Tarp (2002), "Parameter Estimation for a Computable General Equilibrium Model: A Maximum Entropy Approach," *Economic Modeling* 19: 375–98.

A. B. Atkinson and N. H. Stern (1974), "Pigou, Taxation, and Public Goods," *Review of Economic Studies* 41: 119–28.

A. J. Auerbach, L. J. Kotlikoff, and W. Leibfritz (Eds.) (1999), *Generational Accounting Around the World.* Cambridge: National Bureau of Economic Research Project Report.

B. Balassa (1983), "The Adjustment Experience of Developing Economies after 1973," in J. Williamson (Ed.), *IMF Conditionality.* Washington, DC: Institute for International Economics.

C. L. Ballard and D. Fullerton (1992), "Distortionary Taxation and the Provision of Public Goods," *Journal of Economic Perspectives* 6: 117–31.

C. L. Ballard, J. B. Shoven, and J. Whalley (1985), "General Equilibrium Computations of the Marginal Welfare Cost of Taxes in the United States," *American Economic Review* 75: 128–38.

C. Bell and T. N. Srinivasan (1984), "On the Uses and Abuses of Economy-Wide Models in Development Policy Analysis," in M. Syrquin, L. Taylor, and L. E. Westphal (Eds.), *Economic Structure and Performance.* New York: Academic Press, pp. 451–76.

L. Bergman (1989), "Energy, Environment and Economic Growth in Sweden: A CGE-Modeling Approach." Stockholm: Stockholm School of Economics.

F. Bourguignon, J. de Melo, and A. Suwa (1991), "Modeling the Effects of Adjustment Programs on Income Distribution," *World Development* 19(11): 1527–44.

F. Bourguignon, M. Fournier, and M. Gurgand (2001), "Fast Development with a Stable Income Distribution: Taiwan, 1979–1994," *Review of Income and Wealth* 47(2): 139–63.

F. Bourguignon, J. de Melo, and C. Morrisson (1991), "Poverty and Income Distribution During Adjustment: Issues and Evidence from the OECD Project," *World Development* 19(1): 1485–1508.

F. Bourguignon, S. Robinson, and A.-S. Robilliard (2002), "Representative versus Real Households in the Macro-Economic Modeling of Inequality," mimeo, IFPRI.

A. L. Bovenberg (1987), "Indirect Taxation in Developing Countries: A General Equilibrium Approach," *International Monetary Fund Staff Papers*, No. 34.

D. K. Brown (1992), "The Impact of a North American Free Trade Area: Applied General Equilibrium Models," in N. Lustig, B. Bosworth, and R. Z. Lawrence (Eds.), *North American Free Trade: Assessing the Impact*. Washington, DC: Brookings Institution.

E. K. Browning (1987), "On the Marginal Welfare Cost of Taxation," *American Economic Review* 77: 11–23.

M. Burfisher, S. Robinson, and K. Thierfelder (1992), "Agricultural Policy in a U.S.–Mexico Free Trade Agreement," *North American Journal of Economics and Finance* 3(2): 117–40.

(1994), "Wage Changes in a U.S.–Mexico Free Trade Area: Migration Versus Stolper–Samuelson Effects," in J. F. Francois and C. R. Shiells (Eds.), *Modeling Trade Policy: Applied General Equilibrium Assessments of North American Free Trade*. Cambridge: Cambridge University Press.

(1997), "Migration, Prices and Wages in a North American Free Trade Agreement," in R. Rose, C. Tanner, and M. A. Bellamy (Eds.), *Issues in Agricultural Competitiveness, Markets and Policies*, Aldershot: Dartmouth, pp. 375–83.

(2000), "North American Farm Programs and the WTO," *American Journal of Agricultural Economics* 82: 768–74.

(2001), "The Impact of NAFTA on the United States," *Journal of Economic Perspectives* 15(1): 125–44.

D. Cogneau and A.-S. Robilliard (2001), "Growth, Distribution and Poverty in Madagascar: Learning from a Microsimulation Model in a General Equilibrium Framework," IFPRI, Trade and Macroeconomics Division, Discussion Paper No. 61, and DIAL DT/2001/19.

H. Dahl, S. Devarajan, and A. Panagariya (1994), "Revenue-Neutral Tariff Reform: Theory and an Application to Cameroon," *Economic Studies Quarterly* 45(3): 213–26.

K. Dervis, J. de Melo, and S. Robinson (1982), *General Equilibrium Models for Development Policy: A World Bank Research Publication*. Cambridge: Cambridge University Press.

S. Devarajan (1997), "Real Exchange Rate Misalignment in the CFA Zone," *Journal of African Economies* 6(1): 35–53.

S. Devarajan and D. Go (2001), "A Macroeconomic Framework for Poverty Reduction Strategy Papers," Washington, DC: The World Bank.

S. Devarajan, J. D. Lewis, and S. Robinson (1993), "External Shocks, Purchasing Power Parity, and the Equilibrium Real Exchange Rate," *World Bank Economic Review* 7(1): 45–63.

S. Devarajan and S. Hossain (1998), "The Combined Incidence of Taxes and Public Expenditures in the Philippines," *World Development* 26(6): 963–77.

S. Devarajan, S. Suthiwart-Narueput, and K. E. Thierfelder (2001), "The Marginal Cost of Public Funds in Developing Countries," in A. Fossati and W. Wiegard (Eds.), *Policy Evaluation with Computable General Equilibrium Models*. London/New York: Routledge.

S. Devarajan, L. Squire, and S. Suthiwart-Narueput (1997), "Beyond Rate of Return: Reorienting Project Analysis," *World Bank Research Observer* 12(1): 35–46.

M. Dewatripont, W. Grais, and G. Michel (1990), "Foreign Exchange Allocation and Trade Incentives: A General Equilibrium Application for Yugoslavia," in L. Bergman, D. Jorgenson, and E. Zalai (Eds.), *General Equilibrium Modeling and Economic Policy Analysis.* Cambridge: Basil Blackwell, pp. 218–40.

W. E. Diewert and D. A. Lawrence (1994), "The Marginal Costs of Taxation in New Zealand." Report prepared for the New Zealand Business Roundtable by Swan Consultants Pty. Ltd., Canberra, Australia.

P. B. Dixon (2001). Personal Communication to S. Devarajan.

P. B. Dixon, B. R. Parmenter, J. Sutton, and D. P. Vincent (1982), *ORANI: A Multisectoral Model of the Australian Economy.* Amsterdam: North-Holland.

J. F. Francois and C. R. Shiells (1994a), "AGE Models of North American Free Trade," in J. F. Francois and C. R. Shiells (Eds.), *Modeling Trade Policy: Applied General Equilibrium Assessments of North American Free Trade.* Cambridge: Cambridge University Press, Ch. 1.

J. F. Francois and C. R. Shiells (Eds.) (1994b), *Modeling Trade Policy: Applied General Equilibrium Assessments of North American Free Trade.* Cambridge: Cambridge University Press.

D. Fullerton (1991), "Reconciling Recent Estimates of the Marginal Welfare Cost of Taxation," *American Economic Review* 81: 302–8.

A. Gelb (1989), *Oil Windfalls: Blessing or Curse?* London: Oxford University Press.

B. E. Gibson and D. van Seventer (2000), "A Tale of Two Models: Comparing Structuralist and Neoclassical CGEs for South Africa," *International Review of Applied Economics* 14(2): 149–71.

A. Golan, G. Judge, and D. Miller (1996), *Maximum Entropy Econometrics: Robust Estimation with Limited Data.* New York: Wiley & Sons.

A. Golan, G. Judge, and S. Robinson (1994), "Recovering Information from Incomplete or Partial Multisectoral Economic Data," *The Review of Economics and Statistics* 76(3): 541–9.

I. Hansson and C. Stuart (1985), "Tax Revenue and the Marginal Cost of Public Funds in Sweden," *Journal of Public Economics* 27: 331–53.

A. C. Harberger (1964), "The Measurement of Waste," *American Economic Review* 54: 58–76.

T. Hatta (1994), "Uniform v. Non-uniform Tariffs," *Economic Studies Quarterly* 45(3): 196–212.

R. Hinojosa-Ojeda and S. Robinson (1991), "Alternative Scenarios of U.S.–Mexican Integration: A Computable General Equilibrium Approach," Working Paper No. 609, Department of Agricultural and Resource Economics, University of California at Berkeley.

(1992), "Labor Issues in a North American Free Trade Area," in N. Lustig, B. Bosworth, and R. Z. Lawrence (Eds.), *North American Free Trade: Assessing the Impact.* Washington, DC: Brookings Institution.

E. A. Hudson and D. W. Jorgenson (1974), "U.S. Energy Policy and Economic Growth, 1975–2000," *Bell Journal of Economics and Management Science* 5(2): 461–514.

L. Johansen (1960), *A Multisectoral Study of Economic Growth.* Amsterdam: North-Holland. Second edition, 1974.

R. Jones (1965), "The Structure of Simple General Equilibrium Models," *Journal of Political Economy* 73: 557–72.

D. W. Jorgenson (1997), *Tax Policy and the Cost of Capital.* Cambridge, MA: MIT Press.

D. W. Jorgenson and K.-Y. Yun (1986), "The Excess Burden of U.S. Taxation," *Journal of Accounting, Auditing and Finance* 6: 487–509.

KPMG Peat Marwick (1991), "Analysis of Economic Effects of a Free Trade Area Between the United States and Mexico." KPMG Peat Marwick Policy Economics Group, prepared for the U.S. Council of the Mexico–U.S. Business Committee, Washington, DC.

J. D. Lewis and S. Urata (1984), "Anatomy of a Balance-of-Payments Crisis: Application of a Computable General Equilibrium Model to Turkey, 1978–80," *Economic Modelling* 1(3): 281–303.

S. Levy and S. van Wijnbergen (1994), "Agriculture in a U.S.–Mexican Free Trade Agreement," in J. Francois and C. Shiells (Eds.), *Modeling Trade Policy: Applied General Equilibrium Assessments of North American Free Trade*. Cambridge: Cambridge University Press.

N. Lustig, B. P. Bosworth, and R. Z. Lawrence (Eds.) (1992), *North American Free Trade: Assessing the Impact*. Washington, DC: Brookings Institution.

J. Manchester and W. McKibbin (1995), "The Global Macroeconomics of NAFTA," *Open Economies Review* 6(3): 203–23.

A. Manne, R. Mendelsohn, and R. G. Richels (1995), "MERGE: A Model for Evaluating Regional and Global Effects of GHG Reduction Policies," *Energy Policy* 23(17): 17–34.

A. Mansur and J. Whalley (1984), "Numerical Specification of Applied General Equilibrium Models: Estimation, Calibration, and Data," in H. Scarf (Ed.), *Applied General Equilibrium Analysis*. Cambridge: Cambridge University Press.

W. J. McKibbin and J. D. Sachs (1989), "The McKibbon–Sachs Global Model: Theory and Specifications," *NBER Working Paper 3100*, National Bureau of Economic Research.

J. de Melo (1988), "Computable General Equilibrium Models for Trade Policy Analysis in Developing Countries: A Survey," *Journal of Policy Modeling* 10(4): 469–503.

P. K. Mitra (1994), *Adjustment in Oil-Importing Developing Countries*. Cambridge: Cambridge University Press.

N. S. S. Narayana, K. Parikh, and T. N. Srinivasan (1990), *Agriculture, Growth and Redistribution of Income: Policy Analysis with a General-Equilibrium Model of India*, Contributions to Economic Analysis. Amsterdam: North-Holland.

W. Nordhaus (1990), "A General Equilibrium Model of Policies to Slow Global Warming," in David Wood (Ed.), Economic Models of Energy and Environment, Proceedings of a Workshop, Washington, DC.

A. Panagariya (1994), "The Economics of Uniform Tariffs," *Economic Studies Quarterly* 45(3): 227–45.

R. Perot and P. Choate (1993), *Save Your Job, Save Your Country: Why NAFTA Must be Stopped Now!* New York: Hyperion.

A. Powell and R. Snape (1993), "The Contribution of Applied General Equilibrium Analysis to Policy Reform in Australia," *Journal of Policy Modeling* 15(4): 393–414.

J. Rattso (1982), "Different Macroclosures of the Original Johansen Model and Their Impact on Policy Evaluation," *Journal of Policy Modeling* 4(1): 85–97.

S. Robinson (1989), "Multisectoral Models," in Hollis B. Chenery and T. N. Srinivasan (Eds.), *Handbook of Development of Economics*. Amsterdam: Elsevier Press.

    (1991), "Macroeconomics, Financial Variables, and Computable General Equilibrium Models," *World Development* 19(11): 1509–1525.

S. Robinson, M. E. Burfisher, R. Hinojosa-Ojeda, and K. Thierfelder (1993), "Agricultural Policies and Migration in a U.S. – Mexico Free Trade Area: A Computable General Equilibrium Analysis," *Journal of Policy Modeling* 15(5–6): 673–701. An earlier version appeared in U.S. International Trade Commission, *Economy-Wide Modeling of the Economic Implications of a FTA with Mexico and a NAFTA with Canada and Mexico*.

An Addendum to the Report on Investigation No. 332-317 under Section 332 of the Tariff Act of 1930. USITC Publication 2508, May 1992.

S. Robinson, A. Cattaneo, and M. El-Said (2001), "Updating and Estimating a Social Accounting Matrix Using Cross Entropy Methods," *Economic Systems Research* 13(1): 47–64.

D. W. Roland-Holst, K. A. Reinert, and C. R. Shiells (1994), "A General Equilibrium Analysis of North American Integration," in J. F. Francois and C. R. Shiells (Eds.), *Modeling Trade Policy: Applied General Equilibrium Assessments of North American Free Trade.* Cambridge: Cambridge University Press, Chap. 2.

D. E. Sahn (Ed.) (1996), *Economic Reform and the Poor in Africa.* Oxford: Clarendon.

J. B. Shoven and J. Whalley (1984), "Applied General Equilibrium Models of Taxation and International Trade: An Introduction and Survey," *Journal of Economic Literature* 22(3): 1007–51.

A. Snow and R. Warren Jr. (1996), "The Marginal Welfare Cost of Public Funds: Theory and Estimates," *Journal of Public Economics* 61: 289–305.

T. N. Srinivasan (1982), "General Equilibrium Theory, Project Evaluation and Economic Development," in Mark Gersovitz, C. Diaz-Alejandra, G. Ranis, and M. Rosenzweig (Eds.), *The Theory and Experience of Economic Development: Essays in Honor of Sir W. Arthur Lewis.* London: Allen and Unwin, Chap. 14, pp. 229–51.

J. E. Stiglitz and P. S. Dasgupta (1971), "Differential Taxation, Public Goods, and Economic Efficiency," *Review of Economic Studies* 38: 151–74.

C. Stuart (1984), "Welfare Costs per Dollar of Additional Tax Revenue in the United States," *American Economic Review* 74: 352–62.

L. Taylor and F. J. Lysy (1979), "Vanishing Income Redistributions: Keynesian Clues About Model Surprises in the Short-Run," *Journal of Development Economics* 6: 11–30.

U.S. Congressional Budget Office (CBO) (1993), *A Budgetary and Economic Analysis of the North American Free Trade Agreement.* Washington, DC.

U.S. Department of Labor, Bureau of International Labor Affairs (1992), "U.S. Employment Effects of a North American Free Trade Agreement: A Survey of Issues and Estimated Employment Effects," Economic Discussion Paper 40.

(1993), "A Review of the Likely Economic Impact of NAFTA on the United States," Economic Discussion Paper 44.

U.S. International Trade Commission (1992), *Economy-Wide Modeling of the Economic Implications of a FTA with Mexico and a NAFTA with Canada and Mexico.* An Addendum to the Report on Investigation No. 332-317 under Section 332 of the Tariff Act of 1930. USITC Publication 2508, May.

W. J. McKibbin and J. D. Sachs (1989), "*The McKibbin-Sachs Global Model: Theory and Specifications,*" NBER Working Papers 3100, National Bureau of Economic Research, Inc.

D. E. Wildasin (1984), "On Public Good Provision with Distortionary Taxation," *Economic Inquiry* 22: 227–43.

Index